CAMBRIDGE

Books

MW00852245

Classics

From the Renaissance to the nineteenth century, Latin and Greek were compulsory subjects in almost all European universities, and most early modern scholars published their research and conducted international correspondence in Latin. Latin had continued in use in Western Europe long after the fall of the Roman empire as the lingua franca of the educated classes and of law, diplomacy, religion and university teaching. The flight of Greek scholars to the West after the fall of Constantinople in 1453 gave impetus to the study of ancient Greek literature and the Greek New Testament. Eventually, just as nineteenth-century reforms of university curricula were beginning to erode this ascendancy, developments in textual criticism and linguistic analysis, and new ways of studying ancient societies, especially archaeology, led to renewed enthusiasm for the Classics. This collection offers works of criticism, interpretation and synthesis by the outstanding scholars of the nineteenth century.

Notes of a Twelve Years' Voyage of Discovery in the First Six Books of the Eneis

Born in Dublin and classically educated at Trinity College, James Henry (1798–1876) practised as a doctor for more than twenty years before an inheritance allowed him to focus on the close study of Virgil's *Aeneid*. Travelling extensively across Europe, Henry conferred with eminent scholars and consulted numerous manuscripts. After the death of his wife in 1849, he was accompanied and ably assisted in his quest by his sole surviving daughter, Katherine Olivia (1830–72). In 1853 he published in Dresden his textual analysis of the poem's first six books. Reissued here is the version that appeared in Britain in 1859. This painstaking research was in turn incorporated into Henry's monumental multi-volume commentary, *Aeneidea*, published between 1873 and 1892 and now also reissued in the Cambridge Library Collection. The present work throws much light on both the ancient text and the approach of an idiosyncratic and indefatigable Virgilian scholar.

Cambridge University Press has long been a pioneer in the reissuing of out-of-print titles from its own backlist, producing digital reprints of books that are still sought after by scholars and students but could not be reprinted economically using traditional technology. The Cambridge Library Collection extends this activity to a wider range of books which are still of importance to researchers and professionals, either for the source material they contain, or as landmarks in the history of their academic discipline.

Drawing from the world-renowned collections in the Cambridge University Library and other partner libraries, and guided by the advice of experts in each subject area, Cambridge University Press is using state-of-the-art scanning machines in its own Printing House to capture the content of each book selected for inclusion. The files are processed to give a consistently clear, crisp image, and the books finished to the high quality standard for which the Press is recognised around the world. The latest print-on-demand technology ensures that the books will remain available indefinitely, and that orders for single or multiple copies can quickly be supplied.

The Cambridge Library Collection brings back to life books of enduring scholarly value (including out-of-copyright works originally issued by other publishers) across a wide range of disciplines in the humanities and social sciences and in science and technology.

Notes of a Twelve Years' Voyage of Discovery in the First Six Books of the Eneis

JAMES HENRY

CAMBRIDGE
UNIVERSITY PRESS

CAMBRIDGE
UNIVERSITY PRESS

University Printing House, Cambridge, CB2 8BS, United Kingdom

Published in the United States of America by Cambridge University Press, New York

Cambridge University Press is part of the University of Cambridge.
It furthers the University's mission by disseminating knowledge in the pursuit of education, learning and research at the highest international levels of excellence.

www.cambridge.org
Information on this title: www.cambridge.org/9781108064514

This edition first published 1859
This digitally printed version 2013

ISBN 978-1-108-06451-4 Paperback

NOTES

OF A

TWELVE YEARS' VOYAGE

OF DISCOVERY

IN THE

FIRST SIX BOOKS OF THE ENEIS.

BY

JAMES HENRY, M. D.

FELLOW OF THE KING S AND QUEEN'S COLLEGE OF PHYSICIANS IN IRELAND.

WILLIAMS AND NORGATE,
14, HENRIETTA STREET, COVENT GARDEN, LONDON;
AND
20, SOUTH FREDERICK STREET, EDINBURGH.
1859.

PREFATORY REMARKS.

§ I.

MSS. and rare books examined by myself personally, and quoted in the course of this work:

1. The Medicean; in the Laurentian Library in Florence; examined by me personally only with respect to *En. IV. 436*. In all other places I have quoted this MS. from Foggini's fac-simile. The MS. itself is in a state of perfect preservation, except that the ink has become very pale, and that, besides wanting the first Eclogues, it wants also one leaf of the Eneis; happily this leaf is preserved in the Vatican Library in Rome, where I saw it in the year 1850.

2. The oldest Gudian; preserved in the Bibliotheca Guelferbytana at Wolfenbüttel. This MS. is numbered on the back 70, and is so quoted by Heyne. It is numbered 903 in Ebert's *Catal. Biblioth. Guelferb.* I have never seen any MS. so full of alterations and corrections; often, as I think, for the worse. It is difficult to read, and the interlineal and marginal glosses still more difficult, frequently impossible. It does not so generally agree with the Medicean as has been supposed. Both it and the Medicean have been greatly overrated by Nicholas Heinsius, Heyne, and Wagner. I had full opportunity of carefully examining this MS., which was obtained for me from Wolfenbüttel by the kindness of my friend Dr. Klemm, Chief Librarian of the Royal

Library in Dresden. I read the whole of the first six Books of the Eneis in it, and took memorandums of its readings in one hundred and eleven places, a great number of which (not all however) I have quoted in this work.

3. 4. The two Leipzig MSS., viz. Nos. 35 and 36 (Naumann's Catal.). These MSS. were also obtained for me by Dr. Klemm. I carefully collated in these MSS. almost all the important passages in the first six Books of the Eneis, and made one hundred and sixty seven memorandums of the readings of No. 35, and about an equal number of No. 36, and have quoted a great part of these readings in the following work. No. 35 is in much better condition, and much easier to read than No. 36. I will not pretend to say which is the older, or more correct; they do not by any means coincide with each other.

5. The Dresden MS. (D. 134 in Ebert's *Geschichte der kön. Biblioth. zu Dresden)*; a comparatively modern MS., but in several places containing good readings rarely to be found in other MSS. I consider it as deserving of more attention than it has hitherto received. I collated this MS. with the two Leipzig, in the whole of the above mentioned number of places, and have always quoted its readings along with theirs. This MS. has been rarely, if ever, quoted by any of Virgil's editors.

6. 7. 8. 9. The four Gotha MSS., viz. Nos. 54, 55, 56, & 236 (Jacobs's Catal.). My opportunity for collating these MSS. not having been good, I have quoted them only in a few places.

10. 11. 12. 13. The four Munich MSS., viz. Nos. 305, 523, 18059, and 21562 in the Library Catalogue. These MSS. also, and for a similar reason, I have quoted only in a small number of places, viz. twenty two in all They have never, so far as I know, been quoted by any of Virgil's editors.

14. 15. 16. 17. 18. 19. 20. 21. The eight oldest of the MSS. preserved in the Royal Library in Vienna, viz. Nos. 113, 114, 115, 116, 117, 118, 120, 121, in Endlicher's Catal. My quotations from these MSS. in the course of the following work amount to eighty one. These MSS. also have never, so far as I know, been quoted by any of Virgil's editors. The remaining Virgilian MSS. in this library, being more modern, I did not collate at all.

22. A very beautiful MS., preserved in the library of the Convent at Kloster-Neuburg near Vienna. The handsomest, I think of all the Virgilian MSS. I have ever seen; on parchment, folio, and in perfect preservation. It seems to have been wholly unknown to the Virgilian editors. In the Library Catal. it is set down as of the 12th Century. I have quoted the readings of this MS. in fifteen places.

23. 24. 25. The three MSS. preserved in the Ambrosian Library at Milan, viz. Nos. 79 and 107 in the Catal., and the Petrarchian. The first I have quoted in six, the second in two, and the third in twenty two, places. None of these MSS. has been quoted by any of the Virgilian editors. The last mentioned I denominate Petrarchian, because it belonged to Petrarch, who, it is said, caused it to be made for his own use. It contains numerous observations in Petrarch's own hand-writing, which however I found it impossible to decypher. It is not likely that they throw any light whatever on the Virgilian text. This MS. has an allegorical frontispiece said to have been painted by the hand of Simon Memmi.

Besides the above Virgilian MSS. I have occasionally consulted, and on two or three occasions quoted, the MS. of Servius preserved in the Royal Library in Dresden.

Circumstances having prevented me from consulting

the Vatican MSS. I have quoted the Vatican Fragment and the Roman, from Bottari.

In the Laurentian Library in Florence is a copy of the Roman Princeps of Virgil which I have quoted on one occasion only.

The Royal Library at Dresden contains one of the only two existing copies of the edition of Virgil published at Modena in 1475. It is stated by Brunet *(Manuel du Libraire)* that this edition is a mere copy of the Milan Ed. of 1474. This latter edition I have never seen, and am acquainted with only through its *Variantes* as cited by Maittaire; but having compared those *Variantes* with the Modena Ed. I find sufficient discrepancy between them and that edition to make me believe that the latter is, not a copy of the Milan Ed., but an improved edition formed mainly on the Milan Ed. as a basis. In proof of the correctness of which opinion I shall only cite *En. III. 329;* where according to Maittaire, the Milan Ed. reads "me famulamque famulo," but where I find in the Modena Ed. the much better reading "me famulam famuloque." So much care seems to me to have been taken in the formation of the text of the Modena Ed. that I esteem it as of greater authority than many of the MSS. and have accordingly made much use of it, and quoted it very frequently in the course of the following work. I may add that it is a beautifully printed book, and, being at the same time the first book ever printed in Modena, affords astounding evidence of the small progress made in the art of printing beautifully and correctly, I will not say in the art of printing quickly and cheaply, since the first invention of the printing press. This edition seems to have been wholly unknown both to Maittaire and De Bure.

The Dresden Library contains also a copy of that extremely rare book (not even so much as mentioned by Brunet in his enumeration of the works of Pierius)

Castigationes et Varietates Virgilianae Lectionis per Johan. Pierium Valerianum, Romae, 1521 (altered with pen to 1534). When I have had occasion to quote this work, I have taken care to quote the author's own words (never quoted by Burmann or Heyne), believing that very few indeed of my readers will have an opportunity to consult the author himself. The Dresden copy of this extremely rare, and at the same time intrinsically excellent, work belonged to Fabricius, and bears his Autograph: *Georgius Fabricius, Chem. Patavii, mense Julio. M. D. XXXX.* This therefore is the identical copy of Pierius whence Fabricius obtained the *Varietates* which he inserted into his edition of Virgil published at Basle in 1547, a copy of which edition is in the Dresden Library and has been frequently consulted by me for the sake of Donatus's commentary printed in full (for the first time) in that edition, commonly called (from the name of the printer) the Henrico-Petri Edition.

I have frequently had occasion to quote Henry Stephens's Ed. 1583 (the place where printed not stated). The Dresden Library copy (the only one I have ever seen) of this edition belonged to Taubmann, and bears his autograph corrections for his own edition, of which it formed the basis.

I have made much use of Bersmann's Ed. Leipzig, 1596. This edition is valuable in as much as it contains in the margin the *Varietates* of a MS. lent to Bersmann by Louis Camerarius.

I have made constant use of the edition of Daniel Heinsius, Leyden, 1636. This rare book is generally stated to be very incorrect, and to be admired only by book collectors on account of its rarity and the beauty of its typography: "Peu exacte." BRUNET, *Manuel du Libraire.* "Referatur sane illa, si ita placet, inter rariores Elzevirianas; interioris tamen indolis bona habet nulla." HEYNE. This is, I think, an unjust judgment. I have found it to be not only beautifully, but correctly, printed, and I frequently prefer its readings to those of the edition of Nicholas Heinsius; See Comm. *En. I. 744.*

The edition of Nicholas Heinsius which I have used is that of Utrecht, 1704.

The *Epistolae Graecanicae Mutuae,* which I have occasionally quoted, is a collection of Letters attributed to various celebrated Greeks, edited, and furnished with a Latin translation, by Cujacius, and bearing the imprint: Aurel. Allobr. 1606.

The edition of Petronius to which I refer, is that of Hadrianides, Amsterdam, 1669; the edition of Apuleius, that of Hildebrand, Leipzig, 1842.

§ II.

How I have been received by Virgilian editors and other learned men.

In order to obtain further information respecting my Author, I have visited several of his principal living editors. In Sept. 1850, I walked all the way from Utrecht to Helversum and back, in one day, in order to see Peerlkamp. This visit was wholly fruitless. I found a man so entirely engrossed by his own views as to have no room for those of any one else: one of the worst arguers and least rational men, not to be mad, whom I ever met; in one word, exactly what one might *a priori* suppose the editor of Peerlkamp s Virgil to be, a man wholly destitute, not merely of all literary taste, but all literary judgment.

In 1846, I became acquainted with Phil. E. Wagner, at Dresden. I had for four years such intimacy with him as it was possible to have with a man, who however unreserved and incautious in his published criticisms, is, to a remarkable degree, the very opposite in his conversation. I communicated to him freely several of my discoveries respecting the meaning of his and my Author; they made no impression on him. I remember in particular with respect to *En. II. 521,* that he objected to my view of that passage, that the word 'defensor could not be applied to an inanimate object. I produced to him, the very next day, the word 'defensor applied by Cesar to piles sunk in a river in order to break the current. Instead of being pleased or convinced, he replied: "How happy you are in your citations!" Phil. E. Wagner is one of the most minute and accurate of Latin grammarians. His eyes are microscopic. If there is a minute bubble floating on the cup, he is the man to detect it, lay hold on it, and explore its interior with the point of a pin or bristle; but ask him is the wine red or white, new or old, sweet or sour, and he does not know what you mean. To Wagner the Eneis is not a poem, but an accidence for teaching schoolboys Latin. His forty one *Quaestiones Virgilianae* are about what, do you think, gentle reader? about Virgil's splendid imagery? about his extraordinary purity and dignity of diction? about his merits or defects relatively considered to those of Homer, Hesiod, Apollonius, Lucretius, Milton, or Dante? about the plan or scope of the Eneis, or of the Georgics? About Eneas, or Turnus, or Dido, Rome, Carthage, Greece, or Italy? No, gentle reader; they are about 'At', 'Ab', 'Ac', 'Ad', 'Is', 'In', 'Ex', 'Os', 'On', 'Quis', 'Qui', 'Hic, 'Jam', 'Nec', 'Ve', 'Et', 'Qui', 'Tum', 'Tunc', 'Iste', 'Ipse', 'Ille', and whether, and on what occasions, 'Natus' should be spelled with a 'G' prefixed. I neither joke, exaggerate, nor pervert; such, no less in spirit than in letter, are the discussions which Ph. E. Wagner has thought proper to dignify with the misnomer, *Quaestiones Virgilianae*

Dr. A. Forbiger has inserted into his third edition short notices of and extracts from. my observations on the first and second Books, as they were published in the *Classical Museum* (Lond. 1848); also of my observations on the third, fourth, fifth and sixth Books, communicated to him orally in Leipzig in 1851. Forbiger's notices of my views being extremely brief, and my views themselves having been greatly altered and enlarged since 1851, no notion whatever either of the nature and scope, or of the particulars of the following work, can be formed from Forbiger's notices. I found Forbiger ready to admit new light to shine on his Author, even when he himself was not the point of radiation. No other commentator or editor of Virgil whom I have met, would permit of a new planet's throwing its light on the Virgilian Earth.

In 1850 Cardinal Angelo Mai received me in Rome with perfect politeness and as perfect heartlessness; embraced me with both his arms, kissed me on both my cheeks, but, though Head Librarian of the Vatican, stirred no finger on my behalf; afforded me no facilities whatever for my investigations. At my first interview with him I made him a present of my first Virgilian essay, *The first Two Books of the Eneis rendered into Blank Iambic, with new Interpretations and Illustrations.* Remaining in Rome for some months and hearing no word from him, I wrote him a note to the following effect:

"Having become convinced that the book, with which I had the honor some time ago to present your Eminence, and for which I have a great value, is to your Eminence of no value at all, I will esteem it an especial favor if your Eminence kindly return it to me, and so restore his strayed child to the weeping and disconsolate parent."

The Cardinal, it seems, either did not understand the joke, or shut his eyes against satire coming from so obscure a quarter, and returned me the book, accompanied by the usual insincere, complimentary note. When I came to Milan, I heard at the Ambrosian Library, where Mai was well known before his promotion to the Cardinalate (having been there employed by the directors of the Library to publish the Homeric pictures), that I only met from him the treatment to be expected by all persons who know so little of Mai as to suppose that he wishes success to any literary efforts but his own.

I received polite attention from Dr. Dozio, Subprefect of the Ambrosian Library. He presented me with the Commentaries of Cynthius Cenetensis, recently edited by him from a MS. in the Library. The lucubrations of Cynthius Cenetensis like those of Philargyrius, and of the Interpretes Virgilii edited by Mai from the Verona Palimpsest, are utterly worthless; mere grammatical, and not even grammatical, *nugae;* learned dust which were better swept out.

§ III.

Some further particulars relating to this Voyage, to my Six Photographs of the Heroic Times, and to myself

I have been, as the title imports, twelve years, twelve of the fairest years of my life, engaged in this work; encouraged by no one, approved by no one, patronised by no one; receiving no particle of assistance either at home or abroad from any one of all the numerous persons who have with more or less success cultivated the same author, except alone the assistance which I have reared and created for myself in my own daughter, who has already, at the age of twenty two, arrived at such a degree of knowledge of the subject, that I have not printed a single Comment without first submitting it to her censorship. Many and valuable have been the suggestions I have received from her, although I have not specially stated the fact except at *En. II. 683.* The work is entirely original; all the views put forward (unless where the contrary is expressly stated) exclusively my own; wherever I have at first put forward a view as my own, which I have afterwards discovered to have been previously held by any one else, I have expunged the passage. If any such passages remain unexpunged, it is by such mere accident as must occasionally occur in a work of such extensive research. I have even been careful not to quote (unless where I have had new matter to bring forward respecting it) any parallel or illustrative passage which has been previously quoted; and on this account have rarely, if ever, quoted Homer, all the parallelisms of that author having been sufficiently pointed out and discussed by preceding observers.

These Commentaries, however, are not the sole fruit of my twelve years' labor; I have *pari passu* transferred the six Books of the Eneis into my native language. That work has been a more Herculean task than even this. Indeed this arose out of that, and may be considered as a mere appendage of that, all these Commentaries having grown out of the searches which I found it necessary to make into the meaning of each separate sentence before I could honestly undertake to transfer the sentence into English. As I went on, I found that almost every sentence had been more or less misunderstood, and afforded materials for a separate Commentary. Hence the present work. The reader will perhaps think that, the meaning once ascertained, the transference into English followed almost as a matter of course; he is greatly mistaken; a full half of the difficulty remained; viz. to convert that meaning into English poetry; to express myself so that my sentence should give, first, the true meaning of Virgil; secondly, the whole of that true meaning; and thirdly, nothing but that true meaning; and should, at the same time, be easy, free, natural and fluent English poetry. No one had ever succeeded in such attempt either in the English or any other language. In every instance either the sentence became not vernacular poetry, or the meaning not Virgil's. I tried and failed, tried and failed, tried and failed, until I was weary, exhausted and despairing. It was not possible to succeed even in a single sentence. I translated, twice over, the whole of the six Books into English Iambic without rhyme. The two first Books of each of these translations I even printed; I had succeeded tolerably well to express the meaning, but the verse was stiff and un-English, just as Voss's similar translation is stiff and un-German. The work was sure not to be read except by scholars. I was not deterred; I persevered and labored on; tried, like a snake or worm writhing itself out of a hole, to wriggle myself now this way, now that; all in vain; the measure was unyielding, — must have its alternately short and long syllable, — would not be forced to meet Virgil's sense; while, at the same time, Virgil's sense was unyielding, — would not be forced to meet the measure. In this dilemma, I determined at last to change my hand, and to vary the measure — to alter my rythm according to the exigencies of the sense. "The poem," said I to myself, "will be the more agreeable if the rythm be occasionally changed. The chief defect in Virgil's great poem is the monotony inseparable from the uninterrupted succession to each other of ten thousand hexameters; the attention at last wanders involuntarily; the mind roves in search of variety, as the eyes of the spectator soon turn away from the most beautiful picture, tired of its very beauty." I made an infinity of trials, and at last found that I could represent the sense of perhaps two or three pages in succession, in one kind of metre, provided I was then allowed, perhaps for the sake of a single proper name, to take a different. I proceeded in this manner both with greater ease and greater success. I found this new method answer so well that I soon began to vary my measure, even where I was not forced to it, and merely for the sake of preventing the reader's ear from being palled by the long continuance of any one measure. I was the more encouraged to adopt this principle, from having observed the enlivening effect of Shakespeare's intermixture even of prose with his verse, and the soporific effect of Milton's interminable decasyllabics. Cheered by the first results of this method, I went much further; I abandoned the old measures and set about to make new; and, after some trials, fell upon a measure (as far as I know, entirely new and my own invention) which enabled me to convey into English the Virgilian sense, with a certainty and precision, and at the same time with an ease and fluency, wholly unattainable in any other measure or combination of measures. I have used this measure very much in the course of my translation, but principally in the fifth Book, to the liveliness of the subject of which, its liveliness seemed to be peculiarly adapted. The fourth Book alone I have not changed out of the Iambic measure, having translated that Book only twice (both times in Iambic); each of the other Books I have translated three, some of them four, times.

On account of the great variety and continual change of measure, I have thought it advisable to indicate the rythm by means of accents. It is much to be desired that even ordinary poetry were always printed with such helps, without which it is impossible for any one who has not a well practised poetical ear, to know where the ictus of the voice falls, in any measure which deviates, even in the slightest degree, from the accustomed jingle.

It will no doubt, be said that my work is not a translation at all. Very well; I have no objection.

I have not called it a translation myself, and am not desirous it should be so called. There is nothing so very flattering in the reputation of translations that I should be anxious to have my work placed in the same category with them. My *Six Photographs of the Heroic Times* will be found in a volume containing all the poems written by me up to this date, and printed two months ago in Dresden under the title of *My Book.*

I am too well aware of the utter neglect with which authors of works of this kind are usually treated by their contemporaries, to suppose that there lives one individual who will trouble himself to inquire who, or what kind of a man, he *is* who writes these words, and who made this singular voyage; but for the information of the many who are sure, according to the usual fashion of mankind in such cases, to begin, as soon as he is dead, to inquire who and what sort of a man he *was,* I beg to say that most of the important incidents of his life will be found more or less distinctly pictured in the poems which collectively with the *Six Photographs of the Heroic Times* constitute the volume entitled *My Book,* and printed this summer in Dresden.

Warned by the misfortunes of others that a work like this, is neither of the kind voluntarily demanded by the public, nor of the kind forced on the public by that curse and ruin of literature, the Bookselling Trade, I have determined, instead of flinging my work into the barathrum of a publisher's warehouse, to leave a certain number of copies both of this *Voyage* and of *My Book* with Mr. Klemm, Oberbibliothekar of the Royal Library at Dresden, for gratis distribution to such persons in Germany as he shall think fitting, and to send the remainder home, for similar gratuitous distribution in my own country. Both from Mr. Klemm himself, and from Mr. Lossnitzer, Mr. Manitius, and the other officers of the Dresden Library, I have met the most uniform and obliging attention, for which I beg to return my best thanks. In the Dresden Library and in the company of its enlightened directors and officers, have been spent during a series of years many of my happiest hours. I shall never think of it or them but with pleasure and gratitude.

I am indebted to Mr. Moritz Lindemann, author of *De prima quae in Convivio Platonico legitur oratione (Programm des Gymnasiums zu Dresden, 1853)*, not merely for a most careful correction of the printer's proofs, but for many valuable suggestions, and such a general revision of my MS. as has greatly contributed to its accuracy and perfection.

And now — "longarum haec meta viarum" — this is the end of my long voyage, and a happier end than that of the voyage of Eneas; for he, just at the goal, lost his travel's companion — him who was the "levamen omnis curae casusque" — while I have still my fellow traveller at my side, only the more endeared to me, as I to her, by the troubles and pleasures we have shared together on the way. Reader, farewell; and should you be inclined to make a similar voyage through the six Books which I have left unexplored, the greatest happiness and best help which I can wish you, is a similar companion.

JAMES HENRY.

WAISENHAUS-STRASSE, DRESDEN,
July, 1853.

I.

1.

ILLE EGO QUI QUONDAM GRACILI MODULATUS AVENA
CARMEN ET EGRESSUS SILVIS VICINA COEGI
UT QUAMVIS AVIDO PARERENT ARVA COLONO
GRATUM OPUS AGRICOLIS AT NUNC HORRENTIA MARTIS
ARMA VIRUMQUE CANO

IMITATED both by Spenser and Milton:

"Lo! I, the man whose muse whylome did maske,
As time her taught, in lowly shepheard's weeds,
Am now enforst a farre unfitter taske,
For trumpets sterne to chaunge mine oaten reeds,
And sing of knights' and ladies' gentle deeds."
Faerie Queene, st. I.

"I who erewhile the happy garden sung."
Par. Reg v. I.

4.

HORRENTIA MARTIS
ARMA VIRUMQUE CANO TROJÆ QUI PRIMUS AB ORIS
ITALIAM FATO PROFUGUS LAVINAQUE VENIT
LITTORA MULTUM ILLE ET TERRIS JACTATUS ET ALTO
VI SUPERUM SÆVÆ MEMOREM JUNONIS OB IRAM
MULTA QUOQUE ET BELLO PASSUS DUM CONDERET URBEM
INFERRETQUE DEOS LATIO

"CANTO l'armi pietose, e 'l Capitano,
Che 'l gran Sepolcro liberò di Cristo:

Molto egli oprò col senno, e con la mano,
Molto soffrì nel glorioso acquisto;
E in van l'Inferno a lui s' oppose, e in vano
S'armò," &c. * * * * *
* * * * * * * *

"O Musa, tu," &c.

TASSO. *Gerus. Lib., I. 1.*

And such, from the beginning to the end, is the Gerusalemme Liberata; a modernized copy, even to the single stones, of the Virgilian edifice.

HORRENTIA MARTIS ARMA. — MARTIS joined with ARMA is not (as a hasty view has led some commentators to suppose) supererogatory; because *arma* is not a specific term, corresponding to the English *arms,* and, like it, applicable only to *martial weapons,* but a general term applicable to *all kinds of implements, martial, agricultural (Georg. I. 160), nautical (En. V. 15), culinary (En. I. 181),* &c. *Martis* is, therefore, a proper adjunct to *arma,* and in the present instance peculiarly proper, because it was incumbent on the poet well to distinguish between the *arma,* the subject of his present poem, and the *arma* of which he had treated in that former poem, to which, in the passage before us, he makes direct reference. Having formerly defined the *arma* of which he was then treating, as those, "quæ sint duris agrestibus — Queis sine nec potuere seri nec surgere messes" *(Georg. I. 160),* he now defines the *arma* which form his present theme, to be *arma Martis* (compare: *En. I. 549,* where *bello* is added to *armis* in order to show that *armis* means *martial* arms): hence, as from every observation which tends to shew the correctness of their diction, an additional argument in favour of the authenticity of the four introductory lines of the Eneis. For a further argument, derived from the same source, see Comm. *En. II. 247.*

Additional observations on the use of the term *arma* will be found in Comm. *En. V. 15.*

CANO. — Not simply *sing*, as in Dryden's generally received translation, but *sing, in the loud, high, heroic, and oracular style; sound, as on a trumpet;* the poet's present martial song being placed, by the term CANO, in the strongest opposition to the peaceful pastoral which he formerly *lilted,* MODULATUS. Compare:

"Dum non arte canora
Compacta solitum modulatur arundine carmen."
Culex, 98.

and

"Vos, O Calliope, precor, aspirate canenti."
En. IX. 525.

and

"Nec Latiæ cecinere tubæ, nec Graia vetustas."
CLAUD. *de Prob. et Olyb. Cons. V. 198.*

also, Jul. Scalig. Poet. III. 26.

The true sense seems to have been perceived by Voss in his translation:

"Waffen ertönt mein Gesang;"

and by Spenser in his imitation quoted above:

"For trumpets sterne to chaunge mine oaten reeds."

TROJÆ QUI PRIMUS AB ORIS ITALIAM FATO PROFUGUS LAVINAQUE VENIT LITTORA. — The Heynian and Wagnerian punctuation, and Voss's translation, assign FATO exclusively to PROFUGUS:

"Italiam, fato profugus, Laviniaque venit
Littora."

"Kam, durch Schicksal verbannt, gen Italia, und an Lavinums
Wogenden Strand."

This is incorrect. FATO belongs no less to VENIT than to PROFUGUS, the two words PROFUGUS and VENIT being intimately united together, so as to form but one idea, that of *coming as a refugee; taking refuge.* Compare Comment on "*improvida turbat,*" *En. II. 200.* Fate not only drove Eneas from Troy, but (which was principally in Virgil's mind, and formed the subject of his entire poem) brought him to, and planted him in, Italy.

Therefore, fato Italiam Lavinaque littora venit profugus. And so *(En. X. 67)*, "Italiam petiit fatis auctoribus."

SÆVAE MEMOREM JUNONIS OB IRAM. — Sævus, the Greek *δεινος*, is as nearly as possible the English *fell.*

DUM CONDERET URBEM INFERRETQUE DEOS LATIO. — Not *found a, or the, city, and bring the Gods into Latium* (Bis die Stadt er gründet', und Troja's Götter in Latium führte — Voss.), but (LATIO relating no less to CONDERET than to INFERRET), *bring the Gods into Latium, and there found a city.*

URBEM, — sciz. Lavinium, see I. 268; XII. 193, 194.

UNDE, — not with Heyne and Thiel, *quâ ex re, quo factum est;* but, as placed beyond all doubt by the exactly corresponding

> "Alter Atys, genus unde Atii duxere Latini,"
>
> *En. V. 568.*

and

> "Silvius . . . . .
> Unde genus Longa nostrum dominabitur Alba."
>
> *En. VI. 763.*

ex quo Enea, the clause

> "Multum ille et terris jactatus et alto,
> Vi superum, sævæ memorem Junonis ob iram,
> Multa quoque et bello passus, dum conderet urbem,
> Inferretque Deos Latio,"

being only subsidiary or parenthetic. See Comm. *En. III. 571. IV. 484. VI. 84. 741. 882.*

GENUS UNDE LATINUM. — According to the boast of the Romans, that they were the fruit of the mixture of the Trojan and Latin blood, "*ατε δη και γεγονοτες*

> *'Τρωων αγλαα τεκνα μεμιγμενα παισι Λατινων.'*"
>
> PLUTARCH. *Quest. Rom. Ed. Reiskii, p 155:*

and see *En. XII. 823, 837.*

14.

INSIGNEM PIETATE VIRUM.

Pietas is softness, tenderness and goodness of heart in general, whether in man's relation to heaven and in spiritual matters (our piety), or in relation to other men (our brotherly love and charity), in which latter sense it has given origin to the French *Pitié* and the English *Pity*. It is constantly opposed to Justitia, the strict right — the observance of the law. *Pius Eneas* is therefore not Pious Eneas, but kind, gentlehearted, tender and affectionate Eneas, in his conduct and demeanour, both towards heaven and towards his brethern of mankind: who does both toward the Gods and toward mankind not merely what he is bound to do, but what he is prompted by the kindness of his nature to do. Compare:

"Rursus amor patriae ratione valentior omni,
Quod tua texuerant scripta, retexit opus;
Sive pium vis hoc, sive hoc muliebre vocari,
Confiteor, misero molle cor esse mihi."

Ovid. *Ex Ponto. 1. 3. 29.*

"Sed si male firma cubarit
Et vitium coeli senserit aegra sui,
Tunc amor et pietas tua sit manifesta puellae."

Ovid. *Art. Amat. II. 319.*

"Jam legis in Drusum miserabile, Livia, carmen;
Unum, qui dicat jam tibi mater, habes.
Nec tua te pietas distendit amore duorum."

Ovid. *ad Liviam. Aug. 3.*

and especially Virgil himself En. IX. 493.

Figite me, si qua est pietas; in me omnia tela
Conjicite, O Rutuli.

and En. II. 536.

Dii, si qua est coelo pietas, quae talia curet.

See vers. 548 and Comm. & vers. 607 and Comm. also III. 42 & 75 and Comm.

15.

TANTÆNE ANIMIS CŒLESTIBUS IRÆ

OFT imitated line: —

"In heavenly spirits could such perverseness dwell?"
Par. Lost, VI. 788.

"And in soft bosoms dwells such mighty rage?"
Rape of the Lock, I. 12.

"Tant de fiel entre-t-il dans l'ame des dévots?"
BOILEAU, *Lutrin, I. 12.*

Compare *(En. XII. 830):*

"Es germana Jovis, Saturnique altera proles,
Irarum tantos volvis sub pectore fluctus."

16.

URBS ANTIQUA FUIT

FUIT, *was* once, and *is* no longer. See Comment on "Fuimus Troes, fuit Ilium", II. 325; and compare "Campos ubi Troja fuit," III. 11.

23.

PROGENIEM SED ENIM TROJANO A SANGUINE DUCI
AUDIERAT TYRIAS OLIM QUÆ VERTERET ARCES
HINC POPULUM LATE REGEM BELLOQUE SUPERBUM
VENTURUM EXCIDIO LIBYÆ SIC VOLVERE PARCAS

THE third and fourth of these lines are not as supposed by La Cerda, Heyne and other commentators, tautologous of the first and second, but explanatory: POPULUM

LATE REGEM, explaining that the PROGENIEM which was being derived from the Trojan blood, was a great and martial people, (viz. the Romans); and VENTURUM EXCIDIO LIBYÆ informing us, that this great and martial people which was being derived from the Trojan blood, for the sake of overturning Carthage ("Tyrias quae verteret arces,") would actually perform its mission. Compare

"Nunc age, Dardaniam prolem quae deinde sequatur
Gloria, qui maneant Itala de gente nepotes."

En. VI. 756.

where the single Roman people is indicated by the double expression: "Dardaniam prolem," and "Itala de gente nepotes," exactly as it is indicated in our text by the double expression PROGENIEM TROJANO A SANGUINE, and POPULUM LATE REGEM.

QUÆ VERTERET. — Not, *which should or shall overturn* but, *for the purpose of overturning.* Compare "Mittunt legatos qui monerent" (JUSTIN. II. 15), not, *who should or shall admonish,* but *for the purpose of admonishing,* for it might happen that those envoys, though sent for the purpose, might not actually admonish.

HINC. — Not *ex hac progenie,* but *ex hoc Trojano sanguine.* Compare (vers. 238):

"Certe hinc Romanos olim, volventibus annis,
Hinc fore ductores, revocato a sanguine Teucri,"

in which passage, not only exactly similar in structure to our text, but actually containing the very promise of which Juno had heard (AUDIERAT), "hinc" is explained by "revocato a sanguine Teucri", the counterpart of the TROJANO A SANGUINE of our text.

VENTURUM EXCIDIO LIBYÆ. — So (CIC. *Ep. ad Att. VIII. 7)* "subsidio venturus;" and *En. X. 214)* "Ibant subsidio Trojæ." Also:

"Hunc nam fore regi
Exitio vatesque canunt."

VALER. FLAC. *I. 28.*

LIBYÆ. — I cannot agree with the commentators, that there is a particular stress in this word: it seems to me to be used like the immediately preceding TYRIAS ARCES, merely for variety, and to avoid the repetition of the term "Carthago," already employed at verse 17.

SIC VOLVERE PARCAS. — The Parcæ are here said VOLVERE (i. e. volvere vices, *make events roll on, or after each other),* in the same sense as Jupiter is said to do so, verse 266, and III. 375. There is no reference whatever to their spindle, and Voss's translation (so roll' es die Spindel der Parcen) is wrong. — Compare:

"Sic Numina fatis
Volvimur, et nullo Lachesis discrimine sævit."
CLAUDIAN, *Rapt. Proserp. III. 410.*

27.

VETERISQUE MEMOR SATURNIA BELLI.

VETERIS. — Not, *ancient,* but *long exercised, long accustomed, inveterate.* Compare:

"Rursus et in veterem fato revoluta figuram."
En. VI. 449.

"Vetus operis et laboris." TACIT. *Ann. I. 20.* "Vetus regnandi." TACIT. *Ann. VI. 44.*

28.

PRIMA QUOD AD TROJAM PRO CARIS GESSERAT ARGIS.

NOT, with Heyne, *"prius, olim,"* but *foremost, as leader or commander.* Compare: *En. II. 613 & Comm.* I therefore beg to substitute the following, instead of the translation I have given of this passage in my Metempsychosis of the Eneis. Page 3.

The inveterate war
Which she had been foremost
To wage against Troy
On behalf of dear Argos.

32.

ET GENUS INVISUM ET RAPTI GANYMEDIS HONORES

GENUS INVISUM. — Genus Electrae sciz. as placed beyond doubt, not merely by the context, but by the direct testimony of OVID. *Fasti. VI. 41:*

"Tunc me poeniteat, posuisse fideliter iras
In genus Electrae, Dardaniamque domum."

RAPTI. — "Cum contemptu dicitur, ut apud nostrates *entführt,* quod corrumpendi rationem involvit; magna autem est doloris et contemptus conjunctio." — WAGNER. There seems to me to be no sufficient grounds for understanding RAPTI to be here used in a contemptuous sense, RAPTUS being the ordinary expression for the *sudden* & violent removal or carrying off of a person, no matter by what means or for what purpose. Compare OVID. *Ex Ponto I. 9. 1:*

"Quae mihi de rapto tua venit epistola Celso,
Protinus est lacrymis humida facta meis."

where *rapto* is simply, carried off suddenly or violently; viz. by death.

And so in the text, RAPTI GANYMEDIS is simply, Ganymede suddenly or forcibly carried off, viz. by Jupiter, or Jupiter's eagle, see *En. V. 254:*

— quem praepes ab Ida
Sublimem pedibus rapuit Jovis armiger uncis.

where no contempt can be intended, yet the selfsame expression is used.

34.

RELIQUIAS DANAUM ATQUE IMMITIS ACHILLI

So Lycophron; Cassandra; — (*apud Meurs.* tom. V. 972):

Εποψεται δε λειψανον τοξευματων
Του κηραμυντου πευκεως παλαιμονος.

36.

ACTI FATIS

"Si *fatis,* nulla Junonis invidia est. Si Junonis invidiâ fatigabantur quomodo dicit ACTI FATIS? Sed hoc ipsum Junonis odium fatale est. Agebantur *fatis* Junonis, i. e. *voluntate;* vel *fatis,* pro *malis,* ut III. 182." — SERVIUS.

"Non tam quoniam hoc Junonis odium fatale erat, ut Servius; sed potius, quoniam hi ipsi Trojanorum errores fatales erant." — HEYNE.

Not only these two, but all other commentators and translators, as far as I know, have wholly mistaken the meaning of this passage, which is not, *that the Trojans were* jactati, fatigati, or agitati, *harassed, or driven hither and thither by the fates,* (*actus* being never used in the sense assigned to it in such interpretation), but simply that they were *driven onward, or toward Latium, by the fates,* (ACTI FATIS); while at the same time they were *driven backward, or from Latium, by Juno,* (ARCEBAT LONGE LATIO). The result was, MULTOS PER ANNOS ERRABANT MARIA OMNIA CIRCUM: words could not more clearly express the opposition of the forces, between which the Trojans were placed; an opposition on which hangs the whole action of the poem. The *invidia* of Juno, concerning which Servius queries, was manifested by her using her utmost exertions to prevent the Trojans from arriving at the place toward which they were impelled by the fates; i. e. at which it was fated they should arrive.

As ACTI FATIS here, so "fato profugus venit," verse 6; "sedes ubi fata quietas ostendunt," verse 209; "data fata secutus," verse 386; "fata deum vestras exquirere terras imperiis *egere* suis" *(En. VII. 239)*; "fatisque vocantia regna" *(En. V. 656)*; &c.; through all which expressions runs the one constant idea of the fates *calling, forcing, driving* (agentia) the Trojans toward Latium.

42.

ITALIA TEUCRORUM AVERTERE REGEM

NOT merely, turn away, but turn *back*, from Italy; make him turn, so as to show his back. So OVID, of Hercules in the combat with Achelous forcing his adversary round, and then jumping upon his back:

> "Impulsumque manu, (certum mihi vera fateri)
> Protinus avertit; tergoque onerosus inhaesit."
>
> *Metam. IX. 53.*

And Virgil himself *(En. IV. 389)*, of Dido turning her back on Eneas as she goes away and leaves him:

> "— Seque ex oculis avertit et aufert."

and, *En. VIII. 207,* of Cacus driving the oxen from their stable to his cave:

> "Quatuor a stabulis praestanti corpore tauros
> Avertit."

Not merely turns off from their stable, but drives from their stable in the opposite direction. See Comm. *En. I. 572.*

48.

ILLUM EXPIRANTEM TRANSFIXO PECTORE FLAMMAS
TURBINE CORRIPUIT SCOPULOQUE INFIXIT ACUTO

"Turbine. Volubilitate ventorum. Scopulo. Saxo eminenti." — Servius.

"Hub sie im Wirbel empor, und spiesst' an ein scharfes
Gestein ihn."

Voss.

"Ipsum vero Pallas fulmine percussum procellæ vi scopulo etiam allisit." — Heyne.

"Impegit rupi acutæ." — Ruæus.

"Infixit. *Inflixit,* lectionem quorundam MSS. facile prætulissem, et quod statim præcesserit *transfixo,* unde evadit inconcinna cognatæ dictionis repetitio, et quod etiam, *En. X. 303:*

'Namque inflicta vadis, dorso dum pendet iniquo;'

si Sidon. Apoll. v. 197, haud tueretur vulgatam scripturam:

'Fixusque Capharei
Cautibus, inter aquas flammam ructabat Oileus.'"

Wakefield.

To which criticism of Wakefield's, Forbiger adds: "Præterea etiam acuto scopulo *infigendi* voc. accommodatius videtur quam *infligendi.*" And Wagner: "acuto scopulo *infigi* melius." "Erschlug ihn selbst mit dem Blitze, und liess sodann seinen Leichnam von den Wellen an die Klippen spiessen." Ladewig.

This interpretation and these criticisms are founded altogether on a false conception of the meaning of the word *infigere,* which is never to fix *on,* but always either to fix *in,* or to fix *with,* i. e. pierce *with. Scopulo infixit acuto,* pierced *with* a sharp-pointed rock; i. e. hurled a sharp-pointed rock on him, so as to pierce him through. So *(En. XII. 721)* „Cornua obnixi infigunt," fix their horns, not *on*, but *in;* infix their horns; stick their horns into each other; stick each other with their horns: q. d. Cornibus se mutuo infigunt; "Relinquere vero aculeum in audientium animis, is demum potest, qui non pungit, sed infigit." Plin. Jun. Epist. I. 20; and exactly parallel to our text:

"Saturnius me sic infixit Jupiter,
Jovisque numen Mulcibri adscivit manus.
Hos ille cuneos fabrica crudeli inserens,
Perrupit artus: qua miser sollertia
Transverberatus, castrum hoc Furiarum incolo."

Cicero *(translating from Aeschylus) Tuscul. Quaest. II. 10.*

In confirmation of this view of the passage, I may observe: 1st, that it is easier to imagine a man pierced through with a sharp-pointed rock, than flung on a sharp-pointed rock, so as to remain permanently impaled on it; and 2ndly, that the accounts given of the transaction, by Quintus Calaber and Seneca, agree as perfectly with this view as they disagree with the opposite:

Και νυ κεν εξηλυξε κακον μορον, ει μη αρ' αυτω,
ρηξας αιαν ενερθεν, επι προεηκε κολωνην·
ευτε παρος μεγαλοιο κατ' Εγκελαδοιο δαιφρων
Παλλας αειραμενη Σικελην επικαββαλε νησον.
η ῥ' ετι καιεται αιεν υπ' ακαματοιο Γιγαντος,
αιθαλοεν πνειοντος εσω χθονος· ως αρα Λοκρων
αμφεκαλυψεν ανακτα δυσαμμορον ουρεος ακρη,
υψοθεν εξεριπουσα, βαρυνε δε καρτερον ανδρα.
αμφι δε μιν θανατοιο μελας εκιχησατ' ολεθρος,
γαιη ομως δμηθεντα και ατρυγετω ενι ποντω.

Quintus Calab. *XIV. 567.*

And so Seneca; who, having presented us with Ajax clinging to the rock to which he had swum for safety, after his ship had been sunk, and himself struck with lightning, and there uttering violent imprecations against the Deity, adds:

"Plura cum auderet furens,
Tridente rupem subruit pulsam pater
Neptunus, imis exerens undis caput,
Solvitque montem; quem cadens secum tulit:
Terraque et igne victus et pelago jacet."

Agam. 552.

And so also, beyond doubt, we are to understand Sidonius Apollinaris's —

"Fixusque Capharei
Cautibus, inter aquas flammam ructabat Oileus."

Not, with Wakefield and the other commentators, *fixed on* the rocks of Caphareus, but, *pierced with* the rocks of Caphareus, and lying under them. Compare *(En. IX. 701)* "fixo pulmone," the pierced lung; "fixo cerebro" *(En. XII. 537)* the pierced brain; "verubus trementia figunt" *(En. I. 216),* not, fix *on* the spits, but, stick or pierce *with* the spits; and especially (Ovid. *Ibis. 341):*

"Viscera sic aliquis scopulus tua figat, ut olim,
Fixa sub Euboico Graia fuere sinu," —

pierced and pinned down with a rock, at the bottom of the Eubœan gulf.

Turbine. Scopulo. — Not *two* instruments, *a whirlwind and a rock;* but, *one single* instrument, *a whirling rock;* scopulo turbineo; in modo turbinis se circumagente; as if Virgil had said, Solo affixit illum correptum et transverberatum scopulo acuto in eum maxima vi rotato: or, more briefly, Turbine scopuli acuti corripuit, et infixit. Compare:

"Præcipitem scopulo atque ingentis turbine saxi
Excutit effunditque solo."

En. XII. 531.

" . . . . Stupet obvia leto
Turba super stantem, atque emissi turbine montis
Obruitur."

Stat. *Theb. II. 564.*

"Idem altas turres saxis et turbine crebro
Laxat."

Stat. *Theb. X. 742.*

In all which passages turbo is not a whirlwind, or whirling of the wind; but, the whirl or whirling of the just mentioned stone; as at verse 594 of *En. VI.* it is also not a *whirlwind,* but the whirl of the just mentioned thunderbolt.

So understood, 1st, the passage is according to Virgil's usual manner, the latter part of the line explaining and defining the general statement contained in the former; and, 2ndly, Pallas kills her enemy, not by the somewhat roundabout and unusual method of first striking him with thunder, and then snatching him up in a whirlwind, and then either dashing him against a sharp rock, and leaving him impaled there, or, as I have shown is undoubtedly the meaning, impaling him with a sharp rock, but by the more compendious and less out-of-the-way method of first striking him with thunder, and then whirling a sharp-pointed rock on top of him, so as to impale him.

From Milton's imitation of this passage, in his Paradise Lost (II. 180), it appears that even he fell into the general and double error:

> "Caught in a fiery tempest shall be hurled,
> Each on his rock transfixed."

Caro's translation shows that he had no definite idea whatever of the meaning:

> "A tale un turbo
> In preda il diè; che per acuti scogli
> Miserabil ne fe' rapina, e scempio."

Expirantem transfixo pectore flammas. — Breathing, exhaling *out of his mouth,* the flames of the thunderbolt which had pierced his breast. Compare *Stat. Theb. XI. 1.*

> "Postquam magnanimus furias virtutis iniquae
> Consumpsit Capaneus, expiravitque receptum
> Fulmen;"

and Ovid. *Met. VIII. 356;* of the Calydonian boar:

> "Lux micat ex oculis, spiratque e pectore flamma."

50.

AST EGO QUÆ DIVUM INCEDO REGINA JOVISQUE
ET SOROR ET CONJUX UNA CUM GENTE TOT ANNOS
BELLA GERO

INCEDO. — "Wird besonders von der feierlichen, würdevollen Haltung im Gange gebraucht; vers. 500, von der Dido, 'Regina incessit.' Ruhnk. zu TERENT. Andr. I. I. 100. Eun. V. 3, 9. Deshalb der majestätischen Juno eigenthümlich, *Ἡραιον βαδιζειν.* Also nicht für *sum,* sondern ganz eigentlich." — THIEL.

"But I who walk in awful state above."
DRYDEN.

"*Incedere* est *ingredi,* sed proprie cum quadam pompa et fastu." — GESNER.

"Incessus dearum, imprimis Junonis, gravitate sua notus.". — HEYNE.

And so also Holdsworth and Ruæus.

I think, on the contrary, that *incedo,* both here and elsewhere, expresses only the stepping or walking motion generally; and that the character of the step or walk, if inferable at all, is to be inferred only from the context. Accordingly, "Magnifice incedit" (LIV. II. 6); "Turpe incedere" (CATULL. *XXXXII. 8*); "Molliter incedit" (OVID, *Amor. II. 23); "Passu incedit inerti" (OVID, *Metam. II. 772);* "Melius est incessu regem quam imperium regno claudicare" (JUSTIN. VI. *II. 6);* "Incessus omnibus animalibus certus et uniusmodi, et in suo, cuique, genere" (PLIN. *X. 38).*

The emphasis, therefore, is not on INCEDO, but on *regina;* and the meaning is, *I who step, or walk,* QUEEN *of the Gods;* the dignity of the step being, not expressed by INCEDO, but inferable from REGINA. The expression corresponds exactly to "ibit regina" *(En. II. 578);* with this difference only, that "ibit" does not, like INCEDO, specify motion on foot.

JOVISQUE ET SOROR ET CONJUX. — Both the *ets* are emphatic. JOVISQUE *et* SOROR *et* CONJUX.

BELLA expresses the organized resistance which she meets, and the uncertainty of the issue; and, being placed first word in the line, is emphatic.

56.

HIC VASTO REX ÆOLUS ANTRO
LUCTANTES VENTOS TEMPESTATESQUE SONORAS
IMPERIO PREMIT AC VINCLIS ET CARCERE FRÆNAT
ILLI INDIGNANTES MAGNO CUM MURMURE MONTIS
CIRCUM CLAUSTRA FREMUNT CELSA SEDET ÆOLUS ARCE
SCEPTRA TENENS MOLLITQUE ANIMOS ET TEMPERAT IRAS
NI FACIAT MARIA AC TERRAS CŒLUMQUE PROFUNDUM
QUIPPE FERANT RAPIDI SECUM VERRANTQUE PER AURAS
SED PATER OMNIPOTENS SPELUNCIS ABDIDIT ATRIS
HOC METUENS MOLEMQUE ET MONTES INSUPER ALTOS
IMPOSUIT REGEMQUE DEDIT QUI FŒDERE CERTO
ET PREMERE ET LAXAS SCIRET DARE JUSSUS HABENAS

CELSA SEDET ÆOLUS ARCE. — "Celsa in arce, extra antrum, alto in montis cacumine, infra (vers. 144) aula dicta, seu regia." — HEYNE.

"*Celsa arx* est domus regia in cacumine montis instructa." — THIEL.

— "Hoch sitzt auf der Zacke bezeptert
Æolus, sänftigt den Geist, und stillt des Zornes Empörung."

VOSS.

"Ed ei lor sopra, realmente adorno
Di corona, e di scettro, in alto assiso,
L'ira, e gl' impeti lor mitiga, e molce."

CARO.

"*Αιολος αιπεινης δ' απο πετρης σκηπτρα χεριζων.*"

DE BULGARIS.

"High in his hall the undaunted monarch stands,
And shakes his sceptre, and their rage commands."

Dryden.

Eolus is not represented sitting with his sceptre in his hand, on the top or on a peak of the mountain within which the winds are confined, because such a picture were little short of ridiculous. Neither is he represented sitting on a throne inside, and in the midst of the winds, both because *arx* cannot well bear such meaning, and because the actual *carcer,* ill-adapted as it was to be the throne-hall of the king, was still less adapted to be the scene of the interview between the king and Juno

Let us see, if, taking the several words of the passage less literally, and therefore (as I think) less prosaically, we do not obtain a meaning free from all difficulty.

Sceptra tenens. — Not *actually holding his sceptre in his hand,* but *invested with regal power,* in possession of the supreme authority, as (Stat. *Theb. I. 140*):

— "ut sceptra tenentem
"Fœdere præcipiti semper novus angeret hæres."

also (Ovid. *Ex Ponto III. 2. 59.*)

Regna Thoas habuit, Mæotide clarus in ora:
Nec fuit Euxinis notior alter aquis.
Sceptra tenente illo, liquidas fecisse per auras,
Nescio quam dicunt Iphigenian iter."

And separately, sceptra (as in *En. I. 82, 257; IV. 597; VII. 252;* and innumerable passages, both of Virgil and other writers), not, literally *sceptre,* but, *supreme dominion;* and tenens (as in verse 143; II. 505, &c.), not, literally *holding in the hand,* but, *possessing.*

Sedet. — Not, literally *sits,* but, *has his residence, or seat,* (the ordinary "Sedem habet") as En. IX. 4, where see Servius.

Arce. — Neither the mountain containing the dungeon of the winds, nor an elevated throne in the dungeon, but, according to the most common use of the word (compare "Fundantem arces," *En. IV. 260:* "Arcem attollere tectis," *En. III. 134:* "Quas condidit arces," *Ecl. II. 61;* "Cum laceras aries ballistave concutit arces," Ovid, *Met. XI. 509*), strong place, stronghold, burg, keep, schloss, castle, royal palace; viz. in the immediate vicinity of the mountain and dungeon.

Mollit animos et temperat iras. — These words, like sedet and tenens, do not refer particularly to any present act of Eolus, to his soothing the winds with his sceptre, or from his throne, but to the general mollifying effect produced on them by their confinement and restraint, under the command of a governor. The words are connected in the sense with the preceding imperio premit ac vinclis et carcere frænat, as if Virgil had said, Premens imperio suo, et frænans vinclis et carcere, mollit animos, &c. And accordingly we are told (verse 62), ni faciat, unless they were thus mollified, not by that special and personal conciliation generally supposed to be expressed by the words, sceptra tenens sedet mollitque, but, by being kept in prison, and under government, they would, in their untamed violence, sweep the whole world before them; to prevent which consummation, hoc metuens, the provident Father of all placed them under the mollifying influence of confinement and a governor. *Mollio* (to soften) is to be carefully distinguished from *mulceo* and *lenio* (to soothe); the latter being to produce a softening effect by soft measures; *mollio,* to produce the softening effect by any measures, no matter how severe or rigorous; in the passage before us, vinclis et carcere. Compare "Dentibus mollitur cibus" (Cicero, *De Nat. Deor. II. 134.*)

"Usque laborantes dum ferrum molliat ignis"
Hor. *Sat. I. IV. 20.*

The whole passage may be resolved into five parts or clauses: the first of which, hic vasto . . . . . frænat, informs us that king Eolus kept the winds confined in a strong cave. The second, illi indignantes ..... fremunt, more particular, presents us with the prisoners impatient to get out, and roaring about the fastenings or enclosing barriers of their prison. The third clause, CELSA . . . . . IRAS, as particular with respect to the governor as the second with respect to the governed, informs us, that he dwells in a strong burg or castle, and that the object and result of his government is the softening or mollifying of the unruly spirits over which he is placed. The fourth clause, NI FACIAT . . . . AURAS, explains the necessity for these precautionary measures of the Eternal Father. And, finally, in the fifth clause, SED PATER . . . . DEDIT, there is a resumé of the measures, followed by the important corollary, QUI . . . HABENAS (serving as a connecting link between the whole previous description, and the request made by Juno), that the governor had authority to let out his prisoners as occasion required.

In the opinion, that the *arx* of Eolus was separate and distinct from the cavern of the winds, I am supported by the authority of Quintus Calaber, who describes Eolus as going out of his house to the cavern: —

> *Ικετο δ'Αιολιην, ανεμων οθι λαβρον αεντων*
> *Αντρα πελει, στυγερησιν αρηραμεν αμφι πετρησι,*
> *κοιλα και ηχηεντα. δομοι δ'εγχιστα πελονται*
> *Αιολου Ιπποταδαο. κιχεν δε μιν ενδον εοντα*
> *συν τ'αλοχω, και παισι δυωκαιδεκα. και οι εειπεν,*
> *Οπως Αθηναιη Δαναων επιμηδετο νοστω.*
> *Αυταρ ογ' ουκ απιθησε, μολων δ'εκτοσθε μελαθρων,*
> *χερσιν υπ' ακαματοισιν ορος μεγα τυψε τριαινη,*
> *ενθ' ανεμοι κελαδεινοι δυσηχεες ηυλιζοντο,*
> * * * * * * * *
> *βια δ'ερρηξε κολωνην.*
>
> QUINT. CALAB. *XIV. 473.*

and by that of Ovid, whose palace of Eolus *(Heroid. XI. 65)*, has no one character even in the most remote degree indicating an identity with the prison of the winds.

I beg to submit the above, I believe entirely new, explanation of the whole passage, in place not only of the explanations given by previous Virgilian commentators, but in place of that proposed by myself in the 19th No. of the Classical Museum & quoted from that Periodical with conditional approbation by Forbiger in his 3rd Edition.

CLAUSTRA. — Neither, with Caro, *the inclosed place, or prison itself* (chiostri); nor, with Heyne and Forbiger, *the vents or openings* (spiracula); but, primarily and literally, *the locks or other fastenings*, and therefore, secondarily, *the doors or other barriers* by which the passage out was closed (clausum), and made fast. I do not find an instance of *claustra* used in any other sense. The Italians, indeed, designate a place kept locked, or secured by claustra, *chiostri* (cloisters); but such application of the term seems to have been unknown to the classic writers.

Therefore, CIRCUM CLAUSTRA, *about the fastenings*, i. e. about the fast-closed barriers or gates, in momentary expectation of their being opened. Compare:

"Non aliter, moto quam si pater Æolus antro
Portam iterum saxo premat imperiosus, et omne
Claudat iter, jam jam sperantibus æquora ventis."

STAT. *Theb. X. 246.*

"Subtexit nox atra polos; jam claustra rigentis
Æolia percussa sonant, venturaque rauco
Ore minatur hiems."

STAT. *Theb. I. 346.*

— "Sex reserata diebus
Carceris Æolii janua laxa patet."

OVID. *Fasti II. 455.*

ABDIDIT. — "Verbarg." — Voss. No; but, *stowed away*, put away in a place apart, or by themselves: first, because the idea of *hiding* is, notwithstanding the contrary opinion of the lexicographers, foreign from this word, which always means simply *putting away, apart,* (ab-do); compare "abde domo" *(Georg III. 96)*; "lateri capulo tenus abdidit ensem" *(En. II. 553)*, &c. &c.; and secondly, because it was plainly Jupiter's intention to put the winds, not, in a place where they could not be readily seen or found, but, merely in a safe place apart.

73.

INCUTE VIM VENTIS SUBMERSASQUE OBRUE PUPPES

Servius having left his successors their choice between two interpretations of this passage, either to understand VIM to mean strength, and VENTIS the object to which the strength was to be given ("I venti innaspra." ALFIERI.), or to understand VIM to mean violence, and VENTIS to be the instrument by means of which the violence was to be inflicted, viz. on the Trojan fleet, Ruæus, Heyne, Voss and most other commentators have made choice of the former interpretation; I very much prefer the latter; first, because I think *incutio* generally expresses something of aggression or hostility, and therefore although perfectly correct to say *incute metum, terrorem, iram,* into a person or thing, it were less correct to say INCUTE VIM, where no violence or harm of any kind is intended towards the recipient of the *vim.* Secondly, because even if the expression were perfectly unobjectionable, yet the two successive attacks, first on the winds in order to drive or as we might say knock (incutere) power into them, and then, with the winds so strengthened, on Eneas's fleet in order to sink it, were, as it seems to me at least, if not absolutely awkward, certainly not very elegant; thirdly, it is not probable that Juno having taken the utmost pains in the two immediately preceding lines to rivet the attention of Eolus upon his prey, would in the words INCUTE VIM VENTIS, abruptly call off his attention from it in order to fix it upon the winds, in order to inform him what he had first to do with them, before he could be in a fit condition to spring upon the game. How much more probable that she said: — A nation, with whom I am at war, is sailing at this moment on the Tuscan sea; attack them with your winds, sink them or scatter them, &c.

For all these reasons I give a decided preference to Servius's second interpretation, already justified by him by the authority of Ennius, and confirmed as I think by Ovid's

"Improba pugnat hiems, indignaturque quod ausim
Scribere, se rigidas incutiente minas."

Trist. I. II. 41.

If Ovid does not use too bold an expression, when he causes the storm *incutere minas* against him, i. e. against the vessel in which he was sailing, how far from bold is it in Virgil to make the storm *incutere vim* against the fleet of Eneas!

78.

OMNES UT TECUM MERITIS PRO TALIBUS ANNOS
EXIGAT

"Livia sic tecum sociales compleat annos."

OVID. *Trist. II. 161.*

82.

TU MIHI QUODCUNQUE HOC REGNI TU SCEPTRA JOVEMQUE
CONCILIAS TU DAS EPULIS ACCUMBERE DIVUM
NIMBORUMQUE FACIS TEMPESTATUMQUE POTENTEM

"Tuis in me officiis debeo totum hoc ventorum regnum." — WAGNER. *Virg. Br. En.*

"Du hast diese Gewalt, du Jupiters Huld und den Zepter
Mir ja verschafft."

VOSS.

"These airy kingdoms, and this wide command,
Are all the presents of your bounteous hand."

DRYDEN.

No; but the very contrary: *this petty domain of mine;* this domain of mine, such as it is. Compare:

"Tu decus hoc quodcunque lyræ, primusque dedisti
Non vulgare loqui, et famam sperare sepulchro."

STAT. *Silv. V. III. 213.*

TU, TU, TU. — The second person, generally not expressed at all, repeated here three times, is in the highest degree emphatic.

85.

HÆC UBI DICTA CAVUM CONVERSA CUSPIDE MONTEM
IMPULIT IN LATUS

"Egregie dei et potentia et impetuosum obsequium declaratur, uno sub ictu monte non (ut olim accipiebam) in latus dimoto, verum latere montis percusso hasta dei, perrupto et sic patefacto" . . . . "hastam intorquet, immittit, ruptaque rupe viam ventis facit qua erumpant." — HEYNE.

"Ictu sceptri partem montis in latus versus protrudit, ut foramine, hiatu facto, omnes venti simul prorumpere possint." — FORBIGER.

— "Al cavernoso monte
Con lo scettro d'un urto il fianco aperse."

CARO.

— "Hurled against the mountain side
His quivering spear, and all the God applied."

DRYDEN.

"Zum hohlen Gebirg' hinwendend die Spitze
Schlug er die Seit'."

VOSS.

IMPULIT. — "Contorsit." — GESNER.

To all these interpretations there seem to me to be these two decisive general objections: first, that the cave being provided with *claustra* (see verse 60, and Comment), the violent breaking it open, either by pushing the mountain to one side, or by making a breach in its *parietes*, was uncalled for, and in direct violation of the poetic maxim:

"Nec Deus intersit nisi dignus vindice nodus."

Secondly, that it is very unlikely that the poet who describes at such length the forcing open of the door of Priam's palace by Pyrrhus, and of the cave of Cacus by Hercules, would have disposed of Eolus's either removing the whole mountain from its base, or breaking by main force into its cavity, as briefly, in the very same terms, and with no greater emphasis than he might have described the pushing open of a common door.

I therefore reject all these explanations, and, following the strict grammatical construction, understand the meaning to be, *Pushed the hollow mountain on the side with his spear turned towards it;* i. e. turned his spear towards the hollow mountain's side, and pushed the hollow mountain's side with it. See Comm. *En. II. 131.*

CUSPIDE MONTEM IMPULIT. — Not, *flung* his spear against the mountain, because in the few instances which are to be found of *impellere* used in this sense, the object flung is always put in the accusative, not the ablative. Compare:

— "Inque meos ferrum flammasque penates
Impulit."

Ovid, *Metam. XII. 551.*

"Telum ingens avide, et quanto non ante lacerto
Impulit."

Stat. *Theb. VIII. 684.*

but, simply, and conformably with the ordinary meaning of the term, *pushed* the mountain with his spear.

— "Et dextra discedens impulit altam,
Haud ignara modi, puppim"

En. X. 246.

Cavum montem. — The hollow mountain, i. e. that part of the hollow mountain where the *claustra* were, or which formed the *claustra;* this new term being used, not merely for the sake of variety, but to avoid minute particularization.

In latus. — Not, *sideways,* or *to one side,* as (Stat. *Theb. IX. 80*), "Sese dominumque retorsit in latus," but, *on its side,* as *(En. XII. 505),* "Æneas Rutulum Sucronem . . . . excipit in latus;" takes him on the side; wounds him in the side, and so, correctly, De Bulgaris: "*Τυψε πλευροθεν.*" The expression, *latus montis* occurs again in Georg. *IV. 418,* and, as it happens, in connexion with a cave:

— "Est specus ingens
Exesi latere in montis;"

also in Silius Italicus *(IV. 524):*

"Avulsum montis volvit latus."

Conversa. — *Turned towards the mountain;* or, as we would say, with his spear levelled against the mountain. So:

— "In me convertite ferrum."
En. IX. 427.

"Video P. C. in me omnium vestrum ora atque oculos esse conversos." — Cic. in *Catal. IV. 1.*

In confirmation of the above analysis, I may observe further: first, that *impellere* is the word specially employed both by Virgil himself elsewhere and by other Latin writers to express the forcible pushing, or throwing open, of gates or other barriers. See En. VII. 621:

— "Impulit ipsa manu portas."

where observe the exact parallelism, manu portas; cuspide montem; also:

— "Impulsæ patuere fores."
Sil. Ital. III. 693.

and Burmann, ad *Valer. Flacc.* I. 610. And secondly, that it appears from the representations on ancient marbles (see article *Circus* in Smith's Dict. of Greek and Roman Antiquities) that the *carceres* of the circus (of which those of the winds are plainly, as I shall show in Comment on verse 86, an adumbration) were thrown open by forcibly pushing from without inwards.

If it be objected to the whole of the preceding interpretation, that not only Quintus Calaber (see Comment, verse 56), but Statius *(Theb. VI. 108)*, and other Latin poets, represent the cave of the winds as actually broken into, I reply, that in this case, as in so many others, either there were more versions of the story than one, or Virgil's better judgment taught him not to adhere too closely to what was absurd or preposterous in the one only version.

86.

AC VENTI VELUT AGMINE FACTO
QUA DATA PORTA RUUNT ET TERRAS TURBINE PERFLANT

For the sake of rapidity, Virgil connects the rushing forth of the winds immediately with the push of Eolus's spear: IMPULIT AC VENTI. An inferior poet would, no doubt, have told us that the effect of the push was to throw open the barriers, and that, on the barriers being thrown open, the winds immediately rushed forth.*

Compare En. II. 259 where Sinon "laxat claustra," undoes the fastenings, and immediately "patefactus

* This, as I have found since the above commentary was written (in 1852), has been actually done by Alfieri in his translation:

"Disse, e coll' asta al suol rivolta, un cavo
Masso respinse all' un de' canti: appena
Schiusa tal porta, impetuosa fuori
Sgorga dei venti la feroce squadra."

J. H. 1853.

equus" (observe the actual opening of the door and how or by whom opened, is passed over sub silentio for the sake of rapidity) "reddit illos ad auras." Compare also:

> — "Atque illam media inter talia ferro
> Collapsam aspiciunt comites."
>
> *En. IV. 663.*

and Comm.

There can, I think, be little doubt that the whole of this fine picture of the winds indignantly roaring about the *claustra* of the *carcer* in which they are confined, and, upon the opening of those *claustra*, rushing out, and furiously sweeping over land and sea, was suggested to Virgil by the chariot-races of the Ludi Circenses, in which the horses, ready yoked, were kept confined, until the moment of starting, within a *carcer*, separated only from the *spatia* of the circus by *claustra*, for the opening of which the horses used to be seen testifying their impatience by neighing and snorting, and pawing against them with their feet, and on the opening of which they rushed forth (AGMINE FACTO), two, three, or four chariots abreast, and swept the *spatia* with the impetuosity of the whirlwind.

In proof of the correctness of this opinion, I beg the reader, first, to observe, that almost all the words of the description, and notably the words *luctantes, imperio premit, frænat, fremunt, mollit animos, temperat iras, ferant rapidi secum, verrant per auras,* are suitable to the manege; secondly, to refer to *Val. Flaccus* (I. 611), where, in a manifest copy of the scene before us, he will find the winds to be styled, in express terms, *horses rushing from the carcer,* "Fundunt se carcere læti Thraces *equi,* Zephyrusque," &c.; and, thirdly, to compare Virgil's whole description with the description which Sidonius Apollinaris *(Ad Consentium)* has given of the chariot-race:

"Illi (viz. the horses) ad claustra (carceris, viz.)
fremunt, repagulisque
Incumbunt simul, ac per obseratas
Transfumant tabulas, et ante cursum
Campus flatibus occupatur absens:
Impellunt, trepidant, trahunt, repugnant,
Ardescunt, saliunt, timent, timentur,
Nec gressum cohibent, sed inquieto
Duratum pede stipitem flagellant;
Tandem murmure buccinæ strepentis,
Suspensas tubicen vocans quadrigas
Effundit celeres in arva currus;
Non sic fulminis impetus trisulci," &c.

Let him compare, also, Ovid, Metam. II. 153; Lucret. VI. 194; Stat. Theb. VI. 397, et seq.; and Virgil himself, En. V. 144.

Hence new grace and beauty to the whole passage, and proof additional to those adduced above, that the winds were let loose, not through a breach made in the mountain, but through the accustomed *claustra*.

88.

INCUBUERE MARI TOTUMQUE A SEDIBUS IMIS
UNA EURUSQUE NOTUSQUE RUUNT CREBERQUE PROCELLIS
AFRICUS ET VASTOS VOLVUNT AD LITTORA FLUCTUS
INSEQUITUR CLAMORQUE VIRUM STRIDORQUE RUDENTUM
ERIPIUNT SUBITO NUBES CŒLUMQUE DIEMQUE
TEUCRORUM EX OCULIS PONTO NOX INCUBAT ATRA
INTONUERE POLI ET CREBRIS MICAT IGNIBUS ÆTHER

The double action of the winds on the sea is well indicated in this passage.

First, they fall with force, and press on its surface (INCUBUERE) vertically, from above downwards; (compare:

"Incubuere vadis passim discrimine nullo
Turba simul, primique."

STAT. *Theb. IV. 809.*)

forcing their way into it, and, as it were, making a hole in it, and so raising and forcing it up on all sides round: A SEDIBUS IMIS RUUNT.

And secondly, they roll billows to the shores, VOLVUNT AD LITTORA FLUCTUS; such billows being the effect, partly of their direct blowing, and partly of the subsidence of the water from the height to which it had been thrown up by their violent vertical descent; compare *(Georg. II. 310)*:

> "Præsertim si tempestas a vertice silvis
> Incubuit."

where Fea: — "Piomba dall' alto. Arato presso Cicerone (*De Nat. Deor. II. 44.)*

> "Quem summa ab regione Aquilonis flamina pulsant."

Omero referito ma non capito dal Guellio, meglio lo spiega Aulo Gellio *(Lib. II c. 30)*. Venti ab septentrionibus, ex altiore cœli parte in mare incidentes, deorsum in aquarum profunda quasi præcipites deferuntur, undasque faciunt non prorsus impulsas, sed vi intus commotas."

UNA EURUSQUE NOTUSQUE RUUNT CREBERQUE PROCELLIS AFRICUS. —

> — "Nor slept the winds
> Within their stony caves, but rushed abroad
> From the four hinges of the world, and fell
> On the vexed wilderness."
>
> MILTON. *Par. Reg. IV.*

UNA. — Highly emphatic, being placed first word in the line, and repeating the idea already expressed in AGMINE FACTO.

INCUBUERE; INSEQUITUR; ERIPIUNT; INTONUERE. — In order to impart the greatest possible energy to the action, each verb not only contains an intensive particle, but is placed at the commencement of a line, and precedes its nominative. At *vv.* 108 — 109, where the action is still energetic, a similar structure is observable: Franguntur remi; Insequitur mons. And at *v.* 184, where the action is peaceable, exactly the opposite: Æneas conscendit, petit, videat, prospicit; armenta sequuntur, longum pascitur; Æneas constitit, corripuit; fidus gerebat; Æneas sternit, miscet, absistit, fundat, æquet, petit, partitur; bonus onerarat, dederat; Æneas dividit, mulcet. And verse 230: Jupiter constitit, defixit; tristior alloquitur; qui regis, terres; Æneas, Troes potuere; cunctus clauditur; qui tenerent; sententia vertit; fortuna insequitur; Antenor potuit. Then again, in It mare, the change to the rapid construction, indicative of the change to the rapid action; and finally, the placid construction in the placid and final compostus quiescit.

96.

EXTEMPLO ÆNEÆ SOLVUNTUR FRIGORE MEMBRA

The first ground which has been assigned for this extreme emotion of Eneas (considered by many as cowardly and unworthy of Virgil's hero; see in Sir Walter Scott's edition of the Somers Tracts, vol. XII. p. 10, a Tract entitled, "Verdicts of the learned concerning Virgil's and Homer's Heroic Poems"), is that which is expressed in the following lines of Ronsard's Franciade* (c. 2):

> "Hà tu devois en la Troyenne guerre
> Faire couler mon cerveau contre terre,
> Sans me sauver par une feinte ainsi,
> Pour me trahir a ce cruel souci;
> J'eusse eu ma part aux tombeaux de mes peres;
> Ou je n' atten que ces vagues ameres
> Pour mon sepulchre."

* One of those innumerable, once fashionable, but now forgotten poems, which the poetasters of some two hundred years ago used to manufacture out of the Eneis, and pass upon the world as original

To this ground there seems to me to be these two objections: first, that it is insufficient; and secondly, that it is contradicted by verses 104 and 105, which show that Eneas knew that, even if he had died on the plains of Troy, it was by no means certain that his body would have had burial.

The other ground which has been assigned for Eneas's emotion, viz. the reflection that death by shipwreck was death lost and thrown away, death redounding neither to his own honour, nor to the advantage of his country or the world, is probably the true one, because in accordance with the heroic character, with the words of the hero himself, and with the sentiments ascribed to other heroes on similar occasions. See in the Homeric text, of which the passage before us is an almost literal translation:

Τω κ' ελαχον κτερεων, και μεν κλεος ηγον Αχαιοι·
Νυν δε με λευγαλεω θανατω ειμαρτο αλωναι.
Odyss. V. 313.

Compare also Senec. Agam. 518:

"Nil nobile ausos pontus atque undæ ferent?
Ignava fortes fata consument viros?
Perdenda mors est."

And Hercul. Œtæus, 1165: Hercules speaking, —

"Morior, nec ullus per meum stridet latus
Transmissus ensis . . . . . .
. . . . , perdidi mortem, hei mihi!
Toties honestam."

works of their own. It is impossible not to be struck by the resemblance between those professedly original poems, but really semi-translations of the Eneis, and our modern professed translations but really semi-original poems. Both are composed altogether *ad captum vulgi;* in the same easy, flowing, and often sweet style, and with the same total, either ignorance or disregard, of Virgil's meaning; the sole difference between them being the greater antiquity of the language of the former, and such change in the names of the actors, and in the places, times, and order of action, as was necessary to give to the former some colour of originality. — J. H.

If we consider, besides, that it was not his own death alone which Eneas saw impending, but the total destruction of all his surviving friends, and of the last hopes of Troy, we shall, I think, be convinced that nothing could be more becoming or more natural than his deep emotion and pathetic exclamation, — "Better I had died by the hands of my noble enemy on the plains of Troy, fighting bravely for my country before the eyes of my sires, than have lived to see this day, and to meet this fate."

103.

SÆVUS UBI ÆACIDÆ TELO JACET HECTOR UBI INGENS SARPEDON

Observe how the poet surmounts the obvious difficulty of uniting Hector, the principal champion of Troy, and Sarpedon, the son of Jove, in one and the same sentence, without implying a preference for either, without exalting one at the expense of the other; viz., by counterbalancing, by an inferior position towards the end of a line, that advantage of priority of mention, which he must necessarily give to one of them; and by compensating the other for the disadvantage of being placed second in order, by the double advantage of first place in a line, and separation from the rest of the line by a sudden pause.

104.

UBI TOT SIMOIS CORREPTA SUB UNDIS
SCUTA VIRUM GALEASQUE ET FORTIA CORPORA VOLVIT

"Contendit cum Homero *(Il. μ. 22 seq.)*. Potest sane oratio nimis ornata videri ex Eneæ persona; sed innumeris locis poetæ cum epici, tum tragici ac lyrici, sibi indulgent in ornatu, etiam ubi alios loquentes inducunt." — HEYNE.

This stricture, very seasonable in a commentary on Statius or Lucan, is wholly inapplicable to Virgil, a poet remarkable, above all others, for his abstinence from gaudy ornament, and singularly careful to adapt the sentiment to the character and circumstances of the speaker. The words in the text, or some similar words, were indispensable to give full expression to the idea of Eneas; very imperfectly understood either by the annotators, or, with the exception of Caro, by the translators: *Happy those who died on the plains of Troy, in the sight of their sires! O that I, too, had perished there by the hand of Tydides, or been swept away along with so many of my friends by the Simois!*

In justice to the Manes of Virgil, I shall place in juxta-position with this and two other passages, also in the first book of the Eneis, their English representatives; I say their English representatives, because Dryden's may be truly regarded as the only translation of Virgil which is known or read in England. The literal English of the lines in the text is: *Where Simois rolls so many shields and helmets and brave bodies of heroes, snatched under his waves.* There is not one word more or less or different from these in the original; now hear Dryden: —

> "Where Simois rolls the bodies and the shields
> Of heroes, whose dismembered hands yet bear
> The dart aloft, and clench the pointed spear."

Again, *v.* 170: —

> "Fronte sub adversa scopulis pendentibus antrum;
> Intus aquæ dulces vivoque sedilia saxo,
> Nympharum domus.

Under the opposite front, a cave with hanging crags; within, sweet water, and seats of the living stone; house of the nymphs. Hear Dryden: —

"A grot is formed beneath with mossy seats,
To rest the Nereids and exclude the heats,
Down through the crannies of the living walls
The crystal streams descend in murmuring falls."

Once more, *v.* 420:

— "Ubi templum illi, centumque Sabæo
Ture calent aræ sertisque recentibus halant."

Where a temple and hundred altars glow for her, and breathe of fresh garlands. Hear Dryden:

"Where garlands ever green and ever fair
With vows are offered and with solemn prayer;
A hundred altars in her temple smoke,
A thousand bleeding hearts her power invoke."

Such, from beginning to end, with scarcely the exception of a single line, is Dryden's translation of the Eneis — "the most noble and spirited translation," says Pope, "which I know in any language" — that translation, whose very announcement, we are informed by Sir W. Scott (see his Life of Dryden), put all literary England into a ferment of expectation — that translation which Johnson tells us, "satisfied Dryden's friends, and for the most part, silenced his enemies" — that translation which, up to the present day, is the only recognised representative at the court of English Literature, of the sweet, modest, elegant, and always correct muse of Virgil.

106.

TALIA JACTANTI STRIDENS AQUILONE PROCELLA
VELUM ADVERSA FERIT FLUCTUSQUE AD SIDERA TOLLIT
FRANGUNTUR REMI TUM PRORA AVERTIT ET UNDIS
DAT LATUS INSEQUITUR CUMULO PRÆRUPTUS AQUÆ MONS
HI SUMMO IN FLUCTU PENDENT HIS UNDA DEHISCENS
TERRAM INTER FLUCTUS APERIT FURIT ÆSTUS ARENIS

ADVERSA, right in front: in nautical language, *aback.*

INSEQUITUR CUMULO PRÆRUPTUS AQUÆ MONS. — "Præruptus propter altitudinem cumulatæ aquæ." Heyne. No:

Wunderlich is right, that CUMULO depends on INSEQUITUR not on PRÆRUPTUS, for I find no instance of an ablative joined to the latter, while on the other hand the junction of an ablative with the former is of common occurrence. Insequitur lumine: OVID. Metam. XI. 468. Bello insequitur: En. VIII. 146. Infesto vulnere Pyrrhus insequitur: En. II. 529. Morsibus insequitur: OVID. Metam. XIII. 568. And so, INSEQUITUR CUMULO: pursues *with* a heaped up pile of water; i. e. threatening to overwhelm, but not actually overwhelming; as fully shown by the manner in which the thought is carried out: HI SUMMO IN FLUCTU PENDENT, HIS UNDA DEHISCENS; where there is a transition from the single ship of Eneas, and the single mountain wave impending over it, to the entire fleet, some of the vessels of which are similarly situated with the vessel of Eneas, while others are in the exactly opposite situation, i. e. riding on the top of the wave.

Voss and Caro are therefore entirely wrong:

— "Und es stürzt das gebrochene Wassergebirg' ein."
VOSS.

— "E d' acqua un monte intanto
Venne come dal cielo a cader giu."
CARO.

Compare OVID. Metam. XV. 508:

"Cum mare surrexit, cumulusque immanis aquarum
In montis speciem curvari et crescere visus,"

where *cumulus* is the heaped up rising or swelling, not the bursting, pile of water.

FLUCTUS AD SIDERA TOLLIT; INSEQUITUR CUMULO; PRÆRUPTUS AQUÆ MONS; SUMMO IN FLUCTU; PENDENT; are all only different phases of the one idea; the correlative idea begins at HIS UNDA DEHISCENS. FURIT ÆSTUS ARENIS is the complement of the two ideas united. The tumbling in of one of these mountain billows on one of the vessels, and the consequent sinking of the vessel, is described at verse 117.

HIS UNDA DEHISCENS TERRAM INTER FLUCTUS APERIT FURIT ÆSTUS ARENIS. — "Hiante unda et apparente terra vident in imo arenam æstuantem, ac ferventem." — LA CERDA.

"ARENIS; recte Wunderlich explicat in fundo maris, coll. OVID. Metam. XI. 499." — WAGNER.

"ARENIS; auf dem Meeresboden, nicht am Ufer." — THIEL.

— "Dort sinkenden öffnet
Tief die zerlechzende Woge das Land, und es siedet der
Schlamm auf."

VOSS.

— "Ζειε δε αμμος."

DE BULGARIS.

— "Mostra giu il bollente
Letto arenoso suo."

ALFIERI.

— "Or a quei s'apre la terra
Fra due liquidi monti, ove l' arena
Non men ch' a i liti si raggira, e ferve."

CARO.

"Through gaping waves behold the boiling deep."

DRYDEN.

All, as I think, highly incorrect; the last, downright nonsense.

ÆSTUS. — Unless when a *hot* liquid is spoken of, *seething* or *boiling* is a sense foreign from this word, which always means the swell or increment or acme of something which increases progressively, and then progressively diminishes again. "Æstus solis et æstivi temporis flagrantia:" (FEST. *ap. Non. IV. 40*); not, as commonly understood, the heat of the sun, but, if I may so express myself, the swell, or high tide of the sun, or of the sun's heat; i. e. when the temperature is just reaching the maximum. "Propiusque æstus incendia volvunt" *(En. II. 706)*, the conflagration rolls, not the heat nearer, but, its swelling tide nearer. "Jamjam absumor; conficit animam Vis vulneris, ulceris æstus" (CICERO, translating from Sophocles; *Tusc. Quæst.*

II. 7); not, with Gesner, dolor fluctuans, but, the increasing, swelling pain; the tide, acme, or exacerbation of pain. "Sæpe homines ægri, morbo gravi, quum æstu febrique jactantur" (Cic. *Catal. I. 13.*); not the heat, but the paroxysm, access, exacerbation, fit, high tide, of the disease. "Æstus cum ex alto se incitavisset quod bis semper accidit duodecim horarum spatio" (Cæs. *B. G. III. 12*). "Æstus maris accedere et reciprocare, maxime mirum" (Plin. *II. 97).* "Labitur alta secans fluctuque æstuque secundo" *En. X. 687.* The height or acme of the sea; the tide, properly so called. And so in our text, furit æstus, the tide rages; the swelling, tiding sea rages.

Furit arenis. — Rages, not *on* the sands, but, *with* the sands; pulls the sands violently about with it; its rage is so much the more terrible on account of the drifting quicksands which it sets in motion and carries with it. (Æstu miscentur arenæ: *En. III. 557.*) Compare: Ense furens (Valer. Flacc. *I. 144.*); Furentem cæde Neoptolemum *(En. II. 499*). As ense and cæde, added to furens, in these passages, define and enhance the fury of Æson and Neoptolemus, informing us that the former was using his sword, and that the latter was slaughtering all before him, so arenis, in our text, defines and enhances the fury of the sea, informing us that it moved and carried with it the shoaling sands. The allusion is to the Syrtes, the scene of the action, which derived their name from this very liability to be displaced and set in motion by the sea in a storm: "Nam ubi mare magnum esse et sævire cœpit ventis, limum arenamque et saxa ingentia fluctus trahunt; ita facies locorum cum ventis simul mutatur: Syrtes ab tractu nominatæ." — Sall. *Bell. Jugurth. c. 80.* Virgil's *furere arenis* is Sallust's sævire, et trahere arenam.

Compare also Juvenal's cognate expression: Sævire flagellis *(X. 180);* Virgil's own Sævit animis: *(vers. 153);* and stridens aquilone procella, (verse 106, above); Phlegethonta furentem ardentibus undis *(Culex, 270)*; Furit stridoribus: *(Culex, 177)*; and exactly parallel to, and coincident with our text, Valerius Flaccus's Quâ brevibus furit æstus aquis: *(II. 615)*.

FURIT ÆSTUS ARENIS. — The connexion of these words is not with the immediately preceding semi-clause, — HIS UNDA DEHISCENS TERRAM INTER FLUCTUS APERIT which would give the jejune meaning found in the passage by La Cerda and the other expositors "Vident in imo arenam æstuantem ac ferventem," but with the *whole* clause: HI SUMMO IN FLUCTU PENDENT, HIS UNDA DEHISCENS TERRAM INTER FLUCTUS APERIT, of which clause they are the complement, filling up and completing the fine picture; thus: — These vessels here, hang on the crest or ridge of the wave, while those there, descend almost to the ground at the bottom of the trough; the ridge is high, and the trough deep, because the sea is at its acme, i. e. the tide full and swelling; and the raging of the sea is the more terrible on account of the quicksands which it has set in motion and carries along with it. The catastrophe follows at verse 116:

> "Illiditque vadis, atque aggere cingit arenæ."

114.

DORSUM IMMANE MARI SUMMO TRES EURUS AB ALTO
IN BREVIA ET SYRTES URGET

DORSUM. — A reef.

ALTO. — As the adjective *altus* signifies properly neither *height* nor *depth*, but *perpendicular distance*, which may be either *upwards* (suspiciens altam Lunam: *En. IX. 403)*; *downwards* (cum terra araretur, et sulcus altius esset impressus: CIC. *de Divin. II. 23.)*;

or *inwards* (Ferrum haud alte in corpus descendisse: Liv. *I. 41); so altum,* taken substantively, and applied to the sea, is properly neither the ***high sea*** (i. e. the sea considered solely in respect of the height of its surface *above its bottom)*, nor the ***deep sea*** (i. e. the sea considered solely in reference to the *depth of its bottom below the surface*), but (if I may invent a term where the English language possesses none), the ***deep-height*** or the ***high-deep***, i. e. the sea considered in reference to the *perpendicular distance between its two surfaces.* In numerous instances, where (as in the passage before us, and En. I. 7; III. 11) there is no occasion that the reader should be specially informed of the *depth* of the water below the surface; this interpretation (viz. *high-deep*), will, I think, be found to accord better with the context than the ordinarily received interpretation, *the deep.* I may observe, besides, that, unless in this word, the Romans possessed no term for the idea which modern nations express by the terms, *high sea, high water, high flood, high tide, high river, das hohe Meer, die hohe See, &c.*

In brevia et syrtes. — I. e. in brevia syrtium. See En V. 220: In scopulo alto brevibusque vadis.

120.

AST ILLAM TER FLUCTUS IBIDEM
TORQUET AGENS CIRCUM ET RAPIDUS VORAT ÆQUORE VORTEX

"Tre volte il fe' girar con tutte l'acque;
Alla quarta levar la poppa in suso,
E la prora ire in giu, com' altrui piacque,
Infin che 'l mar fu sopra noi richiuso."

Dante, *Infern. XXVI. 139.*

122.

APPARENT RARI NANTES IN GURGITE VASTO
ARMA VIRUM TABULÆQUE ET TROIA GAZA PER UNDAS

"Conspiciuntur passim nantes et arma, h. e. clypei." — Heyne.

"Rings nun schwimmen umher sparsam in unendlicher Meerflut
Waffen des Kriegs und Gebälk und troischer Pomp durch die Brandung."

Voss.

"Gia per l'ondoso mar disperse e rare,
Le navi, e i naviganti si vedevano:
Gia per tutto di Troja a l'onde in preda
Arme, tavole, arnesi a nuoto andavano."

Caro.

"And here and there above the waves were seen
Arms, pictures, precious goods, and floating men."

Dryden.

Not one represents Virgil's meaning; which is, that only an odd swimmer was to be seen here and there (the others having gone to the bottom), while the whole water was thickly strewed with ARMA VIRUM, TABULÆ, ET TROIA GAZA. Compare (Stat. *Theb. IX. 263*):

"Summa vagis late sternuntur flumina telis,
Ima viris."

Rari in gurgite vasto stands in direct contrast with per undas *(everywhere over the water)*. Compare *per antrum: En. III. 631 (everywhere through the cave; through the whole length and breadth of the cave)*. Rari belongs to nantes only; and nantes refers only to the persons. The structure is, *apparent rari nantes in gurgite vasto; apparent fluitantia per undas arma virum tabulæque et Troja gaza*. And so, correctly (with the exception of his interpretation of tabulæ) De Bulgaris:

"Παυροι απειρεσιη δ' εν δινη ορoωντο νεοντες.
Καδ' δ' υδατων οπλα, και πινακες, και γαζα δε Τρωων."

The punctuation of N. Heinsius, Alfieri and the Baskerville should therefore be adopted:

"Apparent rari nantes in gurgite vasto;
Arma virum tabulæque et Troia gaza per undas."

It appears from Foggini that there is in the Medicean a point at VASTO; but the punctuation in that MS is so carelessly performed that unless where it is collaterally supported, great stress cannot safely be laid on it: in proof of which assertion I need only inform the reader, that there is also a point placed after ARMA in that MS.

ARMA VIRUM. — VIRUM added to ARMA (in the same way as *Martis* to the same word, verse 4, where see Comment), shows that the arms meant are no other than those of the warriors themselves, and not, as might possibly, except for this adjunct, have been understood, arms fixed up in the vessel by way of ensign or ornament; still less the oars or other nautical tackling, which (See Comm. *En. V. 15)* were often called *arma.* It is, no doubt, of these same ARMA VIRUM, necessarily laid aside by their owners when they went on board, and began to act as rowers and sailors, and, most probably, hung up out of the way on the aplustre, steersman's baraque, and bulwarks of the vessel, that our author speaks at verse 187, in the words:

— "aut celsis in puppibus arma Caici."

Also, En. VIII. 92:

"Miratur nemus insuetum fulgentia lònge
Scuta virum fluvio pictasque innare carinas."

And En. X. 80:

"Pacem orare manu, præfigere puppibus arma."

TABULÆ. — Not *the planks of the vessel* (for the vessel had not gone to pieces, but foundered and gone down whole), and still less *pictures;* but, *the boards of* such fragile and unessential parts as *the benches of the rowers, steersman's baraque and the aplustre or peaked and lofty taffrel* (for representations of both which, see Vatic. Fragm. apud Bartholi, P. 57. 101. 103. 129. also Smith's Dictionary of Greek and Roman Antiquities: articles Antennæ, Anchora, and Aplustre). How frail these parts were, and how liable to be washed overboard, and to be seen floating about in the water, appears from numerous passages in various writers:

"Per terrarum omneis oras fluitantia aplustra."

Lucr. *II. 556.*

— "Jamque per undas
Et transtra, et mali, laceroque aplustria velo,
Ac miseri fluitant revomentes æquora nautæ."

Sil. Ital. *X. 324.*

"Navibus absumptis fluitantia quærere aplustra."

Cicero's Aratus, *apud Priscian.*

"Inconcussa vehit tranquillus aplustria flatus;
Mollia securo vela rudente tremunt."

Rutilius. *Itin. I. 513.*

where the exception proves the rule, as well as from Virgil himself *(En. V. 858):*

"Et superincumbens cum puppis parte revulsa
Cumque gubernaculo liquidas projecit in undas;"

where the very extremity of the vessel, consisting of the steersman's baraque and the aplustre, is meant, and not that solid part which we are in the habit of denominating poop, or quarter; the breaking off of an integral portion of which could not have been occasioned by the fall of a single man, or, if it could, must have involved the loss of the vessel.

Compare Ovid. *Trist. I. 6. 7:*

"Tu facis ut spolium ne sim, neu nuder ab illis
Naufragii tabulas qui petiere mei."

128.

INTEREA MAGNO MISCERI MURMURE PONTUM
EMISSAMQUE HIEMEM SENSIT NEPTUNUS ET IMIS
STAGNA REFUSA VADIS GRAVITER COMMOTUS ET ALTO
PROSPICIENS SUMMA PLACIDUM CAPUT EXTULIT UNDA
DISJECTAM ÆNEÆ TOTO VIDET ÆQUORE CLASSEM
FLUCTIBUS OPPRESSOS TROAS CŒLIQUE RUINA
NEC LATUERE DOLI FRATREM JUNONIS ET IRÆ
EURUM AD SE ZEPHYRUMQUE VOCAT DEHINC TALIA FATUR
TANTANE VOS GENERIS TENUIT FIDUCIA VESTRI

REFUSA. — According to the peculiar and proper force of the *Re,* pouring or streaming *back,* i. e. out of its proper place (viz. the bottom or depth of the sea); out of the place into which it had been originally put (viz. by Neptune); and so, correctly, LADEWIG: zurückströmend. Compare:

> "Portus erat, si non violentos insula Coros
> Exciperet saxis, lassasque refunderet undas."
>
> LUCAN. *II. 611.*

GRAVITER COMMOTUS. — "Graviter iratus." — RUÆUS.
"Irato." — CARO.
"Mit heftigem Eifer." — VOSS.
"Displeased." — DRYDEN.

No; but, *much disturbed,* put out of his way, discomposed. The identical words are used by Cicero to express the discomposure of mind produced in him by certain unexpected and disagreeable news: "Cum est ad nos allatum de temeritate eorum qui tibi negotium facesserent, etsi graviter primo nuntio commotus sum, quod nihil tam præter opinionem meam accidere potuit; tamen," &c. *(ad. Fam. III. 10).* And Pliny the Younger applies the term *commotus* to the simple circumstance of being moved to write a letter "Quæris fortasse quo commotus hæc scribam" *(Epist. VIII. 23)*

Neptune could not have been correctly represented as *angry* at an occurrence, of the cause and all the circumstances of which he was totally ignorant.

ALTO PROSPICIENS. — "Mari providens." — RUÆUS.

"And fearing for his watery reign."

DRYDEN.

Certainly wrong; because, in the almost identical context:

"Prospiciens, summa flavum caput extulit unda;"

Georg. IV. 352;

the meaning is not figurative, but literal. "Ex fundo maris in quo regia Dei est." — HEYNE. Wrong no less certainly; because, even if a prospect of the sea from its bottom were possible, the addition of the preposition *ab*, or *ex*, were indispensable to enable ALTO to signify the point or stand from which the view was taken. Compare:

— "Quum littora fervere late
Prospiceres arce ex summa;"

En. IV. 409;

where, in order to indicate that Dido took the view, not from the top of the arx, but from within the arx, i. e. from a window or room in the arx, the preposition used is, not *ab*, but *ex:*

"Prospexi Italiam, summa sublimis ab unda;"

En. VI. 357;

where the structure is, not sublimis ab, but prospexi ab; and where, in order to intimate that Palinurus was not *in* the water, but *on the top* of it, viz. floating on the aplustre (see Comment, verse 122), the preposition used is, not *ex*, but *ab;* and:

"Et lætum Æneam classemque ex æthere longe
Dardaniam Siculo prospexit ab usque Pachyno;"

En. VII. 288;

where, in order to define the unusual point of view with the greater accuracy, both prepositions are used together: *ex* to inform us that the view was taken from out the ether, and *ab* that the part of the ether, from out of which the view was taken, was over the promontory Pachynus: that the view was taken *from over* the promontory. ALTO, then, placed thus simply, and without a preposition, is not the stand or point from which the view is taken. Neither is it the object viewed, the object of the view: such object being invariably placed in the accusative after the verb, as *littora fervere,* in the first of the above quotations; *Italiam,* in the second; and *Æneam classemque,* in the third. If, then, ALTO is neither the point from which the view is taken, nor the object viewed, what is it? I reply, *the field of view;* the tract or space over which Neptune looked, in order to discover something which might account for the disturbance in his realms. PROSPICIENS ALTO, looking out *over* the high sea; exactly as Eneas (verse 185) *Prospectum pelago petit,* looks out *over* the sea, in the hope of being able to discern some of his missing ships.

PLACIDUM. — "Temere se torquent interpretes, non intelligentes quomodo graviter commoto caput (os) placidum esse possit. *Graviter commotus* et iratus est Neptunus in ventos et Æolum, sed *placidus* Trojanis." — FORBIGER.

To which explanation there seems to me to be this conclusive objection, that Neptune had raised his head *placidum* above the water before he was at all aware that either Eolus or the Trojans had anything to do with the matter. How, then, explain the apparent contradiction, GRAVITER COMMOTUS, and PLACIDUM CAPUT? I reply, the contradiction is indeed only apparent. Neptune was GRAVITER COMMOTUS (see above); and precisely because he was GRAVITER COMMOTUS, *(a)* CAPUT EXTULIT UNDA, in order to discover something which might explain or account for the tumult; and *(b)* CAPUT EXTULIT UNDA PLACIDUM (for, observe, the structure is not PLACIDUM

CAPUT EXTULIT UNDA, raised his placid head out of the water, but CAPUT EXTULIT UNDA PLACIDUM, raised his head out of the water, placid), in order that the placidity of his countenance might contribute to the restoration of order, or at least that he might not by an angry countenance increase the disorder. The effect is described at verse 158:

> — "Cunctus pelagi cecidit fragor, æquora postquam
> Prospiciens genitor;"

where the repetition of the word PROSPICIENS recalls the recollection of the reader to our text. In the word PLACIDUM lies, not only the chief emphasis of the words, and chief beauty of the picture, but the principal point of resemblance between the God stilling the storm, and the influential man quelling the riot; the effect being, in both cases, produced by the mere look, before a single word is uttered:

> "Conspexere — silent."
>
> — "Cunctus pelagi cecidit fragor, æquora postquam
> Prospiciens genitor."

That the strong pictorial contrast between the God's placidity of aspect, and the turbulence of the storm, was not overlooked by our poet's readers of old, is shown by the terms in which it is referred to by Silius Italicus (VII. 257):

> "Ut cum turbatis placidum caput extulit undis
> Neptunus."

The whole passage is in the strictest and most beautiful conformity with the well-known mythological dogma, that the Gods assume an aspect and demeanour corresponding to the work in which they are engaged: placid and peaceful, if it be one of peace; turbid and sad, displeased, or terrific, if it be the contrary. Compare:

> "Vultu quo cœlum tempestatesque serenat."
>
> *En. I. 259.*

— "Nutuque sereno
Intonuit."
VALER. FLAC. *III. 251.*

"Hæc ubi dicta dedit terras horrenda petivit."
En. VII. 323.

— "Vel qualis in atram
Sollicitus nubem, mœsto Jove, cogitur aer."
CLAUD. *Bell. Getic. 378.*

See also for the application of the same term, not indeed to the aspect, but to the temper (Germ. Stimmung) of the Gods when engaged in a benevolent act, Virgil himself En. III. 265:

— "Dî, talem avertite casum,
Et placidi servate pios."

COELI RUINA. — "Imbribus et conjuncta cum his reliqua tempestatis fœditate." — WAGNER. *Virg. Br. En.*

"Imbre, fulguribus, fulminibus, quæ e cœlo ruunt." — RUÆUS.

The falling, not, as these commentators seem to have understood the passage, of *the contents or discharges of the sky,* but, as understood by Voss, of *the sky itself:* "dem Sturze des Himmels." Compare Ruit arduus æther: *(Georg. I. 324),* and Forbiger on that passage. Also

"Inque fretum credas totum descendere cœlum."
OVID. *Met. XI. 518.*

— "Tremendo
Jupiter ipse ruens tumultu."
HOR. *Carm. I. 16.*

Caro, if we may judge from his translation, misunderstood the word wholly:

— "ch' a la tempesta, a la ruina
E del mare, e del cielo erano esposti."

NEC LATUERE DOLI FRATREM JUNONIS ET IRÆ. — The meaning is not (with Ruæus and Dryden), that Neptune was previously acquainted with the anger and machinations of his sister against the Trojans, but (with

Caro and Heyne), that Neptune, seeing it was the Trojans that suffered, understood at once the cause of the storm, viz. that it had been produced by his sister in order to wreak her vengeance on her enemies. The connexion is, COMMOTUS, PROSPICIENS, VIDET, NEC LATUERE, FRATREM: uneasy at the disturbance and anxious to know its cause, takes a view all round, sees the Trojan ships in distress, and being, from his intimacy with Juno, previously aware of her animosity against the Trojans, understands at once the whole matter. NEC LATUERE DOLI ET IRÆ, i. e. *nec latuit quod tempestas orta sit ex iris et dolis.* Neptune's previous knowledge of the IRÆ and DOLI of his sister is, not expressed by NEC LATUERE, but, implied by FRATREM.

TANTANE VOS GENERIS TENUIT FIDUCIA VESTRI. —

"Magnum et gentile tumentes."

STAT. *Theb. VIII. 429.*

143.

TENET ILLE IMMANIA SAXA
VESTRAS EURE DOMOS ILLA SE JACTET IN AULA
ÆOLUS ET CLAUSO VENTORUM CARCERE REGNET

IMMANIA SAXA. — "Vastum antrum" (*v.* 56). — HEYNE.

No; the reference is not special, but general; not to a particular part of Eolus's empire, but to the whole. First, because the description is in general terms, IMMANIA SAXA, VESTRAS DOMOS, corresponding exactly to the description of Eolia at verse 55:

"Nimborum in patriam, loca fœta furentibus Austris."

Secondly, because it is the *whole* of the empire of Eolus, and not the cave of the winds alone, which should be contrasted with the *whole* of the empire of Neptune, described at verse 142 in the words:

"Non illi imperium pelagi sævumque tridentem,
Sed mihi sorte datum;"

close upon which follows the contrast: TENET ILLE IMMANIA SAXA VESTRAS EURE DOMOS; that wild, rocky Eolia, where the winds had their home; where the cave of the winds was. And thirdly, because the cave of the winds is specified in its proper place in the next verse.

ILLA SE JACTET IN AULA. — ILLA plainly referring AULA to IMMANIA SAXA and VESTRAS DOMOS, and those words being, as just shown, a periphrasis for the country of Eolia, the AULA (Hof or court) in which Eolus is here told to take state on him, is neither, with Heyne, Thiel, and Voss, the *celsa arx* mentioned at verse 60 ("Regia alto in montis cacumine." — HEYNE. "Jene 'celsa arx.'" — THIEL. "Dort üb' im Palaste den Hochmut." — VOSS.) nor, with Dryden (see below), the cavern of the winds, but simply the country of Eolia.

CLAUSO VENTORUM CARCERE REGNET. — The received interpretation, "regnet in clauso ventorum carcere," is erroneous: First, because *regnare,* in order to express reigning *in,* inside, or within a place, must be followed by the preposition *in* expressed, as in "Regnet in aula" *(Georg. IV. 90)*; and

"Inque tua regnant, nullis prohibentibus, aula."
(OVID. *Heroid. I. 89.*);

for I consider *coelo,* in Horace's "cœlo credidimus Jovem regnare" *(Carm. III. v. 1),* and *mundo,* in Seneca's "vacuo regnare mundo" *(Herc. Fur. 67),* to be as certainly the objects of the verb as *oppidis* in Cicero's "In Sicilia Timarchidem omnibus oppidis regnasse" *(In Verr. III. 54).* And secondly, because the command to Eolus to shut himself up in the prison, and reign there among his prisoners, had been a mere *brutum fulmen,* an unmeaning piece of abuse, which Virgil was quite too judicious to put into the mouth of his dignified God of the sea.

The meaning is just the contrary: let him reign as absolute as he likes, but *not* with respect to the prison of the winds. Literally: the prison of the winds being closed, *then* let him reign absolute; or let him close the prison of the winds, and *then* reign absolute; a command, it will be observed, which is, first, compatible with the dignity of Neptune; secondly, imperatively required by the circumstances of the case; and thirdly, in perfect harmony with the delegated authority of Eolus, who might be as despotic as he pleased among the IMMANIA SAXA of Eolia, provided only he did not open or shut the prison of the winds without orders.

> "Regem . . . qui fœdere certo
> Et premere et laxas sciret dare jussus habenas."

The whole force and gist of the passage lies in this word REGNET: which, first, means not merely to *rule,* but *rule as an autocrat* (compare the examples above quoted from Horace, Seneca, and Cicero; also Liv. III. 2, and Gronov. ad Liv. XXIV. 29 and particularly Ovid's

> "Quicquid amor jussit, non est contemnere tutum;
> Regnat, et in dominos jus habet ille Deos."
>
> *Heroid. IV. 11.*)

And secondly, being separated from its conjunction by the sudden pauses preceding and following the ablative absolute, and being, at the same time, the last word in the line and the last word uttered by Neptune, receives the whole ictus of Neptune's voice as he turns and goes away: ET, CLAUSO VENTORUM CARCERE, REGNET. Compare the similar emphasis thrown by Neptune in this very same speech on *venti,* similarly placed at the end of a line, and similarly separated from the preceding context; and the not very dissimilar structure and emphasis at *aras,* verse 113; and the much less strong, (because the sense runs on to the next line) but still somewhat similar, emphasis at *amicum,* verse 614; also, closely corresponding to Virgil's REGNET both in isolated position and independent structure, the *regnat* of Ovid in the passage just quoted.

How good soever, therefore, may be their poetry, the meaning, which the translators have given us for this passage, is exactly the opposite of Virgil's:

> — "Quella è sua reggia
> Quivi solo si vanti, e per regnare,
> De la prigion de' suoi venti non esca."
>
> Caro.

> — "Dort üb im Palaste den Hochmut
> Æolus, und in der Winde verschlossenem Kerker
> gebiet' er."
>
> Voss.

> "His power to hollow caverns is confined;
> There let him reign, the gaoler of the wind;
> With hoarse commands his breathing subjects call,
> And boast and bluster in his empty hall."
>
> Dryden.

> — "*τα δ' ανακτορα ευχεταασθω*
> *Αιολος, ειρκτησιν δ' ανεμων κλειστης αγος εστω.*"
>
> De Bulgaris.

The translators and commentators may, however, plead in extenuation the authority of Servius: "Carcere regnet; licet carcer sit, tamen regnum est Æoli;" a misconception, of a piece with Servius's usual misconceptions of his author's meaning. In Neptune's message to Eolus, not only is there no scoffing allusion to the prison of the winds, or to Eolus's office as gaoler, but the clearest and most marked distinction is drawn between the prison of the winds and Eolus's rocky kingdom of Eolia, in which it was contained; also between Eolus's delegated authority over the winds, and his absolute authority over the rest of the kingdom.

Precisely similar to the absolute CLAUSO CARCERE in our text, is the absolute *clauso Olympo,* vers. 378.

150.

ET VASTAS APERIT SYRTES ET TEMPERAT ÆQUOR
ATQUE ROTIS SUMMAS LEVIBUS PERLABITUR UNDAS

"Via ex arenosis vadis facta, ut naves exire possent; refer ad tres naves, *vv.* 110—111." — HEYNE.

"Viam per arenosa vada facit, ut naves expedire se possint." — WAGNER, *Virg. Br. En.*

"Le tre, che ne l'arena eran sepolte,
Egli stesso le vaste Sirti aprendo,
Sollevò col tridente, ed a se trassele."

CARO.

"Oeffnet durch Sand und Watten die Bahn."

VOSS.

But the addition of VASTAS to SYRTES shows plainly that the action of APERIT is not merely on that part of the Syrtes, where the three ships were imbedded, but on the *vast* Syrtes, or the Syrtes generally. I therefore take the meaning to be, with Servius, that the God opened the Syrtes, i. e. made them *apertas*, open or safe for ships, by levelling them where they had been raised into partial inequalities by the storm, and by spreading the water evenly upon them, of such depth that vessels could sail over them without danger: the three imbedded ships were thus set afloat again. VASTAS APERIT SYRTES, so understood, harmonizes well with TEMPERAT ÆQUOR; for the sea ceased to break on the Syrtes, when they were levelled and deeply covered by the water. It is probable that *apertas* was the term ordinarily applied by seafaring men to express the safe state of the Syrtes, or that state in which they were covered by water of depth sufficient for vessels to sail in, that state in which the sailor might *enter* them, *intraret.* Compare:

— "Madidaque cadente
Pliade, Gætulas intrabit navita Syrtes."
CLAUD. *de Quart. Consul. Honorii. 437.*

And, exactly parallel to our text:

"Pande precor gemino placatum Castore pontum;
Temperet æquoream dux Cytherea viam."
RUTIL. *Itin. I. 155.*

The same term is applied to the sea itself, both in our own language and in Latin; "Aperto mari navigare" (PLIN. *Hist. Nat. I. II. 46*). The poet, having stated the precise manner in which the God removed the other three ships from the rocks, judiciously avoids a similar particularity of description with respect to those which had been imbedded in the sand, leaving his reader to conclude that the ships were not neglected, when the shoals in which they were imbedded were made open and navigable. The account which Sallust *(Bell. Jugurth. 80),* gives of the Syrtes, goes to confirm this explanation: "Duo sunt sinus prope in extrema Africa impares magnitudine, pari natura: quorum proxima terræ præalta sunt; cætera, uti fors tulit, alta; alia in tempestate vadosa: nam ubi mare magnum esse et sævire cœpit ventis, limum arenamque et saxa ingentia fluctus trahunt; ita facies locorum cum ventis simul mutatur: Syrtes ab tractu nominatæ." Sallust's account of the Syrtes, dressed in poetical language, becomes Virgil's, and Virgil's turned into plain prose becomes Sallust's. The historian describes the winds and waves as rendering the Syrtes now *vadosas,* now *altas;* while the poet ascribes the same effect to the agency of Eurus and Neptune, the former of whom "illidit (*naves,* viz.) vadis, atque aggere cingit arenæ," i. e. makes the Syrtes *vadosas*, and dashes the ships upon them; the latter APERIT SYRTES, i. e. makes the *vadosas* (the shallow and impassable, and therefore, closed) *altas* (deep and passable, and therefore, open, *apertas*,) and thus frees and sets afloat the ships. Our author makes a precisely similar use of aperio, En. X. 13:

"Exitium magnum atque Alpes immittet apertas;"

and thus we come round to that very common phrase, and use of the verb aperio, *apertus campus.*

There is a similar application of *pateo,* where the sense requires an intransitive verb: Cuncta maria terræque *patebant.* — Sall. *Bell. Cat. X.*

The connexion is, APERIT, TEMPERAT, ATQUE PERLABITUR: makes the sea on the Syrtes smooth and navigable, and then navigates it himself.

Perlabitur. — *Per:* over the whole of it; from one end to the other, and in every direction over the *vast Syrtes.*

152.

AC VELUTI MAGNO IN POPULO CUM SÆPE COORTA EST
SEDITIO SÆVITQUE ANIMIS IGNOBILE VULGUS
JAMQUE FACES ET SAXA VOLANT FUROR ARMA MINISTRAT
TUM PIETATE GRAVEM AC MERITIS SI FORTE VIRUM QUEM
CONSPEXERE SILENT ARRECTISQUE AURIBUS ADSTANT
ILLE REGIT DICTIS ANIMOS ET PECTORA MULCET
SIC CUNCTUS PELAGI CECIDIT FRAGOR ÆQUORA POSTQUAM
PROSPICIENS GENITOR CŒLOQUE INVECTUS APERTO
FLECTIT EQUOS CURRUQUE VOLANS DAT LORA SECUNDO

Sævitque animis ignobile vulgus . . . genitor. — Ignobile vulgus corresponds with æquora; pietate gravem ac meritis virum with genitor; and the two former contrast with the two latter.

Sævit animis. — Not *sævit in animis,* but *sævit cum animis.* Compare Comm. En. I. 297: II. 418: V. 2 and 739. VI. 825.

Furor arma ministrat. —

— "Quod cuique repertum
Rimanti telum ira facit."

Æn. VII. 507.

Conspexere. — The sudden pause, by which this strong and emphatic word is cut off from the remainder of the line, indicates the sudden pause in the action; the instant stillness of the crowd on a full view (conspexere) of the man, pietate gravem ac meritis. A similar effect is produced by the suddenness of the pause after the three rapid words, pelagi cecidit fragor, in the next verse but one.

Flectit equos, curruque volans dat lora secundo. — One of the numerous instances in which the genuine Virgilian reading, although supported by the consentient authority of all the best manuscripts, has had a narrow escape of being ousted from the text, and having its place supplied by a spurious prosaic substitute, merely because the commentators were not able to understand it.

"Currus secundus qui sit, non satis perspicio; celerem enim poeta hoc vocabulo significare vix potest; et felicem vel propitium cur dixerit non apparet. Servius currum Trojanis obsequentem explicuit, quod loco non convenit; Neptunus enim flectit equos et discedit. Facile esset *cursuque* corrigere, sed conjectura non opus est, cum cod. Rom. aliique *fluctuque* exhibeant, quod reponendum esse videtur." — Jahn.

"Curru secundo, celeri." — Heyne.

Wagner adopts, and in the following words would fain justify, the interpretation of Heyne: Vento utimur secundo, navigamus celeriter; unde celeritatis notio adhærere potuit huic adjectivo.

All these interpretations seem to me to be nearly equally erroneous. *Secundus currus* is not *celer currus:* First, because no instance has been, nor, I think, can be produced, in which *secundus* is used in that sense. Secondly, because, even if *secundus* could bear such meaning elsewhere, it could not well bear it here, where the speed of the chariot has been expressed, quite sufficiently for the occasion, in the immediately preceding VOLANS. Neither is *secundus currus, currus felix,* or *currus propitius;* such expressions bearing no intelligible meaning at all. Neither, finally, is *currus secundus, currus obsequens Trojanis,* for the reason assigned by Jahn. The erroneousness of these interpretations, although, as I have just said, pretty nearly equal, is, however, of two very different kinds, and arises from two perfectly distinct sources: — in the three modern commentators, from a misconception of the sense in which the word is used, not only by Virgil himself elsewhere, but by all other Latin writers; in Servius, who, as might be expected from his having lived so near the time of Virgil, and having possessed a vernacular knowledge of the language, perfectly understood the ordinary meaning of the term, from a false application of the term to the context; the very kind of error into which a man of so narrow and contracted a mind as Servius, and so wholly incapable of understanding and appreciating poetical excellence, was likely, notwithstanding all his knowledge of the language, to fall; and into which he has, in fact, so perpetually fallen.

Having said so much of the false interpretations, let us now see if we cannot ascertain what is the true. And first, with respect to the principal word, *secundus;* this word has, as far as I can discover, but two meanings, either in Virgil or any other Latin writer; first, the primary one of second in rank or order, as in the expressions, secundæ mensæ: *(En. VIII. 283);* Haud ulli veterum virtute secundus: *(En. XI. 441);* and secondly, the secondary meaning (immediately derived from and intimately connected with the primary), of seconding, going, or acting along with another, as a second, not principal, actor. This is its meaning in all such expressions as secundus ventus, secundus amnis, secundus fluctus, secundus clamor, secunda fortuna, secundæ res; wind, river, wave, clamor, fortune, circumstances, seconding you, going along with you: in all which expressions it means exactly the opposite of adversus; adversus ventus, amnis, fluctus, clamor, adversa fortuna, adversæ res, being, wind, river, wave, clamor, fortune, circumstances, opposing you, going directly the opposite way to that which you are going. And so Cæsar *(apud Cicer. ad Attic. X. 8)* "Omnia secundissima nobis, adversissima illis accidisse videntur." Both meanings of *secundus* flow from its root, *sequor;* and, accordingly, it is by a compound of its root that Servius correctly renders it in the passage before us, viz. by obsequens; going readily along with you in the direction you wish, seconding you.

If, then, *secundus* is seconding, going readily along with, or according to the will of, and if the will referred to is not that of the Trojans, whose will is it? Evidently Neptune's. The chariot is *secundus:* seconds the will of the driver, goes readily along with him wherever he wishes, *obsequitur.* If it be objected that *secundus,* in such sense, however applicable to the horses, seems somewhat inapplicable to the insensible chariot, I answer: First, that, even in our own language, we apply the terms, fast, slow, going, running, stopping, driving, and innumerable others, indifferently to carriage and horses. Secondly, that in the Iliad, the term *horses* is so frequently used for *chariot,* as to have given rise to an opinion that the Homeric chiefs fought on horseback; and that there is scarcely one of the ancient writers in which a similar laxity of expression may not be found; of which perhaps the following words in a fragment of Alcæus preserved by Himerius, will serve as well as any other for an example: δους τε επι τουτοις αρμα ελαυνειν (κυκνοι δε ησαν *το αρμα)* —— *ο δε επιβας επι των αρματων, εφη και τους κυκνους εις Υπερβορεους πετεσθαι.* Thirdly, that Pindar's *αρματα πεισιχαλινα (Pyth. II. 21),* seems to be as nearly as possible the exact counterpart of Virgil's *currus secundus,* understood as I have explained it. Fourthly, that the prosaic strictness which forbids the application of *secundus* in this sense to *currus,* must, to be consistent with itself, equally forbid the application to it of *dat lora,* the reins being, in prosaic truth, given loose to the horses, not to the chariot. Should any reader, notwithstanding all these arguments, still entertain a doubt as to the meaning of the passage, I beg to refer him to what I think I may be permitted to call Virgil's own commentary on it, in the last line of the first Georgic:

"Fertur equis auriga, neque audit currus habenas."

FLECTIT EQUOS, CURRUQUE VOLANS DAT LORA SECUNDO. — By these words, which are nearly a repetition of

"Atque rotis summas levibus perlabitur undas,"

(verse 151), the poet brings his readers back to the point at which he had broken off, and left the direct thread of the narrative, in order to enter upon the simile just now completed.

163.

EST IN SECESSU LONGO LOCUS INSULA PORTUM
EFFICIT OBJECTU LATERUM QUIBUS OMNIS AB ALTO
FRANGITUR INQUE SINUS SCINDIT SESE UNDA REDUCTOS
HINC ATQUE HINC VASTÆ RUPES GEMINIQUE MINANTUR
IN CŒLUM SCOPULI QUORUM SUB VERTICE LATE
ÆQUORA TUTA SILENT TUM SILVIS SCENA CORUSCIS
DESUPER HORRENTIQUE ATRUM NEMUS IMMINET UMBRA
FRONTE SUB ADVERSA SCOPULIS PENDENTIBUS ANTRUM
INTUS AQUÆ DULCES VIVOQUE SEDILIA SAXO
NYMPHARUM DOMUS

Est in secessu longo locus. — "Sinu secreto." — Servius. "Sinuoso Libyæ littore." — Heyne. "Tief zurückgezogene Bucht." — Thiel.

"Weit ist zurückgebogen ein Ort."
Voss.

"E di la lungo a la riviera un seno."
Caro.

"Within a long recess there lies a bay."
Dryden.

"There lies a harbour in a long recess."
Trapp.

All wrong; for *secessus* never means *sinus,* or any *shape* or *form* whatever, but always *retreat,* retirement, separation, secession (viz. from the crowd, or hurry of business, or resort of men), *recess*, but only in the sense in which it is used in such expressions as *recess of Parliament, recess between the Law Terms*, not in the sense of retired *place.* "Ille meus in urbe, ille in secessu contubernalis" (Plin. *II. Ep. 13*). "Petis ut libellos tuos in secessu legam" (Plin. *III. Epist. 15).*

"Carmina secessum scribentis et otia quærunt."
Ovid. *Trist. I. I. 41.*

Secessu longo, therefore, describes, not the *shape* of the place, but how it was circumstanced with respect to human intercourse; not that it was a *long creek or inlet,* but that it was *far remote* from the resort of men. The description of the *shape* of the place begins with the words INSULA PORTUM EFFICIT. The mistake of the expositors seems to have arisen from their having confounded *secessus* with *recessus,* which, in many places, and particularly in the following exactly parallel passage of Claudian, has the very sense assigned by the expositors to *secessus* in our text:

> "Urbs, Libyam contra, Tyrio fundata potenti,
> Tenditur in longum Caralis, tenuemque per undas
> Obvia dimittit fracturum flamina collem.
> Efficitur portus medium mare: tutaque ventis
> Omnibus, ingenti mansuescunt stagna recessu."
>
> *Bell. Gildon. 520.*

PORTUM. — The description of the port is contained in four distinct predications: — First, INSULA PORTUM EFFICIT OBJECTU LATERUM; it is a cove sheltered in front by an island. Secondly, HINC ATQUE HINC VASTÆ RUPES GEMINIQUE MINANTUR IN CŒLUM SCOPULI; and lying between two high, steep, threatening-looking, rocky precipices; for this is the entire meaning of this predication, whether, with Heyne, we understand its structure to be VASTÆ RUPES GEMINIQUE SCOPULI MINANTUR; or, as I analyze the passage, *vastæ rupes sunt, et gemini scopuli minantur.* Thirdly, TUM SILVIS SCENA CORUSCIS DESUPER; the clefts and tops of these precipices, thickly set with trees whose branches lean over the water and shimmer in the wind, constitute a woody landscape. Fourthly, FRONTE SUB ADVERSA SCOPULIS PENDENTIBUS ANTRUM; at the far end of the cove, and directly opposite the entrance, a grotto in the face of the rock. Each of these predications has its subsidiary: the first has QUIBUS OMNIS AB ALTO FRANGITUR INQUE SINUS SCINDIT SESE UNDA REDUCTOS; the second has QUORUM SUB VERTICE LATE ÆQUORA TUTA SILENT; the third, HORRENTIQUE ATRUM NEMUS IMMINET UMBRA; and the fourth, INTUS AQUÆ DULCES VIVOQUE SEDILIA SAXO. The words HINC ATQUE HINC, and FRONTE SUB ADVERSA, as well as

HIC (verse 172), and HUC (verse 174), refer back past the subsidiaries to the main subject, PORTUM. That this is the real structure and true analysis of the passage, appears from the fact, that the flow of the sense remains uninterrupted, notwithstanding the omission of any, or all of the subsidiaries, as, for want of a better name, I have termed the helping or dependent sentences. The three principal subsidiaries, QUIBUS OMNIS AB ALTO FRANGITUR INQUE SINUS SCINDIT SESE UNDA REDUCTOS, QUORUM SUB VERTICE LATE ÆQUORA TUTA SILENT, and INTUS AQUÆ DULCES VIVOQUE SEDILIA SAXO, are connected together not merely as dependents on three connected predications, but as together forming one climax: — open sea-shore — sheltered, safe, and quiet haven — still more sheltered, safe, and quiet grotto.

EFFICIT. — Not merely makes ("Che porto un' isoletta Lo fa" — CARO), but according to the proper force of the word (*ef*-ficere), makes completely, effects, accomplishes, makes a complete port of the *locus*. Compare: Capitolium . . . . publice gratis . . . . exædificari atque effici potuit. — CIC. *in Verr. V. 48, c. 19* (STEPH.). Omni opere effecto: — CÆS. *B. G. IV. 18.* "Qui hoc primus in nostros mores induxit, qui maxime auxit, qui solus effecit" CIC. *de Orat. II. 121.*

QUIBUS OMNIS AB ALTO FRANGITUR INQUE SINUS SCINDIT SESE UNDA REDUCTOS. — "Sinus replicabiles." — SERVIUS. "Fracta recedit: tribuuntur et alibi sinus et ipsis fluctibus allisis, qui repulsi sinus faciunt, ut Georg. III., 238." — HEYNE. "In orbes semper longius recedentes dissolvitur fluctus." — WAGNER. *Virg. Br. En.* "Vers 165 nehme ich mit Heyne von den gewölbten Krümmungen, in welche gebrochene Wogen sich formen." — THIEL. It is remarkable that, whilst in all these interpretations so much stress is laid on the mere adjunct REDUCTOS, no notice whatever is taken of the verb SCINDIT SESE, the very word on which, as it appears to me, the whole meaning of the passage hinges. We have only to allow

SCINDIT SESE its due force, and set aside for the moment the deceptive adjunct REDUCTOS, in order to perceive that in the words QUIBUS OMNIS AB ALTO FRANGITUR INQUE SINUS SCINDIT SESE UNDA, Virgil must speak, not of the reflux of the wave or sea, or of the form in which the wave or sea recedes from the shore, but of the advance of the sea forwards between the prominences of the island; for how, except by its flowing up between those prominences, is it possible that it should *divide* itself, or be *divided* by them: FRANGITUR INQUE SINUS SCINDIT SESE. Compare OVID, Metamorph. XV. 739, where, speaking of the insula Tiberina, he says:

> "Scinditur in geminas partes circumfluus amnis,
> Insula nomen habet, laterumque a parte duorum,
> Porrigit æquales media tellure lacertos;"

the sole difference between which view and that given by Virgil is, that here the water is described as divided by the *whole* island, and into two parts only, while in Virgil's view it is described as divided, not by the whole island, but by its several projections or promontories, and therefore into several parts or sinuses. Compare also OVID, Metam. XIV. 51:

> "Parvus erat gurges curvos sinuatus in arcus;"

where the idea is the same as that in the text, except that Virgil's sinuses are sharply re-entrant, while Ovid's are gently curved. This interpretation, long ago proposed by Turnebus, and adopted by Burmann, but forgotten, it would seem, by modern commentators, is so far from being contradicted or invalidated as to be even confirmed by REDUCTOS, which, (first), is not a participle, but an adjective, corresponding exactly to *odoratam (En. VII. 13), inaccessos (En VII. 11),* and numerous other adjectives with participial terminations; nay, is so much an adjective, as to be capable of comparison: "ut qui singulis pinxerunt coloribus, alia tamen eminentiora, alia *reductiora* fecerunt" (QUINCTIL. *Instit. XI. III. 46*); and (secondly) means, as clearly shown by the passage just quoted from Quinctilian, standing backward, or in the back-ground, in comparison of something which is more prominent; precisely the idea which the mathematicians express by the term *re-entrant.* So *reducta valle (En. VI. 703)*, is not a deep or long valley, but a valley standing back or *re-entrant* from the plain; i. e. extending backward from the plain toward the interior between two ranges of hills; not a sunk valley, or one upon which you look down, but one on a level with, and an offset from, the plain, and into which you look from one end. And so also, in the passage before us, the sinuses into which the edge of the sea is divided by the prominences of the island are *reducti, re-entrant between those prominences,* offsets of the sea; or, as expressed by Livy *(Lib. XXVI.)* in his description of the port of Carthago Hispanica: introrsum retracti. Compare Mela, III. 1. "Frons illa aliquamdiu rectam ripam habet; dein modico flexu accepto, mox paullulum eminet; tum *reducta* iterum, iterumque rectâ margine jacens, ad promontorium quod Celticum vocamus, extenditur." Having differed so widely from the above-quoted commentators (and I am not ashamed to add even from my own earlier opinion, expressed in the Classical Museum No. 19, and quoted by Forbiger in his 3rd Edition) in my interpretation of each of the three words, SINUS, SCINDIT, and REDUCTOS, I am inclined to differ from them, besides, in the interpretation of the word UNDA, which I understand to mean here, not *fluctus*, or a great wave or billow rolling in from the deep, and breaking violently on the island, but *the sea,* or, if I may so say, the undulant itself; a sense in which the term is so frequently used, not only by Virgil (ex. gr. *Georg. I. 360, III. 340. &c.)*, but by all other Latin writers. So understood, UNDA seems to me to harmonize better *(a)* with the present quietude of the sea after the miraculous stilling of the storm, and *(b)* with the words, SCINDIT SESE IN SINUS REDUCTOS, the re-entrant sinuses being less properly constituent parts of individual waves than of the sea itself Nor let it be said that FRANGITUR contradicts this idea, and points to billows breaking with great force, for we find the selfsame term used to express the common breaking of the sea upon the shore in calm weather, in the words:

"Qua vada non spirant, nec fracta remurmurat unda."
En. X. 291.

SINUS therefore, in the passage before us, is applied to the sea in the identical sense in which it is applied to it, not only by Virgil himself elsewhere, and other Latin writers, but in the familiar proper names, Sinus Adriaticus, Sinus Tarentinus, Sinus Saronicus, &c.; a sense, it will be observed, directly opposite to that in which it is applied to the female breast, the sails of a ship, or the dress; the term in these latter applications preserving its original meaning of a concavity, hollow, or depression, while in its application to the sea it means a projection corresponding to, and accurately filling up, an opposite concavity or hollow. This remarkable deviation from, or exception to, the original and still general meaning of the word as applied to other objects, has, no doubt, arisen (as in the case of our own *bay*) from its having been found convenient in practice to extend the application of a term, which originally and in strictness signified only a hollow or sinuosity of the shore, to the arm of the sea filling it up. Compare Vossius's definition of the word in his Etymol.— "Sinus de mari dicitur metaphorice, quia ut in homine sinus est quod brachiis comprehenditur, ita et in mari sinus est *maris pars quasi brachiis terræ interjecta*. Græcis est *κολπος;* unde Itali 'golvo' dicunt pro *κολπω*." A similar interpretation will, I think, be found to answer for Georg. IV. 420, where the same words occur again, and where the meaning is: a mountainous promontory runs into the sea, presenting on the exposed side a number of inlets, into which the sea beats, and on the sheltered side the cave of Proteus, and a safe roadstead for ships. Voss and La Cerda understand REDUCTOS SINUS of the two inlets or arms by which the sea communicates round the island with the port behind: an interpretation to which there seems to me to be these two great objections: first, that it is wholly inapplicable to the words where they occur again in the fourth Georgic; and secondly, that we cannot doubt that, if such had been his meaning, Virgil would (like Ovid in his description of the Insula Tiberina, above quoted) have added either *geminos* or *duos,* to indicate that he spoke of two particular inlets, and not of an indefinite number. The mystification under which Caro and Dryden endeavor to conceal their ignorance of their author's meaning amounts almost to nonsense:

"Questa si sporge co' suoi fianchi in guisa,
Ch' ogni vento, ogni flutto, d'ogni lato
Che vi percuota, ritrovando intoppo
O si frange, o si sparte, o si riversa."

CARO.

"Broke by the jutting land on either side,
In double streams the briny waters glide."

DRYDEN.

GEMINIQUE MINANTUR IN CŒLUM SCOPULI. — "Tam alti sunt ut videantur tendere in cœlum: minas murorum, infra IV. 88, muros præaltos dixit." — WAGNER, *Virg. Br. En.* "Minantur *(ire* or *ascensum)* in cœlum: the expression is most poetically beautiful." — TRAPP.

"Rise on each side huge rocks, two o'er the rest
Menace the skies."

BERESFORD.

"Velut respiciat ad gigantum conatus cœlum oppugnantium." — GESNER. This is not the meaning: first, because it is always directly, and not through the medium of a preposition, that *minari* governs the object threatened: compare the numerous examples of the use of this word adduced by the lexicographers; and (especially in point, though not adduced by them) Silius Italicus's "Saxa minantia cœlo" (IV. 2); and Propertius's "Cœloque minantem Cœum" (III. IX. 47); and secondly, because to have described the SCOPULI as threatening the sky had been to introduce an idea foreign from the subject, and distractive of the reader's attention from the main object, the security and privacy of the harbour, to the danger of the sky. I therefore understand MINANTUR in our text to be taken absolutely, i. e. irrespectively of an object, and to mean, rise with a bold, towering, or, if the reader prefer it, threatening aspect. Compare, first, En. VIII. 668, where we have precisely the same predication applied to the identical word *scopulus:*

— "Et te, Catalina, minaci
Pendentem scopulo;"

where the meaning can be no other than a threatening-looking, or, as we say, bold, towering cliff. Compare, secondly, En. II. 628:

— "Illa usque minatur,
Et tremefacta comam concusso vertice nutat;"

where the meaning is not (with Gesner and Dryden) *minatur casum,* but the very opposite: stands boldly; resisting, not yielding to, the attack; as proved by the words, *usque* and *donec; still* preserves its bold, towering, fearless attitude, *until* — &c. in confirmation of which interpretation observe that the word nutat, added here by way of explanation, means where it is again similarly employed by Virgil, viz. En. IX. 682, nod in a menacing manner. Compare, thirdly, En. IV. 88:

— "Pendent opera interrupta, minæque
Murorum ingentes, æquataque machina cœlo;"

not (with Servius) eminentiæ murorum, quas pinnas dicunt, but, the threats of the walls, i. e. the high, towering, threatening-looking walls themselves. And here observe the complementary clause: æquataque machina muro — the machina, not threatening the sky (for Virgil does not indulge in the exaggerated hyperboles of Silius and Statius), but — as high as the sky. And finally, compare En. II. 240:

— "Mediæque minans illabitur urbi;"

glides through the midst of the city, *minans*, i. e. with a bold, towering, threatening mien or aspect. So understood, MINANTUR in our text is well responded to by TUTA in the next verse but one: — the waters repose in safety under the protection of guards, whose threatening, frowning aspect warns not to come too near; an idea thus somewhat less poetically expressed by Statius:

"Qua summas caput Acrocorinthus in auras
Tollit, et alterna geminum mare protegit umbra."
Theb. VII. 106.

IN CŒLUM is added to MINANTUR in order to express, not the object threatened, but the great height to which the threatening object rises, in the same way as *pedes in octo* is added to *protentus* (Georg. I. 171), in order to express the length to which the pole projects; and as *in lucem* is added to *bibit* (Mart. I. 29) and to *cœnat* (Mart. VII. 29), to express the great length of time Acerra drinks, and the great length of time to which Sertorius prolongs his supper. The reader or reciter, first, in order to show that the action of MINANTUR does not pass to CŒLUM, and, secondly, in order to magnify as much as possible the height to which the SCOPULI rise, should take advantage of the separation made by the close of the verse between MINANTUR and IN CŒLUM, and, hanging his voice after MINANTUR, throw that particular emphasis on CŒLUM, for the sake of receiving which the poet has expressly placed it in the beginning of the line: thus —

— "Geminique minantur,
In *cœlum* scopuli."

It is not a little remarkable that not only Ruæus, but Heyne, in his exposition of these words, should have entirely omitted the idea contained in MINANTUR ("Duo scopuli eminent ad cœlum." — RUÆUS. "Duo scopuli eminent." — HEYNE), an omission which, if I may be allowed to speculate, arose from the similar omission in the ordinary text of Servius ("MINANTUR, *eminent.*" — SERVIUS). The credit of the ancient commentator is, however, in this instance (as well, indeed, as in many others) saved by his modern editor, Lion, in whose edition we find the following words supplied: "et ita est, ut quæ eminent, minari videantur." Voss's translation, otherwise correct, is spoiled by the total omission of IN CŒLUM, and the conjunction of RUPES with MINANTUR.

"Links dort drohen und rechts unförmliche Klippen und zwiefach
Starrende Felsen empor."

VOSS.

In place of Virgil's accurately defined and picturesque drawing, Caro presents us with a vague generalization:

"Quinci e quindi alti scogli e rupi altissime;"

and desperately reckless Dryden with barely two rows of rocks:

"Betwixt two rows of rocks a sylvan scene
Appears above, and groves for ever green."

the meaning of which let him guess who can.

TUTA, safe *from the winds;* as rightly rendered by the commentators, and established by the quotation from Claudian, at the beginning of this Comment.

SCENA. — "Inumbratio et dicta *scena, απο της σκιας;* apud antiquos enim theatralis scena parietem non habebat, sed de frondibus umbraculum quærebant. Postea tabulata componere cœperunt in modum parietis." — SERVIUS. And so, after him, Forbiger. However true may be the etymological part of this observation, I have two reasons for thinking that *inumbratio* does not represent the meaning of SCENA in the passage before us: First, because I do not find the word used in this sense on any occasion by any Latin writer whatever, and secondly, because the idea of *inumbration* is expressed unmistakably and fully in the immediately succeeding words: HORRENTIQUE ATRUM NEMUS IMMINET UMBRA.

To Wagner's gloss — "Scena quomodo de longo prospectu accipi possit, non exputo; rectius Isidorus in Glossis, hunc ipsum fortasse locum respiciens, scenam interpretatur *arborum densitatem*" — I make the similar objection; first, that I am not acquainted with a single instance of such a use of the word elsewhere: and secondly that the addition of SILVIS to SCENA is of itself sufficient to show that, in Virgil's mind at least, SCENA did not express the idea of trees at all. I therefore understand SCENA to be here used in its secondary or derived sense, of *a scene,* i. e. a view or prospect similar to that which in theatres used to be, and still is, painted, or otherwise represented, at the back of the stage, viz. on the partition or screen which bounds the view of the spectators, and separates the pulpitum, stage, or proscenium from the part behind the scenes.

This background partition or screen, called in the ancient theatres *Frons scenæ* (— "Cujus quadrati latus est proximum scenæ, præsciditque curvaturam circinationis, ea regione designatur finitio proscenii, et ab ea regione ad extremam circinationem curvaturæ parallelos linea designatur, in qua constituitur frons scenæ." Vitruv. V. 8.) and for plans of which see Holland's Vitruv. Tab. 36 & 37, being always painted so as to represent some view or prospect in harmony with the action of the piece, the term SCENA, originally no more than the actual tent, arbour, or booth (scene), in which the actors performed (See Servius above — for Servius, often as he errs in the application of the fact to Virgil, is generally correct in the fact itself — Vossius, *Etymol.* — Gronov. *Diatrib.* ad Stat. Silv. IV. III. 21. — and Bald. *Lexic. Vitruv.* in voce scena) came afterwards to be applied, first, to this terminal painting, the never-failing accompaniment and most conspicuous object of the SCENA, and then, by a natural transition, to any view or prospect bearing a resemblance to the views usually represented on this terminal painting. Compare Ausonius:

> "Nec solos hominum delectat scena locorum."
>
> *Mosell. 169.*

Compare also Claudian (speaking of the hot springs of Aponus):

> "Viva coronatos astringit scena vapores."
>
> *Eidyll. VI. 45.*

i. e. not such an artificial, painted enclosure as the *Frons scenæ* of the theatre, or the enclosure, similarly ornamented with paintings of scenery, which it was usual to erect about hot baths, but the enclosure formed by the natural slope of the ground, the real living landscape itself: and above all, compare Virgil:

> "Vel scena ut versis discedat frontibus."
>
> *Georg. III. 24.*

where the meaning must be: — how the view (i. e. of the landscape or building or other object painted on the Frons scenæ) departs from before the eyes of the audience as the Frons scenæ turns round and exposes another side, and therefore another picture, i. e. another view, whether of landscape, building, or other object, it matters not. And so, in our text, SCENA is the view that met the eye on entering this natural harbour; which view is defined by the adjunct SILVIS to be a view of woods, a woody landscape; that very species of SCENA or view which we are informed by Vitruvius (ubi supra) was painted on that side of the Frons scenæ which was turned toward the audience during the representation of the pieces called *Satyræ:* "Satyricæ vero ornantur arboribus, speluncis, montibus, reliquisque agrestibus rebus;" a description, it will be observed, exactly coinciding with the SCENA or view presented to us by our author, there being in it not only woods and mountains, but even a cave.

Heyne's explanation, "Scenam nove dixit poeta de prospectu longo inter silvas, h. e. arbores," shows that Heyne had no clear idea of the meaning; the view being neither *long* nor *through trees* (i. e. not being a vista amongst trees), but simply a view *of* trees. Wagner having, in his *Virg. Br. En.* made a second attempt to elucidate the passage, has failed even more signally than before: "Mons ille silvosus, qui portum utrinque claudebat, in modum scenæ theatralis recessisse sinumque effecisse existimandus est," the shape of the place having been already sufficiently defined by the context; and the word SCENA, on the only other occasion on which it has been employed by our author in the singular number, having been employed, as I have already shown, not in this, but a totally different signification. Charles Rann Kennedy (Lond. 1849) has fallen into the same error as Wagner: "The scene is girt with woods." Voss is correct:

— "Auch die Ansicht schaudernder Wälder
Ragt, und schwarzes Gehölz, hoch her mit grauser Beschattung."

CORUSCIS.—"Tremula luce per intervalla micantibus, dum vento moventur." — HEYNE and WAGNER.

"Blinzelnde, bei ihrer Bewegung Lichtstrahlen durchlassende." — THIEL.

An error into which these commentators, in common with the lexicographers, have been led by Servius's gloss *(ad En. II. 173),* "Coruscum alias fulgens, alias tremulum est." *Coruscus* is never fulgens; always has the one invariable meaning, whether applied to light or to whatever other object, viz. that of rapid alternate appearance and disappearance. Compare:

— "In telis et luce coruscus ahena."
En. II. 470.

Telum coruscat — En. XII. 88. Linguas coruscant — OVID, Met. IV. 493. Flamma inter nubes coruscat — CIC. de Orat.

III. 155. 39. In all which instances as well as in every other instance, with which I am acquainted, of the use of this word, the invariable reference is neither to brightness, nor the emission of light, but to movement: to the rapid alternate appearance and disappearance of the object, and that indifferently whether the object be light or any other object. And such is the idea intended to be presented to us by CORUSCIS in our text: that of the alternate appearance and disappearance of the leaves and boughs of the trees from the view of the spectator according as the sunlight does or does not fall upon them, as they move in the wind. Voss's "schaudernder Wälder" expresses the idea of tremulous motion only, not that of alternate appearance and disappearance.

FRONTE SUB ADVERSA. — "Frons; prærupta et ardua pars petræ (Felswand), quam etiam nostri poetæ appellant 'des Berges Felsenstirn.'" — FORBIGER. Correct perhaps, as a description of the locality, but incorrect as a definition of *frons*, which is, generally, the front or face of any thing; that part which presents itself first: and, specially and almost technically, the front or face of land looking toward water — showing a face toward water — or toward other land lower than itself, (the *bluff* of the Americans), without any reference whatever to the material, whether rock or earth or sand, of which that face consists. Compare Mela *(I. 11)* speaking of Asia: "Ipsa, ingenti ac perpetua *fronte* versa ad orientem." . . . . Post se ingenti *fronte* ad Hellesponticum fretum intendit." and again *(III. 1)*, speaking of the coast of Portugal: "Frons illa aliquamdiu rectam ripam habet; dein modico flexu accepto, mox paullulum eminet; tum reducta iterum, iterumque recta margine jacens, ad promontorium, quod Celticum vocamus, extenditur." And so in our text, FRONTE, the front or face of the land; ADVERSA, opposite to those entering the harbour; the rockiness of the face of the land being, not implied in the term *frons,* but deducible perhaps, from the context. The term *frons,* signifying technically not only the face or front of land looking towards water or lower land, but also (see Comment on SCENA above) the fronting partition or scene in the theatre, i. e. the painted partition behind the actors and looking towards the audience, was a term particularly suitable to the description of a locality which might be considered, and which it seems as if the author were actually considering, in the double light of a *frons terræ* and a *frons scenæ.*

The idea contained in *frons* is wholly omitted both by Voss and Caro:

> "Grad' entgegen gewandt ist eine gewölbete Felskluft;"
>
> Voss.

> "D' incontro è di gran massi, e di pendenti
> Scogli un' antro."
>
> Caro.

SCOPULIS PENDENTIBUS ANTRUM. — "In scopulis pendentibus antrum." — THIEL.

"Caverna est in scopulis suspensis." — RUÆUS.

On the contrary the meaning is, I think, a cave *with* hanging rocks, i. e. a cave rocky overhead, a cave with rocks hanging overhead, or in the roof. Compare:

> "Sunt mihi, pars montis, vivo pendentia saxo
> Antra."
>
> OVID. *Metam. XIII. 810.*

> "Fons sacer in medio, speluncaque pumice pendens."
>
> OVID. *Amor. III. 1. 3.*

> "Structaque pendenti pumice tecta subit.'
>
> OVID. *ad Liviam, 252.*

> "Antra vident oculi scabro pendentia topho."
>
> OVID. *Heroid. XV. 141.*

Voss has understood the structure, and translates the expression tolerably correctly "Eine gewölbete Felskluft."

178.

AC PRIMUM SILICI SCINTILLAM EXCUDIT ACHATES
SUSCEPITQUE IGNEM FOLIIS ATQUE ARIDA CIRCUM
NUTRIMENTA DEDIT RAPUITQUE IN FOMITE FLAMMAM

The first part of Servius's Comment on this passage ("RAPUITQUE IN FOMITE FLAMMAM, pæne soloecophanes est; nam cum mutationem verbum significet, ablativo usus est") is erroneous, for there is no *mutatio,* no transference of action, FOMITE not being a new or different object, but the very object just mentioned under the name NUTRIMENTA, and the meaning being, not transferred to a fomes the fire which he had kindled in the ARIDA NUTRIMENTA, but got a flame in the *fomes* formed of or consisting of the ARIDA NUTRIMENTA; got the fomes into flame. And so Servius correctly in the latter part of his note: "RAPUIT, raptim fecit flammam in fomite, i. e. celeriter." The four steps or processes necessary to the kindling of a fire are distinctly specified in the text; first, the striking of a spark (SILICI SCINTILLAM EXCUDIT); secondly, the igniting of tinder by means of the spark (SUSCEPIT IGNEM FOLIIS); thirdly, the making of a *fomes* (ARIDA CIRCUM NUTRIMENTA DEDIT); and fourthly the inflaming of the *fomes* by the ignited tinder (RAPUIT IN FOMITE FLAMMAM).

The two former of these processes are united together into one by the *que* after SUSCEPIT, the two latter into one by the *que* after RAPUIT, and the former pair connected with, and distinguished from, the latter pair by the conjunction *atque.* Compare OVID. Metam. VIII. 641:

> "Inde foco tepidum cinerem dimovit; et ignes
> Suscitat hesternos; foliisque et cortice sicco
> Nutrit; et ad flammas anima producit anili."

a description which corresponds with that in our text as closely as it is possible for the description of the revival of a decayed fire to correspond with that of the original lighting of a fire, there being in both the same ignition (in the one from a spark, in the other from slumbering embers), the same formation of a *fomes,* and the same completion of the process by the production of flame in the *fomes.* Seneca (*Hippol. 962)* makes a not very dissimilar use of the verb rapere:

> "Qui sparsa cito sidera mundo
> Cursusque vagos rapis astrorum,"

The poet not having thought proper to make any allusion, whether direct or indirect, to the method by which Achates RAPUIT IN FOMITE FLAMMAM, the explanations of Wagner (Virg. Br. En.) and Voss — "Celeri vibratione effecit ut fomes........ ardere inciperet." "Schwang in dem glimmenden Reisig die Flamme" — seem as gratuitous as unnecessary.

182.

EXPEDIUNT FESSI RERUM FRUGESQUE RECEPTAS ET TORRERE PARANT FLAMMIS ET FRANGERE SAXO

FESSI RERUM. — "Fatigati casibus." — RUÆUS.

"Mattgequälten." — VOSS.

"Ex calamitatibus et casibus quas subierant (ita *res* poetis) exhausti." — HEYNE.

The meaning is, I think, much stronger. *Tired of every thing; of human affairs; of the world.* For *res* used in this sense, see

> — "Mersis fer opem, mitissima, rebus."
> OVID. *Metam. I. 380.*

> "Jamque caput rerum Romanam intraverat urbem."
> OVID. *Metam. XV. 736.*

> "In rerum dominos movimus arma Deos."
> OVID. *Ex Ponto. II. 2. 12.*

— "Mors ultima linea rerum est."
Hor. *Epist. I. 16. 79.*

"Romanos rerum dominos, gentemque togatam."
En. I. 286.

— "Hæc intentata manebat
Sors rerum."
En. X. 39.

Compare vers. 466 and Comm.

Saxo. — No doubt the *quern* or ancient mortar; the *cava machina* of Ovid.

"Quodcunque est Cereris solidæ cava machina frangat.
Fasti VI. 381.

184.

ÆNEAS SCOPULUM INTEREA CONSCENDIT ET OMNEM
PROSPECTUM LATE PELAGO PETIT ANTHEA SI QUEM
JACTATUM VENTO VIDEAT PHRYGIASQUE BIREMES
AUT CAPYN AUT CELSIS IN PUPPIBUS ARMA CAICI
NAVEM IN CONSPECTU NULLAM TRES LITTORE CERVOS
PROSPICIT ERRANTES HOS TOTA ARMENTA SEQUUNTUR
A TERGO ET LONGUM PER VALLES PASCITUR AGMEN

"Up to a hill anon his steps he reared,
From whose high top to ken the prospect round,
If cottage were in view, sheep-cote or herd;
But cottage, herd, or sheep-cote none he saw,
Only in a bottom saw a pleasant grove,
With chaunt of tuneful birds resounding loud."
Par. Reg. b. II.

Anthea si quem. — *"Si forte quem eorum qui amissi videbantur ut Anthea aut Capyn videat,"* Wagner. No, but simply *aliquem Anthea.* The expression is perfectly English; *If by chance he might see any Antheus or any Capys,* &c. Compare verse 325: mearum si quam sororum; i. e. si quam *(aliquam)* sororem meam.

216.

PARS IN FRUSTA SECANT VERUBUSQUE TREMENTIA FIGUNT
LITTORE AENA LOCANT ALII FLAMMASQUE MINISTRANT
TUM VICTU REVOCANT VIRES FUSIQUE PER HERBAM

VERUBUSQUE TREMENTIA FIGUNT. — Not, fix the junks *on* spits; but, stick or pierce them *with* spits. See Comm. vers. 48. And so, rightly, Ruæus.

FUSI. — Not *scattered,* but *laid at ease.*

"Tu modo fusus humi lucem aversaris iniquam."
STAT. *Silv. II. 1. 170.*

"Forte Venus . . . . .
Densa . . . . sidereos per gramina fuderat artus
Acclinis florum cumulo."
CLAUD. *Epith. Pall. et Celerinæ, v. 1.*

See also Claudian, *ibid.* vers. 35. There is no distributive power in the sentence except what is feebly possessed by the word PER. Compare Fundat humi, verse 197.

220.

POSTQUAM EXEMPTA FAMES EPULIS MENSÆQUE REMOTÆ
AMISSOS LONGO SOCIOS SERMONE REQUIRUNT
SPEMQUE METUMQUE INTER DUBII SEU VIVERE CREDANT
SIVE EXTREMA PATI NEC JAM EXAUDIRE VOCATOS
PRÆCIPUE PIUS ÆNEAS NUNC ACRIS ORONTI
NUNC AMYCI CASUM GEMIT ET CRUDELIA SECUM
FATA LYCI FORTEMQUE GYAN FORTEMQUE CLOANTHUM
ET JAM FINIS ERAT QUUM JUPITER ÆTHERE SUMMO
DESPICIENS MARE VELIVOLUM TERRASQUE JACENTES
LITTORAQUE ET LATOS POPULOS SIC VERTICE CŒLI
CONSTITIT ET LIBYÆ DEFIXIT LUMINA REGNIS
ATQUE ILLUM TALES JACTANTEM PECTORE CURAS
TRISTIOR ET LACRYMIS OCULOS SUFFUSA NITENTES
ALLOQUITUR VENUS

AMISSOS LONGO SOCIOS SERMONE REQUIRUNT. — "Non tam qualis post cœnam esse solet, quam potius multis cum querelis. Vulgari oratione diceres, *multa de sociis amissis inter se conqueruntur.* SIVE EXTREMA PATI NEC JAM EXAUDIRE VOCATOS; h. e. sive *jam esse mortuos. Etrema pati* dicuntur qui crudeli supplicio affecti animam efflant, h. l. simpliciter, qui moriuntur morte violenta, fluctibus submersi. Ad prosaicam subtilitatem debuisset antecedere: num extrema eos *passos esse* credant, et jam conclamatos?" — HEYNE.

"Diversos mores passim confusos videas; alterum solemnibus sepulcralibus peractis, *acclamandi:* alterum, *conclamandi,* si qui morerentur vel mortui essent. Posterior hic intelligendus, nam *Manes* qui invocabantur audientes fingebantur." — WUNDERLICH.

"Hac formula verborum innuunt illos fuisse mortuos." — LA CERDA.

"I. e. nec jam vivere." — TURNEBUS.

"NEC JAM EXAUDIRE VOCATOS. Mos conclamandi mortuos tangitur his verbis." — WAGNER.

Never was clear meaning more completely misunderstood. We have here not an *allusion* to the *conclamatio,* but the *conclamatio* itself: not indeed the mere formal *conclamatio* as usually performed in the case of a person known to be actually dead, but the real *conclamatio* or calling back of the friend who either was missing and it was feared might be dead, or was lying before them in a state of real or apparent death. And such, however it may have afterwards degenerated, was the Roman *conclamatio* in its origin; not a mere empty superstitious ceremony, but a valuable civil and social institution, having the double object, first of ascertaining whether the case were one of real or only of apparent death; and secondly, if it were the former, of making the fact public by the testimony of a sufficient number of witnesses. "Unde putatis inventos tardos funerum apparatus? Unde quod exequias planctibus, ploratu magnoque semper inquietamus ululatu, quam quod *facinus* videtur tam facile credere vel morti?

Vidimus igitur frequenter ad vitam post conclamata suprema redeuntes." Quinctil. Declam. VIII. 10. And (quoted from Τζετζης by De Bulgaris in his note on the passage),

> "Τουτο δ' εδρων ως μνημονες τυγχανοντες φιλιας,
> Και ως ει απελειφθη τις, προς την φωνην συνδραμοι."

And so, in the passage before us, REQUIRUNT: demand back (seek to recover) their missing friends, in the way in which they are usually demanded back (sought to be recovered) on such occasions; viz. *(a)* with much discussion and many conjectures where they are and what has become of them (LONGO SERMONE); *(b)* with frequent calling on them by name in the hope that they might hear and answer (EXAUDIRE VOCATOS); *(c)* with tears and lamentations (PRÆCIPUE PIUS ÆNEAS GEMIT) Compare Valer. Flaccus:

> "Illum (Hylan sciz.) omnes lacrymis, mœstisque reposcere votis,
> Incertique metu, nunc longas littore voces
> Spargere, —
> Ipse —
> Stat lacrymans magnoque viri cunctatur amore."
>
> *III. 601.*

And Statius *(Theb. VIII. 208):*

> "Talia fatidico peragunt solemnia regi.
> Ceu flammas, ac dona rogo, tristesque rependant
> Exsequias, mollique animam tellure reponant.
> Fracta dehinc cunctis, aversaque pectora bello.
> Sic fortes Minyas subito cum funere Tiphys
> Destituit, non arma sequi, non ferre videtur
> Remus aquas, ipsique minus jam ducere venti.
> Jam fessis gemitu paulatim corda levabat
> Exhaustus sermone dolor, noxque addita curas
> Obruit, et facilis lacrymis irrepere somnus."

And especially Sil. Ital. X. 403, where in a line evidently formed upon our text, the term *requirunt* is applied to the funeral lamentation over the actually dead, viz. over those slain in the battle of Cannæ:

"Interdum mœsto socios clamore requirunt:
Hic Galba, hic Piso, et leto non dignus inerti
Curio deflentur; gravis illic Scævola bello:
Hos passim; at Pauli pariter ceu dira parentis
Fata gemunt."

In which passage, as in our text, *Requirunt* is not conqueruntur, but *require back, seek to get back, demand back, call upon to come back;* so Cic. Verr. VII. 70. "Abs te officium tuum debitum generi et nomini *requiro* et flagito;" and Verr. VII. 142. "Omnes hoc loco cives Romani et qui adsunt et qui ubique sunt vestram severitatem desiderant, vestram fidem implorant, vestrum auxilium *requirunt;*" and exactly parallel to our text:

"Quin potius natam pelago terrisque requiris."
Claud. *Rapt. Pros. III. 315.*

Et jam finis erat. — "Vel *epularum,* vel *famis,* vel *malorum.* — Servius.

"*Longi sermonis;* h. e. *querelarum,* aut omnino, *cœnæ factæ.* Pomponius Sabinus *finem diei* interpretatur. Fateor nexum vel transitum mihi non videri felicissimi inventi." — Heyne.

"Sane *sermonis hujus;* est nota transitionis formula, qua expressit Homericum illud *ως οι μεν τοιαυτα προς αλληλους αγορευον.*" — Wagner.

No wonder that Heyne interpreting the preceding passage as he did, should pronounce the connexion awkward. That passage rightly interpreted, the propriety, nay the elegance, of the connexion becomes apparent. Et jam finis erat: and now their search after and lamentations for their missing friends was at an end, when &c. The lamentations of Jason's friends at Jason's departure are concluded by Valerius Flaccus (I. 350) in the selfsame words.

Our heroes' lamentations are not, like those of their Homeric prototypes (*Κλαιοντεσσι δε τοισιν επηλυθε νηδυμος υπνος.* Odyss. 12. 309), continued until night, daylight being necessary for the fine scene immediately subsequent: — QUUM JUPITER ÆTHERE SUMMO &c.

QUUM JUPITER &c. — For Spenser's imitation of this passage, and of Mercury's descent from heaven, see his *Mother Hubbard's Tale,* vers. 1225, and seq. The whole of the interview between Jupiter and Venus has been also copied and greatly amplified by Camoens, *Lusiad. II. 33.*

TERRASQUE JACENTES. — JACENTES, although in the strict grammatical construction connected with TERRAS only, is connected in the sense with all the objects of DESPICIENS, and is to be understood not of low-lying lands as contradistinguished from highlands or mountains, but of the whole prospect lying *(jacens)* under the eye of Jupiter.

SIC VERTICE CŒLI CONSTITIT. — The nominative to CONSTITIT is not JUPITER (vers. 227), but *ille* understood, this being that *αναχολουθος* so usual to Virgil and of which we have already had so remarkable an instance in

> "Id metuens veterisque memor Saturnia belli;"

and the sentence begun at QUUM JUPITER being broken off at POPULOS, and a new one being begun at SIC. Compare the exactly corresponding construction, En. VII. 666:

> "Ipse pedes tegumen torquens immane leonis,
> Terribili impexum saeta cum dentibus albis
> Indutus capiti, sic regia tecta subibat
> Horridus" &c.

where Ipse, like JUPITER in our text, remains absolutely without any corresponding verb, and where a new sentence is begun at *sic.*

The structure should therefore be indicated by a pause longer than that usually placed at POPULOS; viz. by a dash, or (as in Alfieri's text and the Baskerville) by a semicolon.

TRISTIOR ET LACRYMIS OCULOS SUFFUSA NITENTES. — Not (as a mortal might have been drawn) sad and weeping, but, with the most scrupulous regard to the divine decorum (compare Ovid's picture of Ceres lamenting for Proserpine, *Fasti. IV. 521:*

"Dixit, et ut lacrymæ, neque enim lacrymare Deorum est,
Decidit in tepidos lucida gutta sinus.")

somewhat sad, almost sad, and almost weeping; as nearly in tears as a *deity* could be. This is the exact force of TRISTIOR — not quite *tristis* — something less than *tristis*, as obscurior (En. VII. 205) is not quite obscure, something less than obscure, a little obscure, almost obscure.

248.

FONTEM SUPERARE TIMAVI
UNDE PER ORA NOVEM MAGNO CUM MURMURE MONTIS
IT MARE PRORUPTUM ET PELAGO PREMIT ARVA SONANTI

This passage has been hitherto understood in one or other of these two ways. First: it has been supposed to be a description of the river Timavus bursting with immense noise through an embouchure of nine mouths into the sea:

"Tanta vi exit in mare ut etiam resonat mons." — SERVIUS.

— "Den Quell des Timavus:
Wo er, mit dumpfem Getöse des Bergs, neun Schlünden entrollend,
Geht zu brechen das Meer und den Schwall an die Felder emporbraust."
VOSS.

"Where rolling down the steep, Timavus raves
And through nine channels disembogues his waves."
DRYDEN.

"It proruptum in mare; i. e. prorumpit in mare, vel eo decurrit, ubi in mare effunditur." — THIEL.

So understood, the construction must run thus: The fountain of the river Timavus, out of which fountain, it (the river Timavus) runs through nine mouths into the sea. To this interpretation I object *(a)* that FONTEM TIMAVI is not *the fountain of the river Timavus,* but *the fountain Timavus.* Compare URBEM PATAVI in the very next line but two; not *the city of the place, stronghold, or colony Patavium,* but *the city Patavium itself;* also Fons Bandusiæ (HOR. *Od. III. 13*), not *the fountain of the river Bandusia,* but *the fountain Bandusia itself;* and *(b)* that all travellers and geographers, both ancient and modern, are unanimous that the river Timavus never flowed into the sea by more than one mouth. See Mela II. 4. Strabo V. Cluverius. Ital. Antiq. I. 20. Schlözer (who was on the spot in the year 1777) Briefwechsel, II. Theil. p. 340. Göttingen 1778. Valvasor, Ehre des Herzogthums Krain. Fol. Laibach. 1689 B. II. C. 66. & B. IV. C. 44.

The other way in which the passage has been understood is as a description of the river Timavus bursting out with immense noise through nine springs; uniting its nine streams together into one flood or body of water so large as to resemble a sea, and then running through a single opening or embouchure into the sea itself:

"Hi fontes tribus alveis paulo post delati, mox in unum flumen confluunt, quod vix mille passuum viam emensum uno ostio in mare exit..... IT MARE PRORUPTUM: ad maris speciem; magnos fluctus volventis (quod magna aquæ vi prorumpit se, effunditur; ut Pompon.). — HEYNE.

"MARE, maris instar; magnos fluctus volventis." — WAGNER.

This interpretation is liable to precisely the same grammatical objection as the former, and to a not very dissimilar geographical one, for though with the geographers it assigns nine springs and one embouchure to the river Timavus, it magnifies this river (which was no more, even according to Heyne's own admission, than one thousand yards long) into a sea, and not merely into a sea, but into a roaring sea deluging all the country round. No wonder that geographers should have looked in vain in Illyria for a river to which the description in the text might be at all applicable ("Quibus autem in terris fluvius ille quærendus sit, magna fuit inter viros doctos controversia." Heyne in Excurs. ad locum), and should have at last decided that Virgil either had the Po, or, at least, the Brenta, in view, or if the description were really of the river Timavus, indulged on this occasion in a grandiloquence, to say the least of it, very unusual with so discreet a writer.

It is however neither in an unusual grandiloquence of Virgil, nor in a transference of the scene from the north-eastern to the western shores of the Adriatic, that the solution of the difficulty is to be sought, but in a totally different interpretation of the passage; in understanding it, not as a description either of the Po, or of the Brenta, or of the Timavus, or of any other *river* whatever, but of inundations of the sea, taking place occasionally or periodically through the *fountain* or spring, Timavus. Antenor is described as founding his colony of Patavium far up the Adriatic, not only beyond the kingdom of the Liburni, but beyond that remarkable object, the nine-mouthed *fountain* Timavus, through which the sea communicating by subterraneous channels, bursts out from time to time with a great noise, and in such quantity as to flood the neighbouring fields. Hence the immediate juxta position of the words IT and MARE, the verb and its subject, corresponding exactly to Claudian's 'It Venus' (Rapt. Pros. II. 12), Valer. Flaccus's 'It Sthenelus' (V. 90), and 'It tectis Argoa manus' (III. 3), Statius's 'It caput' (Theb. II. 34), Lucretius's

'It ver, et Venus' (V. 736), and Virgil's own 'It comes' (En. VI. 448). *Mare it proruptum,* the sea goes burst forth, i. e. bursts forth. Compare (Georg. IV. 368) "Caput unde Enipeus se erumpit", corresponding almost word for word with our text, *fontem unde mare it proruptum.* Compare also (Sil. III. 51) "Proruptum exundat pelagus." Hence the inundation covers not the shores but ARVA, the inland cultivated fields. Hence the two noises so accurately distinguished by the opposed expressions MAGNO CUM MURMURE MONTIS and PELAGO SONANTI; the former descriptive of the *ground murmur*, or sound of the water rushing through the subterranean passages, and out through their *ora* or apertures; a sound exactly corresponding to, and expressed by the selfsame words as, that of the winds roaring in the caves under the Eolian mountains (verse 59); the latter descriptive of *the resounding of the waves of the flood with which the eruption of the sea through the ora had covered the country.* Hence the remarkable appellations πηγη θαλαττης and μητηρ θαλαττης, by which the place was known in ancient times (Strabo. Lib. V.), appellations preserved and handed down to us in the name Madre del Mare, by which (see Wood on Homer P. 54 and seq.) it was known in the immediate vicinity until very lately. Hence finally the term PELAGO corresponding to Ausonius's *æquoreo amne,* and meaning actually *sea water*, the Fountain Timavus having been actually salt, as testified anciently by Polybius ("πηγας εχει ζ ποτιμου υδατος· Πολυβιος δ' ειρηκε πλην μιας τας αλλας αλμυρου υδατος.") and in more recent times by Cluverius, who in the following account, the result of his own personal and careful observation, not only reconciles the apparent difference between the accounts of Strabo and Polybius, but gives a most lucid and accurate description, both of the place itself, and of the phenomenon which I conceive to be the subject of the

Virgilian picture. "Ceterum de natura septem fontium (Timavi viz.) ita tradentem supra audivimus Strabonem; *Πηγας εχει ζ ποτιμου υδατος· Πολυβιος δ' ειρηκε πλην μιας τας αλλας αλμυρου υδατος.* Utrumque verum est diversi temporis respectu; quippe quum omnis hic tractus inter mare et Frigidum amnem unum perpetuumque sit saxum ('Hohle Kalkfelsen, die die schönsten und wunderbarsten Grotten bilden.' Schlözer; Briefwechsel, II. Theil. p. 340, Göttingen, 1778,) innumeris passim altissimisque antris perforatum, cuniculi quidam a colle saxeo, qui septem Timavi fontibus imminet, ad proximi maris vada pertingunt, per quos incrementum patitur atque decrementum Timavus ex adfluxu refluxuque ejusdem maris; ita ut lenis sine ullo majore strepitu atque mansuetus dulcibus suis aquis per complures fauces defluat amnis ubi mare subsedit ac procul recessit; quam primum vero idem mare æstu suo intumuit, tanto cum impetu prædictis cuniculis infertur fontibusque Timavi permiscetur, ut ingenti cum fragore ac veluti mugitu saxei montis per complura illa spatiosa ora prorumpat, jamque alveo Timavi contineri nequeat, sed adjacentia prata, per quæ ad ostium tendit amnis, longe lateque sæpius inundet, pelagique in speciem plane contegat.......... Hinc *magnum* appellavit Timavum Virgilius in *Eclog. VIII.....* Hinc item *æquoreum* dixit amnem Ausonius, in carmine de claris urbibus, ('æquoreo * non plenior amne Timavus.')......... Tantâ copiâ quum fontibus Timavi permisceatur mare, horum omnium aquas salsedine suâ inficit, impotabilesque reddit, excepto uno quem omnium

---

* If it be alleged that *æquoreus amnis* may possibly mean a river resembling the sea in copiousness, not in saltness, i. e. a large river, not a sea or marine river, I beg to say that I am not aware that *æquoreus* has ever been used in the former sense, while, on the contrary, its use in the latter is placed beyond doubt by that passage in

maximum apud ipsum divi Johannis delubrum erumpere dixi. *Hæc quum ipse egomet coram probe expertus sim*, audacter eos redarguere liceat, qui dulceis perpetuo permanere omnibus fontibus aquas etiam mari cum maxime æstuante, docent." — *Ital. Antiq. I. 20.*

I am indebted to Doctor Wittmann, Director of the Neues Lazareth at Trieste, for the following description and plans of the locality of the Timavus, as it existed in the beginning of the year 1849:

"Ich kenne den Timavo aus eigener Anschauung und muss gestehen, dass der Vergleich dessen, was *ist*, mit dem, was man nach Virgil *erwartet*, ein wenig stark contrastirt. Während er den armen Antenor bei dem FONTEM SUPERARE TIMAVI so sauern Schweiss vergiessen lässt, fährt man jetzt auf der Poststrasse (kaum ein Paar Klafter von den Quellen weg) ganz lustig und bequem über diesen hin, und während man sich auf das Dröhnen der Gebirge und auf Wasserstürze (à la Nilkatarakten) gefasst macht, hört man nichts als das Klappern zweier Mühlen, die der ausströmende Fluss ganz friedlich und gemüthlich in Bewegung setzt.

---

the *Pharsalia*, Lib. VIII. where Lucan, speaking of the sea water used to extinguish Pompey's funeral pyre, says, —

— "Resolutaque nondum
Ossa satis, nervis et inustis plena medullis,
Æquoreâ restinguit aquâ."

From which compared with

"Acta per æquoreas hospita navis aquas."
Ovid. *Fasti I. 340.*

"Qua petit æquoreas advena Tybris aquas."
Ovid. *Fasti. II. 68.*

"Cum socer æquoreus, numerosaque turba sororum
Certarent epulis continuare dies.
Claud. *Epith. Honor. August. & Mariæ. Præf. v. 3.*

and

"Quid? quod ab æquorea numeratur origine quartus."
Ovid. *Met. X. 617.*

it seems certain that Ausonius's *æquoreum amnem* is *a sea river: a river of sea water.*

"Die Quellen des Flusses liegen, wie gesagt, ungefähr 8 bis 10 Schritte abseits der Poststrasse; und beiläufig 9 Fuss über dem Spiegel des Wasserbeckens, welches sie gleich bei der Ausmündung bilden, zieht die Strasse hin, welche am Gebirgsabhange angelegt, ungefähr das nachstehende Profil gibt.

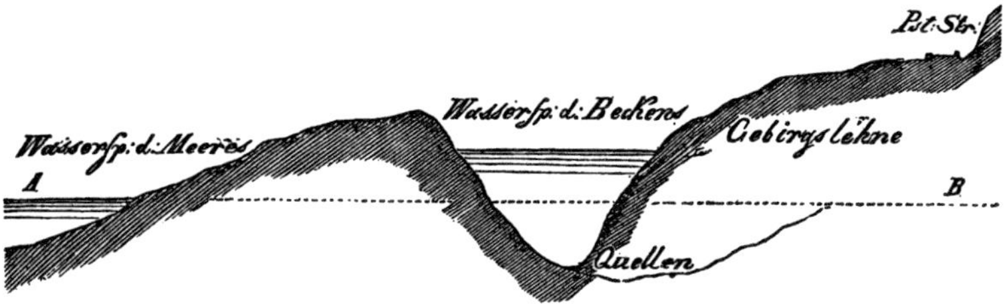

"Die Quellen, deren gegenwärtig sieben sein sollen (auch Strabo gibt nicht mehr an, so dass vielleicht Virgil mit seiner Zahl neun Unrecht hat) sammeln sich an drei Stellen, wo sie' ein durch eine Halbinsel und ein Paar Inselchen durchschnittenes Wasserbecken bilden. Die Ausmündung der Quellen soll ungefähr neun Fuss unter dem Meeresspiegel liegen, die Formation des zwischen dem Becken und dem Meere liegenden Terrains (eine Strecke von höchstens Einer italienischen Miglia) schützt aber die Quellen gegen die Vermischung mit Seewasser. Das Wasser der Quellen ist nicht gesalzen; wird aber, da es, wie natürlich, sehr kalt ist, als fieberverursachend gescheut. Manche behaupten zwar, dass bei ausserordentlich hoher Fluth das Meerwasser bis zu den Quellen hinauf in den Fluss eindringe, die Leute aus den Mühlen haben mir jedoch an Ort und Stelle die Versicherung gegeben, dass dies nicht der Fall ist.

"Ich gebe Ihnen nun hier, zur besseren Orientirung, einen beiläufigen Situationsplan der Gegend.

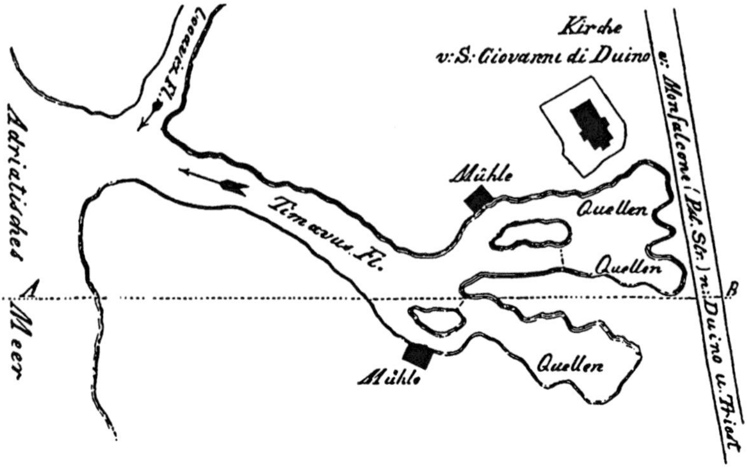

"Sie können also dem Timavo füglich drei Arme zugestehen, die sich, nach kaum hundert bis hundertfünfzig Klafter langem Laufe, zu Einem Flusse vereinigen, der wasserreich genug ist, um ziemlich grosse *Trabacoli* zu tragen, da in der That die Barken, welche das Mehl zwischen S. Giovanni und Triest verführen geradezu bei den im obigen Plane bezeichneten zwei Mühlen anlegen und aus- oder einladen können. Von einem Austreten des Flusses zu einem See, ist heut zu Tage keine Rede mehr. Dagegen gibt es über die Formation der Wässer jener Gegenden im Alterthume eine Menge theilweise auf gründliche Forschung basirte Ansichten, nach welchen einst Wippachfluss und Icongo sich mit dem Timavus vereint und zwischen S. Giovanni und Monfalcone einen förmlichen See gebildet hätten, aus welchen nur die jetzigen Bagni di Monfalcone als Insel hervorgeragt haben.

"Die Benennung *Sorgente e madre del Mare,* welche nach Polybius die alten Bewohner dem Flusse Timavus gegeben haben sollen, mag vielleicht gerade in den grossen Wassermassen ihren Ursprung gehabt haben, welche nach den obenerwähnten Annahmen sich einst in jener Gegend, unter dem Gesammtnamen Timavus, vereiniget haben. Heut zu Tage ist diese Benennung *Madre del mare* den Ortsbewohnern gar nicht mehr bekannt. Hier haben Sie Alles, was ich über den Gegenstand der Frage wusste, oder jetzt in Erfahrung bringen konnte. Das Beste, was man über den Timavus und beziehungsweise über die Ausgleichung der Angaben alter Autoren mit dem factischen Bestande des Flusses an Druckschriften besitzt, soll eine Broschure sein, deren Titel mir so angegeben worden ist, wie ich ihn hier (salvo errore ed ommissione) für Sie ansetze:

Indagine sullo stato del Timavo e delle sue adjacenze al principio dell' era Cristiana, dell' Abbate Giuseppe Berini di Ronchi, di Monfalcone. Udine. Pei Fratelli Mattiuzzi, 1826, nella Tipografia Pecile."

This manifestly accurate and trustworthy description serves to clear up several circumstances in the history of the Timavus which have hitherto been involved in the thickest obscurity. First, it explains at once the reason of the great discrepancy in the accounts which different writers have given of the number of the *ora,* these *ora* being, as appears from both the above plans, overflowed, occasionally at least, by their own waters, which when copious form above them one large basin, pond or tarn (in the plan, "Wasserbecken"), partially subdivided by two small islands and a peninsula; and when scanty, several ponds or basins, corresponding each to one or more *ora,* and entirely separated from each other by the above mentioned peninsula and islands then converted by the lowness of the water into isthmuses. The difficulty of correctly counting the *ora* at the bottom of this basin or these basins, is sufficiently obvious, and is expressed in the description by the words "*sein sollen*" (should be — are said to be), for Dr. Wittmann, though on the spot, does not take upon him to say how many in number these *ora,* being under the water, actually are; in this respect following the example of another visitor to the spot (Schlözer, ubi supra) who having informed us that these *ora* are *holes* (Löcher) in the limestone rock which forms the substratum of this whole district of Carniola, proceeds thus to express himself: "Da nun hier die See immer zunimmt, so findet der ganze Timavus beinahe keinen Abfluss mehr, und das Wasser fängt schon gleich bei seiner Entstehung an zu stehen, zumal in trocknen Zeiten, wo nur die untern *Löcher* der Felsen Wasser geben. Es sind der Löcher mehr als sieben...... Einige haben eine ungeheure Tiefe, andre nicht." Secondly, it explains the meaning of Claudian's remarkable expression "numerantur stagna Timavi" (Paneg. de tert. consulat. Honorii, *v.* 120); 'stagna' being the basins or ponds formed by the springs at their very origin and covering the springs themselves and therefore equivalent to *fontes;* as if he had said the fountain-ponds of Timavus (compare Claudian's account of the spring or *sorgente* of the Aponus seen at the bottom of its own basin, i. e. through the pond formed by itself:

"Consuluit Natura sibi, ne tota lateret;
Admisitque oculos, quo vetat ire calor.
Turbidus impulsu venti cum spargitur aer,
Glaucaque fumiferæ terga serenat aquæ;
Tunc omnem liquidi vallem mirabere fundi:
Tunc veteres hastæ, regia dona, micant:
Quas inter, nigræ tenebris obscurus arenæ,
Discolor abruptum flumen hiatus agit.
Aponus, v. 33.);

and, 'numerantur, *are counted,* these fountain-heads being not only several, but actually varying in number at different times, and so giving rise to a variety of accounts. Thirdly, it shows how easily irruptions of the sea, such as those described in our text, might take place through these *ora* which existing (as testified by Cluverius, Schlözer, Valvasor and others) in a district full of caverns and subterranean passages, and no more than a thousand yards distant from the sea, are besides nine Austrian feet below the sea level. Fourthly, it explains the greatness of the floods caused by such irruptions, the water being prevented by the height of the intervening ground from flowing off immediately and directly into the sea.

Let the reader imagine a large marble basin or bath full of water and flowing over, the water being continually supplied by a number of conduits opening into the bath at different points of its bottom: the openings of these conduits will be Virgil's *ora;* the bath itself (including the *ora*) will be Virgil's *fons,* Claudian's *stagna;* the water overflowing the bath and running off, the river Timavus; and an accidental bursting of the sea out through the bath by means of subterranean communication with the conduits, the inundation described in the text. Phenomena more or less similar to that anciently observed in the fountain Timavus are, we are told, still to be observed in its neighbourhood. At Monfalcone less than a mile distant are warm springs which are said to rise and fall with the flow and ebb of the sea (Filiasi, *Mem. Stor. de' Veneti. cap. XXIX. note,* and Plin. *II. 106*); and from the neighbouring lake of Czirknitz the waters at certain irregular periods run off suddenly through fissures in its bottom (ora), and after an interval return again as suddenly and with a tremendous noise; "avec un bruit épouvantable, semblable à celui du tonnerre." Malte Brun, Livr. 85. The lake, which Dr. Wittmann refers to in the above description as having probably existed in former times in the course of the river Timavus, is laid down in the Carte de Peuttinger (see Malte Brun's Atlas No. 19) and is no doubt the Lacus Timavi of Livy, XXXXI. 5.

An account of the respective positions and names of the seven 'ora Timavi' as they existed in the year 1689 will be found in Valvasor ubi supra.

Compare the description given by Mela *(III. 8)*

of the *os* or *spring* of the Euphrates: "Tigris ut natus est, ita descendens usque in littora permeat: Euphrates immani ore aperto, non exit tantum, unde oritur, sed et vaste quoque decidit; nec secat continuo agros, sed late diffusus in stagna, diu sedentibus aquis piger, et sine alveo patulus, post ubi marginem rupit vere fluvius, acceptisque ripis celer et fremens, per Armenios et Cappadocas occidentem petit." Compare also the account which Claudian *(Eidyl. VI. 40)* gives of the opening or hole, '*hiatus discolor*' (Virgil's *os*), through which the spring or stream which forms the *lacus* or *pond Aponus,* rises, and which *hiatus,* hole or *os,* with the water rising up through it, can be distinctly seen when you look down through the clear water of the pond. Compare also the account given by Pliny *(Ep. VIII. 8)* of the fountain Clitumnus: "Hunc (collem) subter fons exit, et exprimitur pluribus venis, sed imparibus, eluctatusque facit gurgitem, qui lato gremio patescit....... Fons adhuc, et jam amplissimum flumen, atque etiam navium patiens" &c.

That the word *os,* primarily the human mouth, and secondarily any mouth or opening, is the mouth or opening of a spring or source (the hole through which the waters of the spring issue out of the ground) no less than the mouth opening or embouchure of a river into the sea, appears not only from the above quotation from Mela, but from Ovid's

> "Hi (amnes sciz.) redeunt, ac fontibus ora relaxant
> Et defrenato volvuntur æquora cursu."
> *Metam. I. 281.*

and

> "Oraque qua pollens ope sum fontana reclusi
> Sumque repentinas ejaculatus aquas." *Fasti I. 270.*

from Statius's

> "Qualis ubi adversi secretus pabula cœli
> Nilus et Eoas magno bibit ore pruinas,
> Scindit fontis opes, septemque patentibus arvis
> In mare fert hiemes. *Theb. VIII. 358.*

and especially from Virgils own

Ore, Arethusa, tuo Siculis confunditur undis.

En. III. 696.

where *ore* must be *sorgente,* spring, or fountain, Arethusa being not a river, but only a spring or fountain on the sea shore, so near the sea as to require the protection of a pier or embankment against the waves: "qui fluctu totus operiretur, nisi munitione ac mole lapidum a mari disjunctus esset." Cic. *in Verr. III. 53. Ed. Ern.*

252.

GENTI NOMEN DEDIT ARMAQUE FIXIT
TROIA NUNC PLACIDA COMPOSTUS PACE QUIESCIT

"Genti nomen dedit; at quale? dicunt Antenoridarum: apud poetas utique; non vero vulgare nomen; sed Venetorum nomen" &c. — Heyne.

— "Gab Namen dem Volk, und heftete Troja's Rüstungen."

Voss.

"Nomen, Venetorum, ab Henetis Paphlagoniæ, Antenoris comitibus, ut aiunt, ductum." — Wagner, *Virg. Br. En.*

It seems to me however that Virgil so far from leaving us in the dark about the name which Antenor gave his colony, has in the word troia, told us explicitly what that name was: the peculiar position of the word troia — at the close of the sentence to which it belongs and at the same time at the beginning of the next line, and separated from the remainder of the line by a pause — enabling it to embrace in its action not only its own immediate and proper substantive, but the other substantive bound up with it in the same clause. See Comment on,

"*Aerea* cui gradibus surgebant *limina,* nexæque
Aere *trabes.*"

En I. 448.

If instead of the poetical and therefore somewhat irregular TROIA, Virgil had contented himself with the more regular and prosaic Trojæ, the meaning would probably have been less easily mistaken.

The correctness of the above interpretation seems to be placed beyond doubt by the account handed down to us by Livy *(I. 1)* that Antenor actually called the first town which he built on his landing in Italy, Troja.

The above interpretation being adopted, the punctuation should be GENTI NOMEN DEDIT, ARMAQUE FIXIT, TROIA.

NUNC PLACIDA COMPOSTUS PACE QUIESCIT. — "Nunc placidam mortem obiit: *componendi* verbum omnia complectitur, quæ fiunt mortuis." — WAGNER.

> "E quivi han l'ossa sue pace e riposo."
>
> ALFIERI.

I disagree with this interpretation although sanctioned by Handius (ad STAT. *Silv. I. pag. 50*), Jahn, Forbiger and Ladewig. First, for the reason assigned by Peerlkamp: "Venus uti hoc exemplo non potuit, quæ nato suo non placidam mortem, sed felicem vitam optaret"; and secondly, because *componere* is applied both by Virgil himself elsewhere (ex. gr. *En. I. 378, 702*), and very commonly by other authors, to quiet or peace during life:

> "Omnia noctis erant placida composta quiete."
>
> VARRO ATACINUS, *apud Senec. Controv. III. 16.*

> "Redde diem noctemque mihi, da prendere vestes
> Somniferas, ipsaque oculos componere virga."
>
> VALER. FLAC. *VII. 246.*

"Tanto impensius in securitatem compositus, neque loco, neque vultu mutato, sed utsolitum per illos dies egit." TACIT. *Ann. III. 44.* "Dum res firmando Neronis imperio componuntur." TACIT. *Ann. XII. 68.* Compare "Placida cum pace quietus," LUCRET. *VI. 72.* To Heyne's first objection, "At si de *quietis sedibus, rebus placatis, vita tranquilla* agitur, tum fere *res compositæ* memorantur, non *ipsi homines,*" the passage just quoted from Tacitus affords a sufficient answer. To his second objection, "Nam quum pacis otiique significationem contineant vss. praecedentes, non poterit huic rerum statui idem opponi per NUNC, temporum rerumque diversitatem quandam indicans," it may I think be replied that NUNC serves to contrast the present condition of Antenor not with his own previous condition, but with the present condition of Eneas; and that Venus's meaning is not merely that Antenor formerly established himself there, and now enjoys peace and repose there, but that he formerly established himself there, and is enjoying peace there now, at this very moment, while Eneas is still an outcast and the sport of every misfortune; NUNC PLACIDA COMPOSTUS PACE QUIESCIT; NOS, TUA PROGENIES etc. Compare:

"Quam vacet alterius blandos audire susurros
Molliter in tacito littore compositam."

PROPERT. *Eleg. I. 11. 13.*

"Contra vetera fratrum odia et certamina, familiae nostrae Penates rite compossuisse." — TACIT. *Ann. XV. 2.* "Tempus componere gentem." — SIL. ITAL. XVII. 359. "Rebelles barbarorum animos pace componi." — TACIT. *Ann. XIV. 39.*

"At me composita pace fefellit amor."

PROPERT. *Eleg. II. 2. 6;*

and, precisely parallel to our text: "Neque enim dubito esse amoenissimam [villam] in qua se composuerat homo, felicior ante, quam felicissimus fieret." — PLIN. *Epist. V. 18;* and

"Quam tuta possis urbem componere terra."

En. III. 387;

where 'componere urbem', *settle your city,* as in our text COMPOSTUS, *settled.*

259.

VULTU QUO CÆLUM TEMPESTATESQUE SERENAT

See Comment *v. 128.* Page 46. There is a representation of Jupiter Serenus with the inscription "Jovi Sereno sacr." on an ancient lamp in the Passerian Museum. It is stated by Passerius (I know not how truly,) to be the only ancient representation of Jupiter Serenus in existence. See *Lucernæ Fictiles Musæi Passerii, Tom. I. Tab. 33.* It is highly probable that the words of the text allude to some such representation of Jupiter Serenus actually existing, and well known, in the time of Virgil. On Trajan's Column at Rome there is a figure supposed to represent Jupiter Pluvius; see Bartoli, *Colonna Trajana No.133.* Also one on the Column of M. Aurelius Antoninus in the Piazza Colonna in the same city; see Bellorius, Tab. 15. Boissard *(Topog. et Antiq. Urb. Romæ. Pars V. Tab. 24.)* gives a representation of a monument (apparently the pedestal of a statue) bearing the inscription, JOVI SERENO. NUMISIUS ALBINUS. EX VOTO.

279.

INDE LUPÆ FULVO NUTRICIS TEGMINE LÆTUS

"Romulum pro casside lupæ exuvias seu lupinam pellem gessisse narrat." — Heyne, who quotes Prop. IV. 10. 20. But why spoil the picture by limiting the wolfskin 'tegmen' to the head? why not extend it, as the lynxskin 'tegmen', *v. 327,* to the whole person? Compare *En. II. 721; V. 37; VII. 666; VIII. 460.* Had a cap only and not a general covering for the whole person been intended, it would have been distinctly so stated, as *En. VII. 688.*

283.

QUIN ASPERA JUNO
QUÆ MARE NUNC TERRASQUE METU CÆLUMQUE FATIGAT
CONSILIA IN MELIUS REFERET MECUMQUE FOVEBIT
ROMANOS RERUM DOMINOS GENTEMQUE TOGATAM

See the fulfilment of this prophecy, testified by no less authority than that of Juno herself, in Ovid's *Fasti, VI. 41 — 52.*

ROMANOS RERUM DOMINOS GENTEMQUE TOGATAM. — Not merely, the Romans, whose national dress is the 'toga, commanding the world; but the Romans *in their robe of peace, the 'toga'*, commanding the world. Compare: "Me uno togato duce et imperatore." CICERO *in Catil. II. c. 13.* "Quod mihi primum post hanc urbem conditam togato contigit." *In Catil. III. c. 6.* "Erepti (estis) sine cæde, sine sanguine, sine exercitu, sine dimicatione; togati, me uno togato duce et imperatore, vicistis." *In Catil. III. c. 10.* "Et ni multitudo togatorum fuisset, quæ Numidas insequentes mœnibus prohibuit" etc. SALL. *Jugurth. c. 21.* See Comm. *En. VI. 853.*

294.

VOCABITUR HIC QUOQUE VOTIS
ASPERA TUM POSITIS MITESCENT SÆCULA BELLIS
CANA FIDES ET VESTA REMO CUM FRATRE QUIRINUS
JURA DABUNT DIRÆ FERRO ET COMPAGIBUS ARCTIS
CLAUDENTUR BELLI PORTÆ FUROR IMPIUS INTUS
SÆVA SEDENS SUPER ARMA ET CENTUM VINCTUS AHENIS
POST TERGUM NODIS FREMET HORRIDUS ORE CRUENTO

QUOQUE; — i. e. *as well as Eneas himself.* See *v. 263.*

CANA FIDES ET VESTA REMO CUM FRATRE QUIRINUS JURA DABUNT. — The simple meaning is, that *men, ceasing from war, shall live as they did in the good old times, when they obeyed the precepts of Fides, Vesta, and Remus and Romulus* (see below). It is sufficiently evident from *Georg. I. 498* and *II. 533,* that the deities here mentioned were specially associated in the Roman mythology with that primitive epoch of the national history, to which the Romans (sharing a feeling common to all civilised nations that have ever existed) loved to look back as an epoch of peace and innocence; for this reason and no other are they specified as the gods of the returning golden age here announced by Jupiter. I am unwilling so far to derogate from the dignity of this sentiment, as to suppose, with Heyne, that it contains an allusion to the trivial circumstance of the temples of Fides, Vesta, and Remus and Romulus being seated on the Palatine hill near the palace of Augustus; nor do I think it necessary to discuss the opinion advanced by the late Mr. Seward, and preserved by Hayley in one of the notes to his second Epistle on Epic Poetry, that the meaning is, that *civil and criminal justice shall be administered in those temples,* that opinion being based on the erroneous interpretation of JURA DABUNT, pointed out below

The whole of this enunciation of the fates by Jupiter is one magnificent strain of adulation of Augustus. A similar adulation, although somewhat more disguised, is plainly to be read in every word of Venus's complaint to Jupiter, and in the very circumstance of the interview between the queen of love and beauty and the *'Pater hominumque deumque';* that interview having for its sole object the fortunes of Eneas, Augustus's ancestor, and the foundation by him of that great Roman empire, of which Augustus was now the absolute master and head. Nor is the adulation of Augustus confined to those parts of the Eneis, in which, as in the passages before us, there is reference to him by name or distinct allusion; it pervades the whole poem from beginning to end; and could not have been least pleasing to a person of so refined a taste where it is least direct, and where the praise is bestowed, not upon himself, but upon that famous Goddess-born ancestor, from whom it was his greatest pride and boast that he was descended. Not that I suppose, with Warburton and Spence, either that the character of Augustus is adumbrated in that of Eneas, or that the Eneis is a political poem, having for its object to reconcile the Roman nation to the newly settled order of things; on the contrary, I agree with Heyne that there are no sufficient grounds for either of these opinions, and that they are each of them totally inconsistent with the boldness and freedom necessary to a great epic. But, nevertheless, without going so far as Warburton or Spence, I am certainly of opinion that Virgil wrote the Eneis in honor of Augustus: that he selected Eneas for his hero, chiefly because, as Augustus's reputed ancestor, and the first founder of the Roman empire, his praises would redound more to the honor of, and therefore be more grateful to, Augustus, than those of any other hero with which the heroic age could have furnished him; and still further, that he not only purposely abstained from introducing topics which might have been disagreeable to the feelings, or derogatory to the reputation, of Augustus, but also seized every opportunity of giving such tendency and direction to his story, and illustrating it with such allusions as he judged would be best received by him, and shed most honor and glory upon his name. Nor let this be called mere adulation: call it rather the heartfelt gratitude of the partial poet towards his munificent friend and patron, and the fulfilment and realization of his allegorical promise to build a magnificent temple to him by Mincius' side,

— "Viridi in campo templum de marmore ponam
Propter aquam, tardis ingens ubi flexibus errat
Mincius, et tenera prætexit arundine ripas.
In medio mihi Cæsar erit, templumque tenebit."
Georg. III. 13.

CANA FIDES. — "Canam Fidem dixit, vel quod in canis hominibus invenitur, vel quod ei albo panno involuta manu sacrificatur." — SERVIUS.
"La candida Fede." — CARO.

I think rather, with Nonius, Voss, and Heyne, *hoary;* 'die grauende': viz. with age. Compare:

"Si quid longa Fides canaque jura valent."
MART. I. 16. 2.

— "Priscamque resumunt
Canitiem leges."
CLAUD. *Quart. Cons. Honor. 505.*

— "Laxata casside prodit (viz. personified Rome)
Canitiem, plenamque trahit rubiginis hastam."
CLAUD. *Bell. Gildon. 24.*

JURA DABUNT. — *'Jura dare'* is, primarily, *to make and impose laws, to perform the function of lawgiver,* and therefore secondarily, *to rule:* "Cæsar dum magnus ... victor ... volentes Per populos dat jura," *Georg. IV. 560.* "Hospitibus nam te dare jura loquuntur," *En. I. 735.* See also *En. III. 137; V. 758; VIII. 670,* etc.; also

"Det pater hic umbræ mollia jura meæ."
PROP. IV. 11. 18.

It is surprising that Heyne, having correctly interpreted JURA DABUNT in the passage before us by *'præerunt',* should afterwards, at line 511, fall into the common error, and confound *'jura dare'* with *'jus dicere',* the meaning of which is *to expound, explain,* or *lay down what the law is, to perform the office of a judge, to administer justice.* "Ea res a Volcatio, qui Romæ jus dicit, rejecta in Galliam est." CICER. *Fam. Epist. XIII, 14.* "Appius ... quam asperrime poterat jus de creditis pecuniis dicere." LIV. II. 27. "Ipse jus dixit assidue, et in noctem nonnunquam: si parum corpore valeret, lectica pro tribunali collocata, vel etiam domi cubans." — SUET. *Aug. c. 33.* I think also that Heyne confines JURA DABUNT within too narrow limits by subjoining *'imperio Romano'*; and that he should have used some more comprehensive term, such as *'hominibus'*, or *'populis'*, or *'gentibus'*, which would better harmonize with the wide extent of the term SÆCULA, and with the general spirit of the prophecy, that the peace was to be universal, to extend over the whole world.

DIRÆ FERRO ET COMPAGIBUS ARCTIS CLAUDENTUR BELLI PORTÆ. — Heyne has set his seal to the following, which is the universally received, interpretation of this passage: "[belli] *porta dira*, quia dei diri et abominandi, clauditur FERRO ET COMPAGIBUS ARCTIS, seu vinculis, h. e. foribus ferratis." *(Excurs. IX. ad En. I.).* So also Alfieri:

> "Chiuse, e di bronzo sbarrate le atroci
> Porte staranno del guerriero Giano."

It seems almost incredible that neither Heyne nor any of the other commentators should have perceived that this interpretation is not only inconsistent with the well known meaning of the word *'compages'*, but with the plain and obvious structure of the sentence, and with the fairly presumable intention of Virgil. First, with the well known meaning of *'compages'*, which is not *bolts* or *other fastenings*, but *the conjunction* or *colligation of the parts of which a compound object is compacted* or *put together:* as *of the stones* or *bricks of a wall* (LUCAN. III. 491); *of the planks of a ship (En. I. 126)* or *other wooden building*, ex. gr. *the wooden horse (En. II. 51)*; or *of the organs constituting an animal body* (CIC. *de Senect. c. 21*); or *of the several constituent parts of which an empire* (TACIT. *Hist. IV. 74)*, or *the world itself* (AUL. GELL. VI. 1), *consists.* This is the only meaning which the word *'compages'* has either in the Latin language, or in the English, into which it has been adopted from the Latin. Secondly, the received interpretation is inconsistent with the plain and obvious structure, according to which FERRO ET COMPAGIBUS is connected with DIRÆ, not with CLAUDENTUR, in the same way as ORE CRUENTO at the close of the sentence is connected with HORRIDUS, not with FREMET; compare: "Horridus austris Torquet." IX. 670. It is impossible for the reader or reciter to separate FERRO ET COMPAGIBUS ARCTIS from DIRÆ, or ORE CRUENTO from HORRIDUS, without making, at DIRÆ and HORRIDUS, pauses very disagreeable both to the ear and sense. So also, in the sentence "ora modis attollens pallida miris" (*v. 354*), modis miris' is joined with 'pallida, not with 'attollens', as is proved by the corresponding sentence, *Georg. I. 477:* "Simulacra modis pallentia miris." See Comm. *En. I. 641* and *V. 460.* Pliny uses DIRÆ in precisely the same construction (B. V. c. 4): "Sinus vadoso mari dirus." Thirdly, even if it were admitted (which, however, I cannot admit,) that *'compages'* might, in another situation, mean *the bolts* or *fastenings of a gate,* still we must, in justice to the *ars poëtica* of Virgil, refer it in this situation to *the structure of the gate itself,* because it would have been highly incorrect and unpoetical to lay so great a stress on the mere circumstance of the *fastenings of the gate being of iron,* since it appears not only from the celebrated line of Ennius, quoted by Horace, but from Lucan's "Pax missa per orbem Ferrea belligeri compescat limina Jani" (I. 60), and Virgil's own "Belli ferratos rupit Saturnia postes" *(En. VII. 622)*, that *the gate itself was iron;* it is incredible that Virgil should have presented us with the minor picture of the *iron fastenings,* and wholly omitted the greater picture of the *iron gate.* The structure, therefore, is DIRÆ FERRO ET COMPAGIBUS ARCTIS, and these words are the description of the gate itself: DIRÆ expressing the effect which its appearance produced on the mind; FERRO informing us that its material was iron; COMPAGIBUS, that it consisted of several pieces adapted to each other; and ARCTIS, that those pieces were closely joined or compacted together (for, as appears from *En. I. 126,* closeness does not form an essential part of the idea expressed by *'compages'*). It will further be observed, that the emphasis (which by the received interpretation is thrown upon the fastenings of the gate) is by this mode of rendering the passage, thrown upon CLAUDENTUR — the really emphatic word, as containing the principal idea, the *closing* of the temple of Janus in the time of universal peace.

The above interpretation is further confirmed by the point placed in the Medicean MS. between ARCTIS and CLAUDENTUR.

Exactly parallel to FERRO ET COMPAGIBUS ARCTIS, we have *(En. II. 627)* "ferro crebrisque bipennibus," for *crebris bipennibus ferri.*

The turn given by Voltaire to this passage, in his application of it to Elizabeth, Queen of England is as happy as it is truly French:

"Quel exemple pour vous, monarques de la terre!
Une femme a fermé les portes de la guerre,
Et renvoyant chez vous la discorde et l'horreur,
D'un peuple qui l'adore elle a fait le bonheur."

Henriade, C. I

304.

VOLAT ILLE PER AERA MAGNUM
REMIGIO ALARUM

— "Down thither prone in flight
He speeds, and through the vast ethereal sky
Sails between worlds and worlds, with steady wing."

Par. Lost, V. 266

306.

ET JAM JUSSA FACIT PONUNTQUE FEROCIA PŒNI
CORDA VOLENTE DEO

Ferocia is rather our *fierce* than our *ferocious;* compare *En. IV 135;* also the application of the term by Germanicus on his death-bed to the feelings which Agrippina, his wife, entertained toward the persons who were suspected of having been the cause of his death: "Per memoriam sui, per communes liberos oravit, exueret ferociam, sævienti fortunæ submitteret animum." — Tacit. *Annal. II. 72.* See also Hor. *Carm. III. 3. 42:*

— "Stet Capitolium
Fulgens, triumphatisque possit
Roma ferox dare jura Medis;"

also Nep. *Them. c. 2.*

313.

EXACTA REFERRE

"Exacta, quæ explorasset, comperisset." — Heyne. "Diligenter explorata." — Wagner; on which interpretation Wunderlich (without proposing a better) observes: "qua significatione hæc vox rarius (he might have said, 'nunquam') usurpatur. Exacta is simply *facta, transacta;* exacta referre, Anglice, *report proceedings.*

314.

CLASSEM IN CONVEXO NEMORUM SUB RUPE CAVATA
ARBORIBUS CLAUSAM CIRCUM ATQUE HORRENTIBUS UMBRIS
OCCULIT

"Classem occultat sub convexa rupe nemoribus consita." — Heyne. "In convexo nemorum, im Dickicht des

Waldes. Æneas verbirgt seine Schiffe unter einer von Bäumen eingeschlossenen und beschatteten Felsenwölbung." — Ladewig.

Both commentators omit all explanation of the only word in the sentence, which requires explanation, convexo. By understanding this word to mean *a somewhat crescent shaped hollow* or *depression* (i. e. *bay* or *bight*) *in the rocky and wooded side of the cove* we not only obtain at once a clear, simple, and natural meaning for the passage (Eneas fearful that his fleet, if left in the open cove, might be discovered during his absence, puts it into a nook, recess, or offset in the side of the cove, where it is protected by thick branching and shady trees from the view of any boat which might happen to row up the cove, and by the overhanging of the rock from the observation of hunters or stragglers on the cliffs above), but at the same time assign to the word the very sense in which it is used both by Virgil himself elsewhere, and by other Latin writers. Compare *(v. 611):*

> — "Dum montibus umbræ
> Lustrabunt convexa;"

hollows or *depressions among the mountains,* or *on the sides of the mountains.* Also Justin, II. 10: "Montes in planum ducebat et convexa vallium æquabat;" *raised to a level the hollows of the vallies — filled up the vallies till they were on a level with the surrounding country.* Also Pliny, *N. Hist. V. 77:* "Folia erant plantaginis, nisi angustiora essent, et magis laciniosa, convexaque in terram;" *curved downwards,* i. e. so that their concavity was turned towards the ground. Also Ausonius, *Mosell. 247:*

> "Ille autem, scopulis subjectas pronus in undas,
> Inclinat lentæ convexa cacumina virgæ,
> Indutos escis jaciens letalibus hamos."

This is the very sense also in which the term is so commonly applied to the sky in such expressions as 'convexa cæli', 'supera convexa', etc. ("'Supera ad convexa': cæli curvitatem." SERV. *ad En. VI. 241*).

Virgil's

— IN CONVEXO NEMORUM . . . . . .
ARBORIBUS CLAUSAM CIRCUM ATQUE HORRENTIBUS UMBRIS

differs therefore little, except in depth of shade, from Claudian's

— "nemorum frondoso margine cinctus."
De Rapt. Proserp II. 113.

317.

BINA MANU LATO CRISPANS HASTILIA FERRO

"Nitidius verbum et quasi coloratius crispare quam quassare, si id apud Virgilium significat. Crispum enim est non rectum: Quassata hasta curvatur ac crispatur." — SCALIG. *Poet. IV. 1.*

"Crispare ist das bestimmtere Verbum von dem durch Schwingen hervorgebrachten zitternden, blinzenden Scheine des Eisens, von crispus." — THIEL.

"Crispantur, quæ incurvantur, inflectuntur. Est τo πτυσσεσϑαι de hastis. Iliad. ν. 134." — HEYNE.

"Quassans manu." — RUÆUS.

"Vibrans et torquens." — LA CERDA.

"Vibrans." — GESNER.

"Quassando et vibrando micare faciens." — FORCELLINI.

"Zween Wurfspeer' in der Hand, die breit vorschimmerten,
schwenkend."
VOSS.

"Shaking two javelins of broad-pointed steel."
TRAPP.

"Branditi in man duo ben ferrati dardi."
ALFIERI.

To this interpretation I object, first, that no example has been adduced of the use of 'crispare' elsewhere either in this sense, or in any sense at all similar. Secondly, that the act of brandishing or florishing two javelins in the hand (or with the hand) at one and the same time, is not very intelligible; and thirdly, that such brandishing or florishing, if intelligible, is as wholly incompatible with the deep dejection of Eneas *(v. 212)*, his anxiety and want of sleep the preceding night *(v. 309)*, and his present peaceful setting out to explore the neighbourhood, as with the similar peaceful setting out of Turnus (to whom the same words are applied at *v. 165* of the 12th Book) to ratify a solemn truce.

But it will be asked: how is an interpretation possible so long as we retain for CRISPANS its legitimate sense of *curling?* I answer: simply, by understanding 'crispans manu bina hastilia' to be equivalent to crispans manum in bina hastilia, just as in English, *clenching two spears in the hand* is equivalent to *clenching the hand on two spears;* an interpretation which not only preserves to 'crispare' its proper sense of curling, and assigns to Eneas and Turnus an action in perfect harmony with their peaceful intentions, but is, besides, supported by the use which Apulejus makes of 'crispare' to express the folding or bending of the arm at the elbow, and by the use made of the same term by the author of the *Copa* to signify the bending of the side, the bringing of the hip nearer the shoulder: "Jam gestamina longe diversa. Nam dextra quidem ferebat aureum crepitaculum, cujus per angustam laminam in modum baltei recurvatam, trajectæ mediæ paucæ regulæ, *crispante brachio trigeminos jactus,* reddebant argutum sonorem." — APULEIUS, *Metam. Lib. XI.*

"Crispum sub crotalo docta movere latus."

Copa, 2.

So understood the MANU CRISPANS of our text corresponds to the "ferunt" and "læva gerebat" of the exactly parallel passages in the fifth and twelfth Books:

"Cornea bina ferunt præfixa hastilia ferro."
En. V. 557.

— "Uti læva duo forte gerebat
Lenta levis cursu præfixa hastilia ferro."
En. XII. 488;

the latter of which passages shows, first, that these two 'hastilia' used to be carried ("gerebat," "ferunt,") in the left hand, from whence, as from a repository, one might be taken by the right hand whenever required for use; and secondly, that they were a usual equipment for persons going out lightly accoutred on foot, 'levis cursu'; for such, and not, as interpreted by Forbiger, "levi incursu, subito et celeri impetu," is the meaning of 'levis cursu' in this passage, 'cursu' being the dative case, and 'levis cursu' connected, not with 'contorquens dirigit', but with 'gerebat'.

The right understanding of 'manu crispare hastilia' in our text, leads directly to the right understanding of 'crispare conum' in Claudian's *(de III. Cons. Hon. 194):*

"Altum fulminea crispare in casside conum
Festinat Steropes;"

which is not, with Gesner, "conum ex ære parare jubis aut pennis crispis recipiendis aptum," such not being a smith's work, but, *give the cone of the helmet its curl;* the cone, when half made, being a plain, straight piece of brass, when perfected, having a curled shape; its first shape corresponding to the open or expanded hand of Eneas, its second to his hand grasping, or clenched on, the HASTILIA. Compare Stat. *Theb. VIII. 568:*

— "Triplici velaverat ostro
Surgentes etiamnum humeros, et levia mater
Pectora; tunc auro phaleras, auroque sagittas
Cingulaque et manicas (ne conjuge vilior iret)
Presserat, et mixtum cono crispaverat aurum;"

had curled the cone, given the cone its curl.

That clenching, not brandishing, is the true sense of CRISPANS in the passage before us, is further shown by the remarkable fact that 'crispatus' (first changed, of course, into *crespé*) is the very term employed by the French at the present day to express the clenched or curled state of the fingers: "On etablissait egalement que les cheveux trouvés entre *les doigts crespés* de la duchesse et dans la mare de sang ou gisait son corps étaient precisement de la même couleur et de la même longueur que ceux de son mari." — Account of the murder of the Duchess de Choiseul-Prâslin by her husband, in the "Gazette des Tribunaux," Paris, Aug. 20, 1847. And again, in the account given of the same murder by "Le Droit," same date: — *"Les doigts de la main gauche* de la duchesse étaient *crespés,* et retenaient quelques cheveux du meurtrier, arrachés dans cette horrible lutte." It seems to me quite plain that the Latin 'crispare', the French *cresper* and the English *grasp,* not to speak of the still plainer *crisp,* are all but various forms of one and the same word.

318.

CUI MATER MEDIA SESE TULIT OBVIA SILVA
VIRGINIS OS HABITUMQUE GERENS ET VIRGINIS ARMA
SPARTANÆ VEL QUALIS EQUOS THREISSA FATIGAT
HARPALYCE VOLUCREMQUE FUGA PRÆVERTITUR HEBRUM
NAMQUE HUMERIS DE MORE HABILEM SUSPENDERAT ARCUM
VENATRIX DEDERATQUE COMAM DIFFUNDERE VENTIS
NUDA GENU NODOQUE SINUS COLLECTA FLUENTES

Compare the admirable conciseness of this exquisite picture with the (dare I say? tedious) diffuseness of the Spenserian copy, *Faerie Queene, II. 3. 31, and seq.*

Equos fatigat. — Servius has happily preserved the ancient fable which places the meaning of these words beyond all doubt: "Hæc (sciz. Harpalyce), patre propter ferociam a civibus pulso et postea occiso, fugit in silvas, et venatibus latrociniisque vivendo ita efferata est, et hujus velocitatis et exercitii facta est, ut subito ad vicina stabula coacta inopia decurreret, et rapto pecorum fœtu *insequentes etiam equites in celeritate vitaret.*" Even if we had not this fable, the context peremptorily forbids us to entertain Heyne's interpretation ("equo incedit, quod proprium Amazonibus"), the discourse being plainly, not about the speed of an equestrian's horses, but about a pedestrian (in which character, and not in that of an equestrian, Venus appeared to Eneas) so swift of foot as to outstrip not merely horses, but even the swift Hebrus itself. And so Silius's undoubted imitation (II. 73):

> "Quales Threiciæ Rhodopen Pangæaque lustrant
> Saxosis nemora alta jugis, cursuque fatigant
> Hebrum innupta manus."

Heyne referring us for illustration of this passage to the fable preserved by Servius, and at the same time adopting an interpretation wholly inconsistent with that fable, displays a negligence, if not a confusion of mind, which is but too frequently remarkable in his generally excellent and laborious work.

An additional argument if additional argument be required, that not driving in a chariot, or riding on horseback, is here spoken of, but running on foot, may be derived from the costume itself which is that of the female footracer; see below.

Prævertitur hebrum. — The arguments of Wakefield, Wagner and Jahn (ad locum), and of Wakefield ad Lucret. I. 1003, decide me in favor of the received reading hebrum, and against 'Eurum', the reading proposed by Huetius and Rutgersius, and adopted by Brunck, and after Brunck by Heyne. Compare:

"Nec non Autololes, levibus gens ignea plantis,
Cui sonipes cursu, cui cesserit incitus amnis."
SIL. ITAL. III. 306.

I have also myself personally ascertained that HEBRUM or EBRUM is the reading both of Petrarch's MS. and of the MS. No. 79 in the Ambrosian Library at Milan; also of the Kloster-Neuburg MS.; also of the six most ancient MSS. in the Royal Library of Vienna (Nos. 113. 114. 115. 117. 118. 121); also of two MSS. in the Royal Library at Munich (Nos. 18059 and 21562); also of the Gudian, of the Dresden, of the two Leipzig, and of the three (Nos. 54. 55. 56) in the Hof-Bibliothek in Gotha. It is also the reading of both the Heinsii, as well as of H. Stephens and all the ancient editors. It is plain also from Pierius's silence that no other reading was known to him.

DEDERATQUE COMAM DIFFUNDERE VENTIS NUDA GENU. — Such was also, according to Pausanias (*Ηλιακων* A. 16), the costume of the maidens who ran in the races at Elis in honor of Juno: "*Καθειται σφισιν η κομη, χιτων ολιγον υπερ γονατος καθηκει.*"

NODOQUE SINUS COLLECTA FLUENTES. — "Possis intelligere fibulam . . . . . . melius de cingulo accipiemus." — HEYNE. "Rectissime Heyn. non de fibula . . . . . . sed de cingulo capit." — FORBIGER. I understand NODO to mean neither 'fibula', nor 'cingulum', but simply a knot tied on the fullness (SINUS) of her garment, in such a manner as to prevent it from impeding her speed; the fullness of her garment knotted upon itself. For the manner in which the 'sinus fluentes' are thus put out of the way by means of a knot, see the figure of Diana Succincta in the *Mus. Pio Clem. III. Tab. XXXVIII.* See, further, Comm. *En. VI. 300.*

331.

O QUAM TE MEMOREM VIRGO NAMQUE HAUD TIBI VULTUS
MORTALES NEC VOX HOMINEM SONAT O DEA CERTE
AN PHŒBI SOROR AN NYMPHARUM SANGUINIS UNA

"Wer bist du, sprich —" ruft er in Hast,
Starrt an das Wunder, das er schaut —
"Wer bist du, unvergleichlich Weib?
So weit der lichte Himmel blaut,
Nie sah mein Aug' so holden Leib.
Bist du der Elfen eine, sprich,
Die lieblich in der Mondnacht Glanz
Hinwehen im leichten Geistertanz,
Wie? — oder lebst du so wie ich?"

Zedlitz, *Waldfräulein, 4. Abentheuer.*

339.

HAUD EQUIDEM TALI ME DIGNOR HONORE

Not referring specially to 'Multa tibi ante aras' &c., but generally to the whole of Eneas's speech ascribing divinity to her.

343.

GENUS INTRACTABILE BELLO

I am decided by the so similar phrase, 'genus insuperabile bello' *(En. IV. 40)* applied to the 'Gætulæ urbes', to take part with Heyne against Wagner, and refer GENUS INTRACTABILE BELLO, not to *Carthage*, but to the immediately preceding 'fines Libyci'.

353.

ILLE SYCHÆUM
IMPIUS ANTE ARAS ATQUE AURI CÆCUS AMORE
CLAM FERRO INCAUTUM SUPERAT SECURUS AMORUM
GERMANAE

IMPIUS refers, not to ARAS, but to the murder of his sister's husband; and the meaning is, *the unnatural brother-in-law*. Compare Ovid, *Heroid. VII. 127*, of the same murder by the same Pygmalion:

"Est etiam frater; cujus manus impia possit
Respergi nostro, sparsa cruore viri.
Pone deos, et quae tangendo sacra profanas:
Non bene cælestes impia dextra colit."

See Comm. *v. 14*.

360.

CÆCUMQUE DOMUS SCELUS OMNE RETEXIT

So Schiller, *Braut von Messina:*

"Schwarze Verbrechen verbirget dies Haus."

367.

PORTANTUR AVARI
PYGMALIONIS OPES PELAGO

PYGMALIONIS OPES. — These words have been hitherto understood to mean the treasures of which Pygmalion hoped to obtain possession by the murder of Sichæus: "quas ille animo et spe jam præceperat" — HEYNE; whose interpretation has been adopted by succeeding commentators. This interpretation is undoubtedly incorrect: for, first, the peculiar and proper meaning of 'opes' is not treasures, but opulence, and the strength and power consequent upon opulence; so "dives opum," *En. I. 18;* "Trojanas ut opes," *En. II. 4;* "Has evertit opes," *En. II. 603;* "opibus juvabo," *En. I. 575.* Secondly, the possessive PYGMALIONIS cannot without great violence be wrested so as to mean *hope* of possession. Thirdly, supposing the structure to admit of such interpretation, it were unworthy of Virgil, having already employed one sentence in informing us that the ships were seized, and another in informing us that they were loaded with gold, to occupy a third with the statement that the gold sailed. We have only to give to OPES its true signification of *opulential substance,* and to PYGMALIONIS its proper possessive force, and we have a meaning at once simple and worthy of the author, viz. *that the strength and substance of Pygmalion was carried away over the sea.* That this is the true meaning, is further proved by the very next sentence, "dux femina facti," as well as by "Ulta virum, pœnas inimico a fratre recepi," *En. IV. 656.* For, what was the deed achieved by a woman? or what was the revenge which Dido had for her murdered husband? or what was the punishment inflicted upon her hostile brother? Not surely the running away with a treasure which belonged to her own husband, and which Pygmalion had never even so much as possessed; but the emasculating Pygmalion's kingdom, by carrying away (along with the treasure) men, ships, and munitions of war, in sufficient quantity to found a great city and a rival empire. Thus it is not indifferently or *otiose,* that Venus informs Eneas (and Virgil his reader) that the OPES PYGMALIONIS sailed the deep, but expressly for the purpose of preparing him for the display of wealth and power ('opes') with which he is greeted at Carthage; and thus again, the 'nodus' which made it necessary for Venus to appear in person, becomes 'dignior vindice dea'. It may be observed further; first, that the term 'veteres' *(v. 362)* is almost by itself sufficient to show that the 'thesauros' did not belong either to Sichæus or Pygmalion, but were one of those old hoards, of the existence of which no person living was aware, and which it has been from time immemorial the province of ghosts to reveal; and secondly, that OPES must be interpreted as I have proposed, in order to afford a plausible pretext for the apprehension expressed (if not felt) by Dido *(En. IV. 325)*, that Pygmalion would follow her, and make war upon Carthage.

Should the reader still entertain misgivings as to the correctness of this interpretation, let him compare the exactly corresponding passage of Suetonius in *vita Cæsaris, c. 79:* "Fama percrebuit (C. Julium Cæsarem) migraturum Alexandriam vel Ilium, translatis simul opibus imperii." Also the almost express citation of the passage by Ovid, *Heroid. VII. 149:*

"Hos potius populos in dotem, ambage remissa,
Accipe, et advectas Pygmalionis opes."

378.

ANTE DIEM CLAUSO COMPONET VESPER OLYMPO

The allusion is plainly to the ordinary shutting up of a house at the approach of night. Compare:

"Et thalamos clausit Nox atra hominumque Deumque."
SIL. ITAL. XIV. 542.

I find in Pierius: "In codicibus aliquot antiquis non invenuste 'componat' habetur;" which reading, adopted by Wagner in his Heynian Virgil, and with much reason oppugned by Forbiger, has been tacitly abandoned by Wagner in his *Virg. Br. En.*

397.

ADSPICE BIS SENOS LÆTANTES AGMINE CYGNOS
ÆTHERIA QUOS LAPSA PLAGA JOVIS ALES APERTO
TURBABAT CÆLO NUNC TERRAS ORDINE LONGO
AUT CAPERE AUT CAPTAS JAM DESPECTARE VIDENTUR
UT REDUCES ILLI LUDUNT STRIDENTIBUS ALIS
ET CŒTU CINXERE POLUM CANTUSQUE DEDERE
HAUD ALITER PUPPESQUE TUÆ PUBESQUE TUORUM
AUT PORTUM TENET AUT PLENO SUBIT OSTIA VELO

"CAPERE, eligere, ut *(Georg. II. 230):* Ante locum capies oculis. DESPECTARE, i. e. electas jam intentius despicere." — SERVIUS.

"Ii LÆTANTES AGMINE nunc· terras partim e longinquo oculis capere (s. locum ubi considant designare), partim easdem, CAPTAS JAM, ex propinquo spectare videntur (hoc pertinet ad eos, qui sunt in primo agmine, illud ad eos, qui in extremo); factoque in orbem volatu, cum cantu revertuntur." — WAGNER, *Virg. Br. En.* To which interpretation there are these two capital objections: first, that no instance has been produced, nor I think can be found, in which '.capere', simply and without adjunct, signifies *oculis capere, designare;* and secondly, that if CAPERE be *oculis designare,* CAPTAS must be *oculis designatas;* and then what kind of sense does *despectare oculis terras jam oculis designatas* afford? or how could Venus possibly point out, or Eneas possibly observe, a distinction between the fore part of the flock of birds, *despectantes terras oculis,* and the hind part, *designantes terras oculis?*

Another and more generally adopted interpretation of the passage is that of Burmann and Voss: "HAUD ALITER etc. docent partem modo avium jam tenuisse terram, partem vero jam appropinquare et despicere locum, quem capiant. 'Captis' vero est in Mentel. tertio pro varia lectione, et a m. pr. in Regio, sed

CAPTAS rectum est, scilicet jam a prioribus, qui jam descenderant in terram, ut patet ex v. 404, AUT PORTUM TENET, AUT PLENO SUBIT OSTIA VELO: sed scrupulus superest, quomodo, si jam pars in terram delata, alia jam despectare terram et appropinquare videtur, POLUM cinxerint cœtu, quem (i. e. cælum, aëra) jam deseruisse debent intelligi. An liceret solum substituere, quod ab aquila turbatae aves reliquerant, et nunc reduces cingunt ludentes? Sed non addicentibus libris επεχω, et aliis explicandum relinquo." — BURMANN.

"Schaue die zweimal sechs in dem Zug frohlockenden Schwäne,
Die, den ätherischen Höhen entstürzt, erst Jupiters Adler
Wirrt' in entnebelter Luft; nun erdwärts siehst du im Heerzug
Theils sie gesenkt, theils nahend auf schon gesenkte herabschaun.
So wie der Heimkehr jene sich freun mit rauschenden Flügeln,
Wie sie im Schwarm umringten den Pol, und Gesange des Jubels:
So ist dir auch Flotte sowohl, als sämmtliche Jugend,
Theils in dem Port, theils naht sie mit schwellendem Segel der Mündung."

VOSS.

This interpretation is sufficiently condemned by Burmann's own objection, "sed scrupulus superest" etc.

A third interpretation, proposed by Wagner in his edition of Heyne's Virgil, is as follows: "terras partim capere, partim, qui primi terram attigerant, jam rursus in altum sublati despectare videntur."

In all these modes of understanding the passage (and I believe no other mode has ever been proposed) there seems to me to be this radical error, the assumption that the birds are divided by the conjunctions AUT, AUT, into two parties. Let us understand these conjunctions as indicating not two distinct parties, but two distinct acts of the whole number of birds, and all difficulty vanishes at once: *Behold*, says Venus, *those twelve swans: how, having escaped their enemy, they alight one after another* (ORDINE LONGO), *and then, rising again on the wing, wheel round and round in circles, singing their song of triumph and looking down as it were contemptuously* (see Comment on DESPECTARE below) *on the place of shelter for which they have now no longer occasion.*

As the swans are not divided into two parties by the conjunctions AUT, AUT, *v. 400,* so neither is Eneas's fleet divided into two parties by the same conjunctions, *v. 404,* the meaning of *v. 404* being, *are either entering the harbour, or actually safe in it.* The idea of the safety of the fleet would have been equally presented to Eneas, if the swans had been represented merely as alighting or alighted on the ground, and the ships as actually in port, but the picture would have wanted its main beauty, the life and animation bestowed on it by the rejoicing of the birds in airy circles round and round their place of refuge, and by the fleet entering the port in full sail.

NUNC opposes the present safe state of the birds (whether alighting or flying in circles round the place where they had alighted) to their previous state of danger: JAM opposes their last described act of flying round in circles to their immediately preceding act of alighting, of which it is as it were the completion. As if Venus had said: Those birds which you see yonder wheeling round in the air over the spot on which a moment ago they took refuge from the eagle, and from which they have, without resting there, this instant arisen in order to give vent to their joy.

In the words LAETANTES AGMINE Venus describes the present state of the swans, i. e. their state at the moment when she first directs Eneas's attention to them; they are LAETANTES AGMINE, *rejoicing in a body:* in the words ÆTHERIA . . . . . . VIDENTUR she describes their previous misfortune and escape witnessed both by herself and Eneas; and in the words UT REDUCES . . . . . DEDERE returns to their present state, viz. that already expressed by LAETANTES AGMINE, and which has continued unaltered during the time she has been speaking;

the words REDUCES LUDUNT STRIDENTIBUS ALIS, CŒTU CINXERE POLUM, and CANTUS DEDERE, being but a developement of the idea briefly expressed in LÆTANTES AGMINE. Such interruptions (if I may so call them) and resumptions of the direct thread of the discourse are of extremely frequent occurrence in Virgil; compare: "Prospiciens summa placidum caput extulit unda .... Prospiciens genitor cæloque invectus aperto," *v. 131* and *159,* and "rotis summas levibus perlabitur undas .... Flectit equos curruque volans dat lora secundo," *v. 151* and *160.*

CAPERE TERRAS; — as 'capere portum', Cæs. *B. G. IV. 36;* (observe the force and propriety with which Virgil applies to the swans' arrival at their port, the ground, the very term ordinarily used to express a ship's refuging in port); 'capere Italiam', *En. IX. 267;* 'tumulum capit', *En. VI. 754;* 'locum capiunt', *En. V. 315;* and the, if possible, still more exact French parallel, *prendre terre, to land;* with which compare the converse expression of Ovid, *Amor. III. 2. 48:*

"Nil mihi cum pelago; me mea terra capit."

VIDENTUR, — although in the strict construction pertaining equally to CAPERE and DESPECTARE, is (according to the style of which Virgil is so fond — see Comment *v. 420* — and of which see a most remarkable example *En. X. 13)* to be referred in the sense to DESPECTARE alone, as if Virgil had said: *Either alight or seem to look down,* for Eneas could see the swans actually alighting, although he could not see them actually looking down, but only *seeming* as if they looked down.

DESPECTARE. — "Piso vix Tiberio cedere; liberos ejus ut multum infra despectare" TACIT. *Annal. II. 43. 6.* "Despectare omnia terrena." AMMIAN. XIV. 11.

"At tu, seu rapidum poli per axem
Famæ curribus arduis levatus,
Qua surgunt animæ potentiores,
Terras despicis, et sepulchra rides."

STATIUS, *Silv. II. 7. 107.*

I doubt not that DESPECTARE is the true reading, partly because I have found it in the only three MSS. which I have myself personally examined respecting the passage, viz. the two Leipzig and the Dresden, but principally because it is quoted by Donat. ad Terent. *Heaut. II. 3.*

REDUCES, — not *returning,* or *on their way back* ("factoque in orbem volatu, cum cantu revertuntur" — WAGNER), but *actually returned;* first, because such is the ordinary meaning of the term ("Quæ tibi polliceor reduci rebusque secundis," *En. IX. 301.* "Gratatur reduces," *En. V. 40);* and secondly, because the swans cannot well be supposed to celebrate their escape before they have actually arrived in a place of safety.

ET CŒTU CINXERE POLUM CANTUSQUE DEDERE; — i. e. according to the usual manner of swans, *flying and singing together:* "Seine Stimme lässt er (viz. Cycnus musicus) im hohen Fluge ertönen, und ob sie gleich dem *Gak-Gak* der Gänse ähnelt, so ist sie doch weit voller und reiner, und wenn viele zusammen sich hören lassen, klingt es wie ein Glockenspiel, da die Stimme der ältern und jüngern, oder männlichen und weiblichen Vögel höher oder tiefer ist." Reise in Island, Anno 1820, von Thienemann (a most intelligent and accurate observer of nature). Zweite Abth. Zweiter Abschnitt.

I beg to say that I adhere to my interpretation of the above passage, notwithstanding the objections made to it by one of the most judicious and candid of Virgil's commentators, Forbiger; see his third Edition.

407.

DIVINUM VERTICE ODOREM

"*Θειον οδμης πνευμα,*" Hippolytus recognising the presence of a divinity by the odor, EURIP. *Hippol. 1391.*

415.

AT VENUS OBSCURO GRADIENTES AERE SEPSIT
ET MULTO NEBULÆ CIRCUM DEA FUDIT AMICTU

The ancients believed (correctly) that the air was without light in itself, i. e. dark, unless illuminated by the sun's or other light. Compare Lucret. V. 649:

"At nox obruit ingenti caligine terras,
Aut ubi de longo cursu sol ultima cæli
Impulit, atque suos ecflavit languidus ignes,
Concussos itere, et labefactos aere multo;"

also Lucret. V. 695:

"Aut quia crassior est certis in partibus aer,
Sub terris ideo tremulum jubar hæsitat igni,
Nec penetrare potest facile, atque emergere ad ortus."

CIRCUM DEA FUDIT AMICTU. — DEA explains why Venus was able to envelop them in darkness. Compare Propert. II. I. 10:

"Seu cum poscentes somnus declinat ocellos,
Invenio causas mille poeta novas;"

where 'poeta explains why Propertius was able to invent so many explanations. See Comm. *v. 721.*

422.

CORRIPUERE VIAM

Shortened the way, went fast over the road, proceeded quick. Compare: "Erimus ergo ibi dedicationis die, quem epulo celebrare constitui. Subsistemus fortasse et sequenti; sed tanto magis viam ipsam corripiemus." PLIN. *Epist. III. 1.*

— "Tarda necessitas
Leti corripuit gradum."

HOR. *Od. I. 3. 32.*

427.

PARS DUCERE MUROS
MOLIRIQUE ARCEM ET MANIBUS SUBVOLVERE SAXA
PARS OPTARE LOCUM TECTO ET CONCLUDERE SULCO

"Sulco, fossa; civitas enim, non domus, circumdatur sulco." — Servius.

"Concludere sulco, fossam ducere; definire ædium situm ac locum fossa facta, in quam fundamentum immittatur seu crepido. Male de aratro cogitant." — Heyne.

"Fossa facta, qua fundamenta ponantur." — Wagner, *Virg. Br. En.*

"Sed mirum, quod in ipsa Carthagine non solum pars ducere murum aggrediatur, sed

PARS OPTARE LOCUM TECTO ET CONCLUDERE SULCO.

Privatæ itaque ædes eodem Etrusco ritu consecrantur. Quod non revera factum, sed de publico ad privatum solum a Virgilio translatum esse credo. — Lersch, *Antiq. Virgil. p. 30.*

"Durch einen gezogenen Graben den Umfang des künftigen Hauses bezeichnen." — Ladewig.

The fundamental error in all these explanations is the assigning of too restricted a sense to tecto: which here, as 'tectis' in the parallel passage *En. III. 134* (where see Comm.), means not a private house as opposed to the public building, the arx, but *building* generally; locum tecto, i. e. *locum ædificando, idoneum ad ædificandum.* One pars of the working Tyrians is employed in the actual masonry of the city, the arx and walls being the most important parts and representing the whole; the other pars is employed either in choosing sites whereon to erect further buildings (whether of the arx or private houses, is not expressed, and makes small difference); or in enclosing the whole with a 'sulcus'. In plain prose, some of the Tyrians are employed in the laying out, others in the actual building, of the city. The fundamental error corrected, SULCO returns to its proper meaning, *the plough furrow;* drawn as usual, not round a particular private house, but round the whole city, the arx included. So understood the sentence is according to Virgil's usual manner, the last words winding up and rounding the whole. II

Mature consideration has induced me thus to alter the opinion I had previously formed concerning the meaning of this passage, and which, first published in the Classical Museum, has been quoted, and, I am sorry to find, adopted, by Forbiger in the third edition of his excellent work.

OPTARE. — It seems to me by no means certain that this is the correct reading. I find in Pierius: "In veteribus fere omnibus exemplaribus legi aptare locum. *Τουτ᾽ εστι το αρμοζειν.*" A statement strongly confirmed by Burmann: "Aptare etiam omnes fere Heinsio inspecti; et Excerpta nostra, et Grævianus, Francianus, Pugetianus et Ed. Venet." According to Bottari (whose assertion is confirmed by Ambrogi), 'aptare' has been the original reading of the Roman (No. 3867), and has been altered by a different hand into OPTARE (thus: $\overset{\text{O}}{\text{A}}$PTARE). I find 'aptare' in the Dresden MS.; also in the Leipzig No. 35, the 'a' however in the latter having the appearance of being an alteration of the original reading. The other Leipzig MS. (No. 36) has OPTARE; Henry Stephens and Alfieri have 'aptare, the Modena edition of 1475 OPTARE.

430.

JURA MAGISTRATUSQUE LEGUNT SANCTUMQUE SENATUM

The unjust stigma affixed by Heyne to this line has been very properly removed by Wagner. It is quite according to Virgil's usual manner to introduce such, if I may so say, parenthetic passages. See Comments *En. I. 4; III. 571; IV. 484; VI. 83* and *739*. I have myself found the line in the following MSS.: the Gudian, the Petrarchian, the Kloster-Neuburg, three Gothan (Nos. 54, 56 and 236), three Vienna (Nos. 113, 114, 115), also in the two Leipzig and in the Dresden. It is also acknowledged by Servius, and is (according to Foggini) in the Medicean, and (according to Bottari) in the Vatican Fragment. It has also been adopted by both the Stephenses and both the Heinsii, as well as by Burmann, Ambrogi, Brunck, Jahn and Forbiger, and is in Alfieri's text and the Baskerville.

435.

CUM GENTIS ADULTOS
EDUCUNT FETUS

ADULTOS; — having undergone their transformations, and assumed the perfect or adult insect-form, that of 'imago'.

GENTIS; — because "solæ communes gnatos ... habent." *Georg. IV. 153.*

447.

EFFODERE LOCO SIGNUM QUOD REGIA JUNO
MONSTRARAT CAPUT ACRIS EQUI SIC NAM FORE BELLO
EGREGIAM ET FACILEM VICTU PER SÆCULA GENTEM

CAPUT ACRIS EQUI. — See a representation on an ancient Roman lamp in the Passerian Collection, of a war-horse's head transfixed with a spear; set down by Passerius (*Lucernæ Fictiles,* Tom. II. Tab. 27) as an emblem of the conquest of Carthage. See also Ursini (*Virg. Collat.*):

"etiam apud me argenteum numisma Punicis litteris notatum, in cujus altera parte equi caput, et palma percussa est."

FACILEM VICTU. — Ladewig's arguments are not sufficient to induce me to derive VICTU with him from 'vinco', and to take the expression FACILEM VICTU as epexegetic of BELLO EGREGIAM. The description of Carthage in the text seems to me to be exactly parallel to the description of Carthage at the outset of the poem, FACILEM VICTU being equivalent to 'dives opum', and BELLO EGREGIAM to 'studiis asperrima belli'. In reply to the argument of Ladewig, "Auch ist das Pferd nicht Symbol der Fruchtbarkeit und der Fülle," I quote (with De Bulgaris) "*Ιππος γεωργος τ᾽ αγαθος κρατερος τ᾽ αιχμητης.*"

It appears from Ammian (XXII. 16) that, when Dinocrates was building the walls of Alexandria, the future richness and abundance of that city was prognosticated by an omen: "Qui cum ampla mœnia fundaret et pulchra, penuria calcis ad momentum parum repertæ, omnes ambitus lineales farina respersit, quod civitatem post hæc alimentorum uberi copia circumfluere fortuito monstravit."

450.

HIC TEMPLUM JUNONI INGENS SIDONIA DIDO
CONDEBAT DONIS OPULENTUM ET NUMINE DIVÆ
ÆREA CUI GRADIBUS SURGEBANT LIMINA NIXÆQUE
ÆRE TRABES FORIBUS CARDO STRIDEBAT AHENIS

DONIS OPULENTUM ET NUMINE DIVÆ. — Not, *enriched with gifts because of,* or *through the influence of, the 'numen Divae'* ("Potentia Numinis templum donis ditavit, hinc ipsum Divae numine opulentum dicitur" — WAGNER), but, *rich in votive offerings and the 'numen Divae';* the votive offerings together with the 'numen Divae' constituting the riches of the temple. Compare: "Mantua dives avis," *En. X. 201.*

NIXÆQUE ÆRE TRABES. — Heyne, adhering to the vulgar reading 'nexæque', thus explains this passage: "Nexæque liminibus *(adjunctæ et impositæ limini)* trabes *(postes)* surgebant *(erant ex)* ære." On which Wunderlich observes: "Durum est, jungere *surgebant ære.* Nam, ut omittam duplicem structuram *limina surgunt gradibus*, et *trabes surgunt ære,* ea est collocatio verborum ut *nexæ ære* conjungatur audienti. Videtur nectere aliquid aliqua, vel ex aliqua materia, — nam utraque constructio bona est, — esse *fabricari* aliquid de materia; ita ut *nexus ære* pro *æreus* dicatur." The critique on Heyne's gloss is correct and well judged; not so the proposed interpretation, for 'nexae aere', if equivalent to 'aereus', had better been omitted, as embarrassing the construction, without conveying any meaning not already conveyed by ÆREA, the action of which is as full and perfect on TRABES as on LIMINA. Voss's interpretation,

— "und gediegene Pfosten
Strebten mit Erz;"

founded on the same analysis of the structure as Wunderlich's, is liable to the same objection. La Cerda's is the ordinary meaning, *door-posts bound* or *jointed together with fastenings of brass,* and is summarily and justly rejected by Heyne, as wholly unworthy of the picture: "At hoc pro reliqua templi magnificentia quam esset jejunùm!" La Cerda's words declare his distress, and the difficulty he is at to make anything out of the passage: "TRABES; ubi hæ? Refero ad portas templi, vel potius ad postes portarum, qui ex trabibus illigatis innexisque ære. Vel tu mihi indica, ubi essent hæ trabes? nam si ad reliquum opificium templi referas, vix credam, cum Poeta tantum occupatus sit in ornando limine." To these explanations, as well as to all those which have yet been offered, or, so far as I see, can be offered, of the received reading, there is, besides, this capital general objection, that they all so limit Virgil's description as to make it the description, not of a temple, or the facade or portal of a temple, but of a mere door; the sum total of the sense contained in the two lines being, *that there were steps up to the door; the sill, posts, and valves of which were of brass.* I therefore unite with Catrou in rejecting the common reading, as incapable of affording any good sense, and in adopting the reading of the Vatican Fragment (see Bottari) and of those other manuscripts referred to by Servius ("Multi NIXÆ legunt, non nexae") and Burmann, NIXÆQUE. This reading being adopted, the passage becomes disembarrassed of all difficulty, the construction clear, and the meaning harmonious to the context, and worthy of Virgil. LIMINA is not merely the threshold, but the whole *solum* or ground in front of and adjoining the door; TRABES (literally, the great beams, *travi*, of the roof, and particularly the architraves, *architravi:* "Trabes supra columnas et paratatas et antas ponuntur." VITRUV. IV. 2. And again, IV. 7: "Eæque trabes compactiles ponantur, ut tantam habeant crassitudinem, quantæ summæ columnæ erit hypotrachelium") is the roof itself — nor let it be objected, that the object expressed by TRABES must be wooden, for we have (HOR. *Carm. II. 18. 3*) 'trabes' of marble: "Non trabes Hymettiæ premunt columnas;" compare Pliny, Lib. XXXVI. 8; and (CLAUDIAN. *de Rapt. Proserp. I. 242*) 'trabes' actually of brass: "Trabibus solidatur aënis culmen;" — ÆREA SURGEBANT is the common predicate of LIMINA and TRABES: NIXÆ ÆRE *(leaning on brass,* i. e. *brazen columns* — the precise position of the 'trabes as described by Vitruvius —) the special predicate of TRABES; the emphatic words are ÆREA and ÆRE; the structure is, 'cui limina trabesque ære nixæ, surgebant ærea'; and the picture presented is that of the whole facade of the temple, consisting of the *brazen 'limina'*, the *brazen roof-beams* or *architraves* (i. e. *brazen roof: "τον οροφον χαλκουν."* Pausan. *Φωκικα*, cap. V) supported on *brazen columns*, and the *brazen folding* or *valved doors*, all elevated on a flight of steps.

If further confirmation of the reading NIXÆQUE be required, it will be found in the exactly corresponding 'premunt' of Horace, just quoted; in the 'incumbunt' of Statius in his description of the temple of Mars, manifestly a copy of Virgil's temple of Juno:

> "Ferrea compago laterum; ferro arcta teruntur
> Limina; ferratis incumbunt tecta columnis."
>
> *Theb. VII 43;*

in Avienus's

> "Templa Sinopæi Jovis astant nixa columnis."
>
> *Descriptio Terræ, 376;*

in Ovid's

> "Templa manent hodie, vastis innixa columnis;
> Perque quater denos itur in illa gradus."
>
> *Ex Ponto III. 2. 49;*

and in Statius's

> "Pendent innumeris fastigia nixa columnis."
>
> *Silv. I. 2. 152.*

An exact parallel for the expression, 'æreæ surgebant trabes', is supplied by Virgil himself *(Georg. III. 29)*:

> "Navali surgentes ære columnas."

In addition to all which, I may observe, that the omission of columns in the description of so great and magnificent a temple would have been, to say the least of it, very singular and remarkable.

Trabes (*the great beams of the roof*, as, independently of the preceding argument, is sufficiently clear from the etymological tree alone, *trabes, travi, architravi, architraves*) is here used for the whole roof, in the same way as its singular 'trabs' is so often used for the whole ship: ex. gr. En. IV. 566; III. 191; Pers. V. 141; Hor. *Carm. I. 1. 13;* &c.

Conclusive as the above arguments seem to be, I must not conceal from the reader that 'nexaeque' is according to Foggini the reading of the Medicean MS. It is also the reading of both the Heinsii, and of Burmann, although from Burmann's note it would appear that NIXÆQUE was the reading which he had himself intended for his text. I have also found either 'nexaeque' or 'nexae' in all the MSS. which I have myself personally examined with respect to this passage; viz. 'nexaeque' in eight Vienna MSS. (Nos. 113. 114. 115. 116. 117. 118. 120. 121), two Munich (Nos. 18059, 21562), two Ambrosian (viz. the Petrarchian, and No. 79), the Kloster-Neuburg, and both the Leipzig; and 'nexae' in the Gudian, in No. 523 of Munich, and in the Dresden.

It is remarkable that Pierius, no less than Ambrogi, is entirely silent as to the reading of this verse: from which silence I would infer that 'nexaeque' was the only reading known to either; an inference which seems placed beyond doubt as to Pierius at least, by his quotation of 'nexae ære trabes' in the course of his observations on 'auratasque trabes', *En. II. 448.*

In his third Edition Forbiger has adopted NIXÆ, decided thereto (as it would appear from his note) by my arguments in favor of that reading, published in the *Classical Museum (No. XX).* Lond. July, 1848.

466.

SUNT LACRYMÆ RERUM

RERUM; — *human affairs, the world;* as shown by the subsequent "mortalia." See Comm. *v. 182.*

474.

PRIMO QUÆ PRODITA SOMNO
TYDIDES MULTA VASTABAT CÆDE CRUENTUS

Wagner seems to me to err in connecting the words PRIMO SOMNO with VASTABAT, and understanding them to specify simply the time of Tydides's invasion of the camp: "Quem Rhesus prima nocte, postquam ad Trojam venit, capiebat." — *Virg. Br. En.* The words are, I think, connected with PRODITA, and express the instrument or agent by which the camp was betrayed. Compare: "Ipso tacitam se pondere prodit," *Georg. II. 253;* and (SCHILLER, *Braut von Messina*):

— "Des Meers ringsumgebende Welle,
Sie verräth uns dem kühnen Corsaren,
Der die Küste verwegen durchkreuzt."

PRIMO SOMNO, — not the sleep of the first night, but *the beginning,* or *first part, of sleep;* first, because this latter is the meaning of the words both in Phædrus (III. 10. 31):

"Sopita primo quæ nil somno senserat;"

and Silius (IX. 90):

"Ecce sub adventum noctis primumque soporem;"

and (probably) Propert. I. 3. 3:

"Qualis et accubuit primo Cepheïa somno,
Libera jam duris cautibus, Andromeda;"

and of the exactly corresponding phrase 'prima quies' in Virgil himself (II. 268). Secondly, because, so understood, the sense is not only stronger, but more fully explanatory of the subsequent "priusquam Pabula gustassent" &c., viz. *in the early part of the night before they had time to taste* &c. Thirdly, because the fact that the slaughter of Rhesus had taken place on the first night after his arrival at Troy, was so well known as not to require express specification.

The construction is, 'cruentus multa cæde'; not, 'vastabat multa cæde'. See Comm. *v. 294.* Page 103.

478.

PARTE ALIA FUGIENS AMISSIS TROILUS ARMIS
INFELIX PUER ATQUE IMPAR CONGRESSUS ACHILLI
FERTUR EQUIS CURRUQUE HÆRET RESUPINUS INANI
LORA TENENS TAMEN HUIC CERVIXQUE COMÆQUE TRAHUNTUR
PER TERRAM ET VERSA PULVIS INSCRIBITUR HASTA

Compare Hippolytus dragged by his runaway horses and chariot, EURIP. *Hippol. 1236;* also the fabricated story which the messenger tells Clytemnestra of the death of Orestes, SOPHOCL. *Electra, 748.*

Millinghen *(Peintures de Vases Grecs,* Planche 17) gives us a representation, from a Greek vase, of the sepulchral monument of Troilus, authenticated by the inscription of his name upon the *στηλη*, and states that it is the only known artistic memorial of Troilus in existence.

483.

INTEREA AD TEMPLUM NON ÆQUÆ PALLADIS IBANT
CRINIBUS ILIADES PASSIS PEPLUMQUE FEREBANT
SUPPLICITER TRISTES ET TUNSÆ PECTORA PALMIS
DIVA SOLO FIXOS OCULOS AVERSA TENEBAT

Heyne removes the comma placed by preceding editors after FEREBANT, and adds in a note: "Nescio an melius suppliciter ferebant jungas." Wagner restores the comma with the observation: "SUPPLICITER TRISTES; ita jungendum, ut sit supplicantum modo tristes, ut in summo rerum discrimine." Heyne is, I think, nearer the truth than Wagner, but still falls in my opinion far short of a correct understanding of the passage. SUPPLICITER belongs, as it seems to me, neither to TRISTES, nor to FEREBANT, but to the whole of the two verses immediately preceding it, especially to the two verbs IBANT and FEREBANT, but above all to IBANT; as if Virgil had written, *Iliades ibant suppliciter ad templum;* i. e. *crinibus passis, peplum ferentes, tristes et tunsæ pectora palmis.* SUPPLICITER is the emphatic word of the whole sentence, and hence its position at the beginning of the verse, and its separation from both the preceding and the subsequent word by a pause; see Comm. *En. II. 246.* All the predicates, CRINIBUS PASSIS, PEPLUM FEREBANT (for this is no more than a predicate, and equivalent to 'peplum ferentes'), TRISTES, and TUNSÆ PECTORA, are only explanatory or pictorial of SUPPLICITER. The punctuation should therefore be:

INTEREA AD TEMPLUM NON AEQUÆ PALLADIS IBANT
CRINIBUS ILIADES PASSIS, PEPLUMQUE FEREBANT,
SUPPLICITER; TRISTES, ET TUNSÆ PECTORA PALMIS.

As

. . . . IBANT
. . . .
SUPPLICITER;

so *(v. 522):*

. . . . "Ibant
Orantes veniam;"

and *(En. II. 254):*

. . . . "Ibat
. . . .
Littora nota petens."

On the other hand SUPPLICITER and TRISTES are thrown together by the position of the point (viz. after, and not before, TRISTES) both in the Medicean, and in the Vatican Fragm. (see Foggini and Bottari). But as I have already observed (Comm. *v. 122),* small is the stress which can be laid on the punctuation of these MSS.

which seems to have been performed nearly at random; at least wholly at the arbitrement of the scribe.

So much for the structure, and precise meaning; for the general picture, compare: "Antea stolatæ ibant nudis pedibus in clivum, passis capillis, mentibus puris, et Jovem aquam exorabant." PETRON. p. 161.

487.

TER CIRCUM ILIACOS RAPTAVERAT HECTORA MUROS
EXANIMUMQUE AURO CORPUS VENDEBAT ACHILLES

Had killed Hector by dragging him round the walls of Troy, and was now selling the dead body. See Comment on 'tumentes', *En. II. 273.*

498.

HÆC DUM DARDANIO ÆNEÆ MIRANDA VIDENTUR
DUM STUPET OBTUTUQUE HÆRET DEFIXUS IN UNO

"Sed video totum te in illa hærere tabula quæ Trojæ halosin ostendit." PETRON. p. 324.

DARDANIO ÆNEÆ.—Observe the delicate propriety with which the term *Dardan* is applied to Eneas, at the moment when, by the sudden presentation to him, in a strange land, of his own and his country's history, his mind is filled with, and overwhelmed by, *Dardan* recollections.

500.

REGINA AD TEMPLUM FORMA PULCHERRIMA DIDO
INCESSIT

Our author, according to his wont (see Comments *En. II. 18* and *49),* especially on occasions when he wishes to be more than usually impressive, presents us, first, with the single principal idea, and afterwards adds those which are necessary for explanation or embellishment. *The queen comes to the temple; she is of exquisite beauty; and her name is Dido.* REGINA contains the principal idea, because it is the queen, as queen, whom Eneas is expecting and recognizes; it is, therefore, placed first: PULCHERRIMA follows next, because the queen's beauty was almost of necessity the immediately succeeding idea in Eneas's mind; and the name, DIDO, is placed last, as of least importance, and serving only to identify, and connect with the narrative of Venus.

REGINA AD TEMPLUM &c. — Parallel, but (as usual in Shakespeare, and to his great honor) without imitation:

— "The rich stream
Of lords and ladies, having brought the queen
To a prepared place in the choir, fell off
A distance from her, while her grace sat down
To rest a while, some half an hour or so,
In a rich chair of state, opposing freely
The beauty of her person to the people."
Henry VIII. Act IV, sc. 1.

504.

ILLA PHARETRAM
FERT HUMERO GRADIENSQUE DEA SUPEREMINET OMNES
LATONÆ TACITUM PERTENTANT GAUDIA PECTUS

Although I have found the reading 'Deas' in the only four MSS. I have myself personally examined respecting this passage, viz. the Gudian, the Dresden, and the two Leipzig, I feel nevertheless perfectly satisfied that Virgil wrote DEA; first, because of the better sense. Secondly, because such exactly is his usual style; compare:

"At Venus obscuro gradientes aere sepsit
Et multo nebulæ circum dea fudit amictu."

vers. 415.

"At Venus Ascanio placidam per membra quietem
Irrigat, et fotum gremio dea tollit in altos
Idaliæ lucos."

vers. 695.

Thirdly, because there is a peculiar propriety in the connexion of DEA with GRADIENS, the step or gait being one of the most distinguishing attributes of a Goddess; compare:

"Et vera incessu patuit dea."

vers. 409;

(where it will be observed that our author is as little careful not to break Alvarez's head as he is in our text). Fourthly, because the original reading of the Medicean, as appears from Foggini, has been 'Deas upereminet', altered afterwards in red ink into 'Deas supereminet'. Fifthly, because Pierius informs us that DEA is the reading of the Roman and several other ancient MSS. Pierius's words are: "In Romano codice et nonnullis aliis antiquis legere est DEA SUPEREMINET OMNES, ut DEA sit κατ' εξοχην. Nam ipse locus syllabam omnino communem reddit; cæterum hoc in medio sit." Sixthly, because (see Heyne, *V. L.)* DEA is the reading of the oldest Gothan. Seventhly, because Bersmann although himself adopting 'deas', adds in the margin "DEA veteres libri, ut propter incisum 'A' producatur." Eighthly, because it was to be expected that the scribes should, on account of the difficulty presented by the long 'A' in the nominative case, alter DEA into 'deas', and not at all to be expected that they should alter 'deas' into DEA.

LATONÆ TACITUM PERTENTANT GAUDIA PECTUS. —

"These growing thoughts my mother soon perceiving
. . . . inly rejoiced."

Par. Reg. I. 227.

507.

TALIS ERAT DIDO TALEM SE LÆTA FEREBAT
PER MEDIOS INSTANS OPERI REGNISQUE FUTURIS
TUM FORIBUS DIVÆ MEDIA TESTUDINE TEMPLI
SEPTA ARMIS SOLIOQUE ALTE SUBNIXA RESEDIT

"Instans præcipue foribus; et hoc loco distinguendum est; magno enim studio et labore templorum fores fiebant, quas quibusdam insignibant historiis" &c. — SERVIUS. An interpretation which, I should think, requires no comment.

"Man stösst bei FORIBUS und MEDIA TESTUDINE an. Im Vorigen ist gesagt, was sie *ausserhalb* des Tempels that: nun folgt TUM, darauf; FORIBUS DIVÆ, im Innern, *innerhalb,* hineingegangen; MEDIA TESTUDINE, mitten inne des Tempelgewölbes" — THIEL. Scholars will, I think, require the production of some authority for the use of FORIBUS in the sense of *'innerhalb, im Innern',* before they accept an interpretation which assigns to this word a sense diametrically opposed to its ordinary *prima facie* sense of *'ad januam'.*

"MEDIA TESTUDINE TEMPLI; h. e. *medio templo* Latino usu, quatenus *intra fores* consederat. . . . . In templis senatum cogi, ad fores tribunalia poni, notus Romanorum mos, ad quem poeta hoc refinxit." — HEYNE.

"Sub tecto templi testudinato in parte foribus propinqua resedit. . . . . . MEDIA TESTUDINE idem est quod *sub templo."* — WAGNER, *Virg. Br. En.*

If Dido sat, according to the view of these critics, inside the temple, and near its door, first, she must have sat either squeezed up in one of the corners on either hand, or else immediately within the entrance and therefore in the way of those entering; and either with her back to them, in which case no more awkward and ungraceful position could have been chosen, or with her face to them, in which case the principal standing-room must have been behind her. And, secondly, in this position she could have been elevated only by the height of her seat or throne, which, unless so high as to have required for its ascent a flight of steps or a ladder, could not have afforded a sufficient elevation above the crowd. Let us therefore consider whether, adhering strictly to the words of the text, it is not perfectly clear that Virgil has placed Dido not only in an entirely different part of the temple, but in a position at once convenient, conspicuous, and dignified.

And, first, we must carefully distinguish between the Cella and the Temple: the former peculiarly the residence of the Deity (whose image it contained), and, except on particular occasions, accessible to the priests only; the latter no more than the enclosure surrounding the former, sometimes roofed, and sometimes not (in the present instance roofed), and serving for the reception and accommodation of the people who came to worship outside the Cella. "*Το μεν χωριον, εν ῳ θεραπευομεν τους θεους, ιερον και νεως* (the Roman *'Templum'*, and Jewish *Court of the Tabernacle), ενθα δε καθιδρυομεν, σηκος, τεμενος*" (the Roman Cella, and Jewish Tabernacle, *σκηνος*), Pollux, I. 1; this latter the first house or covered residence of the Deity of which we have any record. The Cella was not only the principal object, that on which all the other objects in the temple and the temple itself depended, but at the same time the most conspicuous, occupying the further end of the nave in such a manner that its facade or entrance was directly opposite the entrance of the temple, and (not being immediately under the central opening of the roof, but a little further than it from the temple entrance) was illuminated by the light streaming down from the roof. Such was the conspicuous situation of the Cella, elevated above the floor of the temple, and approached by a flight of steps, the landing-place of which, sometimes adorned with columns in the manner of a portico, afforded a noble entrance to the Cella, visible from all parts of the temple, and even from the outside through the temple-door, and at the same time a convenient, elevated platform or tribunal, from which the priest could address the multitude assembled in the area of the temple, and expound to them the 'mysteries of their religion. The entrance into the Cella from the temple was usually provided with grated iron doors, affording a view of the interior even while they remained shut; and a curtain (velum), for the purpose of excluding the view occasionally, and of protecting the interior of the Cella, and especially the image of the Deity usually placed in a niche at the far end of it, from the weather, as well in those temples which were entirely hypæthral, as in those which, being roofed, had a central opening in the roof for the admission of light and air.

All these particulars can be made out satisfactorily, either from the descriptions given us by ancient writers, or from the still existing remains of the buildings themselves. Particularly to our present purpose is that passage of Pausanias, where, speaking of the temple of Jupiter at Olympia, he informs us that the statue of the God was nearly under the middle of the roof of the temple, and that a portico elevated above the floor of the temple led to it: "*Διος δε αγαλματος κατα μεσον πεποιημενου μαλιστα τον αετον* ("Signo Jovis imminet lacunaris vertex" — Siebelis). *Εστηκασι δε και εντος του ναου κιονες· και στοαι τε ενδον υπερωοι, και προσοδος δι᾽ αυτων επι το αγαλμα εστι*" — Pausan. *Ηλιακων* A. c. X. Compare Servius (ad *Georg. III. 16*): "Quod autem dicit 'in medio', ejus templum fore significat. Nam ei semper sacratus numini locus est, cujus simulachrum in medio collocatur; alia enim tantum ad ornatum pertinent."

In the temple of Bacchus in Pompeii are still to be seen, in a state of considerable perfection, the elevated Cella, the flight of steps leading to it, and the landing-place, which latter Fumagalli considers to be the tribunal described by Vitruvius. See, for a representation of the building, as well as for that of the temple of Isis in Pompeii, in which there are also the elevated Cella, flight of steps, and landing-place (converted by pillars into a portico), Fumagalli's Pompeia, 1 vol. fol. Firenze, 1830.

That it was on this landing-place Dido's throne was placed seems to me to admit of no manner of doubt: first, because we are informed it was placed FORIBUS DIVÆ, *at the door of the Goddess,* i. e. of the Cella which the Goddess inhabited, where her image was kept; and MEDIA TESTUDINE TEMPLI, *under the middle of the vaulted roof of the temple.* And secondly, because the temple offered no site for the throne at all comparable with this, where it was in a good light, where it was conspicuous from all parts, where it was removed from, and elevated above, the crowd, and where, without encroaching on the private domain of the Goddess, it was within the halo of her sanctity, and almost under her very shadow.

With this whole description of the reception of Ilioneus and the Trojan ambassadors by Dido in the temple of Juno, compare the exactly parallel description *(En. VII. 168)* of the reception of the same Ilioneus and his companions by Latinus in the temple of Picus.

SOLIOQUE ALTE SUBNIXA. — 'Subniti' (ἐρείδεσθαι), *to take* or *derive support out of something placed underneath; to lean upon, to rest upon* (without including the idea of repose). And so Gesner, correctly, "*In re tanquam basi niti.*" SUBNIXA operates, not (as gratuitously and most unpoetically supposed by Heyne) on 'scabello', understood, but (as placed beyond all doubt by Claudian's exactly parallel

"Cæsariem tunc forte Venus subnixa corusco
Fingebat solio."

Epith. Honor. et Mariæ, v. 99)

on SOLIO, expressed. Compare: "Parva Philoctetæ subnixa Petilia muro," *En. III. 402;* "Subnixæ nubibus altis," *Ciris, 195;* "Cubito subnixa," *Ciris, 348.* The structure, therefore, is, 'resedit foribus divæ septa armis subnixaque alte solio'. The expression has been borrowed by Hericus, *Vita S. Germani, Lib. VI:*

"Nunc tibi, nunc meritas laudes sacramus, Iesu,
Subnixus solio flectis qui cuncta paterno."

522.

QUID VENIANT CUNCTIS NAM LECTI NAVIBUS IBANT

I have myself personally ascertained that CUNCTIS is the reading of the Leipzig MS. No. 35; also of the Petrarchian; the 's' however in the latter appearing not to have existed in the orginal MS., but to have been added by Petrarch's own hand. It is also, as appears from Bottari, the reading of the Vatican Fragment, the 's' being here added as in the Petrarchian MS. by a corrector. CUNCTIS also affords a better sense than 'cuncti'; for, first, the first object of Eneas's wonder would naturally be, not (with Wagner), "quod ita cuncti venirent," but that they came or were there at all; and secondly, the very next word LECTI shows, as plainly as words can show any thing, that they came not cuncti, but the very opposite, LECTI.

For all these reasons I think that Wagner has done wrong in returning to the reading 'cuncti', adopted by Daniel Heinsius from the Medicean, and already rejected by Nicholas Heinsius.

A full stop should be placed after VENIANT, as in the two above first mentioned MSS., Donatus's quotation of the passage (ad Terent. *Adelph. III. 3*), H. Stephens and N. Heinsius.

Although (as I have myself personally ascertained) the reading in the Gudian is now 'Cuncti nam lecti, it is perfectly plain from the manifest either erasure or decay of the parchment, and the room left for a letter both after 'cuncti' and after 'lecti', that the original reading has been CUNCTIS and 'lectis', of which however the latter must be assumed to have been a mere lapse of the transcriber. In Pierius I find the following: "In Romano Codice et Mediceo (observe, not the Laurentian Medicean quoted above, but the Roman Medicean) 'cuncti' nominativo casu legitur;" which reading I have myself personally found in the Leipzig MS. No. 36.

526.

NOVAM CUI CONDERE JUPITER URBEM
JUSTITIAQUE DEDIT GENTES FRENARE SUPERBAS

These words refer to the two occupations in which Ilioneus and the Trojans have just seen Dido engaged: NOVAM CUI CONDERE JUPITER URBEM to "operumque laborem Partibus æquabat justis" etc. *(v.511)*; JUSTITIAQUE DEDIT etc. to "Jura dabat, legesque viris" *(Ibid.)*.

541.

SUPERANTE SALO

SALO — *the sea in the neighbourhood of the shore — the offing.* Compare: "In salo navem tenuit in ancoris." NEP. *Them. VIII. 7;* where see the Annot. of

Bremi. See also Lamb. Bos. *Exer.* Compare also *En. II. 209.* where the term is again applied to the sea near the shore.

548.

QUO JUSTIOR ALTER
NEC PIETATE FUIT NEC BELLO MAJOR ET ARMIS
QUEM SI FATA VIRUM SERVANT SI VESCITUR AURA
ÆTHERIA NEQUE ADHUC CRUDELIBUS OCCUBAT UMBRIS
NON METUS OFFICIO NEC TE CERTASSE PRIOREM
PŒNITEAT SUNT ET SICULIS REGIONIBUS URBES
ARMAQUE TROJANOQUE A SANGUINE CLARUS ACESTES

'Pietas', *the tender feelings* (see Comm. *v. 14),* is here as elsewhere opposed to 'justitia', *the observance of the strict right,* or *law.* Compare:

"Pyrrhus Achillides, animosus imagine patris,
Inclusam contra jusque piumque tenet."
OVID. *Heroid. VIII. 3.*

SI VESCITUR AURA ÆTHERIA. —

— "Haucht jener des Aethers
Nährende Luft."
VOSS.

"In hoc utroque loco (viz. here, and *En. III. 339)* Wagner *(Quæst. Virg. IX. p. 409)* arbitratur Singularem AURA ob soni elegantiam esse positum, quum hic superior versus et inferior claudatur Ablativo Pluralis, ARMIS — UMBRIS, illic autem antecedentis versus extremum vocabulum sit o r i s. Alibi enim, ubi de a u r a, qua circumfundimur, de aere *(Atmosphære)* sermo est, ubique Plurali utitur Virgilius." — FORBIGER.

No; Virgil uses the singular 'aura here, and *En. III. 339,* not to avoid the *ομοιοτελευτον,* but because he uses 'aura', not in the sense of the air or atmosphere, but in the sense of *the radiance* or *light of the sky* or *ether*, VESCITUR AURA ÆTHERIA not meaning *breathe the ethereal air*, but *see the light of the sky*. See Stat. *Theb. I. 236,* where Jupiter speaking of the blindness of the still living Oedipus, says:

> "Ille tamen Superis æterna piacula solvit,
> Projecitque diem, nec jam amplius æthere nostro
> Vescitur; at nati (facinus sine more) cadentes
> Calcavere oculos."

Compare also: 'Lumina vitæ', *En. VI. 829.*

NON METUS OFFICIO NEC TE CERTASSE PRIOREM PŒNITEAT. — "Vulgata erat lectio, OFFICIO *NEC* TE; in quam mirum est optimum quemque codicem, atque etiam Grammaticos (vid. Heins.), conspirare; est enim manifesto falsa. Sensus quidem qualiscunque extorqueri inde potest; sed occurrit unicuique in oculos, legendum esse, 'non metus, officio *ne* te': *ου φοβος μη. Non metuendum est, ne te pœniteat aliquando beneficiis nos priorem demeruisse.* Et extat hæc lectio in Hamb. a m. sec." — HEYNE. In which reading and argumentation, adopted from La Cerda, Heyne is followed and supported by Wagner, and, as far as I know, by all modern editors with the exception of Jahn.

I have myself personally examined only five MSS. with respect to the reading of this passage, viz. the two Leipzig, the Gudian, the Petrarchian and the Dresden; but in each of the five I have found the reading NEC. It appears also from Foggini, that such is the reading of the Medicean, and further that there is a comma placed in that MS. after METUS, as if expressly for the purpose of isolating the clause (thus, NON METUS,). There can be no doubt also that NEC TE was the reading of all the MSS. examined by Pierius, because although informing us with respect to the former part of the verse that NON METUS is to be assumed as the correct reading, notwithstanding the Medicean (i. e. the Roman Medicean) and some others read, 'Nec metus', he makes no observation on the latter part of the verse, contenting himself with the simple quotation of the verse as follows: NON METUS OFFICIO NEC TE CERTASSE. I am influenced in favor of the reading NEC not less by this undoubted consentient authority of all the MSS. with the exception of the Hamburg alone (in which, besides, NEC appears [see above] to have been the original reading), but by the, with me at least, even stronger argument of the better sense thus obtained, viz. NON METUS, *we have no fear but that all will yet be right with us, and you have no occasion to repent of having shown us kindness.* I consider this a better sense than that obtainable from the reading 'non metus ... ne', first, because the emphatically reduplicated protasis QUEM SI FATA VIRUM SERVANT — SI VESCITUR AURA ÆTHERIA — NEQUE ADHUC CRUDELIBUS OCCUBAT UMBRIS requires a stronger apodosis than the feeble 'non metus ... ne'; and secondly, because it had not been complimentary to Dido thus, not merely to insinuate, but even plainly to express, that Ilioneus thought that Dido did fear, that she would get no reward for showing kindness toward the Trojans.

It is impossible that the protasis QUEM SI FATA VIRUM &c. could have a more fitting apodosis than NON METUS (nobis, sciz.), NEC: If only our brave general survives, we doubt not but we shall get over all our present difficulties — that all will ultimately be well with *us* — and that *you* will have no cause to repent, etc. But if not — "Sin absumpta salus" — if he has perished, and we in consequence (instead of having no fear — NON METUS —) have every reason to fear — to despair entirely (viz. of a happy arrival in Italy), then we will go back to Sicily from whence we came hither, and settle down there among our friends.

In further support of the reading NEC it may be observed that Virgil has elsewhere the identical expression:

"Nec te pœniteat calamo trivisse labellum."

Eclog. II. 34.

NEC is the reading of Burmann, as well as of both the Stephenses and both the Heinsii, although Nicholas Heinsius informs us in his note (see Burmann) that he thinks 'ne' ought to be adopted even against the authority of the MSS. Henry Stephens even places a colon after METUS.

ARMAQUE. — Heyne, whose example has been followed by Wagner, Forbiger, Ladewig and others, has rejected the (up to his time) received reading ARMA, and substituted for it the reading of the Medicean and some minor MSS., 'arva' The following is the reason assigned by Heyne for the change. "ARMA quidem aiunt memorari ad timorem Pœnis incutiendum. At alienum hoc a toto orationis consilio rerumque facie, potiusque ad animos exasperandos idoneum. Eo spectat oratio, ut metum intercipiat, ne in his terris considere velle videantur."

I prefer to adhere to the received reading, which is that of by far the greater weight of MSS., as well as of both the Stephenses and both the Heinsii, and understand ARMA to be added to URBES, not by any means by way of threat, but to explain what kind of cities were meant, viz. 'urbes bellicosæ', cities which were warlike, and therefore able to assist Dido and to become her valuable allies; the clause, SUNT ET SICULIS REGIONIBUS URBES ARMAQUE etc., standing in close connexion with the immediately preceding NON METUS OFFICIO etc.; as if Ilioneus had said: don't lose the opportunity of binding to your interests people who, wretched and needy as they may seem here and under their present circumstances, are powerful and warlike in Sicily, and may become your grateful and valuable friends. The resemblance between this part of Ilioneus's address to Dido and some part of Caractacus's address to the Romans is as great as the difference in the circumstances of the speakers permits: "Præsens sors mea, ut mihi informis, sic tibi magnifica est; habui equos, viros, arma, opes; quid mirum, si hæc invitus amisi?" — TACIT. *Annal. XII. 37.* URBES ARMAQUE, i. e. *armatas urbes:* "viros, arma," i. e. *armatos viros.*

In every one of the seven oldest MSS. (viz. Nos. 115. 116. 117. 118. 119. 120. 121) which I consulted personally in the year 1852 in the Royal Library at Vienna, the reading is ARMA. ARMA is also, as I have personally ascertained, the reading in the Gudian, the two Leipzig, the Dresden, the Kloster-Neuburg, and the Petrarchian. From Pierius's silence as to this verse, it is fairly to be presumed that ARMA was the only reading known to him. Ambrogi, though in his accompanying text he has 'arva', translates from ARMA:

"Anco nella Sicilia armi e cittadi."

560.

NEC SPES JAM RESTAT IULI

"SPES IULI bene pro *Iulo.*" — HEYNE. I think however that the exact and more poetical meaning is, not *if Iulus has perished,* but *if the hope of Iulus* (at his prepresent age nobody, and only the promise, SPES, of a man,) *has perished; if the promise which Iulus gave of being a great man, has been lost to us by his death.* Compare Tacit. *Annal. XIV. 53,* Seneca speaking to Nero: "Ex quo spei tuæ admotus sum;" *from the time I was first placed beside you as tutor when you were not yet a man, but only the promise of a man.* As the subject of Seneca's assertion is not Nero himself, but 'spes' — the hope afforded by Nero's youth that he would yet be a great man — so the loss contemplated by Ilioneus in the words NEC SPES JAM RESTAT (sciz. nobis) IULI, is not that of Iulus (the life of a child being of no consequence to the Trojans), but of the promise which Iulus's youth gave, that if he lived, he would become a great prince, and the successor of Eneas. Compare also Justin, II. 15: "Ut vidit spei urbis invideri;" not *when he saw that the city gave offence*, but *that the promise given by the city that it would become a great city, gave offence*. Also *En. VI. 364:* "Per spem surgentis Iuli;" not *by Iulus himself*, but *by the hope, the apparent promise, that Iulus* (now but a child) *would grow up to be a prince and the successor of his father.*

As here SPES RESTAT, so *En. II. 142:* "Restet fides."

566.

SOLVITE CORDE METUM TEUCRI SECLUDITE CURAS

The testimony of Pierius is very strong in favor of reading 'seducite': "In antiquis plerisque codicibus metus legitur, numero multitudinis: et in longe pluribus seducite curas." SECLUDITE is however quoted by Donatus, ad Ter. *Hec. III. 1.*

572.

NEC TAM AVERSUS EQUOS TYRIA SOL JUNGIT AB URBE

"AVERSUS, h. e. simpliciter *remotus.*" — HEYNE.
"Non tam remoti sumus a sole." — WAGNER, *Virg. Br. En.*
"So weit entfernt von der Stadt." — THIEL.

> "Nicht so entfernt spannt Sol von der Tyrierstadt das Geschirr an."
>
> VOSS.
>
> "Non si lunge da lor si gira il sole."
>
> CARO.

No; but ('aversus' being the opposite of 'adversus', *turned towards*), *does not yoke his horses with his face turned away* (with horror, sciz.) *from Carthage, does not turn his back upon Carthage when he is yoking his horses.* Compare: "Simul hæc dicens, e medio prospectu abscessit, non aversus, sed, dum evanesceret, verecunde retrogrediens, et pectus ostentans." AMMIAN. XVIII. 8. Also:

— "Seque ex oculis avertit et aufert."
En. IV. 389;

and

— "Italia Teucrorum avertere regem."
En I. 42;

where see Comment. And especially compare:

"Aversumque diem mensis furialibus Atrei."
OVID. *Amor. III. 12. 39;*

and

"Exoritur pudibunda dies, cælumque retexens
Aversum Lemno jubar."
STAT. *Theb. V. 296;*

also Sil. Ital. XV. 334, and Lucil. *Etna, 20.*

582.

SI QUIBUS EJECTUS SILVIS AUT URBIBUS ERRAT

Burmann although he has adopted the reading URBIBUS into his text, informs us in his note, that he would prefer 'montibus', the reading of a small number of second rate MSS., on the ground that there must have been but few cities in Africa at this period, and none at all under the dominion of Dido. I have myself personally examined with respect to this word five MSS., viz. the Gudian, the two Leipzig, the Kloster-Neuburg, and the Dresden, and in each of the five I have found URBIBUS; which is also, as appears from Foggini, the reading of the Medicean. URBIBUS has been also adopted by both the Heinsii, as well as by all modern editors, and is further supported by the mention of Getulian cities at *v. 40,* and of great Libyan cities at *v. 173* of 4th Book.

605.

NEC QUICQUID UBIQUE EST
GENTIS DARDANIÆ MAGNUM QUÆ SPARSA PER ORBEM

Besides the settlements which the Trojans made in Italy under Antenor and Eneas, they are also said to have made one in Denmark:

"Quant jadis fut destruite Troie,
. . . .
Plusors qui escaper se porent,
. . . .
Par granz labors par granz perilz
Par plusors terres s' epandirent,
Terres poplerent, citez firent,
Une gent de Troie escaperent,
Ki en Danemarche assenerent."

The alleged origin of the race of Northmans or Normans, who, under Bier and Hasting, invaded and conquered the northwestern part of France, since from them called Normandy. See *Roman de Rou, 157 and seq.*

607.

DI TIBI SI QUA PIOS RESPECTANT NUMINA SI QUID
USQUAM JUSTITIA EST ET MENS SIBI CONSCIA RECTI
PRÆMIA DIGNA FERANT QUÆ TE TAM LÆTA TULERUNT
SÆCULA QUI TANTI TALEM GENUERE PARENTES

SI QUA PIOS RESPECTANT NUMINA. — *If there be any divinities who care for and reward* (not the pious, but) *the tender-hearted and compassionate,* i. e. Dido, for the compassion which she had shown toward the Trojans. See *v. 14.* and Comm.

JUSTITIA. — I entirely agree with Heyne, Wagner and Forbiger, in preferring the reading JUSTITIA to 'Justitiæ'. I have myself personally ascertained that JUSTITIA has been originally the reading of the Gudian (although altered in that MS. by a corrector into 'Justitiæ') and of Dan. Heinsius, and wonder much that Nicholas Heinsius and Burmann should have adopted 'Justitiæ'; which happens however to be the reading of the only other MSS. which I have myself personally examined respecting this word, viz. the Petrarchian, the two Leipzig, and the Dresden, in the latter of which a point is placed after EST; thus expressly connecting MENS SIBI CONSCIA RECTI with DI. In support of the reading JUSTITIA and the consequent deduction that MENS SIBI CONSCIA RECTI is connected, not with DI, but with JUSTITIA, I may adduce the connexion of 'recti' with 'justitia' by Ovid *(Heroid. XX. 169):*

"Si tibi justitiæ, si recti cura fuisset,
Cedere debueras ignibus ipse meis."

QUÆ TE TAM LÆTA TULERUNT &c. —

"Wer bist du, heilig wunderbares Mädchen?
Welch glücklich Land gebar dich? Sprich, wer sind
Die gottgeliebten Eltern, die dich zeugten?"
SCHILLER, *Jungf. v. Orleans, Act I.*

611.

IN FRETA DUM FLUVII CURRENT DUM MONTIBUS UMBRÆ
LUSTRABUNT CONVEXA POLUS DUM SIDERA PASCET
SEMPER HONOS NOMENQUE TUUM LAUDESQUE MANEBUNT
QUÆ ME CUNQUE VOCANT TERRÆ

DUM MONTIBUS UMBRÆ LUSTRABUNT CONVEXA. — "Quod Tibullus, I. 4. 65, nude: 'dum robora tellus .... vehet' hoc ornatius extulit Virgilius: donec in montibus umbrae silvarum convexa montium, h. e. latera et ambitus, obscurabunt, et ornatius, lustrabunt ["obibunt"— Forbiger], umbra pro flexu solis procedente et circumagente se. — Heyne.

"Rem optime expedivisse mihi videtur Heynius." — Wagner.

"Mihi vero, ut Wagnero, Heynii ratio unice vera videtur. Nam etsi alium non memini locum, in quo convexa simpliciter pro vallibus dicatur, convexa tamen vallium legimus apud Justin. II. 10. extr. et 'convexam vallem' apud Plin. *Nat. Hist. V. 5. 5.*" — Forbiger.

This interpretation is liable to these two capital objections: first, that whilst it assigns a subordinate place almost no place at all, in the picture to the mountains, which are expressly and emphatically mentioned (dum montibus umbrae), it awards a principal and prominent position to woods, which are not mentioned at all. In other words, Virgil has committed the error of putting into the picture mountains which might almost, or quite as well, have been absent from it, whilst he has left out woods which are absolutely indispensable to it and perform the chief part — has given us, as it were, the play of Hamlet, the part of Hamlet himself being left out, and that of Othello substituted for it. And secondly, it represents the shadows of the woods as lustrating, going round, obeuntia, circumeuntia, not the woods — which they do actually go round — but the mountains, with respect to which they are, and must be, nearly stationary — Being the shadows of the woods, they must remain where the woods are, going round them as the sun goes round, but remaining with respect to the mountains as stationary, or nearly as stationary, as the very woods themselves. La Cerda's interpretation, "Dum umbrae circumibunt montium ambitus; tuberositas quippe, quae convexa est in montibus, umbram efficit, quae umbra ex diversa solis positione montes lustrat, i. e. circumit ambitque, jam hanc, jam illam partem opacans," although correctly referring UMBRAE to the shadows formed by the mountains themselves, and correctly accounting for the change of place ascribed to the shadows by the word LUSTRABUNT, involves the absurdity of representing the tuberosities of the mountains, the very parts on which the lights fall oftenest and strongest, as the ordinary seat of the shadows.

We have only to understand CONVEXA in its very ordinary sense (see Comm. *v. 314*) of *hollows, crescent-* or *basin-shaped depressions,* and (preserving the remainder of La Cerda's exposition,) we have this very simple and consistent meaning of the sentence: *so long as the shadows of the mountains shall slowly pass along, on,* or *over, the hollows* or *depressions on the sides of the mountains,* or *among the mountains* (i. e. *the hollows imbosomed in the mountains) — so long as the hollows among the mountains shall be traversed by the shadows of the mountains.* Nothing can be more simple than the structure: 'dum in montibus, umbrae (sciz. montium) lustrabunt convexa' (sciz. montium). We have only to add to the idea expressed by Horace *(Carm. III. 6)* in the words,

— "Sol ubi montium
Mutaret umbras," —

the idea of perpetual repetition, and we have the substance of the Virgilian idea: *so long as the sun shall continue to cause the mountain shadows to shift place.*

Although I have not hesitated (with the great majority of MSS. and especially with the Medicean, and Vatican Fragment) to connect CONVEXA with LUSTRABUNT, it is but right to inform my readers that besides the authorities enumerated by N. Heinsius (see Burm. in loc.) for placing a point after LUSTRABUNT and so referring CONVEXA to PASCET, there is also, as I have satisfied myself by personal examination, that of the Petrarchian and the two Leipzig MSS. On the other hand, in the Gudian and the Dresden, as I have satisfied myself by similar personal examination, the line stands thus, without any intermediate point:

LUSTRABUNT CONVEXA POLUS DUM SIDERA PASCET

and Pierius informs us expressly that "In Oblongo Codice, et in aliquot aliis antiquis, post dictionem CONVEXA punctum est .... quae lectio quadrat cum Ti. Donati sententia dicentis .... 'quamdiu solis umbra vel lunae convexa lustraverit montium'."

PASCET. — This is, as I have personally ascertained, the reading of the two Leipzig and the Dresden; also of the Gudian as it now stands, for the original reading in this MS. seems to have been 'pascit', which has been changed into PASCET by the hand of a corrector. I find in Henry Stephens, Bersmann, and the two Heinsii, PASCET.

POLUS DUM SIDERA PASCET. — The stars being supposed to be fiery, or of fire, (see Lucret. V. 518 and seq., Cic. *de Nat. Deor. II. 46. 118)* and fire requiring food, aliment or fuel, the term PASCET in our text, being the term usually applied to the supplying a fire with fuel ("Quae res incendia pascit," LUCIL. *Etna, 220),* is peculiarly appropriate.

QUAE ME CUNQUE VOCANT TERRAE. — "Quocunque abiero, beneficii accepti memor ero." — HEYNE.
"In iis terris, in quibus consedero, ut perennis sit beneficii tui memoria efficiam." — WAGNER.

I am inclined to think that Eneas's nobler meaning is, *no matter whither I may be called — no matter what becomes of ME, YOUR fame will last as long as the world itself.* Compare: "Te tamen oramus, quibuscunque erimus in terris, ut nos liberosque nostros ita tueare" &c. — CIC. *Epist. ad Fam. II. 16.*

The reader will also recognize in the words, QUAE ME CUNQUE VOCANT TERRAE, (VOCANT being in the indicative, not the subjunctive, mood,) a polite and graceful intimation (in answer to Dido's invitation *v. 576)* that Eneas's duty leads him away from Carthage.

617.

OBSTUPUIT PRIMO ASPECTU SIDONIA DIDO

So Propertius (IV. 4. 21), exquisitely, of Tarpeja's first sight of Tatius:

"Obstupuit regis facie et regalibus armis
Interque oblitas excidit urna manus."

634.

NON IGNARA MALI MISERIS SUCCURRERE DISCO

Scarcely less pathetic is our own Sterne: "She had suffered persecution and learned mercy." Nor is Ulysses's sympathy with Ajax (Soph. *Ajax, v. 1381*) less natural and touching, although, as arising, not from recollection of the past, but from expectation of the future, it is somewhat of a different kind:

A. "Αναγκας ουν με τον νεκρον θαπτειν εαν;
O. Εγωγε, και γαρ αυτος ενθαδ' ιξομαι."

Compare also St. Paul, *Epist. to Hebr. IV. 15,* quoted by Peerlkamp: "*ου γαρ εχομεν αρχιερεα μη δυναμενον συμπαθησαι ταις ασθενειαις ημων, πεπειρασμενον δε κατα παντα.*" Also Charlotte Corday, in a letter written on the eve of her execution and published by Lamartine in his *Histoire des Girondins, Liv. 44. ch. VIII:* "Les prisonniers de la Conciergerie, loin de m'injurier comme le peuple dans les rues, ont l'air de me plaindre. Le malheur rend compatissant. C'est ma dernière reflexion.

640.

MUNERA LAETITIAMQUE DEI

The sense of this line (as of 538, 564 and, I believe, of all those which Virgil has left incomplete) is perfect, although the verse is not; MUNERA LAETITIAMQUE DEI, i. e. *Munera laeta Dei;* the particular god intended being sufficiently indicated, *(a)* by the word 'laetitia' (see 'laetitiae Bacchus dator', *v. 738. Διονυσου γανος*, EURIP. *Cycl. v. 414; βοτρυος γανος*, EURIP. *Bacchid. v. 261* and *382; οια Διωνυσος δωκ' ανδρασι χαρμα*, HESIOD, *Shield of Hercules, v. 400)*; and *(b)* by the obvious necessity (observed by La Cerda and others) that wine should form a part of Dido's presents.

I therefore adhere, with Forbiger, to the ordinary reading, and reject with him, as affording a much inferior sense, the reading 'dii', proposed by A. Gellius, and adopted by Heyne, Brunck, Jahn, Wagner, and Thiel. Compare *En. IX. 337,* where Virgil again applies to Bacchus the term 'Deus' without any distinguishing adjunct: "Membra Deo victus;" also, Ovid. *Art. Am. II. 85,* where there is a similar application of the term 'Deus', without distinguishing adjunct, to Phoebus: — "cera Deo propiore liquescit;" also, *En. III. 177:* — "munera libo Intemerata focis," where 'munera intemerata' is the poetic equivalent for *merum vinum;* also, *Georg. III. 526:* "Bacchi Munera;" but, above all, the identical expression of our text in the Letter of Crates to Lysis preserved in the *Epistolae Mut. Graecan.* Aurel. Allobr. 1606. Fol.: "*Οπως αν τοτε δωρον του θεου* (vinum sciz.) *μη ατιμαζοντι εις κεφαλην σοι γενηται.*"

I have myself personally ascertained that DEI is the reading of the Gudian, of the Kloster-Neuburg MS., of two MSS. in the Ambrosian Library (the Petrarchian, and No. 79), of three in the Munich Library (Nos. 18059, 21562, and 305) and of the six principal in the Vienna Library

(Nos. 113. 115. 117. 118. 120. 121), of the two Leipzig, and of the Dresden. I have also found it in both the Heinsii. It is also; as appears from Foggini, the reading of the Medicean, in which, however, the reading has been originally 'De' the final 'i' having been afterwards added in red ink. Finally, in support of this reading we have the weighty testimony of Pierius: "Litem ego quoque sub judice relicturus eram, nisi exemplaria fere omnia vetustiora reclamassent, DEI legendum esse attestantia."

641.

REGALI SPLENDIDA LUXU
INSTRUITUR

The structure is 'splendida regali luxu', not 'instruitur regali luxu'; as in vers. 475, cruentus multa caede', not 'vastabat multa caede' See also Comment on "dirae ferro et compagibus arctis," *v. 297*.

662.

CUPIDO

It is only, as appears from Claudian's beautiful Epithalamium of Honorius and Maria *(v. 73)*, in accordance with the strictest mythological etiquette, that the son of Venus, the great God of Love, himself ("quantus Deus", *v. 723*), should be employed for the ruin of Dido:

"Mille pharetrati ludunt in margine fratres,
Ore pares, similes habitu, gens mollis Amorum.
Hos Nymphæ pariunt: illum (sciz. Cupidinem) Venus aurea solum
Edidit. Ille Deos caelumque et sidera cornu
Temperat, et summos dignatur figere reges;
Hi plebem feriunt."

663.

DONISQUE FURENTEM
INCENDAT REGINAM ATQUE OSSIBUS IMPLICET IGNEM

and 716.

PRAECIPUE INFELIX PESTI DEVOTA FUTURAE
EXPLERI MENTEM NEQUIT ARDESCITQUE TUENDO
PHOENISSA ET PARITER PUERO DONISQUE MOVETUR

There was perhaps more meaning in Eneas's presents than may appear at first sight to the reader. There is reason to think that the double crown was peculiarly the bride's crown; compare Turneb. *Advers. XXIX. 4,* and (quoted there from Donatus) Valerius's "Ipsa suam duplicem Cytherea coronam;" also Gesner in voce 'vitta'. It is certain too that the saffron color was sacred to Hymen, and the saffron colored veil peculiarly the bride's veil:

> "Pars infecta croco velamina lutea Serum
> Pandite, Sidoniasque solo prosternite vestes."
> CLAUD. *Epith. Honor. et Mar. 211.*

See also Catull. in *Nupt. Juliae et Manlii,* Ovid, Martial, Festus, and numerous other writers. Also Claudian, of Proserpine's putting on a garland of flowers:

> "Nunc sociat flores, seseque ignara coronat,
> Augurium fatale tori."
> *De Rapt. Pros. II. 140.*

Nothing could have been more suitable for Venus's purpose, or more likely to produce the effects described in the text, than such suggestive presents conveyed from Eneas to Dido by the hands of Love himself.

666.

ET SUB NOCTEM CURA RECURSAT

Not, as erroneously understood by Wordsworth,

> "The calm of night is powerless to remove
> These cares,"

but *her cares, however they may have been dissipated by the light and cheerfulness of the day, return* (as usually happens with persons whose minds are uneasy) *with the darkness and stillness of returning night, and prevent her from sleeping.* Compare:

> "Quos. jam mente dies, quam saeva insomnia curis
> Prospicio."
>
> VAL. FLACC. I. 329.

> "Talia dicenti curarum maxima nutrix
> Nox intervenit."
>
> OVID. *Met. VIII. 81.*

> "Noxque ruit, soli veniens non mitis amanti.
> Ergo ubi, cunctatis extremo in limine plantis,
> Contigit aegra toros, et mens incensa tenebris,
> Vertere tunc varios per longa insomnia questus,
> Nec pereat quo scire modo."
>
> VAL. FLACC. VII. 3. (of Medea;)

and above all Virgil himself, *En. IV. 529:*

> "At non infelix animi Phoenissa, nec unquam
> Solvitur in somnos, oculisve aut pectore noctem
> Accipit: ingeminant curae."

668.

NATE MEAE VIRES MEA MAGNA POTENTIA SOLUS
NATE PATRIS SUMMI QUI TELA TYPHOEA TEMNIS

Wagner, following N. Heinsius, and followed by Forbiger and Ladewig, has removed from the Heynian text the comma placed between POTENTIA and SOLUS, and connects the two words together so as to obtain the following sense: "Quantumvis magna habeatur vis ac potentia mea, tamen tuo solius numine nititur; nulla est sine te." I not merely replace the pause, but use a semicolon instead of a comma in order to separate the two words more completely;

First and chiefly, because I think we thus obtain a better sense; *son, who ALONE settest at nought the supreme Father's weapons Typhoëan.*

Secondly, because SOLUS is weak coming in at the end of a verse and sentence, to which it seems tacked like an after-thought, while it is extremely strong and emphatic, placed at the commencement of a new sentence, and prefixed to an entire verse.

Thirdly, because it is so separated from the preceding, and connected with the succeeding, sentence by the actual punctuation both of the Medicean and the Vatic. Fragment; see Foggini and Bottari.

Fourthly, because such seems to have been the only punctuation known to Servius, whose words are these: "SOLUS, NATE; id est, qui solus contemnis Jovis fulmina, quæ diis cæteris solent esse terrori."

For all these reasons I join Daniel Heinsius, Burmann, Fabricius, the Baskerville text and Alfieri, in separating SOLUS from the preceding, and attaching it to the succeeding, clause. It was, I have no doubt, the weight of the authority of the Gudian, in which, as I have ascertained by personal examination, there is a semicolon placed after SOLUS, and no pause at all between SOLUS and POTENTIA, which induced N. Heinsius to separate SOLUS from the succeeding context, and connect it with the preceding.

NATE MEÆ VIRES &c. — Compare Venus's similar persuasion of Cupid to wound Medea with the love of Jason: "Ει δ' αγε μοι 'πρόφρων," &c. — APOLLON. RHOD. III. 131. See also (in Gorius, *Mus. Florent.*

Tom. II. Tab. 16, Fig. 1.) a representation, taken from a gem, of Cupid breaking Jupiter's thunder-bolts across his knee.

697.

UBI MOLLIS AMARACUS ILLUM
FLORIBUS ET DULCI ASPIRANS COMPLECTITUR UMBRA

AMARACUS, — specially selected by the poet as sacred to Hymen. See Catull. *in Nupt. Juliæ et Manlii, v. 6:*

"Cinge (Hymen sciz.) tempora floribus
Suaveolentis amaraci."

701.

CUM VENIT AULAEIS JAM SE REGINA SUPERBIS
AUREA COMPOSUIT SPONDA MEDIAMQUE LOCAVIT

AULAEIS. — "Sunt vestes stragulae, spondae et toro injectae." — HEYNE, approved by Ladewig. I think rather (with La Cerda and Alciatus, *Parerg. XII. 10*) *hangings over head;* both because I find no instance of 'aulaea used in the sense thus assigned to it by Heyne, and because otherwise the queen were not sufficiently distinguished from the guests, who are described *(vv. 704. 712)* as reclining on cushions ornamented with crimson embroidery.

COMPOSUIT. — *Settled herself in a becoming position, and adjusted her dress.* Compare: "Idem, quum Graeco pallio amictus intrasset (carent enim togae jure, quibus aqua et igni interdictum est), postquam se composuit, circumspexitque habitum suum." PLIN. *Epist. IV. 11.* "Leviter consurgendum, tum in componenda toga .... paullum est commorandum." QUINCT. II. 3. 156.

MEDIAM LOCAVIT. — To avoid too great minuteness our author states merely that Dido placed herself MEDIAM, i. e. on the middle 'lectus' (corresponding exactly to our *head of the table*), but as there was a middle place, as well as side places, on the middle 'lectus', it is to be understood that Dido occupied, not only the middle 'lectus', but the middle place of the middle 'lectus'.

As it appears clearly from the separate entrances *(v. 703* and *711)* and separate applauses *(v. 751)* of the Trojans and Tyrians, that the two parties sat, to a certain degree, separate and distinct from each other, and as we have just seen that Dido occupied the centre place of the 'medius lectus' (i. e. the centre place at the head of the table), it follows almost certainly that her guests, the Trojans, occupied the 'imus lectus', i. e. that side of the length of the table which was on her right hand, while her own people, the Tyrians, occupied the (opposite) 'summus lectus', or that side of the length of the table which was on her left. Also that Eneas and the simulated Ascanius were placed on Dido's right on the second seat of the 'medius lectus', at the head of the table, having Dido on their left hand, and on their right the right hand corner of the table, and then all along the right side of the table the remainder of the Trojan party. The principal Tyrian nobles would naturally occupy the corresponding place on Dido's left. For a plan of the Triclinium see Doering ad Hor. *Sat. II. 8.* See also *Le Palais de Scaurus XIX,* and Plut. *Symp. VIII. 7.*

As usual in Virgil's sentences, the first placed verb comes last in the order of time: 'mediam locavit, et sese composuit'.

707

ORDINE LONGO

In all the MSS. which I have myself personally examined respecting this passage, viz. the Gudian, the Petrarchian, the Kloster-Neuburg, the Dresden, the two Leipzig, and Nos. 113. 115. 116 in the Royal Library at Vienna, I have found the reading to be LONGO. LONGO is, besides, the only reading recognised either by Servius or Donatus, and is moreover, if Foggini is to be relied on, the reading of the Medicean. I find LONGO also in the younger Heinsius, although in his note (see Burmann) he informs us that the authority of Charisius inclines him in favor of 'longam', contrary to all his MSS. In the elder Heinsius I find 'longam', which has been adopted by Wagner, who, although accustomed to hold himself bound by the single unsupported authority of the Medicean, has on the present occasion most unaccountably and, as it were, for the mere purpose of showing his independance, rebelled against that authority where it is (with one solitary and very doubtful exception) backed by the entire host of Virgilian MSS.

709.

PARES AETATE MINISTRI

It is neither indifferently nor accidentally that Virgil assigns to Dido a number of attendants all of one age. It appears from the following passage of Tacitus *(Annal. XV. 69)* that etiquette did not permit persons of private rank to be waited on by such attendants: "Jubetque praevenire conatus consulis; occupare velut arcem ejus; opprimere delectam juventutem; quia Vestinus imminentes foro aedes, decoraque servitia et pari aetate habebat."

721.

HAEC OCULIS HAEC PECTORE TOTO
HAERET ET INTERDUM GREMIO FOVET INSCIA DIDO
INSIDEAT QUANTUS MISERAE DEUS

"That the word DIDO, after REGINAM and HAEC, is clumsy, and hath a bad effect, will be acknowledged I believe by every poet. I should rather thus: Inscia quantus, Insideat quantus miserae Deus." — JORTIN, *Philol. Tracts.*

On the contrary, the insertion of Dido's name in this position not only gives additional pathos to the passage, but is according to Virgil's manner:

— "Donec regina sacerdos
Marte gravis geminam partu dabit Ilia prolem."
En. I. 277.

"Quos hominum ex facie dea saeva potentibus herbis
Induerat Circe in vultus ac terga ferarum."
En. VII. 19.

See also *En. I. 500* and *695; II. 403;* also the separation of 'Delius' from 'Apollo' *(En. III. 162);* of 'Ithacus' from 'Ulysses' *(III. 628);* of 'Saturnia' from 'Jovis conjux' *(IV. 91);* of 'Deus' from 'Somnus' *(V. 841)*; and the junction of the separated appellatives with separate verbs. The proposed repetition of QUANTUS would have only operated to withdraw the attention from the principal personage, for the purpose of fixing it on one which performs only a secondary part.

Akin to this criticism of the learned Jortin on INSCIA DIDO is that of Steevens, the celebrated editor of Shakespeare, on

"At Venus obscuro gradientes aëre sepsit,
Et multo nebulae circum dea fudit amictu."
En. I. 415:

"Had Virgil lived to have revised his *Eneid,* he would hardly have permitted both of these lines to have remained in his text. The awkward repetition of the nominative case in the second of them seems to decide very strongly against it." — Steevens's Shakespeare, *Romeo and Juliet, Act IV. sc. 1, note.* Hard indeed is the destiny of authors! transcendent excellence, clearness, and beauty of style are as surely accounted awkwardness, clumsiness, and error, by the judges who sit on our critical bench, as, two centuries ago, superior physical knowledge, or even singular blamelessness of life, was received in our criminal courts as proof incontrovertible of communication with the Father of evil.

740.

DIXIT ET IN MENSAM LATICUM LIBAVIT HONOREM

It is remarkable that, although IN MENSAM is the reading of the Medicean, and the only reading recognised either by Servius or Donatus, yet in the only three MSS. which I have myself personally examined, viz. the two Leipzig and the Dresden, as well as in the Modena Ed. of 1475, I have found 'immensum', concerning the antiquity of which reading we have further the testimony of Pierius: "In oblongo codice, quem Pomponii Laeti delicias fuisse dicunt, 'Immensum' legitur; idem in Longobardico et aliquot aliis pervetustis." Maittaire informs us that the Venice Ed. of 1472 reads 'immensum laticis', and the Milan of 1474, 'immensam laticum'. The reading 'immensum' no doubt arose from the accidental corruption of IN MENSAM into 'immensam', and the subsequent intentional change of the latter into 'immensum', in order to make it agree with HONOREM.

744.

CITHARA CRINITUS IOPAS
PERSONAT AURATA DOCUIT QUAE MAXIMUS ATLAS
HIC CANIT ERRANTEM LUNAM SOLISQUE LABORES

Although the Medicean reads 'quem' (which has been adopted by Nich. Heinsius, Jahn and Wakefield), I think Virgil must have written QUAE, first and principally for the reason assigned by Wagner, "Sed illa IOPAS CITHARA PERSONAT flagitant accusativum objecti: ea, quae docuit." Secondly, because from Pierius's words, "In Romano Codice, et quibusdam aliis legere est 'docuit quem maximus atlans'," the plain conclusion is that the majority of Pierius s MSS. read QUAE. Thirdly, because Donatus gives us the express gloss, "Non turpia aut obscoena, sed venientia ex philosophiae fonte, quae docuerat Atlas maximus." Fourthly, because I find QUAE in the Modena Ed. of 1475, and Maittaire testifies that QUAE is the reading both of the Venice Ed. of 1472 and the Milan Ed. of 1474. I have myself personally consulted only three MSS., viz. Leipzig 35, Leipzig 36, and the Dresden. In the first I have found QUAE, in the second q. and in the third 'quem'.

This is one of the numerous instances in which I prefer the much calumniated Daniel Heinsius (who here reads QUAE) to the scarcely less overrated Nicholas. See Prefatory Remarks.

HIC CANIT ERRANTEM LUNAM &c. — The calm and philosophical subject of Iopas's song contrasts finely with the subsequent romantic and exciting narrative of Eneas. In this respect, as in so many others, Virgil has improved upon his master, who, making his minstrel sing, and his hero tell, similarly romantic stories, loses the advantage of contrast. See *Odyss. Books VIII. IX.*

SOLISQUE LABORES. — "Defectus solis." — HEYNE, and so Wagner ad *Georg. II. 478.* I think not, but simply *the toils (diurnal and annual revolutions) of the sun;* for we have in Silius Italicus, XIV. 348:

— "Atque una pelagi lunaeque labores,"

where the adjoined 'pelagi' shews that 'labores' cannot by possibility mean *eclipses* or any thing else but *toils.* ERRANTEM LUNAM SOLISQUE LABORES, i. e. *labores errantis lunae et solis.*

749.

QUID TANTUM OCEANO PROPERENT SE TINGERE SOLES
HIBERNI VEL QUAE TARDIS MORA NOCTIBUS OBSTET
INGEMINANT PLAUSUM TYRII TROESQUE SEQUUNTUR

"TARDIS, non longis, sed aestivis, i. e. tarde venientibus." — SERVIUS.
"Cur dierum spatia decrescant ac crescant per diversas anni vices." — HEYNE.
"Cur aestate breviores sint noctes." — WAGNER.

— "What cause delays
The summer nights, and shortens winter days."
DRYDEN.

Before I accept this interpretation, I beg to be informed where in the whole passage there is any mention of summer, or of any season except winter. If I am told in reply that there is indeed no direct mention of summer, but that summer is to be inferred from the expression TARDIS NOCTIBUS, which can only mean *slowly coming on,* or *late, nights,* I ask again why may not TARDIS NOCTIBUS (as in Ovid, *Ep. ex Pont. II. 4. 25:*

"Longa dies citius brumali sidere, noxque
Tardior hiberna solstitialis erit;")

mean *the slowly moving, slowly departing, nights* of the just mentioned winter, and whether it is not much more simple and natural, and accordant with the usual Virgilian construction, to refer these words to the subject in the sentence of which they form a part, than to suppose, and bring from a distance, a subject to which to refer them? But then I am asked, What is to be done with OBSTET? can it mean any thing else than impediment to the coming on of the nights in summer? Certainly, and much more simply, impediment to the departure or setting, or plunging in ocean, of the nights of winter; the hiatus after the word being supplied (like the subject of TARDIS NOCTIBUS) from the former part of the sentence, thus: OBSTET — quominus eae quoque, praecipitantes caelo (compare *En. II. 8),* se tingant oceano. We have thus this plain and connected meaning of the whole passage: *Why the winter suns are in such haste, and the winter nights so slow, to plunge into the ocean,* or in plain prose, why the winter days are so short and the winter nights so long: NOCTIBUS being opposed to SOLES, TARDIS to PROPERENT, and TINGERE OCEANO and HIBERNI common (according to the usage of Virgil and the best Latin writers) to both clauses of the sentence. The ancients, and particularly the poets, always pictured the night as following the course of the sun or day; rising like him out of the ocean in the east, *En. II. 250,* traversing like him the whole sky, *En. V.835,* and setting like him in the ocean in the west, *En. II. 8.* Compare Comments *En. II. 250; IV. 246.* Also:

"Dum loquor, Hesperio positas in littore metas
Humida nox tetigit."

Ovid, *Metam. II. 142;*

and:

"Sed cur repente noctis aestivae vices
Hiberna longa spatia producunt mora?
Aut quid cadentes detinet stellas polo?
Phoebum moramur: redde jam mundo diem."

Seneca, *Agam. 53;*

and:

"Oscula congerimus properata, sine ordine, raptim;
Et querimur parvas noctibus esse moras."

Ovid, *Heroid. XVIII. 113;*

and exactly parallel to our text:

"Propterea noctes hiberno tempore longae
Cessant, dum veniat radiatum insigne diei."

Lucret. V. 698;

and:

— "Brumamque morantem
Noctibus" —

Auson. *Precat. Cons. Design. v. 49.*

Ingeminant plausum. — Simply, *repeat applause — applaud, and then applaud again.* Compare Ovid *(Metam. III. 368),* of Echo:

— "Tamen haec in fine loquendi
Ingeminat voces, auditaque verba reportat."

The applause is begun by the Tyrians, and only taken up by the Trojans, the Tyrians being at home and the Trojans their guests, and it being customary in entertainments (as appears from Petron. P. 124: "Damus omnes plausum a familia inceptum") that the applause should be commenced by the household. See Comm. vers. 701.

756.

NUNC QUANTUS ACHILLES

"Quam magnus corporis viribus et animi virtute." — HEYNE. I think, not; because such a question bears no resemblance to the other questions asked by Dido, all of which concerned particularities about which a woman was likely to be curious, and which were capable of being answered in a few words, whereas the question, "quam magnus Achilles corporis viribus et animi virtute?" was too comprehensive to be answered in less than an *Achilleis.* The question, I think, relates solely to the great stature for which Achilles was remarkable; see Lycophron *(Cassandra, v. 860):*

> "Πενθειν τον εινaπηχυν Αιακου τριτον
> Και Δωριδος, πρηστηρα δαϊου μαχης."

and Philostratus in *Heroicis:* "υπερφυης δε το σωμα εφαινετο, αυξηθεις τε ρᾳον η τα προς ταις πηγαις δενδρα," quoted by Meursius ad Lycophron *Cassandr.*, Oper. Tom. V. Col. 990. Also Quintus Calaber (III. 60) describing Achilles wounded by Apollo:

> "Ως αρ' εφη, και αϊστος ομου νεφεεσσιν ετυχθη.
> Ηερα δ' εσσαμενος, στυγερον προεηκε βελεμνον,
> Και ε θοως ουτησε κατα σφυρον. αιψα δ' ανιαι
> Δυσαν υπο κραδιην. ο δ' ανετραπετ' ηΰτε πυργος."

Also the account given by the same author (III. 709) of the vastness of the funeral pyre required to burn the corpse of Achilles. Also Horat. *Carm. IV. 6. 9:*

> "Ille (Achilles sciz.), mordaci velut icta ferro
> Pinus, aut impulsa cupressus Euro,
> Procidit late, posuitque collum in
> Pulvere Teucro."

So understood the question is in the most perfect harmony with the context.

Compare Valer. Flacc. V. 209:

— "Quam magnus Enipeus
Et pater aurato q u a n t u s jacet Inachus antro;"

also *En. II. 592:*

— "Confessa deam, qualisque videri
Caelicolis et q u a n t a solet;"

also Prop. II. 7. 51:

— "Et t a n t i corpus Achillei,
Maximaque in parva sustulit ossa manu;

also Polyphemus recommending himself to Galatea:

"Aspice, sim quantus. Non est hoc corpore major
Jupiter in caelo."

Ovid, *Metam. XIII. 842;*

also "Tantus in arma patet," *En. XI. 644.*

II.

1.

CONTICUERE OMNES INTENTIQUE ORA TENEBANT

— "Sieh, wie mit lauschendem Mund
Und weit geöffnetem Auge die Hörer alle passen."
WIELAND. *Oberon* I. 8.

3.

INFANDUM REGINA JUBES RENOVARE DOLOREM

— "Immania vulnera, rector
Integrare jubes, Furias, et Lemnon, et arctis
Arma inserta toris debellatosque pudendo
Ense mares."
STAT. *Theb.* V. 29.

Dante's charming lines, —

— "Nessun maggior dolore,
Che ricordarsi del tempo felice
Nella miseria, e cio sa 'l tuo dottore.
Ma s' a conoscer la prima radice
Del nostro amor tu hai cotanto affetto,
Farò come colui che piange e dice."
Inferno, V. 121.

are a translation of, and, if I may venture so to say, an improvement on, the introductory verses of the Second Book of the Eneis. The poet, who imagines himself visiting the infernal regions in the company, and under the guidance, of the shade of Virgil, meets Francesca di Rimini, and inquires of her in terms parallel to Dido's inquiry of Eneas, (I. 757.) —

"Ma dimmi; al tempo de' dolci sospiri,
A che, e come concedette amore,
Che conosceste i dubbiosi desiri?"

To which he replies in the above-quoted lines, "Nessun maggior dolore, ... E cio sa 'l tuo dottore." 'L tuo dottore, viz. Virgil, who was standing by at the very moment in the capacity of Dante's guide and instructor, and who knew well how great a pain it is to remember in affliction times of past prosperity, having himself so pathetically expressed that sentiment in his famous commencement of the Second Book of the Eneis, INFANDUM REGINA JUBES &c. Francesca then proceeds, almost in the identical terms of Eneas's reply to Dido, —

"Ma s' a conoscer la prima radice
Del nostro amor tu hai cotanto affetto,
(Sed si tantus amor casus cognoscere nostros, &c.)
Farò come colui che piange e dice."

I will do as Eneas did, and weeping tell you the whole story: (Quis talia fando temperet a lacrymis ....: Incipiam.) It seems unaccountable that the plain reference to Virgil's shade in the words "e cio sa 'l tuo dottore," (see no less than two applications of the term *dottore* to Virgil in the 21st Canto of the Purgatory; and compare the exactly corresponding reference to Cato in the exactly corresponding words, "Come sa chi per lei vita rifiuta," *Purgat.* I. 72.), and to the Virgilian INFANDUM REGINA JUBES &c., in "Nessun maggior dolore," should not have been perceived by Dante's commentators; two of the best of whom (Venturi and Biagioli) understand "*'l tuo dottore*" to mean Boëtius, and "*Nessun maggior dolore*" &c., to be a versification of a sentiment which they have found in that philosopher's treatise, *De Consolatione Philosophiae;* whilst a third, (Lombardi,) although correctly referring "'*l tuo dottore*" to Virgil's shade, spoils the whole passage by assigning as the reason of Francesca's special appeal to Virgil's shade, to confirm the truth of the sentiment, "Nessun maggior dolore," &c., that Virgil's shade being, as well as herself, an inhabitant of the infernal regions, had had like experience with herself of the truth of that sentiment; "Trovandosi anch' egli (viz. Virgilio) nella miseria dell' infernale carcere." Beautiful indeed must those lines be, which, even thus distorted, and shorn of half their fine sense and excellence, have yet always been, and still are, quoted as the most beautiful of all the lines of that most beautiful of all the stories in the wonderful work of Virgil's greatest imitator and admirer.

INFANDUM. — The translators (with the exception of Dryden and Sir J. Denham, who never even so much as attempt the true meaning of any of Virgil's words), agree in rendering INFANDUS, *ineffable*, *that cannot be told:* "untellyble" (Douglas); "cannot be told" (Surrey); "past utterance severe" (Beresford); "unaussprechlichen" (Voss). So also Forbiger, in his note on the passage; "*Qui tantus est ut verbis exprimi non possit.*" A very slight observation, however, of Virgil's use of the word in other places, as for instance, *En.* I. 255; II. 132; IV. 85. and 613, is sufficient to show that its meaning is not *ineffable* or *that cannot be told*, but primarily (and according to the proper force of the participle in *dus*), that *should not*, *must not be told*, and therefore, secondarily, *horrible*. So Richardson, in his excellent dictionary, "*Infandous* [Lat. Infandus], That ought not to be spoken; too dreadful to be spoken." And such is Howell's use of the word (quoted by Richardson): "This *infandous* custom of swearing, I observe, reigns in England lately. more than any where else." The wide difference between *infandous* and *ineffable* will be manifest on the substitution of *ineffable* for *infandous* in this sentence.

The Spanish and Italian translators have not fallen into this error.

"La horrible historia y el dolor infando."
VELASCO.

— "Dogliosa istoria,
E d'amara e d'orribil rimembranza."
CARO.

5.

QUAEQUE IPSE MISERRIMA VIDI

QUAEQUE is epexegetic and limitative; the meaning of Eneas being, not that he will describe the taking of Troy, *and* the miseries he had himself witnessed, but that he will describe *so much* of the taking of Troy, and its miseries, *as* he had himself witnessed.

The view thus suggested by the grammatical structure of the introductory sentence, is confirmed by the narrative itself; for Eneas, having briefly mentioned the building of the wooden horse, and the concealment of the Grecian navy at Tenedos, immediately proceeds to say, that he was one of those who issued out of the gates rejoicing, as soon as the news of the departure of the Greeks was bruited abroad; that he saw the horse, and was present at the argument respecting what should be done with it; that he saw Laocoon fling his spear against it, and heard it sound hollow; that his attention was drawn off by the sudden appearance of Sinon, of the whole of whose story he was an ear-witness; that he was one of those who agreed to spare Sinon's life; that he saw the two serpents come across the sea, and destroy Laocoon and his two sons; that he assisted to break down the wall in order to admit the horse into the city; that Hector appeared to him in a dream, and informed him that the city was on fire and could not be saved, — advised him to fly, and committed the Penates to his charge; that on awaking he saw, from the roof of the house, the city in flames; that, flying to arms, he met Pantheus, the priest of Apollo, escaping from the citadel, with his gods' images and the other sacred objects of his religion; that Pantheus informed him that armed men were pouring out of the horse, that Sinon was a traitor and had fired the city, and that the whole Grecian army was entering at the gates; that he united himself with a few friends whom he happened to meet, and falling in with Androgeos, and a party of Greeks, they slew them every one, and clothed themselves with their spoils; that, thus disguised, they for a while carried terror and death everywhere, but at length, in attempting to rescue Cassandra from a party who were dragging her from the temple, were discovered to be Trojans, and attacked by the Greeks, while the Trojans, taking them for Greeks, overwhelmed them with missiles from the top of the temple; that, the greater number of his party having thus perished, he with the small remainder, was attracted by the tumult to Priam's palace, from the roof of which he beheld the door forced, the building set on fire, the women and the aged king driven for shelter to an altar in an interior court, and the king himself slain at the altar in the blood of his son; that, his companions having leaped in despair to the ground, or given themselves up to the flames, he was left alone; that, descending and happening to see Helen where she was hiding, he was about to sacrifice her to the Manes of his country, when his arm was stayed by Venus, who commanded him to seek out his aged parent and his wife and child, and with them fly instantly from Troy; and who, at the same time taking off the veil which clouded his mortal vision, showed him the gods actively and personally engaged in the destruction of the city; that, having returned to his father's house, he saw the encouraging omens of a tongue of fire on the head of Iulus, and a star shooting in the direction of Ida; that he escaped out of the city bearing his father on his shoulders, and leading Iulus by the hand; that Creusa, following behind, was lost on the road; that, returning to seek her, he found his father's house filled with Greeks, and on fire; that, extending his search everywhere, he returned to the citadel, and saw Phenix and Ulysses guarding captives and booty in the temple of Juno; that as he called aloud upon Creusa through the streets and houses, her shade presented itself, and informing him that she was provided for by the mother of the gods, enjoined him to abandon all search for her, and proceed upon his divine mission to found a new empire in Hesperia, where another, and a royal, spouse awaited him; that accordingly he returned to the place where he had concealed his father and son and domestics, and found there a great number of fugitives from the burning city, collected, and prepared to share his fortunes; and that with them and his father and son, he bade adieu for ever to Troy, and made good his retreat to the mountains.

Nothing can be plainer than that this is a mere *personal* narrative of one of the principal sufferers; every circumstance related, with the single exception of the concealment of the Grecian fleet at Tenedos, having been witnessed by the relator, or heard by him on the spot from Pantheus or Sinon. This is, I think, a sufficient answer to those critics who have objected to Virgil's account of the taking of Troy, that it is by no means a full, complete, and strategical account of the taking of a great city; that many circumstances which may be supposed to have happened, and which indeed must have happened on such an occasion, have been either wholly omitted or left unexplained; and that, in short, Virgil, in his second book of the *Eneis*, has evinced his infinite inferiority in strategical science to his great prototype and master, Homer. Many such objections have been urged from time to time by various critics; and, amongst others, by a celebrated personage, whose opinion on any matter connected with military tactics must be received with the greatest deference, I mean the Emperor Napoleon, whose observations on this subject are to be found in a volume published after his death under the following title: Precis des Guerres de César, par Napoléon: écrit par M. Marchand, à l'île Sainte Hélène, sous la dictée de l'Empereur; suivi de plusieurs fragmens inédits. Paris, 1836. 1 vol. 8vo.

It is not my intention to enter into a detailed examination or refutation of all Napoleon's objections, (although I shall probably in the course of these Comments have occasion to refer specially to more than one of them,) but simply to state that the whole of his critique is founded on the assumption that Virgil intended to give, or ought to have given, such a full and complete account of the taking of Troy as was given by Homer of the operations before its walls; such an account as might have been given by a historian, or laid before a directory by a commander-in-chief. On the contrary, it is to be borne carefully in mind, that, Homer's subject being the misfortunes brought by the wrath of Achilles upon the army besieging Troy, that poet could scarcely have given too particular or strategical an account of all that happened before the Trojan walls; while, Virgil's subject being the adventures and fortunes of one man, (as sufficiently evidenced by the very title and exordium of his work,) the taking of Troy was to be treated of, only so far as connected with the personal history of that hero. Virgil, therefore, with his usual judgment, introduces the taking of Troy, not as a part of the action of his poem, but as an episode; and, still more effectually to prevent the attention from being too much drawn away from his hero, and too much fixed upon that great and spirit-stirring event, puts the account of it into the mouth of the hero himself, whom, with the most wonderful art, he represents either as a spectator or actor in so many of the incidents of that memorable night, that on the one hand the account of those incidents is the history of the adventures of his hero, and on the other, the adventures of his hero form a rapid précis of the taking of Troy.

Even if it had been otherwise consistent with the plan of the *Eneis* to have given a full and complete account of the taking of Troy, and to have described, for instance, (as required by Napoleon,) how the other Trojan chiefs, signalised in the *Iliad*, were occupied during that fatal night, and how each defended his own quarter of the city with the troops under his command, such a full account must necessarily, either have rendered Eneas's narrative too long to have been delivered *inter mensas laticemque Lyaeum;* or, to make room for that additional matter, some part of the present story should have been left out; and then, I ask, which of the incidents would the reader be satisfied should have been omitted? — that of Laocoon, the unceasing theme and admiration of all ages, that shuddering picture of a religious prodigy? — that of Sinon, on which the whole plot hangs? — that of the vision, of the inimitable TEMPUS ERAT, the MOESTISSIMUS HECTOR? — that of the Priameian priestess, AD COELUM TENDENS ARDENTIA LUMINA FRUSTRA, LUMINA NAM TENERAS ARCEBANT VINCULA PALMAS? — that of Neoptolemus blazing in burnished brass, QUALIS UBI IN LUCEM COLUBER? — or Hecuba and her daughters flying to the sheltering altar, PRAECIPITES ATRA CEU TEMPESTATE COLUMBAE? — or the good old king, cased in the long-unused armour, and slipping and slain in his Polites' blood? — or Venus staying her son's hand, lifted in vengeance against the fatal spring of all these sorrows? — or the innoxious flame which, playing about the temples of Iulus, foreshowed him the father of a line of kings? — or the TER FRUSTRA COMPRENSA IMAGO of the for ever lost Creusa? Which of all these passages should have been omitted, to make room for the additional matter required by the imperial critic? What reader will consent to give up one, even one, of these most precious pearls, these conspicuous stars in, perhaps, the most brilliant coronet that ever graced a poet's brow? And even if the reader's assent were gained; if he were content with less of Eneas, and more of the other Homeric Trojans; with less of the romance, and more of the art, of war; would such an account have been equally interesting to the assembled guests and the love-caught queen? How coldly would a story in which Eneas played a subordinate part have fallen upon Dido's ear? How would not her thought have wandered from the thing told, to the teller? There was but one way to guard against the double danger, that Dido would forget the story in thinking of Eneas, and that the reader would forget Eneas in thinking of the story; and Virgil adopted that way — he made Eneas speak of himself — QUAEQUE IPSE MISERRIMA VIDI, ET QUORUM PARS MAGNA FUI. With what effect he spoke, we learn in the beginning of the fourth book — HAERENT INFIXI PECTORE VULTUS VERBAQUE, and Dido herself testifies; HEU, QUIBUS ILLE JACTATUS FATIS! QUAE BELLA EXHAUSTA CANEBAT! Or, in the words of another great master of the human heart, —

— "His story being done,
She gave him for his pains a world of sighs:
She swore, — in faith, 'twas strange, 'twas passing strange:
'Twas pitiful, 'twas wondrous pitiful;
She wish'd she had not heard it; yet she wish'd
That heaven had made her such a man; she thank'd him,
And bade him, if he had a friend that lov'd her,
He should but teach him how to tell his story,
And that would woo her."

But let us suppose that the modern commander is right, and the great ancient poet and philosopher wrong: that the error lies not in Napoleon's total misconception, not only of Virgil's general scope and design, but of his meaning in the plainest passages (as, for instance, in the account of the situation of Anchises' house, and of the number of men contained in the horse); let us suppose, I say, that the error lies not in Napoleon's misconception of the poet, but in the poet's ignorance of heroic warfare; and that the episode does, indeed, sin against military tactique (but see Comm. *v.* 604); yet where, in the whole compass of poetry, is there such another episode? so many heart-stirring incidents grouped together, representing in one vivid picture the fall of the most celebrated city in the world, and at the same time, and *pari passu*, the fortunes of one of the most famous heroes of all antiquity, the son of Venus, the ancestor of Augustus, the first founder of Imperial Rome? spoken, too, by the hero himself, at a magnificent banquet, and in presence not only of the princes of his own nation, (the partners of his sufferings, and the witnesses of the truth of all he related), but of the whole Carthaginian court, and at the request of the young and artless queen, who, already admiring his god-like person and beauty, lost her heart more and more at every word he uttered; at every turn of griefs, which,

— "so lively shown,
Made her think upon her own."

Alas, alas, for the cold-blooded criticism which could detect, or, having detected, could dwell upon, errors of military tactique in this flood of living poetry; which would chain the poet with the fetters of the historian; which, frigid and unmoved, could occupy itself with the observation of cracks and flaws in the scenic plaster, while the most magnificent drama ever presented to enraptured audience was being enacted!

13.

INCIPIAM

I feel sure that INCIPIAM here means not to *begin*, but to *undertake* or *take in hand;* —

First, because although it might, strictly speaking, be quite correct for Virgil, having just stated (*v.* 2) that Eneas *began* to speak (ORSUS) with the words INFANDUM REGINA JUBES &c., to cause Eneas almost instantly afterwards to say that he *began* his story with the words FRACTI BELLO &c.; yet it would be highly unpoetical, and evince a barrenness of thought and expression, quite foreign to Virgil.

Secondly, because it is evidently the intention of Eneas not merely to *begin*, but briefly to tell the *whole* story.

Thirdly, because the very word *begin* involves the idea of a long story, and thus, however true in point of fact, contradicts the intention expressed by BREVITER (*v.* 11).

I, therefore, understand INCIPIAM to be here used (as in En. X. 876) in its primary and etymological meaning of *undertaking, taking in hand* [*in capio*]; so understood, it harmonises with ORSUS, with Eneas's intention of telling the whole story, with BREVITER, and with the immediately preceding words, QUANQUAM ANIMUS MEMINISSE HORRET &c. Compare *Disserere incipiam*, LUCR. I. 50; not *begin* or *commence*, but *undertake, take in hand, to discuss;* and (TIBULL. IV. I. 1.)

> — "Quanquam me cognita virtus
> Terret, ut infirmae nequeant subsistere vires,
> *Incipiam* tamen;"

and (HOR. Satir. I. 1. 92.)

> "Denique sit finis quaerendi; quoque habeas plus,
> Pauperiem metuas minus, et finire laborem
> *Incipias,* parto, quod avebas;"

in which latter passage the difficulty pointed out by Mr. John Murray (Original views of passages in the life and writings of the Poet-philosopher of Venusia. Dublin, 1851) in the expression *incipias finire laborem parto* hitherto somewhat absurdly understood to mean *begin to end your labour now that you have gained your object*, is to be got rid of not by interpreting *finire* and *parto* in the manner proposed by Mr. Murray, but simply and at once by restricting *incipias* to its genuine and legimate sense of *setting about*, *taking in hand.* Compare also Virg. himself En. VI. 493.

— "Inceptus clamor frustratur hiantes."

Not, *begins* with a shout and ends with a squeak, but *attempting* to shout, they only squeak. Also Ter. *Andr.* I. 3. 13.

"Nam inceptio est amentium, haud amantium;"

and Id. *Ib.* V. 1. 17.

"Nuptiarum gratia haec sunt ficta atque incepta omnia"

Almost exactly corresponding to ORSUS — INCIPIAM in the passage before us is *adorta* — *orsa* En. VII. 386.

That our own English *begin* had originally and primarily a similar signification, and meant not to *commence*, but to *undertake*, appears both from its German origin (viz. Beginnen, *to undertake* —

"Er würde Freiheit mir und Leben kosten,
Und sein verwegenes *Beginnen* nur
Beschleunigen." — SCHILLER, *Die Piccolom.* I. 3),

and from the use made of the term, not only by the earliest English writers,

("That Eneas *bigan* hys ofspring to Lumbardie first bring."
ROBERT OF GLOUCESTER),

but by Milton, no mean part of the excellence of whose poetry consists in the frequent employment of ordinary and current terms in primitive and obsolete, and therefore extraordinary meanings:

— "If he aught *begin*,
How frequent to desert him, and at last
To heap ingratitude on worthiest deeds."
Sams. Agon. 274.

14.

DUCTORES DANAUM TOT JAM LABENTIBUS ANNIS
INSTAR MONTIS EQUUM DIVINA PALLADIS ARTE
AEDIFICANT SECTAQUE INTEXUNT ABIETE COSTAS

TOT JAM LABENTIBUS ANNIS. — The translators refer LABENTIBUS to the dim and faded past, instead of the vivid and continuing present; for instance, Surrey:

— "All irked with the war,
Wherein they wasted had so many years."

And Phaer:

"Whan all in vaine so many yeeres had past."

— "Da molti anni indarno
Stringevan Troja i condottier de' Greci."

ALFIERI.

Yet the present and continuing force of LABENTIBUS is doubly evident; because the verb *labor* expresses a continuing action, and the present participle a continuing time. It is this continuing sense (observed by Wagner, *Quaest. Virg.* XXIX. 1.) which constitutes the poetical beauty of the passage before us, as well as of Horace's exquisite

— "Eheu, fugaces, Postume, Postume,
Labuntur anni."

Dryden, according to his custom, blinks the meaning altogether.

INSTAR MONTIS EQUUM. — Even in more modern times, cities have been sometimes taken by a similar artifice; for instance, Breda in Holland, in the year 1590, by means of soldiers concealed under turf in a turf-boat, and so introduced into the city; and Luna in Italy, by means of soldiers performing the part of mourners, priests &c. at the pretended funeral of Hasting.

"Le maitre cler cante l'office,
— — — — — — —
Le eveque canta la messe,
Des Paenz fu la turbe epesse" &c.

Roman de Rou, 687.

DIVINA PALLADIS ARTE. — Of the deities favourable to the Greeks, Pallas is, with peculiar propriety, selected to instruct or assist them in building the horse; because, in the heathen mythology, every work of remarkable ingenuity (*e. g.* the building of the ship Argo, VALER. FLACC. *Argon.* L. I.; the construction of the first flute, MART. VIII. 51) was ascribed to Pallas, as the inventress of the arts.

SECTAQUE INTEXUNT ABIETE COSTAS. — The erroneousness of Turnebus's exposition of these words, "Statumina tabulas connexura intus intexunt ei operi" and the correctness of Heyne's observation "tantum ad declarationem ulteriorem *τoυ* aedificant" seems to me to be placed beyond all doubt by the subsequent, "quum jam hic trabibus contextus acernis staret equus," (*v.* 112) quoted by Heyne.

18.

HUC DELECTA VIRUM SORTITI CORPORA FURTIM
INCLUDUNT CAECO LATERI PENITUSQUE CAVERNAS
INGENTES UTERUMQUE ARMATO MILITE CONPLENT

Let not the too prosaic reader, interpreting this sentence according to its literal structure, suppose it to mean that, besides the DELECTA VIRUM CORPORA, which were inclosed in the hollow sides of the horse, the vast caverns of its womb were filled with armed soldiers; or, in other words, that a considerable vacancy, remaining after the selected chiefs were inclosed, was filled up with a large body of common soldiers. On the contrary, the latter clause of the sentence is only explanatory of the former; ARMATO MILITE informing us that the DELECTA VIRUM CORPORA were armed warriors; CAVERNAS INGENTES UTERUMQUE, that by CAECO LATERI was meant the whole interior cavity, or chamber, of the statue; and CONPLENT, that the cavity was completely filled by the persons who were inclosed.

The correctness of this explanation cannot be doubted; first, because it renders a passage, which, as commonly understood, is sufficiently prosaic and mediocre, highly poetical. Secondly, because it is according to Virgil's usual habit (see Comm. *En.* I. 500; II. 51) of presenting in the first clause of his sentence no more than the sketch, or skeleton, of his idea, and then, in the subsequent clause, filling it up and clothing it with flesh and life; and thirdly, because it afterwards appears (*v.* 260 et seq.) that the horse contained only nine persons.

I may add, that I understand the words DELECTA VIRUM SORTITI CORPORA to be equivalent to *delecta ipsorum sortiti corpora*, because SORTITI is predicated of *ductores Danaum*, and we find at *v.* 260 et seq. that the DELECTA CORPORA were of the number of those who were properly comprehended under the term *ductores Danaum.*

Error being fruitful of error, the received erroneous interpretation of this passage has produced the Emperor Napoleon's erroneous criticism (see his essay quoted in Comm. *v.* 5) that the wooden horse, containing so great a number of men, could not have been brought up to the walls of Troy in so short a space of time as is implied in the account given by Virgil. "En supposant," says the Emperor, "que ce cheval contînt seulement cent guerriers, il devait être d'un poids énorme, et il n'est pas probable qu'il ait pu être mené du bord de la mer sous les murs d'Ilion en un jour, ayant surtout deux rivières à traverser." The objection falls to the ground with the erroneous interpretation on which it is founded. See Comm. *En.* II. 299.

23.

STATIO

"*Eine Rhede*, a portu probe distinguenda" Forbiger, correctly. Compare Vell. Pat. II. 72. "Exitialemque tempestatem fugientibus statio pro portu foret."

30.

CLASSIBUS HIC LOCUS HIC ACIES CERTARE SOLEBANT
PARS STUPET INNUPTAE DONUM EXITIALE MINERVAE
ET MOLEM MIRANTUR EQUI PRIMUSQUE THYMOETES
DUCI INTRA MUROS HORTATUR ET ARCE LOCARI
SIVE DOLO SEU JAM TROJAE SIC FATA FEREBANT

CLASSIBUS HIC LOCUS. — In this passage Virgil, according to his custom, (see Comm. *En.* I. 500; II. 18 and 51) presents us first (*v.* 27 and 28) with the general idea, the deserted appearance of the places lately occupied by the Greeks; and then (*v.* 29 and 30) supplies the particulars, in the words of the Trojans pointing out to each other the various localities.

The reader, however, must not be misled by the words CLASSIBUS HIC LOCUS to suppose that there was a place set apart for the ships. Innumerable passages in the *Iliad*, and especially the account of the battle at the ships, (*Iliad.* XIII.) render it perfectly clear that, the ships being drawn up on the shore, the tents were erected beside and amongst them; the ships and tents of one nation forming one group, those of another nation another group, and those of a third nation a third group; and so on, along the entire line of shore occupied by the encampment. CLASSIBUS means therefore, not *the ships, as contra-distinguished from the tents*, but *the ships taken together with their dependencies, the tents;* or in other words, it means *the Grecian encampment*, called *classes* by Virgil, and *αι νηες* by Homer, from its most important and, especially from a distance, most con spicuous part, *the ships.*

Not only Dryden and such like translators, but even Alfieri ("Qui, fitte Eran l'ancore lor") renders CLASSIBUS HIC LOCUS, "here the navy rode," with what understanding of the *Iliad*, or of ancient naval expeditions, (see *En.* III. 71; IX. 69 and 70) or of the Grecian encampment and mode of warfare at Troy, and especially of the battle at the ships, let the reader judge.

DONUM EXITIALE MINERVAE. — "Non quod ipsa dedit, sed quod ei oblatum est." Servius. "Stupor oritur ex dono . . . . quis non stupeat Minervae innuptae dari in donum machinam foetam armis, praegnantem, gravidam." La Cerda. "Donum oblatum Minervae." Wagner. (Virg. Br. En. Ed. 1845.) "Donum perniciosum Graecis consilio suasuque Minervae Trojanis oblatum." Wagner. (Virg. Br. En. Ed. 1849.) "Prius cum Heynio, Wagnero (Virg. Br. En. Ed. 1845) et Thielio interpretatus sum: quod oblatum, destinatum erat Minervae . . . . Quum tamen hoc posterius demum comperiant Trojani (infra *v.* 183) et quum additum sit epitheton *exitiale*, nescio an rectius cum Wagnero in editione minore (Ed. 1849) explices: donum perniciosum a Graecis consilio Minervae (*v.* 15) Trojanis oblatum." Forbiger. Ed. tert.

— "Altri, la mole
Dell' enorme cavallo, in fatal voto
Alla casta Minerva eretto, stanno
Stupefatti ammirando."

ALFIERI.

Forbiger's well founded objection to the interpretation "quod Minervae oblatum est" is unfortunately equally applicable to his own interpretation, for the Trojans were at the present moment quite as ignorant that the horse was a gift "a Graecis consilio Minervae Trojanis oblatum," as that it was a gift "oblatum Minervae." The difficulty is surmounted and a good and satisfactory meaning obtained by understanding DONUM MINERVAE to be applied to the horse in the same general sense as "dona Cereris" to bread, "dona Lyaei" to wine, "dona Veneris" to venereal enjoyments — and to mean neither a gift presented specially to the Trojans by Minerva nor a gift presented by the Greeks to the Trojans according to the advice of Minerva, but simply a work of art, presented, no matter to whom, by the inventress and patroness of the arts; a work so wonderful as to have required for its construction the artistical skill of Minerva; and so precisely (*v.* 15): "Divina Palladis arte aedificant," and Hom. Odyss. VIII. 493. *τον Επειος εποιησεν συν Αθηνη.* Compare: Operum haud ignara Minervae. *En.* V. 284. The meaning seems to have been understood by Schiller:

"Mit Staunen weilt der überraschte Blick
Beim *Wunderbau* des ungeheuren Rosses."

EXITIALE. — The Trojans looking at the horse recognise it as DONUM MINERVAE in the sense just explained, but do not regard it as EXITIALE. This epithet is added by Eneas, from his own after-acquired knowledge, as at *v.* 237 the epithets "fatalis machina" and "foeta armis."

SEU JAM TROJAE SIC FATA FEREBANT. — JAM; *now at last, after so many years of obstinate defence.*

43.

AUT ULLA PUTATIS
DONA CARERE DOLIS DANAUM

Admirably translated by Schiller:

"Ein griechisches Geschenk und kein Betrug verborgen?"

Such masterly touches, promissory of the future splendor of Schiller's genius, occur every now and then in his *Freie Uebersetzung* of the 2d and 4th books of the *Eneis;* which is, however, on the whole, an inferior production, evincing not merely immaturity of poetical power, but a considerable want of perception of the delicacies of Virgil's expressions, and even some ignorance of the Latin language.

49.

QUIDQUID ID EST TIMEO DANAOS ET DONA FERENTES
SIC FATUS VALIDIS INGENTEM VIRIBUS HASTAM
IN LATUS INQUE FERI CURVAM CONPAGIBUS ALVUM
CONTORSIT STETIT ILLA TREMENS UTEROQUE RECUSSO
INSONUERE CAVAE GEMITUMQUE DEDERE CAVERNAE

TIMEO DANAOS ET DONA FERENTES. — In this so oft-quoted sentiment there is nothing new except its application to the Danai: *Εχθρων αδωρα δωρα και ουκ ονησιμα* was a proverb even in the days of Sophocles. See *Ajax Flagellif.* 673.

VALIDIS INGENTEM VIRIBUS. — The great size of the spear, and the force with which it is hurled, are not matters of indifference, but absolutely necessary to the production, on the huge mass of which the horse consisted, of the considerable effect described by the words

UTEROQUE RECUSSO
INSONUERE CAVAE GEMITUMQUE DEDERE CAVERNAE.

Of the five terms most frequently used by Virgil to express the casting of a spear, viz. *jacio*, *conjicio*, *torqueo*, *intorqueo* and *contorqueo*, the two first are the weakest and signify: *jacio*, simply *to throw; conjicio, to throw with the collected force of the individual*, which, however, need not be great, for the term is applied, *v.* 545, to Priam throwing his *imbelle telum sine ictu.* The three latter signify *to hurl; torqueo*, simply *to hurl; intorqueo, to hurl forcibly: contorqueo, with all the collected strength of a powerfully strong man; con*, when applied *in composition* to the act of *one*, being no less intensive than when applied to that of *a number of individuals;*

in the former case, indicating that the act is the result of *the whole collected power of the one*, in the latter that it is the result of *the collected power of the several individuals concerned.*

Impello, although interpreted by Heyne in his gloss on *En.* I. *v.* 86 *intorqueo*, *immitto*, is neither there, nor anywhere else (except under the particular circumstances mentioned in Comm. *En.* I. 85), used in that sense, but always in the sense of *pushing;* either *physically pushing,* as *En.* I. 86; VII. 621; VIII. 239 &c.; or *metaphorically pushing,* as *En.* I. 15; II. 55, 520 &c.

IN LATUS INQUE FERI CURVAM COMPAGIBUS ALVUM. — IN ALVUM is not, as maintained by Thiel, and after him by Forbiger, *into the alvus;* first, because there is much harshness in interpreting the IN before ALVUM so very differently from the IN before LATUS, of which it is the mere repetition. Secondly, because the word RECUSSO, *v.* 52, implies that the interior of the horse was only *concussed,* not *perforated.* Thirdly, because the expression FERRO FOEDARE, *v.* 55, almost expresses that the interior had not been previously *foedata ferro.* Fourthly, because the words *tergo intorserit, v.* 231, limit the lesion made by the *cuspis, v.* 230, to the *tergum,* a term never applied except to the exterior of the body. For all these reasons I reject Thiel's interpretation, and understanding (with Wagner) QUE to be taken epexegetically (see Comm. *En.* I. 500; II. 18) render the passage, *against that part of the side, which was the alvus or belly.* Thus the precise position of the wound is determined to have been in the hinder part of the side, corresponding to the cavity of the belly, not of the chest; and in the lateral part of the belly, not the under part. Virgil chooses this position for the wound, with great propriety, because the portion of the horse's side corresponding to the belly, being much larger than that corresponding to the chest, not only afforded a better mark to Laocoon, but was precisely the part where the enclosed persons were principally situated,

Compare (*En.* VII. 499):

"Perque uterum sonitu perque ilia venit arundo;"

through that part of the *uterus* (belly), which was the *ilia* (loin or flank).

INSONUERE CAVAE GEMITUMQUE DEDERE CAVERNAE. — Not *cavae cavernae insonuere*, but *cavernae insonuere cavae:* QUE is epexegetic, and the meaning is, not that *the hollow caverns both sounded and groaned*, but that *the caverns sounded hollow, and their hollow sound was like a groan.* That such is the structure, is shown not only by the better sense thus obtained, but by the point which, as appears from Foggini, is placed after CAVAE in the Medicean. This point, correctly preserved, in the shape of a comma, by D. Heinsius and La Cerda, has been, as I think, incorrectly, removed by N. Heinsius, whose example has been followed by Burmann and, I believe, all the modern editors. See Comm. *En.* II. 552.

60.

HOC IPSUM UT STRUERET TROJAMQUE APERIRET ACHIVIS

"And open Troye's gates unto the Greeks."
SURREY.

Not literally *open the gates* of Troy, but *procure an entrance* for the Greeks into Troy; *make* Troy *accessible* to them. Compare:

— "Aperit si nulla viam vis."
En. X. 864.

"Theseos ad muros, ut Pallada flecteret, ibat,
Supplicibusque piis faciles aperiret Athenas."
STATIUS. *Theb.* XII. 293.

Also

— "Caeleste reportat
Palladium, ac nostris aperit mala Pergama fatis."
SIL. ITAL. XIII. 49.

65.

ACCIPE NUNC DANAUM INSIDIAS ET CRIMINE AB UNO
DISCE OMNES
NAMQUE UT CONSPECTU IN MEDIO TURBATUS INERMIS
CONSTITIT

DANAUM INSIDIAS. — These words are plainly repeated from Dido's request to Eneas, *En.* I. 758.

INERMIS. — As *arma* means not merely *weapons, whether offensive or defensive*, but *all kinds and means of offence or defence*, so its compound *inermis* means not merely *without weapons*, but *without any means of offence or defence; helpless, defenceless.* The latter is the sense in which I think it is used in the passage before us; because, first, it is not to be supposed that Virgil, having told us that Sinon was a prisoner, with his hands bound behind his back, would think it necessary to inform us almost instantly afterwards that he was *unarmed* or *without weapons.* And, secondly because, even if Sinon had not been bound, weapons could have been of no avail to him against the *agmina* by whom he was surrounded, and therefore the want of them made no real difference in his condition, and could not have been assigned, even by poetical implication, as a reason for his emotion or conduct. It is in this strong sense of *utterly without means of offence or defence*, and not in its literal sense of *weaponless*, that *inermis* is to be understood also *En.* I. 491.

"Tendentemque manus Priamum conspexit inermes;"

because, although it might have contributed to the pathos of the picture, to have represented a *young* warrior's hands as stretched out *weaponless*, it could have had no such effect to have so represented the hands of Priam, who was so old as to be unable to wield weapons, and was equally *inermis* (*helpless and defenceless*), whether he had arms in his hands or not. See *En.* II. 509. 510

et seq. And compare Tacit. Ann. VI. 31. "Et senectutem Tiberii ut inermem despiciens."

The same meaning follows *inermis* into the Italian:

"I semplici fanciulli, e i vecchi *inermi*,
E'l volgo delle donne sbiggottite."
Gerus. Liber. III. 2.

75.

MEMORET QUAE SIT FIDUCIA CAPTO
ILLE HAEC DEPOSITA TANDEM FORMIDINE FATUR
CUNCTA EQUIDEM TIBI REX FUERIT QUODCUMQUE FATEBOR
VERA INQUIT NEQUE ME ARGOLICA DE GENTE NEGABO
HOC PRIMUM NEC SI MISERUM FORTUNA SINONEM
FINXIT VANUM ETIAM MENDACEMQUE IMPROBA FINGET

QUAE SIT FIDUCIA CAPTO. — "Qua fiducia ultro se captivum obtulerit; nam fidens animi se ultro obtulerat (cf. *v.* 59 et seq.)" Forbiger.

I think, however, that there is no particular emphasis either on FIDUCIA or CAPTO. That CAPTO is merely *the prisoner*, and QUAE SIT FIDUCIA, the ordinary inquiry made by judges or persons in authority, what is the defence set up, what is the defendant's case, on what does the accused rely. — QUAE SIT FIDUCIA CAPTO is thus the full explanation of the immediately preceding QUIDVE FERAT, what has he to say for himself?

ILLE HAEC DEPOSITA TANDEM FORMIDINE FATUR. — I cannot agree with the Leyden octavo Edition of 1680, the younger Heinsius, and Burmann, in enclosing this verse between crotchets, and still less with Brunck in expunging it entirely, on the ground that it attributes *fear* to Sinon, whom Virgil but a few lines previously has represented as FIDENS ANIMI, ATQUE PARATUS &c. and must therefore be supposititious. Neither do I plead in its defence, with Heyne and some other commentators, that Sinon first *pretends* to be agitated with fear (TURBATUS), and then *pretends* to lay his fear aside, — "Fingit Sinon et hoc, quasi deposuerit formidinem." Heyne; on the contrary, I think that Virgil, having represented Sinon as entering upon the execution of his plot with boldness and confidence, represents him as *really* TURBATUS (*agitated and frightened*), when he comes to be actually confronted with the danger, and then as *really* recovering from his agitation when he finds that the immediate danger is over, and that the Trojans, instead of putting him to death instantly on the spot, are willing to hear what he has to say.

TURBATUS means *really* agitated, and DEPOSITA FORMIDINE, *really* recovering self-possession, because, first, if Virgil had intended to express by these words only simulated emotion, it cannot be doubted that he would have afforded some clue by which his intention might have been discovered; but he has not only not afforded any such clue, but has actually assigned sufficient cause for real emotion; Sinon is TURBATUS, because he stands INERMIS in the midst of the PHRYGIA AGMINA; and, DEPOSITA FORMIDINE FATUR, because CONVERSI ANIMI, COMPRESSUS ET OMNIS IMPETUS. Secondly, if the words mean only simulated emotion, then Virgil represents Sinon as of such heroic constancy and resolution as to look upon instant violent death without blenching; which is to hold him up, for so far at least, as an object of respect, and even of admiration, to Eneas's hearers as well as to Virgil's readers, and thus to contradict the intention (evidenced by the terms *dolis*, *arte*, *insidiis*, *crimine*, *scelerum tantorum*, *perjuri*), of representing him as a mean-minded man entering upon a dishonorable and dangerous enterprise, with an audacious confidence (FIDENS ANIMI, ATQUE PARATUS &c.) in his own cunning and duplicity. Thirdly, it is altogether unlikely that Virgil should here employ to express *simulated*, the very same words which he employs, *En.* III. 612, in a similar context and similar circumstances, to express *real* emotion. Fourthly, there is a perfect harmony between FIDENS ANIMI ATQUE PARATUS &c. and TURBATUS understood to mean *real* agitation, because a man may enter upon a dangerous undertaking with confidence, and even with courage, (which latter quality, however, it will be observed, is not expressed either by FIDENS ANIMI, or PARATUS &c.) and yet quail before the instant, imminent danger, as exquisitely shown by Homer in his most natural and touching account of Hector's flight before Achilles: how much more, then, the wretch Sinon! Fifthly, TURBATUS means *real*, not *simulated* agitation, because *real* agitation was more likely to move the Trojans to pity than any *simulation* of it. Virgil, therefore, taking the most effectual method of moving the hearts of the Trojans, and recollecting perhaps the advice of his friend Horace,

— "Si vis me flere, dolendum est
Primum ipsi tibi,"

presents Sinon to them in a state of real agitation, pleading for his life with all the eloquence of unaffected fear. So Davos (TER. *And.* IV. 4.) instead of acquainting Mysis with his plot, and instructing her what answers she should give to Chremes, prefers to place her in such a situation, that, speaking the truth, and in entire ignorance of his design, her answers must yet of necessity be the very answers which he desired; and when Mysis afterwards inquires why he had not schooled her as to his intentions, replies:

"Paullum interesse censes ex animo omnia
Ut fert natura facias, an de industria?"

It was inconsistent with Virgil's plot, to make Sinon speak the truth, but he could with perfect consistency, and therefore did, represent him as actuated by real emotion; which *real* emotion is in express terms contrasted with his *false* words at *v.* 107: "Prosequitur *pavitans*, et *ficto pectore* fatur."

The reader will, however, observe that Virgil, always judicious, carefully avoids ascribing *extreme* fear or agitation to Sinon; he is TURBATUS (*agitated*), PAVITANS (*in a flutter*), but he does not, like Dolon, his undoubted original, become *χλωρος υπαι δειους*, nor do his teeth chatter, *αραβος δε δια στομα γινετ' οδοντων*. Such extreme degree of terror, although beautifully consistent with the simple, undisguised confession of Dolon, would have been wholly incompatible with the cunning and intricate web, which Sinon, almost from the first moment he opens his mouth, begins to wrap round the Trojans. It is therefore with the strictest propriety and observance of nature that Virgil represents Sinon, at first bold and confident; then disconcerted and agitated at the prospect of immediate death; then re-assured by the encouragement he received; then again, losing confidence when the Trojans manifest the vehement impatience expressed by the words *Tum vero ardemus scitari* &c. and, with renewed fear and trembling (*pavitans*), pursuing his feigned narrative; and then, finally, when he had received an absolute promise of personal safety, going on, without further fear or hesitation, to reveal the pretended secret of his compatriots.

Throughout the whole story the reader must never forget that, although it was Virgil's ultimate object to deceive the Trojans, by means of Sinon, with respect to the horse, yet he had another object also to effect, (prior in point of time, and not less important than his ultimate object, because absolutely indispensable to the attainment of that ultimate object,) viz. to save Sinon's life, or, in other words, to assign to his reader sufficiently probable and natural reasons why the Trojans did actually spare his life, and did not, as might have been expected, execute such summary judgment upon him as Diomede and Ulysses executed upon Dolon under similar circumstances. Accordingly, the first words which he puts into the mouth of Sinon are a thrilling exclamation of despair, a piteous cry for mercy, HEU! QUAE NUNC TELLUS &c. This has the effect of staying the uplifted sword, of averting the first and instant danger, COMPRESSUS ET OMNIS IMPETUS; they encourage him to speak, to tell who he is, and why he should not meet the captive's doom; Sinon respires, recovers his self-possession, and endeavoring to make good his ground, and strengthen the favourable impression produced by his first words, says, that he was the friend of that Palamedes, of whose unjust condemnation and death they might have heard, and the principal cause of which was the opposition given by him to the undertaking of the war against Troy; and that he had not, like the other Greeks, come to the war out of hostility to the Trojans, or even voluntarily, but had, when a mere boy (and therefore irresponsible), been sent by his father, who was so poor as not otherwise to be able to provide for his son. He then enters upon an account of his quarrel with, and persecution by, Ulysses, their most dreaded and implacable enemy; but, perceiving that they begin to take an interest in what he is saying, suddenly stops short, and artfully begs of them to put him out of pain at once, as he knew that, no matter how great or undeserved his sufferings had been, they could have no pity or forgiveness for one, who was guilty of the crime of being a Greek. The Trojan curiosity is inflamed, and they insist to know the sequel. He proceeds *pavitans*, (whether because he had not yet entirely recovered from his first alarm, or whether alarmed afresh by the vehemence and impatience of the Trojans, or whether from both these causes conjointly,) and relates how, by the villanous concert of the priest Calchas with Ulysses, he was selected to be offered up as a victim to appease the offended Gods; how he escaped from the altar, and lay hid during the night (the preceding night,) in a morass; and then lamenting that his escape from death by the hands of the Greeks had only led him to death by the hands of the Trojans, and that he was never more to see his country, home, or relatives, concludes with a pathetic adjuration, in the name of the Gods above, and of inviolable faith, that they would yet pity such unexampled, such undeserved misery, and spare his life. His tears, his agony of fear, the plausibility of his story, their sympathy with the object of the hatred and persecution of the Greeks and of Ulysses, prevail; they grant him his life; and so closes the first act of the interlude of Sinon.

In nothing is the admirable judgment of Virgil more remarkable, than in the skill with which he has all this while kept the wooden horse, as it were, in abeyance. No act has been done, no word uttered, which could excite in the Trojan mind, or in the mind of the reader, ignorant of the sequel, the slightest suspicion that Sinon has any thing whatsoever to do with the horse, or the horse with Sinon. So careful is the poet to avoid every, even the slightest, ground for a suspicion, which would have been fatal to the entire plot, that it is from a distance, and by the agency of the Trojans themselves, he brings Sinon into the vicinage of the horse; and that, in the whole course of the long history which Sinon gives of himself, and which the reader will observe is now concluded, the horse is never so much as mentioned, or even alluded to, except once, and then so artfully (as it were only for the purpose of fixing a date,) that the mention which is made, while it stimulates the Trojans to question him on the subject, seems less remarkable than absolute silence would have been, inasmuch as it proves that Sinon does not *de industria* eschew all notice of an object, which must have attracted his attention, and of the purport of which he could not but be supposed to have some knowledge.

In the second act of the interlude, or that part which commences with *v.* 152, we find Sinon totally changed; "now more bold, The tempter . . . . New part puts on;" his life secure, guaranteed by the King himself, he is no longer the abject, cringing, hesitating, trembling wretch, but the successful and exulting villain. He loudly and boldly invokes the Gods to witness his abjuration of the Greeks and acceptance of the Trojan covenant; and makes his revelation of the important secret which is to be the rich reward of the Trojan clemency, not, as he had pleaded for his life, in broken passages, leaving off at one place and commencing at another, but *uno tenore*, explaining in uninterrupted sequence, the absence of the Greeks; their intended return; the object for which they built the horse; and why they built it of so large dimensions; the evil consequences to the Trojans if they offered it any injury, and to the Greeks if it were received into the city, &c.; the impostor is fully credited, the generous, unwary, and fate-devoted Trojans are caught in the toils so delicately woven and so noiselessly drawn around them, and the curtain falls.

If the reader happen to be one of those critics, who think the story of the wooden horse deficient in verisimilitude, he will receive with the greater favor an interpretation which tends to increase the verisimilitude, by representing the falsehood and cunning of Sinon as united, not with that quality with which falsehood and cunning are so inconsistent, and so rarely united, heroic fortitude, but with their very compatible and nearly allied quality, audacity.

It is impossible to leave this subject without remarking how favorably to Trojan faith and generosity, (as might be expected, Virgil being the *poeta* and Eneas the narrator,) the conduct of the Trojans towards Sinon contrasts with that of the Greeks towards Dolon. Ulysses and Diomede encourage Dolon, and tell him not to think of death, on which ambiguous pledge he tells the whole truth; they reward him by coolly cutting off his head, as the last word of his revelation passes his lips; Sinon tells the Trojans a tissue of lies, and not only has his life spared, but is treated with kindness and hospitality.

That most rigid and terrific of all the dispensers of the so-called divine retributive justice, Dante, (see *Inferno*,

XXX. 46 et seq.) punishes Sinon in hell with an eternal sweating fever, in company (according to the great poet's usual eccentric manner of grouping his characters,) on the one side with Potiphar's wife, whom he punishes with a similar fever, and on the other with a famous coiner of base money at Brescia, whom he torments with a never-dying thirst and dropsy, and between whom and Sinon ensues a contention in none of the gentlest billingsgate, which of the two is the greater sinner.

FUERIT QUODCUNQUE. — "Quicunque me sequatur eventus." Servius. "Quicquid evenerit, mihique exinde acciderit." Heyne. "*Quodcunque* referendum ad *cuncta*." Wagner. Arguing against which interpretation of Wagner, and in favour of that of Servius and Heyne, Süpfle*) says: "Auch haben schon die Alten, wie Phaedrus im Prologe zum dritten Buche, die Worte anders und wohl richtiger gefasst, nämlich: *was auch daraus werden mag, wie es mir auch ergehen mag (wenn ich in Allem euch die Wahrheit sage)*."

I agree entirely with Wagner, and think the meaning is, *I will confess all whatever it may have been*, *whatever there may have been in it.* The words are not less obscure in the quotation and application made of them by Phaedrus, (see the two-column note on them in Schwabe's edition) than in Sinon's original use of them: a notable proof of the almost hopeless obscurity of the Latin language; an obscurity arising from its brevity, and especially, as it seems to me, from its almost constant omission of pronouns and pronominal adjectives. I am, however, inclined to think that in Phaedrus's quotation the words "Quodcunque fuerit" stand in apposition to "Librum exarabo tertium," and that the meaning of them there as in Sinon's original use of them, is *such as it is*, *good or bad*, *of whatever*

*) Virgilii opera: mit Anmerkungen zur Eneide versehen von Karl Fr. Süpfle. Karlsruhe 1842.

kind it may turn out to be. As if Phaedrus had said: But now as to this third book of mine, ye shall, as Sinon told King Priam, hear the whole of it such as it is, be it good or be it bad. See Comm. I. 82.

FORTUNA . . . FINXIT . . . IMPROBA FINGET. — See Comm. *En.* II. 552.

83.

QUEM FALSA SUB PRODITIONE PELASGI
INSONTEM INFANDO INDICIO QUIA BELLA VETABAT
DEMISERE NECI NUNC CASSUM LUMINE LUGENT
ILLI ME COMITEM ET CONSANGUINITATE PROPINQUUM
PAUPER IN ARMA PATER PRIMIS HUC MISIT AB ANNIS

FALSA SUB PRODITIONE PELASGI. — "*Falsa sub proditione; h. e. sub falso crimine proditionis.*" Servius; followed by Heyne, and all the other commentators and translators. To this interpretation I object,

First, that no authority has been adduced, to show that *proditio* may be used for *crimen proditionis;* the *act* committed, for the *charge* founded upon the commission of the act.

Secondly, that if Virgil had intended to say that the Pelasgi had condemned Palamedes, *on* or *by means of* a false charge of treason, he would more probably have used the words FALSA PRODITIONE, in the same manner as INFANDO INDICIO, without a preposition; or if he had used a preposition, it would have been *per*, not SUB.

Thirdly, that Virgil could scarcely have been guilty of the fade tautology, FALSA, INSONTEM.

Fourthly, that this interpretation represents the whole Greek nation at Troy (PELASGI) as conspiring against Palamedes; which is (*a*) contrary to all verisimilitude; (*b*) deprives INFANDO INDICIO of its force, because, if all were conspiring against Palamedes, it was of small consequence how "infandous" the information or informer was; or, indeed, whether there were any information or informer at all; and (*c*) contradicts the statement (*v.* 90) that it was through the machinations of Ulysses, that Palamedes' condemnation was accomplished.

Rejecting, for all these reasons, the received interpretation, I render FALSA SUB PRODITIONE, *during*, or *at the time of*, *a false or feigned treason; i. e.* when there was an alarm (whether of accidental or concerted origin it matters not,) of treason in the Grecian camp. The words being so interpreted, the meaning of the passage is, not that the Pelasgi brought a *false* charge of treason against Palamedes, and condemned him, *although innocent;* but that the Pelasgi condemned Palamedes on an infandous information, which, being brought against him *at a time when there was an alarm of treason in the camp*, was on that account the more readily credited. In support of this interpretation, I beg to observe,

First, that it restores to PRODITIO its simple, grammatical signification.

Secondly, that the use of SUB in the sense of *during*, or *at the time of*, is familiar to every scholar; thus *sub nocte; sub somno; sub profectione; sub adventu*, &c. Livy (XXVI. 16) has even joined *sub* to the close cognate of *proditio, deditio*, only putting *deditio* in the accusative, because he wishes to express, not the *precise time*, but *about the time* of the *deditio.*

Thirdly, that this interpretation being adopted, INSONS is no longer a tautology of FALSA; the latter expressing only the falsehood of the general rumour of treason, not of the particular charge brought against Palamedes.

Fourthly, that this interpretation represents the Pelasgi, not, unnaturally, in the triple character of conspirators, accusers, and judges, but naturally, in the single character of judges, prevailed upon partly by the prevalent alarm of treason, and partly by the offence they had taken against Palamedes, QUIA BELLA VETABAT, to give credit to an infandous information against him.

Fifthly, that a greater degree of verisimilitude is thus conferred on the words NUNC CASSUM LUMINE LUGENT, because it is more probable that the Pelasgi would lament Palamedes, (as soon as experience had taught them the groundlessness of their dislike to him on account of his opposition to the war,) if they had themselves been deluded into convicting him, on an INFANDUM INDICIUM, than that they would, under any circumstances, lament him, if their hatred to him had been so great as to induce them to convict him on a charge, which they not only knew to be false, but of which they were themselves the concoctors. And,

Sixthly, that Ovid draws an express and strong distinction between the party who *accused*, and the party who *condemned*, Palamedes,

— "An falso Palameden crimine turpe
Accusasse mihi (viz. Ulyssi), vobis (viz. Pelasgis) damnasse decorum est?"
Metam. XIII. 308.

QUEM. — This word (*quem*, and not *illum*) sufficiently shows that Sinon has not yet begun to give any new information to the Trojans, but is employed, as far as the word NECI, in recalling to their recollection facts, with which he knew they were perfectly well acquainted ("incipit a veris." Servius). The words NUNC CASSUM LUMINE LUGENT (see below) are thrown in parenthetically between the exordium in which he thus reminds them of known facts, and the new information which he begins to convey at *v.* 86, ILLI ME COMITEM &c.

Hence a plain reason why Sinon does not specify the precise charge made against Palamedes, his object being not to give a history of that individual, but merely to recall to the mind of the Trojans what they already knew respecting him.

DEMISERE NECI. — Preserved in the old Italian *missono a morte.* See Leopardi's Martirio de' Santi Padri. Cap. II.

NUNC CASSUM LUMINE LUGENT. — *They now* (viz. convinced by experience that it was unwise to have undertaken the war, see *v.* 108) *lament the loss of the prudent counsellor* who "BELLA VETABAT." But this is not the sole force of these words; they serve also to excite the Trojan sympathy, first and directly, for Palamedes (not only innocent, but lamented even by his executioners); and secondly and indirectly, for his friend and companion, Sinon, *afflictus* (see *v.* 92 and Comm.) by his fall; like him, persecuted to the death by the same Ulysses; and (by implication) like him innocent.

CASSUM LUMINE. — Literally without light, dark; compare Lucret. V. 718.

"Nec potis est cerni, quia cassum lumine fertur;"

The use made of "cassum" by the Romans seems to correspond nearly with that made by us of the particle *less* in composition. "Cassum lumine," *lightless*, i. e. *lifeless;* "cassum sanguine" (CIC. *de Divin.* II. 64) *bloodless.*

IN ARMA. — "H. e. *ad bellum.*" Heyne. — I think the meaning is rather, *to the profession of arms; to seek a military fortune.* Compare:

"Sed in Asiam hinc abii propter pauperiem, atque ibi
Simul rem et belli gloriam armis repperi."

TERENT. *Heaut.* I. 1, 59.

PRIMIS . . . AB ANNIS. — See Comm. *En.* II. 138.

92.

AFFLICTUS VITAM IN TENEBRIS LUCTUQUE TRAHEBAM

AFFLICTUS. — Not, *sorrowful*, for that meaning is contained in LUCTU; but *dashed to the ground; beaten down from his prosperity;* viz. by the death of his friend and patron. It is used in this, its primitive sense, on the only other occasion on which Virgil has used the word, *En.*

I. 456; also by Milton, *Par. Lost*, I. 186, *afflicted powers;* and II. 166, *afflicting thunder.*

96.

PROMISI ULTOREM ET VERBIS ODIA ASPERA MOVI
HINC MIHI PRIMA MALI LABES HINC SEMPER ULIXES
CRIMINIBUS TERRERE NOVIS HINC SPARGERE VOCES
IN VOLGUM AMBIGUAS ET QUAERERE CONSCIUS ARMA

ET VERBIS ODIA ASPERA MOVI. — ET is epexegetic, and VERBIS the words in which *promisit se ultorem;* as if Virgil had written *et movi odia aspera verbis, quibus me promisi ultorem;* or *me promittens ultorem.*

LABES. — A stain or spot: compare Ovid. *Metam.* II. 537.

"Nam fuit haec quondam niveis argentea pennis
Ales, ut aequaret totas sine labe columbas."

ET QUAERERE CONSCIUS ARMA. — Wagner's interpretation of these words, viz. that they are a poetical equivalent for "*quaerere conscios*," seems to me to be particularly unfortunate,

First, because Virgil was too good a painter of character to represent the cautious, cunning Ulysses, as going about in search of a number of persons, to whom to communicate his designs against Sinon.

Secondly, because the immediately preceding words CRIMINIBUS TERRERE NOVIS and SPARGERE VOCES, describe Ulysses as proceeding against Sinon by methods, which not only did not require the privity of a number of persons, but were likely to be successful in proportion as their secret object was kept confined to Ulysses' own bosom.

Thirdly, because the extraordinary violence which this interpretation puts upon the words, is not so much as attempted to be supported even by a single authority.

I, therefore, understand ET QUAERERE ARMA to be explanatory of the preceding sentence; and the *arms* (of offence and defence) which Ulysses sought (QUAEREBAT) against Sinon, to be the CRIMINA NOVA, and the VOCES AMBIGUAS. This explanation accords both with Virgil's usual manner (see Comm. *En.* I. 500; II. 18 and 49), and with the ordinary meaning of the terms *quaerere arma;* see *En.* XI. 229. The following are examples of the latitude in which the word *arma* is used by the best Latin writers:

"Persequar aut studium linguae, Demosthenis arma."
PROPERTIUS III. 21. 27.

"Haud ignaro imminet fortuna: video donec arma adversariis tradantur (*means of offence put into the hands of our adversaries through the medium of a new constitution of the state*) differri adversus nos certamen." LIVY III. 54. (Ed. Bipont.)

CONSCIUS, therefore, is not *conspiring with others*, but the very contrary, *he alone conscious; knowing what he was about, but concealing it from others:* for it does not appear that even Calchas had anything to do with the affair until later. Compare (*En.* V. 455) "Conscia virtus" the virtue of which they themselves were conscious; "Formae conscia conjux" (*En.*VIII.393) *conscious* (viz. to herself) *of her beauty;* and (Lucret. VI. 711.)

"Verum aliquid, genere esse ex hoc, quod conscius dicet,
Scimus."

105.

TUM VERO ARDEMUS SCITARI ET QUAERERE CAUSAS

That this is the common hyperbaton: ARDEMUS SCITARI ET QUAERERE CAUSAS, for *ardentes scitamur et quaerimus causas*, is proved by the necessity which exists for some expression, not merely that they *desired* to question him, but that they actually *did* question him. The received interpretation leaves the sense incomplete.

TUM VERO. — *Then indeed* we are all on fire. They were curious before to hear his history, see *v.* 74, but, having heard so far, are now doubly curious. See Comm. *v.* 228; III. 47. and IV. 396. 449. 571.

ARDEMUS. — The force of the verb *ardere* is infinitely more intense than that of its English derivatives; which, having first lost their literal, have at last, as a consequence, almost wholly lost, even their metaphorical sense. The Latin word, on the contrary, where it is not literal, is fully metaphorical. "Tantum est flumen verborum, tam integrae sententiae, ut mihi non solum tu *incendere* judicem, sed ipse *ardere* videaris." Cicer. De Orat. lib. III. c. 45. — "Tanta iracundia incitatus est, ut *arderet*." Argum. ad Terent. Adelph.

110.

FECISSENTQUE UTINAM SAEPE ILLOS ASPERA PONTI
INTERCLUSIT HIEMS ET TERRUIT AUSTER EUNTES

INERCLUSIT operates only on ILLOS; TERRUIT both on ILLOS and EUNTES. INTERCLUSIT ILLOS, *shut them in, rendered it impossible for them even to attempt to go;* TERRUIT EUNTES, *terrified (deterred) them when actually beginning to go.* See Comm. *v.* 552.

121.

CUI FATA PARENT

The meaning is not *cui illi parent fata*, because no suspicion of foul play had yet arisen; but, as rightly interpreted by Burmann, *cui fata parent mortem.*

131.

UNIUS IN MISERI EXITIUM CONVERSA TULERE

CONVERSA TULERE. — "Exquisite pro converterunt." Heyne. No. Converterunt in exitium, would be only, *turned* to my destruction, CONVERSA TULERE IN EXITIUM is not only, *turned* to my destruction, but *turned* and *carried* to my destruction; turned towards and then carried towards.— So: "Furiis incensa feror," *En.* IV. 376, is not merely incendor furiis, *I am fired by the furies*, but *I am fired by the furies and then set in motion*, carried on by them while on fire: in both cases the addition of the verb is required to express the forward motion so necessary to the completeness of the picture. So also, *En.* I. 85.

— "Conversa cuspide montem
Impulit."

Turned his spear towards the mountain and then pushed with it. See Comm. *En.* I. 85.

138.

NEC DULCES NATOS EXOPTATUMQUE PARENTEM

The commentators have always found an insuperable difficulty in this passage. "How," say they, "is it possible to reconcile what Sinon here says, of his having children at home, with what he formerly told us (*v.* 87) of his having been sent to the war by his father, when a mere boy?" In order to get rid of the difficulty, Heyne (who is followed by Wagner, Wunderlich, Forbiger and Thiel,) understands *primis ab annis* (*v.* 87) to mean *ab initio belli;* but this interpretation is inadmissible,

First, because no authority whatever has been adduced in its support; while, on the contrary, there is the authority not only of Ovid (tu comes antiquus, tu *primis* junctus *ab annis*, Ex Ponto, II. 5. 43) and Valer. Flaccus, I. 22. (Haemoniam *primis* Pelias frenabat *ab annis*), but of Virgil himself against it (*primis* et te miretur *ab annis*. En. VIII. 517).

Secondly, because it deprives Sinon's story of its chief pathos; a pathos so necessary to the attainment of his primary object, that of exciting such pity in the breasts of the Trojans as would induce them to spare his life, and, therefore, so necessary to the success of his plot.

Thirdly, because it takes away from Sinon his best excuse to the Trojans for having taken up arms against them, viz. that he had done so in pursuance of a child's duty of obedience to his parent.

Fourthly, because Sinon's informing the Trojans that he had been at the war from the beginning, could serve no other purpose than that of exasperating them the more against him.

How then is the difficulty to be got rid of? I answer, simply by referring NATOS not to Sinon, but to PARENTEM, and by translating the passage, not *my* children and *my* parent, but *the* children and *the* parent, meaning *Sinon's brothers and sisters* (the *Geschwister* of the Germans), *and his and their parent*. All difficulty is thus removed and Virgil's consistency vindicated.

There is a very similar use of *natum*, En. IV. 605, where *natumque patremque* does not mean *my* son and *my* father, but *the* son and *the* father, h. e. *the son and his father*. So also, En. VI. 116. *natique patrisque*, *the* son and *the* father, the son being the speaker himself. Also, En. VIII. 308. rex . . . . . Aeneam . . . . . *natumque* tenebat, "the King kept Eneas and the son, meaning, not his own son, but Eneas's son." See also, En. II. 663. Numerous other instances also might be adduced, in which *natus* is thus referred, not to the speaker, but to its correlative *parens*, or *pater*, or *mater*, expressed. I am aware that it has, on a similiar occasion, been suggested by Forbiger (in his note to *v.* 178): "Virgilium hanc fictam Sinonis narrationem consulto ita composuisse, ut homo iste sibi ipse contradiceret, aut ambigua et obscura proferret;" but this is a suggestion from which I must wholly dissent, because it is evident that, in proportion as Virgil made the story obscure, or inconsistent with itself, it was the less likely to obtain credence with the Trojans; to which if it be replied, that Virgil, as *Poeta*, had it in his power to represent the Trojans as crediting whatever story he thought proper, — I answer, that to represent the Trojans so void of acumen as to credit an unlikely, ambiguous, and, above all, a contradictory story, is to diminish our respect for, and sympathy with, not only the Trojans, but Eneas himself, and thus to contradict the whole scope and design of the poem. And further, I think that the more carefully the story is examined, the more evident does it appear, that Virgil has taken the greatest and most successful pains to fabricate a story for Sinon, which is so consistent with itself, and so extremely like the truth, that it was hardly possible for the Trojans not to be deceived by it.

As a further argument in favour of the above interpretation, I may observe, that it relieves the passage from the manifest awkwardness of the non-mention of Sinon's wife, or of his ever having been married. In the parallel passage, quoted by Ursini (Virg. collat. cum Graecis scriptoribus,) from Lucretius, in which *nati* has the meaning attempted to be fixed on it in the passage before us, there is no such awkwardness, mention being made of the wife along with the children

"Nam jam non domus accipiet te laeta, neque uxor
Optima, nec dulces occurrent oscula nati
Praeripere, et tacita pectus dulcedine tangent."
LUCR. III. 907.

141.

CONSCIA NUMINA VERI

The structure is not (with Heyne and Thiel) CONSCIA VERI, but NUMINA VERI, corresponding exactly with 'Numina Fauni', *Georg.* I. 10. 'Numina Phoebi', *En.* III. 359. 'Numina Palladis', *En.* III. 544. &c. and meaning the Divinity or Divine Power to which truth is sacred; which protects those who speak truth. The object of CONSCIA is — not expressed, but (as in the similar instances of 'conscia agmina' *v.* 267, and 'quaerere conscius arma' *v.* 99) — unterstood from the context: *vos, numina Veri, quae conscia estis quod vera loquor.* Similar to this adjuration of the 'Numina' to whom 'Verum' is sacred, who protect the truth and right, is Eneas's adjuration (*En.* I. 607) of the 'Numina' who protect and reward the tender-hearted and compassionate.

148.

AMISSOS HINC JAM OBLIVISCERE GRAJOS
NOSTER ERIS MIHIQUE HAEC EDISSERE VERA ROGANTI

The elder Heinsius placed a semicolon at GRAJOS and a comma at ERIS. The younger Heinsius, and, after him, Emmenessius and Burmann retain the semicolon at GRAJOS, but substitute a colon for the comma at ERIS; correctly, as I think; NOSTER ERIS being thrown in according to Virgil's usual manner (see Comm. *En.* I. 4. III. 571. IV. 484. VI. 84, 741 and 882) parenthetically between the two connected verbs OBLIVISCERE and EDISSERE, and the sense running thus: *forget the Greeks (for thou shalt from henceforward be ours) and answer me truly these questions.* Wagner, in his Edition of Heyne, returns to the punctuation of the elder Heinsius and observes in his note: "Comma post ERIS ponendum, et quae sequuntur hunc in modum accipienda: ac *proinde* edissere;" thus separating the two similar verbs, and connecting the two dissimilar.

154.

VOS AETERNI IGNES ET NON VIOLABILE VESTRUM
TESTOR NUMEN AIT VOS ARAE ENSESQUE NEFANDI
QUOS FUGI VITTAEQUE DEUM QUAS HOSTIA GESSI
FAS MIHI GRAJORUM SACRATA RESOLVERE JURA
FAS ODISSE VIROS ATQUE OMNIA FERRE SUB AURAS
SI QUA TEGUNT TENEOR PATRIAE NEC LEGIBUS ULLIS
TU MODO PROMISSIS MANEAS SERVATAQUE SERVES
TROJA FIDEM SI VERA FERAM SI MAGNA REPENDAM

VOS AETERNI IGNES ET NON VIOLABILE VESTRUM TESTOR NUMEN AIT. —

— "Caelum hoc et conscia sidera testor."
En. IX. 429.

"Caelum ipsum stellaeque caeligenae omnisque siderea compago Aether vocatur: non, ut quidam putant, quod ignitus sit et incensus (*παρα του αιθειν*), sed quod cursibus rapidis semper rotetur, *παρα του αει θεειν*. Elementum non unum ex quatuor, quae nota sunt cunctis, sed longe aliud, numero quintum, ordine primum, genere divinum et *inviolabile*." Apul. *de Mundo*, cap. I.

VOS ARAE ENSESQUE NEFANDI. — "Neque ullis adpetitus insidiis est, neque devotus hostiae; denique sic de omnibus jurat, ut, per ea quae non fuerunt dans sacramentum, careat objurgatore." *Antiq. Interpr.* (*ap. Maium*). See the similarly equivocating oath of Andromache, SENEC. *Troad.* 604.

FAS MIHI. — The subsequent TENEOR points out the structure; *fas est*, not *fas sit;* i. e. *testor fas mihi esse . . . . . et me teneri.*

SERVATAQUE SERVES. — A common saying, as appears from Petron. P. 155. "Serva me, servabo te."

169.

FLUERE AC RETRO SUBLAPSA REFERRI

"FLUERE; *diffluere, dilabi;* RETRO SUBLAPSA REFERRI; pro prosaico, *retro ferri, labi; de mole, quae in altum erat invecta.*" Heyne. Both explanations wrong, because no example has been, nor I think can be, produced of *fluere* used in the sense of *diffluere, dilabi;* or otherwise than as signifying *to flow like the water in a river;* and because "retro sublapsa referri," where it occurs before (*Georg.* I. 200), is thus explained by Heyne himself: "Non aliter quam is retro sublapsus refertur qui navigium agit atque illum in praeceps prono rapit alveus amni;" an explanation which, even although it had not been, almost totidem verbis, Virgil's own, would have been established beyond the possibility of doubt by the nearly parallel passage of Lucretius, IV. 422.

> "Denique ubi in medio nobis equus acer obhaesit
> Flumine, et in rapidas amnis despeximus undas,
> Stantis equi corpus transvorsum ferre videtur
> Vis, et in advorsum flumen contrudere raptim;
> Et quocunque oculos trajecimus, omnia ferri
> Et fluere adsimili nobis ratione videntur."

The entire sense of the words FLUERE AC RETRO SUBLAPSA REFERRI is therefore expressed by the single English verb *ebb.*

178.

OMINA NI REPETANT ARGIS NUMENQUE REDUCANT
QUOD PELAGO ET CURVIS SECUM AVEXERE CARINIS

— —

As far as my own personal search has extended, *advexere* is the reading only of one MS., viz. one in the Royal Library at Vienna, No. 113 in Endlicher's Catalogue. It has, however, been adopted by Dan. Heinsius and La Cerda, as also by Alfieri from the Baskerville text. On the other hand I have myself personally ascertained that *avexere* is the reading of the oldest Gudian, of No. 116, 117, 121 (Endlicher's Catal.) in the Vienna Library, of No. 18059 in the Munich Library, and of the Kloster Neuburg MS.; it is also the reading, as it appears from Foggini, of the Medicean, and as it appears from Bottari, of the Vatican Fragment: also of N. Heinsius and Burmann; and has been adopted both by Jaeck and Brunck after examination of several MSS. I have found *adduxere* in No. 120 (Endlicher's Catal.) in the Vienna Library, and *vexere* in No. 118 in the same Library.

Taking it for granted, then, that *avexere* is the true reading, what is the sense?

"Nimirum Palladium, quod secum avexere, reducere debent." Burmann.

"Cum ipso Palladio avecto revertendum." Heyne.

"Numen, de simulachro ut *v.* 183." Wagner.

"Indarno i Greci
Stringer d' Ilio le mura, ove novelli
Augurj in Argo non ricerchin pria,
Ove non plachin la furata Diva,
Su i legni loro a forza tratta."

ALFIERI.

"Wenn sie nicht das versöhnte Bild aus Griechenland nach Troja zurückbrachten." Ladewig.

The objection to which interpretation seems to me to be insuperable, viz. that *numen* everywhere else, where it occurs, not only in Virgil, but in all other writers, signifies precisely the opposite; viz. either the actual deity, or the spirit, will, sanction, blessing, or authority of the deity, as opposed to the substantial image or statue. This is true even of the passage cited by Wagner in proof of his contrary opinion, "Numine laeso" (*v.* 183) being (to me at least) clearly spoken, not of the statue, but of the spirit, divinity, or will of Pallas offended by the violence offered to her statue. See Comm. *v.* 182. I, therefore, think it certain that NUMEN is here spoken, not of the Palladium, but as so often elsewhere, of the divine spirit of Pallas and particularly of her grace, good-will and blessing, and that the meaning is: *sail back hither with the same good-will and approbation of the Goddess with which they have now sailed for Greece — obtain her authority for coming back, even as they have now departed and sailed away in obedience to her orders.* And such precisely is the use made of the word by Sinon himself on both the other occasions on which he has used it, *v.* 123 and *v.* 183 where see Comment. Compare also Eneas's setting out with his party in the disguise of Greeks, 'haud numine nostro' (*v.* 396), *without the blessing and good-will of our own accustomed Gods;* and his sailing into the Sicilian port with the *numen Divum* (*En.* V. 56), expressly explained in the selfsame line to mean nothing more than the *mens Divum;* also: "*Εξεπεμψα δε σοι φιλοτης ως αληθως την Ασκληπιαδα νηα, η προσθες μετα του αλιου επισημον και υγιειην, επει κατα δαιμονα τω οντι ιστιοδρομηκε* (prospero numine vela fecit)." Epistolae Graecanicae. Aurel. Allobrog. 1606. Fol. p. 323. "*Πατριδος εσμεν πορρωτερω συν δαιμονι.*" Ibid. p. 133.

In the same way as *numen* is here spoken of as an object which can be carried with persons making a voyage, so it is spoken of (*En.* I. 451 where see Comm.), as constituting along with the 'dona' the opulence of a temple,

— "Donis opulentum et numine Divae."

182.

ITA DIGERIT OMINA CALCHAS
HANC PRO PALLADIO MONITI PRO NUMINE LAESO
EFFIGIEM STATUERE NEFAS QUAE TRISTE PIARET

ITA is emphatic and may be supposed to be accompanied by a significant action of the speaker.

OMINA, not *the* omens (viz. the omens which Calchas has just interpreted), but *omens* generally: *this* is the way in which Calchas explains omens — *this* is what comes of his interpretation of omens; he does not interpret omens for nothing, or to no purpose; in consequence of his omen-interpreting you will, before you know what you are about, have the Greeks on your backs again (improvisi aderunt) with new and recruited forces (arma) and the recovered favor of the Gods (Deos comites — numen reductum): *ITA* DIGERIT OMINA CALCHAS.

DIGERIT — *analyses.* Germ.: *setzt auseinander.*

NUMINE — "signo numinis." Heyne, and so Wagner, and (quoted by Wagner) Wunderlich (ad Tibull.). No; but plainly, *the divine will — sanction — majesty — of the Deity*, offended by the violence offered to the Palladium; compare "numine laeso" *En.* I. 12; also Tibull. I. 3. 79.

"Et Danai proles Veneris quae numina laesit."

See also Comm. *v.* 178.

193.

ULTRO ASIAM MAGNO PELOPEA AD MOENIA BELLO
VENTURAM

"Jam satis valida civitate ut non solum arcere bellum, sed ultro etiam inferre posset." LIV. III. 8. Ed. Bipont.

197.

QUOS NEQUE TYDIDES NEC LARISSAEUS ACHILLES
NON ANNI DOMUERE DECEM NON MILLE CARINAE

"Quem non mille simul turmis, nec Caesare toto
Auferret Fortuna locum, victoribus unus
Eripuit, vetuitque capi."

Luc. VI. 140.

199.

HIC ALIUD MAJUS MISERIS MULTOQUE TREMENDUM
OBJICITUR MAGIS ATQUE IMPROVIDA PECTORA TURBAT

This prodigy is not merely *ominous*, but *typical*, of the destruction about to come upon Troy. The twin serpents prefigure the Grecian armament; which, like them, comes from Tenedos (where, as must not be forgotten, it is lying concealed at the very moment of the prodigy); like them, crosses the tranquil deep; like them, lands; and, going up straight (probably over the very same ground) to the city, slaughters the surprised and unresisting Trojans (prefigured by Laocoon's sons), and overturns the religion and drives out the Gods (prefigured by the priest Laocoon). Even in the most minute particulars the type is perfect: the serpents come abreast towards the shore, like ships sailing together (*Argiva phalanx instructis navibus ibat .... Littora .... petens*); with flaming eyes raised above the waves by the whole length of the neck and breast (*flammas quum regia puppis Extulerat*), and with the hinder part floating and curling along on the surface of the water (*the hinder vessels of the fleet following the lead of the foremost*); and, when their work is done (*the Trojans slaughtered, or, with their Gods, driven out of the city*), take possession of the citadel, under the protection of Pallas (*Jam summas arces Tritonia, respice, Pallas Insedit* &c.).

[Since the above commentary was written (and published in the Classical Museum for 1848), I have found a confirmation of the opinion therein expressed, in Petronius's poem descriptive of the taking of Troy (see his Satyr. P. 328) in one part of which he informs us that the noise, made by the serpents in their passage through the water, was like that of vessels rowing and at the same time cutting their way through the sea,

> "Qualis silenti nocte remorum sonus
> Longe refertur, quum premunt classes mare,
> Pulsumque marmor abiete imposita gemit;"

and in another that the necks and breasts of the serpents, as they came along through the water, resembled tall ships,

> — "Tumida quorum pectora,
> Rates ut altae, lateribus spumas agunt."

J. H. 1853.]

IMPROVIDA PECTORA TURBAT. — "Turbat pectora ita ut fierent improvida: ita enim praecipites egit ea res Trojanos, ut omissa omni cautione facerent, quod Sinon optabat." Wagn. Virg. Br. En. "IMPROVIDA, quae tale quid non praeviderant." Heyne. "Ueberraschte." Weickert. "At quodvis prodigium natura sua inopinatum neque praevideri potest. Ipse IMPROVIDA PECTORA Trojanorum intelligo, qui capti dolis, lacrymisque coactis Sinonis fuisse in prioribus versibus dicti erant." Wunderlich. The simple solution of the difficulty is, I think, to be found in unterstanding the two distinct words IMPROVIDA and TURBAT as standing in close connexion (*Verbindung*) with each other, so as to express the complex idea which we express in English by the single word *alarm*. TURBAT (*disturbs*) IMPROVIDA (*unforeseeing*, *unexpecting*); i. e. *alarms* (Germ. *erschreckt*). Compare 'Gelidus coit', *freezes*, *En.* III. 30. 'Angusti claustra Pelori', *straits of Pelorus, En.* III. 411. 'Aggredior dictis', *accost, En.* III. 358. 'Expediam dictis', *explain, En.* III. 379. 'Profugus venit', *En.* I. 6. 'It proruptum', *bursts forth, En.* I. 250. 'Excussos laxare', *uncoil, En.* III. 267. 'Circumfusa ruit', *En.* II. 64. 'Lapsa cadunt', *En.* VI. 310. 'Vela damus', *sail, En.* III. 191. 'Eques sternet', *ride over, En.* VI. 858. 'Exercet cantus', *sings, Georg.* I. 403. 'Exercet choros', *dances, En.* I. 503. 'Exercent palaestras', *wrestle, En.* III. 281. Heyne and Weickert, although they assign to each of the two words separately taken, its true sense, yet fall short of the exact meaning of the author, because they have not observed the close connexion in which the two words stand to each other, while on the other hand Wagner, who connects the words pretty closely together, unfortunately assigns to them so connected a very artificial, and, as it seems to me, wholly erroneous sense.

203.

ECCE AUTEM GEMINI A TENEDO TRANQUILLA PER ALTA
HORRESCO REFERENS IMMENSIS ORBIBUS ANGUES
INCUMBUNT PELAGO PARITERQUE AD LITORA TENDUNT
PECTORA QUORUM INTER FLUCTUS ARRECTA JUBAEQUE
SANGUINEAE SUPERANT UNDAS PARS CETERA PONTUM
PONE LEGIT SINUATQUE IMMENSA VOLUMINE TERGA
FIT SONITUS SPUMANTE SALO JAMQUE ARVA TENEBANT

HORRESCO REFERENS. — This interjection is not placed indifferently any where in the middle of the sentence, but in its most natural and effective position, after the words GEMINI A TENEDO TRANQUILLA PER ALTA excitatory of expectation; and immediately before IMMENSIS ORBIBUS ANGUES expressive of the actual horrid object. The weaker effect which it would have had, if placed at a greater distance b e f o r e IMMENSIS ORBIBUS ANGUES, is shown by Dryden's translation:

"When, dreadful to behold, from sea we spied
Two serpents, ranked abreast, the seas divide."

and the still weaker which it would have had if placed after, by Surrey's:

"From Tenedon, behold, in circles great
By the calm seas come fleeting, adders twain;
Which plied towards the shore (I loathe to tell)
With reared breast lift up above the seas."

Compare: "Trītonia, respice, Pallas," *v.* 615, and Comm.

PECTORA QUORUM &c.

"Thus Satan, talking to his nearest mate,
With head uplift above the wave, and eyes
That sparkling blazed; his other parts besides
Prone on the flood, extended long and large,
Lay floating many a rood."

Par. Lost, I. 192.

FIT SONITUS SPUMANTE SALO. — The translators, who represent the sound made by the foaming of the brine to have been loud, err doubly; first, in not understanding that SONITUS, without an adjunct expressive of loudness, is not *a loud sound*, but simply *a sound* (see *v.* 732; *Georg.* IV. 79 &c.); and secondly, in not perceiving that propriety of description requires that the sound of foam should not be represented as loud. Dryden, as usual, errs most:

"Their speckled tails advance to steer their course,
And on the sounding shore the flying billows force."

I know but one translated passage, not Dryden's own, which can at all vie with this in incorrectness; it is where Pope, instead of describing Jupiter as seizing Ate by the shining-curled head, in order to fling her from heaven, describes him as snatching her from the top of his own head:

"From his ambrosial head, where perched she sate,
He snatched the Fury-Goddess of debate."

POPE'S *Iliad,* XIX. 125.

ARVA. — There is no occasion to suppose, with Heyne, that ARVA is used "*pro littore*", because, interpreted literally it affords a better meaning, viz. *the fields*, or *cultivated plain inside the beach*, where it is probable the 'solennis ara' stood, at such a distance from the actual shore as to be in no danger from the violence of the sea during stormy weather. Compare: "Pelago premit arva sonanti," *En.* I. 250 and Comm.

213.

ET PRIMUM PARVA DUORUM
CORPORA NATORUM SERPENS AMPLEXUS UTERQUE
IMPLICAT ET MISEROS MORSU DEPASCITUR ARTUS
POST IPSUM AUXILIO SUBEUNTEM AC TELA FERENTEM
CORRIPIUNT SPIRISQUE LIGANT INGENTIBUS

PRIMUM . . . . POST. — There is a most material discrepancy between the account given by Virgil, and the view presented by the sculptor, of the death of Laocoon and his two sons. According to the former, the serpents first (PRIMUM) kill the two sons, and afterwards (POST) seize (CORRIPIUNT) the father, SUBEUNTEM AC TELA FERENTEM, and kill him also; while, according to the latter, the serpents are twined about and kill the father and the two sons simultaneously. Virgil's is the more natural and probable account, because it was more easy for the serpents to conquer Laocoon's powerful strength (see *v.* 50) with the whole of their united force and folds, than with such part only of their force and folds as was not employed upon the sons. There is even some difficulty in understanding (nor does an examination of the sculpture tend much to diminish the difficulty), how two serpents, already twined about, and encumbered with the bodies of two persons, even although those bodies were small (PARVA), could seize, and squeeze to death, a third person, possessed of more than ordinary strength, and armed.

The sculptor, if he had had the choice, would, doubtless, no less than the poet, have represented the killing of Laocoon to have been subsequent to the killing of the sons; but his art failed him; sculpture could not represent successive acts; the chisel could fix no more than a single instant of fleeting time: driven, therefore, by necessity, he places the three persons simultaneously in the folds of the serpents, and his (so much admired) group becomes, in consequence, complicated and almost incomprehensible, and appears in the most disadvantageous contrast with the simple and natural narrative of Virgil.

Such is the infinite inferiority of sculpture (and of painting) to poetry. The sculptor (or painter) labours day and night, and for years together, on one object; and, in the end, his work, representing but an instant of time, fails to present to the mind as many ideas as the poet supplies in half a dozen lines, the work perhaps of half an hour.

Spiris. — 'Spirae' are not merely *coils*, but *spiral coils* — tending upwards, like those of a corkscrew held point-upward. See *Georg.* II. 153 and 154; where Virgil informs us, almost in express terms, that a snake is in orbs ('orbes'), while coiled upon the ground, but in spires ('spirae'), when he raises himself with a motion twisting upwards. The same distinction is observable in the passage before us, where the serpents are said to be in orbs while on the water, and in spires when folded round Laocoon. A right understanding of this word is the more necessary, because it is the only word in the description, except "superant capite et cervicibus altis", which shows that the poet so far agrees with the sculptor, as to represent Laocoon and the serpents twined about him as forming an erect group. With a similar correct precision, our own Milton applies the term spires to the coils of the serpent when erect, or raised upright.

"Not with indented wave
Prone on the ground, as since, but on his rear,
. . . .
With burnished neck of verdant gold, erect
Amidst his circling spires."
Par. Lost, IX. 496.

223.

QUALES MUGITUS FUGIT CUM SAUCIUS ARAM
TAURUS ET INCERTAM EXCUSSIT CERVICE SECURIM

"Qual è quel toro che si slaccia in quella
Ch' ha ricevuto già 'l colpo mortale,
Che gir non sa, ma qua e là saltella;
Vid' io lo Minotauro far cotale."
DANTE, *Inferno*, XII. 22.

"Non altrimenti il toro va saltando
Qualora il mortal colpo ha ricevuto,
E dentro la foresta alto mugghiando
Ricerca il cacciator che l' ha feruto."
BOCCACCIO, *in Filostrato.*

228.

TUM VERO TREMEFACTA NOVUS PER PECTORA CUNCTIS
INSINUAT PAVOR

The words TUM VERO contrast this NOVUS PAVOR — the PAVOR produced by the punishment of Laocoon — with their former terror, viz. that produced by the sight of the serpents themselves. The sight of the serpents had frightened them, "Diffugimus visu exsangues" (*v.* 212), but the punishment of Laocoon smote their consciences — filled them with religious awe and terror; — they saw in it the visible finger of the offended Deity: TUM VERO TRE-

MEFACTA — then indeed they are thoroughly frightened, and this thorough frightening produces the effect which their previous fright (viz. at the sight of the serpents) had failed to do — causes them to cry out with one accord, that the horse must be admitted into the city.

"Ducendum ad sedes simulachrum, orandaque Divae
Numina conclamant."

See Comm. *En.* II. 105; III. 47; IV. 396. 449. 571.

230.

SACRUM QUI CUSPIDE ROBUR
LAESERIT ET TERGO SCELERATAM INTORSERIT HASTAM

"Is it he? quoth one. Is this the man?
By him who died on cross,
With his cruel bow he laid full low
The harmless albatross."
COLERIDGE, *Ancient Mariner.*

236.

STUPEA VINCULA COLLO
INTENDUNT

"Intendunt collo malorum vincula nautae."
AUSON. *Mosell.* 42.

240.

ILLA SUBIT MEDIAEQUE MINANS ILLABITUR URBI

MINANS. — By an error of which none but a French critic could be guilty, Boileau understands this extremely common metaphor literally. "Il (viz. Virgil) ne se contente pas de prêter de la colère a cet arbre (probably referring to and similarly misunderstanding *v.* 53), mais il lui fait faire des menaces a ces laboureurs." *Reflex. Critiques*, XI. Compare *En.* I. 166 and Comm.

242.

IPSO IN LIMINE PORTAE

Our author having expressly informed us (*v.* 234), that the walls were divided for the admission of the horse, PORTA must be, not the *gate of the city*, but *the opening or entrance made by the division of the walls.* Those commentators who understand PORTA to mean *the gate of the city*, are reduced to the forlorn extremity of construing 'dividimus muros' not *divide the walls*, but *enlarge the opening of the gate;* and of understanding 'scandit muros' to be no more than a poetical form of expression for *entering the enlarged gate.* "Scandit muros, h. e. transcendit; major imago, quam si portam intrat, quae, murorum impositorum et attingentium parte dejecta, erat latior facta." Heyne.

246.

TUNC ETIAM FATIS APERIT CASSANDRA FUTURIS ORA DEI JUSSU NON UNQUAM CREDITA TEUCRIS

That CREDITA is predicated, not of Cassandra, but (as in Ovid. *Metam.* XV. 74 — "Primus quoque talibus ora Docta quidem solvit, sed non et credita, verbis"), of ORA, is proved, not only by the stronger poetical sense of the passage so interpreted, but by the emphatic position of ORA, closing the sentence to which it belongs, and at the same time beginning a new line.

I do not know whether it has been observed by any commentator, but I think that a very slight examination of Virgil's style is sufficient to show, that his emphatic words are almost invariably placed at, or as near to as possible, the beginning of the line; that where an increase of emphasis is required, the emphatic word is separated from the immediately succeeding context by a pause in the sense, which allows the mind of the reader, or voice of the reciter, to dwell on the word with a longer emphasis; that, where the word is required to be still more emphatic, it is not only placed at the beginning of the line, and separated from the succeeding context by a pause, but is made to stand at the end of its own sentence, and at the greatest possible distance from the words in that sentence to which it is most immediately related, as ORA, in the passage before us; 'Julius', *En.* I. 292; 'Phoenissa', *En.* I. 718; 'crudelis', *En.* IV. 311; and that when a maximum of emphasis is required, the word thus placed emphatically at the beginning of the line, and with a pause immediately following, is a repetition or reduplication of a word which has already been used in the preceding sentence, as 'lumina', *v.* 406: and I believe it will still farther be found, that, whenever it is possible, not only the reduplicated word, but its original also, is placed in the emphatic position at the beginning of the line; thus 'Nate, nate', *En.* I. 668 and 669; 'Me, me', *En.* IV. 351 and 354; 'Nos, nos', *Bucol.* I. 3 and 4.

In confirmation of the above opinion, that the beginning of the line is, in Virgil's writings, the seat of the emphasis, I may observe that the nominative pronouns (which it is well known are, in Latin, never expressed unless they are emphatic,) are, with few or no exceptions, found at the beginning of lines.

From these principles may be derived a double argument in favour of the authenticity of the four disputed lines at the commencement of the Eneis: first, that the emphatic pronouns 'ille ego' are, according to Virgil's custom, placed in the emphatic position at the commencement of the line; and, secondly, that the words 'arma virumque' are considerably more emphatic towards the close of the sentence, and in connection with 'at nunc horrentia Martis' (and, I may add, contrasted — 'cano' with 'modulatus' — 'arma' with 'silvis' and 'arva' — 'virum' with 'colono') than without connection and contrast, and contrary to Virgil's habitual 'molle atque facetum,' abruptly at the commencement of the sentence and poem.

Having been thus led to speak incidentally of the four introductory lines of the *Eneis*, I shall perhaps be excused if I add, that I entirely dissent from the judgment pronounced on those lines by some of Virgil's most unpoetical poetical commentators, and especially by Dryden; and that I regard those lines (to write which Virgil seems to have taken up the very pen which he had laid down after writing the last eight lines of the last *Georgic*) as not only worthy of Virgil, but as affording (especially in the fine poetical figure, 'coegi arva ut parerent,') the most abundant evidence that they were written by no other hand. See Comm. *En.* 1. 4.

250.

RUIT OCEANO NOX

In as much as the ancients always represented night as following the course of the sun, i. e. as rising in the east, traversing the sky, and descending or setting in the west (see Stat. *Theb.* II. 61; Virg. *En.* II. 8; III. 512), the words RUIT OCEANO NOX, applied to the commencement of night, are to be understood, not as presenting us with the ordinary English image, of night *falling on the ocean*, but as presenting us with the directly reverse image, of personified night *rising* (rushing) *from the ocean.* So Dante, philosophically and following the ancient model:

> "Gia era 'l sole all' orizzonte giunto,
> Lo cui meridian cerchio coverchia
> Jerusalem col suo più alto punto:
> E la notte ch' opposita a lui cerchia,
> Uscia di Gange fuor."
>
> *Il Purgat.* II. 1.

And Shelley (*Prometheus Unbound,* Act. I. sc. 1):

> "And yet to me welcome is day and night;
> Whether one breaks the hoarfrost of the morn,
> Or starry, dim, and slow the other climbs
> The leaden-coloured East."

If it be doubted that 'ruere' can express motion upwards toward the sky, I beg to refer to *Georg.* II. 308:

> — "Ruit atram
> Ad caelum picea crassus caligine nubem;"

and to *En.* X. 256 where the rising of the day is described by the very same term:

> — "Revoluta ruebat
> Matura jam luce dies noctemque fugarat."

See also Comm. *En.* I. 749.

252.

FUSI PER MOENIA TEUCRI
CONTICUERE

"Dispersi per urbem." Forbiger. No; FUSI is, not *dispersi,* but, as rightly interpreted by Forbiger himself at *En.* I. 218, "*prostrati; hingestreckt.*"

255.

TACITAE PER AMICA SILENTIA LUNAE

The silence (i. e. silent time) of the night was favorable to the descent of the Grecians, there being no one in the way to observe their motions. The moon is called tacit, because *she does not tell — does not blab — says nothing about what she sees.* In other words, and connecting the two terms SILENTIA and TACITAE, *nobody sees them but the moon, and she does not tell what she sees — does not betray.* Compare:

> — "Jam Delia furtim
> Nescio quem tacita callida nocte fovet."
>
> TIBULL. I. 6. 6.

Also:

> "Cardine tunc tacito vertere posse fores."
>
> TIBULL. I. 6. 12.

That SILENTIA LUNAE does not mean the 'interlunium', but the time when the moon was actually shining, appears from Stat. *Theb.* II. 58:

> "Inde per Arcturum mediaeque silentia lunae
> Arva super populosque meat."

256.

FLAMMAS QUUM REGIA PUPPIS
EXTULERAT

"Lumina in navibus singula rostratae, bina onerariae haberent: in praetoria nave insigne nocturnum trium luminum fore." LIVY, XXIX. 25.

> "Ecce novam Priamo, facibus de puppe levatis,
> Fert Bellona nurum.'
>
> STAT. *Achill.* I. 33.

'Effero' being the verb employed in Roman military tactics (see Liv. X. 19; XL. 28) to express the raising of the standard, and the carrying it forward out of the camp against the enemy, there can, I think, be little doubt that there is here a tacit comparison of the personified REGIA PUPPIS raising its signal flame, and followed by the 'Argiva phalanx instructis navibus,' to the standard-bearer of an army raising the standard, and followed by the soldiers to battle.

The practice of the admiral's ship carrying a light by night for the guidance of the other vessels of the fleet, having come down to more modern times, is thus humorously alluded to by Shakespeare, *Henry* IV. Part I. Act. III. sc. 3. — *Falstaff* (to Bardolph):— "Thou art our admiral, thou bearest the lantern in the poop — but 'tis in the nose of thee."

259.

LAXAT CLAUSTRA SINON ILLOS PATEFACTUS AD AURAS REDDIT EQUUS

Compare: "Impulit in latus: ac venti" &c., *En.* I. 86 and Comment.

CLAUSTRA. — 'Claustrum;' *that by which any thing is shut either in or out; a shutter; a barrier:* it is, therefore, applied to the moveable pieces (of whatever material), which closed the vents of Eolus's cave, *En.* I. 60 (see Comm. *En.* I. 85); to the high lands on each side, which appeared to close in the straits of Pelorus, *En.* III. 411; to the valve or valves of a door or gate, by which the passage through the door or gate is closed, *En.* II. 491; to mountains, closing or barring the passage from one country into another, Tacit. *Hist* III. 2; and therefore, metaphorically, to the barriers which the laws oppose to the commission of crime, Quintil. XIII. 10; which Nature opposes to the investigation of her secrets, Lucret. I. 71. &c. Claustrum never has any other meaning; not even in the very passages quoted by Forcellini, that prince of laborious and obtuse lexicographers, to prove that its primary meaning is "*repagulum quo janua clauditur.*"

263.

PRIMUSQUE MACHAON

"Molestum h. l. PRIMUS; interim amplector Heynii explicationem: 'qui primus, inter primos, egressus est;' quanquam fateor, ita nescio quid exile inferri orationi." WAGNER, *Quaest. Virg.* XXVIII. 5. I think the meaning is: *the principal or original mover of the whole matter*; *the person playing the first part — taking the lead in the business.* Compare Comm. *En.* II. 612.

267.

ATQUE AGMINA CONSCIA JUNGUNT

CONSCIA. — See Comment, *v.* 96.

268.

TEMPUS ERAT QUO PRIMA QUIES MORTALIBUS AEGRIS INCIPIT ET DONO DIVUM GRATISSIMA SERPIT

"It was the time when rest, soft sliding down
From heaven's height into men's heavy eyes,
In the forgetfulness of sleep doth drown
The careful thoughts of mortal miseries."
SPENSER, *Visions of Bellay*, I.

270.

IN SOMNIS ECCE ANTE OCULOS MAESTISSIMUS HECTOR
VISUS ADESSE MIHI LARGOSQUE EFFUNDERE FLETUS
RAPTATUS BIGIS UT QUONDAM ATERQUE CRUENTO
PULVERE PERQUE PEDES TRAJECTUS LORA TUMENTES

The construction is, *Maestissimus Hector*, *Raptatus bigis* (*ut quondam*), *aterque cruento Pulvere*, *perque pedes trajectus lora tumentes*, *Visus adesse mihi*, *largosque effundere fletus*. The strength and beauty of this passage, consisting mainly in the positiveness of the predication RAPTATUS BIGIS, is wholly lost by those who adopt the interpretation of Wagner, "*Visus est adesse mihi talis, qualis erat*, *quum raptatus esset;*" which has the effect of throwing the emphasis off.the principal words RAPTATUS BIGIS, and placing it upon UT QUONDAM, words which are quite unessential, and introduced solely for the purpose of explaining to Eneas's hearers (and Virgil's readers), that the condition expressed by RAPTATUS BIGIS (viz. *that of having been rapt by a biga*), exactly resembled the condition in which Eneas had formerly seen Hector, after he had been rapt by the 'biga' of Achilles. Or (to make my meaning still clearer), Eneas, during his dream, sees Hector RAPTATUS BIGIS (*presenting the appearance of having been rapt by a biga*), ATERQUE CRUENTO &c., but makes no comparison of that appearance with Hector's real appearance after he had been dragged round the walls of Troy, until he comes to relate his dream; then, as his hearers might not perfectly understand what appearance he meant by RAPTATUS BIGIS, he explains his meaning by a reference (contained in the words UT QUONDAM) to the well-known appearance which Hector had formerly presented, after he had been dragged at Achilles' chariot-wheels. The comma therefore, placed after BIGIS by the more correct judgment of the older editors and removed by Heyne, should be replaced.

I need scarcely point out to the reader, that the words UT QUONDAM, although intended only to illustrate the meaning of RAPTATUS BIGIS, present us also with a natural and philosophical explanation, why Eneas, in his dream, saw Hector quasi RAPTATUS BIGIS; viz. because of the strong impression made upon his mind by the sight of Hector after he had been actually dragged by the 'biga' of Achilles.

Chateaubriand (*Genie du Christianisme*, part II. livre 5. c. 11), instituting a parallel between this dream of Eneas and that in which Athalie (Racine, *Athalie*, II. 5) sees her mother Jesabel, observes: "Quel Hector parôit au premier moment devant Enée, tel il se montre à la fin. Mais la pompe, mais l'éclat emprunté de Jesabel 'pour reparer des ans l'irreparable outrage' suivi tout à coup, non d'une forme entière, mais

"de lambeaux affreux
Que des chiens devorans se disputoient entr'eux,"

est une sorte de changement d'état, de peripetie, qui donne au songe de Racine une beauté qui manque à celui de Virgile. Enfin cette ombre d'une mère qui se baisse vers le lit de sa fille, comme pour s'y cacher, et qui se transforme tout à coup 'en os et en chairs meurtris,' est une de ces beautés vagues, de ces circonstances terribles, de la vraie nature du fantome." In reply to which criticism I shall perhaps be permitted to observe: first, that the absence from Eneas's dream of a 'peripetie,' similar to that which has been so much and so justly admired in the dream of Athalie, so far from being a defect, is rather new evidence of that superior poetical judgment which informed Virgil, that the proper place for such a 'peripetie' was not in the warning, exhorting, encouraging dream of Eneas, but exactly where the poet has placed it, in the horrifying dream of Turnus:

"Talibus Alecto dictis èxarsit in iras" &c.
En. VII. 445.

It was with this similar dream of Turnus — with that Calybe changing into the furious Alecto hissing with all her hydras; or with the similar dream of Eteocles — with that Tiresias converted into the ominous Laius baring his divided throat, and deluging his grandson's sleep with blood ("undanti perfundit vulnere somnum," Stat. *Theb.* II. 124), not with the totally dissimilar Hector of the totally dissimilar dream of Eneas, that Chateaubriand might have correctly compared the Jesabel of Athalie. But lest it should be imagined that I use this plea of dissimilarity as a mere pretext for eschewing a comparison from which my favorite Virgil might perhaps issue with tarnished laurels, I beg to add, secondly, that I prefer Eneas's dream to Athalie's, (*a*) on account of its greater simplicity; the former consisting of a single view or scene, with but a single actor, while the latter is complicated of two scenes, each with its separate actor; and those scenes so far distinct and independent of each other, that Chateaubriand in his parallel has (whether disingenuously or through mere error I will not pretend to say,) assumed and treated one of them as the whole dream, and compared Eneas's dream with that one, without making any, even the least, reference or allusion to the other. (*b*) Because the role assigned to Hector (viz. that of announcing to Eneas the capture of the city and his own immediate personal danger; of urging, and thereby justifying, his flight; of conveying to him the first information that it was he who was to take charge of the 'sacra' of Troy, and establish for them a new and great settlement beyond the sea — that settlement no less than the beginning of that Roman empire whose foundation was the subject and key of the whole poem — and finally of actually committing those 'sacra' into his hands,) confers upon Hector the dignity and importance of a real character — of one of the poet's actual dramatis personae; while Jesabel, whose part rises little, if at all, beyond the production of a certain amount of terror, is a mere phantom, subsidiary to, and making way for, the child Joas; who, as that personage of the dream on which the whole plot and future incidents of the drama hinge, mainly attracts and fixes on himself the interest. (*c*) Eneas's dream is to be preferred to Athalie's, because the former is interwoven with, and forms part of, the narrative; the latter stands separate from it, and is only explanatory, or, at the most, casual. The sailing of the ambushed fleet from Tenedos, Sinon's opening the 'claustra' of the wooden horse, the descent of the chiefs into the city, the throwing wide the gates to the whole Grecian army, Eneas's seeing Hector in a dream, receiving from him the 'sacra' of Troy, waking and hearing the tumult, taking arms &c. are so many mutually dependent and connected parts of the same history, related in one even, uninterrupted tenor by the same narrator, and received by the audience with the same undoubting faith; while on the other hand even Athalie herself does not credit her own dream until she has dreamt it twice over, and even then, when she comes to relate it, thinks it necessary to warn her hearers, in verbiage sufficiently French and tedious, against taking so bizarre an assemblage of objects of different kinds, for the work of chance:

"De tant d'objets divers le bizarre assemblage
Peut-être du hazard vous paroît un ouvrage;
Moi-même quelque temps, honteuse de ma peur,
Je l'ai pris pour l'effet d'une sombre vapeur.
Mais de ce souvenir mon âme possédée
A deux fois en dormant revu la même idée;
Deux fois mes tristes yeux se sont vu retracer" &c.

I should not perhaps have so long dwelt on this comparison, if Racine had not been put forward, not merely by Chateaubriand, but by so many other French critics, and by the French nation generally, as the French Virgil, in his other performances equal, in Athalie superior, to the Mantuan. Alas for that superiority which even here, in this selected passage of this selected work, is guilty, I will not say, of a mere inaccuracy of expression, but of a downright confusion of ideas, in as much as Athalie having made no mention of the real Jesabel, but only of that Jesabel which appeared to her in the dream, the '*son* ombre' intended by Racine to refer to the real Jesabel, must of necessity be referred by the audience or reader to the Jesabel of the dream, and be understood as meaning the shade of that apparition; or, in other words, although Racine undoubtedly wished his audience to understand that the figure which stooped down to embrace Athalie, was no other than the apparition which had just spoken to her; yet as the only correlative in the whole context for the word '*son*' is the preceding '*elle*', the sense which he has actually expressed is, that the figure which stooped down to embrace Athalie, was not that figure which had just spoken to her, but only the shade of that figure, i. e. the shade of a shade: a confusion of ideas, or, to use the milder term, an inaccuracy of expression, for which we in vain seek a parallel even in the least correct of the Latin authors.

TUMENTES. — Dead limbs do not swell in consequence of violence: either, therefore, Virgil means, that the swelling of Hector's feet was the result of putrefaction; or he applies the adjunct TUMENTES in ignorance of the physiological truth; or aware of the truth, falsely, for the sake of effect; or else, he means that both the swelling, and the violence which produced it, were anterior to death.

It is highly improbable that he means that the swelling was the consequence of putrefaction; because, although he might not have felt himself bound by the authority of Homer, who expressly states (*Iliad*, XXIII, XXIV.) that Apollo prevented putrefaction from taking place in the corpse of Hector, yet no poetical advantage was to be gained by suggesting the idea of putrefaction, in as much as that idea was not only revolting in itself, but, by removing our thought so much the further from the living, sentient Hector, directly tended to diminish that sympathy with him, which it was the sole object of the description to excite.

It is still less likely that Virgil, aware of the physiological truth, applied the term falsely, for the sake of effect; the unworthy supposition is contradicted by every thing which is known, or has ever been heard, of Virgil.

The conclusion, therefore, is inevitable, either that Virgil applied the term TUMENTES in ignorance of the physiological truth, that violence inflicted on dead limbs will not cause them to swell; or that the non-Homeric narrative (see Heyne, *Excurs.* XVIII. ad *En.* I.) which he certainly must have followed, when describing Hector as having been dragged round the walls of Troy (and not, as in the Iliad, from Troy to the Grecian tents, and round the tomb of Patroclus), represented Achilles as having bored Hector's feet and dragged him after his chariot before he was yet dead. Nor let the reader, living in times when man has some bowels of compassion for brother man, reject with horror the imputation to Achilles of so atrocious cruelty; let him rather call to mind the boring of the feet of Oedipus, of the feet and hands of malefactors on the cross, the slitting of noses and cropping of ears, the burnings at the stake, and breakings on the wheel, not so very long since discontinued in Christian countries. This latter explanation of the difficulty involved in the word TUMENTES, derives no small confirmation from the words in which Virgil (*En.* I. 487) has described the dragging of Hector round the walls of Troy:

> "Ter circum Iliacos raptaverat Hectora muros,
> Exanimumque auro corpus vendebat Achilles."

There must be some good reason (see Comm. *v.* 552) why in these lines, 'exanimum corpus' is not applied, as might have been expected, to 'raptaverat', but solely to 'vendebat'; and such good reason is at once suggested by the explanation just given of the word TUMENTES; Achilles drags round the Ilian walls Hector (not Hector's 'exanimum corpus', Hector being yet alive); and having thus deprived him of life, sells his corpse ('exanimum corpus') for gold. Compare:

"Ητις σφαγας μεν Εκτορος τροχηλατους
Κατειδον, οικτρως τ' Ιλιον πυρουμενον,"

quoted by Hesselius in his note on the following verses of the Andromache of Ennius:

"Vidi, videreque passa sum aegerrime,
Curru Hectorem quadrijugo raptarier."

If its discrepancy from the Homeric narrative raise any considerable obstacle in the mind of the reader against the reception of this explanation, I beg to refer him for a discrepancy, not merely with an isolated passage, but with a very large and important part of the story of the Iliad, to Euripides's Helen, who never even so much as saw Troy.

[Since the above Comment was written and published (in *The first two books of the Eneis rendered into English Blank Iambic*, Lond. 1845), I have fallen accidentally upon the following passage in the *Ajax* of Sophocles, *v.* 1040 (ed. Eton. 1786):

"Εκτωρ μεν, ῳ δη τουδ' εδωρηθη παρα
Ζωστηρι πρισθεις ιππικων εξ αντυγων,
Εκναπτετ' αιεν εστ' απεψυξεν βιον."

Although these lines, proving the existence of an account of Hector's having been dragged alive after Achilles's chariot, convert almost into certainty the argument which in that Comment I have presented only as a probability, I have yet allowed the Comment to remain unaltered, in order to exemplify the importance and necessity of a closer examination than is usual, of the apparently trivial or supposed well-understood expressions of our author.

Still more lately (January 1853) I have found the following additional evidence that some writers did describe Hector as having been dragged alive after the chariot of Achilles. It is in the account given by Q. Curtius (IV. 28) of Alexander the Great having caused Betis to be fastened alive to a chariot, and so dragged to death: "Per talos enim spirantis lora trajecta sunt, religatumque ad currum traxere circa urbem equi; gloriante rege, Achillem, a quo genus ipse deduceret, imitatum se esse poena in hostem capienda." J. H.]

274.

HEU MIHI QUALIS ERAT QUANTUM MUTATUS AB ILLO
HECTORE QUI REDIT EXUVIAS INDUTUS ACHILLĪ
VEL DANAUM PHRYGIOS JACULATUS PUPPIBUS IGNES

Compare that most touching lamentation in that most pathetic perhaps of all the ancient dramas, the *Electra* of Sophocles, *v.* 1132: "*Ω φιλτατον μνημειον*" &c.

It may perhaps interest the curious in such matters to be informed, that at P. 305 of the third volume of a copy of Clarendon's History of the Rebellion, preserved in Marsh's library in Dublin, may be seen, amongst numerous other autograph annotations of Dean Swift, the words *quantum mutatus* written by the Dean in pencil on the margin, opposite to the following words of Clarendon: "The Duke (viz. of York) was full of spirit and courage, and naturally loved designs, and desired to engage himself in some action that might improve and advance the low condition of the King his brother" (Charles the First).

279.

FLENS IPSE

"Non minus quam ille." Forbiger, correctly; compare Ovid. *Ex Ponto* I. 4. 53:

> "Et narrare meos flenti flens ipse labores."

287.

NEC ME QUAERENTEM VANA MORATUR

Does not delay me by answering my foolish inquiries.

> "Quaesieram multis: non multis ille moratus,
> Contulit in versus sic sua verba duos."
>
> OVID. *Fast.* I. 161.
>
> "Non faciet longas fabula nostra moras."
>
> OVID. *Fast.* II. 248.

296.

MANIBUS VITTAS VESTAMQUE POTENTEM AETERNUMQUE ADYTIS EFFERT PENETRALIBUS IGNEM

Not really, but only in appearance. Compare:

> "Dixit et admota pariter fatalia visus
> Tradere terga manu."
>
> VAL. FLACC. V. 242.

of Phrixus, in the vision, appearing to put the golden fleece into Jason's hands.

298.

DIVERSO LUCTU

'Diversus' indicates *difference*, not *of kind* or *quality*, but *of situation*. 'Diversus luctus': *woe in a quarter of the city at some distance from the house of Anchises*. By this single word thus happily placed at the commencement of the new action, not only is the reader carried at once out of the retired house in which Eneas is sleeping, into the midst of the sacking und burning of the city, but time allowed for the numerous events described by Pantheus (*v.* 325 and seq.) to occur before Eneas is awakened by the noise.

299.

QUAMQUAM SECRETA PARENTIS
ANCHISAE DOMUS ARBORIBUSQUE OBTECTA RECESSIT

One of the objections made by Napoleon (see his *Note sur le deuxième livre de l'Enéide*, quoted in Comm. on *v.* 5) to Virgil's account of the taking of Troy, is, that it was impossible for Eneas, "*dans ce peu d'heures et malgré les combats,*" to have made numerous journeys (*plusieurs voyages*) to the house of Anchises, situated "*dans un bois à une demi-lieue de Troyes.*" This criticism is doubly erroneous; because, first, the house of Anchises was not half a league's distance, nor any distance, from Troy, but in Troy itself, as evidenced by the account (*v.* 730. 753) of Eneas's flight from Anchises' house, out of Troy, through the gate of the city; and, secondly, because Eneas visits the house only twice, and, on one of these occasions (as if Virgil had been careful to guard against any demur being made to so many as even two visits to a house situated, as he here informs us, in a remote part of the town) is miraculously expedited by a goddess.

I know not whether it will be regarded as an extenuation, and not rather as an aggravation, of Napoleon's error, that he has here (as in the other parts of his critique,) depended wholly on Delille's very incorrect translation:

"Déjà le bruit affreux (quoique loin de la ville
Mon père eût sa demeure au fond d'un bois tranquille)."

It was, at least, incumbent on him, before he sent forward to the world, under the sanction of his illustrious name, a condemnation of the second book of the Eneis, both in the general and in the detail, to have taken ordinary pains to ascertain Virgil's true meaning; and to have assured himself that he was not fulminating his condemnation against errors, the greater part of which had no existence except in the false medium through which alone (as sufficiently evidenced both by his own words and his quotations) he had any acquaintance with Virgil.

302.

SUMMI FASTIGIA TECTI

FASTIGIA TECTI; i. e. *tectum fastigatum; a sloping or ridged roof*, such as is commonly used throughout Europe at the present day. That this is the meaning of the term, is placed beyond doubt by the passage in which Livy describes the 'testudo': "scutis super capita densatis, stantibus primis, secundis submissioribus, tertiis magis et quartis, postremis etiam genu nisis, fastigatam, sicut tecta aedificiorum sunt, testudinem faciebant." XLIV. 9.

309.

MANIFESTA FIDES

The expression is preserved in the Italian: "In prova della prima parte si può addurre . . . . queste parole del Convito, che ne fanno manifesta fede." Comment. of Biagioli on Dante, *Infern.* II. 98.

322.

QUO RES SUMMA LOCO PANTHEU QUAM PRENDIMUS ARCEM

On more mature consideration I am inclined to surrender the interpretation which I formerly proposed of this passage (see Class. Museum, XXIV. from which Journal it has been quoted by Forbiger into his third Edition) and to adopt the following: QUO RES SUMMA LOCO? *in what condition is our all — the main chance — that on which everything hinges* — and therefore (by implication) *the State*, 'salus suprema publica'? Compare Forbiger in loc. and C. Nepos in *Eumen.* IX. 2: "Hic omnibus titubantibus et de rebus summis desperantibus." Also: "Periculum summae rerum facere." Liv. XXXIII. 8. And: "Committendum rerum summam in discrimen utcunque ratus." Liv. XXXIII. 7.

QUAM PRENDIMUS ARCEM? — Literally: *if we throw ourselves into the 'arx', what kind of an 'arx' shall we find it to be? is the 'arx' any longer defensible?* PRENDIMUS. — Nearly as in Caesar, *B. C.* III. 112. "Iis autem invitis, a quibus Pharos tenetur, non potest esse propter angustias navibus introitus in portum. Hoc tum veritus Caesar, hostibus in pugna occupatis, militibusque expositis, Pharon prehendit, atque ibi praesidium posuit." Eneas uses the present tense (PRENDIMUS), because he is actually (see *v.* 315) on his way to the 'arx' at the moment when he meets Pantheus.

325.

FUIMUS TROES FUIT ILIUM

The full force of these expressions will be perceived by those readers only who bear in mind, that among the Romans the death of an invidual was, not unfrequently, announced to his friends by the word 'fuit'; see (in Wernsdorf's *Poetae Latini Minores*):

> Mollibus ex oculis aliquis tibi procidet humor,
> Cum dicar subita voce, fuisse, tibi.
> *Elegia incerti auctoris de Maecenat. Morib.*

So also Plautus, *Truc.* I. 2. 93:

> "Horresco misera, mentio quoties fit partionis:
> Ita paene tibi fuit Phronesium."

and *Pseud.* I. 3. 17:

> — "B. Quis est qui moram obcupato molestam obtulit?
> C. Qui tibi sospitalis fuit. B. Mortuus est, qui fuit; qui est, vivos est;"

where there is a play upon this meaning of the word. Compare also Cicero's announcement of the execution of the Catilinarian conspirators: "vixerunt;" and (Schiller, *Mar. Stuart*, Act IV. sc. 11):

> — "Jene hat gelebt,
> Wenn ich dies Blatt aus meinen Händen gebe."

Charlotte Corday in her letter to Barbaroux, written on the eve of her execution and preserved in Lamartine's Histoire des Girondins (Liv. 44, c. 30), refers to this Roman mode of expression: "C'est demain à huit heures que l'on me juge. Probablement à midi j'aurai vécu, pour parler le langage Romain." So also Manzoni, of Napoleon:

> "Ei fu: siccome immobile
> Dato il mortal sospiro
> Stette la spoglia immemore
> Orba di tanto spiro,
> Così percossa, attonita
> La terra al nunzio sta."
> *Il Cinque Maggio.*

From the Latin 'fuit' used in the above sense, come both the Italian 'fu' and the French 'feu', *defunct*, as is placed beyond all doubt by the plural 'furent': "Les notaires de quelques Provinces disent encore, au pluriel, furent, en parlant de deux personnes conjointes et décedées." Trevoux; and to the same effect Furetiere. Corresponding to this use of the past tenses of the verb 'sum', emphatically, to express *death*, i. e. the cessation of existence, was the use of its present tense to express *life*, i. e. the continuance of existence:

"Estis io Superi, nec inexorabile Clotho
Volvit opus."

STAT. *Silv.* I. 4.

"Rachel weeping for her children, and would not be comforted, because they are not (ουκ εισι)." Matth. II. 18. And of its future tense, to express *future* existence, i. e. existence after death: "Nec enim dum ero, angar ulla re, cum omni vacem culpa: et si non ero, sensu omnino carebo." CICER. *ad Fam.* VI. 3.

331.

MILLIA QUOT MAGNIS UMQUAM VENERE MYCENIS

Not only the authenticity, but the precise reading, of this verse is sufficiently defended against Heyne's "totum versum abesse malim," by Ausonius's quotation of it 'ipsissimis literis' in his *Perioch. XX. Iliad.*

I have myself found 'umquam' in the oldest Gudian (No. 70), and 'unquam' in the Leipzig, No. 35 (Naumann); while in the Leipzig, No. 36 (Naumann), and in the Dresden, I have found 'nunquam'. Bersmann, although he has adopted 'nunquam', informs us that in his MS. (the Camerarian) it is 'unquam'. In Daniel Heinsius I find 'numquam', which has been deservedly rejected by Nicholas Heinsius, and 'umquam' adopted instead.

334.

VIX PRIMI PROELIA TENTANT
PORTARUM VIGILES

"Die Posten der ersten Nachtwache." Ladewig. I think Forbiger is more near the truth: "In primo urbis introitu constituti." PRIMI is the emphatic word, and not VIGILES; which latter is only added in order to explain what PRIMI or *persons nearest the enemy* are meant. Compare *v.* 494:

"Fit via vi; rumpunt aditus, primosque trucidant."

Also:

"Discurrunt alii ad portas, primosque trucidant."
En. XII. 577.

And: "Impetus in eosdem factus, et, primis caesis, caeteri in fugam dissipati sunt." LIV. XXXIII. 10.

348.

JUVENES FORTISSIMA FRUSTRA
PECTORA SI VOBIS AUDENTEM EXTREMA CUPIDO
CERTA SEQUI QUAE SIT REBUS FORTUNA VIDETIS
EXCESSERE OMNES ADYTIS ARISQUE RELICTIS
DI QUIBUS IMPERIUM HOC STETERAT SUCCURRITIS URBI
INCENSAE MORIAMUR ET IN MEDIA ARMA RUAMUS

The elder Heinsius incloses all the words from SI, the younger all from QUAE SIT, as far as STETERAT inclusive, in a parenthesis. Both, I think, incorrectly, and to the great detriment of the sense. It seems to me as plain as possible that EXCESSERE OMNES and SUCCURRITIS URBI INCENSAE are parts of one and the same description, viz. of the city deserted by its Gods and on fire. No commentator or editor should have found any difficulty in the passage, which is one of the clearest.

369.

PLURIMA MORTIS IMAGO

"Nothing afraid of what thyself didst make,
Strange images of death."

Macbeth, I. 3.

390.

DOLUS AN VIRTUS

"Das ist das Beste, was zum Ziele führt;
Und was gelungen ist, das ist auch rechtlich."

WERNER, *die Söhne des Thales,* Th. II. A. I. sc. 6.

391.

ARMA DABUNT IPSI

If, as hitherto supposed, IPSI mean *the persons whom Choroebus and his party are despoiling of their arms* ("Die Todten werden Waffen geben"— Schiller), the sentence ARMA DABUNT IPSI is a mere tautology, the same meaning being contained in the preceding 'mutemus clypeos' &c.; for, *let us exchange arms with these persons*, and *these persons shall supply us with arms*, are plainly but different ways of saying the same thing. I therefore refer IPSI to the Danaï; the enemy generally; and understand Choroebus's meaning to run thus: *Let us change shields &c. with these dead fellows here, and, by so doing, compel the Danaï, the invaders themselves* (IPSI), *to furnish us with arms.* The passage being so interpreted, there is, first, no tautology; and, secondly, IPSI has its proper, emphatic force.

The sentiment contained in ARMA DABUNT IPSI is familiar to us in the English proverbial expression, *furnish a rod to whip himself.*

392.

CLIPEIQUE INSIGNE DECORUM

INSIGNE, — *the ensign* or *device on the shield.* Compare:

— "Clipeoque insigne paternum
Centum angues cinctamque gerit serpentibus Hydram."
En. VII. 657.

"At levem clipeum sublatis cornibus Io
Auro insignibat, jam setis obsita, jam bos,
Argumentum ingens, et custos virginis Argus,
Caelataque amnem fundens pater Inachus urna."
En. VII. 789.

— "Clipei non enarrabile textum."
En. VIII. 625.

"Christus purpureum gemmanti textus in auro
Signabat labarum, clipeorum insignia Christus
Scripserat."
PRUDENT. *contr. Symm.* I. 487.

396.

HAUD NUMINE NOSTRO

I think that the structure is, not (with Forbiger and Heyne) numine — haud nostro i. e. *numine averso, non propitio*, but, haud — numine nostro, and that the meaning is, *not with our 'numen'*, i. e. *without our 'numen'; our 'numen' not accompanying us; forsaken by our 'numen'.* Compare exactly parallel (*En.* V. 56):

"Haud equidem sine mente reor, sine numine Divum;"

not without, i. e. *with*, the 'numen' of the Gods. Also (*En*. VIII. 627):

"Haud vatum ignarus, venturique inscius aevi;"

not only, *not ignorant of*, but *well skilled in*, the future.

There cannot, I think, be a doubt but that NUMINE is here to be understood precisely as in the corresponding passage above quoted from the fifth book, and that Servius's second explanation ("Aut quia in scutis Graecorum Neptunus, in Trojanorum fuerat Minerva depicta") is as unfounded, as it is unworthy of Virgil. See Comm. *v*. 178.

The reading in the oldest Gudian being, as I have ascertained by personal examination, 'nomine', a u has been placed over the o by a second hand, thus: 'nomine'.

401.

CONDUNTUR

'Condo' is (strictly), not merely *to hide*, but, the force of 'do' being preserved in its compound (see Comm. *En*. I. 56), *to put or plunge into a place so as to hide*. Hence it is sometimes even joined with a preposition governing the accusative:

"Sol quoque et exoriens, et cum se condet in undas."
Georg. I. 438.

"Ista, mi Lucili, condenda in animum sunt, ut contemnas voluptatem, ex plurium assensione venientem." SENEC. *Epist*. 7.

406.

LUMINA NAM TENERAS ARCEBANT VINCULA PALMAS

The translators understand the words VINCULA ARCEBANT to be equivalent to 'vincula ligabant', and to mean no more than that *chains bound her hands:*

"Her eyen, for fast her tender wrists were bound."
SURREY.

— "Rude fetters bound her tender hands."
BERESFORD.

"Che indegni lacci alla regal donzella
Ambe avvincon le mani."
ALFIERI.

On the contrary, the idea of binding does not extend beyond the word VINCULA; and ARCEBANT has its own proper force of *hindering, keeping away:* bonds (VINCULA) *hindered, kept off* (ARCEBANT) her hands, viz. so that she could not extend them towards heaven.

Our author had probably before his eyes his favorite model:

Αλλ' αντιαζω σ', ω γερον, των σων παρος
Πιτνουσα γονατων (χειρι δ' ουκ εξεστι μοι
Της σης λαβεσθαι φιλτατης γενειαδος)
EURIP. *Androm.* 573.

Our text has been imitated by St. Hieronymus in his marvellous *Mulier septies percussa:* "Oculis, quos tantum tortor alligare non potuit, suspexit ad coelum." *Epist. I. ad Innocent.* §. 3. Also by Ovid (*Metam.* I. 731):

"Quos potuit solos tollens ad sidera vultus;"

and (*Metam.* IV. 681):

— "Manibusque modestos
Celasset vultus, si non religata fuisset.
Lumina, quod potuit, lacrimis implevit obortis."

413.

TUM DANAI GEMITU ATQUE EREPTAE VIRGINIS IRA

Heyne's interpretation, "ira propter ereptam virginem," is proved to be correct, not only by the appropriate sense which it affords, but by our author's use elsewhere of a similar structure, *e. g.* 'Mortis fraternae ira', *En.* IX. 736; 'Grajarum errore jubarum', *v.* 412 above; 'veterum errore locorum', III. 181; 'ereptae amore conjugis', III. 330; also, 'lacrymae rerum', I. 466; and 'lacrymas Creusae', II. 784. For numerous examples of the use of this genitive by other authors, see Dederich on *Dictys Cretens. V.* 4.

GEMITU ATQUE IRA. — Prosaice, *an angry groan; groaning with anger.* IRA is the *feeling;* GEMITU, the *sound* (and, as appears not only from *En.* VII. 15, where the two words are again found united, 'gemitus iraeque leonum', but from *En.* II. 53; III. 555, the *loud sound* or *roar*) by which the *feeling* was expressed.

416.

ADVERSI RUPTO CEU QUONDAM TURBINE VENTI
CONFLIGUNT ZEPHYRUSQUE NOTUSQUE ET LAETUS EOIS
EURUS EQUIS STRIDUNT SILVAE SAEVITQUE TRIDENTI
SPUMEUS ATQUE IMO NEREUS CIET AEQUORA FUNDO

Compare Aeschyl. *Prom. Vinct.* (*v.* 1080, Ed. Blomfield), Prometheus speaking:

> "*Αιθηρ δ'*
> *Ερεθιζεσθω βροντῃ σκαφελῳ τ'*
> *Αγριων ανεμων· χθονα δ' εκ πυθμενων*
> *Αυταις ριζαις πνευμα κραδαινοι,*
> *Κυμα δε ποντου τραχει ροδιῳ*
> *Ξυγχωσειεν, των τ' ουρανιων*
> *Αστρων διοδους.*"

Also Dante, *Inferno*, V. 29:

"Che mugghia, come fa mar per tempesta,
Se da contrari venti e combattuto."

Also Sir Walter Scott in his fine Lyric, the Pibroch of Donald Dhu:

"Come as the winds come
When forests are rended,
Come as the waves come
When navies are stranded."

SAEVITQUE TRIDENTI SPUMEUS ATQUE IMO NEREUS CIET AEQUORA FUNDO. — The structure is, not 'spumeus Nereus saevit tridenti', but 'Nereus saevit tridenti spumeus', and the meaning is, produces a great deal of froth in the operation of stirring up the sea from the bottom with his trident. Compare *En.* XI. 624:

"Qualis ubi alterno procurrens gurgite pontus
Nunc ruit ad terras, scopulosque superjacit undam
Spumeus, extremamque sinu perfundit arenam;"

where, as in our text, 'spumcus' is placed in the emphatic position, and separated, by a pause, from the sequel.

In confirmation of the above interpretation I may add that there is (see Foggini) a point placed after SPUMEUS in the Medicean (see however Comments *v.* 420 and *En.* I. 122), that I have myself found a similar point in the Dresden, and that the comma after SPUMEUS, omitted by modern editors, is to be found in the best old Editions (with the exception of H. Stephens), viz. in the Modena Edition of 1475, in those of the two Heinsii, in Burmann, Brunck, Ambrogi, La Cerda and Bersmann, also in Alfieri and the Baskerville. In the Vatican Fragment (see Bottari) the whole passage is wanting, and, in the Roman, not only the whole passage, but almost the whole of the second Book.

420.

ILLI ETIAM SI QUOS OBSCURA NOCTE PER UMBRAM
FUDIMUS INSIDIIS TOTAQUE AGITAVIMUS URBE
APPARENT PRIMI CLIPEOS MENTITAQUE TELA
AGNOSCUNT ATQUE ORA SONO DISCORDIA SIGNANT

I find in Pierius: "In codicibus aliquot antiquis, eodem membro legas APPARENT PRIMI; disjunctim inde, CLIPEOS MENTITAQUE TELA ADGNOSCUNT. Donatus mavult PRIMI CLIPEOS."

The Medicean, at first sight, appears to sanction the junction of PRIMI with CLIPEOS, a point being interposed in that MS. (see Foggini) between APPARENT and PRIMI; but, as I have had occasion to remark elsewhere (Comm. *En.* I. 122), little is to be concluded from the punctuation either of that or any other ancient MS., the punctuation depending entirely on the arbitrement of their illiterate scribes; and least of all can any conclusion be drawn from the punctuation of the Medicean in the passage before us, the scribe having thought proper to place a point not only after APPARENT, but also after URBE and after CLIPEOS.

ORA SONO DISCORDIA SIGNANT. — SIGNANT, *remark* (compare *En.* V. 317), ORA, *our speech* (compare: "Quod tanta erat commendatio oris atque orationis, ut nemo ei dicendo posset resistere." NEP. in *Alcib.* I. 2, where see Bremi's Annot.; also: "Ego enim dabo vobis os [στομα] et sapientiam." Evang. sec. LUC. XXI. 15), DISCORDIA SONO, *disagreeing in sound*, viz. with our assumed appearance of Greeks, or perhaps simply, sounding differently from the Greek. Contrast Sil. Ital. XVII. 444:

— "Accendunt iras vultusque virorum
Armorumque habitus noti, et vox consona linguae."

432.

NEC TELA NEC ULLAS
VITAVISSE VICES DANAUM

On further consideration I am induced to withdraw the interpretation assigned by me to these words in the Classical Museum, No. XXIV, and quoted by Forbiger in his third Edition. 'Vices', I now think, corresponds exactly with our *turns*, the French *tours*, and the German *Wendungen.* Eneas braved, not only all the weapons, but all the turns, all the *military manoeuvres* of the Danai: and such appears to be the precise meaning of the word in the passages quoted by Forbiger: 'Belli tentare vices', STAT. *Theb.* X. 749. 'Belli vices novisse', SIL. III. 13. 'Martis vices', CLAUD. *IV. Cons. Honor.* 282; neither vicissitudes nor perils, but *evolutions* ('*tours*', Fr.), *tactics.* And so Ovid. *Metam.* XIV. 35:

— "Spernentem sperne, sequenti
Redde vices;"

return his tactics, pay him tit for tat. Compare also *Cul. v.* 209:

— "Acerbas
Cogor adire vices."

For a curious, I cannot say successful, attempt to connect the ancient Latin 'vix, vicis', with the πaξ of the Eleusinian Mysteries, and derive both from the 'Pakscha' of the Brahmins, see Wilford in the *Memoirs of the Asiatic Society*, vol. V, and Ouvaroff, *Etudes de Philologie.* St. Petersburg. 1843.

453.

LIMEN ERAT CAECAEQUE FORES ET PERVIUS USUS
TECTORUM INTER SE PRIAMI POSTESQUE RELICTI
A TERGO

"POSTES RELICTI A TERGO, h. e. porta, quae a tergo erat, opposita illi, quae est in aedium fronte." Heyne. No: A TERGO belongs, not specially to RELICTI, but to the whole sentence; thus: 'A tergo (aedium viz.) erat limen, caecaeque fores, et pervius usus tectorum'; i. e. *at the rear of the house there was an entrance through a secret door:* POSTESQUE RELICTI, *and this door, in the present confusion, was deserted — no longer frequented.*

POSTES RELICTI. — Compare: "Nihil rerum mortalium tam instabile ac fluxum est, quam fama potentiae non sua vi nixa. Statim relictum Agrippinae limen. Nemo solari, nemo adire". TACIT. *Annal.* XIII. 19. Also: "Sedesque astare relictas," *En.* III. 123.

A TERGO LIMEN ERAT &c. — Compare (Plin. *Epist.* II. 17. 5): "A tergo cavaedium, porticum, aream;" and (*Ibid.* 15): "Cingitur diaetis duabus a tergo;" and (*Ibid.* 21): "a pedibus mare, a tergo villae, a capite silvae."

PERVIUS USUS; — *a pervious use*, i. e. made use of as a passage.

458.

EVADO AD SUMMI FASTIGIA CULMINIS

'Evado' (e-vado), *go the whole way through, pass over the entire space* (whether *upward*, *downward*, or *on the level*), *so as to pass out on the far side;* and that, whether *physically*, as in the passage before us, and *En.* XII. 907, or *metaphorically*, as in Terent. *Adelph.* III. 4. 63:

— "Verum nimia illaec licentia
Profecto evadet in aliquod magnum malum;"

and *Andr.* I. 1. 100:

"Quam timeo quorsum evadas."

in both which passages the reference is to the ultimate event, the upshot.

Burmann, in his commentary on this passage, and Forcellini, in his dictionary, interpreting 'evado' by '*ascendo*', transfer to this verb a meaning wholly foreign to it, and contained only (incidentally) in the context.

460.

TURRIM IN PRAECIPITI STANTEM SUMMISQUE SUB ASTRA
EDUCTAM TECTIS UNDE OMNIS TROJA VIDERI
ET DANAUM SOLITAE NAVES ET ACHAIA CASTRA
AGGRESSI FERRO CIRCUM QUA SUMMA LABANTES
JUNCTURAS TABULATA DABANT CONVELLIMUS ALTIS
SEDIBUS IMPULIMUSQUE EA LAPSA REPENTE RUINAM
CUM SONITU TRAHIT ET DANAUM SUPER AGMINA LATE
INCIDIT

IN PRAECIPITI STANTEM. — "In editiore loco positam." Heyne. "In alto." Wagner. "In alto positam." Forbiger. I entirely dissent from this interpretation, first, because 'in praecipiti' never means '*in alto*', but always (not only in Virgil, but in all other Latin authors) *on the edge of a precipice*, or *in such a situation that a headlong fall would be easy and probable.* Secondly, because, if this interpretation be correct, Virgil has committed the double error, (*a*) of stating twice over that the turret was seated in a high situation (first in the words IN PRAECIPITI STANTEM, and then in the immediately succeeding words SUMMISQUE SUB ASTRA EDUCTAM TECTIS), and (*b*) of wholly omitting to state that it was seated (where it certainly must have been seated, or it could not have fallen headlong on the besiegers), viz. *on the edge of the roof, perpendicularly over the front wall.*

IN PRAECIPITI STANTEM being understood to mean *on*

the edge of the roof, the description of the turret becomes simple, clear, and vivid; it was SUMMIS TECTIS, *on the top of the house;* EDUCTAM SUB ASTRA, *raised to a great height above it;* IN PRAECIPITI STANTEM, *standing perpendicularly on the roof edge, above the wall of the palace.*

QUA SUMMA LABANTES JUNCTURAS TABULATA DABANT. — *Where the turret was connected with, and easily separable from, the terrace on the top of the palace.* Heyne and Wagner understand SUMMA TABULATA to mean *the highest story of the turret;* but, admitting that the turret had a number of stories, the Trojans could not have attacked round about with iron the highest story of a turret EDUCTAM SUB ASTRA, without ascending the turret; and having ascended, it seems impossible to comprehend how they could precipitate it on the Greeks, without precipitating themselves along with it; or indeed, how being in or on it, they could precipitate it at all. The words CONVELLIMUS and IMPULIMUS are, of themselves, sufficient to show that the Trojans stood on the roof of the palace, while they *tore up* the turret ALTIS SEDIBUS (*from its high seat*, viz. *on the top of the house*), and *pushed* it forward, so as to cause it to fall on the besiegers. SUMMA TABULATA, therefore, is the flat or terrace on the top of the house (*solarium*, see Palais de Scaurus XV), on which the turret stood. This flat or terrace being a floor (*Tafelwerk*, Germ.) is called TABULATA (see the application of the term by Servius, ad voc. 'Scenam' *En.* I. 168, even to an upright boarding, a perpendicular partition of boards), and being on the top of the house is called SUMMA.

JUNCTURAS what else but the connection or jointings of the tower to the flat terrace on which it stood?

I beg to propose the above interpretation of TABULATA in place of my previous interpretation (*Class. Mus.* XXIV), "the top story of the palace", to which I admit the justice of Forbiger's objection (see his third Edition) that the houses of the ancients had but one story. On the other hand I have found since the above Comment was written, that Forbiger has in his third Edition paid me the compliment of adopting my explanation of IN PRAECIPITI STANTEM, in place of his own previous explanation quoted above.

INCIDIT. — See Comm. *v.* 246 and 505.

471.

QUALIS UBI IN LUCEM COLUBER MALA GRAMINA PASTUS
FRIGIDA SUB TERRA TUMIDUM QUEM BRUMA TEGEBAT
NUNC POSITIS NOVUS EXUVIIS NITIDUSQUE JUVENTA
LUBRICA CONVOLVIT SUBLATO PECTORE TERGA
ARDUUS AD SOLEM ET LINGUIS MICAT ORE TRISULCIS

I doubt if the almost dazzling beauty of this simile considered as a separate and independent picture, is more to be admired than its perfect suitableness and correspondence in every particular to the object which it illustrates. The serpent has lain underground all winter: Pyrrhus, hitherto in abeyance, has not until this moment appeared before Troy. The serpent, poisonless while underground, shows now the first indications of his newly acquired venom (see below): Pyrrhus, hitherto but a boy, and therefore neither dangerous nor dreaded, presents himself for the first time as a formidable warrior and virulent enemy. The serpent, fresh and young and vigorous and agile, lifts his head and breast erect towards the sun, coils his folds, and shimmers with his three-forked tongue: Pyrrhus, no less fresh and young and vigorous and agile, exults and sparkles and flashes in the brazen light of his brandished weapons.

That the comparison is of Pyrrhus hitherto concealed and now at long and last appearing, is evident not only from the emphatic position of the word NUNC (see Comm. *v.* 246), but from Sil. Ital. XII. 6, where the precisely same comparison is applied to Hannibal all the winter shut up in Capua and taking the field again in summer:

— "Ceu condita bruma,
Dum Rhipaea rigent Aquilonis flamina, tandem
Evolvit serpens arcano membra cubili,
Et splendente die novus emicat, atque coruscum
Fert caput, et saniem sublatis faucibus efflat."

MALA GRAMINA PASTUS. — These words are added neither 'otiose', nor yet merely for the sake of heightening the picture, but with a strict regard to the natural history of the serpent, which the ancients supposed to be poisonless during its quiescent state in the winter, and to acquire its poison in spring from certain herbs which it used to eat on leaving its retreat: "omnia secessus tempore veneno orba dormiunt." PLIN. VIII. 59. That this doctrine is, though perhaps too indistinctly to be at once perceptible by us, uninitiated, of modern times, yet certainly contained in Virgil's MALA GRAMINA PASTUS, appears from Statius's imitation:

— "Ceu lubricus alta
Anguis humo verni blanda ad spiramina solis
Erigitur liber senio, et squalentibus annis
Exutus, laetisque minax interviret herbis;
Ah miser, agrestum si quis per gramen hianti
Obvius, et primo siccaverit ora veneno."
STAT. *Theb.* IV. 95.

The structure of the whole passage is of the very simplest; the sentence begun at QUALIS being broken off abruptly at TEGEBAT, and a new sentence begun at NUNC; and IN LUCEM depending neither on the preceding EXULTAT, nor the subsequent CONVOLVIT, but on the verb which was to have followed, if the author had carried on to the end the sentence which he has left unfinished at TEGEBAT. A dash should be placed after TEGEBAT (thus, TEGEBAT —) in order to indicate that such is the structure. See Comm. *En.* I. 220 (Pag. 82).

The punctuation adopted by Brunck and Wagner converts the passage, from one of the simplest into one of the most awkward and perplexed imaginable: "Post TERGA distingui debuit commate. Jungenda enim sunt in lucem convolvit terga." Brunck. "Post TEGEBAT commate tantum interpunxi; distinxi, Brunckium et cod. Medic. secutus, etiam post TERGA; IN LUCEM autem, eodem Brunckio auctore, jungo cum verbo CONVOLVIT." Wagner, *V. L. ad Edit. Heyn.* Heyne though punctuating better, makes by his interpretation a similar hodgepodge of the passage: "IN LUCEM trahendum aut ad EXULTAT, aut ad CONVOLVIT; utrumque parum commode."

479.

IPSE INTER PRIMOS CORREPTA DURA BIPENNI
LIMINA PERRUMPIT POSTESQUE A CARDINE VELLIT
AERATOS JAMQUE EXCISA TRABE FIRMA CAVAVIT
ROBORA ET INGENTEM LATO DEDIT ORE FENESTRAM
APPARET DOMUS INTUS ET ATRIA LONGA PATESCUNT
APPARENT PRIAMI ET VETERUM PENETRALIA REGUM
ARMATOSQUE VIDENT STANTES IN LIMINE PRIMO
AT DOMUS INTERIOR GEMITU MISEROQUE TUMULTU
MISCETUR PENITUSQUE CAVAE PLANGORIBUS AEDES
FEMINEIS ULULANT FERIT AUREA SIDERA CLAMOR
TUM PAVIDAE TECTIS MATRES INGENTIBUS ERRANT
AMPLEXAEQUE TENENT POSTES ATQUE OSCULA FIGUNT
INSTAT VI PATRIA PYRRHUS NEC CLAUSTRA NEQUE IPSI
CUSTODES SUFFERRE VALENT LABAT ARIETE CREBRO
JANUA ET EMOTI PROCUMBUNT CARDINE POSTES
FIT VIA VI RUMPUNT ADITUS PRIMOSQUE TRUCIDANT
IMMISSI DANAI ET LATE LOCA MILITE COMPLENT

All commentators and translators divide this narrative into two distinct parts, making a new paragraph begin at AT DOMUS INTERIOR, and considering the words,

LIMINA PERRUMPIT, POSTESQUE A CARDINE VELLIT
AERATOS,

as descriptive, not of the actual and successful bursting in of the doors, but merely of an attempt to burst them in, which attempt does not succeed until *v.* 492,

LABAT ARIETE CREBRO
JANUA, ET EMOTI PROCUMBUNT CARDINE POSTES.

Heyne's words are: "A CARDINE VELLIT: movet, labefactat, e cardine ut amoveat annititur. Nunc enim adhuc de conatu agitur."

Now this is not according to the usual method of Virgil, who never begins with a hint or shadow of what is about to happen, and then brings gradually forward the event, but on the contrary always places the event full before the eyes first, and then goes back and explains by what means it has been brought about, and then, as it were in a peroration, recapitulates with a re-statement of the event, fuller and grander than at first. And such is the method he has adopted on the present occasion. Having given the brilliant picture of Pyrrhus and his comrades which is contained in the verses 'Vestibulum . . . . jactant', he informs us that Pyrrhus himself (IPSE) at the head of his comrades seizes an axe, bursts through (PER-RUMPIT) the doors, and forces the valves from the hinges. The event, i. e. the complete and successful forcing of the door, is thus in as few words as possible laid before the eyes of the reader. But this could not be done in a moment — required successive steps, which the poet now sets about to describe particularly. First, with the axe Pyrrhus cuts a panel out of the door:

JAMQUE EXCISA TRABE FIRMA CAVAVIT
ROBORA, ET INGENTEM LATO DEDIT ORE FENESTRAM.

This is the first step and is attended by consequences which are described before any mention is made of the second step; the consequences are:

(1) APPARET DOMUS INTUS, ET ATRIA LONGA PATESCUNT;
APPARENT PRIAMI ET VETERUM PENETRALIA REGUM;
ARMATOSQUE VIDENT STANTES IN LIMINE PRIMO.

(2) AT DOMUS INTERIOR GEMITU MISEROQUE TUMULTU
MISCETUR, PENITUSQUE CAVAE PLANGORIBUS AEDES
FEMINEIS ULULANT; FERIT AUREA SIDERA CLAMOR.

TUM PAVIDAE TECTIS MATRES INGENTIBUS ERRANT,
AMPLEXAEQUE TENENT POSTES, ATQUE OSCULA FIGUNT.

The first step and its consequences described, the next step follows:

INSTAT VI PATRIA PYRRHUS; NEC CLAUSTRA,

(viz. the 'claustra' in which he had already made the opening or window with the axe,)

NEQUE IPSI
CUSTODES SUFFERRE VALENT: LABAT ARIETE CREBRO
JANUA, ET EMOTI PROCUMBUNT CARDINE POSTES.

(i. e. the battering ram is brought, and the doors levelled with the ground,) and thus the reader put in full possession of all the particulars necessary to be gone through (and which were actually gone through) in the performance of the act described at *v.* 480 as already performed. This done (and the peroration or winding up made, in the words EMOTI PROCUMBUNT CARDINE POSTES, which it will be observed are only a stronger enunciation of the previously enounced fact, *v.* 480), our author proceeds with the description of the consequences of this fact:

FIT VIA VI: RUMPUNT ADITUS, PRIMOSQUE TRUCIDANT
IMMISSI DANAI, ET LATE LOCA MILITE COMPLENT:

the whole body of Danai burst in, butcher all they meet, and fill the house with soldiers.

Nothing can be more complete and vivid than this picture, nothing more in conformity with Virgil's usual method of painting; on the contrary, nothing more confused and ill imagined, nothing less like Virgil's usual style of painting, than the picture divided into two by the break placed by commentators and translators at PRIMO, and the commencement of a new paragraph at AT DOMUS INTERIOR.

POSTES . . . CARDINE. — The 'postes' of the Romans were (as clearly appears from Lucretius III. 370;

"Praeterea si pro foribus sunt lumina nostra,
Jam magis exemptis oculis debere videtur
Cernere res animus, sublatis postibus ipsis,")

the door itself, which, being always double, i. e. having

two valves meeting in the middle, was expressed by a noun plural. These valves were not fastened either to a door-case, or to the wall of the house or building, but stood in the opening quite detached, and moved on pivots ('cardinibus'), one of which was inserted into the threshold, the other into the lintel. The word 'postes' has passed into the Italian in the form of 'Imposte': "Imposta, Legname che serve a chiudere l'uscio." Voc. Della Crusca.

AERATOS . . . ROBORA. — Observe the effect of these words, placed each in the emphatic position at the commencement of the verse, and separated from the sequel by a pause. VELLIT AERATOS, *tears them down although plated with bronze:* CAVAVIT ROBORA, *scooped out an opening in the door although made of the hardest wood.*

AT DOMUS INTERIOR. — AT contrasts the DOMUS INTERIOR (observe the comparative degree; *farther in*) and what is there happening, not with what is going on at or outside the door i. e. not with the bursting in of Pyrrhus and his comrades, but with the just mentioned DOMUS INTUS (observe the positive degree: *just inside*), ATRIA LONGA, PENETRALIA REGUM, and ARMATOS STANTES IN LIMINE PRIMO. If a contrast with what was going on outside — with the bursting open of the door — had been intended, the word 'interea' would have been added to AT DOMUS INTERIOR.

ATRIA LONGA . . . . DOMUS INTERIOR . . . . CAVAE AEDES. — The two main parts or divisions of which a Roman house consisted (for the plan is taken from a Roman, not a Grecian or Asiatic, house), are here indicated with great distinctness; the front part consisting mainly of the 'atrium', in the words ATRIA LONGA; the inner or back part, the 'cavaedium', in the words CAVAE AEDES. See Becker's *Gallus*, vol. II. The double expression, INTERIOR DOMUS, CAVAE AEDES, reduced to plain prose, becomes the inner or back rooms, that is to say, those surrounding the 'cavaedium' or inner court.

AEDES ULULANT. — "Heule Thor, schreye Stadt!" JESAIA, XIV. 31. (Luther's Bibel.)

AUREA SIDERA. — Compare:

— "Tu proba
Perambulabis astra sidus aureum."
HOR. *Epqd.* 17. 40.

— "Wenn morgen sich die Sterne
Vergolden, Philipp, bin ich fern von dir."
WERNER, *die Söhne des Thales*, Th. I. Act IV. sc. 2.

"Sterne mit den goldnen Füsschen
Wandeln droben bang und sacht,
Dass sie nicht die Erde wecken,
Die da schläft im Schoos der Nacht."
H. HEINE, *neue Gedichte.*

"Wozu sind all die Stern' am Himmel nur gemacht?
Mit goldnem Flitter wol zu schmücken unsre Nacht?"
RUECKERT, *die Weisheit des Brahmanen*, XVII. 44.

496.

NON SIC AGGERIBUS RUPTIS QUUM SPUMEUS AMNIS
EXIT OPPOSITASQUE EVICIT GURGITE MOLES
FERTUR IN ARVA FURENS CUMULO CAMPOSQUE PER OMNES
CUM STABULIS ARMENTA TRAHIT

"Then David said, God hath broken in upon mine enemies by mine hand, like the breaking forth of waters." *I. Chron.* XIV. 11.

"Jene gewaltigen Wetterbäche,
Aus des Hagels unendlichen Schlossen,
Aus den Wolkenbrüchen zusammengeflossen,
Kommen finster gerauscht und geschossen,
Reissen die Brücken und reissen die Dämme
Donnernd mit fort im Wogengeschwemme,
Nichts ist, das die Gewaltigen hemme."
SCHILLER, *Braut von Messina.*

505.

PROCUBUERE

Observe the effect of the emphatic position of this word at the beginning of the verse, and separated from the sequel by a complete and sudden pause. Compare: 'Incidit', *v.* 467; and see Comm. *v.* 246.

507.

CONVULSAQUE VIDIT
LIMINA TECTORUM

CONVULSA. — Viz. 'a sedibus suis'. Compare: "Ac mihi domus ipsa nutare, convulsaque sedibus suis, ruitura supra videtur." PLIN. *Epist.* VII. 19.

521.

NON TALI AUXILIO NEC DEFENSORIBUS ISTIS
TEMPUS EGET NON SI IPSE MEUS NUNC AFFORET HECTOR

NON TALI AUXILIO NEC DEFENSORIBUS ISTIS. — The commentators and translators refer these words to Priam; "DEFENSORIBUS ISTIS, *qualis tu es.*" Forbiger. This is undoubtedly erroneous; for,

First, it is incredible that the exquisite judgment of Virgil would put into the mouth of Hecuba, on such an occasion, words contemptuous of, and offensive to, the aged king, her husband; TALI AUXILIO, *such help as thine;* DEFENSORIBUS ISTIS, *such defenders as thee*, *forsooth!*

Secondly, the passage so understood is utterly inconsistent with the subsequent NON SI IPSE MEUS NUNC AFFORET HECTOR; for the presence of Hector could not render the puny assistance of Priam in the least degree more useful.

Thirdly, the contrast between the assistance brought by Priam, and that assistance, which alone Hecuba considered as of any use, viz. the protection of the altar, is not sufficiently striking.

I therefore refer TALI AUXILIO . . . . DEFENSORIBUS ISTIS to TELIS in the preceding line; so understood, the words are (*a*) perfectly void of offence towards Priam; (*b*) harmonise with NON SI IPSE MEUS NUNC AFFORET HECTOR, the meaning being that arms are now useless, even although Hector himself were here to use them; and (*c*) afford a stronger sense, in as much as the protection of arms contrasts, more strongly than the protection of Priam, with the protection afforded by the altar. Compare Aeschyl. *Supplices*, *v.* 191:

> "*Αμεινον εστι παντος εινεκ', ω κοραι,*
> *Παγον προσιζειν τωνδ' αγωνιων θεων.*
> *Κρεισσον δε πυργου βωμος, αρρηκτον σακος.*"

And Shakespeare, *Coriol.* I. 2:

> — "For the dearth,
> The Gods, not the Patricians make it; and
> Your knees to them, not arms, must help."

Also Stat. *Theb.* IV. 200:

> "Non haec apta mihi nitidis ornatibus, inquit,
> Tempora, nec miserae placent insignia formae
> Te sine, sed dubium coetu solante timorem
> Fallere, et incultos aris adverrere crines."

Also Virgil himself, *En.* VI. 37:

> "Non hoc ista sibi tempus spectacula poscit."

In confirmation of this view, it will be observed that in the description which Virgil has given of Priam, in the immediately preceding verses, it is not so much the mere imbecility of the old man, which he wishes to place before our eyes, as the more affecting picture of that imbecility clothed in, and attempting to wield, arms:

> "A r m a diu senior d e s u e t a trementibus aevo
> Circumdat nequidquam humeris."

And so Hecuba:

"Ipsum autem sumtis Priamum juvenilibus armis
Ut vidit: Quae mens tam dira, miserrime conjux,
Impulit his cingi telis? aut quo ruis? inquit;
Non tali auxilio nec defensoribus istis (viz. istis telis)
Tempus eget."

For examples of 'defensor' applied to an inanimate object see Caes. *de B. G.* IV. 17: "Sublicae et ad inferiorem partem fluminis obliquae adigebantur, ... et aliae item supra pontem ..., ut si arborum trunci, sive naves, dejiciendi operis caussa essent a barbaris missae, his defensoribus earum vis minueretur;" and Claud. *in Rufin.* I. 79:

— "Haec (viz. Megaera) terruit Herculis ora,
Et defensores terrarum polluit arcus."

I crave the pardon of our parliamentary orators for an explanation which shows in what utter ignorance of their true meaning these words are used vituperatively.

529.

ILLUM ARDENS INFESTO VULNERE PYRRHUS
INSEQUITUR JAM JAMQUE MANU TENET ET PREMIT HASTA
UT TANDEM ANTE OCULOS EVASIT ET ORA PARENTUM
CONCIDIT AC MULTO VITAM CUM SANGUINE FUDIT

"PREMIT HASTA, i. e. ferit." Burmann. "PREMIT HASTA, exquisitius quam transfigit. Proprie premit hasta is qui ea transfigit aliquem, ἐρειδόμενος." Heyne. "Durchbohrt ihn mit der Lanze." Ladewig.

I think not; for the following reasons:

First, because in the immediately following words, UT TANDEM ANTE OCULOS EVASIT &c. we are informed that Polites continued to run, which he could not have done, had he been 'pressus hasta' in the above sense, such an expression, if meaning transfixed at all, necessarily meaning transfixed in such a manner as to be entirely overcome, and rendered incapable of doing any thing.

Secondly, because in all the instances with which I am acquainted of 'premere' applied to a fugitive, it means simply, *presses hard*, *hunts* or *drives to extremity:*

— "Apri cursum clamore prementem."
En. I. 328.

"Male rem gerere Darium premique ab Scythis." Nep. *Milt.* III. 3, where Bremi: "Premere und urgere werden häufig von dem gesagt, welcher einen *so in die Enge treibt, dass man sich nicht mehr helfen kann, welcher einem hart zusetzt.*" So also Nep. *Them.* III. 3; *Datam.* VII. 3; *Hannib.* XI. 5. And above all compare Virgil himself, *En.* XI. 545, of Metabus pressed hard by the weapons of the Volsci, when he was fleeing with his daughter Camilla in his arms:

— "Tela undique saeva premebant
Et circumfuso volitabant milite Volsci."

Thirdly, because, similar to Virgil's use of 'premere' in connexion with INSEQUITUR, is Horace's use of the same word in connexion with 'sequitur', in a passage where it can only mean *presses hard:*

"Jam vino quaerens, jam somno fallere curam;
Frustra; nam comes atra premit, sequiturque fugacem."
Satyr. II. 7. 114.

I therefore consider PREMIT in our text to be added to INSEQUITUR, as in the Horatian verse to 'sequitur', not as a new and independent, but as a supplemental, clause, in order to fill up and complete the otherwise imperfect sense: *not only follows him, but presses him hard.* We have thus an explanation why Virgil uses the remarkable expression INSEQUITUR VULNERE; viz. because he is about to complete the sentence with PREMIT HASTA: *follows him with a wound* or *blow* (compare: "Multa viri nequicquam inter se vulnera jactant," *En.* V. 433) *and presses him hard with his spear* — i. e. (VULNERE being explained and completed by HASTA, and INSEQUITUR by PREMIT) *follows him and presses him hard with his spear uplifted and ready to run him through.* The picture then is of the mortally wounded Polites, thus pursued by his enemy with uplifted spear, just arriving in his parents' presence (UT TANDEM ANTE OCULOS &c.), and there dropping down dead — a picture, not only much more pathetic than that afforded by the Heynian interpretation (in as much as Polites is represented as carrying with him during his race, not a slight or trifling, but a deadly and mortal, wound), but of a more unusual kind, the fatal wound being inflicted not within view of the audience, but before the victim makes his appearance on the stage.

It seems almost unnecessary to add that JAM JAMQUE (correctly rendered by Forbiger '*jeden Augenblick*') belongs entirely to TENET and not at all to PREMIT HASTA; also that the clause JAM JAMQUE MANU TENET is parenthetic, and should be separated from ET PREMIT HASTA by a comma.

Compare the picture of the stag pressed similarly close by the hound, *En.* XII. 753:

> — "At vividus Umber
> Haeret hians, jam jamque tenet, similisque tenenti
> Increpuit malis, morsuque elusus inani est."

VULNERE . . . HASTA. — The prosaic 'vulnere hastae', as Hor. *Carm.* I. 27. 11. 'vulnere . . . . sagitta', the prosaic 'vulnere sagittae'.

EVASIT. — See Comm. *v.* 458.

CONCIDIT. — *Falls down all at once and* (as we say) *of a heap;* differs from 'procumbit', which is to lie stretched at full length:

> — "Ante aras ingens ubi victima taurus
> Concidit, abrupta cruor e cervice profusus."
> OVID. *Met.* VIII. 763.

> "Concidit Ancaeus; glomerataque sanguine multo" &c.
> OVID. *Met.* VIII. 401.

533.

HIC PRIAMUS QUAMQUAM IN MEDIA JAM MORTE TENETUR
NON TAMEN ABSTINUIT NEC VOCI IRAEQUE PEPERCIT
AT TIBI PRO SCELERE EXCLAMAT PRO TALIBUS AUSIS
DI SI QUA EST CAELO PIETAS QUAE TALIA CURET

In media morte. — "Inter ipsa mortis confinia." Ammian. XXXI. 13.

At tibi. — I agree entirely with Forbiger in his argument against Wagner, *Quaest. Virg.* XXXVII. 5, that at is here nothing more than a part of the ordinary formula of imprecation. See Hildebrand ad *Apul. Metam.* I. 1, and III. 23.

Si qua est caelo pietas. — There needs no further proof than this single passage, how entirely different the 'pietas' of the Romans was from our piety, how totally opposite 'pius Aeneas' to pious Eneas. See Comments *En.* I. 14 and 607.

545.

RAUCO QUOD PROTINUS AERE REPULSUM
ET SUMMO CLIPEI NEQUICQUAM UMBONE PEPENDIT

Rauco — the ordinary adjunct (compare:

— "An Mauri fremitum raucosque repulsus
Umbonum, et vestros passuri comminus enses?"
Claud. *Bell. Gild.* 433.),

expresses in this case rather the weakness than the strength of the stroke; as if Virgil had said: *made the shield ring, but was unable to penetrate.*

552.

DEXTRAQUE CORUSCUM
EXTULIT AC LATERI CAPULO TENUS ABDIDIT ENSEM

Ensem belongs to both verbs, coruscum only to extulit. Extulit (ensem) coruscum, because the very act of raising and florishing the sword made it flash; abdidit ensem (no longer coruscum), because the very act of plunging it (or stowing it away, see Comm. *En.* I, 56) into the side, caused it to cease to flash.

If it be not mere supererogation to refer to instances of a similar beautiful accuracy of language in a writer, whose language is always super-eminently accurate, I would here refer the reader to the special apposition of 'bellatrix' to 'aurea cingula', and of 'virgo' to 'viris', *En.* I, 497; to the junction of 'Fortuna' with the two verbs 'finxit' and 'finget', and of 'improba' with the latter only, *En.* II, 80; to the similar junction of 'interclusit' and 'terruit' with 'illos', and of 'terruit' alone with 'euntes', *En.* II, 110; and to the precise 'intorserit hastam', 'laeserit cuspide', *En.* II, 230; also to Comm. *v.* 270 and *v.* 689.

554.

HAEC FINIS PRIAMI FATORUM HIC EXITUS ILLUM
SORTE TULIT TROJAM INCENSAM ET PROLAPSA VIDENTEM
PERGAMA TOT QUONDAM POPULIS TERRISQUE SUPERBUM
REGNATOREM ASIAE JACET INGENS LITTORE TRUNCUS
AVULSUMQUE HUMERIS CAPUT ET SINE NOMINE CORPUS

So Ammianus Marcellinus (XIV. 11) finely, of Constantius Gallus Caesar:— "Cervice abscissa, ereptaque vultus et capitis dignitate, cadaver relictum est informe, paullo ante urbibus et provinciis formidatum."

Sine nomine corpus. — "Post totum ignobilitatis elogium, caducae in originem terram, et cadaveris nomen; et de isto quoque nomine periturae, in nullum inde jam nomen, in omnis jam vocabuli mortem." Tertull. *de resurr. carnis, IV.*

The same thought has been beautifully expanded by Bossuet; Oraison funebr. de Mad. Henriette Anne d'Angleterre: "La voilà, malgré ce grand coeur, cette Princesse si admirée et si chérie; la voila telle que la mort nous l'a faite; encore ce reste tel quel va-t-il disparoitre (etiam periere ruinae) . . . La mort ne nous laisse pas assez de corps pour occuper quelque place; et on ne voit la que les tombeaux qui fassent quelque figure. Notre chair change bientôt de nature; notre corps prend un autre nom; même celui de cadavre, dit Tertullian, ne lui demeure pas longtemps: il devient un je ne scais quoi, qui n'a plus de nom en aucune langue; tant il est vrai que tout meurt en lui, jusqu'à ces termes funèbres par lesquels on exprimoit ses malheureux restes."

571.

ILLA SIBI INFESTOS EVERSA OB PERGAMA TEUCROS
ET POENAS DANAUM ET DESERTI CONJUGIS IRAS
PRAEMETUENS

Praemetuens, — "Fürchtete." Voss. "Temendo." Caro. "Dreads." Dryden. All omitting the prae, the force of which is, that her fear anticipated the anger — that she fled without waiting to see whether her fear were well founded or not. Compare:

> "Ovem rogabat cervus modium tritici,
> Lupo sponsore. At illa, praemetuens dolum" &c.
> Phaedr. I. 16. 3.

574.

ATQUE ARIS INVISA SEDEBAT

Invisa, — "Unbemerkt." Ladewig. No; but, as always elsewhere in Virgil, '*odiosa*', *the hateful one*, and therefore 'praemetuens' (*v.* 573) not without reason. That this is the true import of the word, seems to be placed beyond doubt by *v.* 601: "Tyndaridis facies invisa Lacaenae."

583.

NAMQUE ETSI NULLUM MEMORABILE NOMEN
FEMINEA IN POENA EST NEC HABET VICTORIA LAUDEM
EXSTINXISSE NEFAS TAMEN ET SUMSISSE MERENTIS
LAUDABOR POENAS ANIMUMQUE EXPLESSE JUVABIT
ULTRICIS FLAMMAE ET CINERES SATIASSE MEORUM

In the exact coincidence of the sentiments here expressed by Eneas, with those expressed by Aruns when meditating the death of Camilla (*En.* XI. 790 and seq.), Burmann and Heyne might have found a strong additional argument for the authenticity of this fine passage concerning Helen. The reader will, however, observe that the poet, although he has assigned similar sentiments to his hero and the coward Aruns while meditating similar acts, has been careful to draw a sufficiently broad distinction between the actual conduct of the one and that of the other. The hero is immediately diverted from, and relinquishes, his hasty purpose; the coward persists in, and coolly executes, his deliberately formed plan.

591.

CONFESSA DEAM

Jocularly imitated by Petronius: "Modo Bromium, interdum Lyaeum, Euhyumque confessus." P. 143.

608.

HIC UBI DISJECTAS MOLES AVULSAQUE SAXIS
SAXA VIDES MIXTOQUE UNDANTEM PULVERE FUMUM
NEPTUNUS MUROS MAGNOQUE EMOTA TRIDENTI
FUNDAMENTA QUATIT TOTAMQUE A SEDIBUS URBEM
ERUIT HIC JUNO SCAEAS SAEVISSIMA PORTAS
PRIMA TENET SOCIUMQUE FURENS A NAVIBUS AGMEN
FERRO ACCINCTA VOCAT
JAM SUMMAS ARCES TRITONIA RESPICE PALLAS
INSEDIT LIMBO EFFULGENS ET GORGONE SAEVA
IPSE PATER DANAIS ANIMOS VIRESQUE SECUNDAS
SUFFICIT IPSE DEOS IN DARDANA SUSCITAT ARMA

With this fine picture of the Gods giving their personal help towards the destruction of a city, compare the historical narrative: "Adjicitur miraculum, velut numine oblatum; nam cuncta extra, tectis tenus, sole illustria fuere: quod moenibus cingebatur, ita repente atra nube coopertum, fulguribusque discretum est, ut, quasi infensantibus Deis, exitio tradi crederetur." TACIT. *Ann.* XIII. 41.

Independently of the defence, of which Virgil's account of the taking of Troy is otherwise capable (see Comm. *v.* 5), the poet, calling in the hostile Gods, and even Jupiter himself, to aid in the taking and destruction of the city, already (*v.* 351) deserted by its own Gods, seems to be invulnerably armed against the assaults of those critics, who, with Napoleon at their head (see

Comm. *v.* 5), insist that his whole narrative is unstrategical, incredible, impossible.

PRIMA. — *The principal personage, the leader, the mover of the whole matter, 'princeps'.* As Juno, although thus expressly stated to be the leader, the mover of the whole matter (i. e. of the destruction of the city), is yet not mentioned first in order, but placed in the middle between Neptune and Pallas, so Machaon (*v.* 263), also stated to be the 'primus', the mover of the whole matter, the principal actor, or taking the principal part among those enclosed in the wooden horse, is not mentioned first in order, but seventh, or nearly last. The same term 'prima', in the same sense and in a very similar connection, is applied to the same Juno, *En.* I. 27:

> — "Veterisque memor Saturnia belli,
> Prima quod ad Trojam pro caris gesserat Argis."

It is in the same sense also that the same term is applied to Eneas himself, *En.* I. 5:

> — "Trojae qui primus ab oris
> Italiam fato profugus Lavinaque venit
> Littora;"

the principal mover, principal actor, (Germ. 'Urheber',) of the emigration from Troy to Italy; an interpretation perfectly consistent, first, with the fact that Antenor arrived in Italy prior in point of time to Eneas, because Eneas though the 'primus', the 'Urheber', the mover of the whole emigration, and the person who set the example to Antenor, yet, just because he was the principal personage, the principal mover, had special obstacles thrown in his way (these very obstacles being themselves the subject of the poem) which delayed his arrival in Italy until after the arrival of Antenor and those others, who, in undertaking the emigration, had only imitated him, and followed his example; and secondly, this interpretation meets with no contradiction from the words 'Lavinaque littora', the force of the word 'primus' being entirely spent on 'Trojae ab oris Italiam'; of which words 'Lavinaque littora' are but the complement, added for the sole purpose of informing the reader in what precise spot this 'primus', 'princeps', or prime mover of the Trojan emigration to Italy, had actually settled; as if Virgil had said: *Qui profugus ab oris Trojae venit primus ad Italiam, ibique in Lavino littore consedit.*

ARCES PALLAS INSEDIT. — It is with peculiar propriety that Pallas is represented as taking possession of the 'arx', the 'arx' having been her invention, and always (not alone at Troy, but elsewhere) her selected abode. Compare:

— "Pallas, quas condidit arces,
Ipsa colat."
Ecl. II. 61.

"Et Pandionias quae cuspide protegit arces."
CLAUD. *de Rapt. Pros.* II. 19.

"Diva . . . retinens in summis urbibus arces."
CATULL. LXIV. 8.

RESPICE, — not merely *look*, or *see*, but *look behind thee:* 'aspice' (*v.* 604), *look here before thee*, 'respice', *look there behind thee.* Observe also the effective position of the word immediately before the object to which it points, PALLAS; and immediately after the words exciting expectation, JAM SUMMAS ARCES TRITONIA. See Comm. *v.* 203.

LIMBO EFFULGENS ET GORGONE SAEVA. — I have myself personally examined only five MSS. with respect to this passage, viz. the oldest Gudian (No. 70), the two Leipzig, the Dresden, and No. 113 (Endlicher's Catal.) in the royal Library at Vienna, but in the whole five I have found 'nimbo', which (see Foggini) is also the reading of the Medicean, and has been adopted without hesitation or exception, so far as I know, by all the editors and commentators. The explanation which the elder commentators have given us of this word, is *halo* ("nube divina", Servius, La Cerda), against which the objection of Forbiger: "hic voc. nimbi significatus non nisi cadentis Latinitatis," seems to me to be conclusive. The more modern explanation of the word is that adopted by Heyne from Pomponius Sabinus: "nubes obscura qua illa cingitur;" the effulgence of such obscure 'nubes' being ascribed by Heyne to its reflexion of Pallas's aegis, "fulgentem aegidem tenet, a qua relucet nimbus," and by Wagner to its reflexion of the flames of the burning city, "nimbus igitur ille, quem ut iratae deae atrum fuisse consentaneum est, fulgebat et rutilabat ab incendii flammis," an interpretation which has been adopted, and approved of, by Forbiger.

I object, first, that 'nimbus' is never 'nubes', but always that combination of darkness, heavy rain (or hail), wind, thunder and lightning, called in Germany *Gewitter*, and in Italy *temporale*, but for which the English language possesses no more appropriate appellation than *thunderstorm*. See (*En.* V. 317):

"Effusi nimbo similes," —

poured out, surely not *like a cloud*, but *like a thunderstorm*, *a sudden shower of heavy rain.*

— "Toto sonuerunt aethere nimbi."
En. II. 113.

Not, *clouds resounded over the whole sky*, but *thunderstorms resounded.*

— "Insequitur commixta grandine nimbus."
En. IV. 161.

Not, *a cloud mixed with hail*, or *a hail cloud*, *follows*, but *a hailstorm*, *a shower of hail*, *follows.*

"His ego nigrantem commixta grandine nimbum
. . . .
Desuper infundam."
En. IV. 120.

Not, *I will pour a cloud mixed with hail on them*, but *a hailstorm on them.*

Secondly, that there appears no reason, and no reason has ever been assigned, why Pallas should have a 'nimbus' (whether understood to mean a cloud, or a storm) about her on this occasion. Such appendage had been equally useless, either for the purpose of inspiring terror, or for the purpose of concealment, she being (in common with the other Gods introduced on the occasion, and who it will be observed, had no 'nimbi') invisible to all human eyes except those of Eneas alone, from which Venus had miraculously taken away 'omnem nubem quae mortales hebetat visus,' and so rendered them capable of seeing the invisible.

Thirdly, that Pallas could not correctly be represented as 'effulgens nimbo', whether the word be understood to mean (according to Heyne's erroneous definition of it) '*nubes obscura*', or (according to that which I have shown is its only true interpretation), *Gewitter, temporale, thundershower, thunderstorm*, unless we admit the propriety of the expression (in the former case) effulgent with darkness, and (in the latter) effulgent with the obscure cloak in which Gods were used sometimes for particular purposes to wrap themselves up, and hide themselves from observation; compare

— "Venus, obscuro faciem circumdata nimbo."
En. XII. 416.

— "Agens hiemem, nimbo succincta per auras."
En. X. 634.

Despairing therefore of obtaining any good sense from the reading 'nimbo', I look (as in the case of the unintelligible, received reading 'nexaeque' *En.* I. 452) for a different reading, and being informed by Servius that "alii limbo legunt, ut (*En.* IV. 137): Sidoniam picto chlamydem circumdata limbo;" and finding that information confirmed by Heyne ("limbo, Moret. Sec. pro var. Lect."), I adopt LIMBO, and thus at once obtain, not merely an intelligible, but an admirable, sense: *Pallas effulgent*, neither with a dark cloud illuminated by her aegis or by the flames of the burning city, nor with a dark thunderstorm, but *with her 'limbus'* or '*instita*', *and her Gorgon.* Pallas is said to be effulgent with the 'limbus', this part being the most splendid of the whole female dress; see the 'limbus' of Dido, quoted by Servius above, and especially the 'limbus' of the dress put by Thetis (Stat. *Achill.* I. 325) on Achilles when she disguised him as a female, for the court of Lycomedes:

"Aspicit ambiguum genitrix, cogitque volentem,
Innectitque sinus; tunc colla rigentia mollit,
Summittitque graves humeros, et fortia laxat
Brachia, et impexos certo domat ordine crines,
Ac sua dilecta cervice monilia transfert,
Et picturato cohibet vestigia limbo;"

where it will be observed that the whole female dress of Achilles is placed before the eye of the reader by the 'monilia' (representing the upper part), and the embroidered 'limbus' (representing the lower), just as in our text the whole costume of Pallas is represented by the (effulgent) Gorgon above, and the effulgent 'limbus' below.

If it was proper for Statius thus to put forward the 'monilia' and 'limbus' as representatives of the whole of Achilles's petticoats, it was still more proper for Virgil to use a similar representation in the case of Pallas, that Goddess being remarkable for wearing (pace Deae dictum sit!) petticoats so long as to acquire the appellation of 'talares', i. e. of coming down quite to her heels. See almost all her numerous statues, and especially Sidonius Apollinaris's description:

"Squameus ad mediam thorax non pervenit alvum
Post chalybem pendente peplo, tegit extima limbi
Circite palla pedes, qui cum sub veste moventur,
Crispato rigidae crepitant in syrmate rugae."

Panegyr. v. 2409.

I need not point out to the reader either the necessity there was, that Pallas although invisible to all human eyes, should yet wear clothes, or the propriety with which those clothes, when she is rendered visible to Eneas, are described to have been of a splendor suitable to the Goddess (see below), and to the attitude in which she is represented, viz. that of standing mistress of the conquered citadel.

Similar to the effulgence of Pallas's 'limbus' in our text is that of her 'palla' in Claudian, *de Rapt. Pros.* II. 25:

— "Tantum stridentia colla
Gorgonos obtentu pallae fulgentis inumbrat."

and elsewhere I find a similar effulgence ascribed to other parts of the Goddess's equipment; thus (Claudian. *de Rapt. Pros.* II. 226) her spear is so bright as to illuminate the chariot of Dis:

— "Libratur in ictum
Fraxinus, et nigros illuminat obvia currus;"

her chariot (Auson. *Perioch. XVII. Odyss.*) casts a red light over the sky:

"Jam caelum roseis rutilat Tritonia bigis;"

and (Claud. *Gigant.* 91) a similar light is cast by her Gorgon:

— "Tritonia Virgo
Prosilit, ostendens rutila cum Gorgone pectus."

To LIMBO EFFULGENS ET GORGONE SAEVA thus understood as descriptive of the splendor of the Goddess's dress, we have an exact parallel in

— "ipsique in puppibus auro
Ductores longe effulgent ostroque decori."
En. V. 132.

It would appear from the very ancient and remarkable statue of Minerva Polias, now in the Augusteum of Dresden, that the battle of the Giants described by Euripides (*Hecub.* 466), and by the Author of *Ciris* (*v.* 29), as embroidered on the 'peplum' of Pallas, was not spread over the whole 'peplum', but confined to a 'clavus' (limbus?), stripe, or border, represented on the statue as descending down the front of the person from the waist to the feet. For a view of this very striking statue, as well as for a separate view and description of the 'clavus', stripe, or border, descending down the front of its 'peplum', see Becker, *August. Dresd.* Tab. IX and X.

Müller (*Minerva Polias*, pag. 26) informs us, if I understand him right, that there is a similar band, or stripe, on the 'pepla' of all the very ancient statues of the Minerva Polias: "Insignis maxime clavus quidam sive limes caeteris aliquanto latior de medio corpore decurrens, qui etiam apud populos Asiae maxime decorus habebatur."

Saeva is predicated not (according to Servius's second interpretation) of Pallas, but (according to his first interpretation) of the Gorgon; first, because the picture is thus more concentrated, and secondly, because 'saeva' (the Greek *δεινη*) is precisely the term applied to the Gorgon both by Hesiod and Homer·

> "*Παν δε μεταφρενον ειχε καρη δεινοιο πελωρου Γοργους.*"
>
> *Scut. Hercul.* 223.

> "*Εν δε τε Γοργειη κεφαλη δεινοιο πελωρου*
> *Δεινη τε σμερδνη τε, Διος τερας αιγιοχοιο.*"
>
> *Iliad*, V. 741.

626.

AC VELUTI SUMMIS ANTIQUAM IN MONTIBUS ORNUM
CUM FERRO ACCISAM CREBRISQUE BIPENNIBUS INSTANT
ERUERE AGRICOLAE CERTATIM ILLA USQUE MINATUR
ET TREMEFACTA COMAM CONCUSSO VERTICE NUTAT
VULNERIBUS DONEC PAULATIM EVICTA SUPREMUM
CONGEMUIT TRAXITQUE JUGIS AVULSA RUINAM

Minatur; — not *threatens to fall* ("cader minaccia" — Alfieri), but the very contrary, *threatens with violence those who are endeavoring to make her fall; warns those who are endeavoring to make her fall, that she will use violence — attack them in her turn — if they do not immediately desist.* This is not only the only sense of the verb 'minari' used intransitively, but the only sense in which the simile is at all applicable to Troy.

MINATUR ET . . . VERTICE NUTAT. — *Threatens with the nod of her leafy head* as a warrior threatens with the nod of his plumes. Compare *En.* IX. 677:

> "Ipsi intus dextra ac laeva pro turribus adstant
> Armati ferro, et cristis capita alta corusci:
> Quales aeriae liquentia flumina circum,
> Sive Padi ripis, Athesim seu propter amoenum,
> Consurgunt geminae quercus, intonsaque caelo
> Attollunt capita, et sublimi vertice nutant."

See Comm. *En.* I. 163.

CONGEMUIT; — not merely *groaned*, but *groaned loudly;* as it were *with all its force collected into one last effort.* See Comm. *v.* 49.

AVULSA. — "Evulsa." Ruaeus.

> — "Und schmetternd, den Höhn entrottet, hinabkracht."
> VOSS.

> — "E dal suo giogo al fine
> O con parte del giogo si diveglie,
> O si scoscende."
> CARO.

No, but 'avulsa, traxit ruinam jugis', i. e. '*ibi, in jugis*': *torn away with ropes from the stump where the axe had nearly (but not entirely) cut it through, fell there on the mountain.* AVULSA, 'funibus' sciz. Compare:

> — "Labefactaque tandem
> Ictibus innumeris, adductaque funibus arbor
> Corruit, et multam prostravit pondere silvam."
> OVID. *Metam.* VIII. 774.

Thus the cadence (cracked, broken and limping, if the structure be

CONGEMUIT, TRAXITQUE, JUGIS AVULSA, RUINAM)

becomes fluent and sonorous:

CONGEMUIT, TRAXITQUE JUGIS, AVULSA, RUINAM;

the ictus falling full upon VUL.

644.

SIC O SIC POSITUM AFFATI DISCEDITE CORPUS

Positum, — the English *laid out:*

— "Toroque
Mortua componar, positaeque det oscula frater."
Ovid. *Metam.* IX. 502.

Compare Alcimede taking leave of Jason:

— "Et dulci jam nunc preme lumina dextra."
Val. Flacc. I. 335.

648.

EX QUO ME DIVUM PATER ATQUE HOMINUM REX
FULMINIS AFFLAVIT VENTIS ET CONTIGIT IGNI

The ancients believed that thunder was produced by the collision of clouds driven against each other by opposite winds; compare:

— "Caeli quoque nubila vexant
Excutiuntque (*venti* sciz.) feris rutilos concursibus ignes."
Ovid. *Metam.* XI. 435.

The same doctrine will be found laid down at considerable length by Lucretius.

653.

FATOQUE URGENTI INCUMBERE

Not (with Voss), "Gegen das eindringende Schicksal anstreben," but the very opposite, *add his weight to that of the superincumbent Fate.* Compare: "Sed Marium una civitas publice, multique privati, reum peregerunt; in Classicum tota provincia incubuit." Plin. *Epist.* III. 9.

Also: "Id prope unum maxime inclinatis rebus incubuit." Liv. III. 16. *Ed. Bip.*

"Incumbe in iras, teque languentem excita."
SENEC. *Medea*, 902.

"Tollite signa duces, fatorum impellite cursum."
LUCAN. V. 41.

— "Sua quisque ac publica fata
Praecipitare cupit.'
LUCAN. VII. 51.

And, more prosaically, Petron. p. 353 (Ed. Hadrian. Amstel. 1669): "Ne morientes vellet occidere."

CC1.

PATET ISTI JANUA LETO

So Pliny (*Epist.* I. 18): "Illa januam famae patefecit;" and Terent. (*Heaut.* III. 1. 72):

"Quantam fenestram ad nequitiam patefeceris!"

671.

CLIPEOQUE SINISTRAM
INSERTABAM APTANS

INSERTABAM. — This word is peculiarly appropriate, the strap or handle of the shield, through which the arm was passed, being (as we are informed by Cael. Rhod. ad locum) technically denominated 'insertorium'.

683.

NAMQUE MANUS INTER MAESTORUMQUE ORA PARENTUM
ECCE LEVIS SUMMO DE VERTICE VISUS IULI
FUNDERE LUMEN APEX TACTUQUE INNOXIA MOLLES
LAMBERE FLAMMA COMAS ET CIRCUM TEMPORA PASCI

"Apex proprie dicitur in summo flaminis pileo virga lanata, hoc est, in cujus extremitate modica lana est: quod primum constat apud Albam Ascanium statuisse. Modo autem summitatem pilei intelligimus." Servius. "Levem apicem cum Servio de pileo Ascanii, qui ut pueri erat levis, capio." Burmann.

I object to this interpretation, first, that LEVIS seems not to be a very well chosen epithet for a cap; secondly, that if Iulus wore a cap, out of the top of which the flame arose (SUMMO DE VERTICE), the cap would, until itself consumed, have protected Iulus's hair from the fire; at least would have prevented the by-standers from observing what effect the fire had on the hair; unless we imagine, contrary to all verisimilitude, that the flame descending along the sides of the cap, spread from thence to the ringlets about Iulus's temples or on the back of his neck; thirdly, that the first thing to have been done in case of the fire being seated in Iulus's cap, plainly was to have pulled off the cap, not to have poured water on it, and accordingly nothing can be more ridiculous than the figure made by Iulus in the picture in the Vatic. Fragm., where two attendants are represented pouring water on the cap on the top of Iulus's head.

La Cerda is, I believe, the first who, deserting Servius's interpretation, understands APEX to be spoken of the flame itself: "Dicitur ignis ille apex, tum quia in capite, tum quia instar apicis acuminatus ex natura ignis." In which interpretation La Cerda has been followed by Heyne, Wagner (*Virg. Br. En.*) and Forbiger.

This interpretation seems liable to no less formidable

objections than the former; for, **first**, the term 'apex' although of frequent occurence in Virgil, never even so much as once occurs in this sense. **Secondly**, APEX being understood to mean a tongue or cone of fire, becomes the essential part of the prodigy, and should therefore, according to Virgil's usual method, and to produce a suitable impression on the mind of the hearer or reader be placed in the emphatic position at the beginning of the line, exactly where we find FUNDERE LUMEN, words, according to this interpretation, unemphatic and unimportant and a mere appendage to APEX. **Thirdly**, the distinction between FUNDERE LUMEN APEX, and LAMBERE FLAMMA COMAS, is not sufficiently defined, LAMBERE COMAS being almost as fit a predicate for APEX as for FLAMMA, and FUNDERE LUMEN quite as fit for FLAMMA as for APEX.

Rejecting both interpretations therefore, I understand APEX to mean *the tip-top*, and taken in connexion with IULI, *the tip-top of Iulus*. This tip-top of Iulus, consisting of soft, light hair, is called LEVIS; the light which it appears to shed (VISUS *FUNDERE LUMEN* APEX) being the essential part of the prodigy, is with the strictest propriety placed in the emphatic position at the beginning of the line, where in order to render it still more emphatic, it is pointed to by the whole of the immediately preceding verse: ECCE LEVIS SUMMO DE VERTICE VISUS IULI — *FUNDERE LUMEN* APEX; the APEX IULI being a light tuft of hair on the crown of Iulus's head, is correctly and naturally said to pour its light from the crown of the head, SUMMO DE VERTICE; and finally, the distinction between the two wonders, FUNDERE LUMEN APEX, and LAMBERE FLAMMA COMAS, is well preserved, the object which was naturally not luminous, shedding light, and the object which should naturally consume the hair, only licking it without injuring it.

This interpretation, while it thus happily blends all the parts of the description into one harmonious whole, has the further advantage of assigning to APEX a sense in which it has been used by Virgil elsewhere; compare (*En.* X. 270):

> "Ardet apex capiti, cristisque a vertice flamma
> Funditur;"

where light is described as proceeding from the tip-top of Eneas in almost the same terms as in our text from the tip-top of Iulus, the difference being that Eneas having his helmet on at the time, his 'apex' or tip-top is not *a tuft of hair*, but *the crest of his helmet.* Compare also (*Ciris*, 499):

> "Tum qua se medium capitis discrimen agebat
> Ecce repente, velut patrios imitatus honores,
> Puniceam concussit apex in vertice cristam;"

where 'apex' is *the projecting peak* or *point* (*the prominent tuft of feathers*), 'in vertice', *on the crown of the bird's head.* Compare also (*En.* XII. 492):

> — "Apicem tamen incita summum
> Hasta tulit, summasque excussit vertice cristas;"

the spear carried away Eneas's 'apex', i. e. (his helmet being on at the time) *the extreme, highest point of his helmet; the crest.* In every one of which instances it will be observed that 'apex' is, as in our text, *the tip-top, point* or *prominence*, higher than, and rising out of, the 'vertex' itself.

The APEX of our text is therefore *the highest lock* or *tuft of hair* on the 'vertex' of Iulus's head; which if any reader should still doubt, I beg to refer him to the explicit testimony of Claudian (*de Quarto Consulat. Honor.* 192) to that effect:

> — "Ventura potestas
> Claruit Ascanio, subita cum luce comarum
> Innocuus flagraret apex, Phrygioque volutus
> Vertice, fatalis redimiret tempora candor;"

where the sense can be no other than: *the 'apex' of Ascanius's hair showed like blazing fire, yet without being injured.*

If it be not supererogation to add further evidence, that it was Ascanius's hair, and not Ascanius's cap, which seemed to burn, reference may be made to the original from whence Virgil borrowed his prodigy, namely the apparent burning, not of the cap, but of the head, of Servius Tullius: "Puero dormienti, cui Servio Tullio nomen fuit, caput arsisse ferunt, multorum in conspectu. Plurimo igitur clamore inde ad tantae rei miraculum orto excitos reges; et quum quidam familiarium aquam ad restinguendum ferret, ab regina retentum." Livy, I. 39.

I cannot refuse myself the pleasure of informing my readers that the above very new and, as it seems to me, very true explanation of this difficult passage was suggested to me by one, whose zealous assistance and cooperation has all along, not only lightened, but rendered delightful to me, the otherwise almost intolerable labor of this work, I mean my beloved daughter Katharine Olivia Henry.

689.

JUPITER OMNIPOTENS PRECIBUS SI FLECTERIS ULLIS
ASPICE NOS HOC TANTUM ET SI PIETATE MEREMUR
DA DEINDE AUGURIUM PATER ATQUE HAEC OMINA FIRMA

Observe the words JUPITER OMNIPOTENS (expressive of the *power* to relieve, even in so desperate an extremity) joined to all the verbs in the sentence; the word PATER (*moving to exert that power*) joined only to the immediate prayer of the petition, DA DEINDE AUXILIUM, ATQUE HAEC OMINA FIRMA. See Comm. *v.* 552.

ASPICE NOS; HOC TANTUM: This punctuation, which is that of Nich. Heinsius, renders ASPICE NOS, already emphatic by its position at the beginning of the line, still more emphatic by the sudden pause which separates it from the subsequent words; see Comm. *v.* 246. Wagner removes the pause, and connects HOC TANTUM closely with ASPICE NOS: which arrangement — while it has the effect, first, of diminishing as far as in an editor's power the emphasis of the emphatic words ASPICE NOS; and, secondly, of substituting for a simple, pathetic, passionate exclamation, one bound up with a cool, phlegmatic, lawyerlike condition or limitation — is directly opposed to Virgil's usual manner which, as we have so often seen, is first to present us fully and boldly with the main thought — the grand conception — and then to modify, limit, soften down, adapt, or explain, afterwards. And so precisely, on the present occasion, we have first the short, strong, emphatic ASPICE NOS, and then, after a pause, HOC TANTUM: *do but so much and I am sure of all the rest.*

For my opinion of the punctuation of the Medicean, on which Wagner here as well as in numerous other places has laid so much stress, see Comments *En.* I. 122; II. 420. Should, however, the reader, influenced by a respect similar to Wagner's for the punctuation of the Medicean, hesitate to separate words which have been united by the punctuation of that MS., I beg to refer him for a neutralisation of the Medicean punctuation, to the exactly opposite punctuation (ASPICE NOS. HOC TANTUM.) of the Vatican Fragment (Bottari), a MS. of at least equal antiquity and equal authority with the Medicean.

HOC TANTUM. —

"Sed tantum permitte cadat: nil poscimus ultra."
CLAUD. *Bell. Gild.* 314.

693.

ET DE CAELO LAPSA PER UMBRAS
STELLA FACEM DUCENS MULTA CUM LUCE CUCURRIT

Και ιδου, ο αστηρ, ον ειδον εν τη ανατολη, προηγεν αυτους, εως ελθων εστη επανω ου ην το παιδιον. MATTH. II. 9.

In *Saunders's News-Letter*, of July 25, 1844, there is, in an extract from a letter, the following account of a meteor, seen almost on the same spot, and presenting precisely the same appearances as that seen by Eneas:

"Constantinople, July 3. — On Sunday last, five minutes before sunset, we had a splendid sight here. The atmosphere was hazy, but without cloud. Thermometer about 90°. An immense meteor, like a gigantic Congreve rocket, darted, with a rushing noise, from east to west. Its lightning course was marked by a streak of fire, and, after a passage of some forty or fifty degrees, it burst like a bombshell, but without detonation; lighting up the hemisphere with the brilliancy of the noon-day sun. On its disappearance, a white vapour remained in its track, and was visible for nearly half an hour. Everybody thought it was just before his eyes, but it was seen by persons twelve and fifteen miles to the northward, in the same apparent position, and positively the self-same phenomenon. Many of the vulgar look upon it as a very bad omen, whilst others attribute it to the warm weather, which continues. The thermometer stands, at this moment, at 91° in the shade, and in the coolest spot could be selected."

695.

ILLAM SUMMA SUPER LABENTEM CULMINA TECTI
CERNIMUS IDAEA CLARAM SE CONDERE SILVA
SIGNANTEMQUE VIAS TUM LONGO LIMITE SULCUS
DAT LUCEM ET LATE CIRCUM LOCA SULFURE FUMANT

Wagner (*Virg. Br. En.*) and Forbiger, understanding the structure to be 'claram signantemque vias se condere', have removed the pause placed by the two Stephenses, the two Heinsii and Heyne, after SILVA. The pause should undoubtedly be replaced, SIGNANTEM being connected by QUE, not with its unlike CLARAM, but with its like LABENTEM, and it being Virgil's usual method, thus to connect a concluding or winding up clause, not with the immediately preceding clause, but with one more remote. See Comments *v.* 148; III. 571; IV. 484; V. 525.

LIMITE, — *track* or *path.* Contiguous properties being anciently, as still very generally on the continent of Europe, separated from each other, not by a fence, but merely by a narrow intermediate space, along which (in order not to trespass on the ground on either side) it was usual for those who had business in the neighbourhood, to walk, the term 'limes', primarily signifying a boundary or limit, came by a natural and unavoidable transition to signify, *a path*, *way*, or *track.* Compare:

— "Quoties amissus eunti
Limes?"

STAT. *Theb.* XII. 240

how often the way or *path lost.*

703.

VESTROQUE IN NUMINE TROJA EST

"In tua, inquit, pater carissime, in tua sumus custodia." PETRON. p. 354. (Ed. Hadr. Amst. 1669.)

713.

EST URBE EGRESSIS TUMULUS TEMPLUMQUE VETUSTUM DESERTAE CERERIS

"Cujus templum erat desertum vetustate vel belli decennalis tempore." Heyne. No; Wagner's explanation is the correct one: "DESERTAE, quod templum habuit in loco infrequenti." The truth of this interpretation (rested by Wagner solely on the context, and the similar use made of the term 'desertus' by other authors) seems to be established by the testimony of Vitruvius, that religion required that the temples of Ceres should be built outside the walls and in lonely situations: "Item Cereri, extra urbem loco, quo non semper homines, nisi per sacrificium, necesse habeant adire;" in order, no doubt, (see the Emperor Julian's Letter to Libanius, *Epist. Mut. Graecan.* p. 148,) to pay Ceres the especial compliment, that her worship should be apart from all secular concerns, not performed *en passant.*

The temple of Ceres outside Troy was therefore a fit place for the unobserved rendezvous of Eneas and his party; as in real history the temple of Ceres outside Rome was a fit place for Piso (the intended successor to the empire) to wait unobserved until the conspirators should have despatched Nero: "Interim Piso apud aedem Cereris opperiretur, unde eum Praefectus Fenius et caeteri accitum ferrent in castra." TACIT. *Annal.* XV. 53.

725.

FERIMUR PER OPACA LOCORUM

OPACA; — not *dark*, but only *shady;* not so dark but that one could see the way. Compare Plin. *Epist.* VII. 21: "Cubicula obductis velis opaca, nec tamen obscura, facio." Also Plin. *Epist.* VIII. 8: "Modicus collis assurgit, antiqua cupresso nemorosus et opacus."

738.

HEU MISERO CONJUX FATO NE EREPTA CREUSA
SUBSTITIT ERRAVITNE VIA SEU LASSA RESEDIT
INCERTUM

"Excusationes istae ad triplex caput reducuntur; aut ad Deos et fata, quae eripuerunt; aut ad Aeneam, qui non potuit animadvertere; aut ad Creusam, quae disparuit subsistens, errans, sedens prae lassitudine." La Cerda.
"Conjux mihi misero erepta Creusa fatone substitit, an erravit de via, an lassa resedit." Heyne; approved of both by Wunderlich and Forbiger.
"Musste sie nach dem Willen des Schicksals stehen bleiben, um von den Feinden getödtet zu werden." Ladewig.

I agree, however, entirely with Servius: "Fato erepta Creusa, substititne erravitne via." Eneas is certain of one thing and of one thing only, viz. that Creusa was MISERO FATO EREPTA. How it happened that she was MISERO FATO EREPTA, was entirely unknown to him — remained wrapt in obscurity; it might have been that she had stopped short, being afraid to go on, or that she had missed her way, or that she had grown weary, and sat down to rest. He could not tell, in which of these three possible ways it had happened; but certain it was that she had been MISERO FATO EREPTA.

MISERO FATO EREPTA; — "mihi misero erepta fato." Heyne, Wunderlich, De Bulgaris, Forbiger. I have two reasons, however, for thinking that MISERO certainly belongs to FATO, and not to 'mihi' understood: **First**, the personal pronoun is usually expressed when 'miser' is applied to the speaker in the third case; compare:

— "Heu! heu! quid volui misero mihi?"
Ecl. II. 58.

— "Aut quid jam misero mihi denique restat."
En. II. 70.

— "Heu! nunc misero mihi demum
Exitium infelix."
En. X. 849.

seeing that our author has thought it necessary to supply the personal pronoun to 'misero' in these instances, in which there was no ambiguity to be apprehended from its omission, and yet has not supplied it in our text where there was the ambiguity arising from the near vicinity of FATO, I conclude that there is no pronoun at all to be supplied, and that the adjective really belongs (as at first sight it appears to do) to the substantive expressed; compare, only three lines preceding,

"Hic **mihi** nescio quod **treprdo** male numen amicum
Confusam **eripuit** mentem."

And **secondly**, FATO EREPTA, **without** the addition of MISERO, means ***died a natural death*** (see Livy, III. 50: "Quod ad se attineat, uxorem sibi fato ereptam;" also *En.* IV. 696 and Comm.); **with** the addition of MISERO, FATO EREPTA means ***died a violent death;*** compare:

— "Miseri post fata Sychaei."
En. IV. 20.

— "Crudelia secum
Fata Lyci."
En. I. 225.

— "Peribat
. . misera ante diem subitoque accensa furore."
En. IV. 696.

In further support of this interpretation and the consequent junction of NE, in the structure, with SUBSTITIT and not with FATO, I may add that NE stands, as I have had it printed in the text (apart from FATO, and quite as an independent word), both in the Medicean (according to Foggini) and, as I have myself personally ascertained, in the Leipzig No. 35 and in the Dresden. The only other MSS. I have examined respecting the passage, are the Leipzig No. 36 which has 'fatone', and the Gudian (No. 70) which has unaccountably 'fatone a erepta', from which single instance let the uninitiated reader imagine to himself with what myriads of gross errors even the best MSS. abound, and how almost hopeless a task it is to grope among them for the truth. The printed separation of NE from FATO, adopted by several of the ancient editors and, amongst others, by R. Stephens and Ambrogi, as well as by the Modena Ed. of 1475, and fully justified by Servius (see above), is quite necessary to prevent readers from being misled by the mechanical arrangement into a false understanding of the passage.

This, perhaps, is the proper place to observe, that there seems to be no ground whatever for the charge which has so frequently been brought against Eneas, that he deserted, or at least neglected, his wife. It was necessary to divide the party, in order the better to escape observation by the Greeks; and not only the greater imbecility of, but stronger natural tie to, the father and the child, rendered it imperative to bestow the first and chief care on them. If Eneas's direction that Creusa should keep, not merely behind, but far behind ("longe servet vestigia conjux"), excite animadversion, I beg to suggest, that it was indispensable that the separation should be to some considerable distance, not merely in order to ensure its being effectual for the purpose above mentioned, but in order to afford Creusa herself the chance of escape, in case of the miscarriage of those who led the way. With this account of Eneas's loss of Creusa compare Göthe's not less charming description of Epimetheus's loss of Pandora, in his unfinished dramatic piece entitled *Pandora*.

755.

SIMUL IPSA SILENTIA TERRENT

So Tacitus, not less finely of Vitellius: "In palatium regreditur, vastum desertumque . . . . terret solitudo et tacentes loci." *Hist.* III. 84.

"Es schreckt mich selbst das wesenlose Schweigen."
SCHILLER, *Braut von Messina.*

756.

SI FORTE PEDEM SI FORTE TULISSET

"Sive, quod heu timeo! sive superstes eris."
OVID. *Heroid.* XIII. 164.

759.

EXSUPERANT FLAMMAE FURIT AESTUS AD AURAS

"Die Flamme prasselnd schon zum Himmel schlug."
SCHILLER, *Wilhelm Tell,* Act V.

769.

IMPLEVI CLAMORE VIAS MAESTUSQUE CREUSAM
NEQUIDQUAM INGEMINANS ITERUMQUE ITERUMQUE VOCAVI

Compare Orpheus calling on Eurydice in the fourth Georgic, and Pope's fine imitation:

"Eurydice the woods,
Eurydice the floods,
Eurydice the rocks and hollow mountains rung."

781.

ET TERRAM HESPERIAM VENIES UBI LYDIUS ARVA
INTER OPIMA VIRUM LENI FLUIT AGMINE TYBRIS
ILLIC RES LAETAE REGNUMQUE ET REGIA CONJUX
PARTA TIBI LACRYMAS DILECTAE PELLE CREUSAE

UBI LYDIUS ARVA &c. —

"Wo jetzt die Muotta zwischen Wiesen rinnt."
SCHILLER, *Wilhelm Tell*, Act II.

ARVA OPIMA. — "Terra fertilis." Donatus. "Fruitful fields." Surrey. No; 'opimus' is not *fruitful*, but *in prime condition;* in that condition sciz., of which fruitfulness is the consequence. Land is 'opima' (*in prime condition*, or *of the best quality*), before it bears, and even before the seed is put into it; it is not *fruitful*, until it bears. 'Opimus' has precisely the same meaning when applied to animals; viz., *in prime condition;* not, as incorrectly stated by Gesner, Forcellini, and all lexicographers, *fat; fatness* being only one of the qualities necessary to entitle an animal to be styled 'opimus'. This primitive sense of 'opimus' (to which its meanings in the expressions 'spolia opima', 'opima facundia' &c. are but secondary,) is expressed in French by the phrase '*en bon point*'.

Dryden has his reward with the English reader for giving himself no trouble about such niceties, but substituting at once, for the Virgilian thought, whatever idea, suited 'ad captum vulgi', came first into his mind:

"Where gentle Tyber from his bed beholds
The flowery meadows, and the feeding folds."

Virgil is innocent of all but the first three words.

ARVA INTER OPIMA VIRUM. — With Heyne I refer VIRUM to ARVA, and not with Burmann and Forcellini to OPIMA: First, because Virgil, on the other occasions on which he has used the word 'opimus', has used it absolutely. Secondly, because 'opimus' in the forty examples of its use quoted by the industry of Forcellini stands absolute in thirty-eight, and only in two is connected with a case, which case is not the genitive, but the ablative. Thirdly, because, even although it had been the practice of Virgil, or of other good authors, to join 'opimus' to the genitive, the phrase 'opima virum' were neither elegant nor poetic. Fourthly, because OPIMA, taken absolutely, is in perfect unison with the plain intention of the Apparition, viz. to recommend Hesperia to Eneas;. taken in connection with VIRUM, contradicts that intention, a country being the less eligible to new settlers, in the direct ratio in which it is already 'opima virum'.

DILECTAE; — not merely *loved*, but *loved by choice* or *preference*. An exact knowledge of the meaning of this word enables us to observe the consolation which Creusa ministers to herself in the delicate opposition of DILECTAE CREUSAE to REGIA CONJUX PARTA.

785.

NON EGO MYRMIDONUM SEDES DOLOPUMVE SUPERBAS
ASPICIAM AUT GRAJIS SERVITUM MATRIBUS IBO
DARDANIS ET DIVAE VENERIS NURUS

"*Cleop.* Know, sir, that I
Will not wait pinioned at your master's court,
Not once be chastised with the sober eye
Of dull Octavia. Shall they hoist me up,
And show me to the shouting varlotry
Of censuring Rome?

Anton. & Cleop., Act V. Sc. 2.

790.

HAEC UBI DICTA DEDIT LACRYMANTEM ET MULTA VOLENTEM
DICERE DESERUIT TENUESQUE RECESSIT IN AURAS
TER CONATUS IBI COLLO DARE BRACHIA CIRCUM
TER FRUSTRA COMPRENSA MANUS EFFUGIT IMAGO

"This having said, she left me all in tears,
And minding much to speak; but she was gone,
And subtly fled into the weightless air.
Thrice raught I with mine arms to accoll her neck:
Thrice did my hands' vain hold the image escape,
Like nimble winds, and like the flying dream.
So, night spent out, return I to my feres:
And there, wondering, I find together swarmed
A new number of mates, mothers, and men;
A rout exiled, a wretched multitude,
From each-where flock together, prest to pass
With heart and goods, to whatsoever land
By sliding seas, me listed them to lead.
And now rose Lucifer above the ridge
Of lusty Ide, and brought the dawning light;
The Greeks held the entries of the gates beset:
Of help there was no hope. Then gave I place,
Took up my sire, and hasted to the hill."

Such are the concluding words of Surrey's translation of the second book of the Eneis; such the sweet, chaste voice, which the bloody axe of an obscene and ruffian king silenced for ever, at the age of thirty; Diis aliter visum. And this, let the reader observe, is blank verse in its cradle; before it has acquired the sinewy strength, the manly dignity, the high, chivalrous port, of Shakespeare and Milton. Let him, further, compare these lines with the corresponding rhymes of Dryden, and then hear with astonishment (astonishment at the unequal rewards of human deservings), that Surrey's biographer (Dr. Nott) deems it praise, to compare him with that coarse and reckless writer; and that Dr. Johnson, and even Milton, was so little aware, not of his merits only, but almost of his existence, that the former writes in his life of Milton, "The Earl of Surrey is said (is said!) to have translated one of Virgil's books without rhyme;" and the latter (Preface to Paradise Lost) claims for his great poem the (perhaps) only praise to which it is not entitled, that it is "the first example in English, of ancient liberty recovered to heroic poem, from the troublesome and modern bondage of rhyming."

Deseruit. — Observe the tender reproach contained in this word; observe, also, that it is spoken, not of Creusa (on whom the exquisite judgment of the poet is careful not to throw even the shadow of an imputation), but of the apparition, against which it falls harmless, while at the same time it expresses the bereavement of Eneas, and his affection towards his wife, as strongly, nay more strongly, than if it had been spoken directly of Creusa herself. How the word must have sounded in the ears of Dido! Deseruit; *deserted;* therefore left him free to form a new attachment.

Ter conatus ibi collo dare brachia circum &c. —

> "Tre volte dietro a lei le mani avvinsi,
> E tante mi tornai con esse al petto."
>
> Dante, *Purgat.* II. 80.

"Stringebam brachia, sed jam perdideram quam tenebam." St. Ambros. *Orat. de ob. Pat. Frat. Lib.* I. 19.

The Davideis, that wild, unequal, and irregular, but highly poetic, effusion of the neglected Cowley, is a paraphrase, and in many places almost a translation, of the two first books of the Eneis. The Lutrin of Boileau ("qui fait d'un vain pupitre un second Ilion," *Lutrin, c. I.*) is a very elegant, witty and amusing parody of the second.

III.

10.

LITTORA CUM PATRIAE LACRYMANS PORTUSQUE RELINQUO
ET CAMPOS UBI TROJA FUIT

In the more trivial, no less than in the more important, features of his character, Eneas is drawn after Jason: not only is he the daring adventurer, the intrepid navigator, the faithless seducer, but he leaves home weeping:

— "*Αυταρ Ιησων*
Δακρυοεις γαιης απο πατριδος ομματ' ενεικεν."

Apoll. Rhod. I. 534.

See Comm. *En. IV. 143* and *305.*

Fuit. — *Was* once, and *is* no longer. See Comm. I. 16, and II. 325.

18.

AENEADASQUE MEO NOMEN DE NOMINE FINGO
SACRA DIONAEAE MATRI DIVISQUE FEREBAM
AUSPICIBUS COEPTORUM OPERUM SUPEROQUE NITENTEM
CAELICOLUM REGI MACTABAM IN LITTORE TAURUM

— "*Πει. Πρωτον ονομα τη πολει*
Θεσθαι τι μεγα και κλεινον. ειτα τοις θεοις
Θυσαι μετα τουτο.

Aristoph. *Aves, 810.*

Nitentem caelicolum regi mactabam . . . . taurum. — It appears from one of the Emperor Julian's Epistles to Libanius *(Epist. Mut. Graecan.)* that the offering of a 'nitens taurus' to Jupiter was regal: "*Εϑυσα τῳ Διϊ βασιλικως ταυρον λευκον.*" with which compare:

> "*Αυταρ ο βουν ιερευσεν αναξ ανδρων Αγαμεμνων*
> . . . . *Κρονιωνι.*"
>
> Hom. *Il. β. 402.*

34.

MULTA MOVENS ANIMO NYMPHAS VENERABAR AGRESTES
GRADIVUMQUE PATREM GETICIS QUI PRAESIDET ARVIS
RITE SECUNDARENT VISUS OMENQUE LEVARENT

Nymphas agrestes, — *the Hamadryads,* who had the trees under their special protection; see Ovid. *Metam. VIII. 741* and seq. where we have an account of a prodigy similar to that in the text. The same story, scarcely even modernized, cuts a conspicuous figure in Tasso's collection of stolen goods, Canto XIII. St. 41.

Rite secundarent visus. — "Sie möchten segnen meine Augen (den Blick)." Ladewig. I prefer the ordinary interpretation, 'ostentum', 'portentum'; compare: "Jussa numinis, suos Ptolemaeique visus, ingruentia mala, exponit." Tacit. *Hist. IV. 84.*

Omenque levarent. — "'Levare' ist hier 'deflectere', 'avertere', *abwenden, abhalten.*" Süpfle; who quotes (Hor. *Od. II. 17. 27):*

> "Me truncus illapsus cerebro
> Sustulerat, nisi Faunus ictum
> Dextra l'evasset."

Still more appropriate is:

"Nulla relicta foret Romani nominis umbra,
Ni pater ille tuus jamjam ruitura subisset
Pondera, turbatamque ratem, certaque levasset
Naufragium commune manu."

CLAUD. *de IV. Consul. Honor. 59.*

42.

PARCE PIAS SCELERARE MANUS NON ME TIBI TROJA EXTERNUM TULIT

Let not your tender and compassionate hands do an act fit only for brutal hands, viz. disturb the grave of a fellow countryman and relative. See Comments *En. I. 14; III. 75.*

47.

TUM VERO ANCIPITI MENTEM FORMIDINE PRESSUS

ANCIPITI.—"Duplici..... una, quod sepulchrum laeserat: altera, quod metuere coeperat laesum ipsum." Servius. "Von zwiefacher Furcht, veranlasst durch das gesehene Blut und die vernommenen Worte des Polydorus." Ladewig.

"Terror ben altro, a un tal parlar, m' invade
Ed i sensi e la mente."

ALFIERI.

This is wholly erroneous; Eneas had but one fear, viz. that occasioned by the whole prodigy — by the blood and words taken all together — and this fear made him 'anceps'; not know which of two courses he should take; whether persist in his intention of settling in Thrace, or obey the warning voice and blood, and withdraw from that country at once. Thus 'anceps', *hesitating between two courses,* he applies to a council of Chiefs for advice *(v. 58):*

> "Delectos populi ad proceres primumque parentem
> Monstra Deum refero, et quae sit sententia posco."

Tum vero. — The effect on Eneas's mind is accurately proportioned to the cause — increases with the increase of the prodigy. The drops of blood fill him with horror:

> — "Mihi frigidus horror
> Membra quatit, gelidusque coit formidine sanguis;"

but do not deter him from his purpose; on the contrary, excite his curiosity, make him desire to probe the matter further; not so the warning voice; that produces the full effect — makes him not only desist from violating the tomb further, but makes him doubtful whether he ought not altogether to abandon his project of settling in Thrace. The emphatic words tum vero point to this complete effect. Compare:

> "Tum vero tremefacta novus per pectora cunctis
> Insinuat pavor."
>
> *En. II. 228;*

where see Comm. See also Comments *En. II. 105; IV. 396, 449, 571.*

56.

QUID NON MORTALIA PECTORA COGIS
AURI SACRA FAMES

Dante, unaccountably mistaking the bitter reprehension of avarice for an eulogy of thrift, thus paraphrases this passage,

> "Perche non reggi tu, o sacra fame
> Dell' oro, l'appetito de' mortali?"
>
> *Purgat. XXII. 40.*

i. e. *why, O sacred love of gold, moderatest thou not our appetite?* or, in other words, *Would that we had such a proper estimate of the value of money as might restrain the lavish expenditure attendant on the indulgence of sensual and luxurious appetites;* consequently — *as might restrain the appetites themselves.*

This gross misconception, not to say perversion, of his favorite author's meaning in one of his plainest and least mistakable passages, proving, as it does beyond all doubt, that Dante's, like our own Shakespeare's, knowledge of the Latin language and therefore of Classical literature generally, was wholly incommensurate with his poetical genius, affords a striking exemplification of the truth (so consolatory to the humble, and in these days so much despised, scholar and critic) "Non omnia possumus omnes."

63.

STANT MANIBUS ARAE
CAERULEIS MAESTAE VITTIS ATRAQUE CUPRESSO
ET CIRCUM ILIADES CRINEM DE MORE SOLUTAE
INFERIMUS TEPIDO SPUMANTIA CYMBIA LACTE

In Africa "pultes et panis et merum" were brought to the tombs of the martyrs even in the times of St. Augustin and St. Ambrose. The custom was omitted by the latter, "quia illa quasi parentalia superstitioni gentilium essent simillima." See St. August. *Confess. 6. 2.* Throughout continental Europe at the present day, the making of wreaths and garlands for tombs gives employment to a vast number of persons, those wreaths and garlands being periodically renewed during a long series of years by the affection of relatives or friends, or even of strangers. The fresh wreath still hangs on the ancient monument of Abelard and Heloise in the cemetery of Père la Chaise at Paris.

75.

PIUS ARCITENENS

Pius, — *compassionate and affectionate* towards the island on account of its having been his own birth place. See *En. I.-14* and Comm., and *III. 42* and Comm.

79.

EGRESSI VENERAMUR APOLLINIS URBEM

'Venerari', *προσκυνειν*, see Nep. in *Conon. III. 3.* The particular form of the adoration (which it will be observed is repeated on arriving at the temple itself, see *v. 84)* is perhaps now not to be ascertained.

92.

MUGIRE ADYTIS CORTINA RECLUSIS

For information concerning the CORTINA see Cynthius Cenetensis and La Cerda. The word is preserved in the Italian; see *Dizionario della Lingua Italiana,* Livorno 1838; also *Poesie di Giovanni Fantoni; fra gli Arcadi, Labindo;* Italia. 1823. 3 Tom.:

"Lascia di Delfo la vocal cortina
Febo che lavi il biondo crin nel Xanto,
Reca salute alla gentil Nerina
Padre del canto."

Ode ad Apollo, per malattia di Nerina.

'Cortina' is no doubt the root of our English *curtain.*

116.

MODO JUPITER ADSIT

Sciz. in his capacity of God of the weather; compare *Georg. II. 419:*

'Et jam maturis metuendus Jupiter uvis."

123.

SEDESQUE ASTARE RELICTAS

The structure is not 'sedes astare relictas', nor the meaning, *the seats stand abandoned,* but the structure is 'sedes relictas astare', and the meaning, *the seats abandoned* (sciz. by the enemy, as stated in the preceding clause) '*ad*-stant', *stand ready for us — to our hand.* The passage being thus understood, *(a)* there is no tautology; *(b)* the two clauses perfectly correspond, the infinitive being in each the emphatic word; and *(c)* its proper meaning *to stand by,* or *ready,* or *at hand,* is preserved to the compound ASTARE; compare "caeruleus supra caput astitit imber," *v. 194;* "arrectis auribus asto," *II. 303.* "Ego sum Rafael unus ex septem, qui astamus ante dominum." TOBIAS, XII. 15.

126.

OLEARON NIVEAMQUE PARON SPARSASQUE PER AEQUOR
CYCLADAS ET CREBRIS LEGIMUS FRETA CONSITA TERRIS
NAUTICUS EXORITUR VARIO CERTAMINE CLAMOR
HORTANTUR SOCII CRETAM PROAVOSQUE PETAMUS

"Apparet, 'concita', ut lectionem difficiliorem, esse retinendum: nec, si CONSITA legas, commode subjici vss. 128 et 129." Wagner.

I do not agree in this opinion; on the contrary, I think that the 'difficilior lectio is, generally speaking, quite as often incorrect as the 'facilis' and 'vulgaris', and that verses 128 and 129 not only agree with the reading CONSITA, but (see below) go to confirm that reading, and agree much better with it than with the reading 'concita' A better argument for 'concita' is derivable from the almost overpowering weight of MS. authority in favor of that reading. Yet I venture here, as in one or two places elsewhere, and especially in the case of 'Nixae', *En. I. 452,* to go counter to the weight of MS. authority in order to obtain a much better sense. The idea contained in the expression 'freta concita terris', *the seas violently stirred up, greatly excited, put into vehement commotion* (for such is the force of '*con*-cita') *by the lands* (the moveable and moving by the fixed), seems to me so highly incorrect, that I cannot persuade myself that the words are from the pen of Virgil; the more especially as in all the other instances in which Virgil uses this word, he applies it to the moving, not to the resisting, power. Add to this that the words LEGIMUS and "allabimur" imply an easy, skimming, unobstructed motion, and would not have been employed by Virgil to express the motion of the vessels over 'concita freta'. The wind besides was fair, and Crete reached, without difficulty or danger, on the third day. The picture which I think it has been Virgil's intention to place before the reader, has been thus beautifully painted by Avienus:

"Hinc Sporades crebro producunt cespite sese;
Densa serenato ceu splendent sidera caelo."
Descr. Orb. Terrae, 710.

In answer to Heyne's objection ("denique non intelligo, quam poeticum hoc sit, tam accurate Cycladas et Sporadas distinguere, quod vix in geographicis libellis fieri solet") I beg to say, that no such distinction is intended by the poet, as clearly appears from the application of the term SPARSAS (characteristic of the Sporades, see the lexicographers, in voc. 'Sporades', and Mela II. 7) to the Cyclades, under which name are here comprehended all the islands of the Egean; precisely for the purpose of showing which meaning (viz. that not merely one group of islands is intended, but the whole of the islands lying scattered like seed over the face of the Egean,) the supplementary ET CREBRIS LEGIMUS FRETA CONSITA TERRIS is, according to the poet's usual manner, subjoined. The poet is not singular in this general application of the term Cyclades; for Suidas: "*Σποραδες νησοι, ας ενιοι Κυκλαδας λεγουσιν, αι εν τῳ Αιγαιῳ.*" Nor is CONSITA altogether devoid of authority. It is according to Wagner himself the reading of the Palatine; according to Heyne of Moret. 1.; and I have found it in one of the Munich MSS. (No. 523). It has been adopted by both the Heinsii (the younger of whom [see Burmann] pronounces this very strong opinion concerning the rival reading: "Concita, mendose"), by H. Stephens, by Burmann, by Jaeck after the examination of several MSS., and by the Baskerville. It is however but candid to say that I have found 'concita' in the Petrarchian, in the Kloster-Neuburg, in all the Vienna MSS. which I examined, seven in number, and in Nos. 18059 and 21562 of the Munich, in the Gudian, the Dresden, and both the Leipzig.

NAUTICUS EXORITUR VARIO CERTAMINE CLAMOR. — That these words express, not (as has been urged in objection to the reading CONSITA in the preceding line and in favor of 'concita') the clamorous exertions of the sailors contending with rough seas, but simply the clamors and exertions usual among sailors on leaving port, is sufficiently shown, first, by the terms CERTAMINE and CLAMOR which are the very terms used by Virgil in every one of his descriptions of leaving port; see *En. III. 290, 667* (where the exception proves the rule) and *668; IV. 411; V. 778 &c.;* compare also

Apollon. Rhod. I. 1153, where the very quietness of the sea is assigned as a reason for increased exertions of the crew; and secondly, by the words CRETAM PROAVOSQUE PETAMUS, which so indisputably express the mutual exhortations of the sailors *to set out for* Crete according to the instructions and encouragement received from Anchises *(vv. 114. 115 &c.)*, that it has been proposed by Wagner (see Heyne's *V. L.* in loc.), forgetful, as it would seem, of the support which he had found for his reading 'concita' in the subsequent CERTAMINE CLAMOR, to take the whole three verses 128, 129, 130 from their present position, and place them, where, no doubt, they would have been placed by a writer more studious than Virgil of preserving the regular, prosaic order of narrative, sciz. immediately after "pelagoque volamus."

130.

PROSEQUITUR SURGENS A PUPPI VENTUS EUNTES

"Steigender Wind vom Steuer verfolgt die rüstige Meerfahrt."
Voss.

No; but *'begleitet', escorts, convoys, goes along with*, not as of the party, but as an inferior goes along with a superior for the sake of protection, or honor, or some such purpose. Compare:

"His ubi tum natum Anchises unaque Sibyllam
Prosequitur dictis, portaque emittit eburna."
En. VI. 897.

"Nam novum maritum et novam nuptam volo
Rus prosequi (novi hominum mores maleficos)
Ne quis eam abripiat."
PLAUT. *Casin. IV. 2. 3.*

"Prosequitur lateri assultans."
VAL. FLACC. II. 504.

"Ipse viros gradiens ad primi littoris undam
Prosequitur Phineus."

VAL. FLACC. IV. 628.

No notice whatever has been taken of the word either by Caro or Dryden, most probably because neither of them understood it. Ruaeus, more valiant, boldly sets it down, '*propellit*'.

134.

HORTOR AMARE FOCOS ARCEMQUE ATTOLLERE TECTIS
JAMQUE FERE SICCO SUBDUCTAE LITTORE PUPPES
CONNUBIIS ARVISQUE NOVIS OPERATA JUVENTUS

AMARE FOCOS. — Not merely *to love the domestic hearth,* but *to stay close beside it.* Compare *En. V 163* and Comm.; also "Amatque janua limen." HOR. *Carm. I. 25. 4.*

ARCEMQUE ATTOLLERE TECTIS. — "Arx attollatur, quae praesidium sit tectis. Deformant aliqui loci hujus interpretationem, cum poeta nihil aliud dicat quam, hortor, ut domos construant, illisque arcem superimponant." La Cerda. That this criticism is entirely erroneous, and the modern interpretation ("*Tectis,* sexto casu, *adtolli,* eadem ratione dictum qua supra vers. 46 'jaculis increscere'" — Forbiger) correct, is placed beyond all doubt by Statius's exactly parallel expression:

"Jam natat omne nemus; caeduntur robora classi:
Silva minor remis: ferrum laxatur ad usus
Innumeros, quod rostra liget, quod muniat arma,
Belligeros quod frenet equos, quod mille catenis
Squalentes nectat tunicas, quod sanguine fumet,
Vulneraque alta bibat, quod conspirante veneno
Impellat mortes; tenuantque humentia saxa
Attritu, et nigris addunt mucronibus iras.
Nec modus, aut arcus lentare, aut fundere glandes,
Aut torrere sudes, g a l e a s q u e a t t o l l e r e c o n i s."

Achill. I. 428.

Attollere tectis is therefore a poetical equivalent for *build up high,* as 'aggredior dictis' is for *address,* 'expediam dictis' for *explain,* &c.; see Comm. *En. II. 199.* Compare *En. II. 185:*

"Hanc tamen immensam Calchas attollere molem
Roboribus textis caeloque educere jussit."

Connubiis arvisque novis operata juventus. — One of the numerous verses which Peerlkamp thinks should be expunged as unworthy of Virgil. That critic's argument on this occasion, if it does not edify, will at least surprise and amuse, the reader.

148.

EFFIGIES SACRAE DIVUM PHRYGIIQUE PENATES
QUOS MECUM AB TROJA MEDIISQUE EX IGNIBUS URBIS
EXTULERAM VISI ANTE OCULOS ASTARE JACENTIS
IN SOMNIS MULTO MANIFESTI LUMINE QUA SE
PLENA PER INSERTAS FUNDEBAT LUNA FENESTRAS

Confirmatory of the interpretation that effigies and phrygii penates are spoken of the one object, viz. the statues of the Gods Penates, which Eneas had with him in his ship, is that passage of Ovid *(ex Ponto II. 8. 57)* where the poet describes himself as worshipping the imprints of Augustus's family on coins sent to him from Rome, and where there is a similar Endiadys in the case of this same term 'effigies':

"Felices illi, qui non simulacra, sed ipsos,
Quique Deum coram corpora vera vident.
Quod quoniam nobis invidit inutile fatum,
Quos dedit ars votis effigiemque colo."

Jacentis in somnis. — Some editors, and amongst others Heyne in his last edition (1793), read 'insomnis', on the ground that Eneas himself informs us *(v. 173)* that he had not been asleep. That this conclusion is deduced from a false premiss, and that the words, "Nec sopor illud erat." mean, not *that was not sleep,* but *that was not the effect of sleep,* i. e. *was not a mere dream, but a supernatural revelation made during sleep,* appears clearly on a comparison of this vision with the vision *(En. VIII. 26* & seq.) in which Eneas saw the God Tiberinus, and concerning which we are clearly and expressly told, first, that Eneas saw that vision during his sleep, "Procubuit seramque dedit per membra quietem," *v. 30;* and "Nox Aenean somnusque reliquit," *v. 67* (the former of which expressions corresponds exactly with JACENTIS IN SOMNIS in the passage before us); and, secondly, that it was not the effect of sleep, i. e. was not a mere dream; "Ne vana putes haec fingere somnum" *(v. 42),* words as nearly as possible equivalent to "Nec sopor illud erat." Compare also in the sixth Eclogue *(v. 14):* "Silenum somno jacentem." See Comm. *En. III. 173.*

IN SOMNIS is the reading (see Foggini) of the Medicean, and (see Bottari) of the Vatican Fragm. Also of the Modena Ed. of 1475, the two Heinsii, the two Stephenses, Burmann, La Cerda, Brunck, and Jahn. In the MSS. which I have consulted I have found it difficult to determine whether IN SOMNIS or 'insomnis' was intended; it is however plainly the latter in the Vienna MS. No. 116, and in the Petrarchian.

INSERTAS. — To Servius's first interpretation of this term, "clathratas," I object that it seems wholly arbitrary; totally unsupported by any argument. To his second interpretation, "non seratas, ut sit quasi inseratas, i. e. non clausas," I object that INSERTAS cannot be admitted to be the contraction of 'inseratas', first, until it is shown that 'inseratus' was a real word and not one merely supposed or invented by Servius for the explanation of our text; secondly, until it is shown that 'inseratus', if it had really existed, would, according to the genius of the Latin language, have been contracted into 'insertus', and not rather into 'insratus'; and thirdly, until it is shown that windows were usually fastened, like doors, with 'serae'. Neither can I admit the hypallage adopted by La Cerda and Forcellini from the third interpretation proposed by Servius, "quasi lumine suo Luna 'inseruerat,'" *(a)* such interpretation being forced and unnatural, and *(b)* the insertion of the moonlight through the windows being already sufficiently expressed in the words SE FUNDEBAT PER. Rejecting therefore all these interpretations I adopt with Heyne and Wagner the commonly received structure, 'insertas parieti', but think at the same time that the remarkable word INSERTAS is not with Heyne and Wagner merely equivalent to "factas", or "quae sunt in pariete", but has a special reference to the particular kind of window spoken of; which was, neither (with Heyne and Wagner) a mere hole or vacancy left in the wall, nor yet, like our modern windows, a sash thrown across such hole or vacancy, but an actual barrel-shaped tube (or drum open at both ends) which was veritably inserted into the wall, and which, projecting on the outside, protected the apartment from the weather, while it admitted the light and air. Such a window, corresponding exactly to the modern louvers on our roofs, while it is the most suitable which can be imagined for the temporary hut or baraque of a leader of an expedition in the heroic times, agrees perfectly with the two remarkable expressions of our text: first, it is 'inserta', actually *inserted* in the wall, or sloping roof; and secondly, through it as through a tube, canal, or conduit, the full moon SE FUNDEBAT. Compare *(Georg. III. 509)*:

> "Profuit inserto latices infundere cornu
> Lenaeos."

where 'inserto cornu' corresponds exactly to the INSERTAS FENESTRAS, and 'infundere latices' to the SE FUNDEBAT of our text.

INSERTAE FENESTRAE. — Anglice, *louvers*.

173.

NEC SOPOR ILLUD ERAT

Nor was that sleep; i. e. *that was not the effect of sleep, a mere dream, fiction* or *imagination in sleep;* compare *En. VIII. 42:*

"Ne vana putes haec fingere somnum;"

and Stat. *Theb. V. 135:*

— "Nudo stabat Venus ense; videri
Clara mihi, somnosque super;"

i. e. *more clear and plain than mere sleep could present her to me.* Hom. *Odyss. τ. 547:* "ουκ οναρ αλλ' υπαρ εσθλον" ("*non somnium hoc est,* inquit Dea ad somniantem, *sed res vera bona.*" DAMM, in voce υπαρ); also Stat. *Theb. X. 205:*

— "Vanae nec monstra quietis,
Nec somno comperta loquor;"

and Sil. Ital. III. 198:

— "Neque enim sopor ille, nec altae
Vis aderat noctis; virgaque fugante tenebras
Miscuerat lucem somno Deus."

See Comm. on "Jacentis in somnis," *v. 150.*

Strange that St. Jerome in the description which he has given us of his having been snatched up into heaven, and there, before the judgment seat of God, flogged with stripes on account of his addiction to the vain literature of the heathen, should, at the very moment that he relates his solemn renunciation of that literature in the actual visible presence of the Almighty, not only use this heathen argument of Eneas, but even Eneas's very words, to prove that what he saw and heard on that occasion, was not a mere idle dream, but a veritable, heavenly vision. The following is the passage, full of interest and instruction not only for those who do, but for those who do not, believe that it is inconsistent with the christian character and profession to study with delight those ancient heathen authors, whose sayings and admonitions even St. Paul himself did not disdain to mix up with his own in his Epistles to the Christian churches: "Interim parantur exequiae, et vitalis animae calor, toto frigescente jam corpore, in solo tantum tepente pectusculo palpitabat; quum subito, raptus in spiritu, ad tribunal judicis pertrahor ...... Interrogatus de conditione, Christianum me esse respondi. Et ille, qui praesidebat, 'Mentiris', ait; 'Ciceronianus es, non Christianus; ubi enim thesaurus tuus, ibi cor tuum' Illico obmutui, et inter verbera (nam caedi me jusserat) conscientiae magis igne torquebar. ...... Clamare autem coepi, et ejulans dicere, 'Miserere mei, Domine, miserere mei'. Haec vox inter flagella resonabat. Tandem ad Praesidentis genua provoluti qui astiterant, precabantur, ut veniam tribueret adolescentiae .... exacturus deinde cruciatum, si gentilium litterarum libros aliquando legissem. Ego, qui in tanto constrictus articulo vellem etiam majora promittere, dejerare coepi, et nomen ejus obtestans dicere, 'Domine, si unquam habuero codices seculares, si legero, te negavi'. In haec sacramenti verba dimissus, revertor ad superos; et mirantibus cunctis, oculos aperio, tanto lacrymarum imbre perfusos, ut etiam incredulis fidem facerem ex dolore. Nec vero sopor ille fuerat, aut vana somnia, quibus saepe deludimur. Testis est tribunal illud, ante quod jacui; testis judicium triste, quod timui; ita mihi nunquam contingat in talem incidere quaestionem; liventes habuisse scapulas, plagas sensisse post somnum, et tanto dehinc studio divina legisse, quanto non antea mortalia legeram." HIERON. *Epist. XVIII* (ad Eustochium). See concluding Comment *En. IV*.

181.

SEQUE NOVO VETERUM DECEPTUM ERRORE LOCORUM

Heyne, followed by all the modern commentators, rejects the vulgar interpretation of this passage *(deceived by a new, i. e. another or second error respecting the old places)* on the ground that 'novus' cannot here mean *another* or *second,* in as much as Anchises had made no *previous,* error respecting the place where the oracle of Apollo had ordered him to settle: "antea non erraverat Eneas (Anchises Qu.?) in interpretando Apollinis oraculo de antiqua matre et prima tellure exquirenda." Forbiger. In reply I beg to observe that this objection is altogether of the objectors' own creation, exists nowhere but in their own minds; for Anchises does not say that he has made *a new mistake in the interpretation of the oracle,* but *that he has made a new mistake about the old places* (NOVO VETERUM DECEPTUM ERRORE LOCORUM), referring, as I think is clearly shown by the subsequent "Hanc quoque deserimus sedem" *(v. 190),* to the unfortunate landing in Thrace *(v. 13* & seq.), of which there can be no doubt that he, the adviser of all the other movements of the expedition, was the adviser, even if the fact had not been so plainly implied in the words, "Anchises dare fatis vela jubebat" *(v. 9),* followed immediately by the information that they proceeded directly, and in the first place, to Thrace. Contrast the simplicity of the vulgar and obvious interpretation, thus explained, with the subtlety of the far-sought and unnecessary substitutions of the commentators: "'Novus' opponitur tantum 'veteribus locis', quatenus ab eo seriore aevo erratum est circa haec loca interpretanda." Heyne. "Sic solent a poetis jungi contraria, ut alterum alterius illustrandi gratia adjiciatur; ut apud Soph. 'Ω τεκνα Καδμου του παλαι νεα τροφη.'" Wagner. "Ornatum in poeta lubens agnosco, sed non ineptum. Pro NOVO scribamus s u o, etc."

Peerlkamp. See also Valpy's *Classical Journal* (Sept. 1813) for some just observations by Professor Moor of Glasgow on Pearce's ill-judged censure of Virgil for the use of this epithet ("Prae nimio studio proferendi antitheti scripsit NOVO, nullo opinor sensu; NOVO enim VETERUM respondet, sed nihil sententiae addit; imo puerilibus illam ingeniis, quam virilibus, aptiorem efficit." PEARCE, ad Longin. *de Sublim.*), as also for a new and ingenious, but, as it seems to me, very erroneous, interpretation of the passage by the same Professor.

I beg the reader, doubtful of the foregoing explanation, to observe its perfect accordance with the gradation of expression, "Quo Phoebus vocet errantes jubeatque reverti" *(v. 101),* applied to the Trojans after their first or former error, sciz. the landing in Thrace, and *(v. 145):*

"Quam fessis finem rebus ferat; unde laborum
Tentare auxilium jubeat; quo vertere cursus;"

spoken of them, when, after this new or second error, sciz. their landing in Crete, they are hopeless and despairing. See next Comment. The correctness of the above interpretation seems to be further established by the use made by Propertius of the identical words 'novus error', to express a new or second error, i. e. an error similar to one which had preceded:

"Quae tibi sit felix, quoniam novus incidit error;
Et quotcunque voles, una sit ista tibi."
PROP. I. 13. 35.

Compare also *(En. II. 228,* where see Comm.) "novus pavor," *a new*, i. e. *second fear.*

182.

ILIACIS EXERCITE FATIS

The epithet EXERCITE is here peculiarly proper, Eneas's troubles and embarassments having just been twice unnecessarily increased by two so considerable errors of Anchises; see Comm. *v. 181.* Compare Anchises's application of the same term to Eneas when he addresses him on the occasion of the new and unexpected trouble of the burning of his ships by the women, *En. V. 725.*

220.

LAETA BOUM PASSIM CAMPIS ARMENTA VIDEMUS
CAPRIGENUMQUE PECUS NULLO CUSTODE PER HERBAS

Compare: "Lucus ibi, frequenti silva et proceris abietis arboribus septus, laeta in medio pascua habuit, ubi omnis generis sacrum Deae (Laciniae Junoni sciz.) pascebatur pecus sine ullo pastore; separatimque egressi cujusque generis greges nocte remeabant ad stabula, nunquam insidiis ferarum, non fraude violati hominum." LIVY, XXIV. 3.

286.

AERE CAVO CLYPEUM MAGNI GESTAMEN ABANTIS
POSTIBUS ADVERSIS FIGO ET REM CARMINE SIGNO

CAVO. — It appears from the following passage of Ammian that shields were sometimes so hollowed out, i. e. adapted to protect the body not only in front, but on the sides, that they could on an emergency be used somewhat in the manner of boats: "Et miratur historia Rhodanum arma et loricam retinente Sertorio transnatatum; cum eo momento turbati quidam milites, veritique ne remanerent post signum erectum, scutis quae patula sunt et incurva proni firmius adhaerentes, eaque licet imperite regendo, per voraginosum amnem velocitatem comitati sunt navium." AMMIAN. XXIV. 6.

REM CARMINE SIGNO; — i. e. with a verse inscribed on the shield itself. See Hildebrand ad Apul. *Metam. VI. 3.*

297.

ET PATRIO ANDROMACHEN ITERUM CESSISSE MARITO

'Cessisse', as used here, does not at all involve the idea of submission or inferiority; is simply equivalent to *passed to — fell to — became the property of;* compare "Cedat Lavinia," *En. XII. 17, let Lavinia pass to him — become his;* "Morte Neoptolemi regnorum reddita cessit Pars Heleno," *v. 332, passed to Helenus — became Helenus's.* "Uti tum dividua pars dotis posteriori filio, reliqua prioribus, cederet." Apul. *de Magia, 91.*

317.

HEU QUIS TE CASUS DEJECTAM CONJUGE TANTO
EXCIPIT AUT QUAE DIGNA SATIS FORTUNA REVISIT
HECTORIS ANDROMACHEN PYRRHIN CONNUBIA SERVAS

Andromachen is the reading of the Vatican Fragment (see Bottari); and appears from the words of Servius ("Si Andromache, sequentibus junge; si ANDROMACHEN, superioribus") to have been a reading well known and acknowledged in his time. It is also stated by Pierius to be the reading of several of the MSS. which he examined in Rome ("sunt qui et ANDROMACHEN legant"), and by Heyne (who however does not himself adopt it) to be that of two Leyden and of one Hamburg MS. I have myself also found it in one of the Ambrosian MSS. (No. 79).

I prefer this reading for two reasons; first, for that assigned by Ladewig (by whom alone among modern editors this reading has been adopted), viz. that the ordinary reading 'Hectoris Andromache Pyrrhin' connubia servas'? causes Eneas to cast a reproach on Andromache, which the whole drift of his address shows it was not his wish or intention to do. And secondly, because, the words HECTORIS ANDROMACHEN being thus assigned to the clause QUAE DIGNA SATIS FORTUNA REVISIT, that clause is made perfectly to correspond and answer to the clause QUIS TE CASUS DEJECTAM CONJUGE TANTO EXCIPIT? the HECTORIS ANDROMACHEN of the one clause being the CONJUGE TANTO of the other. We have thus the sentence constructed according to Virgil's usual method, the concluding or winding up words, PYRRHIN CONNUBIA SERVAS, not being connected with the immediately preceding clause, but with the whole preceding sense, that whole preceding sense being made up of the first or principal clause (QUIS TE CASUS .... EXCIPIT), explained and completed by the usual subsidiary or parenthetic addition of a second (QUAE DIGNA SATIS ..... ANDROMACHEN). In other words, the two questions, contained in the two first clauses, are reducible to one single one: *In what condition do I find Hector's wife?* and this question is again put in the concluding clause, in the slightly altered form, *Is she still the handmaid of Pyrrhus?* See Comm. *En. III. 571: IV. 483. VI. 83, 739* In the intermediate or parenthetic clause, QUAE DIGNA SATIS ..... ANDROMACHEN, Eneas plainly refers to the report he had just heard of Andromache's new and incredible good fortune, the particular specification of which is with great propriety left to Andromache herself.

Alfieri, following the Baskerville, has endeavored by a change in the punctuation to extract a good sense out of the ordinary reading,

'Hectoris, Andromache, Pyrrhin' connubia servas'?

— "Di Ettórre ancora,
O di Pirro, sei tu?"

This interpretation is liable to the double objection, that it is reproachful to Andromache, and that it asks the absurd question, "are you still married to Hector?" If Virgil had written, not CONNUBIA, but 'fidem', then indeed Alfieri might not have been so far wrong

Having examined, besides the above mentioned

Ambrosian five other MSS., viz. the Petrarchian, Gudian, Dresden, and the two Leipzig, I have found in the whole five 'Andromache'.

330.

AST ILLUM EREPTAE MAGNO INFLAMMATUS AMORE
CONJUGIS ET SCELERUM FURIIS AGITATUS ORESTES
EXCIPIT INCAUTUM PATRIASQUE OBTRUNCAT AD ARAS

Two causes, operating together, impel Orestes to kill Pyrrhus. First, he is in a suitable frame of mind, in consequence of the effect produced on him by his previous murder of his mother: SCELERUM FURIIS AGITATUS; and next, he is specially provoked to the act by the carrying off by Pyrrhus of his beloved spouse: EREPTAE MAGNO INFLAMMATUS AMORE CONJUGIS. That this is the precise meaning, is declared by Ausonius:

"Impius ante aras quem fraude peremit Orestes.
Quid mirum? caesa jam genetrice furens."
Epitaph. Heroum, IX.

INCAUTUM, — sciz. because he was PATRIAS AD ARAS, in other words, *'in penetralibus suis'*, or more simply *'domi suae', at home.* Compare: "Domi suae imparatum confodere" (Ciceronem sciz.). SALLUST. *Catil. 28.* So *En. I. 353:* "ante aras," i. e. κατ' ἐξοχήν, *ante aras patrias; in penetralibus;* where also 'incautum' is applied in the same manner, and for the same reason, as in our text.

377.

PAUCA TIBI E MULTIS QUO TUTIOR HOSPITA LUSTRES
AEQUORA ET AUSONIO POSSIS CONSIDERE PORTU
EXPEDIAM DICTIS

The commentators err doubly with respect to this passage; first misinterpreting the word HOSPITA, and then, to justify the misinterpretation, applying the term otherwise than as intended by Helenus.

"Navigantibus amica, quae navigantes tutos ac salvos remittunt.' Heyne.

"Im Gegensatz des unsichern ('innospitae') Wegs um Unter-Italien." Voss.

Now HOSPITA is not *hospitable;* nor does it apply exclusively to the way round Sicily as contradistinguished from that round 'Unter-Italien', i. e. through the straits separating Italy from Sicily. First, it is not *hospitable; (a)* because in other places (I think I might safely say, in all other places) Virgil uses the term not in this, its derived or secondary, sense, but in its primitive sense of receiving in the manner of a host or inn (compare Dante's "Ahi! serva Italia, di dolore ostello." *Purgat. VI. 76)* without the least reference to the quality (i. e. the goodness or badness, hospitality or inhospitality) of the reception. See vers. 539:

— "Bellum, o terra hospita, portas;"

also Stat. *Silv. V. 1. 252:*

— "Manes placidos locat hospite cymba;"

and Claud. *Epith. Honor. Aug. et Mariae. Praef. v. 2:*

"Nec caperet tantos hospita terra Deos;"

and exactly parallel to our text:

"Ergo ego nunc rudis Adriaci vehar aequoris hospes."
PROP. III. 20. 17.

Compare also:

— "Stupet hospita belli
Unda viros, claraque armorum incenditur umbra."
STAT. *Theb. IX. 228.*

(b) Even if Virgil have elsewhere used the term 'hospita' in the sense of *hospitable,* he has not so used it here; because, if the seas were hospitable ("quae navigantes tutos ac salvos remittunt"), Helenus's directions (quo tutius lustrarentur) were wholly unnecessary. *(c)* That the seas were in point of fact not hospitable, but, on the contrary, in a high degree inhospitable, is proved

by Eneas's subsequent experience; see the storm in the first Book. Secondly, even admitting that HOSPITA may in the passage before us mean *hospitable,* still it cannot apply exclusively to the way round Sicily, in contradistinction to the way through the straits, for, if it do, the meaning of Helenus's words, PAUCA TIBI E MULTIS QUO TUTIOR HOSPITA LUSTRES AEQUORA .... EXPEDIAM DICTIS, can only be: *I will give you such directions as will enable you safely to navigate that course,* whereas in point of fact Helenus gives no directions whatever how or in what way that course is to be navigated, but only that it is to be navigated, and the other, i. e. the dangerous course through the straits, to be avoided.

Let us now see whether interpreting HOSPITA in the sense in which it is used by Virgil at vers. 539, we cannot extract from the passage a meaning, not only consistent with the directions actually given by Helenus, but at the same time compatible with the veracity of the oracle (for it must be borne in mind that Helenus is nothing less than the mouthpiece of the oracle of Apollo; *v. 433).* "I will give you," he says, "a few directions which will enable you to traverse with greater safety (TUTIOR LUSTRES) the seas on which you are about to enter (HOSPITA AEQUORA); the seas which are to receive you; which lie between this and your journey's end." Thus understood the words of Helenus are (first) not only in perfect harmony with the directions which he actually gives *(v. 410* and seq.), directions which amount simply to a warning not to take the course through the Sicilian straits (which course being the shortest, was on that account the most likely to have been taken by Eneas), but to make the circuit of Sicily; and (secondly) in no degree impair the credit of the oracle, the declaration being, not that the way round Sicily was *hospitable, "sicher," absolutely safe,* but that it could be travelled more safely (TUTIOR), with less danger than the other. Gossrau's interpretation *"ignota, fremde Meere,"* is consistent with the real character of the seas, but not conformable to the Virgilian use of the word in other places. Servius's *'vicina'* agrees neither with the character of the seas, nor with the Virgilian use of the word, nor with the context.

As HOSPITA AEQUORA in the text is simply *the host sea*, so the correlative "hospita navis" (OVID. *Fasti, I. 340)* is *the guest ship.*

CONSIDERE PORTU. — CON-SIDERE, not merely with Voss "ruhen," but *settle finally and completely.* Compare Valerius Flaccus (I. 4) of the Argo:

— "Flammifero tandem consedit Olympo."

381.

PRINCIPIO ITALIAM QUAM TU JAM RERE PROPINQUAM
VICINOSQUE IGNARE PARAS INVADERE PORTUS
LONGA PROCUL LONGIS VIA DIVIDIT INVIA TERRIS
ANTE ET TRINACRIA LENTANDUS REMUS IN UNDA
ET SALIS AUSONII LUSTRANDUM NAVIBUS AEQUOR
INFERNIQUE LACUS AEAEAEQUE INSULA CIRCAE
QUAM TUTA POSSIS URBEM COMPONERE TERRA
SIGNA TIBI DICAM TU CONDITA MENTE TENETO

LENTANDUS. — "Flectendus est .... Quidam lentandus nove verbum fictum putant, sed in Annalibus legitur: 'Confricati, oleo lentati, paratique ad arma'." Servius.

"Agendus, sed exquisitius; curvatur enim et flectitur vi undarum et nisu remigis ...... quoniam enim lenta quae sunt, facile flecti possunt, hinc lentus pro flexilis, et lentare, flectere." Heyne.

This is, as it seems to me, all either incorrect in thought, or incorrectly expressed. 'Lentare' is, not 'flectere, *to bend*, but 'flexilem facere', *to render capable of being bent; to make an object supple, so that it will yield* or *bend without breaking.* The root is 'lentus' 'Lentus' (the opposite of 'rigidus') is *bending, pliant, plastic, supple, yielding to force without breaking:* 'lentum vimen', *pliant withe, (En. III. 31);* 'lento argento', *ductile silver, (En. VII. 634);* 'lento marmore' *(En. VII. 28)* not, with Forbiger, "tranquillo, ventis immoto," but *pliable by the oar; that is not broken by the oar, but gives with it.* From this root come 'lentesco', *to grow 'lentus',*

— "Haud unquam in manibus (terra sciz.)
jactata fatiscit,
Sed picis in morem ad digitos lentescit habendo."
Georg. II. 249;

and 'lentare', *to make 'lentus'; to render that which was previously rigid and would break rather than yield, pliable;* see, quoted above by Servius from Ennius's Annals: "confricati, oleo lentati," *rubbed with oil and so made supple;* also:

"Nec modus, aut arcus lentare, aut fundere glandes,
Aut torrere sudes, galeasque attollere conis."
STAT. *Achill. I. 436;*

not, as hitherto understood, *'curvare arcus', bend bows,* but *'facere arcus flexiles', make wood supple and fit for bows,* i. e. *make bows so that when they are drawn they shall bend, not break.* And accordingly in our text, ANTE TRINACRIA LENTANDUS REMUS IN UNDA, not *your oar must be bent in the Trinacrian waters before you reach Italy* (which would only signifiy, you must pass through the Trinacrian waters before you reach Italy), but *your oars are to be rendered supple by rowing in the Trinacrian waters before you reach Italy;* i. e. *you have a long, long voyage to make; your oars will get good practice there — become,* as we say in English, "*well seasoned.*" Catullus's

— "Lentos incurvans gurgite remos."
Epith. Pel. et Thet. 183,

cited by Forbiger as parallel to our text, is therefore not parallel, the meaning of our text being, *make your previously rigid oars 'lentos' by much use of them in a long voyage,* while Catullus's meaning is, *bend your supple,* or *pliant, oars; row with so much force as to bend your pliant oars —, your oars which having previously been 'lentati',* or *made 'lenti', will now not break, but may safely be pulled with the utmost violence.*

393.

IS LOCUS URBIS ERIT

The oracle appoints the place where the white sow is found, as the site of Eneas's new city (viz. his second Troy), because the Latin word 'Troja' (Ital. *Troja,* Fr. *Truie)* signified a sow. Compare *(En. VII. 112* and seq.) the similarly trivial solution of the oracle referred to in the very next words of Helenus: "Nec tu" &c. On such puerilities turned, and (alas, that I should have to say it!) still turn oracles.

402.

PARVA PHILOCTETAE SUBNIXA PETILIA MURO

"Cincta muro modico. Alii, quia imposita est excelso muro, ut Coelius historicus ait." Servius.
"A Philoctete, Herculis comite, condita (hoc enim est SUBNIXA MURO)." Heyne.

No; the reference is to the great strength of the little city: *the little Petilia* — SUBNIXA, *relying on the strong wall by which it was able to defend itself against all assaults.* Compare Liv. XXIII. 30: "Petilia, aliquot post mensibus quam coepta oppugnari erat, ab Himilcone, praefecto Hannibalis, expugnata est. Multo sanguine ac vulneribus ea Poenis victoria stetit; nec ulla magis vis obsessos, quam fames, expugnavit ...... Nec antequam vires ad standum in muris ferendaque arma deerant, expugnati sunt." Our text is a passing compliment to this gallant defence made by the little city.

Subnixa — *relying on;* compare Sil. Ital. II. 397:

— "Galeamque coruscis
Subnixam cristis;"

and VIII. 245:

"Subnixus rapto plebeji muneris ostro
Saevit jam rostris Varro."

For an exactly similar use of 'niti' see Avienus, *Descript. Orb. Terrae, 3:*

— "Per terras qua priscis inclyta muris
Oppida nituntur."

Petilia, — as we would say in English, *Littletown* or *Littleton:* "Petilia a Petilus, quod exile et parvum est *[Petit,* Fr. Qu.?] ut a Rutilo, Rutilius." Turnebus, *Advers. 38. 28.* See also Vossius, *Etym.* in voce.

Parva. — In this instance, as in numerous others, the character of the place, as expressed by its proper name, is repeated by Virgil in his descriptive adjective. Compare:

"Qui Tetricae horrentes rupes montemque Severum."
En. VII. 713.

In like manner our own Rogers, of the Flamingo:

"What clarion winds along the yellow strands?
Far in the deep the giant fisher stands
Folding his wings of flame."

410.

AST UBI DIGRESSUM SICULAE TE ADMOVERIT ORAE
VENTUS ET ANGUSTI RARESCENT CLAUSTRA PELORI

As 'rarus' (the English *thin* and the opposite of 'densus') properly expresses the state of a body whose particles lie not closely compacted, but at some distance from each other, the expression UBI RARESCENT CLAUSTRA PELORI means, *when the barriers of Pelorus after having appeared to you for some time* (viz. so long as they were seen sideways and not in front, or from directly opposite) *to be dense* or *close together, shall begin to grow rare,* i. e. *to shew that they stand at some distance from each other,* or *that there is an interval between them:* or, in other words, *when you shall have proceeded so far round Italy as to be able to see that it is not continuous with Sicily, but separated by a strait.* "Ea est enim procul inspicientibus natura loci (claustrorum Pelori sciz.), ut sinum maris, non transitum putes; quo cum accesseris, discedere ac sejungi promontoria, quae antea juncta fuerant, arbitrere." JUSTIN. IV. 1. (With which compare Valer. Flaccus's description of the Dardanelles:

— "Dirimique procul non aequore visa
Coeperat a gemina discedere Sestus Abydo."

I. 284.)

hardly could more precise description be given of the point at which Eneas was to turn southward.

Compare:

"Rarior hinc tellus, atque ingens undique caelum
Rursus, et incipiens alium prospectus in orbem."

VALER. FLACC. II. 628;

the lands more thinly (widely) scattered: more sea between them.

"Cumque super raros foeni flammantis acervos
Trajicit immundos ebria turba pedes."
PROP. IV. 4. 77.

"Frigidior porro in puteis aestate fit humor,
Rarescit quia terra calore, et semina si qua
Forte vaporis habet propere dimittit in auras."
LUCRET. VI. 841,

(where 'rarescit' corresponds to "putrem," *En. VIII. 596)* *the component particles of the soil grow looser, more separate from each other.* Compare also: "rari nantes" *(En. I. 122);* "raris vocibus" *(En. III. 314),* not *few,* but *at intervals from each other;* or, as in the text, *showing intervals between.* Also: "Gold is so rare as very readily and without the least opposition to transmit the magnetic effluvia, and easily to admit quicksilver into its pores and to let water pass through it." NEWTON.

— "So eagerly the fiend
O'er bog or steep, through strait, rough, dense or rare,
With head, hands, wings, or feet, pursues his way."
MILTON.

CLAUSTRA; — not *the straits* or *actual passage*, but (literally) *the closers, shutters* or *barriers,* i. e. *the approximating headlands between which the very narrow passage, channel, or gut,* technically called *'strait', is left.* See Comment on 'Claustra', *En. I. 60.*

414.

HAEC LOCA VI QUONDAM ET VASTA CONVULSA RUINA

In this and the following verses there seems to be an allusion to the origin of the name Rhegium, as in 'parva', vers. 402, there is to the name Petilia. See Strabo Lib. VI. and Diod. Sicul. IV. 85.

452.

INCONSULTI ABEUNT

Heyne seems to me to err in interpreting INCONSULTI, "Quibus consultum non est, responsum non est;" first, because there is no example of its use in that sense; and secondly, because the inquirers have actually received their answer, although, on account of its being written on leaves, they have not been able to understand it. INCONSULTI is therefore, as always elsewhere, *nullius consilii; qui nesciunt quid facere oporteat; αμηχανοι.* Compare:

— "Turba per urbem
. . . .
Inconsulta ruit."

LUCAN. I. 495.

"Inconsulti homines vitaque erat error in omni."

GRAT. FALISC. *Carm. Venat.* 4;

and especially Cicero, whose words seem almost to be an express gloss upon our text: "Quid est enim praeclarius, quam honoribus et reipublicae muneribus perfunctum senem posse suo jure dicere idem, quod apud Ennium dicat ille Pythius Apollo, se esse eum, unde sibi si non populi et reges, at omnes sui cives consilium expetant,

"Suarum rerum incerti quos mea ope ex
Incertis certos, compotesque consilii
Dimitto, ut ne res temere tractent turbidas."

CIC. *de Oratore, I.* 45.

The Italians preserve the word in the same adjectival sense: *Sconsigliato,* without fixed counsel — not knowing what to think or do. The French too have their *bien conseillé* and *mal conseillé:*

"Les gens bien-conseillés et qui voudront bien faire
Entre eux et les gens fous mettront pour l'ordinaire
Le longueur de ce fil."

LA FONTAINE, *Fables, Le fou qui vend la sagesse.*

482.

NEC MINUS ANDROMACHE DIGRESSU MAESTA SUPREMO
FERT PICTURATAS AURI SUBTEMINE VESTES
ET PHRYGIAM ASCANIO CHLAMYDEM NEC CEDIT HONORE
TEXTILIBUSQUE ONERAT DONIS

HONORE is, as I have myself personally ascertained, the reading of the Gudian (a manu prima), and of the Leipzig No. 35. It is also insisted on by Pomp. Sabinus as the correct reading; and Servius informs us it was the reading of Scaurus. Adopting this reading I arrive at the following interpretation, to me much more satisfactory than any hitherto offered, of this hitherto very obscure passage, and in favor of which I request permission to withdraw the interpretation which I communicated in 1851 to my friend Dr. Forbiger, and which, along with so many other of my suggestions, he has most obligingly inserted in the third Edition of his very valuable work. I consider then, that in the first clause (FERT .... VESTES) Andromache is described generally as bringing apparel splendid with embroidery and thread of gold; that the second and third clauses particularise that this apparel consisted of a Chlamys of the Phrygian fashion, that it was a present for Ascanius, and that Ascanius (naturally, as a young lad) was not loth to receive so splendid a present, does not retire from, decline, the honor (NEC, CEDIT HONORE); and that the fourth clause describes the giving of the Chlamys, the actual putting it on his shoulders. We have thus a sentence constructed according to Virgil's usual manner, the second and third clauses depending on the first, and the last clause referring, not to the immediately preceding clause, but to the whole preceding sense — summing up as it were. The three words NEC CEDIT HONORE thus become a parenthesis very similar to that contained in *v. 661* of *En. V.* and *v. 84* of *En. VI.* where see Comments.

It seems to me no small confirmation of the above interpretation, first, that we have thus the regular *Steigerung,* all the successive steps of the making of the present; Andromache FERT, *brings the garment;* NEC CEDIT HONORE, *Ascanius does not decline,* i. e. *accepts it;* and Andromache ONERAT, *puts it on his shoulders.* And, secondly, that 'honor' is the very term applied, *En. V. 249 & 250,* to a similar present of a 'chlamys aurata':

> "Ipsis praecipuos ductoribus addit honores:
> Victori chlamydem auratam;"

also, *En. VIII. 617,* to the present of arms which Eneas receives from his mother:

> "Ille, deae donis et tanto laetus honore;"

and also to the gold and crimson vest thrown by Eneas over the dead body of Pallas:

> "Tum geminas vestes auroque ostroque rigentes
> Extulit Aeneas, quas illi laeta laborum
> Ipsa suis quondam manibus Sidonia Dido
> Fecerat, et tenui telas discreverat auro;
> Harum unam juveni supremum maestus honorem
> Induit, arsurasque comas obnubit amictu."
>
> *En. XI. 72.*

the resemblance between which description and that of our text is very striking and remarkable. Compare also the application of the same term to Camilla's mantle *(En. VII. 814):*

> — "Ut regius ostro
> Velet honos leves humeros."

With the exception of the Gudian, and Leipzig No. 35, mentioned above, 'Honori' is the reading of all the MSS. (fourteen in number) which I have myself personally examined respecting this passage.

ONERAT, — *loads him with it,* viz. by putting it on his shoulders; compare (TER. *Phorm. V. 6. 4):*

"Sed ego nunc mihi cesso, qui non humerum hunc onero pallio."

where Forcellini: *"mettersi il mantello."*

510.

SORTITI REMOS

"Per sortem divisi ad officia remigandi, qui esset proreta, quis pedem teneret." Servius.

"Qui diem remos agitando exegeramus." Wagner.

Both interpretations seem to me to be very wide indeed of the mark. I feel certain the meaning is, *having divided the oars amongst us to be used as tentpoles;* which interpretation, first suggested to me by Rutilius's

"Littorea noctis requiem metamur arena,
Dat vespertinos myrtea silva focos.
Parvula subjectis facimus tentoria remis;
Transversus subito culmine contus erat."

Itiner. I. 345,

recommends itself at once by the obvious necessity there was that Virgil should supply his navigators with some cover when they left their vessels in order to pass the night on a desolate shore. SORTITI REMOS, *divided the oars* (i. e. by implication, *the tents) among us,* in the same way as *(En. V. 756)* "sortitus domos," *divided the houses.* The 'sortitio remorum' for the purpose of rowing took place only once, viz. at first setting out; and was not repeated at the nightly halts of the expedition, each rower retaining the same oar, 'suus remus', during the entire voyage. See Ap. Rhod. I. 392—5. and *En. VI. 233.*

519.

CASTRA MOVEMUS

Forbiger understands the expression literally. I think it is no more than the ordinary metaphorical expression for *setting out, decamping.* Compare:

— "Cum cerea reges
Castra movent."

CLAUD. *Rapt. Pros. II. 125.*

520.

TENTAMUSQUE VIAM ET VELORUM PANDIMUS ALAS

Velorum pandimus alas. — Not (with Heyne) "extremas velorum partes, lacinias, angulos," because it is not usual to expand the sails to the uttermost immediately at first setting out; but, metaphorically (as "fulminis ocior alis," *En. V. 319;* "alis allapsa sagitta," *En. IX. 578), sails as swift as wings.* Compare, exactly parallel to our text:

"Nec te quod classis centenis remigat alis
Terreat."

Prop. IV. 6. 47.

The same figure (that of young birds attempting to fly) is preserved in both clauses of our text; as if Virgil had said, 'pandimus alas et tentamus volare'.

522.

CUM PROCUL OBSCUROS COLLES HUMILEMQUE VIDEMUS ITALIAM

Obscuros, — *dimly seen; scarcely distinguishable.* "Dubios montes," Lucan. III. 7. Compare:

"Obscuram (Didonem), qualem primo qui surgere mense
Aut videt, aut vidisse putat per nubila lunam."

En. VI. 453;

where see Comment.

531.

TEMPLUMQUE APPARET IN ARCE MINERVAE

Not 'templum Minervae', but 'Arce Minervae', the name of the place being Arx Minervae: "Oppidum vulgari appellatione Castro, quod antiquum illud est Castrum Minervae, sive Arx Minervae, et Minervium." CLUVER. *Ital. Antiq. Lib. IV.* The Arx Minervae is set down in Peutinger's Charta, 'Castra Minerve'.

533.

PORTUS AB EUROO FLUCTU CURVATUS IN ARCUM
OBJECTAE SALSA SPUMANT ASPERGINE CAUTES
IPSE LATET GEMINO DEMITTUNT BRACHIA MURO
TURRITI SCOPULI REFUGITQUE AB LITTORE TEMPLUM

There is a considerable affinity between this picture and that with which we are presented in the first Book *(v. 163)* "insula portum" &c., the subject of each being a natural harbour at the foot of high, rocky cliffs, and sheltered in front, in this case by a ledge of rocks, in that, by an island. The great distinctive difference between the two pictures is, that in the one before us the cliffs are at the far or landward side of the harbour and are crowned by a temple, while in that of the first Book they are seaward, at each side of the harbour's entrance; so that the view in the former case is of a high, rocky hill, the top of which, crowned with a temple, retreats backwards or from the shore, and the lower parts of which advance forwards on each side of the harbour so as to hold (as it were) or embrace it between two arms (GEMINO DEMITTUNT BRACHIA MURO), while in the latter case the view is of two tall cliffs, one on each side of the harbour's entrance, which, becoming lower on the landward side, run round the harbour so as to form its landward boundary, in the perpendicular face of which, directly opposite the entrance, and of course low down near the water's edge, is the grotto of the nymphs.

549.

CORNUA VELATARUM OBVERTIMUS ANTENNARUM
GRAJUGENUMQUE DOMOS SUSPECTAQUE LINQUIMUS ARVA

"Obvertimus, sciz. pelago; nam si e sequ. versu domibus G., h. e. littori, tum potius esset avertere vela, antennas." Heyne.

Exactly what Heyne says is *not* the meaning, *is* the meaning: *We turn* CORNUA ANTENNARUM *towards the* DOMOS GRAJUGENUM *and the* SUSPECTA ARVA. And why is this the meaning? because then the figure contained in the word CORNUA is maintained, and the picture rendered complete and worthy of Virgil; *we turn our horns towards the enemy and so make our retreat; retreat facing the enemy with our horns.* This is undoubtedly the meaning of the passage; first, because 'obvertere' and 'vertere' are the very terms used to express turning the horns against an enemy, facing with the horns:

"Nimisque ego illum hominem metuo et formido male,
Ne malus item erga me sit, ut erga illum fuit.
Ne in re secunda nunc mihi obvortat cornua."

Plaut. *Pseud. IV. 3. 3.*

"Superest ea pars epistolae, quae similiter pro me scripta in memetipsum vertit cornua." Apul. *de Magia 81;* and secondly, because the horns of the 'antennae', and indeed the whole 'antennae', are necessarily, when the vessel sets sail, turned, not like the prows toward the sea, but exactly the opposite way, i. e. toward the land, such being the effect of the fair wind (i. e. of the wind blowing from the land), viz. to force or belly out the sails toward the sea, and of course cause the retaining 'antennae and their horns to point exactly in the same proportion toward land. This effect of the fair wind is to be seen as plainly as possible in the view which the Vatican Fragm. (see Bottari, p. 92) gives of Eneas sailing from Carthage.

551.

HINC SINUS HERCULEI SI VERA EST FAMA TARENTI
CERNITUR

"Hence we behold the bay that bears the name
Of proud Tarentum, proud to share the fame
Of Hercules, though by a dubious claim."
WORDSWORTH.

No; the structure is not 'hinc cernitur sinus Tarenti', for the Bay of Tarentum could not be seen from the port of Castrum Minervae, but HINC, *after leaving this place*, or *next after leaving this place*, SINUS TARENTI CERNITUR, *the Bay of Tarentum is seen by us.*

555.

ET GEMITUM INGENTEM PELAGI PULSATAQUE SAXA
AUDIMUS LONGE FRACTASQUE AD LITTORA VOCES
EXSULTANTQUE VADA ATQUE AESTU MISCENTUR ARENAE

The grandest description with which I am acquainted of perhaps the grandest object in nature, the roaring of an agitated sea. The third Book of the Eneis, lavishly interspersed with these fine descriptive sketches of natural objects and scenery, affords rest and refreshment to the reader's mind between the intensely, almost painfully, concentrated dramatic actions of the second and fourth Books. A similar effect is produced by the interposition of the Ludi of the fifth Book between the fourth and sixth.

The GEMITUM INGENTEM PELAGI is termed by a living

poet (1847) in a fine line, and with a happy extension of the ordinary metaphor,

— "l'hurlo che manda la bocca del mar."

See *Canti Lirici di G. Prati* (of Riva on the Lago di Garda in the Italian Tyrol). Milano, 1843.

FRACTASQUE AD LITTORA VOCES. — The structure is not 'fractas ad littora', but 'voces ad littora'; the voices or sounds were not *broken on*, or *against, the shore,* but *there were at the shore broken sounds.* Compare:

— "Vox
Auditur fractos sonitus imitata tubarum."

Georg IV. 71.

"Hic turpis Cybeles et fracta voce loquendi
Libertas."

Juv. II. 111.

"Mars eminus conspicatus nuptias tenero cum admirationis obtutu languidiore fractior voce laudavit, profundaque visus est traxisse suspiria." MART. CAPELL. IX. 889.

571.

SED HORRIFICIS JUXTA TONAT AETNA RUINIS
INTERDUMQUE ATRUM PRORUMPIT AD AETHERA NUBEM
TURBINE FUMANTEM PICEO ET CANDENTE FAVILLA
ATTOLLITQUE GLOBOS FLAMMARUM ET SIDERA LAMBIT
INTERDUM SCOPULOS AVULSAQUE VISCERA MONTIS
ERIGIT ERUCTANS LIQUEFACTAQUE SAXA SUB AURAS
CUM GEMITU GLOMERAT FUNDOQUE EXAESTUAT IMO
FAMA EST ENCELADI SEMIUSTUM FULMINE CORPUS
URGERI MOLE HAC INGENTEMQUE INSUPER AETNAM
IMPOSITAM RUPTIS FLAMMAM EXSPIRARE CAMINIS
ET FESSUM QUOTIES MUTET LATUS INTREMERE OMNEM
MURMURE TRINACRIAM ET CAELUM SUBTEXERE FUMO

GLOMERAT, — not *forms into a ball,* as shown by Ovid's finding it necessary to add 'in orbes' to 'glomerat' in order to express that idea:

"Sive rudem primos lanam glomerabat in orbes."

Ovid. *Metam. VI. 19;*

but *throws up rapidly one after the other, so rapidly that the objects thrown up seem to be added to each other so as to form one body,* the essential notion of 'glomerare' being *to form into one by successive addition.* Compare "glomerare manum bello," *En. II. 315,* not *to form a round band,* but *to form a band by successive additions.*

FUNDOQUE EXAESTUAT IMO. — These words constitute the grand winding up, the completion of the picture, carrying the reader back beyond the two divisions INTERDUM and INTERDUM, to the commencing statement, HORRIFICIS JUXTA TONAT AETNA RUINIS. And such is the way in which Virgil's most elaborate sentences are usually wrought, the last clause, though in strict grammar connected only with the clause immediately preceding, having yet a connexion in the sense with the outsetting statement, or thesis, and so winding up and rounding the whole. In like manner CAELUM SUBTEXERE FUMO, vers. 582, though in grammatical strictness connected only with INTREMERE OMNEM MURMURE TRINACRIAM, refers back past that clause, to AETNAM RUPTIS EXSPIRARE CAMINIS, with which, and not with INTREMERE OMNEM MURMURE TRINACRIAM, it would have been placed in connexion by an English writer, who instead of saying that Enceladus's flames burst out through Etna, and, as often as he turned, all Trinacria shook and sent up a cloud of smoke, would have said, "the flames and smoke proceeding from the body of Enceladus burst out through Etna, and every time he turned, the whole island shook." In other words, an English writer would have been sure that his readers would have understood him literally if he had said, "Etna threw out the fire, and all Trinacria threw out the smoke." It will be observed that in both the passages not only the sense, but the grammar, remains perfect, if, all the intermediate and filling-up parts being left out, the concluding is subjoined immediately to the commencing clause:

. . . . HORRIFICIS JUXTA TONAT AETNA RUINIS
. . . . FUNDOQUE EXAESTUAT IMO.
. . . . AETNAM
IMPOSITAM RUPTIS FLAMMAM EXSPIRARE CAMINIS
. . . . ET CAELUM SUBTEXERE FUMO.

Compare the exactly similar structure, *En. V. 820:*

"Subsidunt undae, tumidumque sub axe tonanti
Sternitur aequor aquis, fugiunt vasto aethere nimbi;"

where the sense and grammar are both complete, the intermediate filling-up clause being left out:

"Subsidunt undae . . . .
. . . . fugiunt vasto aethere nimbi."

See also Comm. *En. I. 483; III. 317; IV. 483.*

INSUPER AETNAM IMPOSITAM RUPTIS FLAMMAM EXSPIRARE CAMINIS. — The sense is, not that Etna in its present form (i. e. hollowed out and having a passage through it by which the fire, which was consuming Enceladus, might escape) was placed on the top of Enceladus, but that Etna, while it was still a solid mountain, was placed on the top of Enceladus, and that the flames proceeding from him burst a passage through it, *rumpebant caminos; burst out and flamed through the sides of the mountain* as the fire sometimes bursts and breaks out through the sides of a stove. The image is the more correct, in as much as the eruptions of Etna, as well as of other vulcanoes, are apt not to follow the track of previous eruptions, but to make new openings for themselves through the solid sides of the mountain.

CAELUM SUBTEXERE. — Goethe has applied the same idea figuratively with great effect: "Seit der Zeit ist mir's als wäre der Himmel mit einem schwarzen Flor überzogen." *Egmont, Act IV.*

585.

NAM NEQUE ERANT ASTRORUM IGNES NEC LUCIDUS AETHRA
SIDEREA POLUS OBSCURO SED NUBILA CAELO
ET LUNAM IN NIMBO NOX INTEMPESTA TENEBAT

Nox intempesta — precisely the '*Νυξ Κατουλας*' of Apollonius Rhodius:

"*Αυτικα δε Κρηταιον υπερ μεγα λαιτμα θεοντας*
Νυξ εφοβει, την περ τε Κατουλαδα κικλησκουσι,
Νυκτ' ολοην· ουχ αστρα διϊσχανεν, ουκ αμαρυγαι
Μηνης. Ουρανοθεν δε μελαν χαος, ηε τις αλλη
Ωρωρει σκοτιη μυχατων ανιουσα βερεθρων.

Apoll. Rhod. IV. 1694.

606.

SI PEREO HOMINUM MANIBUS PERIISSE JUVABIT

"Sat se beatum, qui manu socia volens occumberet." Apul. *Metam. IV. 2.*

619.

IPSE ARDUUS ALTAQUE PULSAT
SIDERA DI TALEM TERRIS AVERTITE PESTEM
NEC VISU FACILIS NEC DICTU AFFABILIS ULLI

Altaque pulsat sidera. — "Tangit alta astra." Ruaeus. "Sil. Ital. XVII. 651: 'Tangens Tirynthius astra'." Wagner.

— "Un che col capo
Tocca le stelle."

Caro.

"Er selbst hochragend berühret
Hohes Gestirn."

Voss.

And Dryden, more poetical, but not less incorrect:

"Our monstrous host, of more than human size,
Erects his head, and stares within the skies."

The idea is much stronger: *so tall that he knocks, hits, thumps,* or *bumps the stars* (sciz. with his head) *as he walks.* Compare:

"Quod, si me lyricis vatibus inseres
Sublimi feriam sidera vertice."

Hor. *Carm. I. 1. 35.*

The notion of *hitting, knocking,* or *thumping* is inseparable from 'pulsare'.

Nec visu facilis, nec dictu affabilis ulli. — Compare Ovid, *Met. XIII. 760*, speaking of the same Polyphemus:

— "Visus ab hospite nullo
Impune;"

and Pliny, *Paneg. 48,* speaking of Domitian: "Ad haec ipse occursu quoque visuque terribilis — non adire quisquam, non alloqui audebat."

637.

ARGOLICI CLIPEI AUT PHOEBEAE LAMPADIS INSTAR

As large, round, and glaring, as an Argolic shield or the sun. Besides the citations of La Cerda, compare Ammian, XXIV. 2: "Continentem occupant arcem. . . . . . . cujus medietas in sublime consurgens, tereti ambitu Argolici scuti speciem ostendebat, nisi quod a septentrione id quod rotunditati deerat, in Euphratis fluenta projectae cautes eminentius tuebantur." From which passage it appears further that the distinction drawn by La Cerda and the commentators between 'clypeus' and 'scutum' was not very strictly observed by the Latin writers.

646.

CUM VITAM IN SILVIS INTER DESERTA FERARUM
LUSTRA DOMOSQUE TRAHO VASTOSQUE AB RUPE CYCLOPAS
PROSPICIO

AB RUPE belongs to CYCLOPAS, not to PROSPICIO:

First, because the poet has placed it in closer connexion with the former than the latter; jammed in, as it were, between VASTOS and CYCLOPAS, so that it cannot be separated from them without violence. Compare *En. I. 297*, where from the mere position of the words it might be inferred that the structure is, not as hitherto universally supposed 'claudentur ferro et compagibus arctis', but 'dirae ferro et compagibus arctis'.

Secondly, because joined to CYCLOPAS it enhances VASTOS, and so improves the picture; whereas joined to PROSPICIO it weakens VASTOS without strengthening PROSPICIO, and therefore deteriorates the picture.

Thirdly, because, as correctly observed by Heyne, who might have confirmed his observation from Homer, *Odyss. IX. 113:*

"*Αλλ οιγ' υψηλων ορεων ναιουσι καρηνα,*"

the Cyclops are described *(vv. 644, 655, 675)* as frequenting the heights.

I take part therefore with La Cerda and Heyne against Donatus, Wunderlich, Handius, Voss, and Forbiger, in understanding AB RUPE CYCLOPAS PROSPICIO to mean *'prospicio Cyclopas in rupibus, a parte rupium', on the mountain*; a use made of 'ab' not only by Virgil himself, but very commonly by other writers: "Vicino a limite," *Ecl. I. 54;* "Ostendit ab aethere nubem," *En. VII. 143.* "Utrimque ab cornibus positos." Liv. I. 37. "Una pars attingit a Sequanis et Helvetiis flumen Rhenum." Caes. *B. G. I. 1.* "Castra ab decumana porta non munita esse." Caes. *B. G. III. 25.* "Exercitus hostium duo, unus ab Urbe, alter a Gallia, obstant." Sall. *B. Cat. 58.* "Visas nocturno tempore ab occidente faces ardoremque caeli." Cic. *in Catil. III. 8.*

— "Ecce vigil rutilo patefecit ab ortu
Purpureas Aurora fores."

Ovid. *Metam. II. 112.*

Achaemenides concealed in the woods (in silvis) looks out on the Cyclops where they are tending their flocks in the rocky, mountain pastures (ab rupe). On the contrary, if the structure be 'prospicio ab rupe', our author has placed not the Cyclops, but Achaemenides, in the conspicuous situation, and so exposed him to the very object from which he was hiding.

For 'rupes' used in the sense of *mountain*, see *Ecl. VI. 29:*

"Nec tantum Phoebo gaudet Parnassia rupes;
Nec tantum Rhodope mirantur et Ismarus Orphea."

655.

VIX EA FATUS ERAT SUMMO CUM MONTE VIDEMUS
IPSUM INTER PECUDES VASTA SE MOLE MOVENTEM
PASTOREM POLYPHEMUM ET LITTORA NOTA PETENTEM
MONSTRUM HORRENDUM INFORME INGENS CUI LUMEN ADEMTUM
TRUNCA MANU PINUS REGIT ET VESTIGIA FIRMAT

"In Mediceo (Mediceo Romano sciz.) et codicibus aliquot aliis antiq. manu septimo casu legitur. Et ubi 'manum' est quarto casu in cod. MSS. fere passim ultimam contactam: observes. Esset vero sententiae ordo: Pinus trunca manu, vel gestata manu, regit ademptum lumen, et vestigia firmat." Pierius.

This testimony as to the reading is as good and decisive, as this judgment respecting the structure is erroneous; REGIT operates neither, with Pierius, on ADEMTUM LUMEN, nor, with Ladewig and others, on VESTIGIA, but, with Forbiger and Wagner, on eum' understood. I have myself personally examined only three MSS. respecting the passage, viz. the Leipzig Nos. 35 and 36, and the Dresden. In the first I have found MANU with 'manum' superscribed; in the second MANU; in the third 'manum'. Bersmann, although adopting 'manum', informs us that his MS. has MANU. Nicholas Heinsius is, as far as I know, the first editor who has adopted MANU, for which great and manifest improvement, I think Virgil's admirers should be grateful to him.

LUMEN. — Not, as at vers. 635, *the eye*, but, as *En. II. 85* (where see Comm.), *the light of day*.

684.

CONTRA JUSSA MONENT HELENI SCYLLAM ATQUE CHARYBDIM
INTER UTRAMQUE VIAM LETI DISCRIMINE PARVO
NI TENEANT CURSUS CERTUM EST DARE LINTEA RETRO

I think this passage is to be thus unravelled: 'Contra, Heleni jussa monent ni (ne) teneant cursus inter Scyllam atque Charybdim, utramque (et Scyllam et Charybdim), viam leti, discrimine parvo, i. e. viam prope letalem, non multum a leto distantem. Igitur consilium capiunt redeundi, sciz. Cyclopas versus'. While the Trojans are in the very act of fleeing in trepidation from the Cyclops, i. e. out of the port, they find that the wind will certainly carry them up the straits; but that way they dare not take; therefore they determine to put back and face the lesser danger from which they were fleeing. But behold, the wind veers on the instant and carries them away clear of both dangers, and in the very direction of their voyage. *(a)* Utramque, viam leti discrimine parvo is our author's usual parenthetic or subsidiary clause, descriptive of Scylla and Charybdis, and filling up and completing, but not necessary to, the sense, which is perfect the clause being omitted: 'Jussa Heleni monent ne teneant cursus inter Scyllam atque Charybdim'. *(b)* Viam leti discrimine parvo, *the way of death all but a little, almost certainly the way of death;* precisely the 'τυτϑη παραιβασις ολεϑρου' of Apollonius Rhodius speaking of the selfsame dangerous navigation:

— "Αλλ' εχε νηα
Κεισ', οϑι περ τυτϑη γε παραιβασις εσσετ' ολεϑρου."

Apoll. Rhod. IV. 831.

Compare the same Apollonius, IV. 1510:

"Ουδ οσσον πηχυιον ες Αϊδα γιγνεται οιμος."

Also,

— "Tenui discrimine leti
Esse suos."

En. X. 511.

— "Leti discrimina parva."

En. IX. 143.

(c) Viam refers, not to the journey or passage of the Trojans inter Scyllam atque Charybdim, but is applied to leti in the same way as 'janua' to 'leto', *En. II. 661;* as if Virgil had said: 'Utramque (sciz. Scyllam atque Charybdim), januam leti, discrimine parvo', *almost the sure door (way) to death.* *(d)* Servius's observation, "Antiqui Ni pro *ne* ponebant, qua particula plenus est Plautus," and the recognition by Donatus (ad Terent. *Eun. III. 3)* of ni in this very passage ("Ni *ne* significat, et Ne *non.* Ni pro *ne* Virgilius, leti discrimine parvo

NI TENEANT") are, I think, more than a sufficient answer to those who make a difficulty about NI used in the sense of '*ne*'. Virgil seems to have used the ancient form on this occasion (as he has elsewhere used 'olli' for 'illi') for the sake of the more agreeable sound — to avoid the alliteration 'ne-te-ne-'. 'Ne' is the reading of the Gudian (a manû prima).

The reader, even although he decide against this interpretation, and applaud Wagner for having cast the whole three lines out of the text as incapable of any good sense, will at least excuse me for an attempt to preserve to Virgil three entire verses; to the picture, the view of the Trojans putting out of port and immediately putting back again; and to the context, the necessary connecting link between "Praecipites metus acer agit...... secundis," and "Ecce autem Boreas" etc. The three lines being cast out, 'autem' becomes incorrect, and 'ecce autem' doubly so, because then the wind from the direction of the straits agrees with the 'inceptum' of the Trojans, which was to leave port and flee away; the three lines being preserved, 'ecce autem' becomes not only correct, but necessary in order to explain how it happened that they did not sail, as they had determined, directly back into port (CERTUM EST DARE LINTEA RETRO), but, on the contrary, proceeded immediately on their direct voyage forward: "Vivo praetervehor" &c.

TENEANT CURSUS, — simply *steer, sail, hold their voyage;* compare:

"Huc cursum Iliacas vento tenuisse carinas."

En. IV. 46.

So, "Fugam tenuisse," *En. III. 283,* simply, *fled.*

DARE LINTEA RETRO, — simply, *to put back,* viz. into the port which they were upon the point of leaving.

The difficulty, which all the commentators have found in this passage, seems to me to have arisen from their understanding VIAM to be spoken of the *journey* of the Trojans; of the *way past* Scylla, or *past* Charybdis. "Jussa Heleni monent, ne vela teneant cursus inter utramque viam, videlicet inter Scyllam atque Charybdin, parvo leti discrimine." La Cerda. "Viam inter (per) Scyllam et Charybdim utramque (i. e. sive viam per Scyllam, sive per Charybdim elegeris) parvo discrimine esse viam leti, nisi in tempore cursus teneant." Jahn. "Utramque viam inter Scyllam atque Charybdim, sive dextrum littus legentes Scyllae, sive sinistro littori propius navigantes Charybdi appropinquarimus, parvo discrimine leti esse." Forbiger.

"Doch warnt Helenus Wort, dass Scylla hindurch und Charybdis
Beiderlei Weg hinführ' auf des Todes angrenzendem Rande,
Wenn man nicht halte den Lauf."

Voss.

And so the Baskerville punctuation of the passage:

"Contra jussa monent Heleni, Scyllam atque Charybdim,
Inter utramque viam, leti discrimine parvo,
Ni teneant cursus;"

VIAM being joined with LETI and not with UTRAMQUE, and understood in the sense of 'janua leti', *En. II. 661;* 'via mortis', *Georg. III. 482;* 'via salutis', *En. VI. 96,* and the clause UTRAMQUE VIAM LETI DISCRIMINE PARVO being recognised as parenthetic, or subsidiary to the preceding clause, and the following punctuation being adopted, the whole passage becomes at once clear and intelligible:

CONTRA, JUSSA MONENT HELENI SCYLLAM ATQUE CHARYBDIM
INTER (UTRAMQUE, VIAM LETI DISCRIMINE PARVO)
NI TENEANT CURSUS: CERTUM EST DARE LINTEA RETRO.

I agree with both the Heinsii, and almost all the modern editors in rejecting the reading of the Vatican Fragm. 'movent', although I have myself found it in three of the Vienna (viz. 116. 117. 118), in two of the Gotha (viz. 54 & 236), and in No. 18059 of the Munich MSS. I have found MONENT in the Gudian, Petrarchian, Ambrosian (Nos. 79 and 107), Vienna (Nos. 113. 115. 120. 121), Munich (Nos. 21562 and 305), Gotha No. 55,

Leipzig (No. 35, a man. sec., and No. 36), Dresden, and Kloster-Neuburg. What sense it is possible to make out of the reading 'movent', I confess myself unable to discover.

696.

ORE ARETHUSA TUO SICULIS CONFUNDITUR UNDIS

In order to understand this passage, it must be borne in mind that Arethusa is, not a river, but a spring, *sorgente,* or welling fountain, on the very edge of the sea, so near the sea that, if it were not protected by an embankment, it would be entirely covered and overwhelmed by it. See not only the ancient Geographers and modern travellers, but Cicero *in Verrem III. 53* (Ed. Ernesti): "Qui fluctu totus operiretur, nisi munitione ac mole lapidum a mari disjunctus esset." Hence Virgil's expression. 'Qui nunc Siculis undis confunditur ore tuo, Arethusa': *passes out through thy fountain, Arethusa, and immediately mixes with the sea.*

ORE ARETHUSA TUO. — Not, *through thy fountain, O river Arethusa,* but *through thy fountain, O nymph Arethusa,* i. e. *through the fountain Arethusa.* Compare *(En. I. 250):*

> "Unde per ora novem magno cum murmure montis
> It mare proruptum;"

where see Comment.

Alfieri seems wholly to have misunderstood the passage:

> — "Sgorgando l'onda Eléa
> Nel seno stesso, ove tua Sicul' onda
> Sporgi, Aretusa, tu."

716.

SIC PATER AENEAS INTENTIS OMNIBUS UNUS
FATA RENARRABAT DIVUM CURSUSQUE DOCEBAT
CONTICUIT TANDEM FACTOQUE HIC FINE QUIEVIT

RENARRABAT. — "Aut pro simplici et vulgari *narrare* positum, poetarum more, aut ad eum modum formatum, quo *repeti* et *iterari* res, quas narramus, dicuntur." Heyne. ("Hoc verum." Wagner).

On the contrary I think that the compound verb is here used instead of the simple,

First, according to the general principle that a compound verb is stronger and more dignified than its simple, as for instance 'refringo' stronger and more dignified than 'frango', 'rescindo' than 'scindo', 'revello' than 'vello', 'refugio' than 'fugio', 'relinquo' than 'linquo'.

Secondly, because in the particular instance the simple verb was peculiarly ill calculated to confer dignity, in as much as it was generally used in familiar conversation and writing in the sense of 'aio', 'dico', 'loquor': "Narro tibi, haec loca venusta sunt, abdita certe." Cic. *ad Att. XV. 16.* "Narro tibi, plane relegatus videor, postquam in Formiano sum." Cic. *Ib. II. 11.*

Thirdly, because 'narro' in composition with 're' acquiring not the iterative, as most erroneously supposed by Servius, La Cerda, Heyne, Wagner, and others, but the retrospective force, (compare:

— "Ipse alta seductus mente renarrat
Principia irarum."
STAT. *Theb. III. 400;*

and

"Mutuaque exorsae Thebas Argosque renarrant."
STAT. *Theb. XII. 390.)*

was capable of indicating with greater distinctness and certainty that the fates spoken of were not future fates which were yet to be fulfilled, but fates already past and actually accomplished. This retrospective force of the particle 're' is found, more or less strongly marked, in a great many verbs in which it has not been sufficiently distinguished by philologists; ex. gr. "ad poenas *re*poscent," *En. II. 139,* with a retrospect to the previously committed crime; "*re*ferunt thalamo stratisque *re*ponunt," *En. IV. 392,* (with a retrospect to 'suscipiunt famulae'), *render up, give up what they had received.* So also: "Tu pias laetis animas *re*ponis sedibus," Hor. *Od. I. 10. 17,* with a retrospect to his having received the souls in charge. "Finibus Atticis *re*ddas incolumem," Hor. *Od. I. 3. 6,* also with a retrospect to the charge it had received. "Vox *re*ddita fertur ad aures," *En. III. 40,* with a retrospect to the investigations of Eneas. "*Re*dduntur Salio honores," *En. V. 347,* with a retrospect to the honors having been merited and duly earned by Salius, &c. &c.

Similar to the Latin 'renarro' is the Italian *ridico:* "Ch'io ridica Di quel campo ogni duce ed ogni schiera." Tasso, *Gerus. Lib. I. 36.* "Io non so ben ridir com i' v' entrai. Dante, *Inferno, I. 10.*

Quievit, — is not "narrare desiit" (Wagner), because so unterstood it were (as correctly observed by Wunderlich) a mere tautology of conticuit; neither is it (as Burmann and Wunderlich, endeavoring to avoid the tautology, have interpreted it,) "somno se tradidit," because it is wholly incredible that so skilled a master of the poetic art would have called upon his reader to imagine the breaking up of this great entertainment, and the departure of the guests and of Eneas himself, as having taken place in the narrow interval, or, to speak more correctly, in the no interval, between the words facto hic fine and quievit, when he had close at hand (sciz. in the space between the two Books, or, as it were, in the pause between the two acts of his drama) the exactly suitable place and opportunity for such ellipsis.

I reject therefore both interpretations, and understand QUIEVIT in its strictly literal sense of *becoming quiet* or *still.* CONTICUIT, *he whisted* or *became silent;* FACTOQUE HIC FINE, *and having here brought his narrative to a close,* QUIEVIT, *became still.* In the passage so understood there is not only no tautology, but each of the three expressions of which it consists, has its own distinct and appropriate meaning, CONTICUIT signifying his becoming silent, FACTO FINE the conclusion of his narration, QUIEVIT the cessation of his action. Compare Stat. *Theb. IV. 404:*

> — "Sic fata gelatis
> Vultibus, et Baccho jam demigrante, quievit;"

where the words 'gelatis vultibus', and 'Baccho demigrante' sufficiently shew that 'quievit' means, *rested not merely from speaking, but from energetic action.* Compare *En. VI. 226:* "Flamma quievit," *the flame rested from action, ceased to play;* also Liv. III. 58 (Ed. Bipont.): "Manesque Virginiae, mortuae quam vivae felicioris, per tot domos ad petendas poenas vagati, nullo relicto sonte, tandem quieverunt;" *at last rested entirely, became perfectly quiet.* So also *En. VII. 298:* "Odiis aut exsaturata quievi;" *ceased entirely from doing any thing;* and Hor. *Ep. ad Pison. 379:*

> "Ludere qui nescit, campestribus abstinet armis,
> Indoctusque pilae discive trochive quiescit;"

abstains from the game, remains quiet. So also the substantive 'quies' (whether signifying *the quiet of sleep,* or *the quiet of death)* is always cessation, not from speech only, but from all action.

Between this last verse of the third Book and the first verse of the second Book there is a parallelism which seems worthy of observation; there, at the beginning of Eneas's narration, all the company not merely "conticuere," but "intenti ora tenebant;" here, at the close of the narration, Eneas himself not merely CONTICUIT, but, FACTO HIC FINE, QUIEVIT.

IV.

Of all the pictures which it has been the delight of eminent artists to sketch after the model of the 'Infelix Phoenissa', perhaps the loveliest is the Sofonisba of Trissino; the loveliest in the simple dignity of the style, in the unaffected pathos of the sentiments, in the tenderness, resolution and devotion of the unfortunate heroine, and, perhaps not least, in the absence of the wearying monotony of rhyme, the tragedy of Trissino being, I believe, the first example in modern languages (certainly the first of any consideration) of poetry without rhyme. The Sofonisba of Alfieri (also in blank verse, but, like all Alfieri's productions, wholly destitute of pathos) is not cast at all in the mould of Dido.

In the *Oeuvres et meslanges poetiques d'Estienne Jodelle, sieur de Lymodin,* published at Paris in 1583 (and of which a copy, the only one I have ever seen, is preserved with great care in the Bibliotheque du Roi at Paris), is a tragedy entitled *Didon se sacrifiant, Tragedie d'Estienne Jodelle, Parisien.* This tragedy, on the model of the ancient drama, and with choruses, is written in so truly poetic a spirit as to be well worthy of republication, notwithstanding that it is disfigured by such misapprehensions of Virgil's meaning as the following:

— 'qu' alors il ne jouisse
De regne ny de vie, ains mourant a grande peine
Au millieu de ses jours, ne soit en quelque areine
Qu'enterré a demi." ("Mediaque inhumatus arena," *En. IV. 620.)*

The reader will perhaps not be displeased if I present him with a more favorable specimen of the style of this antique and almost forgotten, French poet and dramatist:

"Les dieux ne furent oncq tes parens, ny ta mere
Ne fut oncq celle là, que le tiers ciel tempere,
Le plus benin des cieux; ny oncq (traistre menteur)
Le grand Dardan ne fut de ton lignage auteur;
Le dur mont de Caucase, horrible de froidures,
(O cruel!) t'engendra de ses veines plus dures;
Des tigresses, je crois, tu as sucé le lait,
. . . .
Voyez si seulement, mes pleurs, ma voix, mon deuil
Ont peu la moindre larme arracher de son oeil?
Voyez s'il a sa face ou sa parole esmeuē?
Voyez si seulement il a flechi sa veuē?
Voyez s'il a pitié de cette pauvre amante?" &c.

There is also in the French language another tragedy entitled *Didon;* published by Lefranc in 1734, and preserved in the *Repertoire General du Theatre Français, vol. 30.* Paris, 1822. This work, wholly made up of badly translated 'discerpta membra' of the fourth Book of the Eneis, is remarkable, if for nothing else, at least for the astounding instance it affords of that French sentimentality which finds Shakespeare and Milton (and, as it would seem, even Virgil himself) "un peu trop forts," and dreads nothing so much as the leaving too strong an impression on the mind of the reader. It is in the concluding lines, in which the dying Dido, with her terrible curse of Eneas still quivering on her lips ("Sol, qui terrarum flammis" etc. all which the dramatist formally translates and puts forward as his own; see Comment *En. I. 96),* is made to turn round and apostrophise the hero as follows:

"Et toi dont j'ai troublé la haute destinée,
Toi qui ne m'entends plus, adieu mon cher Enée!
Ne crains point ma colere — elle expire avec moi;
Et mes derniers soupirs sont encore pour toi. *[Elle meurt.]*

Lefranc's tragedy has however been thought worthy of a translation into Italian.

2.

VULNUS ALIT VENIS ET CAECO CARPITUR IGNI

VULNUS . . . . . . IGNI. — Not, *a* wound and *a* fire, but *the* wound and *the* fire of which the reader has heard before, *En. I. 664, 677, 716* &c.

CARPITUR IGNI. — *Is gradually gnawed away, wasted,* or *consumed, by the fire.* So Lucan (VIII. 777), speaking of the tedious consumption of the corpse of Pompey the Great in a weak and insufficient funeral fire:

> "Carpitur, et lentum destillat Magnus in ignem,
> Tabe fovens bustum."

This force of *gradually, by successive steps, bit by bit,* will, I think, be found to adhere closely to 'carpere' in all its various applications. 'Carpere vitales auras', *to breathe — to consume the air by successive respirations;* 'Carpere viam', *to consume the road,* viz. by successive steps; 'Carpere somnos', *to sleep, to consume sleep,* viz. by continuing to sleep on from moment to moment; 'Carpere pensum', *to consume one's task,* i. e. to make it less and less every moment by gradually performing or going through it; 'Carpere herbam', *to graze,* i. e. to crop the grass mouthful by mouthful.

Similar to Virgil's VULNUS ALIT VENIS ET CAECO CARPITUR IGNI is Guarini's

> — "Arde Myrtillo,
> Ma in chiuso foco, e si consuma e tace."
>
> *Pastor Fido, I. 2.*

Also Lamartine's

> — "Mon ame isolée
> Comme un foyer sans air se devorant en moi."
>
> *Jocelyn.*

9.

QUAE ME SUSPENSAM INSOMNIA TERRENT

INSOMNIA, not *wakefulness,* because mere wakefulness had not justified the energy of the exclamation, but *dreams, visions in sleep;* first, because dreams or visions in sleep are frequently of such a nature as to produce both terror (TERRENT), and doubt and anxiety about the propriety of certain conduct (SUSPENSAM); secondly, because this is the sense in which it has been used by Virgil elsewhere, see *En. VI. 897.* Compare Tacit. *Annal. XI. 4:* "Illud haud ambigitur, qualicunque insomnio ipsi fratrique perniciem illatam;" and Ammian, XXIII. 3: "Hic Juliani quiescentis animus, agitatus insomniis, eventurum triste aliquid praesagiebat." And thirdly, because in the original after which Virgil has painted the whole picture, it is expressly *ονειροι:*

> "*Δειλη εγων, οιον με βαρεις εφοβησαν ονειροι.*
> *Δειδια, μη μεγα δη τι φερῃ κακον ηδε κελευθος*
> *Ηρωων. περι μοι ξεινῳ φρενες ηερεθονται.*"
>
> APOLL. RHOD. III. 636.

A right understanding of this word, placed in this prominent position at the commencement of the Book, and forming the subject of Dido's first passionate exclamation to her sister, is essential to the right understanding of almost the whole of the subsequent Drama. A decided color, if I may so say, is thrown on the picture by this first stroke of the pencil, and carefully maintained through the whole, even to the last finish. In this fourth Book of the Eneis as in Bürger's Leonora, the first words are the key to the whole piece. As

> "Lenore fuhr um's Morgenroth
> Empor aus schweren Träumen,"

so Dido after a similar night (probably after the appearance of her deceased husband to her in her sleep,) flies early in the morning to her sister with the exclamation, QUAE ME SUSPENSAM INSOMNIA TERRENT, *what frightful dreams I have had! — I am so distracted I don't know what to do.* As, immediately following Leonora's dreadful dreams, and without other connection than that best of all connections, immediate sequence, comes her exclamation,

> "Bist untreu, Wilhelm, oder todt?
> Wie lange willst du säumen?"

so, immediately following Dido's exclamation of horror at her dreams, comes, without other introduction, or connection, their subject matter: "Quis novus hic hospes" &c. The vehemence of Dido's expressions all through her address to her sister, and especially her tremendous oath or adjuration, "Sed mihi vel tellus" etc., are thus satisfactorily explained. In her distress and agitation between (SUSPENSAM) the impulses of her passion on the one hand, and the terrific (TERRENT) warnings of her dreams on the other, and fearing that the strength of her passion might overcome both her own sense of propriety and the warnings conveyed to her from the dead, or on the part of the dead, through her dreams, she endeavors to strengthen the weakness of her resolution to obey the warnings and conquer her passion, by an oath expressed in the strongest language which it was possible even for Virgil to put into her mouth — and then, the next moment, (her passion conquering both her resolution and her oath) bursts into tears.

The answer of Anna,

> "Id cinerem aut Manes credis curare sepultos?"

goes to confirm the above views; there being in these words, as I think, besides their plain and acknowledged meaning, a special reference to the frightful dreams which Dido had understood to manifest the displeasure of the 'Manes' at her new affection. As if Anna had said: — "Go on with your purpose, and don't mind the dreams which you erroneously suppose the offended Manes to have sent you. Can you indeed believe that your new love is any affair of theirs? that a former husband, once he is dead and buried, cares whether his widow marries again or not?" I am the more inclined to think that there is a reference in the word 'Manes' to the INSOMNIA of Dido, on account of the express connection of 'insomnia' (always, as far as I know, used by the Romans in a bad sense, compare:

"Exercent rabidam truculenta insomnia mentem."
SIL. ITAL. X. 358)

with 'Manes' by Virgil himself, *En. VI. 897,* from which it appears that it was the special province of the Manes to send 'insomnia'. Compare also Dido's threat (vers. 384 & seq.) that, when she is dead and with the 'Manes', she will haunt Eneas 'ignibus atris'.

As here in the first scene, so all through, Dido's part in the drama is deeply tinged with the fine coloring of superstition. Following the advice of her sister, she proceeds immediately to the temples of the Gods, and seeks there for favorable omens to neutralise the bad omens of the INSOMNIA: "Principio delubra adeunt" &c.; later, she threatens Eneas that her ghost will haunt him after her death; and still later, when she has taken the resolution to kill herself, she sees the sanctified wine turn into blood, hears the ominous hooting of the owl, the voice of her dead husband calling to her out of the private chapel she had consecrated to his memory in her palace, and again has her frightful visions — dreams that Eneas is pursuing her, and that, alone and deserted of all, she is wandering through deserts in search of her Tyrians; and finally, when she has actually prepared her funeral pyre, has recourse to the various magical incantations enumerated at vers. 510.

A further confirmation of the above explanation, viz. that Dido, in the words QUAE ME SUSPENSAM INSOMNIA TERRENT, refers to her dead husband having appeared to her in her sleep and warned her not to have any thing to do with Eneas, may be found in Tacit. *Ann. I. 65*, where that writer, having informed us that the Roman General, Cecina, had been terrified by a dream, "Ducemque terruit dira quies" (words corresponding exactly with Dido s QUAE ME SUSPENSAM INSOMNIA TERRENT), proceeds immediately with the explanation: "nam Quinctilium Varum sanguine oblitum et paludibus emersum, cernere et audire visus est velut vocantem" &c. Compare also (vers. 351) the account given by Eneas himself of the frequent terrific warnings he had had from his father Anchises in his dreams:

"Me patris Anchisae, quoties humentibus umbris
Nox operit terras, quoties astra ignea surgunt,
Admonet in somnis et turbida terret imago;"

and observe the exact parallelism, "in somnis turbida terret imago" -- INSOMNIA TERRENT.

22.

SOLUS HIC INFLEXIT SENSUS ANIMUMQUE LABANTEM IMPULIT

LABANTEM IMPULIT. — "Impulit, ut labaret." Forbiger. "Impulit, ut jam labet." Wagner, *Virg. Br. En.*

I think not; but much more simply and naturally, 'impulit animum jam labantem, i. e. invalidum, parum firmum'. Compare:

"Turrim in praecipiti stantem summisque sub astra
Eductam tectis, unde omnis Troja videri
Et Danaum solitae naves et Achaia castra,
Aggressi ferro circum, qua summa l a b a n t e s

2

Juncturas tabulata dabant, convellimus altis
Sedibus impulimusque."

En. II. 460:

also:

— "Agit ipse furentem
In somnis ferus Aeneas."

En. IV. 465;

not, surely, 'agit ut furat'; but 'agit jam furentem, i. e. furiosam .

Impulit. — Highly emphatic, owing to its position. See Comments *En. II. 246; IV. 274.* The same observation applies to 'Abstulit', vers. 29; 'Reppulit', vers. 214; 'Exstruis', vers. 267, and all similarly placed words throughout the whole poem.

27.

ANTE PUDOR QUAM TE VIOLO AUT TUA JURA RESOLVO

Compare *(v. 552):* "Non servata fides" &c. and *(v.596):* "Nunc te facta impia tangunt;" where see Comment.

The chapter of Meursius (Opp. Tom. V. Col. 51) in which he shows from the authority of Festus, Propertius, Valerius Maximus, and Plutarch (he might have added Virgil), and from inscriptions on tombs, that among the Romans, "Honestae matronae, et quibus pudicitiae gloria curae erat, semel tantum viro nubebant," is well worthy the attention of those who discern in the morality of modern civilisation no blemish; in that of ancient, no excellence.

Two years ago, when travelling with a *vetturale* from Rome to Florence, I happened to see in the hands of a Lyonnese gentleman who was in the same carriage, a little volume of poems written not long previously by a Frenchman of humble rank, I believe a working baker of Lyons. In one of the poems of the unpretending little volume I found the sentiment which Virgil here ascribes to Dido, and which does so much honor to ancient Roman morality, expressed with such sweetness and simplicity that I took the trouble to copy the poem; and am sure few of my readers will be offended if I here present it to them entire, in as much as, having neglected to take the name of the author, I am unable to refer them to the work itself; and even if I were able, it is not probable that it could be had except in Lyons:

CONFIDENCE.

LA JEUNE FEMME.

Quelle secrète injure aurais-tu donc reçue?
Pourquoi cette pâleur et ce triste maintien?
Cette larme, qui tombe et craint d'être aperçue,
Me cache quelque chose, et cela n'est pas bien.

LA JEUNE VEUVE.

Il est au fond de l'âme, ô ma douce compagne,
Des peines qu'on ne peut avouer qu'à Dieu seul,
Qu'il faut que le mystère à jamais accompagne,
Et qu'on doit emporter sous son dernier linceul.

LA JEUNE FEMME.

Cependant, ô ma soeur, car le noeud qui nous lie
Me permet envers toi d'user d'un nom si cher,
Parle, tu me connais: dans le sein d'une amie
Le chagrin, que l'on verse, en devient moins amer.

LA JEUNE VEUVE.

Oh! mon Dieu! je croyais dans mon âme oublieuse,
Que la mort nous laissait reprendre notre foi . . . .
Mais non, non: mes aveux te rendraient malheureuse,
Ma soeur; mon amitié n'est plus digne de toi.

LA JEUNE FEMME.

Achève, ma tendresse implore cette epreuve.

LA JEUNE VEUVE.

Ces jours donc, dans le soif de ses enivrements
Je quittai pour le bal mes vetements de veuve,
Et j'y parus le front orné de diamants;

Et le soir, de retour, j'étais devant ma glace,
Et mes yeux me disaient que j'étais belle encor:
Mais, ô terreur! soudain mon image s'efface,
Et je vois apparaître une tête de mort!

Et son front depouille reprend sa chevelure,
Ses yeux vides et creux rallument leur flambeau,
La chair couvre la joue et refait la figure . . . .
Je reconnus les traits d'un epoux au tombeau.

Et dans son ironique et funèbre déboire
Sa levre m adressa de terribles discours,
Que tu n'entendras point . . mais si tu veux m'en croire,
Gardons la foi jurée à nos premiers amours.

Compare the bitter terms of reproach in which the shade of a husband met by Dante in Purgatory complains of his wife's marrying after his death:

"Non credo che la sua madre più m'ami,
Poscia che trasmutò le bianche bende,
Le quai convien che misera ancor brami.
Per lei, assai di lieve si comprende
Quanto in femmina fuoco d'amor dura,
Se l'occhio o'l tatto spesso no'l raccende."

Purgat. VIII. 73.

Compare also the noble sentiment of Böttiger *(die Aldobrandinische Hochzeit, p. 14):* "Das was unsere Sprache so bedeutend ausspricht, als die ihr vielfach verschwisterte griechische (viz. in the word $\gamma\alpha\mu o\varsigma$), die Hochzeit, gehört zu dem Cyclus rein menschlicher Handlungen, und ist das höchste Fest, was im glücklichsten und unbescholtensten Fall jeder Mensch nur einmal feiert." And Statius, *Epicedion in patrem suum, Silv. V. 3. 239:*

"Nec solum larga memet pietate fovebas;
Talis et in thalamos: una tibi cognita taeda
Connubia, unus amor."

And Propert. IV. 11. 36:

"In lapide huic uni nupta fuisse legar."

30.

SIC EFFATA SINUM LACRYMIS IMPLEVIT OBORTIS

SINUM, — *pectoris Didonis.* Peerlkamp refers SINUM to Anna, not to Dido ("credo sinum sororis, in quo sinu caput et vultum reponebat"); contrary to the general principle that an object is to be referred to the nearest person, when there is neither adjunct nor other clear indication to refer it to the more remote; compare: "Vultum lacrymis atque ora rigabat" *(En. IX. 251),* where 'vultus' and 'ora' are those of Alethes, not of Nisus and Euryalus. "Lacrymae volvuntur inanes" *(En. IV. 449),* where 'lacrymae' are the tears of Eneas, not of Dido (see Comm. *v. 449);* and "Nunc te facta impia tangunt" *(En. IV. 596),* where the 'facta impia' are those of Dido, not of Eneas (see Comm. *v. 596).* The examples just quoted are sufficient to shew that the Latin language, verifying the Horatian maxim, "brevis esse laboro, obscurus fio," loses in clearness what it gains in strength and brevity, by its frequent omission of the possessive pronouns. The German language by its similar omission of the possessive pronouns gains and loses in the same manner; see Göthe's *Iphigenia in Tauris,* the plot of which turns on the ambiguity of the expression "Die Schwester," which, applied by the oracle of Apollo to Orestes's sister, is understood by Orestes of Apollo's own sister.

In support of the above interpretation, and against that of Peerlkamp, the following further examples may be adduced. Hypsipyle, speaking of herself (OVID. *Heroid. VI. 70):*

"Huc feror; et lacrymis osque sinusque madent."

Ovid *(Heroid. VIII. 62)* of Medea:

"Perque sinum lacrymae fluminis instar eunt;"

and *(Trist. V. 4. 39):*

"Verba solet, vultumque tuum, gemitusque referre,
Et te flente suos immaduisse sinus;"

also *(Fasti, IV. 521):*

"Dixit; et ut lacrymae (neque enim lacrymare Deorum est)
Decidit in tepidos lucida gutta sinus;"

and above all, the original after which Virgil has, even to the most minute particulars, painted his Dido, Apollonius's Medea, weeping by herself in secret, where there was no bosom to be wet by her tears, but her own:

— "δευε δε κολπους
Αλληκτον δακρυοισι."

APOLL. RHOD. III. 804.

32.

PERPETUA MAERENS CARPERE JUVENTA

The meaning goes hand in hand with the grammatical structure: 'maerens carpere perpetua juventa', *pining, be preyed on by perpetual youth*, i. e. *perpetual celibacy*. The received interpretation, "per totam juventutem tuam maerore carperis" (Forbiger, Wagner, Ladewig), is trebly faulty; first, as substituting a common-place and prosaic, for a new and poetical, idea; secondly, as placing the gist of the thought in MAERENS, and not, as required by the whole context, in JUVENTA; thirdly, as destroying the connexion between this line and the next: *be preyed upon by perpetual youth so as not to know sweet children &c.*, and breaking up this single question into the two dissimilar and unconnected questions: *shalt thou be preyed upon by sorrow during thy whole youth? and shalt thou not know sweet children? &c.* The correct interpretation points out the correct punctuation, viz. a comma instead of the note of interrogation usually placed at JUVENTA.

Virgil's PERPETUA CARPERE JUVENTA is surpassed only by our own Shakespeare's

"Withering on the virgin thorn."

38.

PLACITONE ETIAM PUGNABIS AMORI

"At tu ne pugna cum tali conjuge, virgo."
CATULL. *Carm. LXII. 59.*

52.

DUM PELAGO DESAEVIT HYEMS ET AQUOSUS ORION
QUASSATAEQUE RATES DUM NON TRACTABILE CAELUM
HIS DICTIS INCENSUM ANIMUM INFLAMMAVIT AMORE
SPEMQUE DEDIT DUBIAE MENTI SOLVITQUE PUDOREM
PRINCIPIO DELUBRA ADEUNT PACEMQUE PER ARAS
EXQUIRUNT MACTANT LECTAS DE MORE BIDENTES
LEGIFERAE CERERI PHOEBOQUE PATRIQUE LYAEO
JUNONI ANTE OMNES CUI VINCLA JUGALIA CURAE
IPSA TENENS DEXTRA PATERAM PULCHERRIMA DIDO
CANDENTIS VACCAE MEDIA INTER CORNUA FUNDIT
AUT ANTE ORA DEUM PINGUES SPATIATUR AD ARAS

DESAEVIT. — The DE in DESAEVIT has the force of our English *away;* marks *continuation with reckless vehemence.* DUM PELAGO DESAEVIT HYEMS, *whilst the winter rages away on the sea.* So *(En. X. 569):* "Sic toto Aeneas desaevit in aequore victor," *rages away over the whole plain;* where the expression 'toto aequore' shows the allusion to the *raging away* of a storm over the sea-level. So also *En. II. 215* "Miseros morsu depascitur artus," *feeds away on the wretched limbs.*

En. XI. 59: "Haec ubi deflevit," *when he had wept away.* Ovid, *Fasti, IV. 755:* "Dum degrandinat;" *whilst it hails away.* A similar force will be found to exist in the verbs 'delitigare', 'deproeliare' and some others.

Solvitque pudorem. —

"Cras pudorem, qui latebat veste tectus lignea,
Unico munita nodo non pavebit solvere."

Pervigilium Veneris,
(Pristino nitori restit. Lips. 1852) *v. 21.*

— "*Δη γαρ οι απ' οφθαλμους λιπεν αιδως.*"

Apoll. Rhod. III. 1068.

Bidentes. — "Bidentes autem dictae sunt quasi *biennes;* ..... Sunt etiam in ovibus duo eminentiores dentes inter octo, qui non nisi circa bimatum apparent: nec in omnibus, sed in his quae sunt aptae sacrificiis inveniuntur." Servius. And so Forbiger ad loc. and Gesner in voce.

The observation is highly incorrect; the fact being, as I have satisfied myself by observation, that the sheep, until it has attained the age of one year, has a set of eight primary, or milk, teeth; when the age of one year has been attained, the two central of these eight teeth drop out, and are replaced by the first two teeth of the second or permanent set, which being very large and conspicuous amidst the six remaining milk teeth (originally much smaller, and now greatly diminished by use and absorption) the animal at first sight appears to have only two teeth (sheep never having any teeth at all in the upper jaw); hence the appellation 'Bidens'. This condition of the teeth continues during the whole of the second year, at the end of which, i. e. when the sheep is two years old complete, two more of the milk teeth drop, and are replaced by two large permanent teeth exactly similar to, and one on each side of, the two first; so that from the completion of the second year till the beginning of the third the sheep appears to have a set of four large teeth, and is no longer 'bidens'. 'Bidens' therefore is not 'biennis', but simply 'bi-dens'; i. e. a sheep with two teeth, or, in other words, a sheep in the second year of its age; that is to say, at some period between end of first, and end of second, year.

LEGIFERAE CERERI PHOEBOQUE PATRIQUE LYAEO. — Not only Juno, Venus and Hymen (see Comm. vers. 125) were concerned in matrimonial alliances, but Ceres and Bacchus ("sine Cerere et Baccho friget Venus"), and even Apollo:

"Nec Ceres nec Bacchus absunt, nec poetarum Deus."

Pervigil. Veneris, 43.

"At procul ut Stellae thalamos sensere parari
Latous vatum pater, et Semeleïus Evan,
Hic movet Ortygia, movet hic rapida agmina Nysa;
Huic Lycii montes, gelidaeque umbracula Thymbrae,
Et, Parnasse, sonas; illi Pangaea resultant,
Ismaraque, et quondam genialis littora Naxi."

STAT. *Silv. I. 2. 219.*

"*Απολλωνα φασι μετα τας μεγαλας νικας, ας πληττων την λυραν ηρατο, και κατα παστασδων ηχησαι μελος γαμηλιον.*" HIMER. *Orat. I. 3.*

SPATIATUR AD ARAS. —

— "Sparsis Medea capillis
Bacchantum ritu flagrantes circuit aras."

OVID. *Met. VII. 257.*

65.

HEU VATUM IGNARAE MENTES QUID VOTA FURENTEM
QUID DELUBRA JUVANT EST MOLLES FLAMMA MEDULLAS
INTEREA ET TACITUM VIVIT SUB PECTORE VULNUS

These words cast no reproach either upon soothsaying generally, or upon the soothsayers engaged on this special occasion, their simple meaning being, that Dido's soothsayers little knew the state of Dido's mind — that she was beyond all help — that hers was no case for sacrifice, or propitiation of the Gods — that their art was thrown away upon her. EST MOLLES FLAMMA MEDULLAS INTEREA; so little good is she likely to derive from sacrificing, that, even while she is sacrificing, the internal flame is consuming her. And so Servius: "Non sacerdotes vituperat, quasi nescios futurorum; sed vim amantis exprimit, et inde vituperat sacerdotes. IGNARAE igitur amoris reginae." And so also Apuleius, in his manifest imitation *(Metam. X. 3.* Edit. Hildebr.): "Heu medicorum ignarae mentes! Quid venae pulsus, quid caloris intemperantia, quid fatigatus anhelitus, et utrimquesecus jactatae crebriter laterum mutuae vicissitudines? Dii boni! Quam facilis, licet non artifici medico, cuivis tamen docto, venereae cupidinis comprehensio, cum videas" &c., as if he had said: "Ye may be good enough physicians, but this is not a case for you. What use to examine the state of her pulse, her hurried breathing, her tossing from side to side? It is not illness that is the matter with her; it is not medicine, or a physician, that she requires; she is not sick, but over head and ears in love." Compare also the probable original of our text:

"Ακλειης οδε μαντις, ος ουδ' οσα παιδες ισασιν
Οιδε νοῳ φρασσασθαι, οθ' ουνεκεν ουτε τι λαρον
Ουτ' ερατον κουρη κεν επος προτιμυθησαιτο
Πϊθεῳ, ευτ' αν σφιν επηλυδες αλλοι επωνται."

APOLL. RHOD. III 932.

The doctrine contained in this passage, in that just cited from Apuleius, and in our text, amounts to this: your soothsayers and physicians may be, and I doubt not are, very wise in their respective professions or callings, but beyond those limits they are [like the Pope of the present day] no wiser than their neighbours. Dido's soothsayers, although they could prophesy the future, were blind to the fact which was present and staring them in the face, viz. that Dido was in love; Apuleius's physicians could cure a fever, but could not see that their patient was not sick, but only in love; and Apollonius's Mopsus could vaticinate with unerring skill for Jason and the Argonauts, but had not sufficient discernment to perceive that it was his place to retire when Jason wished to be alone with his sweetheart.

The structure therefore is, not (as at *v. 627, En. VIII.)* 'Ignarae vatum', but 'mentes vatum'; and VATUM is not (with Gossrau) Dido and her sister, but the priests of the temple.

73.

HAERET LATERI LETALIS ARUNDO
NUNC MEDIA AENEAN SECUM PER MOENIA DUCIT
SIDONIASQUE OSTENTAT OPES URBEMQUE PARATAM
INCIPIT EFFARI MEDIAQUE IN VOCE RESISTIT
NUNC EADEM LABENTE DIE CONVIVIA QUAERIT
ILIACOSQUE ITERUM DEMENS AUDIRE LABORES
EXPOSCIT PENDETQUE ITERUM NARRANTIS AB ORE
POST UBI DIGRESSI LUMENQUE OBSCURA VICISSIM
LUNA PREMIT SUADENTQUE CADENTIA SIDERA SOMNOS
SOLA DOMO MAERET VACUA STRATISQUE RELICTIS
INCUBAT

HAERET LATERI LETALIS ARUNDO. — Imitated by many; especially, and with much elegance, by Racine, *Phaedr. II. 2*, Hippolyte speaking:

"Portant partout le trait dont je suis dechiré."

INCIPIT EFFARI MEDIAQUE IN VOCE RESISTIT. —

— "From the tongue
Th' unfinished period falls."

THOMSON, *Spring*.

Nature is ever the same. The whole of Thomson's masterly description of the symptoms of love may serve as a commentary on Virgil's admirable picture of the manifestation of the passion in Dido.

VICISSIM. — Burmann (quoting Hor. *Od. I. 12. 46)* understands VICISSIM of the moon (whose light had been obscured by the sun during the day), obscuring in her turn the light of the stars; an interpretation sufficiently disproved by the words SUADENTQUE CADENTIA SIDERA SOMNOS, which indicate, not that time of night when the moon shines bright among the stars, but that time (towards morning) when both moon and stars become dim. Noehden *(Erklärende Anmerkungen zu Virgil's Aeneis)* renders VICISSIM by '*wechselweise*', and adds the following gloss: "Erst war der Mond hell, LUMEN; dann dunkel, LUNA OBSCURA, i. e. lumen lunae obscuritas vicissim sequitur;" a fade, unmeaning truism, which few readers will permit to be palmed upon Virgil. The interpretation of Wunderlich, "VICISSIM ponitur etiam ubi altera res, quo VICISSIM refertur, non est nominata; tum notat secundum vicissitudinem naturae," although elegant and poetical (as Wunderlich's interpretations almost always are), is yet considerably remote from the truth, for the "altera res, quo VICISSIM refertur" is actually named in the preceding LABENTE DIE; the obvious meaning and connexion of the whole passage being, *Now,* LABENTE DIE *at the close of day, she seeks the same banquets &c. and afterwards,* UBI DIGRESSI, LUMENQUE OBSCURA VICISSIM LUNA PREMIT, SUADENTQUE CADENTIA SIDERA SOMNOS *when the banquet is over, and night too in her turn is near a close,* SOLA DOMO MAERET VACUA &c.; the words LUMEN OBSCURA LUNA PREMIT,

SUADENTQUE CADENTIA SIDERA SOMNOS, in the second clause of the passage, exactly corresponding to the words LABENTE DIE in the first, and expressing, only with an elegant variety of imagery, the exactly similar idea of the night closing, VICISSIM, *in her turn*. Compare (SENEC. *Troad. 1141)*:

— "Astra cum repetunt vices."

Addison, in his beautiful and well known hymn, uses the corresponding English expression in nearly the same manner:

"While all the stars that round her burn,
And all the planets in their turn."

As Virgil in the passage before us speaks of the setting of the moon succeeding the setting of the sun, so Lucan speaks of the shadows of the moon, i. e. the shadows cast by the moon, succeeding to those cast by the sun:

"Sidera prima poli, Phoebo labente sub undas,
Exierant, et luna suas jam fecerat umbras"
LUCAN. V. 424.

Lucan's 'suas' is Virgil's VICISSIM. Compare also the same author, IV, 282:

"Substituit merso dum nox sua lumina Phoebo."

There is a precisely similar use of 'vicissim', *En. V. 827;* where see Comment. So also Claudian, of the alternate succession of night to day:

"Jamque soporiferas nocturna silentia terris
Explicuere vices."
Rapt. Proserp. III. 404;

and, still more apropos to our text, Lucretius (V. 761), where, having first treated of the manner in which the rays of the sun are intercepted from the earth by the moon in a solar eclipse, he proceeds to consider how the earth 'vicissim', *in her turn*, intercepts the solar rays from the moon in a lunar eclipse:

"Et cur terra queat lunam spoliare vicissim
Lumine."

88.

PENDENT OPERA INTERRUPTA MINAEQUE
MURORUM INGENTES AEQUATAQUE MACHINA CAELO

"Torquet nunc lapidem, nunc ingens machina lignum."
HOR. *Epist. II. 2. 73.*

"Sed magnitudo operum, altitudo muri atque turrium, multitudo tormentorum, omnem administrationem tardabat." CAES. (de oppugnatione Massiliae) *B. C. II 2.* From which passages I think it may be safely deduced, first, that OPERA in the text is taken, not in its general, but in its particular, sense, and means, not *the building of the city,* but specially and par excellence, and as we ourselves say in English, *the works,* i. e. *the defences, fortifications of the town.* Compare: "Urbem operibus clausit." C. NEP. *Miltiad. VII. 2.* "Circumdatam operibus Numantiam." VELL. PAT. II. 4. And secondly, that MACHINA is neither (with Heyne) "simpliciter, *moles, aedificium,*" nor (with Gossrau) *"die Gerüste," the scaffolding of the walls,* nor (with Wagner) *"turres* per murum dispositae," for the 'turres' have been mentioned only three lines previously, but *the 'tormenta', or other engines for the defence of the city.* Compare:

"Aut haec in nostros fábricata est machina muros
Inspectura domos venturaque desuper urbi."
En. II. 46;

and:

"Quo molem hanc immanis equi statuere? quis auctor?
Quidve petunt? quae religio? aut quae machina belli?"
En. II. 150;

in both of which passages, as in our text, the great height of the 'machina' is insisted on, height above the enemy being in ancient sieges the quality most requisite in all engines whether of offence or defence.

103.

LICEAT PHRYGIO SERVIRE MARITO
DOTALESQUE TUAE TYRIOS PERMITTERE DEXTRAE

"Vide an PERMITTERE DEXTRAE TUAE sit: tutelae tuae permittere, ut DOTALES ad maritum pertineat." Wunderlich.

Wunderlich is right; but was preceded by H. Stephens, in the margin of whose Edition, opposite to DEXTRAE, I find *'fidei'*. PERMITTERE is the usual term for handing over into the safe keeping of another — transferring to another the power, authority, or jurisdiction over — an object; compare: "Servus quidam, cui cunctam familiae tutelam dominus permiserat suus." APUL. *Met. VIII. 22,* where see Hildebrand.

121.

DUM TREPIDANT ALAE SALTUSQUE INDAGINE CINGUNT

I agree with Servius and Ladewig against Heyne, Wagner, and Forbiger, that ALAE are the *'equites'* and not the *'pinnae'*, or *Federlappen;* and interpret Silius's parallel

— "Subitoque exterrita nimbo
Occultant alae venantum corpora silvis."
SIL. ITAL. II. 418,

not, with Forbiger, "Venantes latebant post alas indaginum," but simply, and, as I think, according to the plain construction, 'alae venantum occultant corpora (sua), i. e. equites venatores occultant se'. Scoppa (in Gruter's *Thesaurus, I. 625)* informs us, on the authority of an ancient fragment, that there were four species of huntsmen: "Investigatores, Indicatores, Insidiatores, et Alati, qui equo feras in casses urgent." Compare Sil. Ital. II. 84:

— "Sed virgine densior ala est."

The term is preserved in Italian; see Manzoni's *Promessi Sposi, Cap. IV.:* "Con gli occhi a terra, col padre compagno al fianco, passò la porta di quella casa, attraversò il cortile tra una folla che lo squadrava con una curiosità poco ceremoniosa, salì le scale, e di mezzo all' altra folla signorile che fece ala al suo passaggio, seguito da cento sguardi, giunse" &c. Also Ibid. Cap. X.: "Si smonto fra due ale di popolo che i servi facevano stare indietro."

125.

ADERO ET TUA SI MIHI CERTA VOLUNTAS
CONNUBIO JUNGAM STABILI PROPRIAMQUE DICABO
HIC HYMENAEUS ERIT

"HIC HYMENAEUS ERIT, i. e. hae erunt nuptiae." Servius.
"Dort sei das bräutliche Fest." Voss.
"HYMENAEUS hier die *solemnia nuptiarum,* die Art und Weise der Verbindung." Thiel.

But first, Virgil, where he uses 'Hymenaeus' in this sense elsewhere, invariably puts it in the plural number; and secondly, HYMENAEUS in this sense is a mere tautology of the preceding line. I therefore understand HYMENAEUS here to mean strictly and properly *the deity Hymen;* as if Venus had said: 'aderimus ego et Hymenaeus'. Compare Ovid, *Metam. VI. 428:*

— "Non pronuba Juno,
Non Hymenaeus adest;"

Heroid. VI. 43:

"Non ego sum furto tibi cognita: pronuba Juno
Affuit, et sertis tempora vinctus Hymen;"

Metam. IX. 761:

"Pronuba quid Juno, quid ad haec, Hymenaee, venitis
Sacra;"

and, above all, *Metam. IX. 795:*

"Postera lux radiis latum patefecerat orbem,
Cum Venus, et Juno, sociosque Hymenaeus ad ignes
Conveniunt, potiturque sua puer Iphis Iänthe."

The three deities whose sanction, as appears from this last passage, was necessary to constitute a perfect marriage, are thus brought to sanction the marriage of Eneas and Dido; viz. Juno and Hymen by their actual presence, and Venus by her CERTA VOLUNTAS, pledged to Juno.

128.

ATQUE DOLIS RISIT CYTHEREA REPERTIS

Not, with Servius and Burmann, "dolis Junonis, quos Venus videbat, deprehendebat;" but, with Heyne and Forbiger, "quos Juno excogitaverat, struxerat." Compare (exactly parallel): "Illic epulante Britannico, quia cibos potusque ejus delectus ex ministris gustu explorabat, ne omitteretur institutum, aut utriusque morte proderetur scelus, talis dolus repertus est." TACIT. *Ann. XIII. 16.*

132.

ODORA CANUM VIS

"Canes robusti." Heyne.

"Voc. VIS et magnum numerum et robur canum indicat." Forbiger.

No: what kind of 'vis' is meant, is clearly pointed out by ODORA. ODORA CANUM VIS, literally *the smelling talent* or *instinct of dogs* — *dogs having the smelling talent* — *keen-scented dogs;* i. e. hounds, *Jagdhunde.* So in Horace, *Epod. VI. 5:*

> "Nam, qualis aut Molossus, aut fulvus Lacon,
> Amica vis pastoribus;"

'vis' is shown by the context not to be the talent of smelling, 'vis odoratus', but *the talent — energy — of fighting,* i. e. strength and courage: that this is the 'vis' meant, is shown by the species of dogs mentioned, the Molossus and Lacon, *bulldog* and *mastiff,* whose 'vis', *innate energy of strength and courage,* is 'amica pastoribus', sciz. because by means of those qualities the sheep are protected from the wolves. In like manner, Petron. p. 321: "Lapidum virgultorumque vis", *the properties of stones and shrubs.*

143.

QUALIS UBI HIBERNAM LYCIAM XANTHIQUE FLUENTA
'DESERIT AC DELUM MATERNAM INVISIT APOLLO
INSTAURATQUE CHOROS MIXTIQUE ALTARIA CIRCUM
CRETESQUE DRYOPESQUE FREMUNT PICTIQUE AGATHYRSI
IPSE JUGIS CYNTHI GRADITUR MOLLIQUE FLUENTEM
FRONDE PREMIT CRINEM FINGENS ATQUE IMPLICAT AURO
TELA SONANT HUMERIS HAUD ILLO SEGNIOR IBAT
AENEAS TANTUM EGREGIO DECUS ENITET ORE

Not only is the hero of the Eneis modelled after the hero of the Argonautics (see Comm. *En. III. 10.),* but he is made the subject of the selfsame comparisons:

> "*Οιος δ' εκ νηοιο θυωδεος εισιν Απολλων*
> *Δηλον αν ηγαθεην, ηε Κλαρον, η ογε Πυθω,*
> *Η Λυκιην ευρειαν επι Ξανθοιο ροησι,*
> *Τοιος ανα πληθυν δημου κιεν* (sciz. *Ιησων*)."

APOLL. RHOD. I. 307.

Hibernam. — "Non δυσχειμερον, sed ευχειμερον (ut vocat Aristot. *Polit. VII.)*, i. e. aptam hiemantibus, ita enim regionis est ingenium." Lemaire, after Servius. I think however, with Heyne, that hibernam is here neither δυσχειμερον, nor ευχειμερον, does not directly express either the clemency, or inclemency, of the Lycian winter or of the Lycian climate, but simply that Lycia was the winter residence of Apollo; *ubi hibernabat.* Of this use of 'hibernus' we have numerous examples: "Sol aut ignis hibernus." Cic. *de Senect. XIV.* "Hibernum cubiculum." Cic. *Ep. ad. Q. Fr. I. 3. 1.* "Hiberna pira." Plin. XXXXVI. 26. "Hibernus calceatus feminarum." Id. ib. c. 8. "Hiberni agni." Id. VIII. 47. Not the sun, fire, chamber, pears, shoeing, lambs, *having the character of winter,* but the sun, fire, chamber &c. *in* or *for the time of winter;* so, in English, winter clothing, winter provisions, winter quarters &c.; and so, in the text, *hibernam* lyciam; not *wintry* (having the character of winter) *Lycia,* but *winter* (the adjective *winter,* i. e. of winter, belonging to the season of winter) *Lycia;* as if Virgil had said, 'hiberna sua in Lycia' Accordingly Servius: "Constat Apollinem sex mensibus hiemalibus apud Pataram, Lyciae civitatem, dare responsa." In which statement however Servius can hardly be perfectly correct, for if Apollo spent one half the year in Lycia and the other half in Delos, when was he to be found in his famous shrine at Delphi? It is much more probable that having spent the winter in Lycia he paid only a passing visit to 'maternam Delon', on his way to spend the summer at Delphi; and accordingly Avienus represents the festivities at Delos in honor of Apollo as taking place early in the spring, 'vere novo':

"Omnes fatidico curant solennia Phoebo.
Nam cum vere novo tellus se dura relaxat,
Culminibusque cavis blandum strepit ales Hirundo,

Gens devota choros agitat, [cratituque] sacrato
Ludunt festa die, visit sacra numen alumnum"

Descript. Orb. Terrae, 705.

Compare the account which Virgil here gives us of the rejoicings with which Apollo was greeted at Delos on his arrival there in the spring, after having passed the winter in Lycia, with the account given us by Himerius *(Orat. XIV. 10),* after Alcaeus, of his festal reception at Delphi in summer on his return from his visit to the Hyperboreans; an account, not only full of beauty in itself, but highly illustrative of the passage before us, and for which, whether it be genuine Alcaic or not, no less than for the numerous other charming fragments, of his own as well as of other authors, which he has handed down to us, I gladly render Himerius the humble tribute of my thanks; and to my thanks would add my recommendation of the fine old rhetorician (easily accessible since the publication of his works at Göttingen by Wernsdorf in 1790) to the attention of scholars, if I did not feel how little likely to be of much effect such recommendation from one less known in the literary world than even Himerius himself.

IMPLICAT AURO. — It appears from Callimachus *(Hymn. in Apoll. 32)* that golden dress and ornaments specially belonged to Apollo:

"*Χρυσεα τῳ 'πολλωνι το, τ' ενδυτον, η τ' επιπορπις,*
Η τε λυρη, το, τ' αεμμα το Λυκτιον, η τε φαρετρη·
Χρυσεα και τα πεδιλα. πολυχρυσος γαρ Απολλων,
Και τε πολυκτεανος."

See also in La Cerda numerous citations to the same effect.

160.

INTEREA MAGNO MISCERI MURMURE CAELUM
INCIPIT INSEQUITUR COMMIXTA GRANDINE NIMBUS
ET TYRII COMITES PASSIM ET TROJANA JUVENTUS
DARDANIUSQUE NEPOS VENERIS DIVERSA PER AGROS
TECTA METU PETIERE RUUNT DE MONTIBUS AMNES
SPELUNCAM DIDO DUX ET TROJANUS EANDEM
DEVENIUNT PRIMA ET TELLUS ET PRONUBA JUNO
DANT SIGNUM FULSERE IGNES ET CONSCIUS AETHER
CONNUBIIS SUMMOQUE ULULARUNT VERTICE NYMPHAE

---

§ I.

The storm not only is the immediate occasional cause of the union between Eneas and Dido, and hides it from the eyes of the company present, but is emblematical of it. There is a union taking place at the same time between Eneas and Dido and between the air and the earth. Compare:

"Tum pater omnipotens foecundis imbribus Aether
Conjugis in gremium laetae descendit, et omnes
Magnus alit, magno commixtus corpore, foetus."

Georg. II. 325.

— "Ipsum in connubia terrae
Aethera, cum pluviis rarescunt nubila, solvo" (Venus sciz.).

STAT. *Silv. I. 2. 185.*

"Cras erit, quo primus Aether copulavit nuptias,
Ut pater totum bearet vernus annum nubibus.
In sinum maritus imber fluxit almae conjugis,
Unde fetus aleret omnes mixta magno corpore."

Pervigilium Veneris, 55.

§ II.

The union of Dido and Eneas is plainly modelled after that of Medea and Jason. Both are brought about specially by Juno herself; both take place in a cave, and the Nymphs officiate at both:

"*Αυτονυχι κουρῃ θαλαμηϊον εντυον ευνην*
Αντρῳ εν ηγαθεῳ . . . .
Ενθα τοτ' εστορεσαν λεκτρον μεγα· τοιο δ' υπερθε

> Χρυσέον αιγλῆεν κωας βαλον, οφρα πελοιτο
> Τιμηεις ο γαμος και αοιδιμος. ανθεα δε σφι
> Νυμφαι αμεργομεναι λευκοις ενι ποικιλα κολποις
> Εσφορεον . . . .
> Αι μεν τ' Αιγαιου ποταμου καλεοντο θυγατρες·
> Αι δ' ορεος κορυφας Μελιτηΐου αμφενεμοντο·
> Αι δ' εσαν εκ πεδιων αλσηΐδες. ωρσε γαρ αυτη
> Ηρη Ζηνος ακοιτις, Ιησονα κυδαινουσα."

APOLL. RHOD. IV. 1130 & seq.

§ III.

DANT SIGNUM. — A signal at the commencement of a ceremony, or when a number of persons is to be set in motion at once, is of obvious necessity, and frequently mentioned by ancient writers. See the Procession in the *Achilleis, II. 153:*

> "Jamque movent gressus; thiasisque Ismenia buxus
> Signa dedit, quater aera Rheae, quater Evia pulsant
> Terga manu."

Also *En. V. 578:*

> — "Signum clamore paratis
> Epytides longe dedit, insonuitque flagello."

And, exactly parallel to our text, Jupiter's giving the signal to the lightnings to play in honor of Probinus and Olybrius's entering on the consular office:

> "Ut sceptrum gessere manu, membrisque rigentes
> Aptavere togas, signum dat summus hiulca
> Nube pater, gratamque facem per inane rotantes
> Prospera vibrati tonuerunt omina nimbi."

CLAUD. *in Prob. et Olybr. Cons. 205.*

§ IV.

It has been generally supposed that our author represents the union of Eneas and Dido as taking place under unlucky omens; that the 'signum' spoken of was an earthquake, and that an earthquake was in a high degree unlucky ("Nihil tam incongruum nubentibus, quam terrae motus vel caeli." Servius), that the flashing of Ether was unlucky ("Cum enim ait fulsisse ignes, infaustum connubium videtur ostendere." Servius).

and finally, that the 'ululatus' of the Nymphs prognosticated death: "Ideo medium elegit sermonem (ululare sciz.) quia post nuptias mors consecuta est." Servius. And so Henry Stephens: "Ulularunt, mortem hoc connubium secuturam significantes." And Alfieri:

— "All' aure
Varj auspicj s'udiro; il suol tremò;"

And Heyne: "Mala nuptiarum omina enarrare debebat poeta et videtur enarrare: motum terrae, aeris fragorem vento concitati, fulmina, et per montium juga auditos clamores vel ululatus; quae omnia, cum tempestate et procella magna interdum conjuncta, nunc praeclare ad deas pronubas Tellurem et Junonem, et ad Nymphas tanquam carmen nuptiale canentes referuntur." And again: "Ululant adeo prae terrore et sensu magni mali."

I hold all this to be not merely incorrect, but directly contrary both to common sense and the author's whole drift and intention. First, the signal given was not the act of Tellus singly (in which case indeed there might have been some grounds for supposing it to be an earthquake), but the act of Tellus conjointly with Juno who in the ancient cosmology has nothing to do with earthquakes, and who besides, being the friend and protectrix of Dido and Carthage, and acting on the present occasion in her special character of Pronuba, in a marriage brought about by her herself for their advantage, cannot be supposed to be a party to the production of a bad omen. The erroneous supposition of an earthquake has no doubt arisen out of the previous erroneous assumption that the Tellus spoken of was the material tellus, *the earth;* this being once assumed, the second error followed as a necessary consequence, there being no conceivable way in which the material earth could give a signal except by motion, i. e. earthquake. Avoiding this error — keeping clear of the manifest absurdity that the solid material earth and the person Juno united to give the signal.

and understanding the meaning to be, that the two personally present Goddesses, Tellus and Juno, gave the signal together, all ground or pretext for an earthquake vanishes, and, with the earthquake, the first of the bad omens. The two Goddesses are to be regarded as giving the signal for the flashings of Ether and the huzzaings of the Nymphs in honor of Dido's wedding, with a simple nod of the head, or waive of the hand, just as in the passage above quoted from Claudian, Jupiter must be imagined to give with a similar nod of the head, or waive of the hand, the signal for the similar manifestations in honor of the entrance of Probinus and Olybrius on their consulate.

§ V.

PRIMA TELLUS. — The epithet PRIMA is applied to Tellus, not (with Wagner) in place of the adverb 'primum' and to signify *"Primum* Tellus et Juno dant signum, *tum* ulularunt Nymphae," (for why should such extraordinary care and emphasis be used to inform us that the signal preceded the act which it commanded), but as declaratory of the character in which Tellus was present at the wedding, viz. as the first spouse, and first mother ("Der Himmel ist der Vater, die Erde die Mutter aller Dinge." CONFUCIUS; see Du Halde, vol. II. p. 349; Klemm, *Cultur-Geschichte, vol. VI. p. 321).* Compare: "primamque Deorum Tellurem" *(En. VII. 136);* where it will be observed further that Tellus is introduced, as in our text, in the company of the Nymphs ("primamque Deorum Tellurem Nymphasque"), and Varro, *R. R. I. 1:* "Itaque quod ii parentes magni dicuntur, Jupiter pater appellatur, Tellus terra mater." Also Hesiod. *Theog. v. 44:*

"Θεων γενος . . . .
Ἐξ αρχης ους Γαια και Ουρανος ευρυς ετικτον."

PRIMA being so understood, each of the two divinities present has a title, not only of honor, but appropriate to the role which she was then playing.

§ VI.

FUISERE IGNES ET CONSCIUS AETHER etc. — Immediately on receiving the signal from Juno and Tellus, Ether (personally present no less than Tellus) lights the nuptial torch (held by Juno herself at the marriage of Peleus and Thetis: "*Αυτη δε σελας χειρεσσιν ανεσχον Νυμφιδιον.*" APOLL. RHOD. IV. 808); compare Himer. *Orat. in Severum Connub*: "*Απτετω τις δαδα μεγαλην.*" and Claudian, *de Rapt. Proserp. II. 230*:

— "Nimbis Hymenaeus hiulcis
Intonat, et testes firmant connubia flammae."

and the Nymphs (also personally present,) raise, not *a melancholy cry* or *howl*, but, as is perfectly plain from the manner in which both Ovid (*Heroid. VII. 95,* Dido herself speaking) and Statius (*Silv. III. 1. 75),* refer to our text and quote the word 'ululare' from it, *the nuptial huzza.* Compare Ovid, *Heroid. II. 117*:

"Pronuba Tisiphone thalamis ululavit in illis;"

(where, the ill omen being solely in the word 'Tisiphone', 'ululare' corresponds, as in our text, to the German *jauchzen.)*

— "Laetis ululare triumphis."
LUCAN. VI. 261.

"Liber adest, festisque fremunt ululatibus agri."
OVID. *Metam. III. 528.*

— "Jam gaudia magnae
Testantur voces, victorque ululatus aderrat
Auribus."
STAT. *Theb. IX. 177.*

and Virgil himself, En. XI. 662:

— "Magnoque ululante tumultu
Feminea exultant lunatis agmina peltis."

Nor let it be objected that it seems somewhat unusual for the Nymphs to be thus brought to rejoice and huzza at a marriage; for not only they, but the Nereids and even wild Pan himself, are brought by Himerius to the wedding of Severus: "*ηγαγον δ᾽αν εκ μεν Αθηνων τας Μουσας ..... τας Νηρηιδας δε εκ του γειτονος, νυμφων τε χορους και Δρυαδων ηχω και Σατυρους σκιρτωντας και Πανα συριζοντα και παντα τον Διονυσου θιασον εντευθεν, οπου τα δρωμενα. . . . . Αλλα που μοι παρθενων, που δε ηιθεων χοροι; Υμιν των λοιπων παραχωρουσιν οι λογοι. Απτετω τις δαδα μεγαλην. ο δε τις ηχειτο. ωδη δε εχετω τα συμπαντα.*" HIMER. *Orat in Severum Connubialis, 20.* And Apollonius (see § II. above) represents Juno as bringing for the especial honor of Jason, "*Ιησονα κυδαινουσα,*" not only the Nymphs of the mountains, but those of the rivers and of the woods, to officiate at his union with Medea.

SUMMO VERTICE. — These words compared with the corresponding words of Apollonius (from whom, see § II. above; the whole scene is very exactly copied), "*Αι δ'ορεος κορυφας Μελιτηιου αμφενεμοντο,*" seem to determine the Nymphs spoken of, to be, not the Hamadryads (who are separately mentioned by Apollonius) but the Oreads or mountain Nymphs: "*Αι μεν οσαι σκοπιας ορεων λαχον.*" APOLLON. RHOD. I. 1226.

§ VII.

So far all has been prosperous. The marriage planned and desired by Juno for the benefit of Dido and Carthage, has been solemnised in the immediate presence of herself and Tellus, the nuptial torch kindled by Ether himself, the nuptial huzza raised by the Nymphs, Venus so far from placing any impediment in the way, actually consenting, and (at vers. 125) giving, as it were, her proxy to Juno; but all is insufficient; Juno's intentions are, as Venus (vers. 128) well knew they would be, all frustrated; the Fates are more powerful than she; what she intended as the first step towards the aggrandizement of Dido and consequently of the Carthaginian empire, is, as we are informed in the very next line, the first step towards Dido's ruin:

"Ille dies primus leti primusque malorum."

the report of what has happened spreads far and near; Iarbas becomes jealous, complains to Jupiter; Mercury is sent down, Eneas hurried off to Italy, and unfortunate and betrayed Dido (betrayed, observe, not by Juno, who is herself disappointed and frustrated, but by Venus and Eneas) kills herself in despair.

178.

IRA IRRITATA DEORUM

"*Χωομενη Διι.*" APOLL. RHOD. II. 40. For the structure see Comments *En. II. 413; III. 181.*

206.

JUPITER OMNIPOTENS CUI NUNC MAURUSIA PICTIS
GENS EPULATA TORIS LENAEUM LIBAT HONOREM
ASPICIS HAEC AN TE GENITOR CUM FULMINA TORQUES
NEQUIDQUAM HORREMUS

Observe the emphasis in NUNC: *now and never before: thy worship having, until introduced by me* (see *v. 199), been unknown to the Maurusian nation."* Compare: "Cui nunc cognomen Iulo," *En. I. 271;* and Peerlkamp's note on that passage.

GENITOR. — Observe Virgil's usual correctness: Iarbas, the son of Jupiter (see *v. 198),* addresses Jupiter not (as Anchises *En. II. 691)* with the ordinary term 'pater', a term so vague and general as to be applicable by any junior or inferior, to any senior or superior (see *En. II. 2),* but with the proper and distinctive appellation 'genitor' ("ο γεννησας πατηρ," SOPH. *Electr. 1432).*

216

MAEONIA MENTUM MITRA CRINEMQUE MADENTEM SUBNEXUS

"Crinem unguentatum subnixum et subligatum habens; aut 'subnixus', fiducia elatus." Servius.
"'Subnixus'. Salmasius, ad Solinum, p. 392, SUBNEXUS, perperam." N. Heins. in Burmann.
"'Subnixus'. Sic membranae nostrae." Brunck.
"Habens subnixum, i. e. subligatum mentum" &c. La Cerda.
"'Subnixus', mento ac crine subnixo, mitra; scilicet mitra subligatum habens mentum ...... Potest 'subnixus', exquisitius dictum videri; quodcunque enim subligatum sibi habet aliquam rem, illud subnixum ea re videri potest." Heyne.
"Pileo quodam incurvo, unde pendebant fasciae, quae subter mentum colligari solebant; itaque 'mentum crinemque madentem subnixus', i. q. mitra subligatum habens mentum" &c. Wagner.
"Leidens Cod. SUBNEXUS .... sed alteram lectionem 'subnixus' recte defendunt Heynius, et Gronov. in *Diatr. Stat. c. 54. p. 543.*" Jahn.

Perhaps in the whole annals of criticism there is no instance of an equal number of scholars agreeing, not merely to accept a solecism from the MSS., but to defend it by argument, while there was at hand a reading not only wholly unobjectionable with respect to grammar, but affording a better, clearer, and stronger sense, and at the same time abundantly confirmed by the use of the author in other places. 'Subnixus', having an active signification, cannot by any possibility exist in connexion with MENTUM; and Virgil must have written not 'subnixus', but, as found in the Leyden MS., SUBNEXUS; a reading, besides, preferable to 'subnixus' (supposing 'subnixus' possible) for these two additional reasons; first, as presenting the idea of *subligation*, or *tying underneath*, an idea not at all expressed by 's u b n i x u s', as is sufficiently shown by Silius's "galeamque coruscis subnixam cristis," where the helmet (which is below) is represented as 'subnixa' on the crests (which are above); and secondly, as the precise word which our author has elsewhere used on two very similar occasions:

— "Fusos cervix cui lactea crines
Accipit, et molli subnectens circulus auro."

En. X. 137.

"Ac primum laxos tenui de vimine circlos
Cervici subnecte."

Georg. III. 166.

Compare Statius, *Silv. V. 3. 115:*

— "Specieque comam subnexus utraque;"

and especially Lucian, *Dial. Deor. XVIII. 1:* "Μιτρᾳ αναδεδεμενος την κομην."

I do not hesitate therefore here, as I have not hesitated at *En. I. 452* (where there is the precisely opposite scriptural error) and at *En. II. 616,* to discard from the text a reading, which, although recommended by the vast majority both of MSS. and of editors, bears a manifest falsehood on its forehead, and to adopt a reading to which there is no other objection than the slender support afforded it either by MS. or printed authority, no MS., so far as I know, being in its favor, except the single Leyden one quoted by Heyne, and no editions except the Baskerville and that of Ruaeus.

237.

NAVIGET

This imperative placed first in the verse, and separated from both preceding and subsequent context by a complete pause, and therefore constituting in itself an entire sentence, is in the highest degree emphatic; see Comments En. II. 246; IV. 274.

242.

TUM VIRGAM CAPIT HAC ANIMAS ILLE EVOCAT ORCO
PALLENTES ALIAS SUB TARTARA TRISTIA MITTIT
DAT SOMNOS ADIMITQUE ET LUMINA MORTE RESIGNAT

§ 1.

DAT SOMNOS ADIMITQUE. — The intimate connexion between these words and the immediately succeeding LUMINA MORTE RESIGNAT will appear more evident if we bear in mind that the coming on of sleep at night and the waking in the morning were in ancient times supposed to be so much under the direction and control of Mercury, that not only were libations made to that deity just before going to bed, but it was usual to have *Ερμινες* or little images of him (corresponding to the little crucifixes which are so generally throughout Christendom hung on or near the bed) either affixed to, or carved on, some part of the bed, in order that they might be the last object beheld by the closing eyes at night, and the first which should salute the opening eyes in the morning. See Schol. ad Hom. *Odyss. ψ. 198.*

Hence appears how even stronger than I have stated in the following section of this Comment, is the parallelism of the one function of Mercury with the other, the closing of the sleeper's eyes at night on the sleeping couch and the opening of them in the morning, with the closing of the dead man's eyes on the deathbed and the opening of them eight days after on the 'lectus funeralis'.

Statius, *Theb. II. 59,* makes a most poetical use of the empire assigned by the ancients to Mercury over sleep:

— "Sopor obvius illi (sciz. Mercurio)
Noctis agebat equos, trepidusque assurgit honori
Numinis, et recto decedit limite caeli."

§ II.

LUMINA MORTE RESIGNAT. — "Claudit, perturbat." Servius. An interpretation which we cannot entertain for one moment, in as much as it is in direct opposition to the constant use of the word, which is never 'claudere', but always 'aperire'.

Forcellini, following a second interpretation of Servius: "resolvere oculos, labefacta eorum structura." Equally inadmissible as Servius's first interpretation, *(a)* because equally opposed to the constant use of 'resignare', and *(b)* because LUMINA MORTE RESIGNAT were then but a repetition of, and much weaker form of expression for, SUB TARTARA TRISTIA MITTIT.

Burmann, unable to unravel, would cut the knot, and following two MSS. of very inferior authority, substitute 'limina' for LUMINA, thus giving us a fade repetition either of SUB TARTARA TRISTIA MITTIT, or of EVOCAT ORCO, or of both; and, not content himself with his own proposition , ingenuously subjoins: "Qui melius se ex hoc loco expedierit, illi lubens accesserim."

Jahn (and Ladewig also) follows Servius, with only a very slight deviation, "Mihi placet ratio, *oculos morte claudit,* ut hujus versus sententia sit, *virga illa dat somnum et mortem.* RESIGNAT enim poeta propter praecedens ADIMIT scripsisse videtur. adimit oculis somnum, et denuo eos (alio tempore) morte occludit," and is answered by the same argument.

"Equidem malim Hemistichium abesse, ET LUMINA MORTE RESIGNAT; quocunque te interpretatione vertas, sententia est a loco aliena." Heyne.

"Hanc esse persuasum habeo sententiam: *lumina aperit jamjam se claudentia;* ut Mercurius dicatur in vitam revocare jam morientes." Wagner. And so Voss: "Vom Tode, vom Todesschlummer entsiegelt; d. i. die schon

Sterbenden in's Leben zurückführt, nicht die Gestorbenen. Es ist Steigerung des vorhergehenden SOMNOS ADIMIT." To which exposition, besides the strong objection raised by Wagner himself, "nihil tale a caeteris scriptoribus (de Mercurio sciz.) traditur," there is the no trifling obstacle, that it represents Mercury as opening the eyes before they are closed.

From all these embroilments it is pleasant to turn to what, to me at least, appears an unobjectionable interpretation, first, I believe, proposed by Turnebus *(Advers. Lib. XXIV.)* and afterwards adopted by that fine old Spanish commentator, La Cerda, whose admirable Virgil lies as much neglected in modern studios as an Irish publication in a London bookseller's shop, and no doubt for the same reason, viz. that so eloquently expressed nearly two thousand years ago in the question, "What good thing can come out of Galilee?" La Cerda's words are brief: "Aperit lumina in rogo; in quo allusum ad morem Romanorum." This interpretation, first, preserves to RESIGNAT its ordinary, well etablished signification of *opening, unsealing;* compare "testamenta resignat" (HOR. *Epist. I. 7. 9) unseals the* (previously sealed, 'signata') *wills.* Secondly, assigns to Mercury no new, unheard-of office, the opening of the dead man's eyes on the pile (probably done originally with the intention that he should be able to see his way to Hades) being naturally placed under the auspices of, or ascribed to, the ψυχοπομπος himself; nay, forming the first and most indispensable step to be taken by him in the discharge of his office. Thirdly, avoids all repetition. Fourthly, makes allusion to a rite which the Romans regarded as of great importance and solemnity: "Morientibus illos (oculos) operire rursusque in rogo patefacere, Quiritium magno ritu sacrum est; ita more condito, ut neque ab homine supremum eos spectari fas sit, et caelo non ostendi." PLIN. XI. 37. In solemn funerals therefore the dead man's eyes remained closed for seven entire days, being closed at the time of death by the hand of one of the family, and opened by the same hand when the body was laid on the pile on the eighth day afterwards: "Octavo incendebatur, nono sepeliebatur." Serv. ad *En. V. 64.* And so Becker, in his excellent romance of *Gallus, oder Römische Scenen aus der Zeit August's* (2nd Ed. 3 Tom. Leipzig, 1849): "Nachdem die Freundschaft dieser Pflicht sich entledigt hatte, setzte der Zug sich wieder in Bewegung, um nach dem Grabmale zu gelangen, das Gallus an der Appischen Strasse sich errichtet hatte. Dort war von trocknen Kieferstämmen, mit Laubgewinden und Teppichen behangen, der Scheiterhaufen errichtet, um welchen rings Cypressen gepflanzt waren. Die Träger hoben den Lectus hinauf, und aus zahlreichen Alabastern gossen Andere köstliche Oele über den Leichnam aus, während Kränze und Weihrauch, als die letzten Gaben der Liebe, von den Anwesenden hinauf geworfen wurden. Dann öffnete Chresimus dem Todten die Augen, welche dieselbe treue Hand zugedrückt hatte (viz. at the time of death eight days previously), dass sie aufwärts zum Himmel schaueten, ergriff unter lautem Klagegesange der Anwesenden und dem Schalle der Hörner und Flöten die brennende Fackel, und hielt sie mit abwärts gewendetem Gesicht unter den Scheiterhaufen, dass die den innern Raum füllenden trockenen Binsen mit heller Flamme emporprasselten." 'Signare', and its diminutive 'sigillare' ("ut signare autem *anulo claudere* est, ita et sigillare quoque pro eodem; nam *sigillum* ex *signo* diminutivum, ut *ligillum* ex *ligno, tigillum* ex *tigno*." SALMASIUS *de modo Usur. p. 455.* Ed. Elzev.) being the very words used by the Romans to express the operation of closing (sealing) the dead man's eyes ("Hae pressant in tabe comas, hae lumina signant," STATIUS *Theb. III. 129;* "Lex Moenia est in pietate, ne filii patribus luce clara sigillent oculos."

Varro; in his lost treatise entitled *Gemini*, quoted by Nonius Marcellus Lib. II. 785), Virgil could not possibly have chosen a more proper, clear, or forcible word to express the unclosing (unsealing) of them than '*re*signare'.

Further still, the allusion to this ceremony could not have been more appropriately placed than immediately after the reference to Mercury's corresponding function of taking away sleep; the taking away of sleep involving the idea of opening the sleeper's eyes, and the idea of opening the sleeper's eyes suggesting that of the well known opening of the dead man's eyes, performed by, or under the auspices of, the same deity; by a reference to which very remarkable and striking rite, the previous account of the office or function of ψυχοπομπος is completed, and forcibly presented, not merely to the imagination, but (in the case of a Roman at least) almost to the very sight. Nor let it be said that Mercury's dominion over sleep is thus made to be thrust in awkwardly between two parts of the office of ψυχοπομπος, such postlocations, if I may use the expression, of part of a preceding idea being (whether in our view graceful or not) of exceedingly common occurence in all parts of the writings of Virgil. See Comments *En. I. 483; III. 317, 571; IV. 483.*

From 'signare' through its diminutive 'sigillare' come the French *sceller* and *desceller* (spelled also *dessiller* and *deciller)*, and our *seal* and *unseal:* all of them, words applied either literally or metaphorically to the eyes:

"Qu' un rayon de clarté vint desiller les yeux."

Voltaire, *Henriade, ch. I.*

In confirmation of the above interpretation I may add that Lucan, in his allusion *(Phars. V. 280)* to the Roman rite of closing the eyes of the recently dead, makes the same use of 'mors' for '*mortuus*' as Virgil in our text:

"Atque oculos morti clausuram quaerere dextram."

245.

ILLA FRETUS AGIT VENTOS ET TURBIDA TRANAT NUBILA

"ILLA FRETUS AGIT VENTOS, i. e. nimia celeritate persequitur, et paene occupat praevenitque." DONAT. ad Ter. *Adelph. III. 2.*

"Ut sessor agit equum quo vehitur, ita Mercurius VENTOS AGIT, idque auxilio virgae, quasi illa ut freno uteretur ad ventos moderandos." La Cerda.

"AGIT *ante se,* quis dubitet? dum volatu per auras fertur." Heyne.

"AGIT VENTOS erklärt Herr Heyne mit 'quis dubitet?' ihm voranzuwehen. Wozu das? Hat denn der Erklärer vergessen, dass er nur eben vorher *(v. 223)* den Wind in die Flügel, also nicht voran, zu hauchen bestimmt? AGIT, *er treibt,* was kann es wohl anders sein, als, er bewegt sie durch die magische Kraft des Stabes, ihm nachzuwehen?" Voss. *Mythol. Br. No. 58.*

"Cosi armato il bel Dio, già fende a volo
Le nubi; e l'aure flagellando, è giunto
A vista" &c.

ALFIERI.

Let us see if a better sense than any of these cannot be made out of the passage. 'Agere' is *to make to move* (hence 'agitare', its frequentative, is *to make to move frequently* or *much, to agitate).* The agent causing the motion may be either in, upon, before, behind, above, below, beside, or in any other conceivable position, with respect to the object put into motion. Thus

— "Agit ipse furentem
In somnis ferus Aeneas."

En. IV. 465;

Eneas, behind, *drives* or *makes to move on, Dido,* before.

"Stridentem fundam ....
Ipse ter adducta circum caput egit habena."

En. IX. 586;

made to move about his head, himself standing steady; *swung about his head.*

> — "Capitolia ad alta
> Victor aget currum."
>
> *En. VI. 837;*

make his chariot move to the Capitol, himself being in the chariot.

> "Velocem Mnestheus agit acri remige Pristin."
>
> *En. V. 116;*

makes the ship move on, himself being in the ship; *regulates the motions of the ship, commands the ship.*

> "Princeps ante omnes densum Palinurus agebat
> Agmen."
>
> *En. V. 833;*

Palinurus, before the squadron, *made the squadron,* behind him, *move on; regulated the motions of the squadron, led the squadron.*

> — "Gubernator sese Palinurus agebat."
>
> *En. VI. 337;*

Palinurus was moving himself, regulating his own motions, moving on.

> "Ecce, Sabinorum prisco de sanguine magnum
> Agmen agens Clausus, magnique ipse agminis instar."
>
> *En. VII. 706;*

> "Hos super advenit Volsca de gente Camilla,
> Agmen agens equitum, et florentes aere catervas."
>
> *En. VII. 803;*

> "Parte alia ventis et dis Agrippa secundis
> Arduus agmen agens."
>
> *En. VIII. 682.*

"Latus vero dextrum Serapion agebat." AMMIAN. XVI. 12. *Clausus, Camilla, Agrippa, Serapion* (how situated with respect to their troops, is not specified) *made their troops move on; regulated at pleasure the motion of their troops.* And so Mercury in our text (how situated with respect to the winds, is not specified, but left to the reader's imagination,) *made the winds move on regulated the motion of the winds; caused the winds to move in such manner and such direction as most facilitated his descent to Libya:* 'vocat (see *v. 223)* et agit ventos; fretus virga', *using his rod in the same manner as a prince or chieftain his sceptre, or a field-marshal his truncheon, either as engine or symbol of authority, or both.*

The reason why the commentators have found this extremely simple sentence, AGIT VENTOS, so unintelligible, is that there is in modern languages no word corresponding to 'agere'; no word which expresses the causing to move on, or the regulating the motions of, an object, without at the same time limiting the mover to some certain position with respect to the object moved.

I agree entirely with Forbiger and Ladewig and Jahn (who has however printed it otherwise in his text) against Wunderlich, that the parenthesis ends at 'resignat', and that the narrative, dropped at 'capit', is resumed, not at 'jamque', but at ILLA.

246.

JAMQUE VOLANS APICEM ET LATERA ARDUA CERNIT
ATLANTIS DURI CAELUM QUI VERTICE FULCIT
ATLANTIS CINCTUM ASSIDUE CUI NUBIBUS ATRIS
PINIFERUM CAPUT ET VENTO PULSATUR ET IMBRI
NIX HUMEROS INFUSA TEGIT TUM FLUMINA MENTO
PRAECIPITANT SENIS ET GLACIE RIGET HORRIDA BARBA

This is not a personification of the mountain Atlas, but a description of the transformed king Atlas—of the the mountain under its former human character. Therefore (vers. 258)

"Materno veniens ab avo Cyllenia proles,"

not *from Mount Atlas,* but *from the man Atlas, Mercury's grandfather.* Compare Ovid's account of the transformation, corresponding almost word for word with our text:

"Quantus erat, mons factus Atlas: jam barba comaeque
In silvas abeunt: juga sunt humerique manusque.
Quod caput ante fuit, summo est in monte cacumen;
Ossa lapis fiunt. Tum partes auctus in omnes
Crevit in immensum (sic Di statuistis) et omne
Cum tot sideribus caelum requievit in illo."

Metam. IV. 657 & seq.

The poetical description agrees with the historical: "Atlas mons e media arenarum consurgit vastitate; et eductus in viciniam lunaris circuli, ultra nubila caput condit: qua ad oceanum extenditur, cui a se nomen dedit, manat fontibus, nemoribus inhorrescit, rupibus asperatur, squalet jejunio, humo nuda nec herbida. .... vertex semper nivalis .... apex Perseo et Herculi pervius, caeteris inaccessus: ita fidem ararum inscriptio palam facit." SOLINUS, *Polyhistor, XXIV.*

JAMQUE VOLANS &c. — We are indebted to Voss *(Mythologische Briefe, Tom. I. Letter 27)* for the best answer which has yet been given to the question, why Mercury should take this apparently very indirect route from Heaven to Carthage. There were three openings or gates affording communication between the residence of the Gods on the heavenly Olympus, and the earth; one in the zenith, immediately above the Thessalian Olympus; one in the east; and one in the west; not to speak of a fourth gate toward the north, mentioned only by Statius *(Theb. VII. 35)* and probably Statius's own invention. From the gate in the zenith or 'vertex caeli', Jupiter takes his survey of the world *(En. I. 229; X. 1)*, lets down his golden chain (HOM. *Il.* ϑ) and hurls his thunder *(Georg. III. 261;* OVID. *Met. I. 175)*. The passage to and from the earth through this gate being inconveniently steep and perpendicular, though the shortest and most direct, a preference was usually given to the eastern or western gate, which, being near the horizon, afforded an easy and convenient passage to the nearest projecting easterly or westerly points (mountain tops) of the earth's surface. Through the eastern gate Sol and Nox, with their respective trains, ascended daily out of the ocean into Heaven, and through the western descended daily out of Heaven into the ocean (Compare *En. I. 749,* and Comm.). Through the eastern gate Eros descended from Heaven to Colchis (Apoll. Rhod. III. 159). And through the western gate, as it may be fairly presumed, Mercury now descends upon Atlas, not only the nearest elevation to that gate, but lying directly in the way between it and Carthage. To render this explanation complete, it is only necessary to add, first, that even supposing the descent by the Thessalian Olympus had been equally gradual and sloping, it would still have been much less suitable than the descent by Atlas for a messenger whose business lay not in Europe, but in Africa; and secondly, that it is scarcely possible to imagine a more appropriate stepping-stone between heaven and earth than the heaven-supporting Atlas.

274.

ASCANIUM SURGENTEM ET SPES HEREDIS IULI
RESPICE CUI REGNUM ITALIAE ROMANAQUE TELLUS
DEBENTUR.

Respice and debentur are both highly emphatic: particularly debentur, the first word of a verse and at the same time the last word of Mercury's speech, and followed by a complete pause. We may suppose both words, especially the last and parting word, accompanied by a significant action: *are his rightful due and must be his.* See Comments *En. II. 246; IV. 22, 237.*

298.

OMNIA TUTA TIMENS

Not, *fearing what was actually safe,* but *fearing because every thing seemed to be safe,* according to the maxim that a reverse is apt to come at the very moment when every thing seems most secure. See the story of Polycrates's ring, Herodot. *Thalia*; also the exclamation of Philip of Macedon when he received three joyful accounts in one day: "*Ω δαιμον, μετριον τι τουτοις αντιθες ελαττωμα.*" PLUTARCH. *Consol. ad Apollon. c. V.* Compare also Seneca *(Troad. 262):*

— "Metuentem Deos
Nimium faventes;"

also the reflection of Chimene (CORNEILLE, *Cid, I. 2),* when informed that her father had given his entire approbation to her marriage with Don Rodrigue:

"Il semble toutefois que mon ame troublée
Refuse cette joie, et s'en trouve accablée;"

also Schiller's

"Darum in deinen fröhlichen Tagen
Fürchte des Unglücks tückische Nähe;"

of which fine passage see the whole *(Braut von Messina,* near the end). This interpretation of OMMIA TUTA TIMENS and that which I have given (see Comm. verse 419) of "Hunc ego si potui tantum sperare dolorem, Et perferre, soror, potero;" are confirmatory of each other.

305—330.

DISSIMULARE ETIAM SPERASTI etc.

Not only the general idea, but most of the particulars, of this fine scene are taken from the dialogue between

Medea and Jason in the fourth Book of the Argonautics. See Comments *En. III. 10; IV. 143.*

It is perhaps not unworthy of remark that while Virgil here (as in his other imitations with scarcely a single exception) greatly improves upon and surpasses his original, those who have recopied from Virgil fall short, not only of the improved model with which he has furnished them, but even of the original itself; compare Tasso's tedious, spiritless and unnatural dialogue of Armida and Rinaldo, in the 16th C. of *Gerusalemme Liberata.*

307.

NEC TE NOSTER AMOR NEC TE DATA DEXTERA QUONDAM
NEC MORITURA TENET CRUDELI FUNERE DIDO
QUIN ETIAM HIBERNO MOLIRIS SIDERE CLASSEM
ET MEDIIS PROPERAS AQUILONIBUS IRE PER ALTUM
CRUDELIS

DATA DEXTERA. — Pledged to Dido, as Jason's to Medea:

"Ως ηυδα, και χειρι παρασχεδον ηραρε χειρι
Δεξιτερην."

APOLLON. RHOD. IV. 99.

CRUDELIS. — This word, compared with the same word *En. I. 411,* affords a striking example of the emphasis acquired to a word by its position at the end of a sentence and at the same time at the beginning of a verse. See *vv. 237, 275, 276,* and Comments; also Comm. En. II. 246. Not only the word itself, but its very position, at the end of the sentence to which it belongs and at the beginning of a verse, is borrowed from Apollon. Rhod. IV. 389:

— "Μαλα γαρ μεγαν ηλιτες ορκον
Νηλεες."

314.

PER EGO HAS LACRYMAS DEXTRAMQUE TUAM TE
QUANDO ALIUD MIHI JAM MISERAE NIHIL IPSA RELIQUI
PER CONNUBIA NOSTRA PER INCEPTOS HYMENAEOS
SI BENE QUID DE TE MERUI FUIT AUT TIBI QUIDQUAM
DULCE MEUM MISERERE DOMUS LABENTIS ET ISTAM
ORO SI QUIS ADHUC PRECIBUS LOCUS EXUE MENTEM

— "And upon my knees
I charm you by my once commended beauty,
By all your vows of love, and that great vow
Which did incorporate and make us one,
That you unfold to me" &c.
SHAKESPEARE, *Jul. Caes. II. 1.* (Portia to Brutus).

321.

TE PROPTER EUNDEM
EXSTINCTUS PUDOR ET QUA SOLA SIDERA ADIBAM
FAMA PRIOR CUI ME MORIBUNDAM DESERIS HOSPES
HOC SOLUM NOMEN QUONIAM DE CONJUGE RESTAT

"Etiamsi aliam non habuissem dignitatem." Wagner. No; but *quam solam habui:* which sole access ad SIDERA (i. e. to a place of honor in heaven), being now closed against her, there is nothing left for her but to die (CUI ME MORIBUNDAM DESERIS?). So *(En. IX. 641)* "Sic itur ad astra." Compare Juvenal speaking of Hercules and Eneas:

"Alter aquis, alter flammis ad sidera missus."
Sat. XI. 63.

Also "Sed jam alter (i. e. Julius Caesar) operibus suis aditum sibi ad caelum instruxerat." VALER. MAX. I. 7. 2.

HOSPES HOC SOLUM NOMEN QUONIAM DE CONJUGE RESTAT. —
"Soror Tonantis (hoc enim solum mihi
Nomen relictum est) semper alienum Jovem
Ac templa summi vidua deserui aetheris."
SENECA, *Hercul. Fur. I. 1.*

327.

SALTEM SI QUA MIHI DE TE SUSCEPTA FUISSET
ANTE FUGAM SUBOLES SI QUIS MIHI PARVULUS AULA
LUDERET AENEAS QUI TE TANTUM ORE REFERRET
NON EQUIDEM OMNINO CAPTA AC DESERTA VIDERER
DIXERAT ILLE JOVIS MONITIS IMMOTA TENEBAT
LUMINA

Nicholas Heinsius, followed by Heyne, Wagner, Forbiger, and most modern editors, has adopted the reading of the Medicean, 'tamen'. The sense so obtained can be no other than this: "I wish I had had by thee some little Eneas, whose resemblance to thee might sometimes remind me of thee — 'tamen', *after all; notwithstanding all that has happened.*" As much as to say: "Even shouldst thou go away as thou hast threatened, the recollection of thee will always be dear to me."

To this sense I object, first, that it expresses more tenderness and affection than is consistent with the highly reproachful, upbraiding character of the rest of the speech, and especially with the epithet PERFIDE *(v. 305)*, and the CAPTA of the immediately succeeding line. Secondly, that it is tautologous, the resemblance to Eneas being sufficiently and unmistakably expressed in the words PARVULUS AENEAS in the very same line. Thirdly, that TE derives an inappropriate emphasis from being thus placed as first syllable of the dactyl 'te tamen'. For all these reasons I prefer the reading TANTUM, and the sense, *some little Eneas,* QUI TE TANTUM ORE REFERRET, *who might resemble thee ONLY in his features;* Dido's wish not being that she might have a little Eneas who would resemble his father in his features, but (the words QUI TE TANTUM ORE REFERRET being entirely limitative) a little Eneas who would not resemble his father in his mind. This sense is not only in the most perfect harmony with the rest of

Dido's speech, but seems to be required by the strongly reproachful expressions PERFIDE and CAPTA, the former of which placed at the beginning, and the latter at the end, of the speech, shows that Dido's feeling remains the same all through, and that there is none of that softening or relenting in it, which would be expressed by 'tamen'. Compare, exactly parallel, *En. XII. 348:*

"Nomine avum referens, animo manibusque parentem;"

like his grandsire only in name.

It appears from Servius's gloss, "Aut illud dicit, optarem filium similem vultui, non moribus tuis," that he was well acquainted with the reading TANTUM, which is that adopted by most of the ancient editors. Maittaire testifies that it is the reading of the Milan Edition of 1474, and I have myself found it in the Modena Ed. of 1475, the Paris Ed. of 1600, both the Stephenses, Bersmann, Daniel Heinsius, La Cerda, and the Baskerville. Pierius's MSS. seem to have been pretty equally divided between the two readings. I have myself personally consulted only the Gudian, the two Leipzig, and the Dresden, respecting the passage; in the latter only I have found TANTUM, in the three former 'tamen'.

IMMOTA TENEBAT LUMINA. — Chateaubriand should have better understood these words, than to found on them a charge against Eneas of meanness of spirit, and a comparison very disadvantageous to him with Bouillon rejecting the seductions of Armida: "Il tient les yeux baissés (IMMOTA TENEBAT LUMINA), il cache son trouble &c. Ce n'est pas de cet air que le capitaine Chretien repousse les adresses d'Armide." *Genie du Christianisme.* IMMOTA LUMINA does not mean *les yeux baissés,* but (as interpreted by Dido herself, vers. 369) *steadfastly fixed;* they are neither cast down in shame ('dejecta', 'demissa'), nor turned away ('aversa'), but simply (as they should be, Eneas's purpose remaining unchanged,) IMMOTA, *unmoved.* The same word is applied in the same sense to Eneas's mind, vers. 449. In this instance, as in so many others, the fault is not in Virgil, but in the commentator; not in the sun, but in the eye of the observer.

356.

NUNC ETIAM INTERPRES DIVUM JOVE MISSUS AB IPSO
TESTOR UTRUMQUE CAPUT CELERES MANDATA PER AURAS
DETULIT IPSE DEUM MANIFESTO IN LUMINE VIDI
INTRANTEM MUROS VOCEMQUE HIS AURIBUS HAUSI

"Es ist des Himmels sichtbarliche Fügung."
SCHILLER, *Die Piccolomini, Act I, sc. 3.*

That it is the commandment of the Deity, is, in the mouth of the moralist, what the cannon is in the hands of princes, the 'ultima ratio', the last and neverfailing justification of whatever act is utterly irreconcilable with the principles of justice, with the best feelings of the human heart; "vatem et insontes deos praetendunt." Compare with Eneas's defence of his perfidious abandonment of the woman whose affections he has gained, and whose honor he has betrayed, Charles the Ninth's justification to himself of his not retaining his friend and favorite, Marsillac, Conte de Rochefaucould, to sleep at the Louvre on the night of the St. Bartholomew, but allowing him to go home to his hotel through the streets of Paris, although he knew he would certainly be murdered on the way: "Je vois bien que Dieu veut qu'il perisse." (Palissot's notes to the *Henriade, C. II.)*. Compare also St. Augustin's defence of his deception and desertion of his mother *(Confess. V. 14. 15)* on this selfsame Carthaginian shore, from whence, by a singular coincidence, he was sailing for the selfsame Italy. However the ingenuous heart may reject the excuses of all three, and refuse to be a party to this shifting of the onus of an iniquity, from the shoulders of the perpetrator to those of the perpetrator's God, still Eneas's excuse is the best, for he sees and hears the present and commanding Deity, while the others without so much as an inquiry

— "Dine hunc ardorem mentibus addunt,
Euryale, an sua cuique Deus fit dira libido?"

assume at once their own strong inclinations, their own mere volitions, to be commandments from Heaven.

362.

TALIA DICENTEM JAMDUDUM AVERSA TUETUR
HUC ILLUC VOLVENS OCULOS TOTUMQUE PERERRAT
LUMINIBUS TACITIS ET SIC ACCENSA PROFATUR

This passage is usually interpreted, *looks at him, rolling her eyes hither and thither, and wanders him all over with silent eyes:*

"Ma già a tai detti, in torvi sguardi incerti,
Ferocemente tacita lo guarda
Da capo a piè, d'ira infiammata, Dido."

ALFIERI.

A little examination, however, affords a sense more exact and more worthy of Virgil. 'Oculus' signifies *the organ, the ball* or *orb of the eye,* considered abstractedly from its function; 'lumen' (as its primary and etymological meaning shows) *the light,* i. e. *the luminous or illuminating part of the eye, the sight* or *function of vision,* corresponding to the German *Augenlicht* ("O öffnet euch, ihr lieben Augenlichter." SCHILLER, *Braut von Messina),* the Italian *luce* ("Com egli alzò le luci al vago viso." TASSONI, *La Secchia Rapita, X. 59),* and, more exactly still, to its own Italian derivative, *lume ("vive faville uscian de' duo' bei lumi."* PETR. *Sonn. 220).* Such being the respective meanings of the two words, Dido is described with great accuracy, first, as rolling her eyeballs hither and thither while she looks at Eneas, and secondly, as wandering him all over with her vision. The second clause of the sentence is thus supplementary to the first, and the whole meaning is: '*tuetur et pererrat totum luminibus tacitis (lumine tacito) oculorum, quos volvebat huc et illuc'*. It were easy to show by numerous examples that the best Latin writers frequently (not always) make this distinction between 'oculos' and 'lumina'. Ex gr.:

"At si tantula pars oculi media illa peresa est,
Incolumis quamvis alioque splendidus orbis,
Occidit extemplo lumen *(the sight is lost)* tenebraeque sequuntur."

LUCRET. III. 414.

See, in the same author, IV. 823. 1137; and especially that fine passage, VI. 1177. Also (CORN. NEPOS, *Timol. IV. 1):* "Sine ullo morbo lumina oculorum amisit," *the light* or *sight of the eyes.* Also (OVID. *Metam. XIII. 561):*

— "Digitos in perfida lumina condit,
Expilatque genis oculos.

Also *Metam. XIV. 200):* "Inanem luminis orbem." Also (CATULL. *Epigr. 49):* "Gemina teguntur Lumina nocte," where it is 'lumina' (not 'oculi'), because it is the *sight* (not the *eyeballs*) that is covered with night; and *(En. II. 210):* "Oculos suffecti," because it is the *balls* (not the *sight*) that are suffused with blood. See also Shakespeare's "There is no speculation (i. e. no '*lumen*', or *observing vision*) in those eyes."

LUMINIBUS TACITIS. — "Ipsa tacita." Servius. "Servii explicatio sequentibus (ACCENSA PROFATUR) refutatur satis. Ego explicarem, non blandis aut amatoriis, sed flammeis et fatentibus ignem." Burmann. "Stiere Augen; quibus nullus inest sensus." Gossrau. "Oculi taciti ad dicendum non pertinent, sed sunt qui iram abdunt." Wagner.

I hold the interpretation of Servius (adopted also

by Heyne) to be the true one; first, on account of the more poetic meaning; secondly, on account of Seneca's "Tacito locum rostro pererrat" *(Thyest. 500)*, where 'tacito', applied to the snout of a hound tracing his game by the scent, can only mean *'ipse canis tacens'*. To which add: "Tacita immurmurat aure", STAT. *Theb. I. 532.* Thirdly, on account of the addition to TUETUR of JAMDUDUM and DICENTEM, words which express as clearly as possible that Dido eyes Eneas over, not (as Burmann thought) during her own reply, but during the latter part of Eneas's speech: *She regards him with a silent scowl until he has finished, and then* ACCENSA PROFATUR. And fourthly, on account of the almost express commentary on the passage, afforded by Statius's

> "Dejecit maestos extemplo Ismenius heros
> In terram vultus, taciteque ad Tydea laesum
> Obliquare oculos, tum longa silentia movit."
>
> *Theb. I 673.*

A similar form of expression is usual in other languages, thus:

> "Doch viel bedeutend fragt ihr stummer Blick."
>
> SCHILLER, *Maria Stuart, A. I. sc. 8.*

"On eût dit qu'il entendait sa chanson dans ses yeux." VICTOR HUGO, *Notre Dame de Paris. B. IX. c. 4.*

365.

NEC TIBI DIVA PARENS GENERIS NEC DARDANUS AUCTOR
PERFIDE SED DURIS GENUIT TE CAUTIBUS HORRENS
CAUCASUS

PERFIDE .... CAUCASUS. — See Comment on 'Crudelis', vers. 311, and Comm. *En. II. 246.*

376.

HEU FURIIS INCENSA FEROR

See Comm. *En. II. 131;* and observe besides that 'fero is the verb appropriated to the carrying of fire, or of a burning object. See vers. 593; also Ovid, de Narcisso *(Met. III. 464):* "Flammas moveoque feroque."

384.

SEQUAR ATRIS IGNIBUS ABSENS
ET CUM FRIGIDA MORS ANIMA SEDUXERIT ARTUS
OMNIBUS UMBRA LOCIS ADERO

"Prosequar te abeuntem absens fumo flammisque rogi mei tanquam malo omine; cf. *v. 661* et seq." Wagner, *Virg. Br. En.*

But, first, the word ABSENS, properly applicable only to a living person, and plainly opposed to the subsequent ET CUM FRIGIDA MORS &c., shows that Dido speaks of something which is to happen not after her death, but during her life; and secondly, it is hardly conceivable that Dido should thus particularly indicate the peculiar manner of her death, not only before its manner had been determined on, but even before she had taken the resolution of dying; see *v. 475.* I therefore understand the ATRIS IGNIBUS with which Dido threatens to pursue Eneas, to be, not *the fires of her funeral pyre,* but *the fires* or *torches of the Furies;* those fires with which Clytemnestra pursues Orestes ("Armatam facibus matrem" *v. 472),* those fires which in the ancient mythology so aptly figure the stings of a guilty conscience; and I take the meaning of the whole passage to be: SEQUAR ABSENS, *I, absent, will follow* (whilst I am yet alive, the recollection of me will pursue you) IGNIBUS ATRIS, *with dark smouldering fires* (the stings of an evil conscience); precisely Ovid's

> "Finge age te rapido (nullum sit in omine pondus)
> Turbine deprendi; quid tibi mentis erit?
> Protinus occurrent falsae perjuria linguae,
> Et Phrygia Dido fraude coacta mori."
>
> *Heroid. VII. 65;*

ET CUM FRIGIDA MORS &c. *and when I am dead, my spectre will haunt you,* sciz. (the idea being supplied from the foregoing SEQUAR ATRIS IGNIBUS ABSENS) *with the same smouldering fires.* The immediately preceding 'pia numina', and the remarkable similarity between Dido's IGNIBUS ATRIS and the "taedas atro lumine fumantes" which Alecto thrust into the breast of Turnus *(En. VII. 456),* seem to place it beyond doubt that in this his commencing sketch of the terrible in Dido, Virgil had in his mind those same avenging Furies, and that same famous pursuit of Orestes by Clytemnestra, which he draws at full shortly afterwards, vers. 471 and sequel.

Our author has here, as in so many other places, improved upon his original, for while Medea threatens that her Furies will pursue Jason,

> — "εκ δε σε πατρης
> Αυτιχ' εμαι γ' ελασειαν Ερινυες."
>
> APOLL. RHOD. IV. 385,

Dido threatens that she will herself become his pursuing Fury; herself (i. e. the recollection of her) hunt him every where with firebrands: SEQUAR ATRIS IGNIBUS ABSENS.

396.

JUSSA TAMEN DIVUM EXSEQUITUR CLASSEMQUE REVISIT
TUM VERO TEUCRI INCUMBUNT ET LITTORE CELSAS
DEDUCUNT TOTO NAVES NATAT UNCTA CARINA
FRONDENTESQUE FERUNT RAMOS ET ROBORA SILVIS
INFABRICATA FUGAE STUDIO
MIGRANTES CERNAS TOTAQUE EX URBE RUENTES

CLASSEM REVISIT; — RE, *again;* sciz. after his long neglect and absence.

TUM VERO. — *Then indeed, and,* by implication, *not till then.* The reference is to the orders previously given (vers. 289) to prepare for sailing, which orders the crews did not seriously set about executing until Eneas himself made his appearance among them. See Comments *En. II. 105, 228; III. 47; IV. 449, 571; V. 659.*

Alfieri, misunderstanding the two words TUM VERO, represents Eneas as finding the Trojans, when he arrives among them, already engaged in performing those acts which Virgil describes them as performing only in consequence of his arrival among them:

— "un Dio,
Che severo lo incalza, e spinge, e sforza
Suoi passi là, dove le navi eccelse
Varando stanno gli operosi Teucri.
Le spalmate carene galleggianti,
E le nuove ali dei trascelti remi,
E, onor de' boschi, le novelle antenne,
Presta ogni cosa Enea trova al far vela."

A translation very much in the reckless style of our own Dryden. It must not be forgotten, however, in any comparison of Alfieri's translation of the Eneis with Dryden's, that Alfieri's so far as it was revised by him (viz. as far as the 656 line of the third Book) is very superior to the above specimen, while Dryden's translation is, from beginning to end, uniformly coarse and reckless, and, except in the story, has little more resemblance to the Eneis, than the Davideis has to Paradise Lost.

FRONDENTESQUE FERUNT RAMOS. — I can hardly doubt that RAMOS (for the MS. authority for which see N. Heinsius's and Burmann's Notes), and not 'remos', is the true reading. Not that I understand (with Peerlkamp) RAMOS to be intended specifically for oars, and ROBORA for masts, but because, first, the expression 'frondentes remos' seems to me to be an expression savoring more of Valerius Flaccus or Statius, than of Virgil, while the expression FRONDENTES RAMOS is not only simple and natural, but of common occurence with our author, see *En. III. 25; VII. 67, 135;* and secondly, because by understanding FRONDENTES RAMOS and ROBORA INFABRICATA as the common Endiadys, we have the excellent sense, *unwrought (uncarpentered) trees, bearing their leafy branches — with their leaves and branches.* Compare *Georg. II. 303—308,* where 'robora', 'frondes', and 'ramos' are, as I think they are in our text, all predicated of the one tree.

Of all the numerous editors of Virgil, whom I am in the habit of consulting, I find the reading RAMOS adopted only by the too much neglected La Cerda. In the three only MSS. which I have myself personally examined respecting the passage, viz. the two Leipzig and the Dresden, I find 'remos'

MIGRANTES CERNAS. — In order to perceive the perfect beauty and correctness of this simile the reader must bear in mind that, as appears from the use of the verb 'cernere', *to discern* or *distinguish from a distance by means of the sight* (compare Venus pointing out to Eneas the distant towers of Carthage, "ubi nunc ingentia cernis Moenia," &c. *En. I. 369;* and, "Ego Catuli Cumanam ex hoc loco regionem video, Pompeianum non cerno; neque quidquam interjectum est, quod obstet; sed intendi longius acies non potest." Cic. *IV. Acad. c. 25)*, and from the still more precise, "prospiceres arce ex summa" (vers. 410), the view is supposed to be taken from a considerable distance. So seen from a considerable distance, the crowds of Trojans hurrying backwards and forwards, and carrying to the ships the various provisions and equipments necessary for their speedy departure and long voyage, could not be compared to any other natural object so correctly and beautifully as to a swarm of ants, "cum populant" &c. Compare Sanct. Basil. in *Hexaemeron. Homil. VI. c. 9.* Edit. Garnier, 1839: "*Ει ποτε απο ακρωρειας μεγαλης πεδιον ειδες πολυ τε και υπτιον, ηλικα μεν σοι των βοων κατεφανη τα ζευγη; πηλικοι δη οι αροτηρες αυτοι; ει μη μυρμηκων τινα σοι παρεσχον φαντασιαν.*"

408.

QUIS TIBI TUNC DIDO CERNENTI TALIA SENSUS
QUOSVE DABAS GEMITUS CUM LITTORA FERVERE LATE
PROSPICERES ARCE EX SUMMA TOTUMQUE VIDERES
MISCERI ANTE OCULOS TANTIS CLAMORIBUS AEQUOR

"*Συ δη, τεκνον, ποιαν μ' αναστασιν δοκεις,*
αυτων βεβωτων, εξ υπνου στηναι τοτε;
ποι' εκδακρυσαι; ποι' αποιμωξαι κακα;
ορωντα μεν ναυς, ας εχων εναυστολουν,
πασας βεβωτας, ανδρα δ' ουδεν' εντοπον,
ουχ οστις αρκεσειεν, ουδ' οστις νοσου
καμνοντι συλλαβοιτο.

Soph. *Philoct. 276.*

415.

NE QUID INEXPERTUM FRUSTRA MORITURA RELINQUAT

FRUSTRA. — "Servius ita accipit, ut FRUSTRA ex poetae judicio sit: ut omnia experiatur, sed frustra! Scilicet turbabat illa vox, cum quaereretur de verborum ordine. Alii jungunt frustra moritura, sc. si quidquam intentatum reliquisset. . . . . . Saltem melior locus τοῦ FRUSTRA in structura exputari nequit." Heyne.

"Brevitatem et poeticam dicendi rationem nota pro vulgari, *ne, si quid inexpertum relinquat, frustra moriatur* Verba a cogitatione Didus pendent." Wunderlich.

In Wunderlich's words lies the whole secret of the constant mal-interpretation of Virgil — poetic brevity: he might have omitted brevity and said simply poetry; for a man of a prosaic, matter-of-fact mind may clearly understand and perfectly explain Tacitus, but let none but a poet ever hope to comprehend, much less successfully expound, Virgil. He will never be able to see the wood for the number of trees.

The best comment on Virgil's NE QUID INEXPERTUM FRUSTRA MORITURA RELINQUAT, is unintentionally supplied us by a poet of no mean order, who speaking of the noblest of her sex, perhaps the most poetic-minded woman that ever lived, uses these words: "Elle (Charlotte de Corday) etudia les choses, les hommes, les circonstances, pour que son courage ne fut pas trompé, et que son sang ne fût pas vain." LAMARTINE, *Hist. des Girondins, Livr. 44. c. VIII.*

419.

HUNC EGO SI POTUI TANTUM SPERARE DOLOREM
ET PERFERRE SOROR POTERO

This is spoken in conformity with the maxim that it is easier to bear an expected, than an unexpected, loss:

"Nur halb ist der Verlust des schönsten Glücks,
Wenn wir auf den Besitz nicht sicher zählten."
GOETHE, *Tasso, Act. III. sc. 2.*

The reader has already had in the words "omnia tuta timens," vers. 298 (where see Comm.), an inkling that Dido had, from the very first, a misgiving that her felicity with Eneas was too great to be of long continuance. POTUI and POTERO are opposed to each other; *have been able* (viz. in the midst of my happiness) *to expect this pain — will be able to endure the pain itself.*

PERFERRE POTERO. —

"Ich kann auch das verschmerzen."
SCHILLER, *Maria Stuart, Act. I. sc. 2.*

435.

EXTREMAM HANC ORO VENIAM MISERERE SORORIS
QUAM MIHI CUM DEDERIT CUMULATA MORTE REMITTAM

"Locus intricatissimus, et ab omnibus vexatus variis conjecturis." Burmann.

"Mihi quidem fateor nondum videri expeditum hunc locum, ac vereor ne in desperatis habendus sit." Wagner.

"Haec nemo unquam intellexit, neque intelliget." Peerlkamp.

As failure can be no disgrace where all have either failed or despaired, I shall hazard a solution of this famous Virgilian 'nodus', adopting as of greatest authority the reading of the Medicean MS. which, without the punctuation, is as follows:

EXTREMAM HANC ORO VENIAM MISERERE SORORIS
QUAM MIHI CUM DEDERIT CUMULATA MORTE REMITTAM

and which I thus interpret: *I entreat of him this last indulgence — pity thy sister — which when he shall have granted me, I will REMIT* (cease to trouble him with my love) *in accumulated death,* i. e. in a condition worse than death.

EXTREMAM HANC ORO VENIAM. — These words are plainly the repetition, at the close of Dido's petition to Eneas ("expectet .... dolere"), of the prefatory words of that petition, "extremum hoc miserae det munus amanti;" Dido herein following the ordinary formula in which a favor is asked: "I have a favor to beg of you; it is so and so .... I entreat you to grant me this favor." So Dido commences with the request: *Let him grant me this last favor;* then explains in the words, "Expectet .... dolere," what the favor is; and concludes with a repetition of her request, EXTREMAM HANC ORO VENIAM. Those who understand these words as spoken of Dido's request to her sister to bear her petition to Eneas, seem not to have observed *(a)* that there is no good reason why the term EXTREMAM should be applied to that request, especially as Dido has just declared that it is her intention to live, and that her object in pressing Eneas to stay is that she may have time to reconcile and accomodate herself to her misfortune. *(b)* That even although there were some good reason why Dido's request to her sister should be called EXTREMAM, this designation of that request in almost the precise terms in which the petition to Eneas had just been designated, were an exhibition of extreme poverty in the poet. *(c)* That the great and undue earnestness, with which, according to this interpretation, Dido presses her request on her sister, implies a doubt of her sister's willingness to oblige her in so small a matter, a doubt wholly inconsistent with the attachment which we are informed subsisted between the two sisters. *(d)* That it never could have been the intention of Virgil thus to withdraw the reader's attention during the whole of the two last lines of Dido's speech, from the main gist and object of the speech, sciz. the petition to Eneas, in order to fix it upon the comparatively unimportant and secondary object, the request to her sister. *(e)* That the termination of Dido's petition to Eneas at the word 'dolere' without at least the ordinary concluding words of a petition, "this is my request, I beg this favor," and especially without any greater inducement held out to Eneas than the prospect of fine weather, were abrupt and inartificial in the poet, and unnatural and unpersuasive in Dido.

REMITTAM — means, not (as hitherto understood by the commentators) *I will repay; (a)* because it were undignified and unbecoming in Dido thus to propose to buy the favor she sought, whether at the hands of Eneas or of her sister; and *(b)* because the words QUUM DEDERIT require that the act expressed by REMITTAM should be performed either at, or not very long after, the time *QUUM* DEDERIT, and not, as those who construe REMITTAM transitively are compelled to understand, at the necessarily remote (see vers. 434) period of Dido s death; but it means *I will remit,* i. e. *cease to trouble him;* a dignified sentiment, suitable to Dido's present situation, in harmony with the prayer of her petition, and an answer in express terms to the concluding words of Eneas's immediately preceding speech,

"Desine meque tuis incendere teque querelis."

as if she had said: *Let him but grant me this last indulgence and I will do what he has required;* i. e. 'desinam queri'.

CUMULATA MORTE. — In these words Dido describes the condition in which she shall be after she shall have entirely renounced Eneas: sciz. as a condition of *accumulated death,* i. e. of misery worse than death. This metaphorical use of the term which usually designates actual death, to express a state of extreme and hopeless misery, is common not only in Latin, but I believe in all languages. See, "Tot funera passis," *En. I. 236.* "Longaque animam sub morte tenebat:" STAT. *Theb. I. 48* (of the blindness of Oedipus); and again, of the same:

— "Saevoque e limine profert
Mortem imperfectam."

Theb. XI. 581.

— "*Συ μεν ζῃς, η δ' εμη ψυχη παλαι*
Τεθνηκεν ωστε τοις θανουσιν ωφελειν."

SOPH. *Antigon. 565.*

See also *Evangel.* MATTH. VIII. 22, and IV. 16; also Shakespeare, *Richard III. Act 1. sc. 2:* "They (sciz. your eyes) kill me with a living death;" and Burmann ad OVID. *Ibin. 16.* 'Cumulata' is added to 'mors', not merely to heighten the expression, but to place it beyond doubt that 'mors' is taken, not in its literal, but in its metaphorical, sense. In the second of the two passages just quoted from Statius, 'mors', used in the same sense, has the exactly corresponding adjunct, 'imperfecta'. "Mors imperfecta," a state of misery *almost equal to death;* 'mors cumulata', a state of misery *exceeding death.* So in *Romeo and Juliet (Act III. sc. 2):*

— "Romeo is banished;
There is no end, no limit, measure, bound,
In that word's death."

The expression 'morte remittere' occurs twice in Sil. Ital. (XIV. 537; XIII. 731):

— "Vix morte incepta remittit."

"Si studium, et saevam cognoscere Amilcaris umbram,
Illa est, cerne procul, cui frons nec morte remissa
Irarum servat rabiem."

The interpretation remains unaltered even although we should so far forsake the guidance of the Medicean

MS. as, with Heinsius, to read 'dederis' instead of DEDERIT: *I beg this last indulgence of him — pity thy sister — which* (obtained from him) *when thou shalt have given me*, i. e. *which when I shall have obtained from him through thy means, I will cease &c.*

Wagner having raised a doubt as to the correctness with which Foggini has represented the reading of this passage in the Medicean, I beg to say that I have myself personally and carefully examined that MS. and found the reading to be precisely as stated by Foggini:

QUAM MIHI CUM DEDERIT. CUMULATA MORTE REMITTA—·

I have also myself personally and carefully examined and ascertained the reading of the passage in the following MSS. and editions:

The Petrarchian, one of the Gotha (No. 236), three of the Vienna (Nos. 116, 118, 120), and the Kloster-Neuburg have

Quam mihi cum dederis cumulata morte remittam

which is the reading adopted by Nicholas Heinsius.

The Gudian has

Quam mihi cum dederis cumulatam morte remittam

but both 'dederis' and 'cumulatam' bear the marks of being alterations of a previous reading.

One of the Gotha (No. 54), three of the Munich (Nos. 18059, 21562, 305), two of the Ambrosian (Nos. 79, 107), three of the Vienna (Nos. 113, 115, 117), one of the Leipzig (No. 35), and the Dresden have

Quam mihi cum dederis cumulatam morte remittam

which is also the reading of the Princeps Ed. Rome 1469, Rob. Stephens, Burmann, Brunck and Jahn.

Two of the Gotha (Nos. 55, 56) and one of the Leipzig (No. 36) have

Quam mihi cum dederis cumulatam morte relinquam

which is the reading of the Venice Ed. of 1470 and the Modena Ed. of 1475; also of H. Stephens, Dan. Heinsius, and the Paris Ed. of 1600.

The Vienna MS. No. 121 has 'dederis cumulatam', but in the case of this MS. I neglected to note the remainder of the line.

Pierius gives little information about this passage; his words are: "'Cumulatam morte relinquam'. In Mediceo, in Porcio, et antiquis aliis codicibus, REMITTAM legitur." From which it would appear that he had not noticed the reading CUMULATA at all.

449.

MENS IMMOTA MANET LACRYMAE VOLVUNTUR INANES
TUM VERO INFELIX FATIS EXTERRITA DIDO
MORTEM ORAT

I take part with Thiel and Voss against Süpfle, in understanding LACRYMAE not of Dido and Anna, but of Eneas; first, because otherwise the words LACRYMAE VOLVUNTUR INANES seem to be a mere filling up of the line, the idea contained in them being already fully expressed in the preceding MENS IMMOTA MANET, and "nullis ille movetur fletibus." Secondly, because the leaves forced from the oak by the blasts of the winds ("Consternunt terram concusso stipite frondes") seem to point to the unavailing tears wrung from Eneas by the importunate distress of his supplicants. Thirdly, because (see Comment, *v. 30)* the object, in the absence of an adjunct expressly referring it to the more remote person, seems generally referrible to the nearer. Fourthly (and I think, conclusively), because we find, on a precisely similar occasion, the same expression applied to similar unavailing tears of pity, *En. X. 464:*

"Audiit Alcides juvenem, magnumque sub imo
Corde premit gemitum, lacrymasque effudit inanes."

Compare also *En. VI. 468* and Comment.

Tum vero infelix fatis exterrita Dido mortem orat. — The mere report of Eneas's preparations for sailing had put her into a fury (vers. 298—300); the certainty that he would sail makes her pray for death: tum vero (i. e. when she had in vain tried every means to dissuade him) mortem orat. See Comments *En. II. 105, 228; III. 47; IV. 396, 571; V. 695.*

464.

MULTAQUE PRAETEREA VATUM PRAEDICTA PRIORUM
TERRIBILI MONITU HORRIFICANT

Of the two readings priorum and 'piorum', both of which are acknowledged both by Servius and Pierius, I give a decided preference to priorum; first, because the epithet 'pius' applied to 'vates' *En. VI. 662,* is applied to 'vates' meaning *poets*, not to 'vates' meaning *prophets*. Secondly, because such epithet, meaning, as it always does, *tender-hearted, gentle* (see Comm. *En. I. 14),* were peculiarly inapplicable to prophets who horrified Dido with terrific admonitions, terribili monitu horrificant. Thirdly, because priorum is on the contrary peculiarly appropriate, it being plainly Virgil's intention to picture Dido as agitated not only by the terror produced by present prodigies, but besides (praeterea) by the recollection of foregone prodigies and the prophetic denunciations founded on them at the time. Fourthly, because in the only four MSS. which I have examined respecting the passage, viz. the Gudian, the two Leipzig and the Dresden, I have found priorum, the reading (as appears from Bottari) of the Vatican Fragment, and (as stated by Maittaire) both of the Venice Ed. of 1472 and of the Milan Ed. of 1474, and which I have myself found in the Modena Ed. of 1475, also in Fabricius, Daniel Heinsius, both the Stephenses, the Paris Ed. of 1600 Ambrogi, La Cerda, Brunck,

Wakefield, and Jahn. Nicholas Heinsius, relying as usual with undue confidence on the Medicean, and deceived (see his note in Burmann) by the application of the term 'pius' to the totally dissimilar 'vates' of the sixth Book, was the first to adopt 'piorum', and his example has been followed by Burmann, Heyne, Wagner, Forbiger, and most modern editors.

It is remarkable that neither N. Heinsius, nor Heyne, nor Wagner, has had the candor to state that the Gudian (a MS. on which all those three critics are in the habit of relying with almost implicit confidence) gives the most direct contradiction to their reading of the passage before us. The reason probably was that the Gudian here contradicts their still more favored Medicean.

471.

AUT AGAMEMNONIUS SCENIS AGITATUS ORESTES
ARMATAM FACIBUS MATREM ET SERPENTIBUS ATRIS
CUM FUGIT ULTRICESQUE SEDENT IN LIMINE DIRAE

My first view of the meaning of this passage is to be found in Forbiger's third Edition. The comment which I had written in support of that view, I think it better to suppress; because, first, my inability to produce an exact parallel for the use of 'scenae' in the sense of *scenes present to the brain only*, i. e. *visions;* and secondly, Ausonius's use *(Epigr. 71)* of the two words 'scenae' and 'agitare' in the very sense in which they are commonly interpreted in the passage before us, compel me, at least for the present, to acquiesce in that common interpretation.

Scenis is the reading of all the MSS. which I have myself personally consulted respecting the passage, viz. six of the Vienna MSS. (Nos. 113. 116. 117. 118. 120

& 121), the Kloster-Neuburg, the Petrarchian, the Gudian, the Dresden, and the two Leipzig. I find the same reading in the Modena Edition of 1475 and all the old editions with which I am acquainted. Pierius alone appears to have found a different reading in some of his MSS. His words are: "In antiquis aliquot codicibus 'Furiis agitatus' legitur. ut rem vero proximiorem faciat, nam quae in scenis representantur, fabulosa esse solent. Verum ego crediderim 'furiis' ex paraphrasi desumptum, et SCENIS inde legitima lectione expuncta, adulterinam suppositam. AGITATUS n. non tantum pertinet ad furias, quae omnino subintelliguntur, verum etiam ad fabulae actionem, quae frequenter s. recitari consuerit."

IN LIMINE. — The peculiar and proper seat of the Furies. Compare (*En. VI. 279*):

— "Mortiferumque adverso in limine bellum,
Ferreique Eumenidum thalami;"

and vers. 555:

"Tisiphoneque sedens, palla succincta cruenta,
Vestibulum exsomnis servat noctesque diesque;

also vers. 574:

— "Cernis, custodia qualis
Vestibulo sedeat? facies quae limina servet?"

also *En. VII. 341:*

"Exin Gorgoneis Alecto infecta venenis
Principio Latium, et Laurentis tecta tyranni
Celsa petit, tacitumque obsedit limen Amatae."

and Ovid, *Metam. IV. 453:*

"Carceris ante fores clausas adamante sedebant,
Deque suis atros pectebant crinibus angues.
Quam simul agnorunt inter caliginis umbras,
Surrexere deae: sedes scelerata vocatur."

See Comments *En. VI. 563* and *574*.

475.

DECREVITQUE MORI

DECREVIT, — *irrevocably determined*, as by a decree of a court of justice. Contrast "mortem orat," *v. 451.*

483.

HINC MIHI MASSYLAE GENTIS MONSTRATA SACERDOS
HESPERIDUM TEMPLI CUSTOS EPULASQUE DRACONI
QUAE DABAT ET SACROS SERVABAT IN ARBORE RAMOS
SPARGENS HUMIDA MELLA SOPORIFERUMQUE PAPAVER

HINC MIHI MASSYLAE GENTIS MONSTRATA SACERDOS. — "*Και γαρ εχω τινα νεωστι γυναικα απο Φρυγιας ηκουσαν εν μαλα τουτων εμπειρον. γαστρομαντευεσθαι δεινην τη των σπαρτων διατασει νυκτωρ και τη των θεων δειξει, και ου δει λεγουση πιστευειν, αλλ ιδειν ως φασι.*" *Γλυκερα Μενανδρῳ.* in *Epist. Mut. Graecan.*

SPARGENS. — "Spargebat in via mella et papaver, quibus advenientes ab horto arceret et poma Hesperidum servaret." Jahn.

This interpretation, of which Wagner, with less than his usual sagacity, observes, "Praeclare, si mel et papaver hunc ad usum adhibuisse veteres ipsorum veterum testimoniis, probasset vir doctissimus," and which it will be observed entirely takes away from the dragon the guardianship of the tree, is founded upon an erroneous view of the construction of the whole passage, which consists, not of two independent statements or propositions, EPULAS DABAT and RAMOS SERVABAT, to the latter of which the winding up or concluding clause, SPARGENS H. M. S. Q. P., especially belongs, but of one proposition only, DABAT EPULAS, of which the second, apparently independent, proposition, SERVABAT RAMOS, is only a parenthetic explanation, and to which the concluding clause, SPARGENS H. M. S. Q. P., looks back as it were, over the parenthesis; thus in plain prose: 'Quae spargens h. m. s. q. p. dabat epulas draconi, atque ita (i. e. per draconem) servabat ramos.' This structure is entirely according to Virgil's usual method, see Comments *En. III. 317, 571; VI. 83, 739.* The structure being established, the question next arises, what is the force of the word SPARGENS? Does it mean (as in Petronius, p. 275: "Quidquid enim a nobis acceperat de coena, latranti [cani sciz.] sparserat") *throwing to him bit by bit, piecemeal?* or does it mean (as in the same Petronius, p. 101, "Glires melle et papavere sparsos") *sprinkling 'mel' and 'papaver' on his food; making his food 'epulae'*, i. e. *a feast, by sprinkling on it 'mel' and 'papaver'?* I adopt the latter view, because it is not likely that Virgil would so soon after using the expression 'dare epulas', have used the similar expression 'spargere mel et papaver' — would have said *gave a feast*, and then explained his meaning by saying *gave 'mel' and 'papaver'*. We obtain, I think, a much better sense by understanding our author to say DABAT EPULAS, *gave a feast*, i. e. according to the proper force of the word EPULAS (compare "rimatur epulis," *En. VI. 599), a treat, dainties, delicacies,* and then by the word SPARGENS to explain how the treat was given, what constituted the treat, wherein the 'epulae' consisted; viz. in 'mel' and 'papaver sprinkled upon the food. The above views being adopted, SOPORIFERUM becomes merely descriptive of the poppy, not at all expressive of an effect intended to be produced on the dragon; and thus the difficulty felt by Servius ("Incongrue videtur positum, ut soporifera species pervigili detur draconi"), as well as by Jahn and some other commentators, is at once and wholly got rid of. For an instance in which even much more stress is laid, and by Virgil himself too, on the soporific properties of the poppy in a case in which yet those properties are not at all called into action, see *Georg. I. 78:*

"Urunt Lethaeo perfusa papavera somno;"

burn the 'papaver somniferum'; as in our text *sprinkle the 'papaver somniferum' on the food.* It will perhaps be said: "All this reasoning is very plausible, but how do we know that the Romans considered 'mel' and 'papaver' sprinkled upon food, to be a great delicacy?" I reply; from many statements of their writers to that effect; from the second of the above quoted passages of Petronius; from the same author's "Omnia dicta factaque quasi papavere et sesamo sparsa;" from Pliny, *Nat. Hist. XIX. 8. 53;* from Horace, *Epist. ad Pison. 375* &c. But it will be rejoined: "The 'papaver' is extremely nauseous and bitter, and, besides, narcotic and poisonous; it is impossible it could ever have been used in the manner you suppose; there is some mistake about the meaning of those passages; it must have been some other plant, perhaps some other poppy, and not the 'papaver somniferum', of which the Romans were so fond, and of which they considered the flavor so sweet and delicate, as to use the phrase, *sprinkled with 'mel' and 'papaver'*, or (even leaving out the 'mel' as only the vehicle) *sprinkled with 'papaver'*, when they wished to express the very highest degree of luscious sweetness ("Omnia dicta factaque quasi papavere et sesamo sparsa." PETRON. p. 5.)." I answer; by no means, there is no mistake at all about the matter; it was this very 'papaver somniferum', and no other, which constituted the Roman delicacy; Pliny's testimony to this effect is conclusive: "Papaveris sativi tria genera. Candidum (our 'papaver somniferum'), cujus semen tostum in secunda mensa cum melle apud antiquos dabatur......" It was, then, our bitter, poisonous, narcotic poppy which the Romans used in their entertainments, and which the Massylian priestess gave as the most dainty delicacy to the dragon; but observe, it was its seeds, which, as most little children of the present day know, and as the reader may satisfy himself by a simple experiment, not only are not nauseous and bitter. but have a very delicate, sweet flavor, and, as any chemist can inform him, are perfectly esculent, and contain none of the narcotic and poisonous properties with which the rest of the plant abounds. We have thus an explanation of the whole matter; the Massylian priestess gave the dragon, not a soporific, but a sweet; the sweetest sweet known before the discovery of sugar; and the dragon, for the sake of obtaining the delicious treat, remained in the garden, and, being excessively fierce towards every person except his benefactress, no one else dared approach the tree. The services of the dragon being thus incidental, not intentional, it is not the dragon, but the priestess who is described as the guardian of the tree, QUAE ..... SERVABAT IN ARBORE RAMOS; and the story acquires a degree of verisimilitude which is quite wanting in those accounts which represent the dragon as watching the tree. It will be observed in further confirmation of the above interpretation that on none of the occasions on which our author produces sleep by means of drugs, is the 'papaper specifically mentioned; see *En. V. 854; VI. 420.* Of all the Virgilian expositors, none, as far as I know, except old Gawin Douglas, suppose poppy seeds to be meant by the word PAPAVER, and he, going into the opposite extreme from those who would administer a narcotic dose to the watch, feels himself under the necessity of attributing to them an exhilarating property, and giving them to the dragon in order to keep him awake and make him lively:

"Strynkland to him the wak hony swete
And sleperye chesbowe sede to walken his sprete."

490.

MUGIRE VIDEBIS
SUB PEDIBUS TERRAM ET DESCENDERE MONTIBUS ORNOS
TESTOR CARA DEOS ET TE GERMANA TUUMQUE
DULCE CAPUT MAGICAS INVITAM ACCINGIER ARTIS
TU SECRETA PYRAM TECTO INTERIORE SUB AURAS
ERIGE ET ARMA VIRI THALAMO QUAE FIXA RELIQUIT
IMPIUS

VIDEBIS — *you shall see, yourself; you shall have ocular demonstration of her power.* Compare the concluding words of the citation from the letter of Glycera to Menander, Comm. *v. 483.*

IMPIUS, — *unfeeling,* to leave his arms hung up in my very chamber. See Comm. *En. I. 14.* The position of the word at the beginning of the verse, and at the close of the clause to which it belongs, renders it emphatic; see Comm. *En. II. 246.*

504.

AT REGINA PYRA PENETRALI IN SEDE SUB AURAS
ERECTA INGENTI TAEDIS ATQUE ILICE SECTA

I adopt Wakefield's punctuation (ERECTA, INGENTI) as affording by far the most elegant structure and most poetical sense, and add to the examples which he has adduced in support of it, the precise parallel from our author himself:

— "Pinguem taedis et robore secto
Ingentem struxere Pyram."

En. VI. 214;

and Seneca's

"Est procul ab urbe lucus, ilicibus niger."

Oedip. 530.

Compare "Cervus cornibus ingens," *En. VII. 483,* and see Comments *En. I. 294; V. 2, 387.*

TAEDIS. — Not *torches,* but *the wood of the Taeda*

tree, the Pinus Taeda of Pliny (XVI. 19), the Pinus Mugho, *Torche-pin*, or *Pin-suif*, of modern naturalists.

Ilice secta. — *Billets*, *σχιδακες*, *of ilex*: "*Και εμελισε το ολοκαυτωμα και επεθηκεν επι τας σχιδακας.*" *Η Παλ. Διαθ. Βασιλ. γ.* 18. 33.

520.

AEQUO FOEDERE

The "*ισῳ ζυγῳ*" of Theocritus (*Idyll. XII. 15*):

"*Αλληλους δ' εφιλησαν ισῳ ζυγῳ. η ρα τοτ' ησαν*
Χρυσειοι παλαι ανδρες, οτ' αντεφιλησ' ο φιληθεις."

and "pari jugo" of Martial (IV. 13. 8).

522.

NOX ERAT ET PLACIDUM CARPEBANT FESSA SOPOREM
CORPORA PER TERRAS SILVAEQUE ET SAEVA QUIERANT
AEQUORA CUM MEDIO VOLVUNTUR SIDERA LAPSU
CUM TACET OMNIS AGER PECUDES PICTAEQUE VOLUCRES
QUAEQUE LACUS LATE LIQUIDOS QUAEQUE ASPERA DUMIS
RURA TENENT SOMNO POSITAE SUB NOCTE SILENTI
LENIBANT CURAS ET CORDA OBLITA LABORUM
AT NON INFELIX ANIMI PHOENISSA NEC UNQUAM
SOLVITUR IN SOMNOS OCULISVE AUT PECTORE NOCTEM
ACCIPIT INGEMINANT CURAE RURSUSQUE RESURGENS
SAEVIT AMOR MAGNOQUE IRARUM FLUCTUAT AESTU

In the *Gerusalemme Liberata* (less an original poem than a splendid adaptation of the *Eneis* to the times of the crusades) we have the following almost exact copy of this fine painting, itself a copy of Apollon. Rhodius's "*Νυξ μεν επειτ'*" (*Argon. III. 744*) or (see Heyne ad *En. VIII. 26*) of Alcman's fragment, "*Ευδουσιν δ' ορεων κορυφαι τε και φαραγγες*" &c.:

"Era la notte, allor ch' alto riposo
Han l'onde e i venti, e parea muto il mondo
Gli animai lassi, e quei che 'l mare ondoso,
O de' liquidi laghi alberga il fondo,
E chi si giace in tana o in mandra ascoso,
E i pinti augelli, nel obblio profondo,
Sotto il silenzio de' secreti orrori,
Sopian gli affanni, e raddolciano i cuori.

Ma nè 'l campo fedel" &c.

Gerusalemme Liberata, II. 96.

The celebrated French minister Turgot (not perhaps generally known to have been a translator of the fourth Book of the Eneis) has thus spiritedly and not unfaithfully rendered the same passage into French hexameters, more agreable, to *my* ear at least, than the wearying sing-song of Delille's rhyming Heroic:

"Dès long-temps la nuit dans les cieux poursuivoit sa carrière;
Les champs, les solitaires forêts, tout se taisoit: et les vents
Suspendoient leur haleine: un calme profond règnoit sur l'onde;
Tous les astres brilloient dans leur tranquille majesté.
Les habitants des airs, des bois, des plaines et des eaux,
Plongés dans le sommeil, réparoient leurs forces épuisées;
Les mortels oublioient leurs soins cuisans. Tout reposoit
Dans la nature: et Didon veilloit dans les pleurs. La nuit paisible
Dans son coeur ne descendra jamais: le sommeil fuit de ses yeux:
Ses ennuis la devorent: l'amour, la fureur, le désespoir
Dans leur flux et reflux orageux font rouler sa pensée."

537.

ILIACAS IGITUR CLASSES ATQUE ULTIMA TEUCRUM JUSSA SEQUAR

Viz. following Medea's example (Apoll. Rhod. IV. 81 and seq.), which if not present in Dido's, was at least present in Virgil's mind when he wrote these words.

551.

NON LICUIT THALAMI EXPERTEM SINE CRIMINE VITAM
DEGERE MORE FERAE TALES NEC TANGERE CURAS

The commentators connecting MORE FERAE with THALAMI EXPERTEM have been obliged either, with Peerlkamp, to put an abomination into the mouth of Dido ("Cur mihi non licuit vivere sine matrimonio et cum quolibet concumbere?") or, with Servius, to seek for a wild animal which after the death of its first mate remains ever after in obstinate widowhood. We have only to connect MORE FERAE, not with THALAMI EXPERTEM, but with VITAM DEGERE, and all difficulty is got rid of at once: 'Non licuit me expertem thalami, vitam degere more ferae;' not, *to live unmarried like a wild animal*, but *continuing unmarried, live like a wild animal;* ex. gr. like a deer that lives free and untamed in the forest; in other words: continue unmarried, and not lose my freedom by submitting to the power of a man; by placing my neck under the matrimonial yoke. Compare the use made by Lucretius and Ovid of the corresponding expressions, 'vita similis ferae', and 'vita more ferarum':

> "Multaque per caelum solis volventia lustra
> Volgivago vitam tractabant more ferarum."
>
> LUCRET. V. 929.

> "Vita ferae similis, nullos agitata per usus."
>
> OVID. *Fasti, II. 291.*

Compare also Seneca's application of the term 'efferatus to the chaste Hippolytus:

> — "Silvarum incola
> Ille efferatus, castus, intactus, rudis."
>
> *Hippol. 923;*

also the application of the terms 'fera' and 'selvatica by the Italians, to express a coy chastity:

> "Bella fera e gentil mi punse il seno."
>
> DELLA CASA, *Son. XII.*

> "Tempo verrà ancor forse
> Ch' al usato soggiorno
> Torni la fera bella e mansueta."
>
> PETR. *Sonn. Part. I. canz. 27.*

"Donna più selvatica di Penelope." LEOPARDI, *Dialogo di Malambruno e di Farfarello* (Opere, 2 Tom Firenze, 1845).

Dido's expressions thus understood stand in the finest contrast with *vv. 58 and 59,* above. It is as if she said: How much happier, if I had continued expers thalami et sine crimine, vitam degens more ferae, 'efferata' and 'selvatica,' not submitting to the institutions of Legifera Ceres, not bowing my neck to the 'vincla jugalia' of Juno! Compare Maximian, *Eleg.* (in Wernsdorf's Poetae Latini Minores):

> "Sed mihi dulce magis resoluto vivere collo
> Nullaque conjugii vincula grata pati."

SINE CRIMINE — is epexegetic of THALAMI EXPERTEM; see, for a similar use of the term, Maximian; *Eleg. IV. 51:*

> "Et nunc infelix tota est sine crimine vita;"

and Ovid, *Heroid. XX. 7:*

> "Conjugium pactamque fidem, non crimina posco;
> Debitus ut conjux, non ut adulter, amo."

and especially, Ovid, *Metam. I. 478:*

> "Multi illam petiere; illa aversata petentes,
> Impatiens expersque viri, nemorum avia lustrat,
> Nec quid Hymen, quid Amor, quid sint connubia, curat.
> Saepe pater dixit: Generum mihi, filia, debes.
> Saepe pater dixit: Debes mihi, nata, nepotes.
> Illa, velut crimen, taedas exosa jugales,
> Pulchra verecundo suffunditur ora rubore;
> Inque patris blandis haerens cervice lacertis,
> Da mihi perpetua, genitor carissime, dixit,
> Virginitate frui."

than which passage there could be no better commentary on our text.

560.

NATE DEA POTES HOC SUB CASU DUCERE SOMNOS etc.

Let the curious reader compare the Fool's anouncement to William the Conqueror, of the conspiracy of his barons:

"U gies Willame? Por kei dors?" &c.

Roman de Rou, 8816.

563.

ILLA DOLOS DIRUMQUE NEFAS IN PECTORE VERSAT
CERTA MORI VARIOQUE IRARUM FLUCTUAT AESTU

CERTA MORI is added, not in order to inform Eneas of Dido's intended suicide, but to magnify the danger to him from a woman, who, being determined to die, would not be prevented by regard for self-preservation from attempting any act no matter how reckless and desperate.

569.

VARIUM ET MUTABILE SEMPER
FEMINA

The oft repeated calumny:

"Mobilior ventis, o femina!" —

CALPURN. *Ecl. III. 10.*

"Elle flotte, elle hesite, en un mot elle est femme."

RACINE, *Athalie.*

"Souvent femme varie;
Bien fol est qui s'y fie."

Quatrain attributed to Francois I. king of Franco.

— "Even to vice
They are not constant, but are changing still
One vice, but of a minute old, for one
Not half so old as that."

Cymbeline, Act II.

Women, as compared with men, are not variable and mutable, but the very contrary; and Dido in particular was unchangeably and devotedly attached to Eneas, whom, if she did not pursue with fire and sword, it was not that *his* inconstancy did not so deserve, but that *her* magnanimity disdained, and *her* still-subsisting passion forbade.

571.

TUM VERO AENEAS SUBITIS EXTERRITUS UMBRIS etc.

TUM VERO. — After the first appearance of Mercury to him *(v. 265)*, Eneas is desirous to go, and makes preparations:

"Ardet abire fuga, dulcesque excedere terras,"

but still hesitates:

"Heu, quid agat? quo nunc reginam ambire furentem
Audeat affatu?" &c.

thoroughly frightened by the second vision, TUM VERO, he actually goes, cannot be off fast enough:

CORRIPIT E SOMNO CORPUS, SOCIOSQUE FATIGAT:
PRAECIPITES VIGILATE VIRI, ET CONSIDITE TRANSTRIS;
SOLVITE VELA CITI . . . .
. . . .
. . . . VAGINAQUE ERIPIT ENSEM
FULMINEUM, STRICTOQUE FERIT RETINACULA FERRO.
. . . .
LITTORA DESERUERE; LATET SUB CLASSIBUS AEQUOR;
ANNIXI TORQUENT SPUMAS, ET CAERULA VERRUNT.

See Comments *En. II. 105, 228; III. 47; IV. 396, 449; V. 659.*

Subitis exterritus umbris. — Umbris, *the vision which Eneas has just seen;* for we are warned, first, by all just poetical sentiment, and secondly, by the exactly parallel expression of Virgil's faithful imitator, "Saguntinis somnos exterritus umbris (Sil. II. 704), not to fall (with Heyne, whom, in this as well as numerous other instances, the other commentators, ex. gr. Thiel and Forbiger, have but too trustingly followed) into the gross error of referring umbris to the natural (and therefore not terrifying) darkness which ensued on the disappearance of the vision. Compare Petronius (p. 368), translating from Epicurus:

"Somnia, quae mentes ludunt volitantibus umbris;"

not, *with darkness*, but *with flitting shades, visions.* See also *En. VI. 894;* also "Quo somnio exterritus," Justin. I. 9.

586.

REGINA E SPECULIS UT PRIMUM ALBESCERE LUCEM
VIDIT ET AEQUATIS CLASSEM PROCEDERE VELIS
LITTORAQUE ET VACUOS SENSIT SINE REMIGE PORTUS
TERQUE QUATERQUE MANU PECTUS PERCUSSA DECORUM
FLAVENTESQUE ABSCISSA COMAS PRO JUPITER IBIT
HIC AIT ET NOSTRIS ILLUSERIT ADVENA REGNIS

Speculis. — Not specially *a watch tower,* but generally *any high situation from which a view might be had; a look-out.* Compare *En. X. 454:*

— "Utque leo, specula cum vidit ab alta
Stare procul campis meditantem in proelia taurum."

This high look-out was probably in the present instance, as at *v. 410,* a window in the arx or royal castle on the top of the hill.

Abscissa. — Fea (ad *Georg. II. 23)* observes (and truly, I think) with respect to abscindo' as distinguished from 'abscido': "'Abscido' significa *separare, dividere un corpo col taglio;* da 'abs' e caedo': 'Abscindo' da 'abs' e 'scindo', *strapparlo, squarciarlo, dividerlo con tutt' altra forza.*" So, *En. V. 685:*

— "Humeris abscindere vestem.

Advena — properly *newcomer,* but here, by implication, *interloper, intruder.* Compare Justin, II. 5: "Quippe conjuges eorum longa expectatione virorum fessae, nec jam teneri bello, sed deletos ratae, servis ad custodiam pecorum relictis nubunt; qui reversos cum victoria dominos, velut advenas, armati finibus prohibent;" and (Just. II. 6): "Soli enim (Athenienses sciz.) praeterquam incremento, etiam origine gloriantur; quippe non advenae, neque passim collecta populi colluvies originem urbi dedit; sed eodem innati solo, quod incolunt, et quae illis sedes. eadem origo est." No more contumelious term could have been applied to Eneas: *this homeless adventurer, who goes about thrusting himself into other people's territories in search of a place to settle in.* Compare the similar contemptuous application of the same term to Eneas by Tolumnius, *En. XII. 261.*

596.

INFELIX DIDO NUNC TE FACTA IMPIA TANGUNT
TUM DECUIT CUM SCEPTRA DABAS

Eneas's sole act of 'impietas' (see Comm. *En. I. 14.*) being his present desertion of Dido, by which it was impossible she could have been affected at the time she admitted him to a share in her sceptre (tum decuit, sciz. factis impiis tangi, cum sceptra dabas), it follows irresistibly that facta impia means, not as seems to have been taken for granted by all commentators, *the 'impietas' of Eneas* ("perfidia Aeneae" — Wagner) but *that of Dido herself,* sciz. in the violation of her vow to Sichaeus; see *v. 24* and seq. also *vv. 322, 547, 552.* The NUNC is emphatic, and the meaning of the whole passage as follows: *Art thou sensible of the 'impietas' of thy conduct only now at last when suffering from its consequences? It had better become thee to have been so when thou wert taking the first step* The FACTA IMPIA with which Dido reproaches herself are precisely the '*κακας μενοινας*' with which her prototype, Medea, reproaches herself, the only difference being that the FACTA IMPIA of Dido were towards her deceased husband, the '*κακαι μενοιναι*' of Medea towards her father:

— "*επει το πρωτον αασθην*
"*Αμπλακιη, θεοθεν δε κακας ηνυσσα μενοινας.*"
APOLL. RHOD. IV. 412.

Compare Cornelia's self-accusation, and application to herself of the selfsame term 'impia', when she first meets Pompey after his infortunate battle at Pharsalia:

"O thalamis indigne meis, hoc juris habebat
In tantum fortuna caput! cur impia nupsi,
Si miserum factura fui."
LUCAN. VIII. 95.

also

"Impia quid dubitas Deïanira mori?"
OVID. *Heroid. IX. 146, 152, 158, 164.*

See Comment vers. 30.

TUM DECUIT CUM SCEPTRA DABAS. — Compare *En. X. 94:*

"Tum decuit metuisse tuis." —

TANGUNT. — Compare *En. I. 466,* and

— "Cura mei si te pia tangit, Oreste,"
OVID. *Heroid. VIII. 15.*

A similar use of the verb *to touch* is familiar in English. The Greeks used *θιγγανω* in the same sense: "*θιγγανει σεθεν τοδε.* EURIP. *Hippol. 310.*

600.

NON POTUI ABREPTUM DIVELLERE CORPUS

"I'll tear her all to pieces."
Othello, Act. III. sc. 3.

608.

TUQUE HARUM INTERPRES CURARUM ET CONSCIA JUNO

Interpres, ... media et conciliatrix. . . . . . Alii, testis, judex, arbitra . . . . . ." Servius. Not only Servius's own examples ("Quae tibi Conditio nova et luculenta fertur per me interpretem." Plaut. *Miles, IV. 1. 5.* "Quod te praesente istic egi, teque interprete." Plaut. *Curcul. III. 64),* but still more Ammian's derivative, 'interpretium' ("Verum quoniam denis modiis singulis solidis indigentibus venumdatis, emerat ipse tricenos, interpretii compendium ad Principis aerarium misit." XXVIII. 1), shows that the former of these meanings is the true one, and that interpres not only here, but at *v. 356, III. 359,* and generally elsewhere, is used, not in the restricted sense of its English derivative, *interpreter,* but in the much wider sense of the English *agent,* and French *commissaire, commissionaire.*

622.

TUM VOS O TYRII STIRPEM ET GENUS OMNE FUTURUM EXERCETE ODIIS

Compare Lucan, *Pharsal. VIII. 283* & seq.

631.

INVISAM QUAERENS QUAMPRIMUM ABRUMPERE LUCEM

"Εχθρον ημαρ, εχθρον εισορω φαος"
EURIP. *Hippol. 355.*

"Horrebant omnia, et ipsa lux." ST. AUGUST. *Confess. IV. 12.*

641.

ILLA GRADUM STUDIO CELERABAT ANILI

I prefer the reading ANILI to 'anilem'; first and mainly, as affording the picture of the flurry of the old woman, entirely lost if we adopt 'anilem'. Secondly, as the only reading which seems to have been known either to Servius or Donatus (see their Comments on the passage). Thirdly as the reading not only quoted, but thus commented on, by Donatus (ad Ter. *Eun. V. 3)*: "Scilicet non re celerabat, sed studio." Fourthly, as the reading of the Medicean (see Foggini and Ambrogi), and of by far the greater number of MSS. ("fere omnes" — Burmann); of the two Heinsii, the two Stephenses, the Paris Ed. of 1600, and La Cerda. When Wagner, in his advocacy of 'anilem', informs us that such is the reading of the Gudian, he seems not to have been aware that 'anile—', the present reading of that MS., is (as it plainly appeared to me from personal examination) a comparatively modern alteration of a different original reading, and therefore probably of ANILI. Besides the Gudian I have examined the Dresden and the two Leipzig MSS., and have found ANILI in the whole three.

649.

PAULUM LACRYMIS ET MENTE MORATA
INCUBUITQUE TORO DIXITQUE NOVISSIMA VERBA
DULCES EXUVIAE DUM FATA DEUSQUE SINEBANT
ACCIPITE HANC ANIMAM MEQUE HIS EXSOLVITE CURIS
VIXI ET QUEM DEDERAT CURSUM FORTUNA PEREGI
ET NUNC MAGNA MEI SUB TERRAS IBIT IMAGO

PAULUM LACRYMIS ET MENTE MORATA. —

"Poi con la tazza in man, sospesa alquanto
Si stette, e disse."

TRISSINO, *La Sofonisba.*

DUM FATA DEUSQUE SINEBANT. — Wagner, not content with ejecting from the Heynian text SINEBANT (the reading, not of Heyne only, but of the Modena Ed. of 1475, Bersmann, the two Stephenses, the Paris Ed. of 1600, the two Heinsii, La Cerda and Burmann) and substituting for it 'sinebat', takes credit to himself for the substitution, as for a restoration of the text to its original purity: "Reposui sinebat." I not only consider the MS. authority for SINEBANT to be even on Wagner's own showing at least equal to that for 'sinebat' (the Vatican Fragment and the Palatine being for the former reading, the Medicean for the latter) but prefer SINEBANT to 'sinebat', first, as affording the simpler and more natural structure; secondly, as fully supported and justified against Wagner's criticism *(Quaest. Virgil. VIII. 3. a)* by the almost exact parallel *(En. VI. 511)*,

"Sed me fata mea et scelus exitiale Lacaenae
His mersere malis,"

and thirdly as the reading acknowledged by Donatus.

VIXI etc. — "I will work the mine of my youth to the last veins of the ore, and then — Good night; I have lived, and am content." BYRON, *Letters.*

Et nunc magna mei sub terras ibit imago. — Not very dissimilar are the reflections of Turnus, *En. XII. 646:*

> — "Vos o mihi Manes
> Este boni; quoniam superis aversa voluntas.
> Sancta ad vos anima atque istius inscia culpae
> Descendam, magnorum haud unquam indignus avorum."

659.

DIXIT ET OS IMPRESSA TORO MORIEMUR INULTAE
SED MORIAMUR AIT SIC SIC JUVAT IRE SUB UMBRAS

§ I.

Os impressa toro. — "Percita furore, salute desperata, et morte vicina. Non enim is erat jam mentis habitus, ut exosculari illas exuvias velle videri posset . . . . . . Ore impresso, prae animi dolore in torum, cui incubat, immisso, haec eloquitur." Heyne.

On the contrary, to have buried her face in the couch, although quite proper for Myrrha (Ovid. *Met. X. 410)*, had been wholly inconsistent with the composure and resolution of Dido; who, in the words os impressa toro, is described merely as bidding an affectionate and impassioned farewell to the "dulces exuviae", *v. 651.* Compare the similar affectionate leave-taking of their couch by Alceste (Eurip. *Alcest. 173* & seq.) and by Medea (Apoll. Rhod. IV. 26), and, for the expression impressa, Horace's

> "Impressit memorem dente labris notam."
> *Carm. I. 13. 12.*

§ II.

Sic sic juvat ire sub umbras. — "Quasi interrogatio et responsio (sic? sic); et placet sic inultam perire, et hoc eam se loco intelligimus percussisse. Unde alii dicunt verba esse se ferientis." Servius.

"Pro *vel sic; vel sic quoque.* Burmann; approved by Voss and Heyne.

"Alii placidius mitiusque morientur, mihi sic ire convenit truculenter et dire." La Cerda.

Sic sic juvat, adeo sive tantum juvat." Wagner, *Virg. Br. En.*

The following meaning seems to me much more energetic and worthy of Dido than any of the above: Sic sic, *hoc ipsissimo modo comparatur quod,* ire sub umbras, *mors* (sciz. *alioquin amara),* juvat, *fit jucunda.* How by this method of dying, ire sub umbras *(death)* juvat *(is rendered pleasant),* is explained in the immediately following words, Hauriat &c. Sic sic juvat ire sub umbras is therefore Dido's cry of triumph and exultation over all the horrors of her situation; horrors which have actually become delightful to her, from the prospect of the punishment inflicted through their means on Eneas. Sic sic juvat ire sub umbras: *O death, where is now thy sting? Thou hast no sting for me now — nothing but sweetness.*

663.

ATQUE ILLAM MEDIA INTER TALIA FERRO
COLLAPSAM ASPICIUNT COMITES ENSEMQUE CRUORE
SPUMANTEM SPARSASQUE MANUS

"Sparsas, conspersas. Vide supra vers. 21." Forbiger.

I feel convinced that this interpretation although sufficiently grammatical, 'cruore' being supplied to sparsas from the preceding line, is yet entirely incorrect; first, because the circumstance that Dido's hands were sprinkled (as no doubt they were) with blood, was too minute to be observed by her attendants, the pyre being very lofty *(vv. 505, 645),* and none of the attendants being upon it *(v. 685).* Secondly, the minute circumstance that the hands were sprinkled, would be more properly mentioned in case of a subsequent inquiry as to the particular mode of her death, and whether or not she had been her own executioner, than on the very first instant of alarm. Thirdly, it is not likely that a poet of Virgil's good taste would have here, in the very midst of his great catastrophe, requested his reader's attention to two different kinds and degrees of bloodiness, indicated, according to this interpretation, by the words SPUMANTEM and SPARSAS, still less that he would have so strongly contrasted these two different kinds of bloodiness by the immediate juxtaposition of the two terms.

I therefore understand SPARSAS to be here applied to MANUS as so often elsewhere to 'capilli' (ex. gr. "Sparsis Medea capillis." OVID. *Metam. VII. 257),* and to mean *hands thrown wide from each other; lying powerless like those of a dead person, one here and another there.* This was a sign of what had happened much more likely to attract the attention of distant spectators then any sprinkling of the hands with blood. They saw first that she had fallen collapsed; secondly, they saw the sword spuming with blood; thirdly, they saw her hands (arms) thrown out; lying without any harmony between them, and like those of a dead, not a living, person. I think it is this meaning which is contained in the latter part of Servius's gloss, "aut perfusas sanguine, aut morte resolutas." This is also, I suppose, the meaning which Lemaire intends to assign to the word when he interprets it "*jactatas;*" and Turgot, when he interprets it "*tombantes.*" Compare Statius, *Achill. II. 440:*

> "Nam procul Oebalios in nubila condere discos,
> Et liquidam nudare (al. *nodare)* Palen et spargere caestus
> Ludus erat, requiesque mihi."

And Valerius Flaccus, I. 420:

"Taurea vulnifico portat caelataque plumbo
Terga Lacon, saltem in vacuos ut brachia ventos
Spargat, et Oebalium Pegaseia puppis alumnum
Spectet, securo celebrantem littora ludo."

FERRO COLLAPSAM, — not, collapsed *on* the sword, in which case the expression would have been 'in ferrum collapsam , but collapsed *with* the sword, *in consequence of the sword wound:* i. e. the attendants see her stab herself and sink in consequence, but the act is so sudden and so immediately followed by its consequence that the observation rests on the consequence, and scarcely perceives the act. Compare *En. I. 85:*

— "Cavum conversa cuspide montem
Impulit in latus, ac venti;"

and see Comment *En. I. 86.*

675.

HOC ILLUD GERMANA FUIT ME FRAUDE PETEBAS
HOC ROGUS ISTE MIHI HOC IGNES ARAEQUE PARABANT
QUID PRIMUM DESERTA QUERAR COMITEMNE SOROREM
SPREVISTI MORIENS EADEM ME AD FATA VOCASSES
IDEM AMBAS FERRO DOLOR ATQUE EADEM HORA TULISSET
HIS ETIAM STRUXI MANIBUS PATRIOSQUE VOCAVI
VOCE DEOS SIC TE UT POSITA CRUDELIS ABESSEM

Thus imitated or rather translated by Trissino, in his address of Erminia to the dying Sofonisba:

"Adunque lassa voi pensate, ch' io
Mi debbia senza voi restare in vita?
Crudele, or non sapete il nostro amore, &c.
. . . .
Ben dovevate ben chiamarmi allora,
Crudel, quando il venen vi fu recato,
E darmi la meta, che morte insieme
Allor saremmo in un medesimo punto."

See Comment on CRUDELIS, below.

HIS ETIAM STRUXI MANIBUS &c. — So Argia, over the dead body of Polynices, STAT. *Theb. XII. 336:*

— "Ipsa dedi bellum, maestumque rogavi
Ipsa patrem, ut talem nunc te complexa tenerem."

CRUDELIS. — I have no doubt that the received interpretation, although supported by the authority of Forbiger, Wagner, and (see above) even of the learned prelate Trissino, errs in referring CRUDELIS to Dido; first, because by its very position, immediately before ABESSEM, CRUDELIS is *prima facie* pointed out as the nominative to that verb, from which it cannot be separated without placing both before and after it a pause that in no small degree impairs the harmony of the versification. Secondly, because CRUDELIS being referred to Dido, Anna's lamentation consists of an uninterrupted series of accusations of her sister, not broken even by so much as one single expression of that self-reproach which is so natural to tender grief. Thirdly, because the change in the structure from questions and wishes addressed to her sister (HOC ILLUD, GERMANA, FUIT? . . . PARABANT? . . . . SPREVISTI? . . . VOCASSES; . . . TULISSET) to questions addressed to herself (STRUXI? . . . VOCAVI?) shows that there is at the latter words a complete transition of thought, and that Anna here passes from the reproach of her sister to the reproach of herself: HIS ETIAM STRUXI MANIBUS (ego sciz.) &c. To have counteracted and made of none effect this natural and exquisitely pathetic self-reproach by mixing up with it a reproachful apostrophe to Dido, would have been unworthy of Virgil's art, and the more unworthy, because unnecessary, Dido having been sufficiently reproached already. Fourthly, because CRUDELIS (which, as an invocation of Dido, would have been better placed somewhere near the beginning of the sentence, at a distance sciz. from SIC TE UT POSITA ABESSEM, see 'Thirdly' above) is placed exactly in the position in which it should be placed if referred by Anna to herself, viz. so as not only to bring the verb and its nominative, the reproach and its cause, as close as possible together, but (see Comm. *En. II. 552*) so as to afford this beautiful and I believe not hitherto observed implication: I might have built the pile for thee; I might have invoked the Gods for thee; I might have aided thee to die; but not to share thy death with thee, that indeed was cruelty. For all these reasons I take part with Donatus and Heyne against the authorities above mentioned, and without hesitation refer CRUDELIS to Anna, Wagner himself suggesting a sufficient justification of her self-reproach: "ut Anna more graviter dolentium culpam fortunae (I would rather have said 'culpam fraudis Didus', see *v. 675)* in se transferat, ac si ipsa in culpa esset."

P.S. Since the above Comment was written, I have met in Silius Italicus an expression applied to Anna which seems to prove that that early student and copyist of Virgil understood CRUDELIS as I do:

> — "Divis inimica sibique (Virgil's CRUDELIS)
> Quod se non dederat comitem in suprema sorori."
>
> VIII. 65.

Compare the parallel passage of the same author (XIII. 655):

> — "Nam cur
> Ulla fuere adeo, quibus a te saevus abessem,
> Momenta?"

also the application to herself of the epithet 'dura by Turnus's sister, *En. XII. 873.* Also Macduff's

> "And *I* must be from thence!"
>
> *Macbeth, Act. IV. sc. 3.*

691.

OCULISQUE ERRANTIBUS ALTO
QUAESIVIT CAELO LUCEM INGEMUITQUE REPERTA
TUM JUNO OMNIPOTENS LONGUM MISERATA DOLOREM
DIFFICILESQUE OBITUS IRIM DEMISIT OLYMPO
QUAE LUCTANTEM ANIMAM NEXOSQUE RESOLVERET ARTUS
NAM QUIA NEC FATO MERITA NEC MORTE PERIBAT
SED MISERA ANTE DIEM SUBITOQUE ACCENSA FURORE
NONDUM ILLI FLAVUM PROSERPINA VERTICE CRINEM
ABSTULERAT STYGIOQUE CAPUT DAMNAVERAT ORCO
ERGO IRIS CROCEIS PER CAELUM ROSCIDA PENNIS
MILLE TRAHENS VARIOS ADVERSO SOLE COLORES
DEVOLAT ET SUPRA CAPUT ASTITIT HUNC EGO DITI
SACRUM JUSSA FERO TEQUE ISTO CORPORE SOLVO
SIC AIT ET DEXTRA CRINEM SECAT

---

§ I.

The ancients (incorrectly, I think) believed the light to be the last object regarded by the expiring person; compare (besides the examples cited by Forbiger) Stat. *Theb. VIII. 650:*

— "Illam unam neglecto lumine caeli,
Aspicit et vultu non exsatiatur amato."

and *Silv. V. 1. 173:*

— "Illum aegris circumdat fortiter ulnis
Immotas obversa genas; nec sole supremo
Lumina, sed dulci mavult satiare marito."

in both which instances the exception proves the rule. Also Eurip. *Alcest. 204.* The opinion is occasionally repeated by more modern writers, and amongst others by Ugo Foscolo, in his beautiful verses entitled *Dei Sepolchri:*

— "Gli occhi del uom cercan morendo
Il sole, e tutti l'ultimo sospiro
Mandano i petti alla fuggente luce;"

and is perhaps alluded to by Gray in those well known lines of his *Elegy in a Country Churchyard:*

"For who, to dumb forgetfulness a prey,
This pleasing, anxious being e'er resigned,
Left the warm precincts of the cheerful day,
Nor cast one longing, lingering look behind?"

Compare *En. X. 898:*

— "Contra Tyrrhenus, ut auras
Suspiciens hausit caelum, mentemque recepit."

§ II.

LUCTANTEM — *Struggling:* sciz. to escape from its connexion with the body (compare "Luctantes ventos;" *En. I. 57), dying slowly;* compare Ovid, *Ibis, 125:*

"Luctatusque diu cruciatos spiritus artus
Deserat; et longa torqueat ante mora."

A somewhat similar thought is thus more lengthily expressed by Goethe: "Ich sterbe, sterbe, und kann nicht ersterben; und in dem fürchterlichen Streit des Lebens und Todes sind die Qualen der Hölle." *Götz von Berlichingen, Act V* Compare also Shirley, *Edward the Black Prince, Act V. sc. 3:*

"Death I have caught: his shaft is in my heart;
It tugs with nature. When shall I get free?"

§ III.

NEC FATO MERITA NEC MORTE, — *neither by a natural death* (death in the natural course of events), *nor by a merited* or *earned death* (death brought upon her by any act of her own; either in mere consequence, or as a punishment): "Decessit Corellius Rufus; et quidem sponte, quod dolorem meum exulcerat: est enim luctuosissimum genus mortis, quae non ex natura, nec fatalis, videtur." PLIN. *Epist. I. 12.* "Habuit et alios multos ex variis matrimoniis regio more susceptos, qui partim fato, partim ferro periere." JUSTIN. IX. 8. "Neque plus hominum ferrum et arma, quam naturalis fatorum conditio raperet." JUSTIN. II. 2. "Si fato concederem, justus mihi dolor etiam adversus Deos esset, quod me parentibus, liberis, patriae, intra juventam praematuro exitu raperent. nunc scelere Pisonis et Plancinae interceptus ultimas preces pectoribus vestris relinquo." Words of the dying Germanicus. ap. Tacit. *Annal. II. 71.*

"At quicumque nefas ausi, prohibente Deorum
Numine, polluerant Pontificale caput,
Morte jacent merita."

Ovid. *Fasti, III. 705.*

"Mortem omnibus ex natura aequalem, oblivione apud posteros vel gloria distingui. Ac, si nocentem innocentemque idem exitus maneat, acrioris viri esse, merito perire." Tacit. *Hist. I. 21.*

— "Et si fata fuissent
Ut caderem, meruisse manu."

En. II. 433.

See Comment *En. II. 738.*

§ IV.

Misera ante diem — answers to nec fato; *not by a natural death, but before her time;* subito accensa furore answers to merita nec morte; *not by the hand of another and in consequence of her previous conduct, but voluntarily and by her own hand, in a fit of fury.*

§ V.

Nondum illi flavum etc. Dextra crinem secat. — Compare:

"*Ιερος γαρ ουτος των κατα χθονος θεων,*
Οτου τοδ' εγχος κρατος αγνισει τριχα."

Eurip. *Alcestis, 76* (Thanatos speaking).

— "Eheu! invidet omnibus
Mors atra, nec scit parcere cuipiam.
Non nemini, ut suadet libido,
Crine caput spolians decorum."

Quoted by Meursius, Tom. V. col. 987.

"*Κολλυς γαρ η θριξ η επι του ακρου ην εφυλλαττον ακουρευτον, θεοις ανατιθεντες.*" *Etymol. Magn.* in voc. *απεσκολυμμενος.* Compare also Himerius's very beautiful allusion to this precious lock of hair, and its fatal shearing: "*Τις απεκειρε δαιμων της εμης εστιας τον χρυσουν βοστρυχον.*" Himerius (on the death of his son), *Orat. XXIII. 7;* where Wernsdorf observes: "Similiter loquitur Demades Rhetor, p. 180: *Απεκειρε την ακμην της Σπαρτης ο Θηβαιος.*" and adds other instances of a similar form of expression.

There can, I think, be no doubt but that the chief reason why the luminous appearance of the apex of Iulus, *En. II. 683,* was considered as portending such extraordinary good fortune, was because it was situated in this charmed lock on the crown of his head. See Comm. *En. II. 683.*

It is this usage which is continued in the consecration of the Roman Catholic nun. The nun's hair is cut off, to signify that she is [devoted to Dis] dead to the world: "On me place a côté du prêtre pour lui presenter les ciseaux .... Sa superbe chevelure tombe de toutes parts sous le fer sacré .... Cependant Amelie n'avoit point encore prononcé ses voeux, et pour mourir au monde il faillait qu'elle passât à travers le tombeau. Ma soeur se couche sur le marbre; on etend sur elle un drap mortuaire; quatre flambeaux en marquent les quatre coins. Le prêtre, l'etole au cou, le livre à la main, commence l'office des morts; de jeunes vierges le continuent"&c. Chateaubriand, *René.*

§ VI.

Ergo iris croceis etc. —Hence, no doubt, Schiller (see the magnificent conclusion of his play of *Die Jungfrau von Orleans)* drew the idea of the appearance of a rainbow in the sky at the moment of Joan d'Arc's death.

Reader, in whose breast may perhaps yet linger some spark of that *mens* at one and the same time *divinior* and *humanior,* which the combined bands of utilitarianism and puritanism are fast sweeping from the face of this fair world, I would ask thee ere thou takest leave of the 'infelix Phoenissa', what thinkest thou? Does it repent thee of the hour thou hast spent with her? of the tear thou hast perhaps shed over her? Does it regret thee, as it did St. Augustin (see his *Confessions),* of so much of thy life lost to the exact sciences, to active occupation, even to thy religion? or dost thou dare to feel that the exercise of thine intellectual faculties in the ennobling, exalting, purifying contemplation of the grand, the beautiful, and the pathetic, whether in the poetical, philosophical, or manuplastic creations of the master spirits of mankind, is not, cannot be of the nature of sin? Thou hesitatest; nor do I wonder; for I too have felt the tyranny of the fashion of the day, the withering oppression of the majority: go then and close thine ears against the music of sweet sounds, thine eyes against the gracious forms of the painter's pencil and the sculptor's chisel; thine heart and understanding against the rushing numbers of the poet, the persuasion of the orator, the irresistible reason of the philosopher; but first hear that same St. Augustin, him who calls himself criminal because he had read and studied and wept over these heathen loves of Dido and Eneas; learn from his own lips what it was that rescued him out of the "Tartarus libidinis et concupiscentiae," what it was that first turned the great luminary of the early Christian church from heathenism to Christianity, from the power of Satan to the one living and only true God. What was it? The narration of an evangelist? the discourse, or the letter, or the visit, of a Christian teacher, or missionary, or apostle? the testimony of a miracle or a martyrdom? No such thing; but the philosophical tract of the prose Virgil of Rome, the pagan Cicero's pagan Hortensius: "Usitato jam discendi ordine (in the usual course of classical studies) perveneram in librum quendam cujusdam Ciceronis, cujus linguam fere omnes mirantur, pectus non ita. Sed liber ille ipsius exhortationem continet ad philosophiam, et vocatur Hortensius. Ille vero liber mutavit affectum meum et ad teipsum Domine mutavit preces meas, et vota ac desideria mea fecit alia. Viluit mihi repente omnis vana spes, et immortalitatem sapientiae concupiscebam aestu cordis incredibili, et surgere coeperam ut ad te redirem ...... Quomodo ardebam, Deus meus, quomodo ardebam revolare a terrenis ad te; et nesciebam quid ageres mecum" etc. St. AUGUSTIN. *Confess. III. 1—7* Go now, reader, and with a rich and noble lord (rich and noble still, for riches and nobility are not the treasures which utilitarianism and puritanism throw away) fling thy classical library into the lake. See Comm. on "Nec sopor illud erat," *En. III. 173.*

V.

"Le cinquieme livre de l'Eneide me semble le plus parfait." Montaigne, *Essais*, II. 10.

The reader will be at no loss for the etiology of this, at first sight, somewhat strange opinion, if he reflect, first, that Montaigne was a Frenchman and therefore, as may be presumed, imbued with his nation's taste (a taste which the French probably inherited from the Romans themselves) for public exhibitions; and secondly, that the celebrated *Essais* from which I have quoted the above criticism, every where afford sufficient evidence that their author was a man wholly devoid of the elevation and tenderness of sentiment necessary for the perception and due appreciation of the nobler, grander and more pathetic parts of Virgil's writings.

1.

INTEREA MEDIUM AENEAS JAM CLASSE TENEBAT
CERTUS ITER FLUCTUSQUE ATROS AQUILONE SECABAT

---

§. I.

Certus. — "Servius minus probabiliter explicat: *itineris sui certus, persistens in consilio proficiscendi in Italiam;* ut igitur sit i. q. IV. 554, "certus eundi". Quod, quum

Aeneas jam in medio sit itinere, minus quadrare perspiciens, rectius Wagner interpretatur: *ad certum locum tendens; recto, non erratico itinere cursum intendens,* coll. "certa hasta", "certa sagitta", et "certa pompa" ap. Tibull. III. 1. 3." Forbiger.

I agree with Servius against both Wagner and Forbiger, and have no doubt that the meaning is *certain, sure, determined;* not, however, *determined on going* ("eundi"), he being already on the way ("in medio itinere"), but *determined on pursuing his voyage;* CERTUS TENEBAT ITER, *was pursuing his voyage with a resolved, steady, determined will.* I am of this opinion for the following reasons:

First, because such is always the meaning of 'certus', even in the very instances quoted by Wagner; "certa hasta," "certa sagitta," being, not *the spear* or *arrow which goes 'recto itinere' to the mark*, but *the spear* or *arrow which goes certainly, surely, determinedly, to the mark.* See *En.* VIII. 39 and seq. for 'certus' used in this (its only) sense, no less than four times within the space of eleven lines; and a little farther on (viz. at vers. 57), the very idea which Wagner has ascribed to CERTUS in our text, (viz. that of *straight* or *direct*), expressed by its proper term, 'rectus'.

Secondly, because Eneas's first, immediate and pressing object was *to sail;* to leave Dido and Carthage, in obedience to the command of Jupiter, conveyed in the single word "Naviget"

Thirdly, because CERTUS so understood refers back to the whole of the latter end of the preceding Book, occupied with the vain efforts of Dido and Juno to make him stay; to make him waver in his resolution of going; to make him 'incertus'.

Fourthly, because CERTUS so understood is finely opposed both to FLUCTUS ATROS AQUILONE SECABAT, and MOENIA RESPICIENS . . . . DUCUNT; as if Virgil had said, *pursuing his voyage steadily and without wavering, although the sea was black with the blasts of winter* (see §. II. below) *and although it was evident that something terrible had just happened in Carthage.*

§. II.

Aquilone. — "Simpliciter pro vento." Heyne, Ruaeus. — "Und schnitt die gedunkelte Fluth in der Kühlung." Voss.

No; aquilone is not merely *the wind*, but specifically *the unfavorable, winter wind, Aquilo;* see not only Dido's reproach (*En.* IV. 310),

"Et mediis properas Aquilonibus ire per altum,"

and her prayer (*En.* IV. 430),

"Expectet facilemque fugam ventosque ferentes,"

but the account in the first Book (verses 106, 395) of Eneas's shipwreck, effected by these 'Aquilones'. Also *En.* III. 285:

"Et glacialis hyems Aquilonibus asperat undas."

Still further; the structure is not, with Voss, 'secabat Aquilone', but 'atros Aquilone'; First, because Eneas could not properly be said to cut his way with a wind which, as we have just seen, was unfavorable to him. Secondly, because there should be some reason assigned why the waves were 'atri'. Thirdly, because we are expressly informed by Gellius (II. 30) that the effect of Aquilo is to render the waves 'atri': "Austris spirantibus mare fieri glaucum et caeruleum, Aquilonibus obscurius atriusque." Fourthly, because we have thus a natural prelude and introduction to the squall at vers. 10. Fifthly, because, as we have already seen (*En.* I. 297 and Comm.), the connexion of the ablative substantive with the adjective, in preference to the verb, is of common occurrence in Virgil. Sixthly, because we have at vers. 696, the exactly corresponding expression, "densis nigerrimus Austris"; and lastly (and leastly), because the passage has been so understood, not only by each of the three ancient commentators, Donatus, Servius, and Pomponius Sabinus, but by H. Stephens.

20.

IN NUBEM COGITUR AER

According to the Physical Philosophy of the Romans, clouds and mists consisted of condensed air. See Cic. *de Nat. Deor.* II. 39: "Exinde mari finitimus aer die et nocte distinguitur: isque tum fusus et extenuatus sublime fertur; tum aútem concretus, in nubes cogitur."

71.

ORE FAVETE OMNES ET CINGITE TEMPORA RAMIS

§. I.

Ore favete. — "Ευφημειτε (i. q. "favete linguis", *Hor. Od.* III. 1. 2), formula satis nota, qua ante sacra instituenda omnes a sacerdote silere et attendere jubentur." Forbiger.

The identity of the Latin with the Greek formula is indeed unquestionable, but that very identity serves to prove, not that the meaning is '*silete, attendite*', but the contrary; for, first, ευφημια being found in the very same sentence with σιγη and connected to it by the conjunction και ("ευφημιαν ανειπε και σιγην στρατω," Eurip. *Iphig. in Aulid.* 1564) must mean something different from σιγη. Secondly, the etymology of ευφημειν informs us intelligibly enough that it does not mean *to be silent*, but on the contrary *to speak well* i. e. '*verba bona, fausta*' (the 'bona verba quaeso' of the comedians). Thirdly, Eschylus confirms this interpretation almost by an actual definition:

> "Ευφημον ημαρ ου πρεπει κακαγγελῳ
> Γλωσσῃ μιαινειν."
>
> *Agam.* 645.

These arguments show, I think, sufficiently clearly,

through the medium of its acknowledged synonyme, *ευφημειτε*, that ORE FAVETE is not '*silete et attendite*', but '*bona verba dicite*'. If a more direct proof be required, it will, I think, be found in the following passage of Ovid (*Fasti*, I. 71):

"Prospera lux oritur: linguis animisque favete;
Nunc dicenda bona sunt bona verba die."

With which compare (OVID. *ex Ponto*, II. 5. 19):

"Tu tamen hic structos inter fera proelia versus
Et legis, et lectos ore favente probas."

So also the corresponding English phrase, "Keep a good tongue in your head" ("*Στομα τ᾽ ευφημον φρουρειτ᾽ αγαθον*," EURIP. *Ion*, 98), means, not *to be silent*, but *to speak only fitting things — neither contradict, nor mock, nor curse:* ("Male nominatis Parcite verbis." HOR. *Od.* III. 14. 11). Should I be required to reconcile the coexistence in the same sentence of two apparently so inconsistent commands as *ευφημειν*, interpreted as I have interpreted it, and *σιγαν* (see Eurip. quoted §. I. above), I beg to observe that these apparently inconsistent commands are really subordinary to each other, the meaning being, not *be absolutely and wholly silent, and at the same time speak good words*, but *cease (be silent from) your idle irreverent, lewd conversations, and speak only what is fitting to the occasion.* A similar double command is frequently found in the Bible, particularly with respect to the sabbath day which the Jews were required to keep holy; holy in act, not merely by abstaining from evil acts, but by performing good acts; holy in word, not merely by abstaining from idle or irreverent speaking, but by speaking words suited to the solemnity of the day: "*Εαν αποστρεψης τον ποδα σου απο των σαββατων, του μη ποιειν τα θηληματα σου εν τη ημερα τη αγια, και καλεσεις τα σαββατα τρυφερα, αγια τω θεω· ουκ αρεις τον ποδα σου επ᾽ εργω, ουδε λαλησεις λογον εν οργη εκ του στοματος σου.*" *Η Παλ. Διαθ. Ησαιας*, LVIII. 13.

§. II.

Ore favete. — *Favor with your mouths; use your mouths so as to further what I am about.* If the speaker is engaged in lamentation, 'ore favete' thus becomes equivalent to *mourn with me;* compare Ovid, *Ibis*, 95:

> "Illum ego devoveo, quem mens intelligit, Ibin;
> Qui se scit factis has meruisse preces.
> Nulla mora est in me; peragam rata vota sacerdos:
> Quisquis ades sacris, ore favete, meis;
> Quisquis ades sacris, lugubria dicite verba,
> Et fletu madidis Ibin adite genis."

If, on the contrary, the speaker is (as Eneas on the present occasion) engaged in rejoicings, 'ore favete' is (as sufficiently shown from the quotations above from Ovid's *Fasti* and *ex Ponto*) equivalent to *rejoice with me; signify with your voices that you participate in my feelings.* Compare: "Inferior miles ..... hastis feriendo clypeos, sonitu assurgens ingenti, uno propemodum ore dictis favebat et coeptis." Ammian. XX. 5.

80.

SALVE SANCTE PARENS ITERUM SALVETE RECEPTI
NEQUIDQUAM CINERES ANIMAEQUE UMBRAEQUE PATERNAE
NON LICUIT FINES ITALOS FATALIAQUE ARVA
NEC TECUM AUSONIUM QUICUNQUE EST QUAERERE TYBRIM

"Jam apud veteres ambiguam fuisse horum verborum interpunctionem, discitur a Servio, qui post iterum distinguendum esse ait, ut est in Mediceo et apud Scholiast. A. Maii: recte puto; verbum recepti enim indicat, respici hic ad id, quod tum secunda fiebat vice." Wagner.

I agree in the conclusion, but from quite different grounds. Iterum is to be joined to salve sancte parens, solely because the history shows that this was Eneas's return to the sepulchre, and therefore his second

'Salve' or salutation. And so, correctly, Mai's Scholiast, quoted above by Wagner: "ITERUM, quia salutaveret quum ad sepulturam mitteret." Both Wagner's arguments are erroneous: First, nothing can be concluded from the Medicean in which ITERUM stands (if only Foggini is to be relied on) with a point immediately preceding, as well as with a point immediately succeeding it, and therefore equally separated both from the preceding and the succeeding context, and as it were in a parenthesis. And secondly, RECEPTI does not refer to any thing which is done now for a second time, but is applied to Anchises in the sense in which it is applied to him *En.* VI. 111. (compare *En.* I. 182, 557, 587), viz. in that of *saved, recovered;* Germ. *gerettet.*

SALVETE RECEPTI NEQUIDQUAM CINERES ANIMAEQUE UMBRAEQUE PATERNAE. — This sentence is entirely epexegetic or parenthetic; as is proved, first, by the necessity for the addition to the salutation SALVE SANCTE PARENS ITERUM of some qualifying expression to show that that salutation was addressed not to a living, but to a dead, person; and secondly, by the singular pronoun TECUM which points past the interposed SALVETE.... PATERNAE, directly to PARENS.

RECEPTI NEQUIDQUAM. — I agree entirely with the ancient commentator in the Gudian (in which MS. I find, over the word RECEPTI, the gloss "*liberati a Troja*") in understanding these words to refer to Eneas's carrying of his father safe off from Troy. RECEPTI NEQUIDQUAM; *umsonst gerettet.* Compare: "nequidquam erepte", *En.* III. 711; also "fruges receptas", *En.* I. 182.

102.

AENA LOCANT ALII

That AENA here, and in *En.* I. 217, are *λοετρα*, *vessels to heat water for the purposes of ablution*, is I think placed beyond all doubt by the exactly corresponding passage of Apollonius Rhodius (*Argon.* III. 271, 299, and seq.):

— "Τοι μεν μεγαν αμφεπενοντο
Ταυρον αλις δμωες· τοι δε ξυλα καγκανα χαλκῳ
Κοπτον· τοι δε λοετρα πυρι ζεον.
. . . .
. . . .
Δμωες δ' οπποτε δη σφιν επαρτεα θηκαν εδωδην,
Αυτοι τε λιαροισιν εφαιδρυναντο λοετροις" etc.

Compare also Soph. *Ajax. Flagell.* 1420:

"Αλλ' οι μεν κοιλην καπετον
Χερσι ταχυνατε, τοι δ' υψιβατον
Τριποδ αμφιπυρον λουτρων οσιων
Θεσθ' επικαιρον."

and (APUL. *Metam.* IV. 7): "In fine sermonis hujus statim se devestiunt; nudatique et flammae largissimae vapore recreati calidaque perfusi, et oleo peruncti, mensas dapibus largiter instructas accumbunt."

118.

INGENTEMQUE GYAS INGENTI MOLE CHIMAERAM
URBIS OPUS

The comparison of a large ship to a city may be excused in a poet, since it has been made even by an historian; see Flor. IV. 11, where speaking of the ships of Mark Antony he says: "Turribus atque tabulatis allevatae castellorum et urbium specie, non sine gemitu maris et labore ventorum ferebantur." For the contrary comparison, viz. that of a city to a ship, see that beautiful passage in Ezekiel, thus rendered in the Vulgate: "O Tyre, tu dixisti: perfecti decoris ego sum, et in corde maris sita. Finitimi tui qui te aedificaverunt, impleverunt decorem tuum. Abietibus de Sanir extruxerunt te cum omnibus tabulatis maris; cedrum de Libano tulerunt, ut facerent tibi malum; quercus de Basan dolaverunt in remos tuos; et transtra tua fecerunt tibi ex ebore Indico et praetoriola de insulis Italiae." EZECHIEL, XXVII. 3.

157.

NUNC UNA AMBAE JUNCTISQUE FERUNTUR
FRONTIBUS ET LONGA SULCANT VADA SALSA CARINA

The simple idea, stripped of its ornament, is that of the two vessels moving on, *abreast in front, and side by side in their length;* and so, no doubt, it would have been expressed by an inferior poet; but Virgil for the sake of variety, and according to his usual custom (see Comm. *En.* IV. 73), alters the latter clause, and instead of saying *with bows abreast and hulls side by side*, says *with bows abreast, and furrow the salt waters with their long keels;* thus used, the epithlet LONGA is, not only not "otiosum", as it has appeared to Peerlkamp, Wagner, and Heyne ("est LONGA prorsus otiosa vox"), but in the highest degree useful and ornamental; (*a*) because it serves to place before the mind not only the length of the vessels (with their consequent size and stateliness), but their parallel position with respect to their length (which latter sense appears more evidently on our supplying UNA from the preceding clause, as suggested by Wagner); and (*b*) because it thus prepares for the succeeding account (vers. 186) of the one vessel passing the other, not by the whole, but only by part of its length:

"Nec tota tamen ille prior praeeunte carina" etc.

That such is really the use and effect of the epithet LONGA will readily appear on suppressing the term and reading the passage without it; SULCANT VADA SALSA CARINA. Compare *En.* X. 197, where the same term is applied to the keel of a vessel with the same happy effect; that of suggesting the idea not merely of a long keel, but of a large and stately vessel. Compare also the similiar use, by another faithful observer of nature, of the same 'epitheton otiosum' (!):

> "The long keel trembles and the timbers groan."
>
> FALCONER, *Shipwreck*, c. III.

Although nautical men of the present day invariably connect the idea of speed with length of keel ("The length of fast ships must be great, 200 feet of keel being requisite to insure with least power a speed of 18 miles an hour, 300 feet of keel to attain 23 miles an hour," etc. See a paper read by Mr. Scott Russell in the Royal Institution, June 2. 1848, and quoted in the *Atheneum* of June 24) it is unnecessary to claim a knowledge of this relation for Virgil, the more obvious relation between length of keel and size and stateliness of vessel, affording a sufficient answer to the charge brought against him, that in applying the term LONGA to a vessel's keel he was guilty of a truism.

A strong confirmation of the views just expressed is afforded by the following passage which I met accidentally in C. Nepos, years after the above was written, and which shows that vessels of war, i. e. the largest, finest, and most stately vessels, were specially and technically denominated 'longae' by the ancients; no doubt because proportionally longer than transports, or merchant vessels. Speaking of the fleet with which Xerxes invaded Greece, Cornelius says: "Hujus enim classis mille et ducentarum navium longarum fuit, quam duo millia onerariarum sequebantur." *Themist.* II. 5; where see Bremi's Annot. So also the same author in *Dion*, V. 3: "Imperium munitum quingentis longis navibus," i. e. *ships of war;* and Justin, II. 4: "Eo igitur profectus longis novem navibus, comitante principum Graeciae juventute, inopinantes aggreditur." So also Caesar (*de Bell. Gall.* IV. 22) opposes "naves longas" to "onerarias". Compare also: "*Ακυλαν . . . επεμψα προς υμας κατασκευαζοντα μοι ναυς στρογγυλας πεντηκοντα, και μακρας διακοσιας*" *Epist. Bruti ad Bithyn.* in the *Epist. Mut. Graecan.*

210.

AT LAETUS MNESTHEUS SUCCESSUQUE ACRIOR IPSO
AGMINE REMORUM CELERI VENTISQUE VOCATIS
PRONA PETIT MARIA ET PELAGO DECURRIT APERTO
QUALIS SPELUNCA SUBITO COMMOTA COLUMBA
CUI DOMUS ET DULCES LATEBROSO IN PUMICE NIDI
FERTUR IN ARVA VOLANS PLAUSUMQUE EXTERRITA PENNIS
DAT TECTO INGENTEM MOX AERE LAPSA QUIETO
RADIT ITER LIQUIDUM CELERES NEQUE COMMOVET ALAS
SIC MNESTHEUS SIC IPSA FUGA SECAT ULTIMA PRISTIS
AEQUORA SIC ILLAM FERT IMPETUS IPSE VOLANTEM

---

§. 1.

PRONA MARIA. — 'Pronus', *declivis in anteriorem partem; sloping downwards and forwards and therefore* (in the case of a fluid) *flowing downwards and forwards.* Compare *Georg.* I. 203:

"Atque illum in praeceps prono rapit alveus amni;"

and *En.* VIII. 548:

— "Pars caetera prona
Fertur aqua;"

carried down with the descending stream, or *current of the river.* Lucan, IV. 429:

"Jamque relabenti crescebant littora ponto;
Missa ratis prono defertur lapsa profundo;"

carried down from the shore towards the deep with the ebbing tide. Also Claudian, *in Eutrop.* II. 28:

"Pronus et in geminas nutavit Bosphorus urbes;"

the tide flowing in opposite directions at the same time. And Lucan, VI. 473, of a river preternaturally flowing upwards or towards its source:

— "Amnisque cucurrit
Non qua pronus erat."

And so in the passage before us, Mnestheus, having reached and rounded the goal, seeks, on his return, to avail himself of the fall in the water towards the land, i. e. of the current or tide setting in shoreward. This interpretation of PRONA is doubly confirmed; (*a*) by the verb DECURRIT (corresponding exactly to '*de*fertur' in the first of the two passages above quoted from Lucan), and (*b*) by the immediately succeeding simile (QUALIS SPELUNCA etc.), in which the pigeon is described as flying, not upwards nor horizontally, but from her nest in the rock downwards towards the fields:

FERTUR IN ARVA VOLANS . . . . . .
. . . . MOX AERE LAPSA QUIETO
RADIT ITER LIQUIDUM, CELERES NEQUE COMMOVET ALAS;

plainly a description of that downward flight of a bird, in which no flapping of the wings is required or used. Compare Dante's exactly similiar description of the downward flying of pigeons from the upper air toward the nest (*Inferno*, V. 82):

"Quali colombe dal desio chiamate
Con l'ali aperte e ferme al dolce nido
Volan per l'aer dal voler portate";

and Biagioli's commentary: "'Con l'ali aperte e ferme;' tale si e l'atto degli augelli volanti d'alto in basso."

Heyne's explanation of this passage ("PRONA MARIA, in quibus cursus *pronus* ac celer sine impedimento fit; idem APERTO PELAGO) is doubly unhappy; first, because to explain 'pronus' by 'pronus' is a mere blinking of the difficulty; secondly, because (see §. III. below)

APERTO PELAGO means something totally different from PRONA MARIA.

Any remaining doubt which the reader may entertain concerning the interpretation of PRONA in the text, must, I should think, disappear before the following examples: Ovid, *Heroid.* XVIII. 121:

> "Hoc quoque si credas; ad te via prona videtur;
> A te cum redeo, clivus inertis aquae."

where 'clivus' and 'inertis' being the opposite of 'prona', 'prona' is plainly not merely *down hill*, but also *running;* i. e. *flowing down toward the shore.*

> "Nec redit in fontes unda supina suos."
> OVID. *Medic. Faciei*, 40;

where the term 'supina', the opposite of 'prona', is applied to water flowing preternaturally upwards; and, Avienus, *Descript. Orb. Terrae*, 197:

> "Hinc arctas inter fauces atque obvia saxa
> Thracius angustas discludit Bosphorus oras;
> Nam vicina sibi stant littora, terraque parci
> Faucibus oris hiat, prona sinus evomit unda;"

i. e. the level of the strait being higher than that of the sea, the former pours *a downward stream of water* ("prona unda") into the latter.

§. II.

PRONA MARIA . . . . PELAGO APERTO . . . . ULTIMA AEQUORA. — The course which the ships had to run (sciz, from the shore to the goal, and this having been turned, see vers. 231, back again to the shore) was, we may presume (the race being one of oars and not of sails), performed in as direct a line as possible. The terms PRONA MARIA, PELAGO APERTO, ULTIMA AEQUORA, indicate therefore not any new parts of the sea, but the very part over which the vessels had passed on their way outward, considered now in relation to their return, and called 'pronum' as inclining downwards in the direction of the shore (see §. I. above), 'apertum' as being free from obstruction (see below), and 'ultimum' as forming the last part of the course.

PELAGO APERTO. — Not, *the open sea* in the sense of *the sea far out from land*, or *farther out than the goal*, but, as sufficiently proved by the sequel, and especially by ULTIMA AEQUORA and "ipso in fine" (vers. 225), *the sea between the goal and the land*, called 'apertum' (see Comment on "Aperit Syrtes", *En.* I. 150), because unobstructed either by the goal itself or by the competing ships; that part of the sea sciz. which for the very same reason is, at vers. 171, called 'tuta'.

§. III.

CUI DOMUS ET DULCES NIDI. — "DULCES, propter liberos." Wagner.

Near, but not exactly, the truth: NIDI is (metaphorically of course) *the 'liberi'; the young themselves;* first, because otherwise it were a mere repetition of DOMUS; secondly, because it is used in this sense not only by other writers, but by Virgil himself elsewhere: "Queruli nidi", SENECA, *Herc. Fur.* 148. "Nidis loquacibus", *En.* XII. 475. "Dulcem nidis immitibus escam", *Georg.* IV. 17. "Implumes nidos", CLAUD. *de Tert. Cons. Honor. Praef.* vers. 5. See also Nonius Marcellus, in voc. Thirdly, because mention of the young is required to complete and vivify the picture, and render the dove's extreme terror natural.

Statius's

— "Cui circum stagna Carysti
Et domus, et conjux, et amantes littora nati."
Theb. VII. 718,

is nearly parallel.

MOX AERE LAPSA QUIETO RADIT ITER LIQUIDUM CELERES NEQUE COMMOVET ALAS SIC MNESTHEUS &C. —

"Behold'st thou not two shapes from the east and west
Come as two doves to one beloved nest,
Twin nurslings of the all-sustaining air,
On swift, still wings, glide down the atmosphere."
SHELLEY, *Prometh. Unbound, Act I.*

220.

ET PRIMUM IN SCOPULO LUCTANTEM DESERIT ALTO SERGESTUM BREVIBUSQUE VADIS

"Scopulus dicitur altus, quia navigantibus e mari conspectus ob prominentiam suam tantae magnitudinis esse videbatur, minime vero quia summae erat altitudinis. Brevia vada sunt loca circa scopulum, aqua carentia, et multam ostendentia arenam." Jacob, *Quaest. Epic. Pars prima*, I. 2.

Both explanations are, I think, erroneous; the former, (*a*) because the rock, according to the description (vers. 124 and seq.), did not rise above the water to a height at all entitling it to the appellation 'altus'; and (*b*) because the height (whether greater or less) of the rock above the water, having nothing whatever to do with the striking of Sergestus's ship (which cannot but be supposed to have been aground on a part of the rock which was below the water), was not likely to have been placed by so accurate a writer as Virgil (see Comment *En.* II. 552) thus prominently before the eyes of the reader in an account, not of the rock, but of the ship's position on it; the latter, because (*a*) a rock situated in the deep sea (vers. 124 and seq.) was not likely to have been surrounded with sandy shallows; (*b*) because a rock so surrounded were the last place Eneas would have chosen for a 'meta'; (*c*) because such surrounding shallows must necessarily have anticipated and prevented the striking of the ship on the rock; and (*d*) because, this interpretation being admitted, the ship must have been aground on the high rock and on the sandy shallows at one and the same time, quod absurdum. I therefore understand ALTO to express the height of the rock (and particularly of that part of it on which the ship was impacted) above the bottom of the sea; and BREVIBUS VADIS to be the shallows formed by that same part of the rock ("saxis procurrentibus," vers. 204) under the water. SCOPULO ALTO BREVIBUSQUE VADIS is thus the ordinary Endiadys for 'brevibus vadis alti scopuli (compare "In brevia et Syrtes," i. e. *in brevia Syrtium, En.* I. 115); and ALTO, graphically opposed to BREVIBUS, explains how it happened that there were shallows in the deep water.

231.

HOS SUCCESSUS ALIT POSSUNT QUIA POSSE VIDENTUR

Heyne and common opinion, VIDENTUR *sibi;* Servius and Voss, VIDENTUR *spectantibus.* I agree with Heyne and common opinion, and believe the author's meaning to be, *their previous success renders them self-confident, and their self-confidence renders them able. Previous success* and *ability* are thus two links of a chain of thought, connected together by the intermediate link, *self-confidence.* The interpretation of Servius and Voss (*their previous success renders them self-confident, and the confidence which the spectators repose in them renders them able,*) cuts the connecting link into two halves, and calling one of the halves *self-confidence*, leaves it in connexion with the left hand link, and calling the other half *the confidence reposed in them by the spectators*, leaves it in connexion with the right hand link; and thus instead of giving us the three mutually connected and dependent ideas, *previous success, self-confidence* and *ability*, presents us with four thoughts, of which the two former, *previous success* and *self-confidence*, stand wholly separate and apart from the two latter, *the confidence of the spectators* and *ability;* and leaving *previous success* and *self-confidence* without their natural and expected consequence, ascribes the consequence to the newly introduced cause, *the confidence of the spectators.*

It is painful to observe the malicious pleasure with which Voss on every occasion on which it is at all possible, deals Heyne a knock on the head either with the awkward cudgel of Servius or with his own far more redoubtable fist. The present occasion is one of the few in which the blow is not accompanied with some such insulting expression as, "So würfeln die drei Herrn, Heyne, Heumann und Bryant über Virgil!" (V. 138). "Albern! wenn man die Regeln des Versbaues kennt." (III. 123). "Ihr heiligen Musen! Das ohrzerreissende exstinxsti trägt epische Würde!" (IV. 682). "Das steht wohl Heyne an, solche Citate zu beekeln!" (IV. 700). "Was sagt der Verwirrte?" (V. 183). "Schön! veniebat veniens." (V. 373). "Der Scharfsinnige!" (VI. 161). "Der feine Spötter!" (VI. 255). "Diese Erklärung ist ihm durch die Elfenbeinpforte gekommen." (VI. 895), and so forth, and so forth; expressions which cannot fail to remind the reader, of the boastful and vituperative language with which a Homeric hero delighted to second his assault on his antagonist, often a better man than himself. It is indeed greatly to be regretted that Voss should have descended from his high status as an accomplished scholar, an acute critic, and a poet able, as proved by his famous Idyl, to compete even with Goethe himself, to these unworthy personalities; directed too against a man distinguished alike for his immense and varied erudition, and for the temperate and becoming language in which he puts forward his own opinions and combats the opinions of others; a man who (his Virgilian labors alone taken into account) has contributed more to the advancement of Classical Literature in Europe than perhaps any man that ever lived. The errors of such a man (and who may hope to discuss without error the meaning of almost every word of Virgil?) are at least deserving of lenity. Servius, the third of the commentators of whom I have here been led to speak, derives from the accident of his having lived so much nearer to the time of Virgil, a double advantage over the other two; viz. a vernacular knowledge of the language, and access to sources of information respecting Virgil, which have since been lost. Notwithstanding these two great advantages Servius (or whoever else may have been the author of the commentaries ascribed to Servius) was, owing to defects in himself, infinitely inferior as a commentator of Virgil, both to Voss and Heyne. Totally destitute of poetical sentiment, and stone-blind to Virgil's fascinating grace and elegance, Servius sees nothing in the Eneis but a mere matter of fact narrative, such as might have come from the pen of an Aratus or an Avienus, and writes comments on it which bear the same relation to those of Heyne and Voss, as we may suppose Critiques upon the dramas of Shakespeare, written some two hundred years ago by the master of a village grammar school in Yorkshire, would bear to those of Schlegel.

244.

TUM SATUS ANCHISA CUNCTIS EX MORE VOCATIS
VICTOREM MAGNA PRAECONIS VOCE CLOANTHUM
DECLARAT VIRIDIQUE ADVELAT TEMPORA LAURO

Eneas in declaring Cloanthus victorious, acts in the capacity, not of head of the expedition and chief of the army, but of Agonotheta, who, having given the games, and furnished the prizes (see vers. 66—70), possesses the right of declaring the victor, and of regulating all matters appertaining to the contest. This right of declaring the victor is always enumerated among the prerogatives of the Christian Agonotheta by the Fathers of the Church when, carrying out the comparison instituted by St. Paul (1. Cor. IX. 24) between the Christian course and a race in the circus, they represent Christ as the Agonotheta of the Christian race: "Ita agnosces ad eundem agonothetam pertinere certaminis arbitrium, qui invitat ad praemium." S. TERTULL. *de fuga in persecutione*, I. 1. "Proponit agonotheta praemium, invitat ad cursum, tenet in manu bravium." S. HIERON. *Lib. I. adv. Jovinian. c.* 12.

252.

INTEXTUSQUE PUER FRONDOSA REGIUS IDA
VELOCES JACULO CERVOS CURSUQUE FATIGAT
ACER ANHELANTI SIMILIS QUEM PRAEPES AB IDA
SUBLIMEM PEDIBUS RAPUIT JOVIS ARMIGER UNCIS

§. I.

Although the change of tense, FATIGAT, RAPUIT, sufficiently points out a change of picture — *here, in this picture, the royal boy is hunting; there, in that one, Jove's bird has seized and carried him up into the air* — and although such representations on the same work of art (whether cloth, plate, or porcelain) of distinct, often successive, acts, are sufficiently common and notorious (witness the shields of Eneas and Achilles, the wedding quilt of Thetis, and the mantle of Jason) yet commentators have not been wanting to accuse Virgil of having here put together (sciz. in a single picture or view) acts which could not by possibility be performed simultaneously: "Virgilius dormitans aliquando: INTEXTUSQUE PUER &c., ubi non exputo, quomodo una in tabula representatus fuerit Ganymedes et venationi intentus, ita ut ipsum currentem videas, et idem sublatus in aerem." Wagner (*Quaest. Virg.*). "Non aliter te expedies ex his tricis, quam fatendo, bonum Virgilium hic dormitasse." Wagner, in Notis ad Virgil. Heyn. Let this palpable error (tacitly acknowledged by Wagner himself in his *Virg. Br. En.*) teach commentators humility, and that the mote is sometimes in their own eyes.

§. II.

QUEM PRAEPES etc.—The commentators, connecting PRAEPES with AB IDA, and displeased with the recurrence here of the same termination of the verse as at vers. 252, propose to read in place of PRAEPES AB IDA, either 'praepes ab alto' (Burmann Jun. ad *Anthol. Lat. Poet.* p. 272) or 'praepes ab aethra', conjectured by Schrader, *Emendat.* p. 154, and actually adopted by Brunck. I am strongly inclined to think that the emendators have entirely mistaken the sense, and that the structure is, not 'praepes ab Ida', but 'praepes armiger sublimem rapuit ab Ida'; first, because I do not elsewhere find 'praepes' connected with 'ab', while on the contrary the connexion of 'rapere' with 'ab' is of usual occurrence ("agnum .... a stabulis rapuit lupus", *En.* IX. 565; "matris ab ubere raptum", *En.* VII. 484); and secondly, because we obtain thus, and thus only, the fine picture of the boy in the talons of the eagle high in the air above the mountain: SUBLIMEM AB IDA RAPUIT.

The word 'praepes' itself seems to me to be neither *flying upwards* nor *flying downwards*, but *flying rapidly forward*, *right ahead;* compare Ausonius (*Epigr.* 146), of a shorthand writer:

"Puer notarum praepetum
Sollers minister, advola;"

and (Ibid):

"Sentire tam velox mihi
Vellem dedisset mens mea,
Quam praepetis dextrae fuga
Tu me loquentem praevenis."

268.

JAMQUE ADEO DONATI OMNES OPIBUSQUE SUPERBI
PUNICEIS IBANT EVINCTI TEMPORA TAENIIS

SUPERBI IBANT. — The identical phrase is preserved in the Italian: "Io andrei sempre superbo di mostrarvi a dito." *Come si diviene Pittore* (Translated by Gar from the Flemish of Constance).

"Le ornasti il crin, che ben puote ir' superba
Del gran figlio la madre."

Carlo Bottari, *Fragment by Louisa Grace* (in the *Monumenti del Giardino Puccini*, Pistoja, 1846).

TAENIIS. — See *Museo Pio-Clementino*, *Tom. VI. Tab. XII* and *XIII*, for busts of Hercules with such Taeniae; also for the observations of Visconti thereon.

317.

SIMUL ULTIMA SIGNANT

Compare Lucian (*De non temere credendo calumniae*): "*Κἀκει γαρ ο μεν αγαθος δρομευς της υσπληγγος ευθυς καταπεσουσης μονον του προσω εφιεμενος και διανοιαν υποτεινας προς το τερμα.*"

323.

EURYALUMQUE HELYMUS SEQUITUR QUO DEINDE SUB IPSO
ECCE VOLAT CALCEMQUE TERIT JAM CALCE DIORES
INCUMBENS HUMERO SPATIA ET SI PLURA SUPERSINT
TRANSEAT ELAPSUS PRIOR AMBIGUUMQUE RELINQUAT

§. 1.

CALCEMQUE TERIT JAM CALCE. — The Virgilian student who happens to be familiar with the very common and even vulgar use in English, of the word 'heel' for the word 'foot' (see Launcelot Gobbo, in *The Merchant of Venice*, II. 2) will smile at the coil which the commentators have made about these words. The "valde dura ratio" (Heyne) which Burmann follows, occupies nearly an entire column of his quarto page, and Peerlkamp having ingenuously confessed that it is impossible to understand how Diores could with his heel have trod upon the heel of Helymus, who was before him, proceeds with the most sober sadness to aver that he trod on him with his toes: "Intellectu difficile est, quomodo Diores calce calcem Helymi triverit. Trivit calcem Helymi digitis pedis." In support of which incontrovertible proposition, the matter-of-fact commentator has unaccountably omitted to quote the matter-of-fact poet:

> — "Instat non segnius acer
> Hesperos, ac prima stringit vestigia planta
> Progressae calcis."
>
> Sil. Ital. XVI. 491.

Poets, beware how ye use figures of speech; they are dangerous, and will infallibly cut your fingers. What will not future commentators say of Thomson's

> "These as they roll, almighty Father, these
> Are but the varied God?"

What has not been already said of "This is my body; this is my blood"? what millions of human lives have not been sacrificed to that one figure? From henceforward for ever let no fugitive presume to take to his heels, far less fly; let no maiden, if she be wise, bestow her hand on her lover; or should she be content to do with one hand for the rest of her life, let her at least not part with her heart; for how exist one single day without the central organ of the circulation, indispensable every moment for forwarding a fresh supply of arterial blood through the arteries, and receiving the old worn-out blood back from the veins.

§. II.

Incumbens humero. — St. Augustin has made a very happy figurative application of this idea: "Et ecce tu imminens dorso fugitivorum tuorum Deus ultionum, et fons misericordiarum simul." *Confess.* IV. 7.

§. III.

Ambiguumque relinquat. — "Ambiguumque Heinsius consensu librorum recepit, quod et pars Pierianorum habebat; ratio tamen et res respuit. Nam si transiisset socium, res non ambigua jam fuisset, uter prior esset. Verius alii editi et scripti 'ambiguumve'." Heyne.

The fault is not in the manuscripts, but in Heyne who did not understand them. Ambiguum relinquat is not a separate event, a second possible consequence of the premiss spatia si plura supersint, such minute subdivision of consequences being, first, mere trifling and littleness, and secondly, not according to Virgil's usual method; but it is, according to Virgil's usual method, a heightening (*Steigerung*) of the single consequence: *Diores would not only pass Helymus by,* transeat elapsus prior, *but leave him completely behind — distance him,* relinquat; 'relinqui' being, as clearly appears from Statius, *Theb.* VI. 344 and 309:

— "Par et concordia voti,
Vincere vel solo cupiunt a fratre relinqui."

— "Stupuere relicta
Nubila, certantes Eurique Notique sequuntur."

the proper, technical term for being *left completely behind, distanced in the race.*

Ambiguum — not *that would be ambiguous when so entirely left behind and distanced in the supposed longer race,* but *that is now in the actual state of the race ambiguous; to whom Diores has come so very close, as to render him (Helymus) ambiguous;* i. e. *doubtful which is actually foremost — actually the winner.* See in Statius's description of the discus-throwing, the distinction made by him between overpassing by so small a space as to leave it doubtful whether one has actually passed by or only come up to (Statius's "dubia junctave meta;" Virgil's AMBIGUUM), and quite distancing and leaving behind, (Statius's "longe super aemula signa consedit;" Virgil's RELINQUAT):

> — "Nec dubia junctave Menesthea victum
> Transabiit meta: longe super aemula signa
> Consedit."
>
> *Theb.* VI. 712.

AMBIGUUM thus becomes the descriptive predicate so often (I may say always where possible) used by Virgil instead of the personal pronoun of prose and prosaic poets.

Wagner (*Quaest. Virg.* XXXVI. 1), although adopting Heyne's reading 've', denies the correctness of Heyne's statement: "'Ambiguumve relinquat'. Sic Codices Heins., non, ut Heynius refert, AMBIGUUMQUE." In this observation as in so many others Wagner is verbally correct, but, as appears to me at least, substantially wrong. Heinsius does indeed say (see his note in Burmann), "'Ambiguumve' codices nostri omnes", and his Leyden Edition of 1671 has 'ambiguumve', but both appear to have been accidental (perhaps typographical) errors; for first, his Utrecht Edition of 1704 has AMBIGUUMQUE; and secondly, the general, almost the universal, reading of the MSS. is actually AMBIGUUMQUE, as I think I may safely state on my own experience, having found that reading in every one of eight MSS. which I consulted expressly concerning this passage, one of those eight being the Gudian, the very MS. on which, above all others, Heinsius was accustomed to rely. The other seven MSS. consulted by me, and in every one of which I found AMBIGUUMQUE, were Nos. 115, 116 and 117 in the Royal Library at Vienna, the Kloster-Neuburg, the two Leipzig and the Dresden. I have also found AMBIGUUMQUE both in the Modena Ed. of 1475 and in Rob. Stephens; it is also the reading of La Cerda and Burmann;

and Bersmann, though himself adopting 'ambiguumve', informs us that AMBIGUUMQUE is the reading of his MS. AMBIGUUMQUE is also (see Foggini) the reading of the Medicean. H. Stephens defends 'ambiguumve' in a long, and, as it seems to me, entirely erroneous disputation, and this reading has been adopted by D. Heinsius.

334.

NON TAMEN EURYALI NON ILLE OBLITUS AMORUM

For some just remarks on Virgil's frequent use of the negation ("les tours négatifs") see Chateaubriand, *Genie du Christianisme*, II. 2. 10.

355.

PRIMAM MERUI QUI LAUDE CORONAM
NI ME QUAE SALIUM FORTUNA INIMICA TULISSET

"Me a primo praemio abstulisset, abduxisset." Heyne. "Ferre h. l. lusum fortunae significat." Wagner.

I dissent from both explications, and think 'ferre' is used here, exactly as in *En.* II. 600 ("Jam flammae tulerint") and *En.* IV. 679 ("Idem ambas ferro dolor, atque eadem hora tulisset"), in the sense of the common English expressions, *make away with*, *make short work of; settle; finish; undo &c.* For a similar use of the same word see (*En.* II. 554):

— "Hic exitus illum
Sorte tulit."

387.

HIC GRAVIS ENTELLUM DICTIS CASTIGAT ACESTES

"GRAVIS, der Würdige. Ein Tadel, der von einem 'vir gravis' ausgeht, hat weit mehr Gewicht, als eine 'gravis castigatio hominis alicujus': darum ist der hier gewählte Ausdruck stärker als wenn es hiesse, 'graviter castigat'." Ladewig.

This observation, abstractedly correct, is misplaced here. The construction is, not 'gravis Acestes castigat Entellum dictis', but 'Acestes castigat Entellum gravis dictis', i. e. *gravibus dictis;* compare (vers. 274) "Gravis ictu," i. e. *gravi ictu*, and see Comments *En.* I. 294; V. 1 (§. II.); IV. 504.

391.

UBI NUNC NOBIS DEUS ILLE MAGISTER
NEQUIDQUAM MEMORATUS ERYX

"Ubi nunc est illa gloria, quod magistro usus es Eryce, quem olim nobis jactabas?" Wagner, *Virg. Br. En.*

I think however that the structure is, not 'memoratus nobis', but 'ubi nunc nobis deus ille Eryx, nequidquam memoratus magister'; NOBIS being the dative ethic, and MAGISTER NEQUIDQUAM MEMORATUS a parenthetic clause: *where now is that God of ours Eryx, vainly vaunted of by thee* (or perhaps even *by us*) *as thy teacher?* Both the sense and the structure are rendered perfectly plain by two commas, one placed after ILLE, the other after MEMORATUS.

Exactly similar to NOBIS in our text is 'vobis', vers. 646:

"Non Beroe vobis, non haec Rhoeteia, matres,
Est Dorycli conjux."

400.

NEC DONA MOROR

"Plausum non moror."
AUSON. *Chilon.* 16.

466.

NON VIRES ALIAS CONVERSAQUE NUMINA SENTIS
CEDE DEO

"VIRES ALIAS, quam putaveras hujus hominis esse, h. e. tuis majores." Heyne.
"VIRES ALIAS, des Entellus." Ladewig.
"VIRES ALIAS, sciz. tibi esse quam ante." Voss.

Neither interpretation pleases me. I think the meaning is declared by the immediately added CONVERSA NUMINA, CEDE DEO, to be *Do you not perceive that the strength against which you are contending, is not that of Entellus, but* VIRES ALIAS, *quite different strength*, *another* or *second strength*, viz. *that of the Gods.* To have said to Dares: "Do you not perceive that the strength of Entellus is quite different (either from what it had been before, or from yours, i. e. greater than yours)," or "Do you not perceive that your own strength is less than it was before," had been to reprove, not to comfort and soothe him ("mulcens dictis," *v.* 464).

481.

STERNITUR EXANIMISQUE TREMENS PROCUMBIT HUMI BOS

Not a mere poetical exaggeration; a similar feat being recorded of Caesar Borgia: "Der schönste Mann; so stark, dass er im Stiergefecht den Kopf des Stiers auf einen Schlag herunterhieb." RANKE, *Die Römischen Päpste, B. I. c.* 2.

487.

INGENTIQUE MANU MALUM DE NAVE SERESTI ERIGIT

"Magna multitudine." Servius.

I think not; first, because the erection of the mast would not require a great body of persons, still less a *very great*, which is the signification of INGENTI placed first word in the verse; see Comm. *En.* II, 246. Secondly, because not only is the epithet 'ingens' elsewhere applied to the person of Eneas (*En.* VI. 413), but Eneas is specially declared to have worked with his own hands at the felling of trees, and such like labor; see *En.* VI. 184.

Compare Statius, *Theb.* VI. 701:

> "Illa manu magna, et multum felicior exit.
> Nec partem exiguam Circi transvecta quievit."

517.

DECIDIT EXANIMIS VITAMQUE RELIQUIT IN ASTRIS

EXANIMIS, not *lifeless*, for then VITAM RELIQUIT becomes tautologous; but *without sense and volition*, either from the physical, or (see "audiit exanimis," *En.* IV. 672; "exanimes magistri," *En.* V. 669) from the mental, effect of the wound, or, as is most likely, from both united. For a remarkable instance of 'exanimis' used, by an equivoque, in these its two different senses at once, see Seneca, *Troad.* 604:

> "Datusque tumulo debita exanimis tulit,"

In order that Andromache may be able to swear these words with a safe conscience, 'exanimis' must mean in her own mind no more than *frightened almost to death,* whilst in Ulysses' ears it means, as she intends it should mean, *actually dead.*

522.

HIC OCULIS SUBITUM OBJICITUR MAGNOQUE FUTURUM
AUGURIO MONSTRUM DOCUIT POST EXITUS INGENS
SERAQUE TERRIFICI CECINERUNT OMINA VATES
NAMQUE VOLANS LIQUIDIS IN NUBIBUS ARSIT ARUNDO
SIGNAVITQUE VIAM FLAMMIS TENUESQUE RECESSIT
CONSUMTA IN VENTOS

§. I.

HIC OCULIS &c. — Our author meaning to express, not *that the object now presented to the eyes was held by the actual beholders to be monstrous*, but *that an object was now presented to the eyes which was afterwards* (i. e. by future generations) *looked upon as monstrous*, says, not 'hic oculis monstrum objicitur, magnoque futurum augurio', but HIC OCULIS OBJICITUR MAGNOQUE FUTURUM AUGURIO MONSTRUM; the latter being tantamount to '*hic oculis objicitur id quod apud posteros erit* (vel *a posteris existimabitur fuisse*) *monstrum augurio magno*'

DOCUIT, — sciz. id verum fuisse monstrum et mali ominis, quod a parentibus falso acceptum erat veluti boni ominis.

SERAQUE TERRIFICI CECINERUNT OMINA VATES. — The omens which the seers afterwards drew from the object now presented to the eyes of the Trojans, were SERA, *late;* or more strictly, *too late* ("Serum dicitur quidquid tardius fit, quam solet, decet, exspectatur, metuitur" — Gesner), because not drawn until after the seers had been taught by the event: DOCUIT POST EXITUS INGENS. That the seers here spoken of are not contemporary, but future seers prophesying after the event, and therefore that Wagner's explanation ("Vates, omen illud interpretantes, aliquanto post gravi cum rerum conversione eventurum canebant") is incorrect, is proved, first, by the position of MONSTRUM after OBJICITUR and FUTURUM (see above); secondly, by the word FUTURUM itself; thirdly, by DOCUIT POST EXITUS INGENS, of which SERAQUE TERRIFICI CECINERUNT OMINA VATES is plainly no more than the complement; and fourthly, by the proper force of SERA, pointed out above. Compare in Statius the similar portent of an arrow returning and falling beside the quiver, and the total ignorance at the time of the nature of the portendment:

> "Quis fluere occultis rerum neget omina causis?
> Fata patent homini: piget inservare, peritque
> Venturi promissa fides. Sic omina casum
> Fecimus, et vires auxit Fortuna nocendi.
> Campum emensa brevi fatalis ab arbore tacta,
> Horrendum visu, per quas modo fugerat auras,
> Venit arundo retro, versumque a fine tenorem
> Pertulit, et notae juxta ruit ora pharetrae.
> Multa duces errore serunt: hi nubila, et altos
> Occurrisse Notos: adverso roboris ictu
> Tela repulsa alii. Penitus latet exitus ingens,
> Monstratumque nefas: uni remeabile bellum,
> Et tristes domino spondebat arundo recursus."
>
> *Theb.* VI. 934.

§. II.

SIGNAVITQUE VIAM FLAMMIS (complementary of ARSIT) is thrown in parenthetically between the strictly cohering clauses NAMQUE VOLANS LIQUIDIS IN NUBIBUS ARSIT ARUNDO, and TENUESQUE RECESSIT CONSUMTA IN VENTOS. Compare Comments *En.* II. 148, 695; III. 571; IV. 483.

LIQUIDIS IN NUBIBUS. — The commentators, perhaps understanding LIQUIDIS to mean *liquid*, and knowing that clouds could not be liquid, inform us that in this place Virgil uses 'nubes' to express *the air*: "Nubes pro aere posuit; nubes enim liquidae esse non possunt." Servius.

"LIQUIDIS IN NUBIBUS: in aere puro." Forbiger. The error is double; NUBIBUS is not '*aer*', but simply, as always elsewhere, *clouds;* and LIQUIDIS, not *liquid* (in the present vernacular sense of that word), but simply, and as, I believe, always in Virgil and the writers of pure latinity, *clear*, *untroubled;* i. e. the reverse of muddy or troubled; ex. gr. *Eclog.* II. 59:

— "Floribus austrum
Perditus, et liquidis immisi fontibus apros;"

where Servius (Dan.): "Qui puros fontes, coenosos efficiant." And Cato, *de Re Rustica*, LXXIII.: "Per aestatem boves aquam bonam et liquidam bibant semper curato: ut valeant, refert."

And so in our text, LIQUIDIS NUBIBUS; *the clouds*, not *turbid* as in bad or wintry weather, but *clear*, *serene, and untroubled* as in the fine weather of summer. In this its proper sense of *clear*, *untroubled*, we find 'liquidus' applied by Virgil to a great variety of objects; amongst others, to oil, *Georg.* II. 466; to fire, *Ecl.* VI. 33; to summer, *Georg.* IV. 59; to the night, *En.* X. 272, and even to the cawing of a crow when less 'rauca' than usual; among which applications of the word the third and fourth are very similar to that in our text.

545—602.

AT PATER AENEAS &C.

§. I.

The examination in detail of the several parts into which this account of the *Trojanum agmen* is, as it were, naturally divisible, will not only facilitate its comprehension as a whole, but place its perfect beauty in a clearer light. First, and according to our author's almost invariable method, there is the general outline or sketch (contained on this occasion in the message to Ascanius, *vv.* 548—551), which, raising and preparing our expectation, informs us almost with the precision of a programme, that Ascanius is about to present a *Ludus*, in which he will perform a principal part himself, and which will consist of the evolutions of a troop of boys mounted on horseback, divided into turms and armed. Secondly, (*vv.* 553—555) the spectacle commences immediately; the boys mounted on bitted horses parade in brilliant array before their parents, and are received by the assembled multitude with loud and wondering approbation. Thirdly, advantage is taken of the time during which the boys make the circuit of the spectators, to give (without interruption to the action) a description (*vv.* 556—574) of their equipment and array. This description is (*a*) g e n e r a l; all have their hair cut short or in a circular crop (see §. I. below); all bear two cornel lances, some quivers besides; all wear the *torques*, a circlet of twisted gold resting on the upper part of the breast and surrounding the neck (see §. VI. below); and the whole *agmen* consists of three turms, not united into one body (as with us several companies into one regiment), but, as the poet is particularly careful to explain (*v.* 562, see §. VII. below), separate and distinct from each other, and each under its own independent leader; and (*b*) p a r t i c u l a r, each leader being described (1) by name, (2) (with the exception of Ascanius in whose case such particularisation was unnecessary) by family, and (3) two of them by their horses, the breeds of which, and in one case even the very color is specified. Fourthly, the description of the equipments and array being finished, the poet returns to the suspended narrative, and taking it up at the very link where he had dropped it (sciz. TRINACRIAE MIRATA FREMIT TROJAEQUE JUVENTUS, *v.* 555, words which are almost repeated in EXCIPIUNT PLAUSU PAVIDOS etc., *v.* 575), goes on to say that the young men (equipped and divided into three turms as described), having made the circuit of the theatre amid the applauses of the spectators, receive the signal from Epytides to begin their evolutions. Fifthly, (*vv.* 580—582) the first evolution: each half of each turm turns round and trots off from its corrèsponding half (as far sciz. as the limits of the theatre permit), and then at the word of command faces about, and charges it; i. e. each half (or choir of six) charges its own corresponding, but now widely separated ('deductum'), half or choir of six (see §. X. below). Sixthly, (*vv.* 583—587) the succeeding evolutions, and the whole sham battle. Seventhly, (*vv.* 588—595) two comparisons; (*a*) the tracks of their courses are as intricate, and impossible to follow, as the mazes of the Cretan Labyrinth; (*b*) the boys themselves as beautiful in their forms, as glancing and brilliant (in their equipment), as swift, agile, and graceful in their motions, as dolphins sporting in the Carpathian or Libyan waters (see §. XII. below).

Perhaps never was so complicated object presented to the mind's eye with so much clearness, precision, and brevity, and at the same time with so much ease and sweetness. We are lost in double admiration; on the one hand of the *ludus* itself, of the youthful beauty and dazzling array of the performers, of their intricate and rapid, but distinct and unconfused, movements; on the other, of the *lucidus ordo*, the perfect and transparent clearness, grace, and fluency of the description. Or rather, our double admiration is one and undivided, we are unable to separate the poet from the performers, the description fròm the thing described. It is not a narrative, but a fact; not a picture, but a real object; so perfectly from beginning to end does every word, every pencil stroke, blend and identify itself with the thing represented. Nor is this all; the *Ludus Troja* has a relative, as well as an intrinsic, excellence; is not only beautiful in itself, but (*a*) beautiful in its novelty; a new species of entertainment, the invention (see §. XIII. below) of the son of the leader of the expedition, and now enacted for the first time, under his own immediate direction, himself taking a principal part; (*b*) beautiful in its sudden and unexpected exhibition (see §. II. below); and (*c*) beautiful in its position at the close of the other games. Those other games had been of a grave and serious description; there was in each of them a contention; a greater or less intermixture of bad passions; there was boasting and rivalry, victory and defeat, misfortune or evil omen, and well nigh death itself. Here on the contrary the contention was only simulated; there was no angry, sullen, or disappointed combatant, no victory dearly bought at the price of a friend's or companion's defeat; all were in harmony, sporting like dolphins through the waves; to the performers, no less than the spectators, it was a real *ludus.* With the greatest propriety therefore, and attention to contrast, was the *Ludus Troja* placed at the end of all the other games; in which position, like the afterpiece of our theatre, it tended by its gaiety, liveliness, and innocence, to obliterate any painful impressions which the more serious character of the preceding pieces might have left upon the mind, and to put all parties concerned, whether actors or spectators, in harmony and good humor with themselves and with each other. Further still; this concluding game, beautiful in itself, beautiful in its novelty, unexpected exhibition, and contrast, had besides a peculiar beauty in the eyes of those for whom our author wrote, the Roman nobility and gentry; whom it reminded, not only of the origin of the Roman empire, and in some instances of the individual founders of their families, but of the performances of their own children in this very *ludus* as reinstituted by Augustus (SUET. *Aug.* 43). Lastly, and perhaps not of least importance to the poet, the description could not fail to be agreeable to Augustus himself, not merely as commemorative of the first beginnings of that power which he now wielded coextensive with the world itself, and of the cradle of his own Julian, heaven-descended race, but especially as affording testimony likely to endure for ever, with what *pietas* towards the Gods, the Romans, and his own family, he had reinstituted the ancient, hereditary game, perfect in every the most minute point and particular, as it could not fail to be, the poet having, with the art of a prophet prophesying after the event, formed the plan and drawn the picture of the ancient game on the model of the reinstituted one.

With Virgil's description of the *Ludus Troja* compare the account given by Apuleius (*Metam.* X. 29) of the Pyrrhic dance: "Puelli puellaeque virenti florentes aetatula, forma conspicui, veste nitidi, incessu gestuosi, Graecanicam saltantes Pyrrhicam, dispositis ordinationibus, decoros ambitus inerrabant, nunc in orbe rotarum flexuosi, nunc in obliquam seriem connexi, et in quadratum patorem cuneati, et in catervae dissidium separati. At ubi discursus reciproci multimodas ambages tubae terminalis cantus explicuit" etc. Compare also Claudian's very happy imitation, if indeed it be imitation, of the passage before us:

"Cum vectaris equo, simulacraque Martia ludis,
Quis molles sinuare fugas, quis tendere contum
Acrior, aut subitos melior flexisse recursus?"
De Quart. Consul. Honor. v. 539.

And the same author's elaborate description of the Pyrrhic dance, in his *Paneg. de sext. consul. Honor. v.* 621 and seq.

§. II.

AT PATER AENEAS NONDUM CERTAMINE MISSO &C. — The following considerations leave no doubt on my mind that this exhibition of the *Trojanum agmen* was presented by Eneas to the assembly unexpectedly and by surprise. First, no such exhibition was mentioned, or even so much as alluded to, by Eneas in his enumeration (*v.* 66 and seq.) of the contests about to be enacted. Secondly, whilst the words connecting the accounts of the other contests plainly intimate that all those contests succeeded each other in regular, expected succession ("Hoc pius Aeneas misso certamine tendit," *v.* 286; "Post, ubi confecti cursus, et dona peregit; Nunc, si cui" &c., *v.* 362; "Protenus Aeneas celeri certare sagitta Invitat," *v.* 485), there is not only no such conjunction of this contest to the preceding, but the disjunction plainly marks the contrast, the transition to something new, of a totally different kind, or out of the regular order. Thirdly, no reason can be assigned why the message was sent to Ascanius secretly (FIDAM AD AUREM) and before the termination of the arrow-shooting (NONDUM CERTAMINE MISSO; see §. III. below), if it were not that the assembly might be surprised by the sudden and unexpected appearance of a new 'certamen' at the very moment they supposed the amusements of the day to be concluded. Fourthly, the wonder of the assembly at the unexpected sight is actually expressed by the word MIRATA (*v.* 555). Fifthly, it was usual for exhibitors of games thus to surprise the people with something unexpected; compare Pliny, *Paneg.* 33: "Quam deinde in edendo (spectaculo sciz.) liberalitatem, quam justitiam exhibuit, omni affectione aut intactus, aut major. Impetratum est, quod postulabatur; oblatum, quod non postulabatur. Institit ultro, et ut concupisceremus admonuit; ac sic quoque plura inopinata, plura subita." Sixthly, thus understood, the beautiful description becomes still more beautiful.

§. III.

NONDUM CERTAMINE MISSO &c. — "CERTAMINE MISSO, ut *αγων*, pro certantium ac spectantium turba dimissa. Sed et pedestri sermone fere sic: ut apud Cicer. "ante ludorum missionem," *Lib. V. ad Div.* 12." Heyne.
"Certantium ac spectantium turba dimissa." Wagner, *Virg. Br. En.*

But first, Virgil has never so much as once throughout this whole description used the singular 'certamen'.

in the sense of 'ludi', while, on the contrary, he has several times employed the plural 'certamina' (*vv.* 66, 114, 596) to signify one single one of those contests whose *tout ensemble* constituted the *ludi.* Secondly, the words 'misso certamine' where they occur before (*v.* 286) are sufficiently proved both by the adjunct 'hoc', and by the context, to refer to the immediately preceding 'certamen', viz. that of the ship-race. Thirdly, the interpretation of Heyne and Wagner being adopted, there must of necessity have been an interval between the termination of the arrow-shooting and the appearance of Ascanius and the *Trojanum agmen* in the circus; and then the difficulty arises, by what means Eneas was able to keep the assembly (which, see §. II. above, was quite unaware that another 'certamen' was in preparation) from breaking up and dispersing at the end of the arrow-shooting. For these reasons I understand NONDUM CERTAMINE MISSO to mean '*sub finem hujus certaminis*' (sciz. sagittarum), or '*antequam hoc certamen missum est*'*;* an interpretation, which (*a*) gives to 'certamen' the same meaning which it has in *v.* 286 already quoted, and (*b*) explains how it was that Eneas was able to bring the *Trojanum agmen* into the circus immediately on its being cleared at the termination of the 'certamen' of the arrows, sciz. by his having despatched the message to Ascanius NONDUM CERTAMINE MISSO, *before the termination of that contest.*

§. IV.

QUOS OMNES EUNTES TRINACRIAE MIRATA FREMIT TROJAEQUE JUVENTUS. — "QUOS . . . . . FREMIT; cum fremitu, i. e. fremente applausu, prosequitur. Fremere Graecorum more cum Accus. rei constructum, quae cum fremitu commemoratur, legitur etiam VII. 460; XI. 132 . . . . . Nullum tamen mihi innotuit exemplum huic loco prorsus simile, ubi Accusativus personae addatur, cui cum fremitu applaudatur." Forbiger.

It seems strange that Forbiger should have thus stopped short just as he was on the very point of discovering the truth; that his observation "nullum tamen mihi innotuit exemplum" &c. did not lead him to the plain consequence that QUOS EUNTES is operated on, not by FREMIT, but by MIRATA. MIRATA FREMIT, i. e. in plain prose '*miratur cum fremitu*'. A precise parallel will be found *En*. VII. 381:

— "Stupet inscia supra
Impubesque manus, mirata volubile buxum;"

where, as in our text, the accusative depends, not (as at *v*. 32 of the second Book) on the intransitive verb, but upon this same transitive participle, 'mirata'.

§. V.

OMNIBUS IN MOREM TONSA COMA PRESSA CORONA. — "Coronati, et quidem, ut infra *v*. 673 intelligitur, corona super galeam imposita; qualis infra VII. 751. Coma tamen vel sic a corona (non a galea) pressa dici potuit, quatenus haec caput ambiebat." Heyne.

But, first, it is impossible that the hair could be, in any sense of the word, PRESSA by a chaplet placed outside the helmet; and secondly, it is incredible that Virgil, if his meaning had really been that *the young men wore chaplets on their helmets*, should not have afforded a clue to the discovery of that meaning by making some mention of, or, at least, some allusion to, the helmets, when speaking of the chaplets. I reject therefore this interpretation notwithstanding the authority by which it comes recommended; and, with a pleasure appreciable only by the Virgilian student who beholds a bright and unexpected ray suddenly illuminate a hitherto hopelessly obscure passage of his favorite author, turn to the suggestion of Gesner that TONSA CORONA is, not *a crown* or *chaplet* of any kind, but *the circular cut* or *tonsure by which* (COMA PRESSA) *the hair was pressed, restrained*, or *kept within bounds*, i. e. *shortened*. The following arguments present themselves to my mind in favor of this suggestion: first, it entirely relieves the passage from the above mentioned difficulty, viz. the non-mention of the helmets, which, as appears from *v.* 673, were certainly worn on the occasion. Secondly, the sense which it assigns to 'premere', is not only highly poetical, but, as well observed by Gesner, the very sense in which Horace (*Od.* I. 31. 9) has used that word when speaking of the analogous operation of pruning the vine; and, as Gesner might have added, the very sense in which Virgil himself has used it, *Georg.* I. 157: "Ruris opaci, Falce premes umbras;" also Pallad. *de Re Rustica,* XII. 9, and Vegetius, *Vet.* I. 56. Compare "Pressae quietis," Apul. *Metam.* IV. 25, interpreted by Hildebrand: "pressae, i. e. adstrictae, compressae, et sic brevis; ut, passim, pressa oratio, vox, sermo." Thirdly, we find in St. Jerome's translation of Ezekiel (XLIV. 20), as well as in his commentary on the same, the expression 'comas ad pressum tondere', which is so close an approximation to the Virgilian TONSA COMA PRESSA CORONA that it may almost be taken for its express gloss, or prosaic equivalent. Fourthly, the term 'corona' (generally applicable, as every scholar knows, to whatever has the form of, or surrounds in the manner of, a crown or coronet) is specially applicable to the horse's fetlock (Columel. *de Re Rustica,* VI. 15 and 29), and to the hair of the human head when made by art to assume a circular form, whether that of the monkish or clerical tonsure, see Sidonius, *Lib.* VII. *Ep.* 8; *Concil. Toletan.* (held A. C. 633) IV. c. 41, and Du Cange in voc. 'Corona'; or that of the poll commanded to the Jewish priests (Ezekiel, XLIV. 20); see article *Haar* in the *Deutsche Encyclopaedie* (Frankf. a. M. 1788); which poll seems to have been as nearly as possible the short crop worn by the Roman boys. Fifthly, the Italians of the present day actually use the term *corona* in this very sense: "Diciamo degli alberi, Tagliarli o scapezzarli a corona quando si taglian loro tutti i rami; *ebrancher un arbre.*" Antonini. Sixthly, in the ordinary interpretation of the passage,

IN MOREM must mean, *according to the habitude of the game* ("e more hujus ludi" — Forbiger), and thus directly contradicts *v.* 596 and seq. which, informing us emphatically that Ascanius introduced into Latium the very 'mos' (HUNC MOREM, *v.* 596) of the game as now enacted before Eneas, intimate plainly that the game had no previous 'mos', i. e. that it was now enacted for the first time, and that this its first enactment was the type of all future. On the contrary, the interpretation suggested by Gesner, by enabling us to understand IN MOREM as equivalent to '*in morem puerorum*', not only avoids this contradiction, but gives us the following excellent meaning for the entire sentence: *All had the luxuriance of their hair restrained by a clipped coronet* or *circle*, i. e. (TONSA CORONA being tantamount to '*tonsura coronaria* seu *circulari*') *by a circular crop* or *circular clipping, according to the fashion of boys* (the well-known fashion of the Roman boys at the time when Virgil wrote being transferred by his usual prolepsis to the Trojan boys in the time of Eneas); see Suet. *Aug.* 45: "Histrionum licentiam adeo compescuit, ut Stephanionem togatarium, cui in puerilem habitum circumtonsam matronam ministrasse compererat, per trina theatra virgis caesum relegaverit."

The reader, well weighing all these arguments, will I think hesitate little to agree with me that Gesner's suggestion affords the clue to the true exposition of this so long and so greatly misunderstood passage, and that OMNIBUS IN MOREM TONSA COMA PRESSA CORONA is in plain prose nothing more than '*coma omnium circumtonsa erat in morem puerorum Teucrorum*'.

The trope, used by Virgil in the passage before us, is precisely the converse of that used by Statius (*Silv.* III. 4. 2) in his expression "auro coronato;" the object CORONA being substituted by the former for the predicate 'coronato' (i. e. *coronario*), and the predicate "coronato" by the latter for the object 'corona', while the predicate

TONSA is employed by the former in place of the object 'tonsura', and the object "auro" by the latter in place of the predicate 'aureo': TONSA CORONA, *circular tonsure;* "auro coronato," *golden circle.*

I do not know whether it will be regarded as a further confirmation of the above interpretation that Ausonius, making use of this verse for the construction of a line of one of his centos (a line, by the way, in which he has broken Alvarez' head) connects 'tonsa' with 'coma':

"Quatuor huic juvenes, totidem innuptaeque puellae:
Omnibus in morem tonsa coma. Pectore summo
Flexilis obtorti per collum circulus auri."
Eidyll. XIII;

where Floridus: "Capillus est tonsus iis omnibus more solito." Compare Pliny, *Epist* V. 6: "Ambit hunc ambulatio pressis varieque tonsis viridibus inclusa."

§. VI.

IT PECTORE SUMMO . . . . . PER COLLUM. — An accurate description of the manner in which the Romans wore the *torques;* neither on the neck, tight and close like a collar, nor yet suspended from the neck so as to hang down in an oblong shape on the front of the chest like a chain or necklace; but round the neck, and at the same time on the top of the breast; i. e. resting on the top of the breast, surrounding and near to, but still at a little distance from, the neck, somewhat in the manner of the upper hem of the garment in which Christ is usually painted, or of the chemise of Titian's mistress.

FLEXILIS OBTORTI . . . . CIRCULUS AURI. — A description of the Roman *torques* is here poetically substituted for the name; 'obtortum aurum, i. e. *torques aureus*'. Compare Isidor. XIX. 31.

§. VII.

TRES EQUITUM NUMERO TURMAE TERNIQUE VAGANTUR DUCTORES. — TERNI is merely '*tres*' (as, *En.* VII. 538, 'quina' is merely '*quinque*'), the ordinal being used in place of the numeral in order to give variety, and avoid the repetition of the same word.

VAGANTUR. — The beautiful term 'vagari', corresponding almost exactly to the German *wandeln*, is simply *to go about here and there without aiming at a certain point* or *destination.* It has, I believe, no precise English equivalent, excluding, as it does, the idea of *not knowing where one is*, included in *wander;* of *fickleness,* included in *rove;* of *eccentricity* or *going beyond bounds*, included in *ramble;* and of *indolence* or *idleness,* included in *saunter.*

AGMINE PARTITO FULGENT PARIBUSQUE MAGISTRIS. — Let not the reader, falling into the general error, suppose that these words are no more than an unmeaning repetition of the preceding TRES EQUITUM NUMERO TURMAE, TERNIQUE VAGANTUR DUCTORES. On the contrary, the addition of these words was indispensably necessary in order to define and specify the meaning of TRES EQUITUM NUMERO &c. sciz. that these three turms, although in their aggregate constituting the *Trojanum agmen*, *vv.* 549, 602,, were however not actually compacted into one body (as, with us, several companies into one regiment), over which each of the TERNI DUCTORES had a general coordinate command, but constituted three distinct and separate bodies, each under its special and independent leader.

§. VIII.

VESTIGIA PRIMI ALBA PEDIS. — "Primorum pedum vestigia." Servius.

"Sed ubi istae maculae? . . . In pede dextro, me interprete." La Cerda.

I think however that PRIMI means *the first part* or *beginning of the leg* (PEDIS), i. e. *the pastern;* and that the pasterns (the VESTIGIA PRIMI PEDIS) of the whole four feet of the horse were white. Compare *En.* I. 545:

— "Primaque vetant consistere terra;"

the beginning, first part, or *edge*, *of the land.*

"At tu vix primas extollens gurgite palmas."

PROPERT. II. 20. 11;

raising the beginnings or *tops of the hands out of the water;* it had been too minute to specify fingers. So in our text it had been trivial and jockey-like to specify pastern joint, and therefore the poet says *first part* or *beginning of the foot*, or *leg*, PEDIS. Compare Ausonius's imitation (*Descriptio Egredientis Sponsae*):

— "Vestigia primi
Alba pedis;"

the first, or *fore*, *part of the foot; the toes and instep* as opposed to the heel.

§. IX.

EXCIPIUNT PLAUSU PAVIDOS GAUDENTQUE TUENTES DARDANIDAE. — "'Ruentes' edidit D. Heinsius, quod vitio librariorum contigit, et hinc Masvicius ut vulgatam lectionem habuit, quia et Emmenessius expresserat." Burmann.
"'Ruentes' vitium ed. Dan. Heins., vide Burm." Heyne (Wagner's Ed.).

Both Burmann and Heyne have here confounded Daniel with Nicholas Heinsius, for I find TUENTES in Daniel Heinsius (Leyden, 1636), and 'ruentes' in Nicholas Heinsius (Utrecht, 1704). And this explains why Emmenessius also has 'ruentes', his text being always taken from Nicholas, not Daniel, Heinsius.

§. X.

OLLI DISCURRERE PARES ATQUE AGMINA TERNI DIDUCTIS SOLVERE CHORIS. — "Ternis diversis turmis, quas choros appellat, discedunt." Heyne.
"Postquam consessum spectantium conjuncto agmine lustraverunt, solvunt agmen ita, ut in tres pares numero turmas discedant." Wagner, *Virg. Br. En.*
"Singuli in diversas partes abeunt; nam si quaeque turma in tres partes divideretur, aut si terni aveherentur, ut duodecim essent catervae, trium unaquaeque puerorum (quae Heynii est sententia), confusum praeberetur spectaculum." Forbiger.

But the young men are already in ternis turmis', each turm led by its own chief who is mentioned separately and by name See *v.* 560 and seq. In these three turms AGMINE PARTITO FULGENT, and in these three turms they must be presumed to be (no mention having been made to the contrary), when, having exhibited themselves to the eyes of the whole consession (*v.* 577), they receive the signal from Epytides to begin their evolutions. The description therefore (from OLLI as far as CHORIS) is not that of the formation of the three turms, but of their first movement or evolution, and the words are as precise as possible to that effect: OLLI *they,* TERNI *being* (as already described, *v.* 560) *in three* (sciz. three turms), DISCURRERE PARES ATQUE &C.

The meaning of TERNI having been established, the remainder of the sentence presents no serious difficulty: OLLI TERNI, *they, the three turms,* DISCURRERE, *have trotted off different ways* or *asunder* ('currere' being the generic term for quick motion of any kind whether on foot or horseback, whether on land or water; see "Quorum aequora curro," *v.* 235), PARES, *equal* (i. e. in two equal parts), ATQUE AGMINA SOLVERE, *and* (sciz. by so trotting off different ways) *have dissolved,* AGMINA, *the solid bodies* (of which sciz they, the three turms, consisted), DIDUCTIS CHORIS, *by forming out of them widely separated 'chori'*, or, more literally, *their 'chori' becoming widely separated.* Let us call the turms respectively

a x
b y
c z

The halves *a, b, c,* trotting off to the left, and the halves *x, y, z,* trotting off to the right, become the widely separated 'chori'

a			*x*
b	*m*	*n*	*y*
c			*z*

which, at the word of command, CONVERTERE VIAS INFESTAQUE TELA TULERE, *wheel about and charge each other over the space m n.* The picture therefore, which Virgil has here drawn in a few and appropriate strokes, is that of the three turms first parading before the assembled people, and then dividing into six 'chori' (sciz. each turm into halves), which 'chori' trot off to some distance from each other, and then, at the word of command, face about and charge each other, sciz. three 'chori' against three 'chori'.

§. XI.

ALTERNOSQUE ORBIBUS ORBES IMPEDIUNT PUGNAEQUE CIENT SIMULACRA SUB ARMIS. — "IMPEDIUNT, id est, miscent." Donatus.

"Tum in varios orbes equitant ita inter se implicatos (IMPEDIUNT), ut, dum unum agmen in orbem fertur, alterum agmen eum orbem suo orbe secet (ALTERNOS ORBES)." Wagner, *Virg. Br. En.*

No; the picture is not thus confused and indeterminate, but clear and definite, and 'impedire' is not '*implicare*', but, as always elsewhere, simply *impede*, *let*, *hinder*. The youths make not a number of implicated or complicated circles, but each band (viz. of those on one side of the arena) wheels round in one circle, suppose from East to West, while the corresponding opposite band (ADVERSIS SPATIIS) wheels round in another circle, suppose from West to East, and the two circles (or two bands in circular motion) meeting in the middle of the 'spatia', IMPEDIUNT, *stop*, *impede*, *hinder*, each other; *prevent* each other from getting on, from completing their respective circles, and then fighting, or pretending to fight, for passage, PUGNAE CIENT SIMULACRA SUB ARMIS. Thus the picture is clear and defined, and its invariable meaning of *let*, *hinder*, *impede*, preserved to IMPEDIUNT. Compare:

"Euryalum tenebrae ramorum onerosaque praeda
Impediunt."

En. IX. 384.

"Interdum genua impediunt, cursumque recusant."

En. XII. 747.

Wagner's "secet" expresses exactly the opposite idea, viz. that of one band intersecting, or passing through, the other. A right understanding of the word IMPEDIUNT is indispensable to the right comprehension of the picture; out of this IMPEDIUNT, out of this *hindering, thwarting, and stopping each other*, arise the SIMULACRA PUGNAE:

IMPEDIUNT, PUGNAEQUE CIENT SIMULACRA SUB ARMIS.

And so again, *v.* 593:

IMPEDIUNT, TEXUNTQUE FUGAS ET PROELIA LUDO.

Not only this repetition of the word, but its emphatic position in both cases, in the beginning of the line (see Comm. *En.* II. 246), and its similar explanations in both cases (in the one case, PUGNAEQUE CIENT SIMULACRA SUB ARMIS; in the other case, TEXUNTQUE FUGAS ET PROELIA LUDO) show the great stress which is laid on it — that it is in fact the key to the entire passage. 'Impedire', literally *to entangle the feet so as to disable them from getting on*, is exactly the opposite of 'expedire', literally *to disentangle the feet so as to enable them to get on.*

ORBIBUS ORBES. — There being six 'chori' (or half turms), each consisting of six horsemen, and each pair of opposite 'chori' making two ORBES, which impeded or obstructed each other where they met in the middle of the 'spatia' or *lists*, there were in all six ORBES.

§. XII.

UT QUONDAM CRETA &c. DELPHINUM SIMILES &c. — Two comparisons of the *Trojanum agmen* taken, as the reader will not fail to have observed, in two different and distinct points of view; first, in respect of the course or track of its movements (sciz. as it would be marked on a chart); and secondly, in respect of the beauty, brilliancy and agility of the persons of whom it consisted. The double comparison gives richness, the double point of view, variety, to the description; the former shows the teeming fertility, the latter the correct judgment of the poet. The first comparison (viz. that of the *swiftly moving Trojan agmen* with the *immovable labyrinth*) absolutely required the addition of the second, and for the second no object could have been better chosen than the swift and playful dolphins; see below. For a similarly, although less distinctly, double comparison, see the ship-race in the commencement of this Book, where the starting ships are likened to chariots starting for the race; the rowers bending over their oars, to the charioteers leaning with their whole bodies over the reins and lash.

DELPHINUM SIMILES. — The reader, comparing the description which the unfortunate Falconer (a poet who, it must not be forgotten, always wrote from actual observation) has given of the sporting of a shoal of dolphins in the water, will perceive with what perfect propriety the boys composing the *Trojanum agmen* are likened (sciz. in the triple respect of beauty, brilliancy, and graceful agility) to dolphins:

"But now, beneath the lofty vessel's stern,
A shoal of sporting dolphins they discern,
Beaming [LUCENT, FULGENT], from burnished scales, refulgent rays,
Till all the glowing ocean seems to blaze:
In curling wreaths they wanton on the tide,
Now bound aloft, now downward swiftly glide;
A while beneath the waves their tracks remain,
And burn in silver streams along the liquid plain."

The Shipwreck, c. II.

Compare Pliny, *Nat. Hist.* IX. 8: "Velocissimum omnium animalium, non solum marinorum, est delphinus, ocior volucre, acrior telo."

§. XIII.

QUO PUER IPSE MODO &c. — These words seem to me plainly to ascribe the origin and invention of the *Trojanum agmen* to Ascanius. See §. V. above.

TROJAQUE NUNC PUERI TROJANUM DICITUR AGMEN. — The two Heinsii, Maittaire, Heyne, Wagner, and Forbiger, divide this line into two parts by a comma placed after NUNC. The effect of this punctuation is, first, wholly to destroy the cadence of the verse; and secondly, to outlaw and place beyond the grammatical pale both sections of the line; the first section presenting a subject without verb or predicate; the second a superfluous subject yoked to a verb in a totally different regime. I shall not pretend to say where, or with whom, this punctuation originated, but I find it first in Dan. Heinsius. The other five above mentioned editors have all adopted it, and in so doing have abandoned their usual favorite guide, the Medicean, which, if only Bottari is correct, places the pause not after NUNC, but after PUERI. Nor is the punctuation of the Medicean peculiar to that MS.; I have myself found the same in the Gudian, and both the Leipzig; Maittaire also gives it as the punctuation of the Venice Ed. of 1472, and I find it in the Paris Ed. of 1600. Some editors, ex. gr. Henry Stephens, Burmann, Brunck, and Alfieri, place a comma both before and after PUERI, and others, as the Modena editor of 1475, La Cerda, and Robert Stephens, leave the line, as it is in the Dresden MS., entirely unbroken; but the division of the line into two (to me at least) wholly unintelligible fragments by a single comma placed after NUNC, seems to have been first performed either by, or about the time of, Dan. Heinsius. The comma being placed (with the Medicean, and other above mentioned MSS.) after PUERI, we obtain, first, a pause which not only does not shock, but is agreeable to, the ear; and secondly, the simple and natural structure 'pueri nunc (dicuntur) Troja; agmen dicitur Trojanum'.

The statement PUERI NUNC (dicuntur) TROJA is expressly confirmed by several ancient historians; especially by Suetonius, *Jul. Caes.* 39: "Trojam lusit turma duplex majorum, minorumque puerorum."

609.

ILLA VIAM CELERANS PER MILLE COLORIBUS ARCUM

ILLA VIAM CELERANS &c. — The virgin Iris hastily descending her rainbow path towards the Trojan ships never fails to recall to my recollection the island maiden Haidee (*Don Juan*, *Canto II*) hastening down the hillside towards Juan's cave:

"And down the cliff the island virgin came,
And near the cave with quick, light footstep drew,
While the sun smiled on her with his first flame,
And young Aurora kissed her lips with dew,
Taking her for a sister."

The absence from which picture, of that splendid ornament of the Virgilian, the rainbow, is well compensated by "The sun smiling on her with his first flame," and "Aurora kissing her lips with dew, taking her for a sister." Pity that these happy touches are (with the exception of the early cantos of *Don Juan* and the early cantos of *Childe Harold*) of but rare occurence in Lord Byron's numerous and, generally speaking, hastily drawn, ill proportioned and unnatural sketches.

MILLE COLORIBUS ARCUM. — The rainbow, like the taking fire of Acestes's arrow, was a bad omen. See Tzetzes, *Antehom.* 212:

"*Τρωσι δ' αρ' Ιρις εφαινεν, Αρηος σημα κακοιο,*
Ουρανοθεν πυκινως φαεινομενη, πολυχροιος·
Σημα γαρ ηγε τετυκται χειματος ηε αρηος,
Αστρασιν ουρανιοις επιλαμπεσιν ισα κομηταις."

See also the same, *v.* 314.

618.

ERGO INTER MEDIAS SESE HAUD IGNARA NOCENDI
CONJICIT ET FACIEMQUE DEAE VESTEMQUE REPONIT
FIT BEROE TMARII CONJUX LONGAEVA DORYCLI
CUI GENUS ET QUONDAM NOMEN NATIQUE FUISSENT

HAUD IGNARA NOCENDI. — "I. e. nocitura; cum consilio nocendi." Forbiger.

No; but *not inexperienced in*, *not unpractised in*, *not unskilled in*, *not a novice in*, '*nocendo*'; as (*En*. I. 634) "Non ignara mali."

FIT BEROE TMARII CONJUX &c. — I have myself personally examined four MSS. respecting this passage, viz. the oldest Gudian, the Dresden, and both the Leipzig. In the two former I have found TMARII, in the two latter 'marii'. In the Gudian the final E of BEROE is connected (according to the usual manner of that MS.) with the following word; thus: BERO &MARII; whence no doubt the origin of the reading of the Leipzig MSS., 'marii'. I can further add to the arguments of Nicholas Heinsius and Wagner in favor of TMARII, that Bersmann, although adopting 'Ismarii', informs us that in his MS. the reading is 'Marii'.

To Pierius's argument in favor of 'Ismarii', "Quamvis in Longobardico codice, in Mediceo, et plerisque aliis, pro 'Ismarii' duabus minus literis 'Marii' legatur, nemo tamen ex eruditis est cui non potius 'Ismarii' faciat satis. Nam quid ad ea tempora Marii nomen?" the answer will be found above, viz. that 'Marii' has arisen from &MARII, the form in which TMARII, preceded by the final E of BEROE, is actually found written in the Gudian. I may add besides that I find in Daniel's *Servius* (Paris, 1600): "TMARII; Tmarus enim mons Thraciae."

CUI. — "Sive ad Doryclum, sive ad Beroen referas, parum interest. Hoc alterum forte melius, siquidem in feminae auctoritate res posita. Vix tamen feminae NOMEN tribui potest. Praestat ergo ad maritum referre." Heyne. To which Forbiger adds: "Ideoque etiam CUI rectius ad Doryclum refertur." The conclusion falls to the ground with the false premiss; for (see *En.* VII. 581):

— "Neque enim leve nomen Amatae;"

and (*En.* XI. 340):

— "Genus huic materna superbum
Nobilitas dabat."

Besides, even without insisting that CUI is better referred to the whole preceding clause than to its unimportant fragment DORYCLI, the authority of Beroe ("Bene suadentis commendatur auctoritas" — Servius) is much greater, if inherent, than if only derived from that of her husband. So also, we have the clear and appropriate division; in the first line, the statement who Beroe is; in the second, the reasons why she had influence, and was therefore a fit person for Iris's purpose. And still further, if any *still further* be required, Doryclus being dead (see Hom. *Il.* β), the term QUONDAM could not with propriety be applied to him.

658.

INGENTEMQUE FUGA SECUIT SUB NUBIBUS ARCUM

"Secando aerem fecit arcum" Wagner, *Virg. Br. En.*

I look upon this interpretation with more than suspicion; first, because it appears from *v.* 609, that the bow was already in the clouds; and secondly, because "ventos secabat," *En.* IV. 257, must be, not '*secando aerem faciebat ventos*', but '*iter faciebat per ventos*'. SECUIT ARCUM is therefore '*iter fecit per arcum*', and the whole phrase FUGA SECUIT ARCUM no more than the prosaic '*fugit per arcum*', dressed up in a poetical garb.

Compare Ovid (*Metam.* XI. 632), of the same Iris:

— "Remeat per quos modo venerat arcus."

659.

TUM VERO ATTONITAE MONSTRIS ACTAEQUE FURORE
CONCLAMANT RAPIUNTQUE FOCIS PENETRALIBUS IGNEM
PARS SPOLIANT ARAS FRONDEM AC VIRGULTA FACESQUE
CONJICIUNT

ATTONITAE MONSTRIS ACTAEQUE FURORE (matres) is the subject not merely of CONCLAMANT and RAPIUNT, but of CONJICIUNT; first, because such parenthetic structure is usual in Virgil (see *En.* VI. 83, 739, and Comments); and secondly, because Virgil could never have intended to limit the throwing of the fire to those who supplied themselves from the altars. All the women shout, and all fling flaming brands and combustibles which some procure FOCIS PENETRALIBUS and some from the altars; FRONDEM AC VIRGULTA FACESQUE referring equally to FOCIS PENETRALIBUS and ARAS. In order to guide the reader to the sense, it will be necessary to enclose PARS SPOLIANT ARAS between marks indicative of a parenthesis, and to substitute a comma for the semicolon placed at IGNEM by all the editors, not even excepting the two Heinsii.

TUM VERO, — here, as every where else, expresses the production of the full effect. The flinging of the first brand by the pretended Beroe had the minor effect of rousing and exciting and astonishing the matrons:

— "Arrectae mentes, stupefactaque corda
Illadum;"

Pyrgo's speech had the further effect of making them consider whether it might not be right to follow Beroe's advice and example:

"At matres primo ancipites, oculisque malignis
Ambiguae spectare rates" &c.

The manifestation of the Goddess removes all doubt; decides them at once; produces the full effect:

ATTONITAE MONSTRIS ACTAEQUE FURORE
CONCLAMANT, RAPIUNTQUE FOCIS &c.

The whole of Wagner's disputation on these words (*Quaest. Virg.* XXV. 6.d) is erroneous; the words 'tum vero' do not indicate in one place "alacritatem gaudiumque;" in another place "dolorem," in another "furorem et iram," in another "curam, terrorem, pavorem," in another "omnino rem tristem horridamque;" but always simply the production, at last, of that full effect which preceding minor causes had failed to produce — that full effect which was *then indeed*, 'tum vero,' produced. See Comments *En.* II. 105, 228; III. 47; IV. 396, 449, 571.

666.

RESPICIUNT ATRAM IN NIMBO VOLITARE FAVILLAM

"On the low hills to westward
The Consul fixed his eye,
And saw the swarthy storm of dust
Rise fast along the sky."
MACAULAY, *Lays of ancient Rome, Horat.* XX.

704.

TUM SENIOR NAUTES UNUM TRITONIA PALLAS
QUEM DOCUIT MULTAQUE INSIGNEM REDDIDIT ARTE
HAEC RESPONSA DABAT VEL QUAE PORTENDERET IRA
MAGNA DEUM VEL QUAE FATORUM POSCERET ORDO
ISQUE HIS AENEAN SOLATUS VOCIBUS INFIT

§. I.

"Nautes RESPONSA HAEC DABAT, quae mox exponit: "Nate Dea." Respondit autem et interpretando vaticinatus est ea, quae vel ira Deum portenderet vel fatorum ordo posceret, ostento hoc incensarum navium." Heyne. ("Vera haec interpretatio." Wagner.)

"IRA DEUM, quae cernebatur in incendio classis." Wagner, *Virg. Br. En.*

To this interpretation I object: first, that it leaves wholly unexplained in what respect Pallas had rendered Nautes INSIGNEM; whether, as Goddess of the arts, she had inspired him with superior mechanical skill, or, as Goddess of wisdom, with superior foresight. Secondly, that, according to this interpretation, the address of Nautes to Eneas should contain in it an explanation either of what was portended by the IRA DEUM, or of what was required by the ORDO FATORUM, or of both; whereas, on the contrary, it contains not even one single word concerning either the one or the other, and consists wholly in advice to Eneas, what, according to Nautes's opinion, was best to be done in the present difficulty. Thirdly, that, if this advice of Nautes to Eneas had consisted (as, according to this interpretation, it should have consisted) of the authoritative commands of the Gods, of RESPONSA what the IRA DEUM, or FATORUM ORDO, or both, demanded, there was in that case no necessity, no 'dignus vindice nodus', for the appearance of the Shade of Anchises, to repeat almost *totidem verbis* the oracular response.

All these objections are got rid of at once, by understanding our author, immediately after mentioning the name of Nautes, TUM SENIOR NAUTES, to proceed, according to his usual manner (see Comm. *En.* VI. 83) to explain who this Nautes was, viz. that he was one whom Pallas had rendered INSIGNEM MULTA ARTE, and then again, in like manner, after the words INSIGNEM MULTA ARTE, to proceed further to explain what he meant by those words, viz. that Pallas was in the habit of giving Nautes responses when he inquired of her respecting future events. The sentence thus contains two parentheses; one (viz. from UNUM to ARTE inclusive) dependent on NAUTES; the other (viz. from HAEC to ORDO inclusive) dependent on INSIGNEM MULTA ARTE, and the narrative, broken off at

NAUTES, and interrupted by the two parentheses, is resumed at ISQUE.

§. II.

HAEC RESPONSA DABAT. — These words account (see §. I. above) for that 'multa ars', or superior wisdom, for which Nautes was remarkable, and which rendered him a fit person to advise Eneas: HAEC, viz. Pallas, RESPONSA DABAT; not *gave him responses on the present occasion*, but, according to the peculiar force of DABAT, *used to give him*, *was in the habit of giving him*, *responses;* and accordingly those responses are defined, not specially, or as having relation to the burning of the ships or to the present circumstances, but generally; Pallas was in the habit of answering him as to both of the great classes into which all future events were divisable; not only as to those fixed and immutable events which were decreed by the Fates (that class of events to which, for instance, Eneas's arrival in Italy, and establishment of a great empire there, belonged), but as to those, if I may so say, uncertain and precarious events which were produced by the special intervention of offended Deities (that class of events of which the storm in the first Book and all Eneas's subsequent misfortunes afford examples). To these two great classes into which, according to the philosophy of the Romans, all future events were divisable, and not, as supposed by Heyne and Wagner, to the burning of the ships by the Trojan women and the founding of the city of Acesta, is reference made in the words VEL QUAE PORTENDERET IRA MAGNA DEUM VEL QUAE FATORUM POSCERET ORDO. Compare Claudian's precise parallel:

"Frigida ter decies nudatum frondibus Haemum
Tendit hiems vestire gelu; totidemque solutis
Ver nivibus viridem monti reparavit amictum,
Ex quo jam patrios gens haec oblita Triones,
Atque Istrum transvecta semel, vestigia fixit
Threicio funesta solo; seu. fata vocabant,
Seu gravis ira Deum, seriem meditata ruinis."

De Bell. Getic. 166.

§. III.

Nautes, having, from the frequent revelations made to him by Pallas respecting future events, acquired a reputation for superior wisdom and foresight, was a fitting person to advise, and accordingly did advise, Eneas; but, observe, only advised; gave him no oracle, no oracular response received from Pallas on this particular occasion; as appears (*a*) from the total absence in his address to Eneas of any reference to an oracle, or consulted or commanding Deity; (*b*) from the several expressions, "sequamur," "solatus," "incensus dictis senioris amici," all of them expressions such as would naturally be used by, or applied to, a friend advising a friend; (*c*) from the immediately subsequent appearance of the Shade of Anchises to give weight and authority to, and make imperative on, Eneas the advice he had just received from his friend Nautes; and (*d*) from the words of the Apparition expressly characterising the counsels of Nautes, not as the declaration of an oracle or the commands of Heaven, but simply as sound and excellent advice:

> "Consiliis pare, quae nunc pulcherrima Nautes
> Dat senior."

I am even inclined to go a step further and to entertain an opinion that the words

> UNUM TRITONIA PALLAS
> QUEM DOCUIT, MULTAQUE INSIGNEM REDDIDIT ARTE,
> HAEC RESPONSA DABAT,

are not to be taken as literally meaning that the Goddess Pallas in *propria persona* taught Nautes, or gave him RESPONSA; but that they are rather a mere poetical personification for that superior *Minerva* or good sense of Nautes which enabled him to see his way through the misty future with a keener vision than his neighbours; see for a not very dissimilar personification (in the case too of this selfsame Pallas), *En.* II. 15:

> "Instar montis equum divina Palladis arte
> Aedificant;"

and Homer, *Odyss.* VIII. 493:

— "*Τον Επειος εποιησεν συν Αθηνη.*"

If this last view be correct, as I am strongly inclined to think it is, the expressions

UNUM TRITONIA PALLAS
QUEM DOCUIT MULTAQUE INSIGNEM REDDIDIT ARTE,

and

HAEC RESPONSA DABAT,

are of the same nature as (*v.* 662):

— "Furit immissis Vulcanus habenis
Transtra per et remos et pictas abiete puppes;"

and (Statius, *Theb.* IV. 404):

— "Sic fata gelatis
Vultibus, et Baccho jam demigrante quievit."

751.

ANIMOS NIL MAGNAE LAUDIS EGENTES

There can be little doubt but that EGENTES, the reading of the Medicean (a man. sec.) and of all the editions, is the true reading, Donatus having so quoted the passage, ad Ter. *Eun.* IV. 6. It is also EGENTES in two of the only three MSS. I have examined respecting the passage, viz. the two Leipzig. In the third (the Dresden) I have however found 'agentes'. The use of 'egere' in the passage before us, as well as its precisely similar use *Georg.* II. 28 ("Nil radicis egent"), proves the exact correspondence between the Latin 'egere' and the English *to want*, each verb having the two closely related, but at the same time very dissimilar, meanings: (*a*) of *lacking* (Gr. *δεω*), and (*b*) of *requiring*, *desiring* (Gr. *δεομαι*, German *verlangen*).

767.

QUIBUS ASPERA QUONDAM
VISA MARIS FACIES ET NON TOLERABILE CAELUM

I adopt CAELUM, instead of the generally received reading 'numen', for the following reasons:

First and principally, because I do not find elsewhere any recognition of a 'numen' or *divine authority* inherent in the sea, the meaning of the expression "numen habere maris," *En.* X. 221, being plainly *to be deities of the sea, to have divine authority* OVER *the sea.*

Secondly, because I do not know of the application elsewhere to 'numen', of an epithet at all parallel to NON TOLERABILE.

Thirdly, because we have in Virgil himself expressions very similar to NON TOLERABILE CAELUM; especially "non tractabile caelum," *En.* IV. 53, where observe the great similarity of the context to our text:

"Dum pelago desaevit hiems et aquosus Orion
Quassataeque rates, dum non tractabile caelum."

Compare also the expression "se credere caelo," *En.* VI. 15; and the constant junction of the 'minae caeli' with the 'minae maris':

"Illc meum comitatus iter, maria omnia mecum
Atque omnes pelagique minas caelique ferebat
Invalidus, vires ultra sortemque senectae."
En. VI. 112;

(where again observe the similarity to our text).

"Vim cunctam atque minas perfert caelique marisque."
En. X. 695.

— "Saepe furores
Compressi et rabiem tantam caelique marisque."
En. V. 801.

Fourthly, the authority of the Medicean in favor of 'numen' is greatly invalidated by the fact that the original reading of that MS. is not 'numen', but 'nomen', afterwards altered into 'numen'.

Fifthly, the testimony of Bottari that CAELUM is the reading of the Roman MS., is fully confirmed by Pierius: "In Romano codice CAELUM: non 'numen' habetur. Superius enim ferre se tam diu freta tot, et inhospita saxa, sideraque lamentabantur."

Sixthly, CAELUM is, as we are informed by Burmann, the reading of the Parrhasian MS., and I have myself found it in the Dresden.

I have personally examined only three other MSS. respecting this passage, viz. the Gudian and the two Leipzig, but in the whole three I have found 'numen', which reading is also recognised both by Servius and Donatus. Daniel Heinsius has 'numen', Nicholas Heinsius 'nomen'; the Modena Ed. of 1475, both the Stephenses, Burmann, and La Cerda 'numen'. Heyne's good taste led him to prefer CAELUM (see his *V. L.*), but not finding sufficient MS. authority for that reading, and objecting, as I do, to 'numen', he adopted 'nomen'. Wagner has brought back the previous 'numen', and justified it by arguments which seem to me any thing but convincing.

785.

NON MEDIA DE GENTE PHRYGUM EXCIDISSE NEFANDIS URBEM ODIIS SATIS EST

I would not believe, even although we had not the weighty authority of the Vatican Fragment for EXCIDISSE, that Virgil, who has always elsewhere used one or other of the two expressions 'excidere urbem' or 'exscindere urbem', has on this single occasion chosen in preference the coarse and extravagant expression 'exedere urbem'. Having myself personally consulted only three MSS. respecting the passage, viz. the Leipzig 35, the Leipzig 36, and the Dresden, I have found in the first EXCIDISSE, in the second 'exidisse', and in the third alone, 'exedisse'. The reading EXCIDISSE seems further to be confirmed by the observation of Donatus (ad loc.): "Leve quiddam se existimans perfecisse, quia supersunt Trojanorum aliqui, et vivunt aliqui post excidium Trojae;" and again: "Tam saeva extitit Juno, ut post excisum (observe, not exesum) Ilium, perditosque diversa caede Trojanos, persequatur reliquos" etc.

796.

QUOD SUPEREST ORO LICEAT DARE TUTA PER UNDAS
VELA TIBI LICEAT LAURENTEM ATTINGERE TYBRIM

"QUOD SUPEREST, nämlich: *zu sagen;* also: *schliesslich.*" Ladewig.

I think not; but *all that is now possible for us to obtain from you in this our distressed condition.* Compare (*vers.* 691):

> "Vel tu, quod superest, infesto fulmine morti,
> Si mereor, demitte;"

all that is left for you to do, in order to complete the work you have begun. Also Statius, *Achill.* I. 48:

> "Ibo tamen, pelagique Deos, dextramque secundi,
> Quod superest, complexa Jovis;"

my only remaining resource. And Sil. Italic. XII. 258:

> "Macte Antenoride; nunc, inquit, rapta petamus,
> Quod superest, Libyci rectoris tegmina;"

all that remains to be done.

LICEAT DARE TUTA PER UNDAS VELA TIBI. — "Sicher die Segel dir anzuvertrauen auf dem Meere." Ladewig.

No; TIBI is not the Dative depending on DARE, but the ethical Dative, as *En.* I. 467; VI. 773; and in this place is nearly equivalent to *Be so good as; please:* LICEAT DARE TUTA VELA, TIBI, *be so good as to allow us to sail safely;* the two words DARE VELA express, not the two distinct ideas of giving and sailing, but the one single idea of sailing. Compare "vela damus," *En.* III. 191, and see Comm. *En.* II. 199.

814.

UNUS ERIT TANTUM AMISSUM QUEM GURGITE QUAERES

I prefer QUAERES to 'quaeret'; first, because it is (see Foggini) the reading of the Medicean, and (see Bottari) of the Vatican Fragment. Secondly, because we have the following strong testimony of Pierius in its favor: "In exemplaribus omnibus antiquis, quotquot habui, QUAERES persona secunda legitur. Quod Venerem ostendit pro salute omnium aeque laborare." Thirdly, because having myself personally consulted only three MSS. respecting the passage, viz. the two Leipzig and the Dresden, I have in the two former found QUAERES; in the latter alone 'quaeret'. Fourthly, because Bersmann informs us that QUAERES is the reading of his MS. Fifthly, because I find QUAERES in the Modena Ed. of 1475, and in the Ed. of Rob. Stephens; and Maittaire testifies it to be the reading of the Venice Ed. of 1472 and the Milan Ed. of 1474.

Nicholas Heinsius, although informing us in his note in Burmann that he thinks QUAERES is the true reading, yet in his edition most unaccountably adopts 'quaeret', which has been adopted also by Dan. Heinsius, H. Stephens, Burmann, La Cerda, Heyne, Wagner, and Forbiger; Wagner justifying the reading by the observation: "sed ea cura magis attingit Aeneam quam Venerem" (an observation which he might also have applied to Venus's "sic nos in sceptra reponis," *En.* I. 257), and Forbiger by the not sufficiently considered (see preceding part of this Comm.) assertion that 'quaeret' is the reading of the best authorities: "optimorum potius quam plurimorum Codd. auctoritatem sequi maluimus."

827.

BLANDA VICISSIM
GAUDIA

Bland joys in their turn, viz. after his previous anxieties; see *vv.* 700 and 720; also Comm. *En.* IV. 73.

VI.

1.

CLASSIQUE IMMITTIT HABENAS

This is the ordinary metaphor (as *En. V. 662; *Lucret. V. 784; Ovid. *Met. I. 280)*; but is here peculiarly appropriate, the 'habenae' of a ship being its 'rudentes' *(sheets)*, which required to be let loose, or slacked, in order to allow the sails to be filled with the wind and the vessel to go at full speed. *En. X. 229:*

— "Velis immitte rudentes."

---

9 — 157.

AT PIUS AENEAS ARCES etc.

---

§ I.

I shall lay before the reader in as few words as possible the picture which this description presents to my mind. The principal object, and, as being well known, supposed rather than specially described by our author, is the hill of Cumae, a nearly circular or orbicular hill rising from the plain, and on one side overhanging the sea. The lower part of this hill, on one of the sides not next the sea, sloping and thickly planted with a sacred grove (TRIVIAE LUCOS, vers. 13); the upper or central part or kernel of the hill very rocky and almost perpendicular (EUBOICAE LATUS INGENS RUPIS, vers. 42); on the sloping part of the hill an hypaethral temple

(ARCES QUIBUS ALTUS APOLLO PRAESIDET, vers. 9; AUREA TECTA, vers. 13; IMMANIA TEMPLA, vers. 19; ALTA TEMPLA, vers. 41) having the sacred grove on both sides and in front; in the front, sculptured doors (FORIBUS, vers. 20); in the fourth, or hinder side, consisting merely of the bare perpendicular rock of the hill, a number of other doors (ADITUS CENTUM, OSTIA CENTUM, vers. 43 and 81; LIMEN, vers. 45; FORES, vers. 47; MAGNA ORA DOMUS, vers. 53) leading into a vast cave (ANTRUM IMMANE, vers. 11; SECRETA SIBYLLAE, vers. 10; ANTRO, vers. 77; ADYTO, vers. 98; ANTRUM, vers. 157) in the substance of the rock. In front of these last mentioned doors an altar (ARAS, vers. 124).

§ II.

JAM SUBEUNT TRIVIAE LUCOS ATQUE AUREA TECTA. — The way to the cavern lying through the sacred grove and the temple, opportunity is taken to relate by whom, and on what occasion, the latter was built, and particularly to describe the subjects of the carvings on its doors; IN FORIBUS LETUM ANDROGEI &c. Whilst Eneas is admiring these carvings, Achates, who had been despatched by him to inform the Sibyl of his having come to consult the oracle, returns accompanied by her, and she invites Eneas and the Trojans with him to enter the temple — VOCAT ALTA IN TEMPLA SACERDOS — and conducts them straight through it to the entrance of the cave in its further side, VENTUM ERAT AD LIMEN. Here the priestess begins to be inspired by the nearer presence of the Deity, NUMINE PROPIORE DEI, and having informed Eneas that the doors (sciz. of the 'antrum' or 'adytum') will not open until he has made his vows and prayers, enters the cavern by a private passage, and leaves him and the Trojans standing before its still closed doors; whilst Eneas prays and vows, the inspiration of the priestess within the cavern arrives at its full height, and he has scarcely finished when the doors spontaneously flying open give passage to the oracular responses; which terminated, Eneas retires, that is to say, leaves the spot where he was standing before the 'adytum', and returns by the way by which he had arrived, viz. through the temple.

§ III.

The above view (§ I, II) of the position of the Sibyl's cave being adopted, viz. that it was neither under the temple (Voss), nor outside and at a distance from it (Heyne and Wagner), but opening into it through the perpendicular face of the rock which formed its posterior wall, Virgil's description, hitherto found so perplexed and obscure, not to say unintelligible, becomes all at once simple, clear, graphic, and consistent with the use in other oracular temples; compare Lucan, V. 71 and seq. where we have the similar hill, 'Jugum Parnassi' ("Mons Phoebo Bromioque sacer"), with its similar 'rupes' or rocky side containing the similar 'antrum'; the similar 'templum' entirely dependent on, more modern than, and affording access to, the 'antrum'; the identical term 'limen' applied, as not only in the text, but *En. III. 371,* to the entrance, not of the temple, but of the 'antrum'; and as if to remove all doubt after what original the whole drawing is made, the express comparison:

"Qualis in Euboico vates Cumana recessu" &c.

vers. 183.

§ IV.

The Hill of Cumae is thus described by the Canonico Andrea de Jorio, in his *Guida di Pozzuoli e Contorni, col suo Atlante* (Napoli, 1830): "Lo stato attuale del promontorio di Cuma, che sotto a' tuoi occhi trionfa la spiaggia nel mezzo della vasta pianura, e il seguente. Egli e un piccolo promontorio volcanico della piu remota antichità, ed inaccessibile da tutti i lati menoche da mezzogiorno. Gran parte del colle essendo di tufo, e traforato con moltiplici e vaste grotte. Una di esse securamente era quella della Sibylla." So convinced was the Canonico that the Sibyl's cave was to be found among these caverns, as to spend some money and much time and trouble in exploring them, until at last, as he informs us, his guide, or, as perhaps the malicious reader will be inclined to think with me, not only the guide but the good Canonico himself, becoming alarmed at the increasing gloom and depth of the cavern, and the sight of some human bones lying on its floor, made a precipitate retreat and abandoned the undertaking. The Canonico seems not to have recollected that we have the authority of Agathias *(Hist. Lib. I.)* for the fact that the Sibyl's cave was destroyed nearly 1300 years ago by Narses when besieging Aligernus and the Goths, who had retreated into Cumae with much treasure and fortified themselves there.

§ V.

HORRENDAEQUE PROCUL SECRETA SIBYLLAE. — The immediate juxtaposition of PROCUL and SECRETA SIBYLLAE has given rise to the strange notion that the cave of the Sibyl was at some distance (greater or less, according to the precise idea which each expositor had of the force of the word PROCUL) from the temple of Apollo. Hence inextricable confusion in the views which have been taken, and the accounts which have been given, of Eneas's visit to the Sibyl. The simple solution of the whole matter is, that PROCUL belongs, not to SECRETA, but to PETIT, the construction being: Aeneas petit procul (far from, or more properly, apart from those of his companions who were engaged in procuring fire and water, see preceding lines) arces, quibus Apollo praesidet, secretaque Sibyllae. A false understanding of this word no longer leading us astray, we perceive at once (see § IV above) that the 'antrum' of the Sibyl was not at any distance, greater or less, from the temple of Apollo, but was a part of it; actually constituted (as might *a priori* have been expected) the 'adytum' out of which the Sibyl delivered the responses of the God, whose priestess she was, and who presided over the temple.

Exactly similar to the words PROCUL . . . . PETIT in our text, only twice as widely separated from each other, are the words "deinde . . . . dividit," *En. I. 199.*

§ VI.

ALTUS APOLLO. — "Contendit ad Apollinem, cujus templum situm in sublimi parte Cumarum; ideo ipse Apollo, ALTUS: ideo templum ARCES." La Cerda.

"ARCES; erat templum in montium jugis: hinc Apollo, altus; et praesidet arci, quatenus templum tuetur, et cum eo urbem." Heyne.

No; ALTUS has reference, not to the high situation of the temple, but to the dignity of the God; Compare Ovid, *Metam. III. 284:*

> — "Quantusque et qualis ab alta
> Junone excipitur;"

also *Metam. XII. 505:*

> — "Qui tantus erat, Junonis ut altae
> Spem caperet;"

also

> "Da veniam coepto, Jupiter alte, meo."
> OVID. *Ars Am. II. 38.*

> "Ut rediit animus, Da certa piamina, dixit,
> Fulminis, altorum rexque paterque Deum."
> OVID. *Fasti, III. 333.*

and especially Virgil himself, *En. X. 875:*

> "Sic pater ille Deum faciat, sic altus Apollo."

DELIUS INSPIRAT VATES. — *Apollo;* the VATES of Jove. as the Sibyl was of Apollo. Compare *(En. III. 251):*

> "Quae Phoebo pater omnipotens, mihi Phoebus Apollo,
> Praedixit, vobis Furiarum ego maxima pando;"

and Lucan (V. 93), of the oracular cavern of Apollo at Delphi:

— "Forsan terris inserta regendis,
Aere libratum vacuo quae sustinet orbem,
Totius pars magna Jovis, Cirrhaea per antra
Exit, et aetherio trahitur connexa Tonanti.
Hoc ubi virgineo conceptum est pectore numen" &c.

CONTRA ELATA MARI RESPONDET. — "RESPONDET, *aspicitur,* nam contra Athenas est posita." Servius. "In unis forium valvis expressas puta Athenas,..... in alteris valvis Cretam" &c. Heyne.

These explanations express the meaning of CONTRA but wholly omit that of RESPONDET, which is, that the two views were what is technically called *companions, matches,* or *pendants,* i. e. similar or related in subject, and of the same size and general appearance; *corresponded.*

NON HOC ISTA SIBI TEMPUS SPECTACULA POSCIT. — Compare "Non tali auxilio" &c. *En. II. 521* and Comment.

§ VII.

VOCAT ALTA IN TEMPLA SACERDOS. — "Fallunt viros doctos ALTA TEMPLA, quae nunc non sunt Apollinis aedes, sed antrum Sibyllae." Heyne.

This criticism is certainly incorrect; first, because the Sibyl could not be properly said to call the Teucri (IN) *into* a temple, at which neither she nor they had yet arrived (see VENTUM ERAT AD LIMEN, four verses later) and whose doors were not only shut, but would not open until after a certain process had been gone through *(v.52);* and secondly, because it cannot be believed that Virgil would have applied the same term, TEMPLA, within the space of a few lines, to two objects so wholly dissimilar as the stone or marble temple of Apollo built by Daedalus (POSUITQUE IMMANIA TEMPLA, *v. 19),* and the cavern of the Sibyl. See § I. above.

§ VIII.

EXCISUM EUBOICAE LATUS &c. — The whole cast of this sentence, nay the very rythm of the verses, shows that it is not, as supposed by Heyne and Wagner, a mere epexegesis of the preceeding ALTA TEMPLA, but the commencement of a new description, viz. of the description of the ANTRUM SIBYLLAE to which the Teucri accompanied by the Sibyl, having entered the ALTA TEMPLA, are now approaching. Happily for the literary credit of his costly edition of Heyne's Virgil, Wagner did not put into execution the purpose about which he informs us he for some time hesitated, viz. that of substituting a comma for the period at SACERDOS, and thus pressing his readers, nolentes volentes, into the adoption of his and Heyne's views of the meaning of ALTA TEMPLA.

QUO LATI DUCUNT ADITUS CENTUM OSTIA CENTUM. — "ADITUS; puta, *subterranei meatus*; συριγγες, ut in Aegypto appellabantur: hos meatus, statuendum est duxisse ad unum aliquod penetrale, cujus est limen, *v. 45,* et fores *v. 47,* et ora *v. 53,* ostia *v. 81.* Quod si itaque in interiore antro, adyto, Sibylla vaticinia effaretur, remeabat vox per infinitos hos canaliculos seu spiramina et exitus, quae res ad religiosum horrorem valde accommodata esse debuit." Heyne.

To this view of Heyne, viz. that the CENTUM ADITUS are numerous subterranean passages leading to numerous doors (OSTIA CENTUM) which opened directly into the 'adytum' or interior part of the cavern, at the 'limen' of one of which doors Eneas and the Sibyl are described as arriving in the words VENTUM ERAT AD LIMEN *(v. 45),* there seems to me to be these strong objections; first, that the poet was bound in common propriety to have furnished Eneas and the Sibyl with light, when he placed them thus together at the further and closed end of a subterraneous passage. Secondly, that we are informed at *v. 40,* that the inquirers heard the responses issuing through CENTUM ADITUS, OSTIA CENTUM, whereas, if Heyne's interpretation be correct, they reached Eneas through only one ostium, and no aditus. Thirdly, that ADITUS is not meatus' (whether subterranean or above ground), but the *approach* to a place, through a 'meatus', door, gate, or other opening: the *access* afforded by a road, passage or opening, not the road, passage, or opening, itself. Compare: "Quo neque sit ventis aditus," *Georg. IV. 9.* "Rumpunt aditus," *En. II. 494;* not *break the door* or *road,* or *opening,* but *a passage through it; force an entrance; burst in.* Also (Cic. *de Oratore I. 204*): "Sic ego intelligo, si in haec, quae patefecit oratione sua Crassus, intrare volueritis, facillime vos ad ea, quae cupitis, perventuros ab hoc aditu januaque patefacta;" i. e. *by the passage through this opened door.* And so in our text, *into which there is access through a hundred wide doors;* as if Virgil had written, 'in quod itur per centum ostia lata'. Compare, exactly parallel (Ammian. XVII. 4): "Urbem (Thebas sciz.) .... portarum centum quondam aditibus celebrem;" *celebrated for its hundred entrances through a hundred gates.* Even Servius and La Cerda seem to have been of this opinion: "Non sine causa et aditus dixit et ostia: nam Vitruvius, qui de Architectonica scripsit, ostium dicit per quod ab aliquo arcemur ingressu, ab *ostando* dictum: aditum ab *adeundo,* per quem ingredimur." Servius. "Aditus, ostia; non est tautologia, ut multi volunt, sed elegans oppositio vocum. Nulla in Virgilio tautologia." La Cerda; who then goes on to quote Servius as above. In the following line we have the exactly similar structure, totidem voces responsa sibyllae: responsa being the explanation of voces, as in our text ostia is of aditus. Compare *En. XI. 525:*

"Angustaeque ferunt fauces aditusque maligni;"

where the meaning is, not *that the place was approached through narrow gorges* and *other difficult passages,* but *that the approach to the place being through a narrow gorge, was on that account difficult.* See § V above.

There seems to me to be no ground whatever for the view which some commentators (amongst others Süpfle and Ladewig) have taken of the CENTUM OSTIA, viz. that by one of these OSTIA only the cave communicated with the temple, while by the others it communicated with the exterior, i. e. with the open country. Not only had such a structure of the Sibyl's cell been totally inconsistent with the mystery and sanctity so indispensable to an oracle, but we are told expressly, *vv. 81, 82,* that the answer to Eneas's question was returned through all the doors. Can any sane man believe that this answer, returned through all the doors, was conveyed to Eneas through only one, and through the remainder carried out quite beyond the precincts of the holy place, and published to the whole world?

§ IX.

VENTUM ERAT AD LIMEN. — "Quod sane non potuit esse centum ostiorum, sed tantum unius." Heyne. The continuation or sequel of the error pointed out in § VIII above. LIMEN is the threshold neither of CENTUM OSTIA nor of "unum ostium", but of ANTRUM; to which it refers past the two immediately preceding lines, which being merely descriptive of ANTRUM, may be regarded as parenthetic; as if Virgil had said:

EXCISUM EUBOICAE LATUS INGENS RUPIS IN ANTRUM.
VENTUM ERAT AD LIMEN.

See Comments *En. I. 4; III. 571; V. 522* (§. II.), *659; VI. 83, 431, 739.* Accordingly while Eneas stands here AD LIMEN, or as expressed in vers. 47, ANTE FORES, the CENTUM OSTIA fly open, and he hears the responses issuing out through them and then borne through the open air (PER AURAS) to where he is standing 'sub dio', within the temple, *ιερον*, or sacred enclosure of Apollo. See § I above.

52.

NEQUE ENIM ANTE DEHISCENT
ATTONITAE MAGNA ORA DOMUS

"ATTONITAE: stupendae, non stupentis. Ergo, facientis attonitos." Servius, followed by H. Stephens, La Cerda and all the older commentators.
"Der von des Gottes Gewalt erschütterten Kluft." Voss, *Randglossen.*
"Ut rei inanimatae tribuatur sensus idem, qui est in iis, qui repente revelli fores audiunt. ("Hoc probo, ut in re magna et horrenda." Wagner.) . . . . . . Scilicet debebat esse attonito tibi propter fores, ubi revellentur; transfertur doctius epitheton ad fores." Heyne.

No, just the contrary; ATTONITAE is applied strictly and specially to the DOMUS, which being 'attonita', will not, or cannot, open its mouth; remains with closed mouth, like a man who is so astounded that he cannot speak. That this is the true interpretation, is shown, first, by the more appropriate sense thus obtained. Secondly, by the terms DEHISCENT (compare *En. III. 314)* and ORA, plainly personifying the DOMUS. Thirdly, by the peculiar and proper force of the word 'attonitus', which is *to be so astounded as to be deprived of the power of speech and motion.* Compare "Attonitis inhians animis." *En. VII. 814.* "Attonitis haesere animis." *En. V. 529.* "Huic me operi attonitum clara lux oppressit." APUL. *Met. IV. 22;* and Hildebrand ad Apul. *Met. XI. 14:* "Attonitus enim, quaqua significatione usurpatur, semper primariam habet stupendi notionem de eo, qui ita quasi defixus in re vel conspicienda vel perficienda est, ut discedere ab ea nequeat." And fourthly, by the use which the Italians still make of the word in this precise sense:

"Ei fu; siccome immobile,
Dato il mortal sospiro,
Stette la spoglia immemore
Orba di tanto spiro,
Così percossa, attonita
La terra al nunzio sta."

MANZONI, *Il cinque Maggio.*

Compare the application of the term by Valer. Flaccus (I. 43) to a table at which a murder was committed:

"Hunc ferus Aeëtes, Scythiam Phasinque rigentem
Qui colit, (heu magni Solis pudor!) hospita vina
Inter, et attonitae mactat solemnia mensae."

[The actual junction by Lucan of 'tacuere' to 'attonitae domus' in the following passage (which I have accidentally met since the above Comment was written) proves to a demonstration, that the meaning of ATTONITAE DEHISCENT in our text is precisely that which I have declared it to be:

— "Sic funere primo
Attonitae tacuere domus, cum corpora nondum
Conclamata jacent," —

LUCAN. II. 21.]

69.

TUM PHOEBO ET TRIVIAE SOLIDO DE MARMORE TEMPLA INSTITUAM

Wagner prefers 'templum', the reading of the Medicean; and, never at a loss to assign an unworthy origin to a good reading, considers the reading TEMPLA to have arisen from the form (templu¯) in which 'templum' is found written in the Medicean. I prefer TEMPLA (in the sense of a single temple; as

"Templa dei saxo venerabar structa vetusto."

En. III. 84.

— "Teucros vocat alta in templa sacerdos."

En. VI. 41.

"Ultus avos Trojae, templa et temerata Minervae."
En. VI. 841.

"Ipse tibi ad tua templa feram solemnia dona."
En. IX. 626;

and, precisely parallel:

"Aurea tunc mediis urbis tibi templa dicabo
Collibus."
STAT. *Theb. II. 728),*

first, because the plural is more dignified than the singular. Secondly, because it is adopted by Pierius, although at the same time informing us that he found templum' both in the Rom. and the Longobard. Thirdly, because I have myself found TEMPLA not only in the only three MSS. I have personally examined, viz. the two Leipzig and the Dresden, but in the Modena Ed. of 1475, Dan. Heinsius, Bersmann, both the Stephenses, the Paris Ed. of 1600, and La Cerda. Fourthly because, as appears from Maittaire, TEMPLA is the reading both of the Venice Ed. of 1472 and of the Milan of 1474.

Nich. Heinsius, as usual preferring (with Wagner) the authority of the Medicean to all other, has templum

---

77.

AT PHOEBI NONDUM PATIENS IMMANIS IN ANTRO
BACCHATUR VATES MAGNUM SI PECTORE POSSIT
EXCUSSISSE DEUM TANTO MAGIS ILLE FATIGAT
OS RABIDUM FERA CORDA DOMANS FINGITQUE PREMENDO

FINGITQUE PREMENDO. — "Dura prius argilla, cera, digitis premitur, subigitur et fingitur atque ita ad formam componitur." Peerlkamp.

Altogether erroneous; first, because Sibylla was not patient and plastic like potter's clay, or wax, but resistant and rebellious; and secondly, because it is perfectly plain, from *vv. 100, 101,* and *102,* that the image is that of a wild horse undergoing the manege; and so, correctly, the other commentators.

83.

O TANDEM MAGNIS PELAGI DEFUNCTE PERICLIS
SED TERRAE GRAVIORA MANENT IN REGNA LAVINI
DARDANIDAE VENIENT MITTE HANC DE PECTORE CURAM
SED NON ET VENISSE VOLENT

The words SED TERRAE GRAVIORA MANENT (as wholly parenthetic as MITTE HANC DE PECTORE CURAM in the next line, and "non indebita posco regna meis fatis," vers. 66) express an idea suggested by the just preceding PELAGI, but not forming a part of the current thought, which passes from PERICLIS to IN REGNA LAVINI DARDANIDAE VENIENT. The period at MANENT, which I find in all the editions down to Ladewig, should therefore be removed, as splitting the body into two exactly in the middle, leaving the head and shoulders on the left hand, and the tail on the right; i. e. leaving on the left hand, *O thou who hast gone through the sea's great perils, but land's greater perils yet await thee;* and leaving on the right hand, *The Dardanidae shall come into the Lavinian realms.* Nothing has contributed more to the complete misunderstanding and consequent misrepresentation of our author than the ignorance manifested by Virgil's best commentators of this, the usual, structure of his sentences. See Comments *En. I. 4; III. 571; V. 522 (§ II), 659; VI. 739.*

TERRAE. — I have no doubt at all that this, which I have myself found in the Leipzig MS. No. 36, is the correct reading. I have examined only two other MSS. respecting the passage, viz. the Leipzig No. 35, and the Dresden. The former has 'terra', the latter 'terris In the Dresden copy of the Modena Edition the a of 'terra has been altered into æ' by the same ancient hand which has made numerous glosses and corrections through the whole of the volume Nicholas Heinsius also has adopted TERRAE in place of the 'terra' of Daniel Heinsius.

90.

NEC TEUCRIS ADDITA JUNO
USQUAM ABERIT

Compare Schiller, *Maria Stuart, Act IV,* where Elizabeth, speaking of Mary, says:

"Sie ist die Furie meines Lebens; mir
Ein Plagegeist, vom Schicksal angeheftet."

This sense is however solely derivable from the context, not at all contained in ADDITA, a word employed indifferently whether the meaning intended to be conveyed is good or bad:

"Salve, vera Jovis proles, decus addite divis."
En. VIII. 301,

which single instance is to me sufficient to prove the incorrectness of the whole of Heyne's disputation on the passage, and how erroneously the ADDITA of our text is rendered by Macrobius, "affixa, et per hoc infesta," and by Servius, "inimica." Compare Statius, *Theb. I. 22:*

— "Tuque o Latiae decus addite famae"

167.

ET LITUO PUGNAS INSIGNIS OBIBAT ET HASTA

"Volker, der kühne Spielmann, also genannt weil er fiedeln konnte und fechten mit gleicher Meisterschaft." *Kriemhilde's Rache, von Alfred Reumont.*

186.

SIC ORE PRECATUR

Pierius says: "In Rom. cod. legere est 'voce', in Longobardico, ORE." Either reading affording an equally good sense, I have adopted ORE, which I have myself found in the Leipzig No. 36. The following is Servius's opinion of the third reading 'forte': "Vacat 'forte'; et est versus de his, qui tibicines vocantur, quibus additur aliquid ad solam metri sustentationem ..... Nec enim possumus intelligere eum fortuitu rogasse." This opinion, instead of preventing Wagner from ousting out of the Heynian text the excellent reading 'voce' and substituting for it the unmeaning, and worse than unmeaning, 'forte', has been used by him as a means of bastardising the ousted reading: "Apparet hoc Servii judicium causam aliis exstitisse, ut experirentur, qua ratione emendarent versum; hinc alii ORE, alii 'voce' substituerunt." It is fortunate that we have the testimony of Pierius (quoted above) that these readings emanate from MSS. of equal authority with Servius himself.

I find either ORE or 'voce in H. Stephens, the Paris Ed. of 1600, La Cerda, Bersmann, Burmann, Nich. Heinsius and Brunck. 'Forte' is the reading of the Medicean (see Foggini), and on the authority of that MS. and of its recognition in the very severe criticism of Servius quoted above, has been adopted by Wagner, Forbiger and several other modern commentators. I have myself also found it in the Modena Ed. of 1475 and the only two MSS. (excepting the Leipzig No. 36) which I have examined respecting the passage, viz. the Leipzig 35, and the Dresden. It is also the reading of Dan. Heinsius, and of Rob. Stephens.

202.

TOLLUNT SE CELERES LIQUIDUMQUE PER AERA LAPSAE
SEDIBUS OPTATIS GEMINAE SUPER ARBORE SIDUNT
DISCOLOR UNDE AURI PER RAMOS AURA REFULSIT

GEMINAE, and not 'gemina', is the correct reading; first, because it is according to Virgil's custom thus to repeat his subject just before the verb; see Comm. *En. I. 504.* Secondly, because the repetition of the subject in the word GEMINAE places the picture of the two birds perched on the tree, vividly before the eyes. Thirdly, because the double nature of the tree is sufficiently described in the following line. Fourthly, because on every one of the forty other occasions on which Virgil uses this word, it means, not *of two different natures,* but *twins, two in number.* Thus "geminum solem" *(En. IV. 470)* is *two suns;* "geminum honorem" *(En. V. 365) two prizes;* "geminam prolem" *(En. I. 278) two offsprings, two children;* "gemino muro" *(En. III. 535) two walls;* &c. &c. Fifthly, because the words 'gemina arbore', where they occur in Statius, *Theb. X. 841:*

"Gemina latus arbore clusus
Aerium sibi portat iter,"

mean, not *one tree of two different natures,* but *two distinct trees;* viz. the pair of trees, which form the two upright sides or poles of a ladder. Sixthly, because Pierius informs us, "In Longobardico GEMINAE legitur, ut sit de columbis." Seventhly, I find in the Dresden copy of the Modena Edition of 1475 GEMINAE written in, in the same ancient hand I have before spoken of, over 'gemina', the reading of the Edition. Eighthly, because we are informed by Maittaire that GEMINAE is the reading of the Venice Ed. of 1472. Ninthly, because I have myself found GEMINAE in the Leipzig MS. No. 36; also in Burmann and La Cerda, who defend the reading in their notes; also in Brunck. The other Leipzig MS. (No. 35) has 'gemina'; and the Dresden, 'gemina sub'.

214.

PRINCIPIO PINGUEM TAEDIS ET ROBORE SECTO
INGENTEM STRUXERE PYRAM

I entirely agree with Wakefield that this passage is to be thus punctuated:

PRINCIPIO, PINGUEM TAEDIS, ET ROBORE SECTO
INGENTEM, STRUXERE PYRAM.

See Comment *En. IV. 504.*

242.

UNDE LOCUM GRAII DIXERUNT NOMINE AVERNUM
QUATUOR HIC PRIMUM NIGRANTES TERGA JUVENCOS
CONSTITUIT FRONTIQUE INVERGIT VINA SACERDOS
ET SUMMAS CARPENS MEDIA INTER CORNUA SETAS
IGNIBUS IMPONIT SACRIS LIBAMINA PRIMA

The first of these verses has been marked with a stigma as spurious by most of the modern editors, and summarily ejected out of the text by others (ex. gr. by Brunck and Wagner). I think however that it is genuine; first and principally, because it is according to Virgil's usual habit thus to explain the origin of names of places; compare *En. I. 113* and *536; III. 702; V. 718; VI. 234* and *381; VII. 1;* &c. &c. Secondly, because Pierius (see below) found it in all the MSS. examined by him. Thirdly, because I have myself found it in the following: the Gudian, the Dresden, No. 36 of the Leipzig, No. 56 of the Gotha, and the Petrarchian; also in Nos. 113 and 115 of the Vienna MSS., in which two latter, however, it has been written in, in a later hand. The verse is entirely absent from the Leipzig No. 35.

Avernum. — I have myself found this reading in the Dresden, No. 36 of the Leipzig, the Petrarchian, and Nos. 113 and 115 of the Vienna (see above). Bottari informs us that it is the reading of the Roman, and Pierius says expressly: "Inolevit his temporibus consuetudo, ut 'Aornum' scribatur etiam a litteratis viris. Sed enim in antiquis codicibus omnibus, quotquot habui, avernum notatum observavi." I find avernum also in the Modena Edition of 1475. 'Aornon', the reading of Daniel Heinsius, I have never seen in any MS.; 'Aornum', the reading of Nicholas Heinsius, I have found only in the Gudian.

Hic. — That it was usual to offer sacrifices at the lake of Avernus, appears from Livy, XXIV. 12 (of Hannibal): "Cum cetero exercitu ad lacum Averni per speciem sacrificandi, re ipsa ut tentaret Puteolos, quodque ibi praesidii erat, descendit."

Libamina prima. — Compare Statius, *Theb. VI. 193:*

"At genitor, sceptrique decus, cultusque Tonantis
Injicit ipse rogis, tergoque et pectore fusam
Caesariem ferro minuit, sectisque jacentis
Obnubit tenuia ora comis, ac talia fletu
Verba pio miscens: Alio tibi, perfide, pacto,
Juppiter, hunc crinem voti reus ante dicaram,
Si pariter virides nati libare dedisses
Ad tua templa genas;"

and Statius, *Theb. II. 253:*

— "Hic more parentum
Iasides, thalamis ubi casta adolesceret aetas,
Virgineas libare comas, primosque solebant
Excusare toros."

260.

INVADE VIAM

'*In*-vadere viam' (exactly the opposite of '*e*-vadere viam', *En. II. 731;* and see Comm. *En. II. 458)* is *to enter upon a journey, set out.*

269.

PERQUE DOMOS DITIS VACUAS ET INANIA REGNA
QUALE PER INCERTAM LUNAM SUB LUCE MALIGNA
EST ITER IN SILVIS UBI CAELUM CONDIDIT UMBRA
JUPITER ET REBUS NOX ABSTULIT ATRA COLOREM
VESTIBULUM ANTE IPSUM PRIMISQUE IN FAUCIBUS ORCI
LUCTUS ET ULTRICES POSUERE CUBILIA CURAE

"O ye interminable, gloomy realms
Of swimming shadows and enormous shapes."
BYRON, *Cain, II. 2.*

INCERTAM LUNAM. — "Nubilo caelo." Heyne. "Cujus lux nubibus incerta et dubia redditur, quae modo splendet, modo nubibus obscuratur." Forbiger.

No: first, because without some limitative or qualifying adjunct the general and indefinite term INCERTAM cannot be taken in this special sense, the supposed parallel, "incertos caeca caligine soles" *(En. III. 203)*, not being parallel at all, in as much as in that passage 'soles' means, not *suns*, but *days,* and 'incertos', not *clouded*, but, as determined by the adjunct 'caeca caligine', literally *uncertain*, i. e. *uncertain whether days or nights.* And secondly, because the light by which

Eneas and the Sibyl were walking, was, not sometimes bright and sure, and sometimes dim, but always dim and unsure.

I therefore understand INCERTAM in our text to be used in its ordinary general sense of *uncertain, unsure, not to be depended on,* and to express generally the character of the moon, or moonlight, as compared with that of the sun, or daylight. Compare:

"But westering Sol bids us make haste,
And not our precious minutes waste
In too contemplative a gaze
On various Nature's wondrous ways,
When on night quarters we should think
And something get to eat and drink;
And hints that though his sister Di
May do for lovers to swear by,
She 's not to be depended on
By two who, by themselves alone,
Travel on foot a land unknown."

My Journey, My Book, Dresden, 1853.

Our author having thus, according to his usual custom (see Comments *En. I. 48, 500; V. 157, and 323, § III),* commenced with the general statement QUALE PER INCERTAM LUNAM, proceeds inmediately to limit and define, informing us in the words SUB LUCE MALIGNA EST ITER IN SILVIS that the moonlight of which he speaks is not such light as the moon shows in the open country, but the insufficient, unfavorable light (MALIGNA) which she affords to travellers in a wood. To Servius's reading, 'inceptam,' I object, first, with the editors and commentators, that the MS. authority on which it rests (and for which see the notes of Nich. Heinsius and Burmann) is much inferior to that of the Medicean, and Vatican Fragment, both of which read INCERTAM; and secondly, that travellers by night in a wood during the new moon, have not even so much as the dim light which Virgil allows Eneas and the Sibyl, but are in total darkness.

Of the three only MSS. which I have myself personally examined, I have found INCERTAM in two (viz. the two Leipzig), 'incoeptam' in one (viz. the Dresden).

I should therefore myself, in my *Six Photographs of the Heroic Times,* have interpreted this passage, not, according to the reading of Servius,

By the créscent moon's twilight,

but, according to that of the Vatican Fragment and Medicean,

By the moon's unsure twílight,

The 'luna' spoken of here, as well as at vers. 454, being plainly the material moon, not the Goddess Luna, the word in both places should be spelled with a small initial letter, not, as most unaccountably both by Heyne and Wagner (by the latter even in his *Virg. Br. En.),* with a capital.

VESTIBULUM ANTE IPSUM &c. — Compare *(En. VII. 177):*

"Quin etiam veterum effigies ex ordine avorum
Antiqua e cedro; Italusque, paterque Sabinus
Vitisator, curvam servans sub imagine falcem,
Saturnusque senex, Janique bifrontis imago
Vestibulo astabant."

282.

IN MEDIO RAMOS ANNOSAQUE BRACHIA PANDIT
ULMUS OPACA INGENS QUAM SEDEM SOMNIA VULGO
VANA TENERE FERUNT FOLIISQUE SUB OMNIBUS HAERENT

SOMNIA — must be understood to be in the form of birds; compare Silius Italicus, XIII. 595:

"Dextra vasta comas nemorosaque brachia fundit
Taxus, Cocyti rigua frondosior unda.
Hic dirae volucres, pastusque cadavere vultur,
Et multus bubo, ac sparsis strix sanguine pennis,
Harpyiaeque fovent nidos, atque omnibus haerent
Condensae foliis: saevit stridoribus arbor."

300.

STANT LUMINA FLAMMA
SORDIDUS EX HUMERIS NODO DEPENDET AMICTUS

"Flamma stat (est) in oculis." Heyne.

No; the meaning is infinitely stronger; *his eyes are a mass of fire.* Compare:

— "Jam pulvere caelum
Stare vident;"

En. X. 407.

the sky is thick with dust; is one cloud of dust, one mass of dust.

"Vides ut alta stet nive candidum
Soracte;"

HOR. *Carm. I. 9. 1.*

how Soracte is one mass of deep, white snow.

"Verbreitete das Gerücht, Wien stehe in Flammen." *Allgemeine Zeitung, Nov. 1. 1848;* not (as Heyne's interpretation of our text would lead us to understand the words) *there were flames in Vienna,* but *Vienna was on fire, was one mass of fire.*

With this idea of fulness or quantity, is combined, I have no doubt, the primary idea of the term, viz. that of immobility; compare:

"Sunt avidae volucres, non quae Phineia mensis
Guttura fraudabant, sed genus inde trahunt:
Grande caput, stantes oculi, rostra apta rapinae."

OVID. *Fasti, VI. 131.*

"Stat nunquam facies." —

LUCAN. V. 214.

I do not at all doubt but FLAMMA, the corrected reading of the Medicean (see Foggini), and the reading of the Modena Edition of 1475, the two Stephenses, Dan. Heinsius, Bersmann, La Cerda, and the Paris Edition of 1600, is correct. Nich. Heinsius's note (in Burmann) in support of FLAMMA, is richer and fuller than Nich.

Heinsius's notes usually are; it is therefore the more surprising that his own edition (at least that of Utrecht 1704, the only one to which I have access at present) has 'flammae', which reading I have found in the four only MSS. I have myself personally examined, viz. the Gudian, the Dresden, and the two Leipzig.

NODO. — *Tied, in a slovenly manner,* IN *a knot over his shoulder; not fastened with a clasp or button, as usual with those who were careful about their personal appearance.* See Comment *En. I. 318.*

429.

ABSTULIT ATRA DIES ET FUNERE MERSIT ACERBO

See Muret. *Var. Lect. Select.* (a Kraft, Lipsiae, 1830) *Lib. XIII. c. 2.*

431.

NEC VERO HAE SINE SORTE DATAE SINE JUDICE SEDES
QUAESITOR MINOS URNAM MOVET ILLE SILENTUM
CONCILIUMQUE VOCAT VITASQUE ET CRIMINA DISCIT

These three wholly and plainly parenthetic lines afford a good instance of that remarkable peculiarity of Virgil's style to which I have had occasion so frequently elsewhere to call the reader's attention; see Comments *En. I. 4; III. 571; IV. 484; V. 522* (§ II.) and *659; VI. 83, 739.*

438.

FATA OBSTANT TRISTIQUE PALUS INAMABILIS UNDA ALLIGAT

MS. authority is nearly equally divided (see Heyne, *V. L.)* between the two readings FATA OBSTANT and 'Fas obstat' I prefer FATA OBSTANT; first and principally because Virgil, although elsewhere using the word 'fas' twenty two times, has never even so much as once used it as *forbidding, prohibiting,* or *opposing;* always on the contrary in the sense of *permitting.* Secondly, because he uses the precise expression "Fata obstant," *En. IV. 440.* Thirdly, because the verse of the Medicean containing the reading 'Fas obstat', is in other parts manifestly incorrect, and is besides marked with stigmas (see Foggini). Fourthly, because Pierius, although informing us that the Roman MS. and Servius both have 'Fas', himself cites and adopts the reading received in his time, FATA OBSTANT. Fifthly, because, having myself personally examined only three Virgilian MSS. respecting the passage, I have in two of them, viz. the Dresden and No. 35 of the Leipzig, found FATA OBSTANT, and in the third, viz. No. 36 of the Leipzig, 'fatum obstat'. Sixthly, because in the Dresden MS. of Servius I have found FATA OBSTANT, which is also the reading of the Modena Ed. of 1475, Bersmann, the two Stephenses, Fabricius, the Paris Ed. of 1600, Daniel Heinsius and La Cerda.

INAMABILIS — is to be preferred to 'innabilis'; first, on account of the more poetic sense. Secondly, because it is the only reading recognised either by Servius, or Donatus, or Pomponius Sabinus. Thirdly, because Pierius testifies thus strongly in its favor: "INAMABILIS UNDA ..... sunt et qui legant 'innabilis', a No, nas; quod in veteribus exemplaribus non memini me legere." Fourthly, on account of the parallels adduced by N. Heinsius in his note (see Burmann). 'Innabilis' however is not wholly without authority. I have myself found it in the two Dresden MSS., viz. both in the Virgil and in the Servius, and it has been adopted both by Bersmann (who however informs us that his MS. reads INAMABILIS) and by La Cerda, who has not been able to adduce any sufficient argument in its favor.

447.

HIS LAODAMIA
IT COMES ET JUVENIS QUONDAM NUNC FEMINA CAENEUS
RURSUS ET IN VETEREM FATO REVOLUTA FIGURAM

I have found CAENEUS in all the MSS. which I have myself personally examined, viz. the Petrarchian, the Gudian, the Dresden, and the two Leipzig; and it is certain from the silence both of Pierius and Heinsius that neither of those diligent investigators found any other reading. The meaning afforded by this reading seems to me not only unobjectionable, but excellent: *here was also the youth Ceneus restored to his primitive female sex.* Those critics who, objecting with Brunck, Heyne, Peerlkamp, Jahn and Ladewig to the application of the feminine predicate REVOLUTA to the masculine noun CAENEUS, substitute Caenis for CAENEUS, not only substitute a purely conjectural reading for one in which the MSS. are unanimous, but deprive the passage of its whole pith and marrow, which consists in this very application of the feminine adjective to the masculine name formerly owned by the now remetamorphosed female, and in placing this remetamorphosed female (the QUONDAM JUVENIS CAENEUS), under her masculine name, in the company of the other females enumerated.

I find CAENEUS also in the Modena Ed. of 1475, and in all the old editions. 'Caenis' makes its first appearance in Brunck, who says "CAENEUS REVOLUTA, foedus soloecismus." In the Dresden MS. of Servius I find: NUNC·FEMINA CENEUS; Coeneus virgo fuit, quae &c., the 'i' having been placed over the u by some grammarian to whom the feminine predicate attached to the masculine name, was as great an abomination as it was to Brunck.

Compare Ovid, *Metam. IV. 279:*

"Nec loquor, ut quondam naturae jure novato
Ambiguus fuerit modo vir, modo femina, Scython."

451.

QUAM TROIUS HEROS
UT PRIMUM JUXTA STETIT AGNOVITQUE PER UMBRAM
OBSCURAM QUALEM PRIMO QUI SURGERE MENSE
AUT VIDET AUT VIDISSE PUTAT PER NUBILA LUNAM
DEMISIT LACRYMAS DULCIQUE AFFATUS AMORE EST

The error into which the Medicean MS. has led all the ancient editors, and Wagner among the modern, is, not that of reading UMBRAM, but that of connecting UMBRAM with OBSCURAM by means of a pause placed after the latter. Placing the pause before, instead of after, OBSCURAM, the latter word becomes referrible to Dido equally whether we read (with the Medicean) UMBRAM, or (with the Leyden and other MSS. quoted by N. Heinsius) 'umbras', and the question raised by the commentators as to the reading (whether UMBRAS or 'umbram') ceases to be of any importance. That OBSCURAN certainly belongs to Dido, even although we should follow the Medicean so far as to read UMBRAM, is I think sufficiently proved by this single argument, viz. that the predicate of a substantive which closes a verse is never placed by Virgil first word in the following line and separated from the sequel by a pause, unless (as in the case of 'exiguam', *v. 493),* for the purpose of expressing a very strong emphasis (see Comm. *En. II. 246);* and a very strong emphasis on OBSCURAM, considered as the predicate of UMBRAM, would express such a degree of darkness as would not only have prevented Eneas from seeing Dido, QUALEM &c., but would have been quite inconsistent with the explicit statement (at *v. 270)* that there was a degree of light present, resembling moonlight in a wood.

Having myself personally examined only three MSS. respecting the passage, viz. the two Leipzig and the Dresden, I have found UMBRAM in the Leipzig No. 35, and the Dresden; 'umbras' in the Leipzig No. 36.

OBSCURAM — *dimly seen, scarcely distinguishable;* see Comment *En. III. 522.*

467.

TALIBUS AENEAS ARDENTEM ET TORVA TUENTEM
LENIBAT DICTIS ANIMUM LACRYMASQUE CIEBAT
ILLA SOLO FIXOS OCULOS AVERSA TENEBAT
NEC MAGIS INCEPTO VULTUM SERMONE MOVETUR
QUAM SI DURA SILEX AUT STET MARPESIA CAUTES

"Duncan fleeched and Duncan prayed:
Ha, ha, the wooing o't!
Meg was deaf as Ailsa Craig;
Ha, ha, the wooing o't!"

BURNS.

LACRYMASQUE CIEBAT. — "Er suchte ihr Thränen zu entlocken als Zeichen der eingetretenen weicheren Stimmung." Ladewig, and so Peerlkamp.

Nothing could be further from the meaning, or less poetical. LACRYMAS CIEBAT is simply *wept;* see vers. 476, and Comments *En. IV. 30 and 449.*

477

INDE DATUM MOLITUR ITER

"DATUM; simpl. accipe, *qua via patet, ducit.*" Heyne. "Viam patentem ac se quasi offerentem progredienti." Wagner. *Virg. Br. En.*

Both wrong; the meaning being (as *vers. 537; III. 255, 501; IV. 225; VII. 313) 'datum a fatis';* and so, rightly, Voss. Compare Terent. *Heaut. II. 3:* "Datur modo: fruere dum licet;" and Terent. *Eun. III. 1:*

— "Est istuc datum
Profecto, ut grata mihi sint quae facio omnia;"

where Donatus: "Fato decretoque concessum."

535.

ROSEIS AURORA QUADRIGIS
JAM MEDIUM AETHERIO CURSU TRAJECERAT AXEM

According to the poets, Aurora performed the same diurnal journey as Phoebus, rising like him in the East, traversing the whole sky, and sinking in the West. See Voss, *Mythol. Briefe, Band II, Brief 46.* Also Voss, *Beiträge zum Comm. der Ilias, II. 48.*

542.

AT LAEVA MALORUM
EXERCET POENAS ET AD IMPIA TARTARA MITTIT

As we would say in English, *the penal road*, or *the convicts road;* i. e. the road from the court house to the jail. So, in Venice, The Bridge of Sighs, celebrated by Lord Byron.

546.

MELIORIBUS UTERE FATIS

"Usus Caesar virtute et fortuna sua Perusiam expugnavit." VELL. PAT. II. 74.

559.

CONSTITIT AENEAS STREPITUMQUE EXTERRITUS HAUSIT

With his usual inordinate confidence in the Medicean MS. Wagner has been here, as so often elsewhere, but too forward in correcting the Heynian text. STREPITUMQUE EXTERRITUS HAUSIT is to be preferred to 'strepituque exterritus haesit'; first, because the picture of Eneas listening with horror to the sound is finer than that of Eneas only horrified and not listening; compare Statius, *Silv. II. 7. 116*:

"Seu magna sacer et superbus umbra
Nescis Tartaron, et procul nocentum
Audis verbera."

Secondly, because the sound was not a sudden crash, over at once. but a mixed sound, all the component parts of which are minutely described by our author, and which continued and was heard by Eneas so long as he was in the neighbourhood; and thirdly, because STREPITUM HAUSIT is the reading recognised by Servius.

I have myself examined only three MSS. with respect to the passage, viz. the two Leipzig and the Dresden, but in the whole three I have found STREPITUM HAUSIT. I find the same reading in the Modena Edition of 1475, both the Stephenses, Bersmann, the Paris Edition of 1600, Fabricius, Burmann, and both the Heinsii.

563.

NULLI FAS CASTO SCELERATUM INSISTERE LIMEN

SCELERATUM. — "Sceleribus contaminatum, adeoque impurum, incestum." Heyne.

No; but *par excellence* SCELERATUM ("sedes scelerata," OVID. *Met. IV. 456)*, because the seat of the Furies. See Comm. *En. IV. 471.*

566.

GNOSIUS HAEC RHADAMANTHUS HABET DURISSIMA REGNA

The meaning is, not *that Rhadamanthus dwelt* or *had his criminal court IN Tartarus*, because we shall see, at vers. 573, that it was necessary that the gates of Tartarus should be opened for the admission of criminals coming from his judgment seat, but the meaning is *that he was the supreme lord* or *ruler over this Infernal bridewell*, dwelling, no doubt, in a castle or 'arx' in the neighbourhood, just as we have seen (Comm.

En. I. 56) that Eolus, the ruler of the 'carcer' of the winds, did not reside amongst his prisoners, but ruled them from his castle or 'arx' in the vicinity.

Any doubt, which may have lingered in the reader's mind of the correctness of the opinion expressed in the Comment just referred to, viz. that the 'arx' of Eolus was outside the 'carcer' of the winds, will probably vanish on his observing the parallelism between the two rulers and the two 'carceres':

— "Hic vasto rex Aeolus antro
Luctantes ventos tempestatesque sonoras
Imperio premit, ac vinclis et carcere frenat."
En. I. 56

GNOSIUS HAEC RHADAMANTHUS HABET DURISSIMA REGNA,
CASTIGATQUE AUDITQUE DOLOS &c.

574.

CERNIS CUSTODIA QUALIS
VESTIBULO SEDEAT FACIES QUAE LIMINA SERVET
QUINQUAGINTA ATRIS IMMANIS HIATIBUS HYDRA
SAEVIOR INTUS HABET SEDEM TUM TARTARUS IPSE
BIS PATET IN PRAECEPS TANTUM TENDITQUE SUB UMBRAS
QUANTUS AD AETHERIUM CAELI SUSPECTUS OLYMPUM

Nothing can be worse or more prosaic than the new elucidation of this passage proposed by Süpfle, and adopted by Ladewig; viz. that the line QUINQUAGINTA.... HYDRA is the answer to the question CERNIS .... SERVET, that a new sentence begins at SAEVIOR, and that Virgil represents the gate of Tartarus as watched outside by one Hydra and inside by another. No; the CUSTODIA which sits in the vestibule, the FACIES which watches the door, is the 'ultrix Tisiphone' herself, in her bloody 'palla', and armed with her snaky lash (see *vv. 555, 570:* also Comm. *v. 563; IV 471):* and the *Steigerung* the three degrees of horror are: outside, Tisiphone; inside, the enormous Hydra gaping with its fifty gullets; and, immediately beyond, the abyss of Tartarus itself, TARTARUS *IPSE*

618.

PHLEGYASQUE MISERRIMUS OMNES
ADMONET ET MAGNA TESTATUR VOCE PER UMBRAS

Dante also has his Phlegyas, calling too, though in a somewhat different manner:

"Corda non pinse mai da se saetta,
Che si corresse via per l'aere snella,
Com' i' vidi una nave piccioletta
Venir per l'acqua verso noi in quella,
Sotto 'l governo d'un sol galeoto,
Che gridava: 'or se' giunta, anima fella?'
'Flegiàs, Flegiàs, tu gridi a voto,'
Disse lo mio signore, 'a questa volta:
Più non ci avrai, se non passando il loto.'"
Inferno, VIII. 13.

620.

DISCITE JUSTITIAM MONITI ET NON TEMNERE DIVOS

"Lernet gewarnt recht thun, und nicht missachten die Götter."
Voss.

— "Il retto
Imparate a conoscere per prova,
E a riverir gli Dei."
ALFIERI.

This, like most literal translations, does not give the real meaning of the passage, which is not *Be just in your dealings with men, and respectful toward the Gods,* but *Be just in your dealings with men, and do not sup-*

pose that ye can with impunity disobey the command of the Gods to that effect, viz. the command to be just; the only virtue enjoined by the line being that of justice. The meaning of the passage once understood, we see the propriety of the expression NON TEMNERE: *set not at naught the divine commandment to be just.* Compare *En. I. 546,* where Ilioneus having demanded justice of Dido — having required her to deal with him and the Trojans according to the immutable principles of justice — reminds her of the sanction of the Gods, and warns her not to despise that sanction; 'non temnere Divos':

"Si genus humanum et mortalia temnitis arma,
At sperate deos memores fandi atque nefandi."

Also Apollon. Rhod. IV. 1098, where Alcinous expresses almost in the very terms of our text his fear of the divine retribution if he should be guilty of an act of injustice:

"*Αρητη, και κεν συν τευχεσιν εξελασαιμι*
Κολχους, ηρωεσσι φερων χαριν, εινεκα κουρης.
Αλλα Διος δειδοικα δικην ιθειαν ατισσαι."

Compare also (above, vers: 565):

"Ipsa deum poenas docuit, perque omnia duxit.
Gnosius haec Rhadamanthus habet durissima regna,
Castigatque auditque dolos, subigitque fateri,
Quae quis apud superos, furto laetatus inani,
Distulit in seram commissa piacula mortem;"

where precisely the same doctrine is conveyed in somewhat different terms, 'furto laetatus inani' informing us that, however we may contemn human retribution, whatever success we may have in escaping punishment among men ('apud superos'), the retribution of the Gods is 'non contemnenda'; we shall certainly have to undergo after death the 'poenas deum', for not having hearkened in time to the divine precept *Be just.*

The above interpretation is fully confirmed by the position of our text, viz. in the middle, as it were, of an assize calendar of culprits, who have violated the laws, sinned against the eternal principles of justice, and so have drawn down upon themselves the threatened vengeance of the Gods. In the very middle of such a calendar stands our text, on one side "Hic quibus invisi fratres" &c., on the other "Vendidit hic auro patriam" &c.

I do not flatter myself that the right understanding of its meaning will tend to increase the admiration in which this famous text has been so long held. The extreme of human admiration is generally bestowed on objects which are either not at all or only half understood. See last three lines of Comment *En. II. 521.*

648.

HIC GENUS ANTIQUUM TEUCRI PULCHERRIMA PROLES

That the structure is 'genus Teucri', not 'proles Teucri', is shown by the point placed after TEUCRI in the Medicean, and still more by the parallel:

"Hic genus antiquum Terrae, Titania pubes."

vers. 580.

658.

INTER ODORATUM LAURI NEMUS UNDE SUPERNE
PLURIMUS ERIDANI PER SILVAM VOLVITUR AMNIS

"Eridanus SUPERNE, h. e. *ex editiore loco,* VOLVITUR, *venit.*" Heyne.

— "Wo von der Höhe
Vollgedrängt durch den Wald des Eridanus Strom sich herabwälzt."

Voss.

"SUPERNE zeigt an, dass der Lorbeerhain auf einem Bergabhange liegt." Süpfle.
"Der Lorbeerhain lag also auf einem Bergabhange." Ladewig.
"SUPERNE, *ex altiore loco.* Lauri nemus igitur in colli leviter edito quaerendum." Forbiger.

No; as 'inferne', the adverbial form of the adjective 'infernus', is never *from below upwards,* but always simply *below, at the under part,* so 'superne', the adverbial form of the adjective 'supernus', is never *from above downwards,* but always *aloft, above, at the upper part.* Compare:

— "Ut turpiter atrum
Desinat in piscem mulier formosa superne."
HOR. *Epist. ad Pis. 3.*

— "Album mutor in alitem
Superne."
HOR. *Carm. II. 20. 10.*

"Argentum superne innatat, ut oleum aquis." PLIN. *H. N. XXXIII. 6.*
In loose writing indeed 'superne' can mean *'sursum',* as our own aloft can mean *upwards:* "Solum enim hoc genus superne tendit, non, ut cetera, in terram." PLIN. *H. N. XIX. 5;* but I am not acquainted with even so much as one single instance in which it bears the sense assigned to it in our text not only by all the commentators, but by all the lexicographers.

SUPERNE rightly understood, the true interpretation of the passage follows as a matter of course: UNDE, *from which laurel grove,* i. e. rising or taking its spring out of which laurel grove, *the Eridanus rolls,* PLURIMUS, *in a great body of water,* PER SILVAM, *through the wood,* SUPERNE, *above in the world* ("ad superos" — Servius). Or shortly and simply (PLURIMUS PER SILVAM VOLVITUR being merely a description of Eridanus as it was known above in the world) *the laurel grove where Eridanus (that mighty Italian river) has its spring.*

Thus we have an explanation at once simple and in perfect conformity with the cosmology of the ancients:

> "Multaque sub tergo terraï flumina tecta
> Volvere vi fluctus, submersaque saxa putandum est."
>
> LUCRET. VI. 540;

and especially of Virgil himself, who informs us that Aristeus, when he descended under ground, saw the sources of many of the great rivers of the world, and amongst others that of this very Eridanus:

> "Omnia sub magna labentia flumina terra
> Spectabat diversa locis, Phasimque Lycumque,
> Et caput, unde altus primum se erumpit Enipeus,
> Unde pater Tiberinus, et unde Aniena fluenta,
> Saxosusque sonans Hypanis, Mysusque Caicus,
> Et gemina auratus taurino cornua vultu
> Eridanus, quo non alius per pinguia culta
> In mare purpureum violentior effluit amnis."
>
> *Georg. IV. 366;*

where observe the exact parallelism to our text: The Eridanus rises deep *under ground,* 'sub magna terra', and then, *above ground,* flows 'quo non alius violentior per pinguia culta in mare purpureum'; and: *The Eridanus rises in a laurel grove in the underworld, and then* SUPERNE, *above ground, in the world above,* PLURIMUS PER SILVAM VOLVITUR. Who can doubt that the two views are of one and the same object, seen only under different lights?

677.

CAMPOSQUE NITENTES

Literally *sleek and glossy* (as cattle from good feeding and caring, vers. 654); the opposite of 'horridus' There is no corresponding term applicable to land in in the English language.

687.

VENISTI TANDEM TUAQUE EXSPECTATA PARENTI
VICIT ITER DURUM PIETAS

To the arguments advanced by Wagner against the reading of the two Heinsii and Burmann, as well as of most printed editions, 'spectata', and in favor of the reading of the great majority of MSS. EXSPECTATA, I may add that I have found that reading in two of the only three MSS. which I have myself personally examined respecting the passage, viz. in both the Leipzig. In the third MS. which I have examined, viz. the Dresden, the reading is 'exoptata'. I find also EXSPECTATA in the Modena Edition of 1475, in Bersmann, the Paris Ed. of 1600, and both the Stephenses. In the Dresden copy of Henry Stephens EXSPECTATA has been altered into 'spectata' by the hand of Taubmann, to whom the book formerly belonged. Pierius having taken no notice of the passage, and EXSPECTATA being the undoubted reading of the Vatican Fragment (see Bottari), it may be presumed almost to a certainty that Pierius found that reading in all the MSS examined by him.

727.

MAGNO SE CORPORE MISCET

"Per totum mundum didita est anima mundi." Heyne.

That the words MAGNO CORPORE mean, not the 'mundus', universe, or *Weltall*, but simply the *Earth*, is shown, not merely by the use of the term in the *Pervigilium Veneris, 55*:

"In sinum maritus imber fluxit almae conjugis,
Unde fetus aleret omnes mixta magno corpore;"

but by our author's own use of it, *Georg. II. 325:*

"Tum pater omnipotens fecundis imbribus Aether
Conjugis in gremium laetae descendit, et omnes
Magnus alit, magno commixtus corpore, fetus."

733.

HINC METUUNT CUPIUNTQUE DOLENT GAUDENTQUE NEQUE AURAS RESPICIUNT CLAUSAE TENEBRIS ET CARCERE CAECO

---

§ I.

AURAS. — "Lucem." Heyne. Wagner.

The reader, who, taking the trouble to cast his eye over the Heynian Index, shall have observed that in no one of the other ninety four instances in which it has been used by Virgil, does the word 'aurae' bear the meaning of 'lux', will hardly require to be informed by me how little likely it is that 'lux' should be the correct interpretation of AURAE in the passage before us. From the slightest examination of those ninety four instances it is perfectly clear that (omitting the metaphorical "Populares aurae" of *En. VI. 817)* Virgil never uses the word 'aurae' except in one or other of the two following senses, or, to speak more accurately, in one or other of the two following varieties of the same general sense; either, first, to express those *airs* which we feel blowing upon us, the gentler currents of that atmosphere by which we are immediately surrounded; or, secondly, those remoter parts of the same atmosphere, which, high above our heads, and beyond our reach or touch, and made known to us only by our sense of sight, we denominate *the sky*. In the former of these senses the word is to be understood in all such expressions as the following: "Crebrescunt optatae aurae," *En. III. 530;* "Vocat carbasus auras," *En. IV. 417;* "Zephyri tepentibus auris," *Georg. II. 330;* &c. &c. Examples of its use in the latter sense are: "Omnia ferre sub auras," *En. II. 158;* "Furit aestus ad auras," *En.. II. 759;* "Sub auras erigit fluctus," *En. III. 422;* "Saxa sub auras glomerat," *En. III. 576;* "Assurgere in auras," *Georg. III. 109,* "Auras suspiciens," *En. X. 898.* Often, but by no means always, when 'aurae' is used in this second sense, an adjective is added in order to give force and clearness: "Auras aetherias," *Georg. II. 291;* "Superas auras," *En. V. 427;* "Aerias auras," *En. V. 520,* not, surely, *aerial air*, or *aerial light,* but *aerial sky.* It is in this, its second, sense, that AURAE is used in the passage before us. The souls, shut up in the dark prison of the body, lose their fine perception, become brutalized, and cease to look back to, or have any regard for, their celestial origin, the 'caelum', sky, or 'aurae' ('superae aurae'), from whence they originally came. The German *Luft* (whence our English *lift,* the sky) corresponds to the Latin 'aurae', not merely in the first of these significations, but, as appears from the following example, in the second also:

"Es dünkte ihm, als schaut' er unsern Erdball
Gleich einer ungeheuren grünen Kugel,
Die zwischen Meer und Luft gehänget war."
WERNER, *Die Söhne des Thales, Theil II. Prolog.*

This double Virgilian use of the word 'aurae' once clearly established, we immediately perceive the true meaning of that generally misunderstood passage in the first Eclogue *(v. 57),* "Canet frondator ad auras; not *will sing to the air,* which were as much as to say, *will sing to no purpose, will throw away his song* (see "partem volucres dispersit in auras," *En. XI. 795;* where 'volucres' is added to show that 'auras is used in the former of the two senses given above), but *will sing to the sky, his only company — will sing alone,* or, as correctly rendered by Fea, *da se.*

§ II.

RESPICIUNT, the reading of the Palatine (Heyne) and recognised by Donatus (ad Terent. *Andr. V. 4. 34)*, is to be found in almost all the old editions, and has been found by myself in Fabricius, Bersmann, both the Stephenses, the Paris Edition of 1600, La Cerda, and Daniel Heinsius. For this reading N. Heinsius has substituted 'Dispiciunt'; and this substitution, of which Heyne says "'Dispiciunt praeclare Heins. restituit," has been adopted by most modern editors. I object to it, first, that the word 'dispicere' is not elsewhere to be found in Virgil. Secondly, that the memorandum I have of the reading of the Gudian (the principal foundation of Heinsius's substitution) is to the following effect: "RESPICIUNT; but the reading seems to have been originally 'despiciunt' and to have been altered into RESPICIUNT." Heinsius therefore, if my memorandum be correct, made his emendation neither from the present reading of the MS. nor from that which appeared to me, on personal examination, to have been the original reading. Thirdly, that the meaning afforded by 'dispiciunt ("proprie dicitur de iis, qui caeci fuerant, aut in tenebris versantes primum vident lucem" — Wagner) is inappropriate, the (as I think) plain drift and intention of Virgil, as shown by the whole context, being to say, not *cannot distinctly see (distinguish),* but *do not care to see, have acquired a disinclination to see;* precisely the meaning contained in the vulgar reading RESPICIUNT, rejected by N. Heinsius: NEQUE AURAS RESPICIUNT, *no longer look towards*, or *care for, those 'aurae', that sky* (see § I. above), *from which they originally came.* Compare, *En. IV. 236:*

"Nec prolem Ausoniam et Lavinia respicit arva."

I have myself examined, besides the Gudian, only three other MSS. respecting this passage, viz. the Leipzig No. 35, the Leipzig No. 36, and the Dresden; in the first alone I have found 'dispiciunt', in the second and third 'despiciunt. In Pierius I find: "In antiquis omnibus codicibus quos viderim, eodem exemplo legitur, 'neque auras despiciunt'; alicubi etiam RESPICIUNT habetur." Still further, 'despiciunt' (not 'dispiciunt') is the reading, as appears from Foggini, of the Medicean, and, as appears from Bottari, of the Vatican Fragment. In the Modena Edition of 1475 I find 'Suspiciunt', which (see Maittaire) is also the reading of the Milan Ed. of 1474.

737.

PENITUSQUE NECESSE EST
MULTA DIU CONCRETA MODIS INOLESCERE MIRIS

I reject Fea's conjecture, 'abolescere', and adhere to the vulgar reading and interpretation; first, because of the excellent sense thus obtained; secondly, because both reading and interpretation are confirmed both by Claudian in his account of the condemnation of the shade of Rufinus by Rhadamanthus:

— "En, pectus inustae
Deformant maculae vitiisque inolevit imago."
In Rufinum, II. 504;

and by Silius (VIII. 582):

"Nunc Silarus quos nutrit aquis, quo gurgite tradunt
Duritiem lapidum mersis inolescere ramis."

Thirdly, because neither Pierius nor N. Heinsius gives us even a hint of his having found any other reading; and fourthly, because in the only five MSS. I have myself personally examined, viz. the Petrarchian, Kloster-Neuburg, Dresden, and two Leipzig, I have found INOLESCERE. The 'mollescere' of the Casanata MS. quoted by Fea has evidently arisen from the IN of INOLESCERE being mistaken for M; I find the same error in the Modena Ed. of 1475.

739.

ERGO EXERCENTUR POENIS VETERUMQUE MALORUM
SUPPLICIA EXPENDUNT ALIAE PANDUNTUR INANES
SUSPENSAE AD VENTOS ALIIS SUB GURGITE VASTO
INFECTUM ELUITUR SCELUS AUT EXURITUR IGNI
QUISQUE SUOS PATIMUR MANES EXINDE PER AMPLUM
MITTIMUR ELYSIUM ET PAUCI LAETA ARVA TENEMUS
DONEC LONGA DIES PERFECTO TEMPORIS ORBE
CONCRETAM EXEMIT LABEM PURUMQUE RELINQUIT
AETHERIUM SENSUM ATQUE AURAI SIMPLICIS IGNEM

The insuperable difficulties which the commentators have found in this passage (and for a detailed account of which see Heyne and Forbiger ad loc.) have arisen, as it appears to me, principally from their having read the whole passage *uno tenore,* and not perceived that the two lines from QUISQUE as far as TENEMUS are intercalatory, inserted for the purpose of explaining, on the spot and in the very middle of the sentence, a difficulty which has just presented itself, and the explanation of which would have been deferred by any other writer till the sentence had been completed. The difficulty is this; if the souls of the dead required such purification, how did it happen that not only Anchises himself, but the other Trojan heroes, dead so short time, were already in possession of Elysium? This difficulty is explained in the two parenthetic lines QUISQUE . . . . TENEMUS: *As there are different degrees of impurity among men, so there are different degrees of purification required after death; the more pure requiring a less, the less pure a greater, degree; therefore you see me and your other Trojan friends here in Elysium already.* This explanation given, the account of the purification, broken off at EXURITUR IGNI, is resumed in the words DONEC LONGA DIES &c.; *the purification by water, air, or fire, goes on until such time as the earthly stains are thoroughly purged out &c.* We have thus not only a happy reconciliation of the two, at first sight discordant and contradictory, facts (the necessity of the purgation described in the preceding verses, and the actual presence of Anchises and the other Trojan heroes, so soon after their deaths, in the Elysian fields), but we have the sentence constructed after Virgil's usual manner (see Comments *En. I. 4; III. 317, 571; IV. 483; V. 522 (§ II)* and *659; VI. 83);* and still further, we get rid of the palpable absurdity of the doctrine embraced by Fea and Thiel, and indeed necessarily flowing from the conjunction of DONEC with the immediately preceding clause, viz. that Elysium served the purpose of a second Purgatory. The intercalatory nature of the two lines in question, even if such intercalation had not been according to Virgil's usual habit, is rendered sufficiently clear by the sudden introduction of the first person with those lines, the carrying on of that person through them, and the sudden dropping of it at their termination. A further proof, if further proof were wanting, of the entirely intercalatory nature of these lines, is unwittingly supplied by the commentators themselves, some of whom (Heyne, for instance) think that the text would be better without them, and others of whom (Brunck, for instance) actually remove them out of their position in order to place them after vers. 747. The genius of modern languages not permitting so considerable a parenthesis in the middle of a sentence, I have found it absolutely necessary in my translation of the passage (see, among my poems, *Six Photographs of the Heroic Times)* to adopt with respect to the English, the plan which Brunck has thought it necessary to adopt with respect to the Latin, and transferring the parenthetic lines to the end of the sentence, embody them with the context.

INANES. — "Ein gewöhnliches Beiwort des Windes." Ladewig; and so, as appears from their citations, it has been understood both by Wagner *(Virg. Br. En.)* and Forbiger. I disagree, and, referring the epithet to ALIAE, understand the sense to be, *are hung up* INANES, *to the winds*, i. e. *are hung up for the winds to blow through their unsubstantial forms.*

PANDUNTUR SUSPENSAE AD VENTOS. — La Cerda's arguments convince me of the correctness of his shrewd guess that these words are periphrastic of crucifixion.

763.

SILVIUS ALBANUM NOMEN TUA POSTUMA PROLES
QUEM TIBI LONGAEVO SERUM LAVINIA CONJUX
EDUCET SILVIS REGEM REGUMQUE PARENTEM

Begotten in your old age (LONGAEVO), *and therefore too late* (SERUM), *and born after your death* (POSTUMA).

780.

VIDEN UT GEMINAE STANT VERTICE CRISTAE
ET PATER IPSE SUO SUPERUM JAM SIGNAT HONORE

Anchises points out Romulus already wearing the double-crested helmet (GEMINAE VERTICE CRISTAE), the honor or mark of distinction (HONORE) which he is to wear in the upper world, i. e. on earth (SUPERUM), and with which honor he is already (JAM) stamped (SIGNAT) by the Father himself (IPSE PATER), i. e. Jupiter. The two clauses thus form one connected thought, the second clause being explanatory of the first.

PATER IPSE — not (with Servius) *Mars*, but, as Virgil's 'Pater ipse' always is when without adjunct, *Jupiter:*

"Ipse pater, media nimborum in nocte, corusca
Fulmina molitur dextra."

Georg. I. 328.

"Ipse pater statuit, quid monstrua luna moneret."

Georg. I. 353.

"Ipse pater Danais animos viresque secundas
Sufficit."

En. II. 617.

SUPERUM — is not, with Donatus, La Cerda, Voss, Heyne, and Forbiger, the abbreviation for superorum', and dependent on IPSE PATER; first, because it is distinctly separated from IPSE PATER by the intervening suo; and secondly, because SIGNAT requires it for object. It is the accusative of the adjective 'superus', and means, not (with Servius) *'deum'*; but *in the upper world,* i. e. (the speaker being in the under-world) *on earth, become a man, an inhabitant of earth.*

HONORE — is not (with Wagner) "ea dignitate oris. quae in ipso Jove exsplendescit;" first, because Virgil had too good taste to pay Romulus an extravagant compliment, wholly unwarranted even by any tradition that Romulus's personal appearance was of such extraordinary dignity; and secondly, because the term 'signare' points plainly, not to any general dignity of the whole appearance, but to some special mark or stamp, and what special mark or stamp more probable than that just mentioned, the GEMINAE CRISTAE, by which periphrasis the poet has, for the sake of greater effect, thought proper to designate the helmet always worn by Romulus: "ipsa galea perpetuum, quantum memini, Romuli insigne." Heyne Compare the application of this very term 'honos , to the purple crest on the crown of the head of Minos,

"Tum qua se medium capitis discrimen agebat,
Ecce repente, velut patrios imitatus honores,
Puniceam concussit apex in vertice cristam."

Ciris, 498;

and for proof that it was as perfectly consistent with religious etiquette among the ancients, as the 'Rex Dei gratia witnesses it to be among the moderns, to represent human and earthly honors as special gifts of the supreme Deity, compare the exactly parallel

"Quem pater ipse deum sceptri donavit honore."

Ciris, 268.

I think it probable, though I am not in a condition categorically to prove the facts, first, that a double-crested helmet was an ensign, or peculiar equipment, of Mars; compare Valer. Maximus, I. 6: "Cognitum pariter atque creditum est, Martem patrem tunc populo suo adfuisse. Inter caetera hujusce rei manifesta indicia galea quoque duabus distincta pinnis, qua caeleste caput tectum fuerat, argumentum praebuit." And secondly, that Romulus, as his son, wore a similar helmet; whence a peculiar propriety in the term 'Mavortius', vers. 778.

782.

EN HUJUS NATE AUSPICIIS ILLA INCLYTA ROMA
IMPERIUM TERRIS ANIMOS AEQUABIT OLYMPO
SEPTEMQUE UNA SIBI MURO CIRCUMDABIT ARCES
FELIX PROLE VIRUM QUALIS BERECYNTIA MATER
INVEHITUR CURRU PHRYGIAS TURRITA PER URBES
LAETA DEUM PARTU CENTUM COMPLEXA NEPOTES
OMNES CAELICOLAS OMNES SUPERA ALTA TENENTES

Byron, in one of the happiest of his passages, gives us the reverse of this fine simile; also applied to Rome:

"O Rome! my country! city of the soul!
The orphans of the heart must turn to thee,
Lone mother of dead empires! and control
In their shut breasts their petty misery.
. . . .
. . . .
The Niobe of nations! there she stands
Childless and crownless, in her voiceless woe;
An empty urn within her withered hands,
Whose holy dust was scattered long ago."

Childe Harold's Pilgrim. IV. 78 & 79.

Pity, that Lord Byron was not equal to sustain this unusually fine image. The very next line spoils it all by the confusion which it makes between the real urn of which it speaks and the figurative urn of the lines immediately preceding:

"The Scipios' tomb contains no ashes now;
The very sepulcres lie tenantless
Of their heroic dwellers: dost thou flow,
Old Tyber, through a marble wilderness?
Rise, with thy yellow waves, and mantle her distress!"

otherwise the comparison of Rome, in her present desolate state, to Niobe, is quite equal to Virgil's comparison of her, in her palmy state, to Cybele. His previous comparison (Stanza 2 of same Canto) of Venice to the turret-crowned Cybele is one of a different kind:

"She looks a sea Cybele, fresh from ocean,
Rising with her tiara of proud towers
At airy distance with majestic motion,
A ruler of the waters and their powers:
And such she was: — her daughters had their dowers
From spoils of nations, and the exhaustless East
Poured in her lap all gems in sparkling showers:
In purple was she robed, and of her feast
Monarchs partook, and deemed their dignity increased;"

the resemblance in the case of this comparison being only between the domes of Venice and the turret crown of the Goddess, and not extending, as in the case of Virgil's, to the children of the Goddess and the nations affiliated to the city. Byron's idea was borrowed, as he himself informs us, from Sabellicus *de Venetae Urbis situ narratio* (Taur. 1527), *Lib I. fol. 202*: "Quo fit, ut, qui superne urbem contempletur, turritam telluris imaginem medio oceano figuratam se putet inspicere."

811.

PRIMAM QUI LEGIBUS URBEM
FUNDABIT

"Primum dare leges urbi." Wagner.

I think, rather 'qui per leges Romam reddet urbem; qui aedificabit urbem supra legibus quasi supra fundamento'; *who will by means of laws make, as it were, a new city;* compare Justin, II. 7: "Sed civitati (Athenis sciz.) nullae tunc leges erant; quia libido regum pro legibus habebatur. Legitur itaque Solon .... qui velut novam civitatem legibus conderet." Wagner has however, I think, done well in rejecting Heyne's reading 'primus' and substituting PRIMAM; to his arguments in favor of which reading I can add that I have found it in the three only MSS. which I have myself personally examined respecting the passage, viz. the two Leipzig and the Dresden; also that Bersmann informs us that it is the reading of his MS.

The passage seems to have been present to the recollection of Calpurnius, when he wrote the following lines *(Eclog. I. 65):*

"Altera regna Numae, qui primus ovantia caede
Agmina, Romuleis et adhuc ardentia castris
Pacis opus docuit, jussitque silentibus armis
Inter sacra tubas, non inter bella, sonare."

813.

CUI DEINDE SUBIBIT
OTIA QUI RUMPET PATRIAE RESIDESQUE MOVEBIT
TULLUS IN ARMA VIROS ET JAM DESUETA TRIUMPHIS
AGMINA.

Observe the fine effect, first, of the postponement of the name until after the introductory CUI ..... MOVEBIT, and then of its position in the beginning of the new line and in close connexion with IN ARMA. You almost see Tullus calling out the soldiers, you almost hear their rallying cry — "Tullus! Tullus!" See Comm. *En. II. 246.*

817.

POPULARIBUS AURIS

"Quem neque periculi tempestas neque honoris aura potuit . . . . de suo cursu . . . . demovere." CIC. *Sext. 47. extr.*

844.

PARVOQUE POTENTEM

FABRICIUM

"*Reich in der Armuth.* Bezeichnung des Genügsamen." Ladewig.
"Qui etiam in parva re domestica ob parsimoniam et continentiam dives est." Forbiger.

I have no doubt however that the true meaning is *powerful on a little; possessed of small means but great power.* This meaning is not only stronger, but harmonises better both with the history of Fabricius, and the peculiar force of the word 'potens', which, like our English *powerful,* expresses, not what the person is in himself, or absolutely considered, but what he is in relation to others. Compare *(En. I. 668):* "Mea magna potentia;" *by means of whom I am able to command the world.* "Hoc maxime convenire in Alcibiadem videbatur, quod et potentior et major, quam privatus, existimabatur: multos enim liberalitate devinxerat, plures etiam opera forensi suos reddiderat." Nep. *Alcib. III. 4;* where see Bremi's Annot.

"Habet bene ac pudice eductam, ignaram artis meretriciae.
Mea est potens, procax, magnifica, sumptuosa, nobilis."
Ter. *Heaut. II. 1. 14:*

where Perlet: "Potens, *amatori imperans.*" Also

"Sic te Diva potens Cypri."
Hor. *Od. I. 3. 1;*

and *En. I. 84.*

850.

CAELIQUE MEATUS
DESCRIBENT RADIO ET SURGENTIA SIDERA DICENT

"Caeli meatus, h. e. siderum cursus." Heyne.

I think not, the stars being specifically mentioned in the next line; but the 'Circuli', or *great heavenly Circles,* thus enumerated by Germanicus Caesar in his *Aratea:* "Lacteus, Tropicus Cancri, Tropicus Capricorni, Aequinoctialis, Zodiacus." That these Circles are the meatus caeli of Virgil, is further rendered probable, first, by the remarkable circumstance that Germ. Caesar, after the description of these Circles, passes immediately to the description of the 'orientia et occidentia' ('sidera'), just as in our text Virgil passes from the caeli meatus to the surgentia sidera; secondly, by the fact that one of these 'Circuli' (viz. Zodiacus) is actually denominated by the same Germanicus, 'via solis':

"Una via est solis bissenis lucida signis."
Fragm. III. 1;

and thirdly, by the application of the term 're-meare by the same author to the annual re-turn of the sun to that point in his circle, from whence he had set out:

— "Namque anno solem remeare videbis,
Moverit unde suos currus per signa volantes."
Fragm. III.

Compare Apoll. Rhod. of the Circles on the armillary sphere:

"Χρυσεια μεν οι κυκλα τετευχαται."

Argon. III. 137.

853.

PACISQUE IMPONERE MOREM

"Pacis praeferrem, cujus mos est, ut stipendia et tributa imponantur victis gentibus et provinciis et ita pax concilietur, liberatis ab regio et alieno jure." Burmann. "Leges pacis ponere, ferre, ut Aen. I. 264 (268): 'moresque viris et moenia ponet'." Heyne, *V. L.*

The former of these interpretations is wholly erroneous; the latter an approach, a distant approach to the truth; a pale, meagre shadow of the strong and manly original. 'Imponere' is not 'ponere, ferre', nor does the sentence correspond to "moresque viris et moenia ponet." And first, 'imponere' is not 'ponere, ferre', because it is always and invariably *to IM-pose, to place* or *set one thing over another thing;* and generally in such a manner that the former commands the latter, dominates. So

— "Has leges aeternaque foedera certis
Imposuit Natura locis."

Georg. I. 60.

— "Dominumque potentem
Imposuit."

En. VI. 621.

— "Imponent montibus arces."

En. VI. 774.

"Quodque virum toti properans imponere mundo."

LUCAN. III. 393.

"Quibus rebus effectum est, ut .... Philippus ...... regnum Macedoniae. Graeciae et Asiae cervicibus, velut jugum servitutis, imponeret." JUSTIN. VI. 9. And so in the passage before us, *impose* MOREM PACIS *upon the conquered nations* ('debellatis populis'); *set* MOREM PACIS ('velut jugum') *upon them;* in plain prose, *compel them to cultivate the arts of peace.* Secondly, the words quoted by Heyne from the first Book, "moresque viris et moenia ponet," are not parallel; *(a)* because 'mores in that context may, and most probably does, comprehend 'mores belli' (compare "Mos erat Hesperio in Latio" &c. *En. VII. 601)* as well as 'mores pacis'; i. e. means *the entire manners of the nation; (b)* because those 'mores' were not imposed upon conquered nations, but laid down for his own people, and therefore *(c)* use made, not of the strong '*imponere*', implying *compulsion,* but of 'ponere', a term so mild as to be equally applicable to 'mores' and 'moenia'.

The Italians preserve in their *imporre* the Latin term in its original sense: "Sul quale (sciz. séggio) è assiso il Pàpa in contegnó composto insieme di dignità e di bontà in atto di stendere il braccio destro, e nella mossa d'imporre, consigliare, e proteggere; azione che il Milizia nelle sue lettere paragona a quella maestosa del Marco Aurelio." NIBBY, *Roma Moderna, Part. I. p. 116.*

In the three only MSS. which I have myself personally examined, viz. the Leipzig 35, the Leipzig 36, and the Dresden, I have found PACIS, the s being however in the first mentioned a correction. PACIS is also, as we are informed by Maittaire, the reading of the Venice Ed. of 1472, and has been adopted by Daniel Heinsius, Robert Stephens, and Burmann. On the contrary, the Modena Ed. of 1475, Henry Stephens, N. Heinsius and Bersmann have 'paci'; the latter however informing us that his MS. has PACIS. Pierius says: "'Pacique imponere morem'. In Longobardico et quibusdam aliis codicibus vetustis PACIS legitur,....

quam lectionem Servius agnoscit." All which considered, PACIS seems to me, notwithstanding the contrary authority of the by far too much esteemed Medicean, to be undoubtedly the true reading.

Between our text so read and understood, and the

"Romanos rerum dominos gentemque togatam"

of the first Book, there is an exact parallelism, the fundamental idea of both passages being that of the Romans commanding the whole world *in peace*. See Comment *En. I. 283*.

858.

HIC REM ROMANAM MAGNO TURBANTE TUMULTU
SISTET EQUES STERNET POENOS GALLUMQUE REBELLEM

Heyne's two Comments, "EQUES, ad majorem dignitatem pro *bellator, dux*." . . . . "Alii distinguunt post SISTET EQUES; nil refert," and Voss's translation,

"Der wird das Römische Heil in dem Sturm des grossen Tumultes
Halten zu Ross, und den Poener zerstreun" &c.,

not only show how little those scholars understood the passage, but make nonsense of it; EQUES belongs to STERNET only, and with it expresses the compound idea *ride over*. Compare (PROP. IV. 3. 38) "currat eques," *ride;* and see Comm. *En. II. 199*. *Marcellus*, EQUES STERNET POENOS, *will tread the enemy under his horse's hoofs, and, by so doing,* SISTET REM ROMANAM, *firmly re-establish the tottering Roman State.* SISTET is opposed to STERNET, and is rendered emphatic by its position, viz. in the beginning of the line and followed by a sudden pause; see Comm. *En. II. 246*.

866.

QUIS STREPITUS CIRCA COMITUM QUANTUM INSTAR IN IPSO

There are two opinions concerning the meaning of INSTAR in this passage:
First, that of Servius, which has been adopted by Pomponius Sabinus, Wagner, Forbiger, and Voss: "INSTAR; Similitudo." Servius. "QUANTUM INSTAR; quanta similitudo." Sabinus. "INSTAR, similitudo cum illo ipso Claudio Marcello quinquies Consule." Wagner *(V. Br. En.);* and to the same effect, Forbiger and Voss.
The other, that of Donatus, adopted by Heyne: "Placet mihi instar ejus, h. e. corporis forma; sed cur tenebrae caput ejus fuscaverint, nosse cupio." Donatus. "Verisimile fit, nove h. l. INSTAR positum esse pro exemplo magnae dignitatis, specie augusta corporis." Heyne.

I am hardy enough not only to disagree with both opinions, but to think that 'instar' never has either of the two meanings thus assigned to it, but always and in every instance, the one, single meaning, *amount:*

> "Instar montis equum."
>
> *En. II. 15;*

not, *a horse like a mountain,* but *a horse the amount of a mountain,* i. e. *equal to — equivalent to — a mountain.*

> "Insulsissimus est homo, nec sapit pueri instar
> Bimuli."
>
> CATULL. XVII. 12;

not *like a two-year-old child,* but *the amount of a two-year-old child; as much as a two-year-old child; equal to — equivalent to — a two-year-old child.*

> "Hastaque terribili surgens per nubila gyro
> Instar habet silvae."
>
> CLAUD. *Rapt. Pros. II. 24;*

not *like a wood,* but *the amount of a wood; equi-*

valent to a wood, or, as is vulgarly said in English, *as good as a wood.*

"Cujus (equi sciz.) instar pro aede Veneris Genitricis postea dedicavit." SUETON. *Jul. Caes. 61;* i. e. *a statue,* not merely *like* or *of the same form,* but *of the same size, as the horse; a counterpart of the horse.*

"Sed scelus hoc meriti pondus et instar habet."
OVID. *Heroid. II. 30;*

not *a crime like a merit,* but *a crime which counts as a merit, which has the weight and value (amount, 'Werth', 'Gehalt') of a merit.*

"Cujus viri magnitudo multorum voluminum instar exigit." VELL. PATERC. II. 29; *requires,* not *the likeness of many volumes,* but *the amount of many volumes.*

"Ambitus terrae totius, quae nobis videtur immensa, ad magnitudinem universitatis instar brevis obtinet puncti." AMMIAN. XV. 1.

The precise meaning of 'instar' in the last of which passages, and, by consequence, in all the others (viz. that it signifies simply *amount)* seems to me to be placed beyond doubt by Macrobius's "Physici terram ad magnitudinem circi, per quem volvitur sol, puncti modum obtinere docuere." *Somn. Scip. I. 16;* the meaning remaining unaltered in Ammian, if you substitute 'modum' for 'instar', and in Macrobius, if you substitute 'instar' for 'modum'. And such precisely is the meaning of INSTAR in our text: QUANTUM INSTAR IN IPSO, *what an amount in himself! how much in him!*

The error into which lexicographers and commentators have fallen, of understanding 'instar' to mean *'similitudo',* has, I think, plainly arisen from the accidental circumstance that generally to the word 'instar *(amount)* was added (as in all the above cited examples) a genitive expressive of the *greatness* of the amount; such form of expression not being usual in modern languages, expositors fell naturally into the error of understanding 'instar' to mean, not *the absolute amount* (German *Gehalt) of the object spoken of,* but *its similitude* or *proportion to some other object.* On the contrary, and as I think the above quoted examples sufficiently show, 'instar' is always and in itself *the absolute amount, 'Gehalt', 'modus', of the object spoken of,* and is totally devoid of comparative force, unless when, as in the above cited examples, an object (in the genitive) is placed beside it, with which to compare the 'instar' of the subject spoken of; and accordingly in our text, there being no genitive, no object of comparison, INSTAR is simply *amount (Gehalt):* QUANTUM INSTAR IN IPSO, *how great an amount in himself! how much in him!*

879.

HEU PIETAS HEU PRISCA FIDES INVICTAQUE BELLO
DEXTERA NON ILLI SE QUISQUAM IMPUNE TULISSET
OBVIUS ARMATO SEU CUM PEDES IRET IN HOSTEM
SEU SPUMANTIS EQUI FODERET CALCARIBUS ARMOS

Not spoken of the virtues actually possessed by Marcellus, but of the virtues he would have exhibited, had he lived; as if Virgil had said: *mourn for the loss in the bud, of a flower which, if suffered to grow, would have been so lovely.* The words from NON ILLI as far as ARMOS are but an amplification, or filling up, of the idea already shortly set before the reader in the three emphatic words INVICTA BELLO DEXTERA.

883.

HEU MISERANDE PUER SI QUA FATA ASPERA RUMPAS
TU MARCELLUS ERIS MANIBUS DATE LILIA PLENIS
PURPUREOS SPARGAM FLORES ANIMAMQUE NEPOTIS
HIS SALTEM ACCUMULEM DONIS ET FUNGAR INANI
MUNERE

HEU MISERANDE PUER SI QUA FATA ASPERA RUMPAS TU MARCELLUS ERIS. — "SI QUA via ac ratione FATA RUMPAS, ... tam durum fatum effugere tibi liceat, tu ad M. Marcelli, b. Punico II. clari, nomen ac gloriam es perventurus." Heyne.

"Vide, an in fine vs. 883 rectius posueris exclamandi signum, ut hoc dicat poeta: utinam rumpas aliquo modo fata aspera! Sic efficietur, ut nomen Marcelli, — non jam illius, qui bello Punico secundo magnas res gessit, sed ipsius filii Octaviae — hic demum positum singularem habeat vim ad miserationem movendam." Wagner.

Each critic is half right and half wrong; Wagner is right that the person meant by MARCELLUS is *the son of Octavia*, but wrong that SI QUA FATA ASPERA RUMPAS is an exclamation. Heyne is right that the words SI QUA FATA ASPERA RUMPAS express the condition on which the lad will become Marcellus, viz. if he does not die prematurely, but wrong that MARCELLUS means *a Marcellus, a second Marcellus*, and not properly *Marcellus, the son of Octavia.* The whole meaning is certainly and beyond doubt: *Ah! boy to be pitied, only live and thou shalt be the gentle knight, the man of sterling worth and honesty, the invincible warrior; in one word, thou shalt be Marcellus.* The gist of the passage is that the 'puer', the young son of Octavia, would be only (see Comm. *En. I. 560)* the 'spes Marcelli', *the promise of Marcellus,* not be really Marcellus, not deserve to be called Marcellus until grown up: but he was fated not to grow up; was not to break through his FATA ASPERA, and therefore Anchises (in imagination) throws flowers upon his tomb; observe, not on Marcellus's tomb, but upon the tomb NEPOTIS, of Anchises' descendant, the young son of Octavia.

MANIBUS DATE LILIA PLENIS PURPUREOS SPARGAM FLORES &c.

"With roses and the lily buds,
Ye nymphs, her grave adorn,
And weeping tell, thus sweet she was,
Thus early from us torn."

Allan Ramsay's beautiful *Ode sacred to the memory of Anne, Duchess of Hamilton.*

898.

HIS UBI TUM NATUM ANCHISES UNAQUE SIBYLLAM
PROSEQUITUR DICTIS PORTAQUE EMITTIT EBURNA
ILLE VIAM SECAT AD NAVES SOCIOSQUE REVISIT
TUM SE AD CAJETAE RECTO FERT LITTORE PORTUM

"Quae postquam multa perpessus nocte Cupido
Effugit, pulsa tandem caligine somni
Evolat ad superos, portaque evadit eburna."

The words 'pulsa tandem caligine somni' in this plain imitation of our author by the learned and elegant Ausonius *(Cupid. Cruc. 101)*, leave no doubt on my mind that Virgil means to describe, in the words of our text, not alone Eneas's return from the underworld, but, at the same time, his awaking out of the dream in which only (as the poet would now at last intimate) his visit to the under-world had been paid.

Notwithstanding the strong reprobation, with which this termination of the sixth Book of the Eneis has been visited by Heyne, and others whose opinions have weight with the public, I think it impossible to imagine any *denouement* more simple, natural, and (even in Virgil's own time and before it had become classical from his use of it) classical and poetical.

LITTORE. — In this instance as in some few others I justify Wagner's deviation from the Heynian reading. LITTORE is to be preferred to 'limite', first, because required in order to show that the journey from Cuma to Cajeta was made (as the following verse, no less than the necessity of the case, shows it was made) by sea (RECTO LITTORE, *right along the shore, coastwise,* i. e. *coasting);* and secondly, because it is not only the reading (according to Foggini) of the Medicean, and (according to Bottari) of the Vatican Fragment, but is recognised besides both by Servius (ad *Aen. III. 16)* and Donatus, the former however alone understanding the passage correctly, the latter, by some egregious blunder, supposing that Eneas walked along the shore all the way to Cajeta, and only there at last met his fleet. I have myself examined only the two Leipzig and the Dresden MSS. respecting the passage. In both the former I have found LITTORE, in the latter 'limite'. LITTORE is also the reading of the Modena Ed. of 1475, of both the Heinsii, both the Stephenses, and Bersmann; also of Burmann and La Cerda. The silence of Pierius shows that he found no variety of reading. Compare, *En. VIII. 57:* "Ripis et recto flumine;" *straight along the river's bank.*

ADDENDA ET CORRIGENDA.

I. p. 1. Line 3 from bottom, complete the verse by adding: GENUS UNDE LATINUM

I. p. 2. Line 3 from bottom, instead of *247,* read *246.*

I. p. 2. *Dele* the two last lines.

I. p. 4. Line 7 from bottom, instead of *484. VI. 84. 741. 882,* read *483; VI. 83, 739.*

I. p. 5. After line 3 from bottom, add:
and Statius's personified Pietas

Saevum . . . . Jovem, Parcasque nocentes
Vociferans, seseque polis, et luce relicta
Descensuram Erebo, et Stygios jam malle Penates:
'Quid me', ait, 'ut saevis animantum, ac saepe Deorum
Obstaturam animis, princeps natura, creabas?'
Theb. XI. 462.

I. p. 9. First line, instead of Metempsychosis of the Eneis, read *Six Photographs of the Heroic Times,*

I. p. 16. Line 6 from bottom, instead of *step, or walk,* read *step, walk,* or *go,*

I. p. 16. Line 3 from bottom, substitute a period for the semicolon; and *dele* the whole of the subsequent clause.

I. p. 20. Line 3 from bottom, after Period add: For an additional argument that the *arx* of Eolus was outside the *carcer* of the winds, see Comm. *En. VI. 566.*

I. p. 26. Line 13 from bottom, instead of *Catal.,* read *Catil.*

I. p. 32. Line 19 from top, instead of *313,* read *311.*

I. p. 67. Line 15 from top, instead of Catalina, read Catilina,

I. p. 110. Line 7 from bottom, instead of *568,* read *565:*

I. p. 111. After line 11 from bottom, add:
P. S. No light is thrown upon the word 'crispare' by Ammian's use of it, XIV. 2, in connexion with 'tela'; XX. 4, in connexion with 'missilia'; and XXVII. 10, in connexion with 'hastas'. In each of the three places the sense is equally good whether with his editors, J. A. Wagner and Erfurdt, we understand it to mean *'vibrare,'* or, as I have ventured to explain it in our text, *to grasp; hold firmly grasped in the hand.*

I. p. 123. After last line insert the following:

423.

JAMQUE ASCENDEBANT COLLEM QUI PLURIMUS URBI
IMMINET ADVERSASQUE ASPECTAT DESUPER ARCES

"Και πριν μεν ελθειν τηνδε γην Τροιζηνιαν,
Πετραν παρ' αυτην Παλλαδος, κατοψιον
Γης τησδε, ναον Κυπριδος καθεισατο."
EURIP. *Hippol.* 29.

"Φαιδρα δια το καλλος ερασθεισα αυτου τοτε μεν απελθοντος εις Τροιζηνα ιδρυσατο ιερον Αφροδιτης παρα την Ακροπολιν, οθεν ην καθοραν την Τροιζηνα." DIOD. SICUL. IV. 62.

I. p. 125. Line 6 from bottom, instead of 'Alfieri', read 'the Baskerville'. [Note. Alfieri wrote his Translation of the Eneis on the margin of a Baskerville's Virgil, which, happily, is still preserved in the Laurentian Library, in Florence. Having seen and examined the volume when I was in Florence in 1850, and observed that it contained many corrections of the text in the handwriting of Alfieri (ex. gr. at vers. 436 of the fourth Book, the 'dederis' of the Baskerville text has been altered into 'dederit', and the note "i. e. Enea" appended in the margin), I took it for granted that the text affixed side by side to Alfieri's Translation (in his *Opere,* Brescia, 1809), was this Baskervillian text so corrected by Alfieri himself, and have accordingly, in the earlier part of these Commentaries spoken of an "Alfieri's text" as distinct and separate from the Baskervillian. It was not long however before I discovered my error, and observed that the text affixed to Alfieri's Translation is not the Baskervillian so corrected by Alfieri, but the original Baskervillian. I have therefore to request my readers to consider the text which in the early part of these Commentaries,

I speak of as Alfieri's and distinct from the Baskerville, to be neither more nor less than the Baskerville itself, and to excuse an error into which I have been led by Alfieri's editors themselves, who, publishing his Translation after his death, have, I know not whether to say ignorantly or negligently, but certainly very injuriously to the Translator, affixed to his Translation a text often materially different from that from which he translated; as, for instance, in the passage already cited, and at vers. 429 of Book I, where, while Alfieri himself translates from 'optare', his affixed text has 'aptare'].

I. p. 137. Line 5 from bottom, after Period add: Ninthly, because it is 'Dea ...... supereminet omnes' in the exactly corresponding passage of Ovid *(Metam. III. 178)*:

> "Sicut erant, viso nudae sua pectora Nymphae
> Percussere viro, subitisque ululatibus omne
> Implevere nemus, circumfusaeque Dianam
> Corporibus texere suis. Tamen altior illis
> Ipsa Dea est, colloque tenus supereminet omnes."

I. p. 147. Line 6 from bottom, after Period add: That such precisely is the meaning of the emphatic (see Comm. *En. II. 246)* ARMAQUE, seems to me to be placed beyond doubt by the corresponding passage in the address of Jason to Aeetes, of which Ilioneus's address to Dido is a copy:

> — "*Και δε τοι ηδη*
> *Προφρονες ειμεν Αρηϊ θοην αποτισαι αμοιβην,*
> *Ειτ' ουν Σαυροματας γε λιλαιεαι, ειτε τιν' αλλον*
> *Δημον σφωϊτεροισιν υπο σκηπτροισι δαμασσαι.*"
>
> APOLLON. RHOD. III. 392.

I. p. 150. Top line, *dele* the words enclosed in parenthesis; and after line 19 from top, add:

The form of expression has been borrowed by Statius, *Theb. I. 683:*

"Nec sic aversum Fama Mycenis
Volvit iter;"

a road so entirely turned away from Mycenae.

I. p. 163. Last line, after Period add: Compare *(En. VI. 567):*

"Castigatque auditque dolos, subigitque fateri,"

where the order of time is exactly the reverse of the order of statement. See (below, in these Addenda) Comment on that passage.

I. p. 168. Line 12 from top, after *toils,* add: also in Statius *(Theb. III. 2):*

"Nocte sub ancipiti, quamvis humentibus astris
Longus ad Auroram superet labor."

II. p. 41. Line 5 from bottom, instead of 484. VI. 84, 741 and 882, read 483; V. 522 (§ II); VI. 83, 739.

II. p. 55. After line 8 from top, add: (compare "Hunc neque divisis cepissent Pergama muros." Stat. *Silv. I. 1. 11).*

II. p. 75. Line 11 from top, instead of I. 4. read I. 4. 1.

II. p. 109. Line 18 from top, after Period add: See also the use made by Apollonius Rhodius (IV. 940) of the exactly corresponding Greek term, πεζα, to express the whole skirt, or petticoat part, of the female dress:

"Αυτιχ' ανασχομεναι λευκοις επι γουνασι πεζας."

and the confirmatory statement of Nonius, that the term 'limbus' was applied not merely to the sewed-on border, but to the garment itself on which the border was sewed: "Limbus, muliebre vestimentum quod purpuram in imo habet."

II. p. 110. After line 19 from top, insert: Nay, she is even represented by Apollon. Rhodius (IV. 1309) as issuing παμφαινουσα out of the head of Jupiter:

— "Αι ποτ' Αθηνην,
Ημος οτ' εκ πατρος κεφαλης θορε παμφαινουσα,
Αντομεναι Τριτωνος εφ' υδασι χυτλωσαντο."

II. p. 118. After line 19 from top, add:
There cannot, I think, be a doubt but that the preternatural light on the head of Iulus was considered as of the happiest omen, not so much because it was a preternatural light on his head, as because it had its seat in his APEX, i. e. in the topmost, talismanic lock on the crown of his head; see *En. IV. 698* and Comment *IV. 691, § V.*

II. p. 121. Line 15 from top, instead of 484; V. 525. read 483; V. 522, § II.

II. p. 125. Line 20 from top, after Period add:

"Si quaeras, ubi sit formosi mater Iuli:
Occidit, a duro sola relicta viro."

OVID, *Heroid. VII. 83.*

III. p. 26. Line 7 from top, *dele* from 'lento marmore' as far as *gives with it* (line 10) inclusive.

III. p. 27. After line 8 from top, add:
P. S.[1] It will perhaps be asked: "If the radical meaning of 'lentus' be, as stated in the above Comment, *pliant, supple, ductile*, and if 'lentare arcus, remos,' be *to render bows and oars supple, to take the rigidity out of bows and oars*, viz. by frequent straining and tugging of them, how are we to explain such expressions as Virgil's "lentus in umbra" *(Ecl. I. 4)*, Horace's "lentus spectator" *(Epist. II. 1. 178)*, and Silius's "lentando fervida bella" (VIII. 11)?" To this question I reply that in all these instances, and I believe in every other instance which may be adduced of a similar use of 'lentus' and 'lentare', these terms retain more or less of the primitive sense assigned to them in the above Comment; that Virgil's "lentus in umbra" and Horace's "lentus spectator" express the state opposite to that of exertion, tension and rigidity (German, *Spannung)*, that state in which the muscles, or, if you please, the mind, or more probably in each of the just mentioned instances, both body and mind,

the whole individual, is in a relaxed, unexerted, inactive, listless state; in that state which as near as possible approaches to that of a bow in its unstrung ('lentus') state, and that "lentando fervida bella" applied by Silius to Fabius Cunctator, expresses the well known tactics of that General, his rendering wars, which had been previously vehement ('concita', 'fervida'), languid and relaxed; his depriving them of their tension and rigidity, unstringing them as it were, and reducing them to a state of pliant listlessness; making them dull and slow.

The difficulty which commentators and lexicographers have found in explaining 'lentus' (and *a fortiori* in explaining 'lentare') has arisen from there being no corresponding term in modern languages; no word used to express, according to circumstances, both active and passive pliancy; both the active pliancy (suppleness) of the serpent's spine (Ovid. *Metam. III. 66),* of the wrestler or warrior (see Servius's quotation from Ennius above), of Neaera's arms (Hor. *Epod. XV. 6),* and the passive pliancy of wax, birdlime, the willow, the ductile and malleable metals, oars, bows, dying Camilla's neck, the listless spectator in the theatre, and the indolent sleeper or lounger in the shade; I might add, of the sea in a calm, when the oars "in lento luctantur marmore" *(En. VII. 28),* struggle with difficulty through the water, which has become listless and inactive ("maria pigro fixa languore." Senec. *Agam. 161)* and no longer helps the oars on by its own proper motion.

III. p. 33. After line 9 from bottom, add:
'Cedere honore', as *(En. IX. 620)* "cedite ferro". For numerous examples of this use of 'cedere' (sciz. with the ablative of the thing ceded from) see Weber, ad Lucan. VIII. 693; and for the precise expression 'honore cedere', though in a slightly different sense, see (Plin. *Panegyr. 94):* "Tu clara judicii tui signa misisti, cum

proficiscenti ad exercitum tuo nomine, tuo honore, cessisti."

III. p. 38. After line 14 from top, add: Compare (exactly parallel) Cicero, *De Natura Deorum II. 44:* "Capiti autem Equi proximat Aquarii dextra, totusque deinceps Aquarius .... Hinc autem aspicitur

Ut sese ostendens emergit Scorpius alte

.... Deinde Delphinus .... Quem subsequens

Fervidus ille Canis stellarum luce refulget.

Post Lepus subsequitur;" where 'Hinc' is not, *from this place,* but *next after this.*

III. p. 45. After line 9 from bottom, add: Compare "Cyclopia saxa," *En. I. 205;* and

— "Aeriamque educere molem,
Cyclopum scopulos ultra."

STAT. *Silv. V. 3. 48.*

III. p. 47. After line 11 from bottom, add: and Seneca, *Medea, 301:*

"Audax nimium, qui freta primus
Rate tam fragili perfida rupit;
Terrasque suas post terga videns,
Animam levibus credidit auris;
Dubioque secans aequora cursu,
Potuit tenui fidere ligno,
Inter vitae mortisque vias
Nimium gracili limite ducto."

IV. p. 26. After line 10 from bottom, add: MATERNAM. — "Sein Muttergefild'" Voss. No, not *where he was born,* but *belonging to his mother, sacred to his mother.* See "materna myrto," *En. V. 72;* "maternas aves," *En. VI. 193; myrtle, birds, belonging to his mother, sacred to his mother;* the only sense in which the word has ever been used by Virgil.

IV. p. 35. Line 18 from top, after *κομην.*" add: and *(Copa, vers. 1):*

"Copa Syrisca, caput Graia redimita mitella."

IV. p. 48. After line 6 from bottom, add: and especially Cicero, *Tuscul. Quaest. I. 30:* "Ita enim censebat, itaque disseruit (Socrates sciz.): duas esse vias, duplicesque cursus animorum e corpore excedentium. nam qui se humanis vitiis contaminavissent, et se totos libidinibus dedidissent, quibus caecati, vel domesticis vitiis atque flagitiis se inquinavissent, vel republica violanda fraudes inexpiabiles concepissent, iis devium quoddam iter esse, seclusum a concilio deorum: qui autem se integros castosque servavissent, quibusque fuisset minima cum corporibus contagio, seseque ab his semper sevocassent, essentque in corporibus humanis vitam imitati deorum: his ad illos, a quibus essent profecti, reditum facilem patere."

IV. p. 56. After line 11 from bottom, add: Compare *En. III. 331;* and Liv. I. 48 (of Tullia): "Agitantibus Furiis sororis et viri."

IV. p. 69. After last line but one, add:
and Seneca, *Herc. Oet. 609:*

"Tenet auratum limen Erinnys,
Et cum magnae patuere fores,
Intrant fraudes, cautique doli,
Ferrumque latens."

IV. p. 74. Line 9 from bottom, read

— "Pinguem taedis, et robore secto
Ingentem, struxere pyram."

VI. p. 23. After line 10 from top, add:

395.

TARTAREUM ILLE MANU CUSTODEM IN VINCLA PETIVIT
IPSIUS A SOLIO REGIS TRAXITQUE TREMENTEM

Here, as at *v. 214,* and *IV. 505,* I entirely agree with Wakefield's punctuation:

IN VINCLA PETIVIT
IPSIUS A SOLIO REGIS,

and to Wagner's "Ego Mediceum secutus, et post PETIVIT et post REGIS interpunxi," reply that the sense is always a better guide to the punctuation than the authority of any scribe; see Comments *En. I. 122; II. 420.* The removal of the pause placed by the Medicean after PETIVIT has the advantage, not only of strengthening and defining PETIVIT, but of referring IPSIUS A SOLIO REGIS equally to both verbs, to the complement of PETIVIT no less than to PETIVIT itself. The same MS. whose guidance Wagner follows in placing a pause after PETIVIT, places (see Foggini) a similar pause after 'armatus', *v. 388,* after 'viva', *v. 391,* and after 'euntem', *v. 392.* If the guide be safe, why has not Wagner followed him on these so near, and so similar, occasions?

VI. p. 31. After line 15 from top, add:
CASTIGATQUE AUDITQUE DOLOS SUBIGITQUE FATERI &c. — The *υστερον προτερον* observed by Servius in this passage is not accidental; first, because it is according to Virgil's usual manner thus to reverse in his statement the order of time (see Comm. *En. I. 701);* and secondly, because in this particular instance it has the (manifestly intended) effect of bringing the explanation and thing explained, into as close apposition as possible: DURISSIMA REGNA, CASTIGAT. It being the invariable practice (as it is the no small excellence) of Virgil to place the principal idea first, and the minor or subsidiary ideas second (see Comments *En. I. 500, 701; II. 96),* and the principal idea being frequently the latest in order of time, the *υστερον προτερον* comes necessarily to be of frequent occurrence in Virgil.

VI. p. 44. Line 8 from top, after Period add: Compare the application by Ausonius of this same term 'suspensus' to Cupid crucified by the Heroines in Hades:

> "Hujus in excelso suspensum stipite Amorem
> Devinctum post terga manus, substrictaque plantis
> Vincula moerentem, nullo moderamine poenae
> Affigunt."
>
> AUSON. *Cupido Cruci Affixus, 59.*

FURTHER ADDENDA.

II. p. 110. After line 2 from top, add:

That LIMBO in the text means *the whole Peplum* of Pallas (the sewed-on stripe being put by the usual Synechdoche for the whole dress) is further shown by that passage of Statius in which Apollo Musagetes is described as putting off (as soon as he has done playing on the lyre) the embroidered 'limbus', i. e. the gown with embroidered border, which he had worn while playing:

> "Dumque chelyn lauro, textumque illustre coronae
> Subligat, et picto discingit pectora limbo."
>
> *Theb. VI. 366;*

where 'limbo' is, not *the sewed-on border,* but *the whole dress* or *gown;* first, because it was not the border, but the whole dress which Apollo put off; and secondly, because the term 'discingere', where elsewhere used, applies not to the border, or 'limbus' properly so called, but to the whole dress, as shown by the Roman proverb, "Discincta vestis, discinctus animus," quoted by Desprez, ad Hor. *Epod. I. 34.*

Any doubt which may remain on the reader's mind that LIMBO in the text, is *the whole female dress, skirt* or *petticoat* of Pallas, will I think disappear on a comparison of the above passage of the *Thebaid,* in which Apollo is described as putting the 'limbus' off his chest, with the passage in the *Achilleis* quoted in my Commentary above, in which the 'limbus' is described as confining the step of Achilles when Thetis has dressed him in petticoats. The embroidered 'limbus' which Apollo undoes from about his breast. and the embroidered 'limbus' which confined the freedom of Achilles's step, can be nothing else but *the whole female skirt* or *petticoat.*

III. p. 26. Line 14 from bottom, instead of *make wood supple and fit for bows*, read *make bows supple,*

Page 65, of the *Addenda.* After line 8 from bottom, add:

Ancient Bas-reliefs and statues often represent Cupid and other personages in the act 'lentandi arcum'; See *Mus. Capitolin. III. 4;* also Clarac, *Musée de Sculpture, Tom. III. Tab. 281, 282.* In order to perform this act, the bow (previously unstrung) is held firmly in the left hand by the middle, with the convexity toward the person; one horn of the bow is then caught with the right hand and drawn forcibly backwards towards the person; the bow having been thus rendered nearly straight, the right hand is gradually relaxed and the bow allowed to return to its bowed condition. By the frequent repetition of this manoeuvre the bow 'lentatur', *is made supple, and fit for use.* 'Lentare arcum' and 'flectere arcum' therefore, so far from being, as supposed by the commentators and lexicographers, synonimous terms, or both expressive of the act of bending the bow, are terms diametrically opposed to each other; 'flectere arcum being *to strain the bow in the direction of its curve, to shoot with the bow;* 'lentare arcum' *to strain the bow in the opposite direction*, i. e. *against its curve, and then allow it to return by its natural spring to its bent position;* the effect of the frequent repetition of such manoeuvre being to supple the bow.

Át this hóur on this same évening
Lást year Í was gáy and háppy,
Hére alóng this grássy róadside
Sáuntering with my néwly wédded.

Únderfóot the sprı́ngy dáisy,
Óverhéad the táll elm bránches,.
Ón this róadside wé were wálking
Ánd this háwthorn hédge admíring.

Rich it wás as nów with blóssoms,
Ánd as nów gilt with the slánt beams
Óf yon slówly sétting Máy sun,
Ánd the déw as nów was fálling.

Ón this spót, where nów I'm stánding,
Árm in árm we stóod and listened
Tó the trilling óf the bláckbird;
Ín the sáme bush nów he 's trilling.

Ánd these swállows, thát have since then
Séen far lánds and séas and cíties,
Pást us tó and fró that évening
Smóoth and swift as nów were gliding.

Háwthorn hédge and sétting Máy sun,
Trilling bláckbird, glíding swállows,
Déwy róadside, élms and dáisies,
Áll are hére as ón that évening;

Bút my néwly wédded 's lýing
Ín her cóffin, ín the chúrchyard,
Whére I 'd ráther bé besíde her
Thán here wándering bróken hearted.

WAISENHAUS-STRASSE, DRESDEN, July 10, 1853.

Féar not Déath; Death 's bút a cípher;
Á mere blánk, a nón-existence;
Whén thou díest, thóu bút retúrnest
Tó the státe in which thou láyest
Únobstrúcted, únmolésted,
Áll the past etérnal áges,
While all things that líved were súffering.

Féar to líve; it 's Lífe that súffers;
All things róund are Life's torméntors;
Living, súffering, bút two different
Wórds expréssive of the sáme thing;
Í and Thóu but things that súffer
Till we 're Í and Thóu no lónger;
Déath an énd to Í and Thóu puts,
Ánd with I and Thóu to súffering.

Thóu that diest, féar to die not;
Nót even Life thou lósest, dýing;
Tó have lóst, thou múst survive Death;
Lóss belóngs but tó the líving.

WAISENHAUS-STRASSE, DRESDEN, July 31, 1853.

CPSIA information can be obtained at www.ICGtesting.com
Printed in the USA
LVOW08s1930230913

353754LV00001B/49/P

9 781108 064514